SECOND EDITION

READINGS IN U.S H

AFRICAN-AMERICAN EMPHASIS

KEITH R.V. HENINGBURG

Kendall Hunt
publishing company

Cover image © Shutterstock, Inc.

www.kendallhunt.com
Send all inquiries to:
4050 Westmark Drive
Dubuque, IA 52004-1840

Copyright © 2008, 2015 by Keith R. V. Heningburg

ISBN 978-1-4652-8237-8

Printed in the United States of America

Contents

Section One

African Slavery

CHAPTER 1

The Era of The Slave Trade

It is one of the ironies of African history that the end of isolation, made possible through the maritime revolution, should have led in hardly more than two centuries to a new commerce in which Africa's chief export was its own people. Historians have long disputed the causes and consequences of the slave trade—both for Africa and for the world—and the debates are far from finished.

Recent research nevertheless makes it possible to dismiss some of the older myths about the slave trade, myths that originated is the eighteenth- and nineteenth-century European image of Africa with all its racist overtones. Where the slave trade was once explained by the "primitive" condition of African societies and the "natural docility" of the Africans, it is now clear that Africa was not primitive and African slaves were far from docile. Slave revolts were a standard feature in the American tropics. Not only were the Afro-Americans of Saint Domingue (now the republic of Haiti) the first non-Europeans to overthrow colonial rule; other, less known, revolts were also successful. Communities of runaways and rebels were scattered through the back country of South America and in the tangled mountains of the larger Caribbean islands. Several such communities maintained their independence of European control until the end of slavery itself ended their need for isolation.

The Origins of Negro Slavery

Other research helps to explain why Africans came to make up the majority of slaves in the Western world. In southern Europe—unlike northern Europe, where the slavery of the Roman period changed gradually into various forms of inequality generally categorized as serfdom—slavery continued throughout the Middle Ages and down to the eighteenth century in some places. Mediterranean slavery had nothing to do with the race of the slaves. It was a matter of religion; Christians enslaved Muslims, and Muslims enslaved Christians. Black Africans were present among the Mediterranean slaves, but not in large numbers until the fourteenth century. Before that time, the principal external source of slaves for Christian Europe was the northern and eastern coasts of the Black Sea.

In the fourteenth and fifteenth centuries, slavery in southern Europe served three purposes—to furnish domestic service, to provide oarsmen for the galleys that were the principal naval craft, and to concentrate people for new enterprises. Wherever mines or plantations were established in places with an insufficient supply of labor, the institution of slavery was a convenient way of mobilizing labor, especially for sugar plantations on the Mediterranean islands, southern Spain, or Portugal.

Even before the discovery of America, Europeans began to set up similar plantations on Atlantic islands like the Canaries or Madeira. By the early sixteenth century, they had moved as far as São Thomé in the Gulf of Guinea, and these moves were followed later in the century by similar establishments in the Caribbean and Brazil. At each step, the existing population was too small to provide enough workers for a labor-intensive crop like sugar, and the previously isolated populations lived in disease environments that lacked many of the common diseases of Africa and Europe. This meant that the people had no immunities derived from childhood infection or inheritance. With the introduction of Afro-European diseases, they passed through a series of devastating epidemics of diseases like measles, smallpox, typhus, malaria, or yellow fever. The result was a population disaster, sometimes ending in the effective extinction of the original population, especially in the tropical lowlands of the Americas—the region best suited for plantation agriculture. Europeans already had the institution of slavery as a way of forcing labor mobility; they used it in the Atlantic just as they had done in the Mediterranean.

Some form of slavery or forced labor was useful for other reasons as well. The natural conditions of a frontier region, with plenty of land and few people, made for high wage rates, and high labor costs made for labor-extensive use of the land—often pastoralism or simply hunting wild cattle. It was tempting in these conditions to use force in order to make people work some of the land more intensively. As the Indian populations declined in Mexico and Peru, the Spanish turned increasingly to various forms of peonage. On the eastern frontiers of Europe, the landed class tightened the bonds of serfdom. The solution found for America's tropical lowlands was slavery.

But Africans were not the only enforced immigrants to the New World. Convicts, unsuccessful rebels against the government, and indentured workers who bound themselves more or less voluntarily to serve for a period of years were shipped off to the Americas in large numbers. Indians were also enslaved and used for plantation agriculture, especially in Brazil. Of the three sources of labor—Africa, America, and Europe—it was soon clear that the Africans survived best in the tropical American environment. At the time, African superiority is this respect was attributed to some special quality of the Negro race, but modern knowledge of epidemiology shows that early environment rather than race is the true explanation. Europeans died in large numbers is the American tropics, just as they died in even larger numbers in the African tropics. Indians also died on contact with Afro-European diseases, but Africans were comparatively immune both to tropical diseases and to the ordinary range of diseases common on the Afro-Eurasian land mass. Migration from Africa to the Americas brought higher death rates for the first generation, but lower rates than those of Europeans who made the equivalent move.

Given the choice of slavery as a labor system and the fact that Africans were the most efficient workers, the problem of supply remained. A large-scale slave trade would have been impossible if Africa had been truly primitive; European death rates on the coast guaranteed as much. But Africa was not primitive.

Developed commercial networks were already in existence before the discovery of America, both in West Africa and the southern savanna. African rulers often enslaved war prisoners, and the prisoners were sold into the slave trade—often for shipment to distant places where escape was less likely. Some were exported across the Sahara to North Africa, and the Portuguese were briefly in the business of buying slaves in one part of Africa and selling them in another, even before the demand from American plantations drew the focus of the slave trade across the Atlantic.

But slavery in Africa was different from slavery on an American plantation. A slave was without rights at the moment of his capture; he could be killed or sold. He continued without rights until he was sold to an ultimate master in Africa—or else to the Europeans for transportation overseas. If he ended up on an American plantation, his rights would be few and he was treated as a mere labor unit. But in Africa, slavery was not mainly an economic institution. The object in buying a slave was to increase the size of one's own group, more often for prestige or military power than for the sake of wealth. Women were therefore more desirable than men, but men and women alike were assimilated into the master's social group. They had rights as well as obligations. In many cases, a second-generation slave could no longer be sold. And slaves belonging to important people could often rise to positions of command over free men.

The Slave Trade in Africa

The Atlantic slave trade thus tapped an existing African slave trade, but in doing so it sent people into a very different kind of slavery. Over the centuries, it diverted increasing numbers to the coast for sale to Europeans. The organization of this trade varied greatly from one part of Africa to the next. In some regions, Europeans built trade forts; twenty-seven were constructed on the Gold Coast over a distance of only about 220 miles. African authorities allowed the Europeans to exercise sovereignty within the forts themselves, but they often charged rent for the land the fort stood on. Other trading posts were nothing more than a few unfortified houses onshore for the storage of trade goods and a tightly fenced yard for slaves awaiting shipment. In that case, the Europeans who stayed onshore between ships' visits did so with the permission of the African ruler, and under his protection. Another form of trade was the "ship trade," in which Europeans sailed down the coast, calling at likely ports, but without leaving European agents permanently stationed onshore.

Whatever the point of trade, elaborate customary procedures had come into existence by the end of the sixteenth century. Trade normally began with a payment to the local authorities, partly a gift to demonstrate good will and partly a tax. Each section of the coast had its own trade currency of account—the "bar" (originally an iron bar), the "ounce" (originally an ounce of gold dust), a form of brass currency called manillas, or cowrie shells from the Indian Ocean. Various European commodities were customarily valued at so many bars or ounces. Bargains were struck in terms of the number of bars or ounces to be paid for a slave and then once more in terms of the "sorting" of different European goods that would be used to make up that value.

The internal trade to the coast was more diverse. In some African kingdoms, such as late-eighteenth-century Dahomey, the slave trade was a royal monopoly, tightly controlled for the profit of the state. Other states, such as Futa Toro on the Senegal River, sold few slaves themselves but charged heavy tolls for the privilege of shipping slaves through the country on the way to the coast. Still other states expanded by conquest in order to be able to control the passage of slaves. The kingdom of Akwamu followed a pattern of expansion in the late seventeenth century, moving to the east and west of the Volta River in present-day Ghana, but some distance back from the coast. After a period of growing strength based on revenue from the flow of trade across the kingdom, Akwamu was able to reach down to the coast itself in the 1680s and dictate terms to the coastal trading states and the European garrisons alike.

Other African societies adjusted to the demand for slaves, changing their own social and political institutions. Along the fringes of the Niger delta, the Ijo had been settled for centuries as fishermen and exporters of salt to the interior. Early in the eighteenth century, a series of new city-states like Nembe, Bonny, and Kalabari came into existence, with a commercial and political organization designed expressly to serve the demand for slaves. Each city-state was divided internally into a series of "canoe houses," in effect a commercial firm based on the extended family plus domestic slaves.

The houses operated large trading canoes, vessels that might have fifty to a hundred paddlers and mount a small cannon. Trade was highly competitive between houses, and within a house command went to the most successful traders. A slave might rise to become head of the house. The Ijo canoes on the creeks of the delta were supplied, in turn, by other trade networks leading to the waterside, The Aro subgroup among the Ibo, for example, had small colonies of Aro settled in towns throughout Iboland. Slaves were passed from one Aro community to another until they were sold to the Ijo and finally to the Europeans. The Aro enjoyed this special position partly because they also controlled an important religions shrine, and many of the slaves they collected were originally given as sacrifices at the shrine, though in fact they ended in the Americas.

African societies south of the tropical forest also adjusted to the trade in slaves. By the late seventeenth century, the Imbangala, who had first appeared as destructive raiders a century earlier, turned to commerce. Their kingdom, inland from the Portuguese post at Luanda, drew slaves from a wide range of central Africa. A little later, the Ovimbundu in the hinterland of Benguela took the same course. Bihé and Mbalundu in particular among the Ovimbundu states became wealthy on the basis of trade routes reaching far into the interior, ultimately as far as the present Shaba province of Zaire. Like Imbangala to the north, the Ovimbundu states were far too strong to be threatened by Portuguese power on the coast. In time, a rough alliance came into existence, in which the Portuguese acquiesced to the trade monopoly of the inland kingdoms for the sake of having a regular and plentiful supply of slaves delivered to the coast.

East Africa also made a small contribution to the slave trade, especially the hinterland of Mozambique City. (To the north of Cape Delgado, slaves from the Swahili coast were almost all directed toward Arabia and Persia, though this trade was small until the early nineteenth century.) The principal African carriers of the trade within southeastern Africa were the Yao from the vicinity of Lake Malawi. They first went into the long-distance ivory trade and then shifted to slaves as demand increased in the course of the eighteenth century. For southeastern Africa, the most important destination of that period was the Mascarene Islands in the Indian Ocean, where the French developed sugar plantations on the pattern of the West Indies. A few thousand nevertheless found their way around the Cape of Good Hope into the slave trade of the Atlantic.

The Growth and Incidence of the Slave Trade

The European demand for slaves grew slowly and steadily; over many decades African institutions adapted to meet the demand. From an annual average of less than 2000 slaves imported into the Americas each year in the century before 1600, the trade grew to about 55,000 a year for the eighteenth century as a whole. The peak decade for the whole history of the trade was the 1780s, with an annual average of 88,000 slaves arriving in the Americas each year; deliveries reached more than 100,000 in a few individual years. At least for the crucial period from 1701 to 1809, it is possible to estimate the drain of population from various regions of Africa by taking the combined estimates of the exports carried by the three most important carriers—England, France, and Portugal. (See Fig. 8.) While the map represents the origins of the vast majority of all those carried, it also leaves out some important aspects of the trade. During that century, the sources of the trade shifted dramatically from one part of the coast to another. The Gold Coast, for example, supplied 20 percent of exports in the 1740s, but only about 9 percent in the 1790s. Meanwhile, the Bight of Biafra rose with the development of the Ijo-Aro trade network from about 1 percent of the trade in the 1730s to almost a quarter of the whole in the 1790s. Or again, the exports from central Africa doubled between the 1770s and the 1780s. In short, while the demand for slaves was relatively steady, it was met by rapid shifts from one source of supply to another, depending on African political conditions or the development of new trade routes from the interior.

North Americans, with a view of world history that centers on their own country, often think of the slave trade as a flow of people from Africa to the United States. In fact, about one third of all slaves landed in the Americas went to Brazil; about a half went to the Caribbean islands and mainland; no more than a twentieth came to the United States. Yet the Afro-America population of the United States today is one of the largest in the New World. The explanation lies in a sharp and important demographic distinction between North America and the American tropics. While the Negro population of the North American colonies began to grow from natural increase at a very early date, the slave population of the tropical plantations suffered an excess of deaths over births. This meant that the slave trade could not be a one-shot affair, importing a basic population that could then maintain its own numbers. It had to be continuous merely to maintain the existing level of population; any growth of the plantation economy required still more slaves from Africa.

Several factors help to account for this demographic peculiarity. Disease environment was important in the first generation, since both morbidity and mortality rates were higher among slaves raised in Africa than they were among the American-born. Planters also imported about two men for every woman, and they worked the women in the fields along with the men, preferring to have their labor rather than creating the kind of social setting in which they would be willing to have children.

The planters may have been correct, on strictly economic grounds, in believing that it was cheaper to import new labor from Africa than to allow the leisure, additional rations, and other privileges that might have encouraged a high birth rate among the slaves. The real cost of slaves was very small indeed before the middle of the eighteenth century. In 1695, for example, a slave could be bought in Jamaica for about £20 currency, or about the same value as sis hundred pounds of raw sugar sold on the London market, or the European cost of sixteen trade guns for sale in Africa. All things being equal, a new slave could be expected to add more than six hundred pounds to the plantation's production in a single year. Yet a prime slave on the coast of Africa cost only about eight guns or a half ton of iron in bars—little enough to allow a handsome profit on the slave trade itself.

But the real price of slaves in Africa rose steadily during the eighteenth century. One result was to make planters think twice about their policy of importing slaves, rather than allowing them to breed naturally. By the 1770s, several Caribbean planters began to readjust by balancing the number of men and women on their estates, granting special privileges to child-rearing mothers and time off for child care. It is uncertain how generally these new polities were applied, but some of the older colonies, such as Barbados, began to achieve a self-perpetuating slave population by about 1800. Even where slaves were still imported, the demand tended to drop as the local birth rate rose, and the total number imported dropped in each decade from 1790 to 1820. When the United States, Great Britain, and Denmark abolished their own part of the slave trade in the first decade of the nineteenth century, the planters complained, but the really serious need for continued slave imports was nearing its end—at least in the older plantation areas.

The slave trade nevertheless reached its peak in the early nineteenth century. In spite of British efforts to halt the trade by a partial blockade of the African coast—and by diplomatic pressure on Portugal, Brazil, and Spain—a sugar boom in Cuba and a coffee boom in southern Brazil brought a new demand for slaves from places where the plantation economy was newly introduced in that century. The slave trade therefore lasted until Brazil decided, in 1850, to enforce its own anti-slave trade laws and Spain made a similar decision for its Cuban colony in the 1860s.

The Impact of the Slave Trade on Africa

Leaving aside the unanswerable question of what Africa might have become over these centuries without the slave trade, some evidence for assessing the impact of the trade is available. We know that most of the slaves sent to the Americas were captured in war. Some warfare took place in order to supply slaves to the trade, and all warfare produced captives who could be sold. Thus, the rise and fall of African states, contested successions, or periods of chronic warfare between states attracted slave dealers who followed the armies and purchased the prisoners. Famine was another cause of enslavement in the regions of unreliable rainfall, where a series of bad harvests forced people to sell their domestic servants, or even their kin and themselves. Judicial condemnation for crime or political dissent also sent some people on their way to the Americas.

But the knowledge that warfare was the principal cause of enslavement in Africa is not as useful for assessing the impact of the trade as one might suppose. If a war took place with the specific and sole aim of capturing slaves, then the slave trade can be blamed for the damage to society at large. When, however, people were enslaved in the course of wars that took place for other reasons, the slave trade was a neutral factor. It might even have been beneficial; all wars are destructive, but a war fought so as to

maximize the number of prisoners might well he less destructive than most. Our present knowledge is enough to indicate that both types of warfare took place in Africa, but not enough to tell which type was more common. On one side, historians can point to spectacular events like the collapse of the empire of Oyo in present-day Nigeria, a political change which led to a whole series of wars lasting for many decades is the early nineteenth century. It is clear that these wars were fought over real issues, not merely to supply the slave trade—yet they supplied more slaves to the trade than any other source in their time. In other cases, historians have detected what appears to have been a "gun-slave cycle," where an African state armed itself with guns, used them to capture unarmed neighbors, who were sold for still more guns. Once caught in this cycle, it was hard to escape. Sooner or later, the neighboring peoples would have guns as well; at that point, slave raiding to buy guns might be necessary for survival. Cases can be found where African states, like Dahomey in the late eighteenth century, reorganized as a military machine for the supply of slaves. But the gun-slave cycle may have been comparatively rare. The long reloading time of the typical eighteenth-century muzzle-loader limited its advantage against rapid-fire bowmen in the forest or wooded savanna. In the open savanna, cavalry was still the dominant military arm far into the nineteenth century.

Still another problem in assessing the impact of the trade is the obvious variation from one African society to another. Some societies were completely destroyed, others may have become wealthy by selling their neighbors to the Europeans, still others were never seriously involved in the trade at all—either as sellers or as victims. We might be able to arrive at a better assessment if we knew more about the level of African populations during the period of the trade; we could thus make some estimates as to the per capita drain of population. But it could still be argued that the underlying influence of the trade was far more profound than any mere drain of population or change in the incidence of warfare. Having been isolated from the intercommunicating zone, the Africans of the western coasts had, in the arrival of seaborne Europeans, both an opportunity and a challenge. If they had responded by seeking new products to sell in return for the Indian textiles and European hardware offered by the maritime trade, they might well have been led to new economic institutions, technological innovations, and a more rapid rate of economic development than ever before. As it was, the Europeans wanted slaves, and the challenge of meeting this demand diverted African creativity to an essentially unproductive enterprise. When the slave trade finally ended, African societies took up the challenge of supplying products rather than people, but time was already running out; the European invasions came before the adjustment could be completed. It seems clear from this point of view that, at the very least, the slave trade forestalled some of the positive fruits of more intense contact with the outside world.

On the other hand, it is hard to sustain the view that the slave trade destroyed African civilization or set Africa back on its path to progress. African civilization was not destroyed, and Africa made progress during this period in spite of slave trade. Literacy spread in the western sudan with the spread of Islam. Literacy in English and Portuguese spread along the coast, where slave dealers learned to read and write and sometimes sent their children to Europe for education. Recent studies of African states like Ashanti show a continuous development from small-scale, kinship-based political units to the institutions of a large state, capable of assimilating its conquered territories and exercising administrative control that was at least as effective as that of feudal monarchies in western Europe before the thirteenth, century. Metallurgy and textile production also improved, and hand-loomed cotton cloths were sold into world trade during the eighteenth century, before the cheaper machine-made cloth from Europe drove them from the market. In short, measured by technology, there is no doubt that African societies advanced during the period of the slave trade, though it is equally certain that the advance was too slow to close the gap between African technology and that of the intercommunicating zone.

Section Two

Slavery in Colonial America

CHAPTER 2

The First Blacks Arrive in Virginia

John Rolfe to Sir Edwin Sandys, January? 1619/20.

About the latter end of August, a Dutch man of Warr of the burden of a 160 tunes arriued at Point-Comfort, the Commando[rs] name Capt Jope, his Pilott for the West Indies one M[r] Marmaduke an Englishman. They mett w[th] the Trer in the West Indyes, and determyned to hold consort shipp hetherward, but in their passage lost one the other. He brought not any thing but 20 and odd Negroes, wth the Governor and Cape Marchant bought for victualle (whereof he was in greate need as he p[re]tended) at the best and easyest rate they could. He hadd a lardge and ample Comyssion from his Excellency to range and to take purchase in the West Indyes.

***** ***** ***** ***** *****

Slavery Becomes a Legal Fact in Virginia

[1630]

September 17th, 1630. Hugh Davis to be soundly whipped, before an assembly of Negroes and others for abusing himself to the dishonor of God and shame of Christians, by defiling his body in lying with a negro; which fault he is to acknowledge next Sabbath day.

Statutes 1:146

[1640]

Robert Sweet to do penance in church according to laws of England, for getting a negroe woman with child and the woman whipt.

Statutes 1:552

[1659–60]

Act XIV.
An Act for repealing an Act for Irish Servants.

Whereas the act for Irish servants coemeing in without indentures enjoyning them to serve six yeeres, carried with it both rigour and inconvenience, many by the length of time they have to serve discouraged from coemeing into the country, And by that meanes the peopling of the country retarded, And these inconveniencies augmented by the addition of the last clause in that act, That all aliens should be included, *Bee it therefore enacted and confirmed*, That the whole act be repealed and made void and null, And that for the future no servant coemeing into the country without indentures, of what christian nation soever, shall serve longer then those of our own country, of the like age: *And it is further enacted*, That what alien soever arrive here before that clause was inserted and that hath been by vertue of that last clause inforced to serve any time longer then the custom of the countrey did oblige them to shall be allowed competent wages by their severall masters for the time they have overserved, Any act, order of court or judgment to the contrary notwithstanding, Provided alwaies that all such aliens as came in servants during the time that the said clause was in force shall serve according to the tenor of that act.

Statutes 1:538–39

[1659–60]

Act XVI.
An Act for the Dutch and all other Strangers for Tradeing to this Place.

Whereas the restriction of trade hath appeared to be the greatest impediment to the advance of the estimation and value of our present only commodity tobacco, *Bee it enacted and confirmed,* That the Dutch and all strangers of what Xtian nation soever in amity with the people of England shall have free liberty to trade with vs, for all allowable comodities, And receive protection from vs to our vtmost powers while they are in our jurisdiction, and shall have equall right and justice with our own nation in all courts of judicature, *Provided* they give bond and pay the impost of tenn shillings per hogshead laid vpon all tobacco exported to any fforreigne dominions and give bond according to act, *Alwaies provided,* That if the said Dutch or other forreiners shall import any negro slaves, They the said Dutch or others shall, for the tobacco really produced by the sale of the said negro, pay only the impost of two shillings per hogshead, the like being paid by our owne nation.

Statutes 1:540

[1660–61]

Act XXII.
English running away with negroes.

Bee itt enacted That in case any English servant shall run away in company with any negroes who are incapable of making satisfaction by addition of time, Bee it enacted that the English so running

away in company with them shall serve for the time of the said Negroes absence as they are to do for their owne by a former act.

Statutes 2:26

[1661–62]

Act CII
Run-aways.

Whereas there are diverse loytering runaways in this country who very often absent themselves from their masters service and sometimes in a long time cannot be found, the losse of the time and the charge in the seeking them often exceeding the value of their labor: *Bee it therefore enacted* that all runaways that shall absent themselves from their said masters service, shalbe lyable to make satisfaction by service after the times by custome or indenture is expired (vizt.) double their times of service soe neglected, and if the time of their running away was in the crop or the charge of recovering them extraordinary the court shall lymitt a longer time of service proportionable to the damage the master shall make appeare he hath susteyned, and because the adjudging the time they should serve is often referred untill the time by indenture is expired, when the proofe of what is due is very uncertaine, *it is enacted* that the master of any runaway that intends to take the benefitt of this act, shall as soone as he hath recovered him carry him to the next commissioner and there declare and prove the time of his absence, and the charge he hath bin at in his recovery, which commissioner thereupon shall grant his certificate, and the court on that certificate passe judgment for the time he shall serve for his absence; and in case any English servant shall run away in company of any negroes who are incapable of making satisfaction by addition of a time, *it is enacted* that the English soe running away in the company with them shall at the time of service to their owne masters expired, serve the masters of the said negroes for thier absence soe long as they should have done by this act if they had not beene slaves, every christian in company serving his proportion; and if the negroes be lost or dye in such time of their being run away, the christian servants in company with them shall by proportion among them, either pay fower thousand five hundred pounds of tobacco and caske or fower yeares service for every negro soe lost or dead.

Statutes 2:116–17

[1662]

Act XII.
Negro womens children to serve according to the condition of the mother.

Whereas some doubts have arrisen whether children got by any Englishman upon a negro woman should be slave or ffree, *Be it therefore enacted and declared by this present grand assembly*, that all children borne in this country shalbe held bond or free only according to the condition of the mother, And that if any christian shall committ ffornication with a negro man or woman, hee or shee soe offending shall pay double the ffines imposed by the former act.

Statutes 2:170

[1667]

Act III.
An act declaring that baptisme of slaves doth not exempt them from bondage.

Whereas some doubts have risen whether children that are slaves by birth, and by the charity and piety of their owners made pertakers of the blessed sacrament of baptisme, should by vertue of their baptisme be made ffree; *It is enacted and declared by this grand assembly, and the authority thereof*, that the conferring of baptisme doth not alter the condition of the person as to his bondage or ffreedome; that diverse masters, ffreed from this doubt, may more carefully endeavor the propagation of christialnity by permitting children, though slaves, or those of greater growth if capable to be admitted to that sacrament.

Statutes 2:260

[1670]

Act V.
Noe Negroes nor Indians to buy christian servants.

Whereas it hath beene questioned whither Indians or negroes manumited, or otherwise free, could be capable of purchasing christian servants, *It is enacted* that noe negro or Indian though baptised and enjoyned their owne ffreedome shall be capable of

any such purchase of christians, but yet not debarred from buying any of their owne nation.

Statutes 2:280–81

[1670]

Act XII.
What tyme Indians to serve.

Whereas some dispute have arisen whither Indians taken in warr by any other nation, and by that nation that taketh them sold to the English, are servants for life or terme of yeares, *It is resolved and enacted* that all servants not being christians imported into this colony by shipping shalbe slaves for their lives; but what shall come by land shall serve, if boyes or girles, untill thirty yeares of age, if men or women twelve yeares and no longer.

Statutes 2:283

[1680]

Act X.
An act for preventing Negroes Insurrections.

Whereas the frequent meeting of considerable numbers of negroe slaves under pretence of feasts and burialls is judged of dangerous consequence; for prevention whereof for the future, *Bee it enacted by the kings most excellent majestie by and with the consent of the generall assembly, and it is hereby enacted by the authority aforesaid*, that from and after the publication of this law, it shall not be lawful] for any negroe or other slave to carry or arme himselfe with any club, staffe, gunn, sword or any other weapon of defence or offence, nor to goe or depart from of his masters ground without a certificate from his master, mistris or overseer, and such permission not to be granted but upon perticuler and necessary occasions; and every negroe or slave soe offending not haveing a certificate as aforesaid shalbe sent to the next constable, who is hereby enjoyned and required to give the said negroe twenty lashes on his bare back well layd on, and soe sent home to his said master, mistris or overseer. *And it is further enacted by the authority aforesaid* that if any negroe or other slave shall presume to lift up his hand in opposition against any christian, shall for every such offence, upon due proofe made thereof by the oath of the party before a magistrate, have and receive thirty lashes on his bare back well laid on. *And it is hereby further enacted by the authority aforesaid* that if any negroe or other slave shall absent himself from his masters service and lye hid and lurking in obscure places, comitting injuries to the inhabitants, and shall resist any person or persons that shalby any lawfull authority be imployed to apprehend and take the said negroe, that then in case of such resistance, it shalbe lawfull for such person or persons to kill the said negroe or slave soe lying out and resisting, and that this law be once every six months published at the respective county courts and parish churches within this colony.

Statutes 2:481–82

[1691]

Act XVI.
An act for suppressing outlying Slaves.

Whereas many times negroes, mulattoes, and other slaves unlawfully absent themselves from their masters and mistresses service, and lie hid and lurk in obscure places killing hoggs and committing other injuries to the inhabitants of this dominion, for remedy whereof for the future, *Be it enacted by their majesties lieutenant governour, councell and burgesses of this present generall assembly and the authoritie thereof, and it is hereby enacted,* that in all such cases upon intelligence of any such negroes, mulattoes, or other slaves lying out, two of their majesties justices of the peace of that county, whereof one to be of the quorum, where such negroes, mulattoes or other slave shall be, shall be impowered and commanded, and are hereby impowered and commanded to issue out their warrants directed to the sherrife of the same county to apprehend such negroes, mulattoes, and other slaves, which said sherriffe is hereby likewise required upon all such occasions to raise such and soe many forces from time to time as he shall think convenient and necessary for the effectuall apprehending such negroes, mulattoes and other slaves, and in case any negroes, mulattoes or other slave or slaves lying out as aforesaid shall resist, runaway, or refuse to deliver and surrender him or themselves to any person or persons that shall be by lawfull authority employed to apprehend and take such negroes, mulattoes or other slaves that in such cases it shall and may be lawfull for such person and persons to kill and distroy such negroes, mulattoes, and other slave or slaves by gunn or any otherwaise whatsoever.

Provided that where any negroe or mulattoe slave or slaves shall be killed in pursuance of this act, the owner or owners of such negro, or mulatto slave shall be paid for such negro or mulatto slave four thousand pounds of tobacco by the publique. And for prevention of that abominable mixture and spurious issue which hereafter may encrease in this dominion, as well by negroes, mulattoes, and Indians intermarrying with English, or other white women, as by their unlawfull accompanying with one another, *Be it enacted by the authoritie aforesaid, and it is hereby enacted,* that for the time to come, whatsoever English or other white man or women being free shall intermarry with a negroe, mulatto, or Indian man or woman bond or free, shall within three months after such marriage be banished and removed from this dominion forever, and that the justices of each respective countie within this dominion make it their perticular care, that this act be put in effectuall execution. *And be it further enacted by the authoritie aforesaid, and it is hereby enacted,* That if any English woman being free shall have a bastard child by any negro or mulatto, she pay the sume of fifteen pounds sterling, within one moneth after such bastard child shall be born, to the Church wardens of the parish where she shall be delivered of such child, and in default of such payment she shall be taken into the possession [of] the said Church wardens and disposed of for five yeares, and the said fine of fifteen pounds, or whatever the woman shall be disposed of for, shall be paid, one third part to their majesties for and towards the support of the government and the contingent charges thereof, and the other third part to the use of the parish where the offence is committed, and the other third part to the informer, and that such bastard child be bound out as a servant by the said Church wardens untill he or she shall attaine the age of thirty yeares, and in case such English woman that shall have such bastard child be a servant, she shall be sold by the said Church wardens, (after her time is expired that she ought by law to serve her master) for five yeares, and the money she shall be sold for divided as is before appointed, and the child to serve as aforesaid.

And forasmuch as great inconveniences may happen to this country by the setting of negroes and mulattoes free, by their either entertaining negro slaves from their masters service, or receiveing stolen goods, or being grown old bringing a charge upon the country; for prevention thereof, *Be it enacted by the authority aforesaid, and it is hereby enacted,* That no negro or mulatto be after the end of this present session of assembly set free by any person or persons whatsoever, unless such person or persons, their heires, executors or administrators pay for the transportation of such negro or Negroes out of the countrey within six moneths after such setting them free, upon penalty of paying of tenn pounds sterling to the Church wardens of the parish where such person shall dwell with, which money, or so much thereof as shall be necessary, the said Church wardens are to cause the said negro or mulatto to be transported out of the countrey, and the remainder of the said money to imploy to the use of the poor of the parish.

Statutes 3:86–88

CHAPTER 3

Early Negro Petitions for Freedom, 1661–1726

Herbert Aptheker, ed.

Individual Negroes quite frequently petitioned governmental bodies for freedom prior to the American Revolution. Three examples of such petitions are given below. The first, dated 1661, was in Dutch and was addressed to the colony of New Netherlands (later New York). Its prayer was granted. The second, dated 1675, was the work of a Virginia Negro and what decision was made in regard to it does not appear. The third petition, dated 1726, was addressed to the North Carolina General Court and was denied.

＊＊＊＊＊

[a]

New Netherlands Petition, 1661

To the Noble Right Honorable Director-General and Lords Councillors of New Netherlands

Herewith very respectfully declare Emanuel Pieterson, a free Negro, and Reytory, otherwise Dorothy, Angola, free Negro woman, together husband and wife, the very humble petitioners of your noble honors, that she, Reytory, in the year 1643, on the third of August, stood as godparent or witness at the Christian baptism of a little son of one Anthony van Angola, begotten with his own wife named Louise, the which aforementioned Anthony and Louise were both free Negroes; and about four weeks thereafter the aforementioned Louise came to depart this world, leaving behind the aforementioned little son named Anthony, the which child your petitioner out of Christian affection took to herself, and with the fruits of her hands' bitter toil she

reared him as her own child, and up to the present supported him, taking all motherly solicitude and care for him, without aid of anyone in the world, not even his father (who likewise died about five years thereafter), to solicit his nourishment; and also your petitioner [i.e., Emanuel] since he was married to Reytory, has done his duty and his very best for the rearing . . . to assist . . . your petitioners . . . very respectfully address themselves to you, noble and right honorable lords, humbly begging that your noble honors consent to grant a stamp in this margin of this [document], or otherwise a document containing the consent and approval of the above-mentioned adoption and nurturing, on the part of your petitioner, in behalf of the aforementioned Anthony with the intent [of declaring] that he himself, being of free parents, reared and brought up without burden or expense of the [West Indian) Company, or of anyone else than your petitioner, in accordance therewith he may be declared by your noble honors to be a free person: this being done, [the document] was signed with the mark of Anthony Pieterson.

———

Manuscript in New York State Library, Albany. The editor is indebted to Professor Margaret Schlauch formerly of New York University and Professor Adriaan Barnouw of Columbia University for the translation. Ellipses indicate illegible portions of the document; bracketed words are the editor's.

[b]

Virginia Petition, 1675

To the R[T] Hon[ble] Sir William Berkeley, Knt., Gover[r] and Capt. Genl. of Virg**a**, with the Hon. Councell of State.

The Petition of Phillip Corven, a Negro, in all humility showeth: That yo[r] pe[tr] being a servant to M[rs] Annye Beazley, late of James Citty County, widdow, deed. The said M[rs] Beazley made her last will & testament in writing, under her hand & seal, bearing date, the 9th day of April, An. Dom. 1664, and, amongst other things, did order, will appoint thatyo[r] pe[tr] by the then name of Negro boy Phillip, should serve her cousin, Mr. Humphrey Stafford, the terme of eight yeares, then next ensueing, and then should enjoy his freedome & be paid three barrels of corne & a sute of clothes, as by the said will appears. Sonne after the makeing of which will, the said M[rs] Beazley departed this life, yo[r] pe[tr] did continue & and abide with the said Mr Stafford, (with whome he was ordered by the said will to live) some yeares, and then the said, Mr. Stafford sold the remainder of yo[r] pe[tr] time to one Mr. Charles Lucas, with whom yo[r] pe[tr] alsoe continued, doeing true & faithfull service; but the said M[r]. Lucas, coveting yo[r] pe[trs] service longer then of right itt was due, did not att the expiracon of the said eight yeares, discharge yo[r] pe[tr] from his service, but compelled him to serve three years longer than the time set by the said M[rs]. Beazley's will, and then not being willing yo[r] pe[tr] should enjoy his freedome, did, contrary to all honesty and good conscience with threats & a high hand, in the time of yo[r] pe[trs] service with him, and by his confederacy with some persons compel yo[r] pe[tr] to sett his hand to a writeing, which the said M[r] Lucas now saith is an Indenture for twenty yeares, and forced yo[r] pe[tr] to acknowledge the same in the County Court of Warwick.

Now, for that itt please yo[r] Hon[r], yo[r] pe[tr], who all the time of the makeing the said forced writing, in the servicee of the said M[r]. Lucas, and never discharged from the same, the said M[r] Lucas alwaies unjustly pretending that yo[r] pe[tr] was to serve him three yeares longer, by an order of Court, w[h] is untrue, which pretence of the said Mr. Lucas will appeare to yo[r] hon[r] by ye testimony of persons of good creditt

Yo[r] Pe[tr] therefore most humbly prayeth yo[r] hon[rs] to order that the said M[r] Lucas make him sattisfaction for the said three yeares service above his time, and pay him corne & clothes, with costs of suite.

And yo[r] pe[tr] (as in duty bound) shall ever pray, &c.

———

Wm. P. Palmer, ed., *Calendar of Virginia State Papers,* I (Richmond, 1875), pp. 9–10.

[c]

North Carolina Petition, 1726

To the Honoble Christopher Gale Esqr Chief justice of the General Court February the third one thousand Seven hundred & twenty Six

The Complaint and petition of peter Vantrump a free Negro Sheweth that yor Complainant being a free Negro and at his own voluntary disposall & hath hired himself to Service Sundry times particularly in New York and other places and being at St Thomas's this Summer past one Captain Mackie in a Brigantine from thence being bound (as be reported) to Europe Your Honors Complainant agreed to go with him in Order to gett to Holland but instead of proceeding the Sayd Voyage the Sayd Mackie came to North Carolina where combining with one Edmund porter of this province and fearing the Sayd Mackie not to be on a lawfull Trade Yor Complainant was desirous to leave him and the Sayd porter by plausible pretences gott Your Complainant to come away from the Sayd Mackie with him although Your Complainant often told the Sayd porter that he was not a Slave but a free man Yet nevertheless the Sayd porter now against all right now pretends Your Complainant to be his Slave and hath held and used him as Such wherefore Your Complainant prays he may be adjudgd & declard free as in justice he ought to be & Signd Peter Vantrump.

———

Wm. Saunders, ed., *The Colonial Records of North Carolina,* (Raleigh, 1886), pp. 702–03.

Statements of Slave Rebels, 1741

Herbert Aptheker, ed.

The history of American Negro slavery was marked by very many conspiracies and revolts on the part of the Negroes. The colonial period was no exception to this. The New York City slave plot of 1741, during which many buildings were destroyed by fire, was one of the major events of this character. It provoked hysteria leading to exaggeration of the extent of the actual conspiracy, but that one existed is clear. To obtain direct statements from contemporary Negroes themselves concerning these events is not easy. Below appear the confessions of two Negroes made in New York City on the afternoon of May 30, 1741, while chained to stakes before a howling, impatient mob. Following these confessions, the slaves were burned alive. In addition, twenty-nine other Negroes were executed as were four whites including, among the latter, two women.

The recorder of the slaves' confessions takes us to the scene of the execution.

✳ ✳ ✳ ✳ ✳

Mr. Moore, the deputy secretary, undertook singly to examine them both, endeavoring to persuade them to confess their guilt, and all they knew of the matter, without effect, till at length Mr. Roosevelt came up to him, and said he would undertake Quaco, whilst Mr. Moore examined Cuffee; but before they could proceed to the purpose, each of them was obliged to flatter his respective criminal that his fellow sufferer had begun, which stratagem prevailed; Mr. Roosevelt stuck to Quaco altogether, and Mr. Moore took Cuffee's confession, and sometimes also minutes of what each said; and afterwards upon drawing up their confessions in form from their minutes, they therefore intermixed what came from each.

Quaco's confession at the stake. He said—

1. That Hughson was the first contriver of the whole plot, and promoter of it; which was to burn the houses of the town; Cuffee said, to kill the people.

2. That Hughson brought in first Caesar, Varack's; then Prince, Auboyneauls; Cuffee, Philipse's; and others, amongst whom were old Kip's Negro; Robin, Chambers'; Cuffee, Gornez's; Jack, Codweis's, and another short Negro, that cooks for him.

3. That he (Quaco) did fire the fort; that it was by a lighted stick taken out of the servant's hall, about eight o'clock at night; that he went up the back stairs with it, and so through Barbara's room, and put it near the gutter, betwixt the shingles and the roof of the house.

4. That on Sunday afternoon, a month before the firing of the fort, over a bowl of punch, the confederates at Hughson's (amongst whom were the confederates above named, Albany and Tickle, *alias* Will, Jack and Cook, Comfort's; old Butchell, Caesar, and Guy, Horsfield's; Tom, Van Rant's; Caesar, Peck's; Worcester, and others voted him, (Quaco), as having a wife in the fort, to be the person who should fire the fort; Sandy and Jack, Codweis's; Caesar and Guy, Horsfield's; were to assist him in it.

5. That Hughson desired the Negroes to bring to his house what they could get from the fire, and Hughson was to bring down country people in his boat to further the business, and would bring in other Negroes.

6. That forty or fifty to his knowledge were concerned, but their names could not recollect. (The mob pressing and interrupting.)

7. That Cuffee, Gomez's; and Caesar, Peck's, fired Vant Zant's storehouse.

8. That Mary Burton had spoke the truth, and could name many more.

9. Fortune, Wilkins's, and Sandy, had done the same; and Sandy could name the Spaniards, and say much more, which Cuffee particularly confirmed.

10. Being asked what view Hughson had in acting in this manner? he answered, to make himself rich.

11. That after the fire was over, Quaco was at Hughson's house, Jack, Comfort's, a leading man, Hughson, wife, and daughter present, and said the job was done, meaning the fire; that he went frequently to Hughson's house, and met there Tickle and Albany.

12. Quaco said his wife was no ways concerned, for be never would trust her with it; and that Denby knew nothing about the matter. [The wife was the governor's cook; Denby his domestic.]

13. Jamaica, Ellis's not concerned that he knew of, but was frequently at Hughson's with his fiddle.

14. Said he was not sworn by Hughson, but others were.

——— ——— ———

Daniel Horsmanden, *The Negro Conspiracy in the City of New York, in 1741* (N.Y., 1851), pp. 87–89.

SECTION THREE

AMERICAN REVOLUTION AND US CONSTITUTION

CHAPTER 4

The Revolutionary War as a Black Declaration of Independence

Benjamin Quarles

During the summer of 1777 Capt. William Whipple, a soldier from Portsmouth, New Hampshire, noted that his slave, Prince, was quite dejected. Asked by Whipple to account for his moodiness, Prince explained, "Master, *you* are going to fight for your *liberty*, but I have none to fight for." Struck by the essential truth of Prince's complaint, Whipple lost no time in freeing him.[1]

Before his emancipation Prince had been one of the oarsmen who rowed George Washington and his party across the ice-choked Delaware River in a blinding snow and sleet storm Christmas night 1776. But even had Prince Whipple not taken part in one of the most significant battles of the Revolutionary War, there was nothing unusual about his longing to be free. This yearning for freedom was common among those in bondage and its roots ran deep. The contagion of liberty had long infected blacks, reaching epidemic proportions with the outbreak of the war against England. As was the case for other Americans, regional differences characterized Afro-American culture, and within each regional group status determinants such as occupation and skin color further divided both slave and free blacks. Moreover, in ever-changing early America the patterns of black life were not static from one generation to another.[2] But regardless of these distinctions, all blacks during the Revolutionary era shared a common goal—the pursuit of freedom and equality.

The exchange between Captain Whipple and his slave illustrated another major characteristic of Revolutionary War blacks, their tendency to differ with whites in interpreting the rhetoric and the meaning of the war itself. When whites, for example, accused England of trying to enslave them, they had in mind such measures as stamp acts and trade restrictions, royal decrees and Parliamentary legislation. To white Americans the war meant freedom and liberty in a politico-economic sense rather than in the sense of personal bondage. Admittedly, the Revolutionary War did have its social overtones, as J. Franklin Jameson reminded us half a century ago.[3] And, as Jesse Lemisch, Alfred F. Young, and others have pointed out more recently, various underprivileged white groups, including women, had distinctive reactions to the war, each of them viewing it as an opportunity for advancement.[4]

With all due credit for its pivotal role in the history of human freedom, the American Revolution fell considerably short of the egalitarian goals it proclaimed. Like many subsequent armed outbreaks, it was essentially a colonial war of liberation; it was waged, however, against a country not unlike America itself. White Americans claimed that they were fighting for the rights of Englishmen—rights that they had long enjoyed but that the Crown had tried to abrogate; they struggled to retain freedom rather than to acquire it.

Although white patriots might not have cared to acknowledge it, the American Revolution bore the overtones of a civil war; indeed, it was more a war of independence than one of revolution.

Berlin, Ira, and Ronald Hoffman, eds. *Slavery and Freedom in the American Revolution*, pp. 283-301. © 1983 by the Rector and Visitors of the University of Virginia. Reprinted by permission of the University of Virginia Press.

Moreover, unlike other colonial wars of liberation, as Moses Coit Tyler pointed out, it was "directed not against tyranny inflicted, but only against tyranny anticipated."[5] Its inherent conservatism limited the revolutionary potential of the American War for Independence.

Slaves saw the matter differently. In its impact on them the war was truly revolutionary. Seizing the opportunity, they gave a personal interpretation of the theory of natural rights and to the slogans of liberty and independence. Such a patriotic exhortation as "Give me liberty or give me death" carried special meaning to people in bondage.

The desire of blacks for freedom did not, of course, originate with the American Revolution. In one of his midweek lectures to Boston slaves, delivered on May 21, 1721, Cotton Mather denounced the "*Fondness for Freedom* in many of you, who lived Comfortably in a very easy Servitude." Obviously not alluding to religious freedom, Mather had in mind a freedom of the person which, in his opinion, was not the state God had ordained for the assembled bonds people.[6] Half a century later, on the eve of the Revolutionary War, this fondness for freedom had become even more prevalent. The number of blacks had multiplied, and they had become more at home in provincial America and more responsive to its ways of life, particularly those tinged with egalitarianism of substance, tone, or spirit.

The special circumstances of Afro-American life sharpened the desire to be free. In sheer numbers blacks composed in 1774 a larger proportion of the total population than they ever would again, 500,000 out of 2,600,000, nearly 20 percent. These half-million blacks had become Afro-Americans in the true sense of the hyphenated word. Reinforced by more recent arrivals from overseas, they retained strong spiritual and aesthetic ties with their ancestral homelands, their rich cultural heritage already working its way into American music, dance, folk literature, and art. Indeed, in reference to Americans from Africa the term *acculturation* lacks precision; it would be better to use *transculturation*, a process of exchange and not a one-way street. Despite the persistence of their African heritage, however, most blacks by 1774 had undergone a transition from Africans to Afro-Americans and were no longer the "outlandish" blacks slave traders had deposited in the New World.

Their Americanization had resulted from a complex of influences, economic, socioreligious,

and genetic. They certainly had been integrated economically, as a vital source of labor. Slaves in the southern colonies, numbering 90 percent of the total slave population, produced the agricultural staples of the late colonial period, tobacco, rice, and sugar. A plantation required skilled laborers as well as field hands, and these too were black. As Marcus W. Jernegan pointed out, "It is hard to see how the eighteenth-century plantation could have survived if the Negro slave had not made his important contribution as an artisan."[7] In South Carolina, Peter H. Wood has noted, slaves not only engaged in the full range of plantation activities "but were also thoroughly involved wherever experiments were made with new products;" such as the development of silk culture.[8] North Carolina's blacks likewise performed complex and essential tasks. "If their status often forced them into menial labor," observed Jeffrey J. Crow, "they still contributed skills and know-how to the colony's agriculture and crafts."[9]

The northern provinces also had their component of slaves with industrial skills. Slave workers in New York, as described by Edgar J. McManus, "showed proficiency in every field of human endeavor."[10] Lorenzo J. Greene, another authority on blacks in the colonial North, painted a similar picture of the slave in New England who might be called upon "not only to care for stock, to act as a servant, repair a fence, serve on board ship, shoe a horse, print a newspaper, but even to manage his master's business."[11] And in New England, as elsewhere, slave women were proficient spinners, knitters, and weavers.

Daily contacts between black worker and white owner inevitably led to a sociocultural interaction between the parties, with the slaves becoming familiar with and sometimes adopting the beliefs and behavior patterns of their owners. Such personal contacts were most frequent when a master owned only one or two slaves. The pattern of person-to-person association between the races was less pervasive on the larger plantations, but even there one would find a corps of domestic slaves, whose children, it may be added, tended to play with the children of the master.

In the absence of a slave row with its separate quarters, the slaves in New England and the middle colonies were in close and constant contact with their owners. In the cities above the Potomac, Ira Berlin has argued, the acculturation of blacks "was a matter of years, not generations."[12] If somewhat slower, the process also went on in the northern countryside. Traveling in rural Connecticut in 1704, Sarah Kemble Knight took note of white masters who permitted what she termed a "too great familiarity" vis-à-vis their slaves, dining at the same table with them. A terse entry in Madame Knight's diary bespoke her displeasure: "Into the dish goes the black hoof as freely as the white hand."[13]

Out of such white-black proximity, North and South, emerged another force in the Americanization of blacks—their conversion to Christianity. Although many masters considered it imprudent, the idea of bringing slaves to Christ gained momentum throughout the eighteenth century. The movement was led by the London-based Society for the Propagation of the Gospel in Foreign Parts (S.P.G.), an Episcopal organization that operated mainly in the southern colonies. A handful of Puritans and Quakers, more often laboring individually than in organized groups, also took up evangelical work across the color line. In 1740 the conversion of blacks assumed major proportions with the religious revival known as the Great Awakening, with its central theme of equality before God. Negroes entered the churches in unprecedented numbers, imbibing the "New Light" ideas that characterized the crusade. Writing in 1743, Charles Chauncy, a cleric critical of the Great Awakening, complained that it permitted "women and girls; yea Negroes . . . to do the business of preachers."[14]

A significant by-product of this eighteenth-century evangelistic impulse was the emergence of a small but steadily increasing contingent of blacks who could read and write, a case of religion with letters. The S.P.G. established several schools for blacks, one of which, in Goose Creek Parish, South Carolina, employed two black teachers, the first of their race in colonial America.[15] The Quakers were especially notable for their efforts to provide education for blacks, their zeal spurred by Anthony Benezet, the leading abolitionist of his day. In 1750 Benezet established in Philadelphia a night school for blacks that was still in operation, and with an enrollment of forty-six, when the Revolutionary War broke out.[16] In New England many slaves received training in the "three R's," not only so they could read the Bible but also because literate slaves brought a higher price on the market.

The close relationship between religion and literacy among blacks was reflected in the two best-known poetic publications of the period, one by Jupiter Hammon and the other by Phillis Wheatley. Hammon's work, a broadside of eighty-eight lines, bore the revealing title "An Evening Thought. Salvation by Christ, with Penetential Cries: Composed by Jupiter Hammon, a Negro belonging to Mr. Lloyd, of Queen's Village, on Long Island, the 25th of December, 1760." Far more celebrated than her predecessor, Phillis Wheatley at the age of twenty-three became in 1773 only the second woman in colonial America to publish a volume of poetry. The title of her path-breaking work, *Poems on Various Subjects, Religious and Moral,* conveys the basic outlook and orientation of a writer who had in 1771 been baptized in Boston's Old South Meeting House.

If Hammon and Wheatley personified the religious acculturation of Afro-Americans, the scientist Benjamin Banneker personified another characteristic of white-black proximity, the mixing of bloodlines. Banneker's white English grandmother had freed and married one of her slaves, Bannaky, a former African chief. As Banneker's ancestry illustrates, blacks in the thirteen colonies were by no means of exclusively African stock. Early Virginia permitted white-black marriages, but even after all the southern colonies, as well as Pennsylvania and Massachusetts, outlawed racial intermixing, miscegenation remained extensive, as evidenced by the large numbers of mulattoes, some of them blue-eyed and red-haired. "It is impossible," Winthrop D. Jordan has argued, "to ascertain how much intermixture there actually was, though it seems likely that there was more during the eighteenth century than at any time since."[17] It is hardly necessary to add that blacks, like whites, also mingled their blood with that of Indians.

As a result of the white-black contacts previously mentioned—economic, socioreligious, and sexual—the half million Afro-Americans of 1774 had begun to experience a sense of distinct identity, a race-conscious identity if you will, but one that reflected the essential values of the Revolutionary era. Watered by the Revolutionary War, this sense of self-identity would flower into a collective sense of community, the latter too an affirmation of the most cherished values of the early republic.

The Revolution, with its slogans of liberty and equality, inevitably appealed to a group such as the blacks. If this were the credo of the new America, they would joyfully make the most of it. As a class black Americans were not strong on theory and would hardly have been prepared to discuss the ideological origins of the war. But they could readily understand propositions to the effect that all men were created equal and that everyone was entitled to personal freedom. Themselves short on worldly goods, most blacks did not consider private property, particularly the ownership of slaves, a basic natural right.

Like other Americans, blacks viewed the war in terms of their own interests and concerns. Perceiving what they regarded as an inescapable inconsistency between the ideals of the Revolution and the institution of slavery, they redoubled their efforts for emancipation, their methods including freedom suits, petitions to state legislatures, and military service. In states like Massachusetts that considered them not only property but also persons before the law, slaves instituted suits for freedom. Such actions cast the master in the role of defendant, obliged either to defend the validity of his title or to answer the charge that slavery itself was illegal or unconstitutional.

The effect of a judicial decree extended only to the litigants immediately involved in the case. Hence blacks seeking freedom collectively rather than individually drafted petitions to their state legislatures. Typical of such pleas was that sent in November 1779 to the New Hampshire assembly by nineteen slaves from Portsmouth. Contending that "the God of nature gave them life and freedom," the petitioners asserted that freedom "is an inherent right of the human species, not to be surrendered but by consent."[18]

Slaves in the Revolutionary War South, denied recourse to the courts or the legislatures, expressed their protests more directly. Exhibiting an insubordinate disposition, they became harder to handle. Ronald Hoffman concluded in his study of Revolutionary Maryland that the Eastern Shore centers of black population "were severe sources of strain and worry during the Anglo-American conflict."[19] By way of example, Hoffman cited a late 1775 dispatch from the Dorchester County Committee of Inspection reporting that "the insolence of the Negroes in this country is come to such a height that we are under a necessity of disarming them. We took about eighty guns, some bayonets, swords, etc."[20]

Slave discontent was further evidenced in the marked increase of runaways. To escape-minded blacks the war was a godsend; the number of fugitive slaves reached flood proportions during the conflict. Thomas Jefferson estimated that during the war more than 30,000 Virginia slaves took to their heels.[21] Attesting to their numerical strength, runaway slaves in Revolutionary Georgia established communities of their own.

Blacks' desire for freedom found its greatest fulfillment in wartime service as arms-bearers. British overtures and American military necessity enabled slaves to join the armed forces and thereby win freedom with their muskets. The invitation to blacks to join the British ranks was first offered in the early months of the war by Lord Dunmore, Virginia's last royal governor. In June 1779 Commander in Chief Sir Henry Clinton issued the most sweeping of the slave-freeing proclamations by the British command. It promised blacks their freedom and stipulated that they would be given their choice of any occupation within the British lines. Blacks welcomed such overtures, their motivation being more pro-freedom than pro-British.

By 1779 the Americans too were welcoming blacks to their armies. In the early stages of the war American military and civilian authorities had adopted a policy of excluding Negroes, a policy based on the mistaken supposition that the war would be over quickly. By the summer of 1777, with the war dragging into its third year, a policy reversal began when the northern colonies and Maryland decided to enlist blacks whatever the risks.

Slaves needed no second invitation. Recruiting agents had only to mention or hint at that magic word *freedom* to bring them into the fighting forces. It is striking, for example, that of the 289 identifiable blacks in the Connecticut army, five reported "Liberty" as their surname when they signed on, and eighteen reported "Freedom" or "Freeman."[22]

Free blacks also welcomed the coming of the Revolutionary War. Just as their lot was akin to that of the slaves, so was their response. Like the slaves, the free blacks drafted petitions and joined the army, Prince Hall, for example, did both. Led by the Cuffe brothers, blacks in Massachusetts lodged an official protest against the denial of their right to vote even though they paid taxes. In a 1780 petition to the state legislature they invoked the patriotic slogan "No taxation without representation."[23]

Free blacks who joined the army were variously motivated. They shared the common hope, however, that the high-sounding affirmations of the Revolution were more than hollow rhetoric. With a touch of the wishful thinking not uncommon to those who are reform-minded, black Americans tended to take seriously the proclaimed goals of the patriots.

Hence in assessing the temper and spirit of the Revolutionary War blacks, one finds that, slave and free alike, their loyalty was not to a locality in which they were propertyless, not to an assembly in which they could not sit, and not to a social order that denied their worth. They reserved allegiance for whoever made them the best and most concrete offer in terms of man's inalienable rights, which is only to say that the loyalty of black Americans centered on the fundamental credos upon which the new nation was founded.

The hope of black Americans for a new day of equality was not realized; it was a dream deferred. True, the Revolutionary War had it positive side. It was imbued with a strong moral overtone, leading some whites to question an institution such as slavery, no matter how time-honored. To whites of a reformist turn of mind the war had exposed the inconsistencies and contradictions in American thought about the rights of man, particularly those of the black man. But if heightened sensitivity to the presence of an underprivileged black group characterized some whites, they were far outnumbered by those who detected no ideological inconsistency. These white Americans, not considering themselves counterrevolutionary, would never have dreamed of repudiating the theory of natural rights. Instead they skirted the dilemma by maintaining that blacks were an outgroup rather than members of the body politic. They subscribed to an equation of equality that excluded nonwhites, regarding them as outside the sociopolitical community encompassed by the Revolutionary War tenets of freedom and equality.

Black Americans, not unexpectedly, gave an entirely different reading to these war-spawned concepts. To them freedom was everyone's birthright; everyone had certain inalienable rights. In black circles the feeling of independence that these beliefs had fostered outlasted the roar of the guns. Still unspent, the spirit of '76 found new outlets among blacks. The Revolutionary War as a black Declaration of Independence took on a power of its own, fueled by residual Revolutionary rhetoric and sustained by the memory of fallen heroes and the cloud of living black witnesses. To black Americans the theory of natural rights did not lose its relevance with the departure of the British troops. Blacks were

left no choice other than to oppose all efforts to de-revolutionize the Revolution.

However complacent and self-congratulatory their white countrymen may have been after expelling the British, the less euphoric black Americans turned their thoughts to the unfinished business of democracy. Their sense of self-identity, forged in the colonial period and honed by the Revolutionary War, now gave way to a sense of community, of cooperative effort in a cause that was no less true-blue Americanism simply because its advocates were dark-skinned. Their problems pressing, their resources meager, black Americans took heed of the Revolutionary War slogan "Unite or die." They were brought together not so much by a blood knot or a common Old World heritage as by a shared experience, particularly during the war, and by a shared pursuit of the goals articulated by Jefferson in 1776.

Free blacks assumed the leadership roles as keepers of the flame; in 1790 they numbered nearly 60,000. The 700,000 slaves were hardly in a position to become spokesmen for the new freedom, although a growing number of skilled and literate slaves were more likely to resort to extreme measures as they recalled wartime slogans of liberty. As Gerald W. Mullin pointed out, it was just such a freedom-inspired, literate skilled slave, the blacksmith Gabriel Prosser of Richmond, who planned one of the most ambitious slave conspiracies in United States history.[24] St. George Tucker, a Virginian and a contemporary of Prosser's, observed that there was a difference between the slaves who responded to Lord Dunmore's proclamation in 1775 and those who took part in Gabriel's plot in 1800. The slaves of 1775 fought for freedom as a good, said Tucker, whereas those of 1800 claimed freedom as a right.[25]

The dwindling component of slaves in the post-Revolutionary War North, however, found it unnecessary to resort to overt rebellion; time was on their side and gradual emancipation the vogue, especially with the increased availability of white workers. But, like those to the south, northern slaves were not the same after the war. Even the pacifist-minded bondsman Jupiter Hammon was affected. In February 1787 he published "An Address to the Negroes in the State of New York," a poignantly worded leaflet. "That liberty is a great thing," wrote Hammon, "we may know from our own feelings, and we may likewise judge from the conduct of the white people in the late war. How much money has been spent, and how many lives have been lost to defend their liberty. I must say that I have hoped that God would open their eyes, when they were so much engaged for liberty, to think of the state of the poor blacks, and to pity us."[26]

With northern slaves quiescent in their expectation of emancipation and southern slaves under surveillance, free blacks led the movement for racial unification and solidarity. As might be expected, such leadership fell largely to those living above the Mason-Dixon line. Their counterparts in the South were not entirely stripped of citizenship rights, but their limited opportunity for independent reformist action is suggested by the title of Ira Berlin's perceptive study of their marginal status, *Slaves without Masters.*[27]

Out of this impulse toward organized independence in the North came the mighty fortress of the independent black church, a church that preached the equality of all human beings before God and had its own interpretation of the Christian theme of the apocalypse. It was a church whose mission of reconciliation was not only between God and man but also between man and his own noblest ideals, a church that envisioned a new earth as logically ancillary to a new heaven. By the end of the century the pattern of racially separate churches had been firmly fixed.

In the South small independent black Baptist churches first appeared during the Revolutionary War years. Many of these churches were offshoots of white congregations which, for a time, exercised a nominal "watch-care" over them. As in the religious services held by slaves, a characteristic feature of these black churches was the singing of spirituals. If these Negro spirituals had their escapist, otherworldly overtones, they also abounded in code words and double meanings, many of them striking a note of social protest and carrying a barely concealed freedom ring. It was during the late eighteenth century that blacks began to sing one of the greatest of these spirituals with a hidden or double meaning:

> Go down, Moses,
> Way down in Egypt land.
> Tell ole Pharoh
> Let my people go.[28]

In the North, Richard Allen, a former slave who had purchased his freedom, led the movement for the independent black church. In 1786 Allen attempted to establish a separate congregation of Negro Methodists in Philadelphia. Rebuffed in this effort by an official of St. George's Methodist Episcopal Church, Allen withdrew his membership a year later when, at a Sunday morning worship service, a white trustee ordered him and two other black communicants to hie themselves to the gallery. They would never return to St. George's.[29]

By then Allen who, in the words of biographer Carol V. R. George, had "imbibed the philosophical preferences of Revolutionary America" had come to the conclusion that an independent black church and a gospel of social deliverance would be mutually supportive.[30] Deeply religious, he would never lose sight of "that city called Heaven." But to him, to his co-workers who founded Bethel Church in 1794, and to succeeding generations of black churchgoers, the theology to which they subscribed was a theology of liberation in which God spoke out in thunder tones against chattel slavery and sharply condemned other forms of injustice inflicted upon any of His children. Thus the black church was not only a spiritual fellowship; it was also a social unit, and for this reason represented a fusion of redemptions, religious and racial.

In whatever sphere it operated, however, a given church tended to confine its immediate services to members of its own congregation, its own denomination. Hence the movement toward black independence also led to the establishment of organizations that cut across denominational ties, even while retaining a broadly Christian orientation. During the early years of the republic a number of societies and organizations emerged to promote black solidarity, self-help, and self-improvement. Blacks certainly played their part in making post-Revolutionary War America a nation of joiners.

The earliest of these black secular organizations was the African Union Society of Newport, Rhode Island, founded in November 1780; it was followed seven years later by the Free African Society of Philadelphia. The 1790s witnessed the birth of the Brown Fellowship Society, located in Charleston (1790),[31] the African Society of Providence, Rhode Island (1793), the African Society of Boston (1796), and the Friendly Society of St. Thomas, in Philadelphia (1797).[32] A sense of racial identity and pride accounts for the frequent use of the word *African* in the naming of these groups.

As might be expected, the major emphases of these organizations were mutual aid programs, such as supporting one another in sickness and in want, and requirements that their members lead upright lives, minding their morals and their manners. If these goals appeared to be limited exclusively to the welfare of their own participants, however, such was not their overall design. The societies were bent on demonstrating that blacks as a class were, if given the opportunity, prepared to assume the full responsibilities of freedom and citizenship, thus disputing the argument that blacks had never amounted to anything except as slaves, and never would. In a 1794 public letter Richard Allen, founder (with slaveborn Absalom Jones) of the Free African Society, urged his fellow blacks to fulfill "the obligations we lie under to help forward the cause of freedom." A special obligation, Allen insisted, fell upon those who themselves had tasted the cup "of which the slave has to drink."[33]

The wider concerns of these early societies are revealed by their interest in Africa, particularly in establishing a black Christian presence among their brethren abroad. This missionary impulse to uplift the Africans and at the same time strike an indirect blow against slavery, was particularly strong in the Rhode Island societies. In Newport the movement was led by Newport Gardner, in Providence by Bristol Yamma, both literate former slaves born in Africa.[34] The efforts of these eighteenth-century black emigrationists were unsuccessful, but later blacks would echo their call, although with additional reasons, including disillusionment with the American dream.

In company with church and secular groups, the roster of late eighteenth-century Afro-American organizations included the first black secret fraternal order in this country, the Masons. If black Masonry can be said to have had a single founder, it was Prince Hall of Boston, a Revolutionary War veteran and, to use a present-day term, a civil rights activist. Determined to establish a black Masonic lodge and rebuffed by white Masonic authorities in America, he succeeded after a ten-year struggle in obtaining a charter from the British Grand Lodge. On May 6, 1787, African Lodge No. 459 (its charter number) was formally organized with Prince Hall as Master. Ten years later Hall, now bearing the title of Grand Master, established lodges in Providence and Philadelphia, in the latter instance installing Absalom Jones as Worshipful Master.[35]

In common with other black self-help and self-improvement organizations, the Masons placed great emphasis on formal education, especially reading and writing. If blacks of the colonial period deemed such education a privilege, blacks of the Revolutionary War era thought of it as an American entitlement, if not an inherent right of man. "Let us lay by our recreations, and all superfluities, so that we may . . . educate our rising generation," Prince Hall urged in an address to the African Lodge on June 25, 1792. And in the same breath Hall berated the selectmen of Boston for taxing blacks while not permitting them to attend the public schools.[36]

In Philadelphia, Absalom Jones established a school for blacks in 1799. "It is with pleasure that I now inform you that the school was opened on the 4th day of March," Jones wrote to the Pennsylvania Abolition Society, expressing "unfeigned thanks for the encouragement you were pleas[ed] to give me."[37] As a result of the sacrificial efforts of such black leaders as Hall and Jones and the extensive educational operations of white-membered abolitionist societies, the pursuit of formal education became a mainspring in black life during the formative years of the new nation.

Blacks of the Revolutionary War era could work independently as in their churches, or cooperatively with whites, as in providing schools. But neither by independent nor cooperative action could they make any headway in winning suffrage, a right so vital to the "created equal" concept in the Declaration of Independence. In the New England colonies during the colonial period, slaves had been permitted to establish mock Negro governments, electing their own "governors." Primarily a form of diversion, these slave "elections" were occasions for feasting and merriment, but as Lorenzo Greene has argued, the "governments" they set up "acted as a sort of political school wherein slaves received the rudiments of political education which could be drawn upon once they were enfranchised."[38]

Five of the thirteen states forming the new nation—New York, Pennsylvania, Delaware, Maryland, and North Carolina—did not exclude blacks from voting. Indeed, in one of these states, Maryland, a black candidate ran for public office in 1792, very likely the first of his color ever to take this bold step. Thomas Brown, a horse doctor, sought one of the two seats allotted to Baltimore in the House of Delegates. In a September 24, 1792, public letter addressed "To the virtuous, free and independent electors of Baltimore-Town," Brown asserted that he had "been a zealous patriot in the cause of liberty during the late struggle for freedom and independence, not fearing prison or death for my country's cause." Brown closed his somewhat lengthy letter with a pledge that "the corpulency of my body shall be no clog to the exercise of my genius, and agility of my limbs, which shall be kept in perpetual motion for the good of the state."[39] His vote so minuscule as not to have been recorded, Brown was defeated in his bid for office, a circumstance reflecting the times. In but a few scattered instances were blacks a political factor during the eighteenth century, and black enfranchisement in post-Revolutionary America was generally short-lived. In fact after 1810 Thomas Brown himself could not even have voted, Maryland having barred blacks from the polls as of that year. Politically minded blacks could hope for little when property-less whites were subject to disfranchisement.[40]

Postwar blacks resorted to another form of political participation, the right to petition for redress of grievances. On December 30, 1799, as the Revolutionary War era was drawing to a close, a group of seventy-four blacks from the Philadelphia area addressed a petition "To the President, Senate, and House of Representatives," requesting abolition of the overseas slave trade and modification of the fugitive slave law so as to prevent the kidnapping of free blacks. The document concluded with a plea that blacks might "be admitted to partake of the liberties and unalienable rights" to which they were entitled.[41] Although invoking the language and the spirit of the Declaration of Independence and the Constitution, the appeal was couched in the most respectful and conciliatory of tones, and it issued from a city in which the Liberty Bell once had rung, heralding the birth of the new nation. But the House of Representatives did not prove to be liberation-minded; the Congressmen rejected the petition by a chilling vote of eight-five to one.[42]

This rejection of Revolutionary principles, like others, did not deter blacks from pressing for the Revolution's goals of freedom and equality. Determined and patient, they would hardly have heeded J. R. Pole's observations that "revolutions by the nature of the historical process are always incomplete" and that a revolution tends to raise hopes that it cannot satisfy.[43] Blacks of the Revolutionary War era would have been more receptive to the contention of jurist Benjamin N. Cardozo that a principle has a tendency "to expand itself to the limit of its logic."[44] For them the war and the freedom concepts it sprouted bore their own seeds of regeneration.

In fine, the Revolutionary War can be termed a black Declaration of Independence in the sense it spurred black Americans to seek freedom and equality. The Afro-Americans of that era stood wholeheartedly among those who viewed the war as an ongoing revolution in freedom's cause. To a degree approaching unanimity, they clothed the War for Independence with a meaning and a significance transcending their own day and time and not confined to the shores of the new republic. To them the full worth of the American Revolution lay ahead.

Endnotes

1. Charles W. Brewster, *Rambles about Portsmouth: Sketches of Persons, Localities, and Incidents of Two Centuries: Principally from Tradition and Unpublished Sources* (Portsmouth, N.H., 1859, p. 153.
2. On this point see Ira Berlin, "Time, Space, and the Evolution of Afro-American Society in British Mainland North America," *American Historical Review* 85 (1980):44–78, and idem, "The Revolution in Black Life," in Alfred F. Young, ed., *The American Revolution: Explorations in the History of American Radicalism* (DeKalb, Ill., 1976), pp. 351–82.
3. *The American Revolution Considered as a Social Movement* (Princeton, 1926).
4. Jesse Lemisch, "The American Revolution Seen from the Bottom Up," in Barton J. Bernstein, ed., *Towards a New Past: Dissenting Essays in American History* (New York, 1968), pp. 3–29; Young, *American Revolution*.
5. *The Literary History of the American Revolution, 1763–1783*, 2 vols. (1897; reprint ed., New York, 1957), 1:8.
6. *Tremenda: The Dreadful Sound with Which the Wicked Are to Be Thunderstruck . . .* (Boston, 1721), quoted in Lawrence W. Towner, "'A Fondness for Freedom': Servant Protest in Puritan Society," *William and Mary Quarterly*, 3d ser. 19 (1962):201. For a penetrating analysis of Mather's views on slavery, see Daniel K. Richter, "'It Is God Who Has Caused Them To Be Servants': Cotton Mather and Afro-American Slavery in New England," *Bulletin of the Congregational Library* 15 (1979):3–13.
7. *Laboring and Dependent Classes in Colonial America, 1607–1783* (Chicago, 1931), p. 23.
8. *Black Majority: Negroes in Colonial South Carolina from 1670 through the Stono Rebellion* (New York, 1974), p. 199.
9. *The Black Experience in Revolutionary North Carolina* (Raleigh, N.C., 1977), p. 12.
10. *A History of Negro Slavery in New York* (Syracuse, N.Y., 1966), p. 47.

11. *The Negro in Colonial New England* (New York, 1942), p. 101.
12. Time, Space, and the Evolution of Afro-American Society," p. 49.
13. *The Private Journal of Sarah Kemble Knight: Being the Record of a Journey from Boston to New York in the Year 1704* (1825; reprinted, Norwich, Conn., 1901), p. 52.
14. *Seasonable Thoughts on the State of Religion in New England* (Boston, 1743), quoted in Eldon J. Eisenbach, "Cultural Politics and Political Thought: The American Revolution Made and Remembered," *American Studies* 20 (1979):74.
15. Frank J. Klingberg, An Appraisal of the Negro in Colonial South Carolina (Washington, D.C., 1941), pp. 111 and 114–15
16. George S. Brookes, *Friend Anthony Benezet* (Philadelphia, 1937), p. 45.
17. *White over Black: American Attitudes toward the Negro, 1550–1812* (Chapel Hill, N.C., 1968), p. 137.
18. Petition reproduced in Isaac W. Hammond, "Slavery in New Hampshire in Olden Time," *Granite Monthly* 4 (1880): 108–10.
19. "The 'Disaffected' in the Revolutionary South," in Young, *American Revolution*, p. 281.
20. *A Spirit of Dissension: Economics, Politics, and the Revolution in Maryland* (Baltimore, 1973), p. 148.
21. John Chester Miller, *The Wolf by the Ears: Thomas Jefferson and Slavery* (New York, 1977), p. 26.
22. David O. White, *Connecticut's Black Soldiers, 1775–1783* (Chester, Conn.,1973), pp. 57–64.
23. Petition reproduced in Roger Bruns, ed., *Am I Not a Man and a Brother: The Antislavery Crusade of Revolutionary America, 1688–1788* (New York, 1977), pp. 454–56.
24. *Flight and Rebellion: Slave Resistance in Eighteenth-Century Virginia* (New York, 1972), pp. 140–63.
25. Ibid., p. 157.
26. Oscar Wegelin, *Jupiter Hammon, A Negro Poet: Selections from His Writings and a Bibliography* (Miami, Fla., 1969), p. 27.
27. *Slaves without Masters: The Free Negro in the Antebellum South* (New York, 1974).
28. Miles Mark Fisher, *Negro Slave Songs in the United States* (Ithaca, N.Y., 1953), p. 40.
29. Charles H. Wesley, *Richard Allen: Apostle of Freedom* (Washington, D.C., 1935), pp. 52–53
30. *Segregated Sabbaths: Richard Allen and the Rise of Independent Black Churches, 1750–1840* (New York, 1973), p. 9.
31. E. Horace Fitchett, "The Traditions of the Free Negro in Charleston, South Carolina," *Journal of Negro History* 25 (1940): 144.
32. Floyd J. Miller, *The Search for a Black Nationality: Black Emigration and Colonization, 1787–1863* (Urbana, Ill., 1975), pp. 8, 16, and 34.
33. Dorothy Porter, ed., *Negro Protest Pamphlets* (New York, 1969), p. 23.
34. Miller, *Search for a Black Nationality*, pp. 7–9, and 15–20.
35. Harles H. Wesley, *Prince Hall: Life and Legacy* (Washington, D.C., 1977), pp. 124 and 142. For a facsimile of the charter from the British Grand Lodge, see p. 49.
36. "A Charge Delivered to the Brethren of the African Lodge . . . in Dorothy Porter, ed., *Early Negro Writing, 1760–1837* (Boston, 1971), p. 67.
37. Jones to Pennsylvania Abolition Society, Mar. 11, 1799, Papers of the Pennsylvania Society for Promoting the Abolition of Slavery, and for the Relief of Free Negroes Unlawfully Held in Bondage, and for Improving the Condition of the African Race, Pennsylvania Historical Society, Philadelphia.
38. Greene, *Negro in Colonial New England*, p. 255.
39. *Baltimore Daily Repository*, Sept. 26, 1792.
40. Indeed, down to the Civil War era blacks wielded little power as voters except for a twenty-year span, 1800–1820, when the Federalist party wooed their vote, See Dixon Ryan Fox, "The Negro Vote in Old New York," *Political Science Quarterly* 32 (1917): 252–75. No black would hold elective office until 1854, when the voters of Oberlin, Ohio, chose John Mercer Langston as township clerk.
41. Petition in Porter, *Early Negro Writing*, pp. 330–32.
42. U.S., Congress, House, *Congressional Record*, 6th Cong., Jan. 3, 1800, pp. 244–45.
43. *The Pursuit of Equality in American History* (Berkeley, Calif., 1978), p. 325.
44. *The Nature of the Judicial Process* (New Haven, 1932), p. 51, quoted in A. Leon Higginbotham, Jr., *In the Matter of Color: Race and the American Legal Process* (New York, 1978), pp. 383–84.

Slaves Petition for Freedom During the Revolution, 1773–1779

Herbert Aptheker, ed.

The ferment preceding and accompanying the Revolutionary War, stimulated many Negro people, collectively and individually, to make public pleas against slavery and to point out to the less than two and a half million American white people the incongruity and the danger of shouting 'Liberty or Death' while enslaving 750,000 human beings. There follow five examples of such statements covering the years from 1773 through 1779.

✳ ✳ ✳ ✳ ✳

[a]

Province of the Massachusetts Bay To His Excellency Thomas Hutchinson, Esq; Governor; To The Honorable His Majesty's Council, and To the Honorable House of Representatives in General Court assembled at Boston, the 6th Day of *January*, 1773.

The humble PETITION of many Slaves, living in the Town of Boston, and other Towns in the Province is this, namely

That your Excellency and Honors, and the Honorable the Representatives would be pleased to take their unhappy State and Condition under your wise and just Consideration.

We desire to bless God, who loves Mankind, who sent his Son to die for their Salvation, and who is no respecter of Persons; that He hath lately put it into the Hearts of Multitudes on both Sides of the Water, to bear our Burthens, some of whom are Men of great Note and Influence; who have pleaded our Cause with Arguments which we hope will have their weight with this Honorable Court.

We presume not to dictate to your Excellency and Honors, being willing to rest our Cause on your Humanity and justice; yet would beg Leave to say a Word or two on the Subject.

Although some of the Negroes are vicious, (who doubtless may be punished and restrained by the same Laws which are in Force against other of the King's Subjects) there are many others of a quite different Character, and who, if made free, would soon be able as well as willing to bear a Part in the Public Charges; many of them of good natural Parts, are discreet, sober, honest, and industrious; and may it not be said of many, that they are virtuous and religious, although their Condition is in itself so unfriendly to Religion, and every moral Virtue except *Patience*. How many of that Number have there been, and now are in this Province, who have had every Day of their Lives imbittered with this most intollerable Reflection, That, let their Behaviour be what it will, neither they, nor their Children to all Generations, shall ever be able to do, or to possess and enjoy any Thing, no, not even *Life itself*, but in a Manner as the *Beasts that perish*.

We have no Property! We have no Wives! No Children! We have no City! No Country! But we have a Father in Heaven, and we are determined, as far as his Grace shall enable us, and as far as our degraded contemptuous Life will admit, to keep all his Commandments: Especially will we be obedient to our Masters, so long as God in his sovereign Providence shall suffer us to beholden in Bondage.

It would be impudent, if not presumptuous in us, to suggest to your Excellency and Honors any Law or Laws proper to be made, in relation to our unhappy State, which, although our greatest Unhappiness, is not our Fault; and this gives us great Encouragement to pray and hope for such Relief as is consistent with your Wisdom, Justice, and Goodness.

We think Ourselves very happy, that we may thus address the Great and General Court of this Province, which great and good Court is to us, the best Judge, under God, of what is wise, just and good.

We humbly beg Leave to add but this one Thing more: We pray for such Relief only, which by no Possibility can ever be productive of the least Wrong or Injury to our Masters; but to us will be as Life from the dead.

Signed,

FELIX

————

The Appendix: or, some Observations on the expediency of the Petition of the Africans, living in Boston, &c., lately presented to the General Assembly of this Province. To which is annexed, the Petition referred to. Likewise, Thoughts on Slavery with a useful extract from the Massachusetts Spy, of January 28, 1773, by way of an Address to the Members of the Assembly. By a Lover of Constitutional Liberty. (Boston, E. Russell, n.d.) pp. 9–11. Copy in the *Boston Athenaeum.*

[b]

Boston, April 20th, 1773

Sir, The efforts made by the legislative of this province in their last sessions to free themselves from slavery, gave us, who are in that deplorable state, a high degree of satisfaction. We expect great things from men who have made such a noble stand against the designs of their *fellow-men* to enslave them. We cannot but wish and hope Sir, that you will have the same grand object, we mean civil and religious liberty, in view in your next session. The divine spirit of *freedom* seems to fire every humane breast on this continent, except such as are bribed to assist in executing the execrable plan.

We are very sensible that it would be highly detrimental to our present masters, if we were allowed to demand all that of *right* belongs to us for past services; this we disclaim. Even the *Spaniards,* who have not those sublime ideas of freedom that English men have, are conscious that they have no right to all the services of their fellow-men, we mean the Africans, whom they have purchased with their money; therefore they allow them one day in a week to work for themselves, to enable them to earn money to purchase the residue of their time, which they have a right to demand in such portions as they are able to pay for (a due appraizement of their services being first made, which always stands at the purchase money.) We do not pretend to dictate to you Sir, or to the Honorable Assembly, of which you are a member. We acknowledge our obligations to you for what you have already done, but as the people of this province seem to be actuated by the principles of equity and justice, we cannot but expect your house will again take our deplorable case into serious consideration, and give us that ample relief which, as men, we have a natural right to.

But since the wise and righteous governor of the universe, has permitted our fellow men to make us slaves, we bow in submission to him, and determine to behave in such a manner as that we may have reason to expect the divine approbation of, and assistance in, our peaceable and lawful attempts to gain our freedom.

We are willing to submit to such regulations and laws, as may be made relative to us, until we leave the province, which we determine to do as soon as we can, from our joynt labours procure money to transport ourselves to some part of the Coast of *Africa,* where we propose a settlement. We are very desirous that you should have instructions relative to us, from your town, therefore we pray you to communicate this letter to them, and ask this favor for us.

In behalf of our fellow slaves in this province, and by order of their Committee.

Peter Bestes,
Sambo Freeman,
Felix Holbrook,
Chester Joie.

For the Representative of the town of Thompson.

————

Printed leaflet, original in library of New York Historical Society; photostat in Boston Public Library. The last word in this leaflet—Thompson—was written in ink.

[c]

To his Excellency Thomas Gage Esq. Captain General and Governor in Chief in and over this Province.
To the Honourable his Majestys Council and the Honourable House of Representatives in General Court assembled May 25 1774

The Petition of a Grate Number of Blackes of this Province who by divine permission are held in a state of Slavery within the bowels of a free and christian Country

Humbly Shewing

That your Petitioners apprehind we have in common with all other men a naturel right to our freedoms without Being depriv'd of them by our fellow men as we are a freeborn Pepel and have never forfeited this Blessing by aney compact or agreement whatever. But we were unjustly dragged by the cruel hand of power from our dearest frinds and sum of us stolen from the bosoms of our tender Parents and from a Populous Pleasant and plentiful country and Brought hither to be made slaves for Life in a Christian land. Thus we are deprived of every thing that hath a tendency to make life even tolerable, the endearing ties of husband and wife we are strangers to for we are no longer man and wife than our masters or mistresses thinkes proper marred or onmarred. Our children are also taken from us by force and sent maney miles from us wear we seldom or ever see them again there to be made slaves of for Life which sumtimes is vere short by Reson of Being dragged from their mothers Breest Thus our Lives are imbittered to us on these accounts By our deplorable situation we are rendered incapable of shewing our obedience to Almighty God how can a slave perform the duties of a husband to a wife or parent to his child How can a husband leave master to work and cleave to his wife How can the wife submit themselves to there husbands in all things How can the child obey thear parents in all things. There is a great number of us sencear . . . members of the Church of Christ how can the master and the slave be said to fulfil that command Live in love let Brotherly Love contuner and abound Beare yea onenothers Bordenes How can the master be said to Beare my Borden when he Beares me down whith the Have chanes of slavery and operson against my will and how can we fulfill our parte of duty to him whilst in this condition and as we cannot searve our

God as we ought whilst in this situation. Nither can we reap an equal benefet from the laws of the Land which doth not justifi but condemns Slavery or if there had bin aney Law to hold us in Bondage we are Humbely of the Opinion ther never was aney to inslave our children for life when Born in a free Countrey. We therfor Bage your Excellency and Honours will give this its deer weight and consideration and that you will accordingly cause an act of the legislative to be pessed that we may obtain our Natural right our freedoms and our children be set at lebety at the yeare of twenty one for whoues sekes more petequeley your Petitioners is in Duty ever to pray.

———— ——

Collections, Massachusetts Historical Society, 5th Series, III (Boston, 1817) pp. 432–37 for above and the following petition.

[d]

To the Honorable Counsel & House of [Represental tives for the State of Massachusetts Bay in General Court assembled, January 13, 1777

The petition of A Great Number of Blackes detained in a State of slavery in the Bowels of a free & Christian Country Humbly sheweth that your Petitioners apprehend that they have in Common with all other men a Natural and Unaliable Right to that freedom which the Grat Parent of the Unavers hath Bestowed equalley on all menkind and which they have Never forfeited by any Compact or agreement whatever—but that wher Unjustly Dragged by the hand of cruel Power from their Derest friends and sum of them Even torn from the Embraces of their tender Parents—from A populous Pleasant and plentiful country and in violation of Laws of Nature and off Nations and in defiance of all the tender feelings of humanity Brough hear Either to Be sold Like Beast of Burthen & Like them Condemnd to Slavery for Life—Among A People Profesing the mild Religion of Jesus A people Not Insensible of the Secrets of Rational Being Nor without spirit to Resent the unjust endeavours of others to Reduce them to a state of Bondage and Subjection your honouer Need not to be informed that A Live of Slavery Like that of your petioners Deprived of Every social privilege of Every thing Requisit to Render Life Tolable is far worse then Nonexistence.

[In imitate]ion of the Lawdable Example of the Good People of these States your petitiononers have Long and Patiently waited the Evnt of petition after petition By them presented to the Legislative Body of this state and cannot but with Grief Reflect that their Sucess hath ben but too similar they Cannot but express their Astonishment that It have Never Bin Considerd that Every Principle from which Amarica has Acted in the Cours of their unhappy Dificultes with Great Briton Pleads Stronger than A thousand arguments in favours of your petioners they therfor humble Beseech your honours to give this petion its due weight & consideration & cause an act of the Legislatur to be past Wherby they may be Restored to the Enjoyments of that which is the Naturel Right of all men—and their Children who wher Born in this Land of Liberty may not be heald as Slaves after they arive at the age of twenty one years so may the Inhabitance of this Stats No longer chargeable with the inconsistancey of acting themselves the part which they condem and oppose in others Be prospered in their present Glorious struggle for Liberty and have those Blessing to them, &c.

[e]

To the Honbl. General Assembly of the State of Connecticut to be held at Hartford on the Second Thursday of Instant May [1779]—The Petition of the Negroes in the Towns of Stratford and Fairfield in the County of Fairfield who are held in a State of Slavery humbly sheweth—

That many of your Petitioners, were (as they verily believe) most unjustly torn, from the Bosom of their dear Parents, and Friends, and without any Crime, by them committed, doomed, and bound down, to perpetual Slavery; and as if the Perpetrators of this horrid Wickedness, were conscious (that we poor Ignorant Africans, upon the least Glimering Sight, derived from a Knowledge of the Sense and Practice of civilized Nations) should Convince them of their Sin, they have added another dreadful Evil, that of holding us in gross Ignorance, so as to render Our Subjection more easy and tolerable. may it please your Honours, we are most grievously affected, under the Consideration of the flagrant Injustice; Your Honours who are nobly contending, in the Cause of Liberty, whose Conduct excites the Admiration, and Reverence, of all the great Empires of the World; will not resent, our thus freely animadverting, on this detestable Practice; altho our Skins are different in Colour, from those whom we serve, Yet Reason & Revelation join to declare, that we are the Creatures of that God, who made of one Blood, and Kindred, all the Nations of the Earth; we perceive by our own Reflection, that we are endowed with the same Faculties with our masters, and there is nothing that leads us to a Belief, or Suspicion, that we are any more obliged to serve them, than they us, and the more we Consider of this matter, the more we are Convinced of our Right (by the Laws of Nature and by the whole Tenor of the Christian Religion, so far as we have been taught) to be free; we have endeavoured rightly to understand what is our Right, and what is our Duty, and can never be convinced that we were made to be Slaves. Altho God almighty may justly lay this, and more upon us, yet we deserve it not, from the hands of Men. We are impatient under the grievous Yoke, but our Reason teaches us that it is not best for us to use violent measures, to cast it off; we are also convinced, that we are unable to extricate ourselves from our abject State; but we think we may with the greatest Propriety look up to your Honours, (who are the fathers of the People) for Relief. And we not only groan under our own burden, but with concern, & Horror, look forward, & contemplate, the miserable Condition of our Children, who are training up, and kept in Preparation, for a like State of Bondage, and Servitude. We beg leave to submit, to your Honours serious Consideration, whether it is consistent with the present Claims, of the united States, to hold so many Thousands, of the Race of Adam, our Common Father, in perpetual Slavery. Can human Nature endure the Shocking Idea? can your Honours any longer Suffer this great Evil to prevail under your Government: we entreat your Honours, let no considerations of Publick Inconvenience deter your Honours from interposing in behalf of your Petitioners; we ask for nothing, but what we are fully persuaded is ours to Claim. we beseech your Honours to weigh this matter in the Scale of justice, and in your great Wisdom and goodness, apply such Remedy as the Evil does require; and let your Petitioners rejoice with your Honours in the Participation with your Honours of that inestimable Blessing, Freedom and your Humble Petitioners, as in Duty bound shall ever pray &c.

dated in Fairfield the
11th Day of May AD 1779—

Signed in Presence of
Jonth Sturges.

in Behalf of
themselves and
the other Petioners

prime a Negro man
servant to Mr.
Vam A. Sturge
of Fairfield
his
Prince X a Negro man
mark
servant of Capt. Stephen Jenings
of Fairfield——

———

Photostat of original document in Archives, Connecticut State Library. Dr. Lorenzo J. Greene, of Lincoln University, Jefferson City, Missouri, very kindly lent this photostat to the editor.

Gaining Freedom During the Revolution, 1779–1784

Herbert Aptheker, ed.

The Revolution itself made it possible for many Negroes to gain their freedom in a number of ways. Two such methods, one stemming from the fight of a Tory master and the other from faithful service by the Negro in the Revolutionary Army, are illustrated in the two documents below of the years 1779 and 1784. The second method, service in the Revolutionary Army, was a very common one, since some five thousand Negroes fought in that Army, of whom many were slaves.

* * * * *

[a]

To the Honble the General Assembly of the Governor and Company of the State of Connecticut Now Sitting at Hartford in said State—

The memorial of Pomp a Negro man Slave belonging to the Estate of Jeremiah Leaming late of Norwalk in the County of Fairfield in said State— Clerk now absconded and with, the Enemy at open war with the United States of America and under their protection humbly shewith—

That on the 11th Day of July last past the said Jeremiah Leaming with his Family Voluntarily join'd the British Troops in said Norwalk and with them then went over to Long Island and New York and hath ever since their [sic] continued under their protection—

That your Honors Memorialist being unwilling to go with his said master over to the Enemy made his Escape from him while the said Troops were in said Norwalk and is held and Considered as a part of the Estate of his said Master and forfeited to the said State of Connecticut—

That the said Jeremiah Leamings Estate hath been a Special County Court held at Fairfield with and for the County of Fairfield on the 4th Tuesday of September last past Declared and adjudged forfeit to said State and since Administration hath been granted thereon to Samuel Gruman of Sd. Norwalk who is now about to Inventory the same wherein your Honors Memorialist must be included and considered a part of his master('s) Estate as your Honors Memorialist is advised notwithstanding your Honors Memorialist at the Time of his Sd. Master(')s joining the Enemy veryly tho't and believed by his remaining in said Norwalk and preventing by his Escape as aforesd. his masters taking him with him over to the Enemy he should have obtained his Freedom from Slavery and that your Honors Memorialist is about Thirty Years of Age and of a firm and healthy Constitution and able to well-provide for himself and a Wife and Child and that his Wife is a free woman and your Honors Memorialist is advised that he cannot be Emancipated without your Honors Consent as he is now become the property of the Sd. State altho the Selectmen of Sd. Norwalk judge your Honors Memorialist a proper Subject of Freedom— Wherefore your Honors Memorialist humbly prays your Honors to take his Case into your wise Consideration and resolve that he be freed from his State of Slavery or in such other way grant him such relief in the premises as your Honors in your great

Wisdom shall judge proper and he as in Duty Bound shall Ever pray Dated at Norwalk the 20th Day of October A.D. 1779

his

Pomp X

mark

———

Archives, Connecticut State Library. Photostat kindly provided the editor by Dr. Lorenzo J. Greene.

[b]

To The General Assembly of the State of North Carolina

The Petitioner of Ned Griffin a Man of mixed Blood Humbley Saieth that a Small space of Time before the Battle of Gilford a certain William Kitchen then in the Service of his Countrey as a Soldier Deserted from his line for which he was Turned in to the Continental Service to serve as the Law Directs—Your Petitioner was then a Servant to William Griffin and was purchased by the said Kitchen for the purpose of Serving in His place, with a Solom Assurance that if he your Petitioner would faithfully serve the Term of Time that the said Kitchen was Returned for be should be a free Man— Upon which said Promise and Assurance your Petitioner Consented to enter in to the Continental Service in said Kitchens Behalf and was Received by Colo: James Armstrong At Martinborough as a free Man Your Petitioner furter saieth that at that Time no Person could have been hired to have served in said Kitchens behalf for so small a sum as what I was purchased for and that at the Time that I was Received into Service by said Colo: Armstrong said Kitchen Openly Declared me to be free Man— The Faithfull purformance of the above agreement will appear from my Discharge—some Time after your Petitioners Return he was Seized upon by said Kitchen and Sold to a Certain Abner Roberson, who now holds me as a Servant—Your Petitioner therefore thinks that by Contract and merit he is Intitled to his Freedom I therefore submit my case to your Honourable Body hoping that I shall have that justice done me as you in your Wisdom shall think I am Intitled to and Desarving of & Your Petitioner as in duty bound Will Pray

N Carolina	his
Edgecomb County	Ned X Griffin
April 4th 1784	mark

———

MS. in archives of the North Carolina Historical Commission, Raleigh, North Carolina. Photostat in editor's possession. Published by the editor in *The Negro History Bulletin*, November, 1949.

Negroes Protest against Taxation without Representation, 1780

Herbert Aptheker, ed.

Seven Negroes of Dartmouth, Massachusetts, including Paul Cuffe and his brother John, protested on February 10, 1780, in a petition to the revolutionary legislature of their state, against the fact that they were subjected to taxation without the right to vote. In 1793, by court decision, Negroes subject to taxation were declared to be entitled to the suffrage.

The Paul Cuffe involved in this petition became a successful ship captain and merchant. In 1815 he pioneered in the actual colonization of West Africa by American Negroes, transporting at his own expense thirty-eight Negroes for this purpose.

*****

To The Honouerable Councel and House of Representives in General Court assembled for the State of the Massachusetts Bay in New England— March 14th A D 1780—

The petition of several poor Negroes & molattoes who are Inhabitant of the Town of Dartmouth Humbly Sheweth—That we being Chiefly of the African Extract and by Reason of Long Bondag and hard Slavery we have been deprived of Injoying the Profits of our Labouer or the advantage of Inheriting Estates from our Parents as our Neighbouers the white people do haveing some of us not long Injoyed our own freedom & yet of late, Contrary to the invariable Custom & Practice of the Country we have been & now are Taxed both in our Polls and that small Pittance of Estate which through much hard Labour & Industry we have got together to Sustain our selves & families withal—We apprehand it therefore to be hard usag and [one word is illegible here— ed.] doubtless (if Continued will) Reduce us to a State of Beggary whereby we shall become a Berthan to others if not timely prevented by the Interposition of your justice & power & yor Petitioners farther sheweth that we appreband ourselves to be Aggreeved, in that while we are not allowed the Privilage of freemen of the State having no vote or Influence in the Election of those that Tax us yet many of our Colour (as is well known) have cheerfully Entered the field of Battle in the defence of the Common Cause and that (as we conceive) against a similar Exertion of Power (in Regard to taxation) too well Known to need a recital in this place—

That these the Most honouerable Court we Humbley Beseech they would to take this into Considerration and Let us aside from Paying tax or taxes or cause us to Be Cleaired for we ever have Been a people that was fair from all these thing ever since the days of our four fathers and therefore we take it as aheard ship that we should be so delt By now in these Difficulty times for their is not to exceed more then five or six that hath a cow in this town and theirfore in our Distress we send unto the peaceableness of thee people and the mercy of God that we may be Releaved for we are not alowed in voating in the town meating in nur to chuse an oficer Neither their was not one ever heard in the active Court of the General Assembly the poor

Dispised miserable Black people, & we have not an equal chance with white people neither by Sea nur by Land therefore we take it as a heard ship that poor old Negroes should be Rated which have been in Bondage some thirty some forty and some fifty years and now just got their Liberty some by going into the serviese and some by going to Sea and others by good fortan and also poor Distressed mungrels which have no larning and no land and also no [one word illegible — ed.] Neither where to put their head but some shelter them selves into an old rotten hut which thy dogs would not lay in

Therefore we pray that these may give no offence at all By no means But that thee most Honouerable Court will take it in to consideration as if it were their own case for we think it as to be a heard ship that we should be assessed and not be a lowed as we may say to Eat Bread therefore we Humbley Beg and pray thee to plead our Case for us with thy people O God; that those who have the rule in their hands may be mercyfull unto the poor and needy give unto those who ask of thee and he that would Borrow of thee turn not away empty: O God be mercyfull unto the poor and give unto those who give ought unto the poor therefore we return unto thee again: most honouerable Court that thou wouldst Consider us in these Difficut times for we send in nur come unto thee not with false words Neither with lieing Lips therefore we think that we may be clear from being called tories tho some few of our Colour bath Rebelled and Done Wickedly however we think that their is more of our Collour gone into the wars according to the Number of them into the Respepiktive towns then any other nation here and [one word illegible — ed.] therefore We most humbley Request therefore that you would take our unhappy Case into your serious Consideration and in your wisdom and Power grant us Relief from Taxation while under our Present depressed Circumstances and your poor Petioners as in duty bound shall ever pray &c

———

Manuscript in Archives Division, Massachusetts Historical Society; photostat in editor's possession.

Thomas Jefferson and the Problem of Slavery*

William Cohen**

It seems paradoxical that Thomas Jefferson, one of the enduring heroes of American democracy, should have been the owner of more than 180 slaves at the very time when he was proclaiming that all men were created equal and that they were "endowed by their Creator" with the "unalienable Rights" of "Life, Liberty and the pursuit of Happiness." Moreover, throughout his life he continued to hold that slavery was unjust and immoral. In 1785 he had used the phrase "avarice and oppression" to characterize the slaveholding interest, and he contrasted this with the "sacred side" of emancipation. A year later, he marveled at the fact that American patriots who had endured beatings, starvation, and imprisonment at the hands of their British oppressors could inflict "on their fellow men a bondage one hour of which is fraught with more misery than ages of that which he rose in rebellion to oppose." In the final year of his life, he reiterated his belief that it was unlawful for "one man to appropriate to himself the faculties of another without his consent."[1]

Most Jefferson scholars have dealt with this contradiction by ignoring it, or by citing his views on abolition and holding that his role as an owner of men was entailed upon him. Born into a slave system, they argue, he could not in good conscience abandon his black charges; he made the best of a bad situation by behaving as a benevolent and indulgent master. Indeed, the most competent and scholarly biographer of Jefferson contends that "if the master himself erred [in handling his slaves] he did so on the side of leniency."[2]

This argument is supported by Jefferson's own remarks. The most famous of these comments is his reply to a letter from Edward Coles, a Virginia slaveholder, who, in 1814, urged him to take the leadership of the abolition cause and described his own plan to move to a free state. Jefferson answered by agreeing with Coles' sentiments and saying:

> The love of justice and the love of country plead equally the cause of the people [slaves], and it is a moral reproach to us that they should have pleaded it so long in vain, and should have produced not a single effort, nay I fear not much serious willingness to relieve them and ourselves from our present condition of moral and political reprobation.[3]

Jefferson then described his own idea of a practical plan for abolition, but, taking note of the fact that he was now an old man, he left the antislavery enterprise to the young "who can follow it up." He urged Coles not to shirk his responsibility to his slaves by leaving Virginia and added:

> until more can be done for them, we should endeavor with those whom fortune has thrown on our hands, to feed and clothe them well, protect them from all ill usage, require such reasonable labor only as is performed voluntarily by freemen, and he led by no repugnancies to abdicate them, and our duties to them .[4]

This view of Jefferson as a proto-abolitionist master came under attack in 1961. Robert McColley's *Slavery and Jeffersonian Virginia* depicted the author of the Declaration of Independence as a man who believed in Negro inferiority and whose public actions frequently favored the slave system. Devoted to showing that the institution of slavery actually gained strength during the post-Revolutionary era, this work often used Jefferson as an example of the

* Original version published in The Journal of American History, no. 3: Dec, 1969. The Portuguese translation was published in Revista Estudos Avançados, no. 38: Jan.-April, 2000.
** William Cohen is research associate at the Center for Urban Studies, University of Chicago.

planter class and argued that political expediency and racist ideology prevented him from working effectively against the system.[5]

More recently, Winthrop Jordan devoted a chapter of his study to an analysis of the contradiction within Jefferson's thought on the subject of black servitude. Accepting the traditional formulation that the Virginian was trapped by a system he abhorred, Jordan defined Jefferson's central dilemma as being that he "hated slavery but thought Negroes inferior to white men." Taking note of Jefferson's daily personal involvement with the slave system, Jordan concluded that "his heartfelt hatred of slavery did not derive so much from this harassing personal entanglement in the practicalities of slavery as from the system of politics in which he was enmeshed mentally."[6]

Jordan treated the problem almost exclusively in terms of Jefferson's ideas and emotions, and his perceptive account described the confusion which emerged from the clash of the contradictory tendencies within the Virginian's thought. First, his belief in a single creation and in a universe governed by natural law led him inexorably toward the view that the concept of natural rights applied to Negroes by virtue of the fact that they were human beings too. Second, Jefferson also held an intuitive belief in the inferiority of the blacks, which he tried to cover up with an appeal to science, but which actually stemmed from the interaction between his own psychological makeup and the mores of the society which surrounded him. Jefferson's refusal to accept an environmentalist explanation for the apparent inferiority of the blacks led to a confusion which Jordan termed "monumental." For if the Negroes were innately inferior, then Jefferson must have "suspected that the Creator might have in fact created men unequal; and he could not say this without giving his assertion exactly the same logical force as his famous statement to the contrary."[7]

Jordan's work is valuable for its analysis of Jefferson's intellectual entanglement with slavery, but it does not delve into Jefferson's day to day relationship with slavery. This is important because Jefferson's practical involvement with the system of black bondage indicates that, while his racist beliefs were generally congruent with his actions, his libertarian views about slavery tended to be mere intellectual abstractions. This is particularly true for the years after 1785; and to a somewhat lesser degree, it holds true for the earlier period as well.

Upon the death of his father in 1757, Jefferson inherited more than 5,000 acres of land and twenty slaves. By 1774, natural increase, purchases, and the deed of all Negroes owned by his mother brought this number to forty-two. At this time he acquired (on his wife's behalf), 11,000 more acres and 135 slaves as his share of the estate of his father-in-law, John Wayles. Debts on this property caused the sale of about half the new land, but even so, he was left with more than 5,000 acres which, when added to his own land, gave him an estate of more than 10,000 acres; and it remained at about this size until his death.[8]

As a result of the inheritance, Jefferson owned 187 men, women, and children, but the figure changed from year to year with births, deaths, purchases, and sales. In 1783, despite the loss of thirty slaves to the British, it rose to 204. By 1798, he owned only 147 Negroes because he had sold over fifty bondsmen to pay off his debts. The number increased to 197 in 1810; and, by 1822, it reached 267. After 1774, Jefferson's holdings in land and Negroes made him the second wealthiest man in Albemarle County and one of the richest men in Virginia.[9]

This new status did not prevent him from advocating the abolition of the slave trade and even of slavery itself during the years 1774–1784, but the extent of this activity should not be exaggerated. In 1774, as opposition to Britain increased, Jefferson indicted the British monarch for the disallowance of Virginia laws which would have ended the African slave trade in the colony. Putting the blame on the British government without condemning those who currently perpetuated the system, he wrote:

> For the most trifling reasons, [. . .] his majesty has rejected laws of the most salutary tendency. The abolition of domestic slavery is the great object of desire in those colonies where it was unhappily introduced in their infant state. But previous to the enfranchisement of the slaves we have, it is necessary to exclude all further importations from Africa. Yet our repeated attempts to effect this [. . .] have been hitherto defeated by his majesty's negative.[10]

As the crisis with England deepened, Jefferson became more positive in his opposition to the slave trade. The draft he wrote in 1776 of a constitution for Virginia contained a provision that "No person hereafter coming into this country [Virginia] shall be held in slavery under any pretext whatever."[11] The document was not adopted, but Jefferson continued to attack the slave trade; and in his draft of the Declaration of Independence he included a paragraph reminiscent of the remarks he had made in 1774. George III, he charged:

> waged cruel war against human nature itself, violating its most sacred rights of life and liberty in the persons of a distant people who never offended him [. . .] This piratical warfare, the opprobrium of *infidel* powers, is the warfare of the *Christian* king of Great Britain. Determined to keep open a market where MEN should be bought and sold, he has prostituted his negative for suppressing every legislative attempt to prohibit or to restrain this execrable commerce [. . .][12]

Jefferson made this onslaught despite the fact that his fortune was founded partly upon profits derived from the slave trade. His father-in-law had engaged in this commerce, and several of the bondsmen inherited by Jefferson bore African names. Moreover, the locations of the Negro quarters were indicated in his "Farm Book" by such appellations as Angola and Guinea.[13]

Of far greater significance, however, was Jefferson's charge that the slave trade violated the "most sacred rights of life and liberty in the persons of a distant people." These words show clearly that, when he spoke of man's "unalienable Rights," he meant black men too. This is not to imply that he believed the races to be equal in endowment. In 1784, Jefferson expressed the "suspicion" that Negroes were inherently inferior to whites; and he seems to have retained this view throughout his life. The apparent contradiction between his belief in equal rights and his position that Negroes were not on a par with whites is partly explained by remarks he made in 1809 when he argued that "whatever be their degree of talent it is no measure of their rights. Because Sir Isaac Newton was superior to others in understanding, he was not therefore lord of the person or property of others."[14]

In 1778, Virginia outlawed the slave trade. There is no evidence that Jefferson participated directly in securing the passage of the law, but there can be little doubt that, at the very least, he helped to create the climate for it.[15] Nevertheless, the bill did not lead to the emancipations that Jefferson had indicated would follow in the wake of such an action. Indeed, there was no necessary connection between opposition to the trade and support of slavery itself. In the case of Jefferson, it is quite likely that there was a link between his opposition to this commerce

and his distaste for slavery, but other masters might oppose it for a wide variety of other reasons including a realization of the fact that the price of slaves would rise if the trade were cut off.

Jefferson was more circumspect in dealing directly with the question of abolition. In 1769, during his first term in the House of Burgesses, he seconded a motion for the adoption of a law which would permit masters to manumit their slaves, but it did not pass. When such a law was adopted in 1782, Jefferson failed to free his own bondsmen.[16] In three other instances Jefferson proposed specific plans which called for emancipation, but he was less than vigorous in pressing for their adoption and only the Ordinance of 1784 was actually brought before a public body for consideration.[17]

In November 1776, Jefferson was chosen as a member of a committee whose task was to revise, modernize, and codify the statutes of Virginia. Among his assignments was the job of drawing up the legislation dealing with slaves. He later described this bill, which he completed in 1778, as a "mere digest" of the existing legislation on the subject, and to a certain extent this was true. The bill did contain a strengthened version of a law which prohibited the slave trade, and Jefferson was merely codifying previous laws when he included provisions barring Negroes from testifying against whites and forbidding slaves to possess arms or to leave the property of their masters without a pass. Jefferson's measure also included the usual penalty of whipping for such slave offenses as rioting, presenting seditious speeches, and running away, but here, too, he was copying earlier legislation.[18]

Nevertheless, the bill was more than a digest of earlier codes and it contained some significant additions which were designed to prevent the increase of the state's free Negro population. It was to be illegal for free Negroes to come into Virginia of their own accord or to remain there for more than one year after they were emancipated. A white woman having a child by a Negro would be required to leave the state within a year. The individual who violated these regulations would be placed "out of the protection of the laws."[19] This would have left them subject to re-enslavement or even to murder at the whim of their neighbors and was, therefore, a most severe punishment.

It has been argued that Jefferson may have included these provisions in the belief that slavery would gradually die out because of an absence of new recruits to replenish the stock. This may have been his reason, but it seems unlikely in view of his own personal knowledge of the ratio of births to deaths on his plantation. During the years 1774–1778 there were at least twenty-two births and twelve deaths among his Negroes.[20] It must have been obvious to him that preventing further importations and limiting the growth of the free-Negro population would not stop the increase of the slave population due to natural causes. Another, and more reasonable, explanation is that Jefferson feared that a sizeable population of free Negroes would be an incitement to unrest among the slaves.

In 1784, Jefferson described his amendment to the Bill Pertaining to Slaves. It would have freed all bondsmen born after the passage of the act. Significantly, the amendment also provided that after a suitable period of education these blacks "should be colonized to such place as the circumstances of the time should render most proper," for he could not envision the two races living together peacefully on a plane of equality. When the bill was sent to the legislature for final action in 1785, the amendment did not accompany it because Jefferson "found that the public mind would not yet bear the proposition." He must have had grave doubts all along about its acceptability; there is no independent evidence (outside of Jefferson's own statement) of its existence, and he did nothing to help create a favorable reception for his proposed revision.[21] Moreover, his use of the words "such place as the circumstances of the time should render most proper" seems to suggest that he did not really believe his suggestion would be adopted in the immediate future.

The single most important antislavery act in Jefferson's career was writing a clause for the Ordinance of 1781 which would have barred slavery from the western territory (North and South) after 1800.[22] In this proposal is the germ of the free-soil doctrine of the nineteenth century, which accepted the existence of slavery where it had already taken root and attempted to stop its extension to new areas. Like many of his free-soil successors, Jefferson was seeking to protect whites from the baneful effects of slavery; and he certainly did not believe that the blacks could, or should, become equal partners in the building of these new western communities. The entire body of Jefferson's writings shows that he never seriously considered the possibility of any form of racial coexistence on the basis of equality

and that, from at least 1778 until his death, he saw colonization as the only alternative to slavery.[23]

Jefferson's proposal certainly foreshadowed these aspects of the free-soil doctrine, but he can scarcely be credited with originating the portion of the doctrine which held that, if slavery were prevented from further expansion, it would die a natural death. If such thoughts were in his mind in 1784, he certainly had repudiated them by 1820; and, when the Missouri question was dividing the nation, he wrote:

> Of one thing I am certain, that as the passage of slaves from one State to another would not make a slave of a single human being who would not be so without it, so their diffusion over a greater surface would make them individually happier, and proportionally facilitate the accomplishment of their emancipation, by dividing the burden on a greater number of coadjutors.[24]

The Ordinance of 1784 failed of adoption by one vote, but even if it had become law, bondage would have been legal in the area for sixteen years; and it seems likely that, if the institution of slavery had been allowed to get a foothold in the territory, the prohibition would have been repealed. Even after the Ordinance of 1787 banned slavery from the Northwest Territory, there was widespread sentiment in favor of rescinding the exclusion clause; and in 1802 a convention was held in Indiana under the auspices of Governor William Henry Harrison to petition Congress for its revocation. The request was denied, but, if slavery had been given a sixteen-year grace period in the entire western territory, Congress probably would have been forced to yield.[25] Thus, the Northwest Ordinance of 1787 was significantly different from Jefferson's proposal because, by providing for immediate freedom in the area, it rendered the possibility of a later repeal less likely. The Ordinance of 1784 marked Jefferson's last public attempt to limit or end slavery. Thereafter, he restricted his opposition to private letters directed to men whose views appeared to be in substantial agreement with his own. In these communications he deplored slavery and advocated expatriation as the only solution to this difficult problem.[26] One theme that emerges with great clarity from an evaluation of Jefferson's antislavery career is his steadfast opposition to the slave trade. On this issue public opinion was with him, and he did not temporize or take a moderate stand.

On the whole, however, there was a significant gap between his thought and action with regard to the abolition question. He fully believed that it was morally and politically evil to hold another man in slavery, but he continued to do so. Believing that bondage should be abolished, he wrote an amendment which would have accomplished this gradually. But lie kept it a secret for fear the public was not ready. Meanwhile, he codified Virginia's slave law and added to it harsh provisions aimed against free Negroes. He agreed to the desirability of keeping slavery out of the western territory, but his proposal would have allowed the disease a sixteen-year incubation period.

The contradiction in Jefferson's intellectual position stemmed in large part from his equivocal stance on the question of racial equality.[27] Jefferson's only systematic account of his views on race is to be found in *Notes on the State of Virginia*. Even here, the ambiguity of his position is pointed up by his attempts to prevent the work from being made public because he feared that the terms in which he spoke of slavery and the constitution of Virginia might "produce an irritation which will revolt the minds of our countrymen against reformation in these two articles and thus do more harm than good."[28] Moreover, Jefferson must have been aware that such statements might harm his political career by provoking the ire of his fellow southerners.

Despite his attempt to prevent the publication of the book, Jefferson's remarks were generally moderate. In discussing the "revisal" of Virginia's laws, he described his proposed amendment to "emancipate all slaves born after the passing [of] the act" and then explained why wholesale manumissions would have to be accompanied by the expatriation of the freed Negroes. It would be impossible "to retain and incorporate the blacks into the State," he argued, because white prejudice and black memories of past wrongs would lead to disorders.[29] Jefferson also discussed the physical and moral barriers which he believed would prevent the two races from living together harmoniously in a condition of freedom.

He made a series of observations about the physical and behavioral differences between the races which suggested that Negroes were cruder and more animalistic than whites. He found greater beauty in the flowing hair and variable coloration of the Caucasians than in the "immovable veil of black" which covered the emotions of the Negroes, and noted that they themselves seemed to prefer the whites. Since the factor of superior beauty was considered to be worthy of attention in the propagation

of domestic animals, he asked, "why not in that of man." He observed that Negroes sweat more and urinate less than whites, which results in their having a "strong and disagreeable odor." They seemed to need less sleep and to have grieves that were "merely transient." Furthermore, they were "more ardent after their female; but love seems with them to be more an eager desire, than a tender delicate mixture of sentiment and sensation."[30]

Jefferson found that the blacks were equal in memory to the whites, but far inferior in their ability to reason. In imagination they were "dull, tasteless and anomalous." He saw little to praise by objective standards in the works of the Negro writers which had come to his attention. Referring to the Negro poetess, Phillis Wheatley, he lauded the effect of religion upon her sentiments, but held that her compositions were "beneath the dignity of criticism."[31] In 1791, Jefferson expressed high regard for the elegant geometrical solutions of Benjamin Banneker, a free Negro mathematician. In 1809, however, he voiced the suspicion that Banneker's attainments had been made with white assistance. He went on to add that a letter from the mathematician showed him to have "a mind of very common stature indeed."[32]

In *Notes on the State of Virginia*, and elsewhere as well, Jefferson's remarks were usually conveyed in the dispassionate tones of the scientific investigator. Clearly aware of the environmentalist argument, he earnestly expressed the wish that future evidence might prove that the Negroes' inferiority was the result of their condition rather than their nature.[33] Nevertheless, he did not seem to have much hope that this would be the case; and his appeal to science may, as Jordan points out, have been a veneer which covered the already formed conclusion that "it is not their condition then, but nature which has produced the distinction" between the intellectual attainments of blacks and whites.[34] But he finally contented himself with a more tentative statement: "I advance it, therefore, as a suspicion only that the blacks, whether originally a distinct race, or made distinct by time and circumstances, are inferior to the whites in the endowments both of body and mind."[35]

There was, however, one highly significant area in which Jefferson held that Negroes were every bit the equal of the whites: they possessed a "moral sense." As Jordan points out, for Jefferson to deny this would have been tantamount to excluding Negroes from membership in the human species; it was this faculty which, the Virginian believed, separated man from the animals. Although Jefferson may have doubted that all men were created equal, he did not deny that the blacks were men.[36] Curiously, Jefferson, who was unable to view environment as responsible for the differences he observed between the intellectual abilities of the races, turned to this interpretation to explain the Negroes' lapses from white standards of morality. He defended the blacks against the charge that they were congenitally thievish and ascribed this trait to their situation rather than to "any depravity of the moral sense"; and he went on to remark:

> the man in whose favor no laws of property exist, probably feels himself less bound to respect those made in favor of others. When arguing for ourselves, we lay it down as a fundamental, that laws, to be just, must give a reciprocation of right; that, without this, they are mere arbitrary rules of conduct, founded in force, and not in conscience; and it is a problem which I give to the master to solve, whether the religious precepts against the violation of property were not framed for him as well as his slave?[37]

Jefferson then pointed out that he had found numerous instances of rigid integrity among the Negroes and that benevolence, gratitude, and fidelity were seen as often in slaves as in masters.[38]

Jefferson's views on slavery and race suggest that his libertarian sentiments were more than counterbalanced by his conviction that Negroes were members of a race so alien and inferior that there was no hope that whites and blacks could coexist side by side on terms of equality. Jefferson's libertarian views, however, had virtually no impact upon his actions after 1784, and his belief in the inferiority of the slaves was completely congruent with his behavior as both a planter and a politician.

In his daily life there were few differences between Jefferson's behavior as an owner of men and that of Virginia plantation masters who opposed his antislavery speculations. His bondsmen were well fed and clothed, and their work load was comparable to that of white freemen.[39] In this regard their lot may have been easier than that of many other slaves in the state. Nevertheless, when he dealt with runaways, sales of slaves, breeding, flogging, and manumissions, his behavior did not differ appreciably from that of other enlightened slaveholders who deplored needless cruelty, but would use whatever means they felt necessary to protect their peculiar form of property.

During Jefferson's adult lifetime, more than forty of his Negroes attempted to escape.[40] Thirty of these were mentioned by him in a letter to an Englishman, Dr. William Gordon, who had fought on the American side in the Revolution and returned to Great Britain in 1786. Jefferson described the depredations of Lord Cornwallis and his troops when they overran his estate in 1781 and added: "he carried off also about thirty slaves; had this been to give them their freedom, he would have done right, but it was to consign them to inevitable death from the smallpox and putrid fever then raging in his camp."[41]

This account differs markedly from the cold facts recorded in his "Farm Book" when these events took place. In that document, which was not intended for the public eye, he listed the names of the slaves that he had lost and described what had befallen them.

Next to eight entries in a group he wrote: "fled to the enemy and died." Another two slaves were said to have "joined the enemy and died"; while four more, "joined the enemy, returned and died." Beside three names he wrote laconically: "joined enemy"; and it is presumed that they managed to survive the war. One slave, Barnaby, was described as having "run away, returned and died." Four slaves were said to have "joined the enemy, but came back again and lived."[42] Nowhere in this account is the term "carried off" seen, and Jefferson's later use of the phrase glosses over the fact that more than one seventh of his blacks chose to desert him.

Jefferson's statement that Cornwallis would have done right if he had taken the Negroes to free them is at variance with the Virginian's behavior both before and after 1781. In 1769 he placed an advertisement in the Virginia Gazette asking for the return of a runaway slave named Sandy.[43] Throughout his life Jefferson hired slave catchers and asked his friends to keep an eye peeled for his thralls when they struck out for freedom. In early September 1805, Jame Hubbard, a stout Negro who worked in the plantation nail factory, ran away, but was soon apprehended and returned. About five years later, he escaped again. A year passed before Jefferson learned that Hubbard was living in the area of Lexington and dispatched Isham Chisolm to retrieve the bondsman. It was too late, however; Hubbard had departed only a few days earlier for parts unknown. When Chisolm returned emptyhanded, Jefferson offered him a bonus of twentyfive dollars to go after the man a second time. This time Hubbard was caught and brought back in irons, and Jefferson reported: "I had him severely flogged in the presence of his old companions. . ." He then added that he was convinced that Hubbard "will never again serve any man as a slave. the [sic] moment he is out of jail and his irons off he will be off himself." Before Jefferson could implement plans to have him sold out of the state, Hubbard disappeared again.[44]

In the abstract Jefferson did not believe one man had a right to own another, and, hence, no man had a right to sell another. He repeatedly expressed his dislike for this commerce, and he tried to avoid selling his human property except for misbehavior or at their own request.[45] Nevertheless, slaves were sold when he was pressed for cash, regardless of their wishes in the matter. In 1787, deeply in debt as the result of obligations which he had inherited from his father-in-law, Jefferson wrote to his plantation manager:

> The torment of mind I endure till the moment shall arrive when I shall not owe a shilling on earth is such really as to render life of little value. I cannot decide to sell my lands. I have sold too much of them already, and they are the only sure provision for my children, nor would I willingly sell the slaves as long as there remains any prospect of paying my debts with their labor. In this I am governed solely by views to their happiness which will render it worth their while to use extraordinary exertions for some time to enable me to put them ultimately on an easier footing, which I will do the moment they have paid the debts due from the estate, two thirds of which have been contracted by purchasing them.'[46]

These remarks may appear to confirm the view that Jefferson's primary concern was the welfare of his bondsmen, but just the opposite is true. The underlying assumption in this letter is that the slaves owe him a living and that, if they do not provide it, they will be the ones to suffer. A second implication is that he has the right to dispose of them as he thinks best. Acting upon this view in the years 1783–1794, he reluctantly sold about fifty slaves.[47]

When selling slaves, Jefferson did his best to keep families together if it did not entail a financial hardship for him. In 1792, he sold two males named York and Jame and offered to throw their superannuated parents, Judy and Will, into the bargain if they wished to go along with their sons. His gesture might have saved him money by taking from his shoulders the burden of caring for the old couple who were no longer good for much work. That Jefferson did not let scruples about breaking up families interfere with his business is shown by the fact that in the same lot of slaves with Jame and York was Dilcey, a twenty-three-year-old woman, whose valuable parents remained his property.[48]

The eleven males to be sold in this lot were insufficient in number to make a sale by themselves, and Jefferson instructed his agents to carry them "to some other sale in that part of the country to be sold." Jefferson had yet another reason for selling them elsewhere: "I do not (while in public life) like to have my name annexed in the public papers to the sale of property."[49] Whether he was referring specifically to slave property or to property in general is not clear.

Whenever it could be done without seriously inconveniencing himself, Jefferson tried to unite husbands and wives; and he would buy or sell one partner of a marriage to enable the two of them to live together. He expressed himself as "always willing to indulge connections seriously formed by those people, where it can be done reasonably."[50] In 1792, when he needed to sell a few more slaves to pay his debts, Jefferson offered to sell a slave and her children to his brother who owned her husband. The bonds-woman had been asking to be united with her husband for some time, but her wishes in the matter had had to await Jefferson's convenience.[51]

In November 1806, Jefferson noted that he had always intended to buy the wife of his slave, Moses, when he could "spare the money," but he could not do so at that time. He said he was willing to hire her, but feared that she had not been brought up to field labor. However, he told his manager that it would be permissible to employ her if she could earn her keep. She was not hired, and Moses and his wife remained apart for the next six months. At the end of that time, however, Jefferson did purchase the woman and her children.[52]

It may be argued that, although Jefferson deplored the institution of slavery and particularly the buying and selling of men, the purchases and sales he made were impossible to avoid, since they were for the purpose of paying off debts or uniting families. But in 1805, he said that he was "endeavoring to purchase young and able negro men" for his plantation.[53] Clearly then, he was not merely engaged in a holding operation designed to protect his slaves from a cruel and inhospitable world.

Like any other entrepreneur, Jefferson was concerned with the problem of increasing his capital assets—land and Negroes. Because he was always short of cash, it was difficult for him to increase his land holdings; and he never did. Slaves, however, increased of their own accord, and Jefferson took pains to make sure that this source of profit was not lost through shortsightedness. In 1819 he instructed his manager:

> I have had no reason to believe that any overseer, since Griffin's time has over worked them, accordingly, the deaths among the grown ones seems ascribable to natural causes, but the loss of 5. little ones in 4 years induces me to fear that the overseers do not permit the women to devote as much time as is necessary to the care of their children: that they view their labor as the 1st object and the raising their child but as secondary. I consider the labor of a breeding woman as no object, and that a child raised every 2. years is of more profit than the crop of the best laboring man. in this, as in all other cases, providence has made our interests and our duties coincide perfectly [. . .] I must pray you to inculcate upon the overseers that it is not their labor, but their increase which is the first consideration with us.[54]

Between 1810 and 1822, about 100 slaves were born to Jefferson's "breeding women"; while only a total of thirty Negroes died, were sold, or ran away.[55]

Throughout his life, Jefferson appears to have emancipated only two slaves; and one of them bought his freedom in 1792 at the price of .£60. Upon his death in 1826, Jefferson manumitted five more Negroes and willed over 260 bondsmen to his heirs. Of the total of seven slaves that he freed, at least five were members of a mulatto family named Hemings; and it seems well established that these favored individuals were directly descended from Jefferson's father-in-law. Nevertheless, several of them remained in servitude after Jefferson died. In 1822, two Hemings girls, tired of waiting for their freedom, ran away to Washington.[56]

Apparently, Jefferson's unwillingness to manumit his bondsmen arose, at least in part, from his reluctance to alter his standard of living and to bring his practices into line with his principles. He took much pride in the fine wines, good hooks, and generous hospitality to be found at Monticello; and he went to great lengths to preserve intact this inheritance for his posterity.[57] It may be argued that Jefferson did not believe in emancipation unless it

was accompanied by colonization, and this is true enough. But if this had been the only obstacle to the emancipation of his slaves, he could have made arrangements for the expatriation of those who might choose freedom.

Although manumissions were infrequent in Virginia at this time, they were by no means unknown. When George Washington died in 1799, he gave his slaves their freedom, and so did Jefferson's mentor, George Wythe, who passed away in 1806. Coles, a young planter who had served as private secretary to President James Madison, went still further and in 1819 migrated to Illinois with his slaves and gave 160 acres of land to each family along with its freedom. When the eccentric John Randolph of Roanoke died in 1833 (seven years after Jefferson), his will contained a provision for the emancipation of his 400 bondsmen.[58]

If self-interest played a major role in determining Jefferson's behavior as a plantation owner, it was equally important in shaping his stance as a national leader on questions involving slavery. After 1784, he refrained from discussing the issue publicly for political reasons, but the matter came up occasionally in the course of his official duties. As ambassador to France, he zealously sought to justify the American claim to compensation for slaves taken by the British in 1783; and he continued to press for satisfaction on this issue when he served as secretary of state. He then pressured the Spanish government into denying sanctuary in Florida to fugitive slaves from Georgia.[59]

Although Jefferson embraced the French Revolution, he shuddered with fear in August 1791 when slaves on the island of Santo Domingo revolted for their liberty, and he approved a grant of arms and ammunition to their embattled Gallic masters. The situation grew more complicated when it became apparent that a second and larger grant might provoke the resentment of the French mother country; and Jefferson insisted that future applications for aid be routed through Paris. Nevertheless, he continued to sympathize with the island aristocracy; and, when in 1793 many of them fled to the United States, he argued that they be generously aided. True to his states' rights convictions, he denied the power of the federal government to apply money to such a purpose, but he denied it "with a bleeding heart." He implored James Monroe to urge the government of Virginia to make a large donation to the refugees and said: "never was so deep a tragedy presented to the feelings of men."[60]

The upheaval in Santo Domingo struck a responsive chord in Jefferson, for he feared that Virginia would eventually see the same kind of murderous violence. He warned Monroe that "it is high time we should foresee the bloody scenes which our children certainly, and possibly ourselves . . . [will] have to wade through, and try to avert them." Four years afterward, in 1797, he again urged that "if something is not done and soon done we shall be the murderers of our own children."[61]

Three years later, his worst fears seemed about to be realized when a Virginia slave revolt, which may have involved as many as 1,000 Negroes, was aborted. Monroe informed Jefferson that ten of the rebels had already been hanged and wondered what to do about the remaining conspirators. Jefferson, advising against any further executions, cautioned that "the other states and the world at large will forever condemn us if we indulge a principle of revenge, or go one step beyond absolute necessity. They cannot lose sight of the rights of the two parties, and the object of the unsuccessful one." This was good advice, but it did not prevent the execution of about twenty-five more Negroes involved in the plot.[62]

Within a few months Jefferson became President, and he failed to use his office to avert the bloody scenes which he had predicted. Deeply worried by the slave revolt of 1800, the Virginia legislature requested Governor Monroe to consult with the President about means of deporting Negroes involved in future outbreaks. Jefferson, a longtime colonizationist, then asked the American minister to England to negotiate with the Sierra Leone Company for the "reception of such of these people as might be colonized thither." After learning that the Company was unwilling to consider the proposal, the President abandoned his colonization efforts for the duration of his term.[63]

Jefferson's proslavery actions were particularly evident in the area of foreign policy, and the treaty which granted the Louisiana Territory to the United States contained a provision protecting the right of the Spanish and French inhabitants in the area to keep their slaves. The French insistence upon such a condition was understandable, and so was its acceptance by the United States, but the author of the Ordinance of 1784 made no move to limit the further introduction of bondage into the area.[64]

Napoleon had given up Louisiana largely because of his inability to crush the rebel forces on Santo Domingo. By 1806, he again entertained the hope of reconquering the island, and he asked the American government to cooperate by cutting off all trade with the black nation. Jefferson complied with this request and commended the measure to Congress, where it passed in the House by a vote of 93–26. The President supported France in this venture because he hoped that Napoleon would reciprocate by aiding the United States to acquire Florida, but Jefferson was surely aware of the fact that if the plan succeeded it would destroy the island's Negro regime, which stood as a beacon of hope to American slaves.[65]

Despite these actions, the dominant theme of Jefferson's administration on the subject of slavery was discreet silence. When citizens in the Indiana Territory were demanding that slavery be permitted throughout the Northwest Territory, the President made no comment.[66] Although Jefferson privately continued to represent himself as a foe of human bondage and on rare occasions during his presidency voiced such sentiments in letters to men who shared his views, he was exceedingly careful to keep these thoughts from reaching the public. When he received an emancipation tract from Thomas Brannagan, a slave trader-turned-abolitionist, Jefferson did not directly reply to the author's request for an endorsement. Instead, he wrote to Dr. George Logan:

> The cause in which he embarks is so holy, the sentiments he expresses in his letter so friendly that it is highly painful to me to hesitate on a compliance which appears so small. But that is not its true character, and it would be injurious even to his views, for me to commit myself on paper by answering his letter. I have most carefully avoided every public act or manifestation on that subject. Should an occasion occur in which I can interpose with decisive effect, I shall certainly know and do my duty with promptitude and zeal.[67]

In fact, by the time he wrote these words, Jefferson had already given up "the expectation of any early provision for the extinguishment of slavery among us," and his actions appear to have been designed more to mute the issue than to resolve it.[68]

Ten years after he left office, as the Missouri issue was dividing the nation, Jefferson again demonstrated his ability to mix vague abolition sentiments with a position that worked to the advantage of the slave states. Recognizing that the dispute over the admission of Missouri heralded an era of increasing national division over the slavery issue, he likened the controversy to a "fire bell in the night" and warned of impending disaster for the

Union. Speaking of slavery, he implicitly endorsed the moral position of the North when he described the dilemma of the South: "We have the wolf by the ears and can neither hold him, nor safely let him go. Justice is in the one scale, and self-preservation in the other." He indicated his willingness to give up his bondsmen if any *"practicable"* way of achieving their "emancipation and *expatriation*" could be found.[69]

Nevertheless, he endorsed the southern position and charged the Federalists with creating a geographical division based on an ostensibly moral question as a means of regaining their influence. He then denied that morality was involved because the limitation of the area of bondage would free no one. He also denied that the federal government could regulate the "condition of different descriptions of men composing a State," and he ruled out the only practical means by which emancipation might eventually have been brought about.[70]

It may be argued that Jefferson's position on the Missouri issue and also his inactivity as President may have been dictated by his strict construction of the Constitution. When the object was large enough, however, Jefferson could be quite flexible; and he did not allow such scruples to prevent the acquisition of the Louisiana Territory. Moreover, he believed that the expatriation of America's blacks was a subject which merited a similar elasticity.

Despite his support for the southern position on the issue of Missouri, in 1821 Jefferson could still write: "Nothing is more certainly written in the book of fate than that these people are to be free, Nor is it less certain that the two races, equally free, cannot live in the same government."[71] Thus, in the last years of his life he continued to insist that emancipation must be accompanied by expatriation. Nevertheless, he lacked enthusiasm about the plan to resettle the Negroes in Africa and believed that the distance of that continent would make it impossible for such an operation to succeed.[72]

In 1824 Jefferson argued that there were a million and a half slaves in the nation and that no one conceived it to be "practicable for us, or expedient for them" to send all the blacks away at once. He then went on to calculate:

> Their estimated value as property, in the first place, (for actual property has been lawfully vested in that form, and who can lawfully take it from the possessors?) at an average of two hundred dollars each . . . would amount to six hundred millions of dollars which must be paid or lost by somebody.

To this add the cost of their transportation by land and sea to Mesurado, a year's provision of food and clothes, implements of husbandry and of their trades, which will amount to three hundred millions more . . . and it is impossible to look at the question a second time.[73]

Since African colonization seemed an impossibility, Jefferson suggested a plan which entailed "emancipating the afterborn, leaving them, on due compensation, with their mothers, until their services are worth their maintenance, and putting them to industrious occupations until a proper age for deportation."[74] The individuals who would be "freed" immediately after their birth would eventually be sent to Santo Domingo which, according to the newspapers, had recently offered to open its doors to such persons. In effect, Jefferson was proposing that the federal government buy all newborn slaves from their owners (at twelve dollars and fifty cents each) and that it pay for their "nurture with the mother [for] a few years." Beyond this, the plan would not cost the government anything, for the young blacks would then work for their maintenance until deported. Santo Domingo had offered to bear the cost of passage.

Jefferson noted that a majority of Americans then living would live to see the black population reach six million and warned that "a million and a half are within their control; but six millions, . . . and one million of these fighting men, will say, 'we will not go.' " The Virginia statesman concluded his proposal by urging that neither constitutional problems nor human sentiment ought to be allowed to stand in its way:

> I am aware that this subject involves some constitutional scruples. But a liberal construction, justified by the object, may go far, and an amendment of the constitution, the whole length necessary. The separation of infants from their mothers, too, would produce some scruples of humanity. But this would be straining at a gnat, and swallowing a camel.[75]

Thus, only two and a half years before his death, Jefferson reiterated his long held belief that emancipation was imperative for the sake of the nation, but that it must be accompanied by colonization. Even here, however, his theory differed from his practice; and in this case his inconsistency would follow him beyond the grave for he did not offer to free his slaves on the condition that they leave the country. On the contrary, in his will he requested the Virginia legislature to grant special permission to the five slaves he manumitted to continue to live in the state.[76]

Jefferson was a man of many dimensions, and any explanation of his behavior must contain a myriad of seeming contradictions. He was a sincere and dedicated foe of the slave trade who bought and sold men whenever he found it personally necessary. He believed that all men were entitled to life and liberty regardless of their abilities, yet he tracked down those slaves who had the courage to take their rights by running away. He believed that slavery was morally and politically wrong, but still he wrote a slave code for his state and opposed a national attempt in 1819 to limit the further expansion of the institution. He believed that one hour of slavery was worse than ages of British oppression, yet he was able to discuss the matter of slave breeding in much the same terms that one would use when speaking of the propagation of dogs and horses.

From an intellectual point of view, his strong "suspicion" that the Negroes were innately inferior is probably of great significance in explaining his ability to ignore his own strictures about their rights. Thinking of them as lesser men, he was able to convince himself that his behavior toward them was benevolent and humane; and indeed it was, when judged by the traditional assumptions of the slaveholders. It is a mistake, however, to treat Jefferson's relationship to slavery in intellectual or psychological terms alone, for the institution shaped the warp and woof of life at Monticello and his abstract speculations about human freedom carried little weight when balanced against the whole pattern of his existence there.

Interacting with one another as both cause and effect to produce Jefferson's proslavery behavior was a complex set of factors which included his belief in Negro inferiority, a societal environment which took for granted the enslavement of one race by another, and the fact that he owned 10,000 acres of land and over 200 slaves.[77] His wealth, his status, and his political position were tied to the system of slavery, and never once did he actively propose a plan that would have jeopardized all this. More often than not, the actions he took with regard to slavery actually strengthened the institution. This can be seen in his authorship in 1778 of Virginia's slave code, in his support of the plantation owners of Santo Domingo, and in his position on the Missouri question.

Monticello was the workshop of the maker of the "agrarian dream." It was here that Jefferson conducted his agricultural and scientific experiments and offered a generous hospitality to visitors. It was here that he lived a bustling, but gracious life far from the money changers in the cities of the North. This was the life that he sought to preserve against the incursions of the forces of commerce and industry. But it should not be forgotten that Jefferson's world depended upon forced labor for its very existence.

Endnotes

1. Thomas Jefferson to Edward Everett, April 8, 1826, Paul Leicester Ford, ed., *The Works of Thomas Jefferson* (12 vols., New York, 1904–1905), XII, 469. T. Jefferson to Richard Price, Aug. 7, 1785; T. Jefferson to Jean Nicolas Demeunier [June 26, 1736], Julian P. Boyd, ed., and Lyman H. Butterfield and Mina R. Bryan, associate eds., *The Papers of Thomas Jefferson* (17 vols., Princeton, 1950–1965), VIII, 357, X, 63.

2. Dumas Malone, *Jefferson and His Time* (3 vols., Boston, 1948–1962), III, 212. Dumas Malone is the most prominent advocate of the view which holds that, although T. Jefferson disliked his role as an owner of men, it was entailed upon hint. Henry S. Randall took a similar view. A New Yorker, writing with family authorization, Randall handled the slavery issue gingerly; and the picture of plantation life which emerges is idyllic in the extreme. Henry S. Randall, *The Life of Thomas Jefferson* (3 vols., New York, 1858), I, 552–53, III, 667–69.

   Marie Kimball, *Jefferson: The Road to Glory, 1743–1776* (New York, 1943), and Gilbert Chinard, *Thomas Jefferson: The Apostle of Americanism* (2nd ed. rev.; Ann Arbor, 1957), both describe his antislavery opinions in glowing terms, but fail to come to grips with the contradiction between these ideas and his role as a plantation owner. The same holds true for Adrienne Koch, *Jefferson and Madison: The Great Collaboration* (New York, 1950). After describing Jefferson's emancipation plan of 1778, she dismisses the inconsistency in his position: "one can speculate on the consequences to American History had the enlightened legislation of the liberal Jefferson been adopted, but such speculation is resisted here on the condition that Jefferson's intention be noted by all who remember him as a 'slaveholding Virginia planter.'" Koch, *Jefferson and Madison*, 13.

   Nathan Schachner, *Thomas Jefferson: A Biography* (New York, 1951), gives little space to the problem of Jefferson and slavery. When he does deal with it, he is either neutral or somewhat critical. In treating Jefferson's plan to colonize free Negroes and slave criminals Ile notes that the plantation owner "saw nothing wrong with this sudden wrenching from their homes of free Negroes." Schachner, *Thomas Jefferson*, 704.

Albert Jay Nock, *Jefferson* (Washington, D.C., 1926), is in many respects a sensitive and perceptive portrayal of the Virginian, but it accepts without question Jefferson's role as a slaveholder. Taking note of the wastefulness of the Negro children who toiled in Jefferson's nail factory, Nock wrote: -but what better could be done with these boys. . . It was to no purpose to educate them beyond their slave status; and even if one killed them off, their place would be taken almost immediately by others precisely like them." Nock, *Jefferson*, 68.

3. T. Jefferson to Edward Coles, Aug. 25, 1814, Ford, ed., *Works of Thomas Jefferson*, XI, 416.

4. *Ibid.*, 419.

5. Robert McCulley, *Slavery and Jeffersonian Virginia* (Urbana, 1964), 124.

6. Winthrop D. Jordan, *White Over Black: American Attitudes Toward the Negro, 1550–1812* (Chapel Hill, 1968), 429, 431.

7. *Ibid.*, 453.

8. Malone, *Jefferson and His Time*, I, 439–44.

9. For an assessment of T. Jefferson's comparative wealth in Albemarle County, see *ibid.*, 441. The data on slaves is from T. Jefferson's "Farm Book," 5–9, 24, 57, 128–31. A facsimile reproduction of the "Farm Book" is printed in Edwin Morris Betts, ed., *Thomas Jefferson's Farm Book: With Relevant Commentary and Extracts From Other Writings* (Princeton, 1953). Since the "Extracts" and the "Farm Book" are numbered separately and each begins with 1, references to the facsimile will be cited as T. Jefferson, "Farm Book," and references to "Extracts" will he cited as Betts, ed.. *Thomas Jefferson's . . . Writings.*

10. Thomas Jefferson, "A Summary View of the Rights of British America," Boyd, ed., *Papers of Thomas Jefferson*, I, 129.130.

11. *Ibid.*, 353. This document was written before June 13, 1776.

12. Carl L. Becker, *The Declaration of Independence: A Study in the History of Political Ideas* (New York, 1942), 212.

13. T. Jefferson, "Farm Book," 7.9; Boyd, ed., *Papers of Thomas Jefferson*, I, 96n.

14. T. Jefferson to Henri Gregoire, Feb. 25, 1809, Ford, ed., *Works of Thomas Jefferson*, XI, 100. See also Jordan, *White Over Black*, 429–81; McColley, *Slavery and Jeffersonian Virginia*, 124–32.

15. In his autobiography, T. Jefferson asserted that in 1778 he brought in a bill to prevent the further importation of slaves into Virginia. Paul L. Ford disputes this claim and notes that Jefferson was not in the legislature when the bill was debated and adopted. Ford, ed., *Works of Thomas Jefferson*, I, 60, 60n-61n. The editors of the Jefferson papers believe that he was probably responsible for the bill, and they point nut that his absence does not necessarily prove that the bill was not the product of his labors. Boyd, ed., *Papers of Thomas Jefferson*, II, 23n.

16. Randall, *Thomas Jefferson*, I, 58; Ford, ed., *Works of Thomas Jefferson*, I, 7. In a footnote Ford indicates that a diligent search of the *Journal of the House of Burgesses* failed to reveal any trace of this effort. The editors of the Jefferson papers refer to this motion as -an extension of the protection of certain laws to Negroes,- and they point out I hat the motion may have been made -in the committee of the whole or in some other manner not requiring a record." Boyd, ed., *Papers of Thomas Jefferson*, II, 23n.

17. These attempts were an amendment in the Virginia legislature, 1778 to the bill pertaining to slaves; the Ordinance of 1784; and 'r. Jefferson's 1784 draft of a revised constitution for Virginia. This last document provided that all slaves in the state would be free after December 31, 1800. Boyd, ed., *Papers of Thomas Jefferson*, VI, 298.

18. This was Bill No. 51 of those prepared by the Committee of Revisors. *Ibid.*, II, 470–72. Ford, ed.. *Works of Thomas Jefferson*, I, 77.

19. Boyd, ed., *Papers of Thomas Jefferson*, II, 471–72, 473n. As finally passed by the legislature in 1785 the bill omitted these provisions.

20. T. Jefferson, "Farm Book," 21–22, 28. The figures for 1776 do not appear in the -Farm Book" and are unknown. T. Jefferson said that it was a known fact that slaves multiply as rapidly as free inhabitants. Thomas Jefferson, *Notes on the State of Virginia* (New York, 1961), 136. The argument that T. Jefferson believed slavery would gradually die out if the free Negro population were reduced is advanced in Boyd, ed., *Papers of Thomas Jefferson*, II, 473n.

21. Jefferson, *Notes on . . . Virginia*, 132–33; Boyd, ed., *Papers of Thomas Jefferson*, II, 472n.

22. Boyd, ed., *Papers of Thomas Jefferson*, VI, 604.

23. T. Jefferson's immediate motive for incorporating the exclusionary clause in the Ordinance is unclear, but he may have written it more for the purpose of halting the slave trade than of weakening the institution of bondage itself. Writing in 1819, James Madison claimed that the prohibition of slavery which appeared in the Northwest Ordinance of 1787 had been adopted as a means of restraining the trade by narrowing the potential market for bondsmen. He doubted that such a provision would have even been proposed if the power to abolish the trade already had been vested in Congress. While Madison's remarks were clearly directed to the Ordinance of

1787, it seems likely that they applied to the earlier version as well. With Spanish slave traders infesting the lower Mississippi area, the threat from this quarter certainly required attention. Madison to Robert Walsh, Nov. 27, 1819, Gaillard Hunt, ed., *The Writings of James Madison: Comprising His Public Papers and His Private Correspondence, Including Numerous Letters and Documents Now for the First Time Printed* (9 vols., New York, 1900–1910), IX, 9–10. See also McCulley, *Slavery and Jeffersonian Virginia*, 171.

24. T. Jefferson to John Holmes, April 22, 1820, Ford, ed., *Works of Thomas Jefferson*, XII, 159; Boyd. ed., *Papers of Thomas Jefferson*, VI, 604.

25. McCulley, *Slavery and Jeffersonian Virginia*, 125, 178–80; T. Jefferson to Madison. April 25, 1781, Boyd, ed., *Papers of Thomas Jefferson*, VII, 118–19.

26. On T. Jefferson's reluctance to speak out publicly about slavery, see T. Jefferson to [General] Chastellux, June 7, 1785, Boyd, ed., *Papers of Thomas Jefferson*, VIII, 184; and T. Jefferson to George Logan, May 11, 1805, Ford, ed., *Works of Thomas Jefferson*, X, 141–42. For his advocacy of expatriation, see T. Jefferson to Jared Sparks, Feb. 4, 1824, *ibid.*, XII. 334–39.

27. This analysis of T. Jefferson's thought on the race question was written before the publication of *White Over Black*. It has subsequently undergone extensive revision, and this newer version reflects many insights gained from Jordan's important work.

28. Jefferson to James Monroe, June 17, 1785, Boyd, ed., *Papers of Thomas Jefferson*, VIII, 229.

29. Jefferson, *Notes on . . . Virginia*, 132–33.

30. *Ibid.*, 133–34.

31. *Ibid.*, 134–35.

32. T. Jefferson to Joel Barlow, Oct. 8, 1809, T. Jefferson to the Marquis de Condorcet, Aug. 30, 1791, T. Jefferson to Benjamin Banneker, Aug. 30, 1791, Ford, ed., *Works of Thomas Jefferson*, XI, 121, VI, 311, 309–10.

33. Although environmentalism has only come into its own in recent years, there were many, even in Jefferson's time, who subscribed to this position; and he was keenly aware of their views. T. Jefferson, *Notes on . . . Virginia*, 134–38. Abbe Raynal, Adam Smith, and Alexander Hamilton were among those who believed that the degraded condition of the blacks was due exclusively to the effects of their situation. John C. Miller, *Alexander Hamilton: Portrait in Paradox* (New York, 1959), 41–42; David Brion Davis, *The Problem of Slavery in Western Culture* (Ithaca, 1966), 420–21, 456.

34. Jefferson. *Notes on . . . Virginia*, 137.

35. *Ibid.*, 138; Jordan, *White Over Black*, 438–39.

36. Jordan, *White Over Black*, 431–32, 439–40.

37. Jefferson, *Notes on . . . Virginia*, 137.

38. *Ibid.*, 138.

39. Betts, ed., *Thomas Jefferson's . . . Writings*, 5–7.

40. This includes thirty slaves who went over to the British in 1781 and cases involving one or more runaways mentioned in the following sources: advertisement for a runaway named Sandy in the *Virginia Gazette*, Sept. 7, 14, 1769, George Wythe to T. Jefferson, Dec. 31, 1781, Boyd, ed., *Papers of Thomas Jefferson*, VI, 144; Daniel Bradley to T. Jefferson, Oct. 6, 1805, T. Jefferson to Joseph Daugherty, July 31, 1806, T. Jefferson to Mary Dangerfield, July 31, 1808, T. Jefferson to Jeremiah Goodman, July 26, 1813, noel Yancey to T. Jefferson, May 22, 1821, Betts, ed., *Thomas Jefferson's . . . Writings*, 21, 22, 27, 36, 46. Two other runaways, Beverly and Harriet [Hemings] are listed in Jefferson, "Farm Book," 130. The figure of forty is probably conservative as it is based solely on a study of readily available sources.

41. T. Jefferson to William Gordon, July 16, 1788, Boyd, ed., *Papers of Thomas Jefferson*, XIII, 363–64.

42. T. Jefferson, "Farm Book," 29. Albert J. Nock quotes both the Gordon letter and the "Farm Book" entry, but he does not explore the contradiction between them. Nock, *Jefferson*, 63–64.

43. *Virginia Gazette*, Sept. 7, 14, 1769, Boyd, ed., *Papers of Thomas Jefferson*, I, 33.

44. Jefferson to Bradley, Oct. 6, 1805, T. Jefferson to Reuben Perry, April 16, 1812. Sqq. 3. 1812, Betts, ed., *Thomas Jefferson's . . . Writings*, 21, 34–36.

45. T. Jefferson to John W. Eppes, June 30, 1820, T. Jefferson to Craven Peyton, Nov. 27, 1815, T. Jefferson to Thomas Mann Randolph, June 8, 1803, *ibid.*, 45. 40, 19.

46. T. Jefferson to Nicholas Lewis, July 29. 1787, Ford, ed., *Works of Thomas Jefferson*, V, 311. This letter is also given in Boyd, ed., *Papers of Thomas Jefferson*, XI, 640, but in place of the word "exertions," Boyd substitutes the word "cautions."

47. Malone, *Jefferson and His Time*, III, 207, I, 443–44. References to sales of slaves appear in T. Jefferson to Alexander McCall% Jan. 4, 1787, Boyd, ed., *Papers of Thomas Jefferson*, 10; sad T. Jefferson to James Lyle, April 25, 1793, Ford, ed., *Works of Thomas Jefferson*, VII, 27R.

48. T. Jefferson to Bowling Clarke, Sept. 21, 1792; Betts, ed., *Thomas Jefferson's . . . Writings*, 13; T. Jefferson, "Farm Book," 9, 24, 30. Bess was known as Betty in 1774. In 1795 T. Jefferson wrote the word -old-beside the names of Judy and Will indicating that they were not useful for labor anymore.

49. T. Jefferson to Clarke, Sept. 21, 1792, Betts, ed., *Thomas Jefferson's . . . Writings*, 13.

50. T. Jefferson to John Jordan, Dec. 21, 1805, *ibid.*, 21.

51. T. Jefferson to Randolph Jefferson, Sept. 25, 1792, *ibid.*, 14.

52. T. Jefferson to Edmund Bacon, Nov. 21, 1806, T. Jefferson to Randolph Lewis, April 21, 1807; Account Book for 1807, *ibid.*, 24–27.

53. T. Jefferson to Jordan, Dec. 21. 1805, Betts, *ibid.*, 21.

54. T. Jefferson to Yancey, Jan. 17, 1819, *ibid.*, 43. Writing to Eppes on June 30, 1820, T. Jefferson said: "1 know no error more consuming to an estate than that of stocking farms with men almost exclusively. I consider a woman who brings a child every two years as more profitable than the best man of the farm. What she produces is an addition to capital, while his labors disappear in mere consumption." *Ibid.*, 45–46. T. Jefferson's keen awareness of the profit to be derived from the natural increase of his slaves is also shown in his observation that "our families of negroes double in 25 years which is an increase of the capital invested in them, 4. per cent over and above keeping up the original number." See Jordan, *White Over Black*, 430.

55. These figures are based on T. Jefferson, "Farm Book," 130–31.

56. *Ibid.*, 130. For the freedom papers of Robert and James Hemings (dated Dec. 12, 1794 and Feb. 5, 1796 respectively), see Betts, ed., *Thomas Jefferson's . . . Writings*, 15. For T. Jefferson's will, dated March 1826, see Ford, ed., *Works of Thomas Jefferson*, XII, 482. The relationship of the Hemings family to Jefferson and his relatives is discussed in Merrill D. Peterson, *The Jefferson Image in the American Mind* (New York, 1960), 185–86. See also Jordan, *White Over Black*, 464–68.

57. In his will the Virginian went to elaborate lengths to see that his estate went to his daughter Martha and not to the creditors of her husband. Ford, ed., *Works of Thomas Jefferson*. XII, 479; McColley, *Slavery and Jeffersonian Virginia*. 23: Randall, *Thomas Jefferson*, III, 112.33; Nock, *Jefferson*, 59.

58. John Alexander Carroll and Mary Wells Ashworth, *George Washington: First in Peace* (New York, 1957), 585. "George Wythe," *Dictionary of American Biography* (11 vols., New York, 1957), XI, 588; "John Randolph," *ibid.*, VIII, 366.

59. Amplification of Subjects Discussed with Vergennes [ca. Dec. 20, 1785], Jefferson to John Jay, April 23, 1786, Boyd, ed., *Papers of Thomas Jefferson*, IX, 111, 403–04; 'I. Jefferson to British Minister, May 29, 1792, Dec. 15, 1793, T. Jefferson to Governor of Florida, March 10, 1791, T. Jefferson to Governor of Georgia, March 26, 1791, Ford, ed., *Works of Thomas Jefferson*, VII, 41–46, VIII, 95–97, VI, 212, 226–27.

60. T. Jefferson to Monroe, July 14, 1793, T. Jefferson to the Chargé d'Affaires in France [William Short], Nov. 24, 1791, Ford, ed., *Works of Thomas Jefferson*, VII, 149–50, VI, 331–32.

61. T. Jefferson to St. George Tucker, Aug. 28, 1797, T. Jefferson to Monroe, July 14, 1793, *ibid.*, VIII, 334–36, VII, 449–50.

62. T. Jefferson to Monroe, Sept. 20, 1800, *ibid.*, IX, 146. Herbert Aptheker, *American Negro Slave Revolts* (New York, 1943). 219–27. T. Jefferson's desire to avoid further executions appears to have stemmed in part from a genuine respect for the rebels. While investigating the possibility that such Negroes might be banished to Africa and colonized there, he observed that "they are not felons or common malefactors, but persons guilty of what the safety of society, under actual circumstances, obliges us to treat as a crime, but which their feelings may represent in a far different shape. They are such as will be a valuable acquisition to the settlement already existing [in Africa] . . . and well calculated to cooperate in the plan of civilization." T. Jefferson to Rufus King, July 13, 1802, Ford, ed., *Works of Thomas Jefferson*, IX, 385.

63. Ford, ed., *Works of Thomas Jefferson*, IX, 383–86. The quotation is to be found in T. Jefferson to John Lynch, Jan. 21, 1811, *ibid.*, XI, 179. The request of the Virginia legislature also asked that the matter of finding a place to which free Negroes could be sent should also be investigated.

64. McColley, *Slavery and Jeffersonian Virginia*, 125.

65. *Ibid.*, 112.

66. *Ibid.*, 178–80.

67. T. Jefferson to Logan, May 11, 1805, Ford, ed., *Works of Thomas Jefferson*, X, 141.

68. T. Jefferson to William A. Burwell, Jan. 28, 1805, *ibid.*, X, 126.

69. T. Jefferson to John Holmes, April 22, 1820, *ibid.*, XII, 159.

70. *Ibid.*, T. Jefferson to Albert Gallatin, Dec. 26, 1820, *ibid.*, XII, 187–89.

71. *Ibid.*, I, 77.

72. T. Jefferson to Jared Sparks, Feb. 4. 1824, *ibid.*, XII, 334–35.

73. *Ibid.*, XII, 335–36.

74. *Ibid.*, XII, 336.

75. *Ibid.*, XII, 339.

76. T. Jefferson's March 1826, *ibid.*, XII, 483.

77. This listing is not meant to exclude the effect of T. Jefferson's psychological make-up as a factor which influenced his behavior with regard to slavery. Jordan convincingly suggests that the Virginian's belief in Negro inferiority was partially rooted in his inner mind. See Jordan, *White Over Black*, 457–81.

CHAPTER 5

Articles of Confederation, 1777

To all to whom there Presents shall come, we the undersigned Delegates of the States affixed to our Names, send greeting

WHEREAS the Delegates of the United States of America, in Congress assembled, did, on the 15th day of November, in the year [1777]. . . . agree to certain Articles of Confederation and perpetual Union between the States of. . . . in the words following, viz.:

Articles of Confederation and perpetual Union between the states of New Hampshire, Massachusetts Bay, Rhode Island and Providence Plantations, Connecticut, New-York, New-Jersey, Pennsylvania, Delaware, Maryland, Virginia, North-Carolina, South-Carolina, and Georgia.

✳ ✳ ✳ ✳ ✳

I.   The stile of this Confederacy shall be 'The United States of America'.

II.   Each state retains its sovereignty, freedom, and independence, and every power, jurisdiction, and right, which is not by this Confederation expressly delegated to the United States, in Congress assembled.

III.   The said states hereby severally enter into a firm league of friendship with each other, for their common defence, the security of their liberties, and their mutual and general welfare, binding themselves to assist each other, against all force offered to, or attacks made upon them, or any of them, on account of religion, sovereignty, trade, or any other pretence whatever.

IV.   The better to secure and perpetuate mutual friendship and intercourse among the people of the different states in this union, the free inhabitants of each of these states, paupers, vagabonds, and fugitives from justice excepted, shall be entitled to all privileges and immunities of free citizens in the several states; and the people of each state shall have free ingress and regress to and from any other state, and shall enjoy therein all the privileges of trade and commerce, subject to the same duties, impositions and restrictions as the inhabitants thereof respectively, provided that such restriction shall not extend so far as to prevent the removal of property imported into any state, to any other state, of which the owner is an inhabitant; provided also that no imposition, duties or restriction shall be laid by any state, on the property of the United States, or either of them.

If any person guilty of, or charged with treason, felony, or other high misdemeanor in any state, shall flee from justice, and be found in any of the United States, he shall, upon demand of the Governor or executive power of the state from which he fled, be delivered up and removed to the state having jurisdiction of his offence.

Full faith and credit shall be given in each of these states to the records, acts and judicial proceedings of the courts and magistrates of every other state.

V.   For the more convenient management of the general interests of the United States, delegates shall be annually appointed in such manner as the legislature of each state shall direct, to meet in Congress on the first Monday in November, in every year, with a power reserved to each state to recal its delegates, or any of them, at any time within the year, and to send others in their stead for the remainder of the year.

No state shall be represented in Congress by less than two, nor by more than seven members; and no person shall be capable of being a delegate for more than three years in any term of six years; nor shall any person, being a delegate, be capable of holding any office under the United States, for which he, or another for his benefit receives any salary, fees or emolument of any kind.

Each state shall maintain its own delegates in a meeting of the states, and while they act as members of the committee of the states.

In determining questions in the United States in Congress assembled, each state shall have one vote.

Freedom of speech and debate in Congress shall not be impeached or questioned in any court or place out of Congress, and the members of Congress shall be protected in their persons from arrests and imprisonments, during the time of their going to and from, and attendance on Congress, except for treason, felony, or breach of the peace.

VI. No state, without the consent of the United States in Congress assembled, shall send any embassy to, or receive any embassy from, or enter into any conference, agreement, alliance or treaty with any king, prince or state; nor shall any person holding any office of profit or trust under the United States, or any of them, accept of any present, emolument, office or title of any kind whatever from any king, prince or foreign state; nor shall the United States in Congress assembled, or any of them, grant any title of nobility.

No two or more states shall enter into any treaty, confederation or alliance whatever between them, without the consent of the United States in Congress assembled, specifying accurately the purposes for which the same is to be entered into, and how long it shall continue.

No state shall lay any imposts or duties, which may interfere with any stipulations in treaties, entered into by the United States in Congress assembled, with any king, prince or state, in pursuance of any treaties, already proposed by Congress, to the courts of France and Spain. . . .

The United States in Congress assembled shall also be the last resort on appeal in all disputes and differences now subsisting or that hereafter may arise between two or more states concerning boundary, jurisdiction or any other cause whatever. . . .

The United States in Congress assembled shall also have the sole and exclusive right and power of regulating the alloy and value of coin struck by their own authority, or by that of the respective states—fixing the standard of weights and measures throughout the United States—regulating the trade and managing all affairs with the Indians, not members of any of the states, provided that the legislative right of any state within its own limits be not infringed or violated—establishing or regulating post-offices from one state to another, throughout all the United States, and exacting such postage on the papers passing thro' the same as may be requisite to defray the expences of the said office—appointing all officers of the land forces, in the service of the United States, excepting regimental officers—appointing all the officers of the naval forces, and commissioning all officers whatever in the service of the United States—making rules for the government and regulation of the said land and naval forces, and directing their operations.

The United States in Congress assembled shall have authority to appoint a committee, to sit in the recess of Congress, to be denominated 'A Committee of the States', and to consist of one delegate from each state; and to appoint such other committees and civil officers as may be necessary for managing the general affairs of the United States under their direction—to appoint one of their number to preside, provided that no person be allowed to serve in the office of president more than one year in any term of three years; to ascertain the necessary sums of money to be raised for the service of the United States, and to appropriate and apply the same for defraying the public expences—to borrow money, or emit bills on the credit of the United States, transmitting every half-year to the respective states an account of their sums of money so borrowed or emitted—to build and equip a navy—to agree upon the number of land forces, and to make requisitions from each state for its quota, in proportion to the number of white inhabitants in such state. . . .

The United States in Congress assembled shall never engage in a war, nor grant letters of marque and reprisal in time of peace, nor enter into any treaties or alliances, nor coin money, nor regulate the value thereof, nor ascertain the sums and expences necessary for the defence and welfare of the United States, or any of them, nor emit bills, nor borrow money on the credit of the United States, nor appropriate money, nor agree upon the number of vessels of war, to be built or purchased, or the number of land or sea forces to be raised, nor appoint a commander in chief of the army or navy, *unless* nine states assent to the same: nor shall a question on any other point, except for adjourning from day to day be determined, unless by the votes of a majority of the United States in Congress assembled. . . .

X.   The Committee of the States, or any nine of them, shall be authorized to execute, in the recess of Congress, such of the powers of Congress as the United States in Congress assembled, by the consent of nine states, shall from time to time think expedient to vest them with; provided that no power be delegated to the said Committee, for the exercise of which by the Articles of Confederation, the voice of nine states in the Congress of the United States assembled is requisite. . . .

XIII.   Every state shall abide by the determinations of the United States in Congress assembled, on all questions which by this confederation are submitted to them. And the Articles of this Confederation shall be inviolably observed by every state, and the union shall be perpetual; nor shall any alteration at any time hereafter be made in any of them; unless such alteration be agreed to in a Congress of the United States, and be afterwards confirmed by the legislatures of every state.

And Whereas it hath pleased the Great Governor of the World to incline the hearts of the legislatures we respectively represent in Congress, to approve of, and to authorize us to ratify the said articles of confederation and perpetual union. Know ye that we the undersigned delegates, by virtue of the power and authority to us given for that purpose, do by these presents, in the name and in behalf of our respective constituents, fully and entirely ratify and confirm each and every of the said articles of confederation and perpetual union, and all and singular the matters and things therin contained; And we do further solemnly plight and engage the faith of our respective constituents, that they shall abide by the determinations of the United States in Congress assembled, on all questions, which by the said confederation are submitted to them. And that the articles thereof shall be inviolably observed by the states we respectively represent, and that the union shall be perpetual. In Witness whereof we have hereunto set our hands in Congress. Done at Philadelphia in the state of Pennsylvania the ninth day of July, in the year of our Lord one Thousand seven Hundred and Seventy-eight, and in the third year of the independence of America.

The Constitution of the United States

As Presented by the Federal Convention in 1787 and Adopted in 1788

We the People of the United States, in Order to form a more perfect Union, establish justice, insure domestic Tranquility, provide for the common defence, promote the general Welfare, and secure the Blessings of Liberty to ourselves and our Posterity, do ordain and establish this Constitution for the United States of America.

✳ ✳ ✳ ✳ ✳

Article I

SECTION 1. All legislative Powers herein granted shall be vested in a Congress of the United States, which shall consist of a Senate and House of Representatives.

SECTION 2. The House of Representatives shall be composed of Members chosen every second Year by the People of the several States, and the Electors in each State shall have the Qualifications requisite for Electors of the most numerous Branch of the State Legislature.

No Person shall be a Representative who shall not have attained to the Age of twenty five Years, and been seven Years a Citizen of the United States, and who shall not, when elected, be an Inhabitant of that State in which he shall be chosen.

Representatives and direct Taxes shall be apportioned among the several States which may be included within this Union, according to their respective Numbers, which shall be determined by adding to the whole Number of free Persons, including those bound to Service for a Term of Years, and excluding Indians not taxed, three fifths of all other Persons. The actual Enumeration shall be made within three Years after the first Meeting of the Congress of the United States, and within every subsequent Term of ten Years, in such Manner as they shall by Law direct. The Number of Representatives shall not exceed one for every thirty Thousand, but each State shall have at Least one Representative; and until such enumeration shall be made, the State of New Hampshire shall be entitled to chuse three, Massachusetts eight, Rhode-Island and Providence Plantations one, Connecticut five, New - York six, New jersey four, Pennsylvania eight, Delaware one, Maryland six, Virginia ten, North Carolina five, South Carolina five, and Georgia three.

When vacancies happen in the Representation from any State, the Executive Authority thereof shall issue Writs of Election to fill such Vacancies.

The House of Representatives shall chuse their Speaker and other Officers; and shall have the sole Power of Impeachment.

SECTION 3. The Senate of the United States shall be composed of two 3

Senators from each State, chosen by the Legislature thereof, for six Years; and each Senator shall have one Vote.

Immediately after they shall be assembled in Consequence of the first Election, they shall be divided as equally as may be into three Classes. The Seats of the Senators of the first Class shall be vacated at the Expiration of the second Year, of the second Class at the Expiration of the fourth Year, and of the third Class at the Expiration of the sixth Year, so that one third may be chosen every second Year; and if Vacancies happen by Resignation, or otherwise, during the Recess of the Legislature of any State, the Executive thereof may make temporary Appointments until the next Meeting of the Legislature, which shall then fill such Vacancies.

No Person shall be a Senator who shall not have attained to the Age of thirty Years, and been nine Years a Citizen of the United States, and who shall not, when elected, be an Inhabitant of that State for which he shall be chosen.

The Vice President of the United States shall be President of the Senate, but shall have no Vote, unless they be equally divided.

The Senate shall chuse their other Officers, and also a President pro tempore, in the Absence of the Vice President, or when he shall exercise the Office of President of the United States.

The Senate shall have the sole Power to try all Impeachments. When sitting for that Purpose, they shall be on Oath or Affirmation. When the President of the United States is tried, the Chief Justice shall preside: And no Person shall be convicted without the Concurrence of two thirds of the Members present.

Judgment in Cases of Impeachment shall not extend further than to removal from Office, and disqualification to hold and enjoy any Office of honor, Trust or Profit under the United States: but the Party convicted shall nevertheless be liable and subject to Indictment, Trial, Judgment and Punishment, according to Law.

Section 4. The Times, Places and Manner of holding Elections for Senators and Representatives, shall be prescribed in each State by the Legislature thereof; but the Congress may at any time by Law make or alter such Regulations, except as to the Places of chusing Senators.

The Congress shall assemble at least once in every Year, and such Meeting shall be on the first Monday in December, unless they shall by Law appoint a different Day.

Section 5. Each House shall be the Judge of the Elections, Returns and Qualifications of its own Members, and a Majority of each shall constitute a Quorum to do Business; but a smaller Number may adjourn from day to day, and may be authorized to compel the Attendance of absent Members, in such Manner, and under such Penalties as each House may provide.

Each House may determine the Rules of its Proceedings, punish its Members for disorderly Behaviour, and, with the Concurrence of two thirds, expel a Member.

Each House shall keep a journal of its Proceedings, and from time to time publish the same, excepting such Parts as may in their judgment require Secrecy; and the Yeas and Nays of the Members of either House on any question shall, at the Desire of one fifth of those Present, be entered on the Journal.

Neither House, during the Session of Congress, shall, without the Consent of the other, adjourn for more than three days, nor to any other Place than that in which the two Houses shall be sitting.

Section 6. The Senators and Representatives shall receive a Compensation for their Services, to be ascertained by Law, and paid out of the Treasury of the United States. They shall in all Cases, except Treason, Felony and Breach of the Peace, be privileged from Arrest during their Attendance at the Session of their respective Houses, and in going to and returning from the same; and for any Speech or Debate in either House, they shall not be questioned in any other Place.

No Senator or Representative shall, during the Time for which he was elected, be appointed to any civil Office under the Authority of the United States which shall have been created, or the Emoluments whereof shall have been encreased during such time; and no Person holding any Office under the United States, shall be a Member of either House during his Continuance in Office.

Section 7. All Bills for raising Revenue shall originate in the House of Representatives; but the Senate may propose or concur with Amendments as on other Bills.

Every Bill which shall have passed the House of Representatives and the Senate, shall, before it become a Law, be presented to the President of the United States; If he approve he shall sign it, but if not he shall return it, with his Objections to that House in which it shall have originated, who shall enter the Objections at large on their Journal, and proceed to reconsider it. If after such Reconsideration two thirds of that House shall agree to pass the Bill, it shall be sent, together with the Objections, to the other House, by which it shall likewise be reconsidered, and if approved by two thirds of that House, it shall become a Law. But in all such Cases the Votes of both Houses shall be determined by Yeas and Nays, and the Names of the Persons voting for and against the Bill shall be entered on the Journal of each House respectively. If any Bill shall not be returned by the President within ten Days (Sundays excepted) after it shall have been presented to him, the Same shall be a Law, in like Manner as if he had signed it, unless the Congress by their Adjournment prevent its Return, in which Case it shall not be a Law.

Every Order, Resolution, or Vote to which the Concurrence of the Senate and House of Representatives may be necessary (except on a question of Adjournment) shall be presented to the President of the United States; and before the Same shall take Effect, shall be approved by him, or being disapproved by him, shall be repassed by two thirds of the Senate and House of Representatives, according to the Rules and Limitations prescribed in the Case of a Bill.

SECTION 8. The Congress shall have Power To lay and collect Taxes, Duties, Imposts and Excises, to pay the Debts and provide for the common Defence and general Welfare of the United States; but all Duties, Imposts and Excises shall be uniform throughout the United States;

To borrow Money on the credit of the United States;

To regulate Commerce with foreign Nations, and among the several States, and with the Indian Tribes;

To establish an uniform Rule of Naturalization, and uniform Laws on the subject of Bankruptcies throughout the United States;

To coin Money, regulate the Value thereof, and of foreign Coin, and fix the standard of weights and measures;

To provide for the Punishment of counterfeiting the Securities and current Coin of the United States;

To establish Post Offices and post Roads;

To promote the Progress of Science and useful Arts, by securing for limited Times to Authors and Inventors the exclusive Right to their respective Writings and Discoveries;

To constitute Tribunals inferior to the supreme Court;

To define and punish Piracies and Felonies committed on the high Seas, and Offences against the Law of Nations;

To declare War, grant Letters of Marque and Reprisal, and make Rules concerning Captures on Land and Water;

To raise and support Armies, but no Appropriation of Money to that Use shall be for a longer Term than two Years;

To provide and maintain a Navy;

To make Rules for the Government and Regulation of the land and naval Forces;

To provide for calling forth the Militia to execute the Laws of the Union, suppress Insurrections and repel Invasions;

To provide for organizing, arming, and disciplining the Militia, and for governing such Part of them as may be employed in the Service of the United States, reserving to the States respectively, the Appointment of the Officers, and the Authority of training the Militia according to the discipline prescribed by Congress;

To exercise exclusive Legislation in all Cases whatsoever, over such District (not exceeding ten Miles square) as may, by Cession of particular States, and the Acceptance of Congress, become the Seat of the Government of the United States, and to exercise like Authority over all Places purchased by the Consent of the Legislature of the State in which the Same shall be, for the Erection of Forts, Magazines, Arsenals, dock-Yards, and other needful Buildings; –And

To make all Laws which shall be necessary and proper for carrying into Execution the foregoing Powers, and all other Powers vested by this Constitution in the Government of the United States, or in any Department or Officer thereof.

SECTION 9. The Migration or Importation of such Persons as any of the States now existing shall think proper to admit, shall not be prohibited by the Congress prior to the Year one thousand eight hundred and eight, but a Tax or duty may be imposed on such Importation, not exceeding ten dollars for each Person.

The privilege of the writ of habeas corpus shall not be suspended, unless when in the case of rebellion or invasion the public safety may require it.

No Bill of Attainder or ex post facto Law shall be passed.

No Capitation, or other direct, Tax shall be laid, unless in Proportion to the Census or Enumeration herein before directed to be taken.

No Tax or Duty shall be laid on Articles exported from any State.

No Preference shall be given by any Regulation of Commerce or Revenue to the Ports of one State over those of another: nor shall Vessels bound to, or from, one State, be obliged to enter, clear, or pay Duties in another.

No Money shall be drawn from the Treasury, but in Consequence of Appropriations made by Law; and a regular Statement and Account of the Receipts and Expenditures of all public Money shall be published from time to time.

No Title of Nobility shall be granted by the United States: And no Person holding any Office of Profit or Trust under them, shall, without the

Consent of the Congress, accept of any present, Emolument, Office, or Title, of any kind whatever, from any King, Prince or foreign State.

SECTION 10. No State shall enter into any Treaty, Alliance, or Confederation; grant Letters of Marque and Reprisal; coin Money; emit Bills of Credit; make any Thing but gold and silver Coin a Tender in Payment of Debts; pass any Bill of Attainder, ex post facto Law, or Law impairing the Obligation of Contracts, or grant any Title of Nobility.

No State shall, without the Consent of the Congress, lay any Imposts or Duties on Imports or Exports, except what may be absolutely necessary for executing it's inspection Laws: and the net Produce of all Duties and Imposts, laid by any State on Imports or Exports, shall be for the Use of the Treasury of the United States; and all such Laws shall be subject to the Revision and Controul of the Congress.

No State shall, without the Consent of Congress, lay any Duty of Tonnage, keep Troops, or Ships of War in time of Peace, enter into any Agreement or Compact with another State, or with a foreign Power, or engage in War, unless actually invaded, or in such imminent Danger as will not admit of delay.

Article II

SECTION 1. The executive Power shall be vested in a President of the United States of America. He shall hold his Office during the Term of four Years, and, together with the Vice President, chosen for the same Term, be elected, as follows

Each State shall appoint, in such Manner as the Legislature thereof may direct, a Number of Electors, equal to the whole Number of Senators and Representatives to which the State may be entitled in the Congress: but no Senator or Representative, or Person holding an Office of Trust or Profit under the United States, shall be appointed an Elector.

The Electors shall meet in their respective States, and vote by Ballot for two Persons, of whom one at least shall not be an Inhabitant of the same State with themselves. And they shall make a List of all the Persons voted for, and of the Number of Votes for each; which List they shall sign and certify, and transmit sealed to the Seat of the Government of the United States, directed to the President of the Senate. The President of the Senate shall, in the Presence

of the Senate and House of Representatives, open all the Certificates, and the Votes shall then be counted. The Person having the greatest Number of Votes shall be the President, if such Number be a Majority of the whole Number of Electors appointed; and if there be more than one who have such Majority, and have an equal Number of Votes, then the House of Representatives shall immediately chuse by Ballot one of them for President; and if no person have a Majority, then from the five highest on the List the said House shall in like Manner chuse the President. But in chusing the President, the Votes shall be taken by States, the Representation from each State having one Vote; A quorum for this Purpose shall consist of a Member or Members from two thirds of the States, and a Majority of all the States shall be necessary to a Choice. In every Case, after the Choice of the President, the Person having the greatest Number of Votes of the Electors shall be the Vice President. But if there should remain two or more who have equal Votes, the Senate shall chuse from them by Ballot the Vice President.

The Congress may determine the Time of chusing the Electors, and the Day on which they shall give their Votes; which Day shall be the same throughout the United States.

No Person except a natural born Citizen, or a Citizen of the United States, at the time of the Adoption of this Constitution, shall be eligible to the Office of President; neither shall any Person be eligible to that Office who shall not have attained to the Age of thirty five Years, and been fourteen Years a Resident within the United States.

In Case of the Removal of the President from Office, or of his Death, Resignation, or Inability to discharge the Powers and Duties of the said Office, the Same shall devolve on the Vice President, and the Congress may by Law provide for the Case of Removal, Death, Resignation or Inability, both of the President and Vice President, declaring what Officer shall then act as President, and such Officer shall act accordingly, until the Disability be removed, or a President shall be elected.

The President shall at stated Times receive for his Services, a Compensation, which shall neither be increased nor diminished during the Period for which he shall have been elected, and he shall not receive within that Period any other Emolument from the United States, or any of them.

Before he enter on the Execution of his Office, he shall take the following Oath or Affirmation:— "I do solemnly swear (or affirm) that I will faithfully execute the Office of President of the United States, and will to the best of my Ability, preserve, protect and defend the Constitution of the United States."

SECTION 2. The President shall be Commander in Chief of the Army and Navy of the United States, and of the Militia of the several States, when called into the actual Service of the United States; he may require the Opinion, in writing, of the principal Officer in each of the executive Departments, upon any Subject relating to the Duties of their respective Offices, and he shall have Power to grant Reprieves and Pardons for Offences against the United States, except in Cases of Impeachment.

He shall have Power, by and with the Advice and Consent of the Senate, to make Treaties, provided two thirds of the Senators present concur; and he shall nominate, and by and with the Advice and Consent of the Senate, shall appoint Ambassadors, other public Ministers and Consuls, judges of the supreme Court, and all other Officers of the United States, whose Appointments are not herein otherwise provided for, and which shall be established by Law: but the Congress may by Law vest the Appointment of such inferior Officers, as they think proper, in the President alone, in the Courts of Law, or in the Heads of Departments.

The President shall have Power to fill up all Vacancies that may happen during the Recess of the Senate, by granting Commissions which shall expire at the End of their next Session.

SECTION 3. He shall from time to time give to the Congress Information of the State of the Union, and recommend to their Consideration such Measures as he shall judge necessary and expedient; he may, on extraordinary Occasions, convene both Houses, or either of them, and in Case of Disagreement between them, with Respect to the Time of Adjournment, he may adjourn them to such Time as he shall think proper; he shall receive Ambassadors and other public Ministers; he shall take Care that the Laws be faithfully executed, and shall Commission all the Officers of the United States.

SECTION 4. The President, Vice President and all civil Officers of the United States, shall be removed from Office on Impeachment for, and Conviction of, Treason, Bribery, or other high Crimes and Misdemeanors.

Article III

SECTION 1. The judicial Power of the United States, shall be vested in one supreme Court, and in such inferior Courts as the Congress may from time to time ordain and establish. The Judges, both of the supreme and inferior Courts, shall hold their Offices during good Behaviour, and shall, at stated Times, receive for their Services, a Compensation, which shall not be diminished during their Continuance in Office.

SECTION 2. The judicial Power shall extend to all Cases, in Law and Equity, arising under this Constitution, the Laws of the United States, and Treaties made, or which shall be made, under their Authority;—to all Cases affecting Ambassadors, other public Ministers and Consuls;—to all Cases of admiralty and mari time jurisdiction;—to Controversies to which the United States shall be a Party;—to Controversies between two or more States; between a State and Citizens of another State;—between Citizens of different States,—between Citizens of the same State claiming Lands under Grants of different States, and between a State, or the Citizens thereof, and foreign States, Citizens or Subjects.

In all Cases affecting Ambassadors, other public Ministers and Consuls, and those in which a State shall be Party, the supreme Court shall have original jurisdiction. In all the other cases before mentioned, the supreme Court shall have appellate jurisdiction, both as to Law and Fact, with such Exceptions, and under such Regulations as the Congress shall make.

The Trial of all Crimes, except in Cases of Impeachment, shall be by jury; and such Trial shall be held in the State where the said Crimes shall have been committed; but when not committed within any State, the Trial shall be at such Place or Places as the Congress may by Law have directed.

SECTION 3. Treason against the United States, shall consist only in levying War against them, or in adhering to their Enemies, giving them Aid and Comfort. No Person shall be convicted of Treason unless on the Testimony of two Witnesses to the same overt Act, or on Confession in open Court.

The Congress shall have Power to declare the Punishment of Treason, but no Attainder of Treason shall work Corruption of Blood, or Forfeiture except during the Life of the Person attainted.

Article IV

SECTION 1. Full Faith and Credit shall be given in each State to the Public Acts, Records, and judicial Proceedings of every other State. And the Congress may by general Laws prescribe the Manner in which such Acts, Records and Proceedings shall be proved, and the Effect thereof.

SECTION 2. The Citizens of each State shall be entitled to all Privileges and Immunities of Citizens in the Several States.

A Person charged in any State with Treason, Felony, or other Crime, who shall flee from justice, and be found in another State, shall on Demand of the executive Authority of the State from which he fled, be delivered up, to be removed to the State having jurisdiction of the Crime.

No Person held to Service or Labour in one State, under the Laws thereof, escaping into another, shall, in Consequence of any Law or Regulation therein, be discharged from such Service or Labour, but shall be delivered up on Claim of the Party to whom such Service or Labour may be due.

SECTION 3. New States may be admitted by the Congress into this Union; but no new States shall be formed or erected within the Jurisdiction of any other State; nor any State be formed by the Junction of two or more States, or Parts of States, without the Consent of the Legislatures of the States concerned as well as of the Congress.

The Congress shall have Power to dispose of and make all needful Rules and Regulations respecting the Territory or other Property belonging to the United States; and nothing in this Constitution shall be so construed as to Prejudice any Claims of the United States, or of any particular State.

SECTION 4. The United States shall guarantee to every State in this Union a Republican Form of Government, and shall protect each of them against Invasion; and on Application of the Legislature, or of the Executive (when the Legislature cannot be convened) against domestic Violence.

Article V

The Congress, whenever two thirds of both Houses shall deem it necessary, shall propose Amendments to this Constitution, or, on the Application of the Legislatures of two thirds of the several States, shall call a Convention for proposing Amendments, which, in either Case, shall be valid to all Intents and Purposes, as Part of this Constitution, when ratified by the Legislatures of three fourths of the several States or by Conventions in three fourths thereof, as the one or the other Mode of Ratification may be proposed by the Congress; Provided that no Amendment which may be made prior to the Year One thousand eight hundred and eight shall in any Manner affect the first and fourth Clauses in the Ninth Section of the first Article; and that no State, without its Consent, shall be deprived of its equal Suffrage in the Senate.

Article VI

All Debts contracted and Engagements entered into, before the Adoption of this Constitution, shall be as valid against the United States under this Constitution, as under the Confederation.

This Constitution, and the Laws of the United States which shall be made in Pursuance thereof, and all Treaties made, or which shall be made, under the Authority of the United States, shall be the supreme Law of the Land; and the judges in every State shall be bound thereby, any Thing in the Constitution or Laws of any State to the Contrary notwithstanding.

The Senators and Representatives before mentioned, and the Members of the several State Legislatures, and all executive and judicial Officers, both of the United States and of the several States, shall be bound by Oath or Affirmation, to support this Constitution; but no religious Test shall ever be required as a Qualification to any Office or public Trust under the United States.

Article VII

The Ratification of the Conventions of nine States, shall be sufficient for the Establishment of this Constitution between the States so ratifying the Same.

Done in Convention by the Unanimous Consent of the States present the Seventeenth Day of September in the Year of our Lord one thousand seven hundred and Eighty seven and of the Independance of the United States of America the Twelfth. In witness whereof We have hereunto subscribed our Names,

G° WASHINGTON

President and Deputy from Virginia

Delaware
Richard Bassett
Gunning Bedford Jun
Jaco: Broom
John Dickinson
C--- Reed

North Carolina
Wm Blount
Richd Dobbs Spaight
Hu Williamson

South Carolina
Pierce Butler
Charles Cotesworth Pinckney
Charles Pinckney
J. Rutledge

Georgia
Abr Baldwin
William Few

New Hampshire
Nicholas Gilman
John Langdon

Maryland
DanL Carroll
Dan of St Thos Jenifer
James McHenry

Massachusetts
Nathaniel Gorham
Rufus King

Connecticut
Wm Saml Johnson
Roger Sherman

New York
Alexander Hamilton

New Jersey
David Brearley
Jona: Dayton
Wil: Livingston
Wm Paterson

Virginia
John Blair
James Madison Jr.

Pennsylvania
Geo. Clymer
Thos FitzSimons
B Franklin
Jared Ingersoll
Thomas Mifflin
Gouv Morris
Robt Morris
James Wilson

The U.S. Bill of Rights

The Preamble to The Bill of Rights

Congress of the United States
begun and held at the City of New-York, on Wednesday the fourth of March, one thousand seven hundred and eighty nine.

THE Conventions of a number of the States, having at the time of their adopting the Constitution, expressed a desire, in order to prevent misconstruction or abuse of its powers, that further declaratory and restrictive clauses should be added: And as extending the ground of public confidence in the Government, will best ensure the beneficent ends of its institution.

RESOLVED by the Senate and House of Representatives of the United States of America, in Congress assembled, two thirds of both Houses concurring, that the following Articles be proposed to the Legislatures of the several States, as amendments to the Constitution of the United States, all, or any of which Articles, when ratified by three fourths of the said Legislatures, to be valid to all intents and purposes, as part of the said Constitution; viz.

ARTICLES in addition to, and Amendment of the Constitution of the United States of America, proposed by Congress, and ratified by the Legislatures of the several States, pursuant to the fifth Article of the original Constitution.

Note: The following text is a transcription of the first ten amendments to the Constitution in their original form. These amendments were ratified December 15, 1791, and form what is known as the "Bill of Rights."

Amendment I

Congress shall make no law respecting an establishment of religion, or prohibiting the free exercise thereof; or abridging the freedom of speech, or of the press; or the right of the people peaceably to assemble, and to petition the Government for a redress of grievances.

Amendment II

A well regulated Militia, being necessary to the security of a free State, the right of the people to keep and bear Arms, shall not be infringed.

Amendment III

No Soldier shall, in time of peace be quartered in any house, without the consent of the Owner, nor in time of war, but in a manner to be prescribed by law.

Amendment IV

The right of the people to be secure in their persons, houses, papers, and effects, against unreasonable searches and seizures, shall not be violated, and no Warrants shall issue, but upon probable cause, supported by Oath or affirmation, and particularly describing the place to be searched, and the persons or things to be seized.

Amendment V

No person shall be held to answer for a capital, or otherwise infamous crime, unless on a presentment or indictment of a Grand Jury, except in cases arising in the land or naval forces, or in the Militia, when in actual service in time of War or public danger; nor shall any person be subject for the same offence to be twice put in jeopardy of life or limb; nor shall be compelled in any criminal case to be a witness against himself, nor be deprived of life, liberty, or property, without due process of law; nor shall private property be taken for public use, without just compensation.

Amendment VI

In all criminal prosecutions, the accused shall enjoy the right to a speedy and public trial, by an impartial jury of the State and district wherein the crime shall have been committed, which district shall have been previously ascertained by law, and to be informed of the nature and cause of the accusation; to be confronted with the witnesses against him; to have compulsory process for obtaining witnesses in his favor, and to have the Assistance of Counsel for his defence.

Amendment VII

In Suits at common law, where the value in controversy shall exceed twenty dollars, the right of trial by jury shall be preserved, and no fact tried by a jury, shall be otherwise re-examined in any Court of the United States, than according to the rules of the common law.

Amendment VIII

Excessive bail shall not be required, nor excessive fines imposed, nor cruel and unusual punishments inflicted.

Amendment IX

The enumeration in the Constitution, of certain rights, shall not be construed to deny or disparage others retained by the people.

Amendment X

The powers not delegated to the United States by the Constitution, nor prohibited by it to the States, are reserved to the States respectively, or to the people.

Section Four

Slave Resistance,
the Abolition Movement,
Manifest Destiny, and
Women's Rights

CHAPTER 6

The Hypocrisy of Whites, 1829

David Walker

David Walker (1785–1830) was a North Carolina free black who relocated in 1825 to Boston, where he ran a secondhand clothing store. An agent for *Freedom's Journal,* the nation's first black newspaper, and an influential member of Massachusetts General Colored Association, Walker was a self-taught intellectual whose wide experiences made him a leader in the African-American community. He financed three editions of his *Appeal,* which first appeared in September 1829.

In this militant essay, Walker lambastes the moral failure of whites, including colonizationists, to extend their religious and political principles to blacks. Near the end of his four-part pamphlet, he concludes in Old Testament terms that divine retribution awaits the nation and its failure to honor the full meaning of the Declaration of Independence. In part, he is assailing Thomas Jefferson, the author of the Declaration, who not only held numerous slaves at Monticello but also strongly suggested in *Notes on Virginia* that blacks were racially inferior. With impassioned rhetoric, Walker extends a Lockean right of revolution to the slaves: "Brethren, arise, arise! Strike for your lives and liberties. Now is the day and the hour." The appearance of the *Appeal* in southern ports led to restrictions on black sailors and the proscription of Walker. In 1830 he died suddenly. Black tradition has it that he was poisoned, though no concrete evidence of murder exists.

* * * * *

A Declaration Made July 4, 1776

It says,[1] "When in the course of human events, it becomes necessary for one people to dissolve the political bands which have connected them with another, and to assume the Powers of the earth, the separate and equal station to which the laws of nature and of nature's God entitle them. A decent respect for the opinions of mankind requires, that they should declare the causes which impel them to the separation.—We hold these truths to be self-evident—that all men are created equal, that they are endowed by their Creator with certain unalienable rights: that among these, are life, liberty, and tile pursuit of happiness that, to secure these rights, governments are instituted among men, deriving their just powers from the consent of the governed; that when ever any form of government becomes destructive of these ends, it is the right of the people to alter or to abolish it, and to institute a new government laying its foundation on such principles, and organizing its powers in such form, as to them shall seem most likely to effect their safety and happiness. Prudence, indeed, will dictate, that governments long established should not be changed for light and transient causes; and accordingly all experience hath shewn, that mankind are more disposed to suffer, while evils are sufferable, than to right themselves by abolishing the forms to which they are accustomed. But when a long train of abuses and usurpations, pursuing invariably the same object, evinces a design to reduce them under absolute despotism, it is their right it is their duty to throw off such government, and to provide new guards for their future security." See your Declaration Americans! ! ! Do you understand your own language? Hear your language, proclaimed to the world, July 4th, 1776—"We hold these truths to be self evident—that ALL MEN ARE CREATED EQUAL! ! that they are endowed by their Creator with certain unalienable rights; that among these are life, liberty, and the pursuit of happiness! !" Compare your own language above, extracted from your Declaration of Independence, with your cruelties and murders inflicted by your cruel and unmerciful fathers and yourselves on our fathers and on us—men who have never given your fathers or you the least provocation! ! ! ! !

Hear your language further!—"But when a long train of abuses and usurpation, pursuing invariably the same object, evinces a design to reduce them under absolute despotism, it is their right, it is their duty, to throw off such government, and to provide new guards for their future security."

Now, Americans! I ask you candidly, was your sufferings under Great Britain, one-hundredth part as Cruel and tyrannical as you have rendered ours under you? Some of you, no doubt, believe that we will never throw off your murderous government and "provide new guards for our future security." If Satan has made you believe it, will he not deceive you?[2] Do the whites say, I being a black man, ought to be humble, which I readily admit? I ask them, ought they not to be as humble as I? or do they think that they can measure arms with Jehovah? Will not the Lord yet humble them? or will not these very coloured people whom they now treat worse than brutes, yet under God, humble them low down enough?

Endnotes

1. See the Declaration of Independence of the United States.
2. The Lord has not taught the Americans that we will not some day or other throw off their chains and hand-cuffs, from our hands and feet, and their devilish lashes (which some of them shall have enough of yet) from off our backs.

To the Public, 1831

William Lloyd Garrison

Born in Newburyport, Massachusetts, William Lloyd Garrison (1805–1879) was deserted by an alcoholic father and raised by a poor but pious mother. His early family life may well have inclined a devout Garrison to seek moral perfection as well as social recognition, creating the tension between the spiritual and secular that characterized his reform career. He was a printer in Boston before joining the Quaker Benjamin Lundy in Baltimore as co-editor of the *Genius of Universal Emancipation*, an antislavery newspaper. In 1829 Garrison denounced colonization, breaking with Lundy's gradualism, though he also found the militancy of David Walker's *Appeal* injudicious. Yet Garrison's own rhetoric landed him in jail the next year for libeling a Newburyport merchant as a slave trader. After being bailed out by philanthropist Arthur Tappan, Garrison returned to Boston. There on January 1, 1831, he began publication of *The Liberator,* defiantly declaring, "I will be heard." Sustained by loyal black subscribers and a nucleus of white supporters, Garrison was increasingly heard, launching his journal on a thirty-five-year career dedicated to immediate abolitionism.

The following statement of purpose appeared on page one in the first issue of *The Liberator.*

* * * * *

In the month of August, I issued proposals for publishing *The Liberator* in Washington City; but the enterprise, though hailed in different sections of the country, was praised by public indifference. Since that time, the removal of the *Genius of Universal Emancipation* to the seat of government has rendered less imperious the establishment of a similar periodical in that quarter.

During my recent tour for the purpose of exciting the minds of the people by a series of discourses on the subject of slavery, every place that I visited gave fresh evidence of the fact, that a greater revolution in public sentiment was to be effected in the free states— —than at the South. I found contempt more bitter, opposition more active, detraction more relentless, prejudice more stubborn, and apathy more frozen, than among slaveowners themselves. Of course, there were individual exceptions to the contrary. This state of things afflicted, but did not dishearten me. I determined, at every hazard, to lift up the standard of emancipation in the eyes of the nation, *within sight of Bunker Hill* and in the birthplace of liberty. That standard is now unfurled; and long may it float, unhurt by the spoliations of time or the missiles of a desperate foe— yea, till every chain be broken, and every bondman

set free! Let Southern oppressors tremble—let their secret abettors tremble—let their Northern apologists tremble—let all the enemies of the persecuted blacks tremble.

I deem the publication of my original prospectus unnecessary, as it has obtained a wide circulation. The principles therein inculcated will be steadily pursued in this paper, excepting that I shall not array myself as the political partisan of any man. In defending the great cause of human rights, I wish to derive the assistance of all religions and of all parties.

Assenting to the "self-evident truth" maintained in the American Declaration of Independence, "that all men are created equal, and endowed by their Creator with certain inalienable rights—among which are life, liberty and the pursuit of happiness," I shall strenuously contend for the immediate enfranchisement of our slave population. In Park-Street Church, on the Fourth of July, 1829, in an address on slavery, I unreflectingly assented to the popular but pernicious doctrine of *gradual* abolition. I seize this opportunity to make a full and unequivocal recantation, and thus publicly to ask pardon of my God, of my country, and of my brethren the poor slaves, for having uttered a sentiment so full of timidity, injustice, and absurdity. A similar recantation, from my pen, was published in the *Genius of Universal Emancipation* at Baltimore, in September, 1829. My conscience is now satisfied.

I am aware that many object to the severity of my language; but is there not cause for severity? I will be as harsh as truth, and as uncompromising as justice. On this subject, I do not wish to think, or speak, or write, with moderation. No! no! Tell a man whose house is on fire to give a moderate alarm; tell him to moderately rescue his wife from the hands of the ravisher; tell the mother to gradually extricate her babe from the fire into which it has fallen;—but urge me not to use moderation in a cause like the present. I am in earnest—I will not equivocate—I will not excuse—I will not retreat a single inch—and I will be heard. The apathy of the people is enough to make every Statue leap from its pedestal, and to hasten the resurrection of the dead.

It is pretended, that I am retarding the cause of emancipation by the coarseness of my invective and the precipitancy of my measures. The charge is not true. On this question my influence, humble as it is,—is felt at this moment to a considerable extent, and shall be felt in coming years—not perniciously, but beneficially—not as a curse, but as a blessing; and posterity will bear testimony that I was right. I desire to thank God, that he enables me to disregard "the fear of man which bringeth a snare," and to speak his truth in its simplicity and power. And here I close with this fresh dedication:

> Oppression! I have seen thee, face to face,
> And met thy cruel eye and cloudy brow;
> But thy, soul-withering glance I fear not now—
> For dread to prouder feelings cloth give place
> Of deep abhorrence! Scorning the disgrace
> Of slavish knees that at thy footstool bow,
> I also kneel!—but with far other vow
> Do hail thee and thy herd of hirelings base:—
> I swear, while life-blood warms my throbbing veins,
> Still to oppose pose and thwart, with heart and hand,
> Thy brutalizing sway—till Afric's chains
> Are burst, and Freedom rules the rescued land,—
> Trampling Oppression and his iron rod:
> Such is the vow I take—so help me God!

William Lloyd Garrison
Boston, January 1, 1831

The Emergence of Political Abolitionism, 1837–1839

Elizur Wright

Widespread anti-abolitionism, including northern mobs, forced immediatists to reevaluate their means and ends, resulting in a three-way schism in their ranks. By 1840 nonresistant Garrisonians in Boston controlled the American Anti-Slavery Society, whereas church-oriented abolitionists led by Lewis Tappan in New York City formed the rival American and Foreign Anti-Slavery Society. A third group, centered in upstate New York, turned to political action and organized the Liberty party.

The following private correspondence of Elizur Wright (1805–1885), the domestic secretary of the American Anti-Slavery Society from 1833 to 1839 and then editor of the anti-Garrisonian *Massachusetts Abolitionist* from 1839 to 1840, illustrates the factionalism among abolitionists. Wright's 1837 letter to Garrison assails the doctrine of nonresistance. In an 1838 letter to Amos Phelps, an antislavery agent and Congregational minister who bridled at the Grimkés' defiance of decorum, Wright complains that the "woman question" is "tying a tin kettle to the tail of our enterprise." And to Henry B. Stanton, an officer of the national society, Wright in 1839 stresses that the American Anti-Slavery Society must nominate abolitionist candidates for president in order to refocus the cause. This confidential letter inadvertently came into Garrison's possession, adding to the acrimony among abolitionists.

＊＊＊＊＊

To William Lloyd Garrison
November 6, 1837

. . . My last letter, I hope, has convinced you that I do not wish to *gag* you on any subject. Still do I beg of you, as a brother, to let other subjects alone till slavery is finished, because this is the work you have taken in hand, it is the most pressing, and needs your whole energy. What if you do not live to communicate to the world your peculiar views of peace, Human Government, Theology, &c., will wisdom die with you? God is not so poverty stricken in regard to the means of accomplishing any of his designs as to be frustrated for the want of any man. You say 'truth is *one*, and not conflictive and multitudinous.' True; but the people are conflictive, and moreover they cannot receive and unitedly act upon more than one great truth at once. Again, abolitionists do not agree on many points not embraced in their Declaration of Sentiments. Hence it is no more than right that those persons and papers that are 'conspicuously identified' with them as a body, and are understood to speak a language common to all, should confine themselves to subjects on which all agree, or rather on which they do not seriously differ. Here is no restriction of liberty more than is due to truth and righteousness. God, by the very nature of things, has forbidden us to attempt everything at once.

But it does appear to me that *your* 'truth' that human government has no rightful authority, does conflict with *our truths*, as expressed in our

Declaration of Sentiments as well as with the most important measures by which we seek to accomplish our object. In the Declaration we maintain that 'the slaves ought instantly to be set free and brought under the *protection of law*,' and that 'Congress has the *right* and is solemnly bound to suppress the domestic slave trade' &c. What miserable falsehood if human government has no *right* to exist! You impeach my Christianity, because I 'cannot cease looking to man for *protection* and redress;' how can it consist with your Christianity to demand for others 'the *protection of law*'? If you follow out your doctrine, surely you must cease having anything to do with Congress and State Legislatures. Our action upon them in the direction of humanity, not only recognizes, but tends to confirm their power, for human governments are never so strong as when the weakest enjoy their protection. Having this view of the bearing of your Peace doctrines upon the dear cause of the slave, could I do less than to beg of you to suppress them till our contest is over? I have no fear of the prevalence of your opinions provided they make their home in their own tub—and that stands distinctly on its own bottom. What I fear is that they will suck *you* into a vortex of spiritual Quixotism, and thus absorb energies which might have shaken down the citadel of oppression.

As to the doctrine of 'perfect holiness,' I have not much to say. My observation of men concurs with the little study I have been able to bestow on the Old and New Testaments, in convincing me that men are not completely freed from sin by the grace of God, in this life. The final victory is over the banks of the Jordan. That a marvellous change does take place by the blessing of God upon Gospel truth, I joyfully believe; but that a man, while in the body, is placed by it beyond the power of temptation, I must be allowed to doubt. The history of Christianity is far from furnishing any proof to this effect, and the passages of scripture you quote, when taken in their connection, and with the allowances, exceptions and reservations to which all general propositions, not *founded on strict definitions*, are subject, do not seem to me to prove that a man cannot be holy in his general character without being altogether sinless. He cannot of course be holy and sinful in the same act, and how many times and how far he may sin and yet repent and be forgiven I shall not undertake to decide. There are a great many things that I don't know. But, I must believe the testimony of my own senses, in preference to anybody's interpretation of scripture, for Scripture itself after all rests on the testimony of sense—and according to that testimony I have never yet met with a man who was free from sin. I am obliged to reject your own claim to sinlessness. Your very letter refutes it. Hence, I am obliged to reject your theory, or to believe that the Gospel has never done its appropriate work within the range of my observation. If your theory could be established from scripture, it would only make me an infidel, for I cannot receive a revelation which asserts that which my senses pronounce to be false, nor one which visibly fails to accomplish its object. On your theory I must either believe that the Gospel has been in the world eighteen hundred years for nothing; or I must believe that pride and vanity, flattery and slander are holy affections and righteous acts! To be sure I may be saved from the dilemma by more evidence, but so far as what I have goes, I am transfixed on one horn or the other. Still therefore am I obliged to mourn over your theological position as 'down right fanaticism' and I pronounce it so with about the same confidence that I pronounce slaveholding a sin, but with far different feelings toward the subject of it.

Your theory of perfection, of course, takes away my hopes of salvation, which are not founded as you intimate on the law, but on *God's free grace to sinners*, who, believing in Christ, *desire to be saved from sin*. But I have said more than I intended—more than I shall every say again. I am sick unto death of the selfish, luxurious, good for nothing sort of religion which is eternally inquiring what will become of ME! If there are any men in the world who deserve to be damned, they are your very religious men whose anxiety is, not *to do right*, but to *escape hell*. They libel their Maker and disgrace his Saviour. Let us do what needs to be done to promote the welfare of all within our reach and leave our *salvation* to God.

To Amos A. Phelps
July 11, 1838

. . . Now for a word on the 'woman question'—for I am in a hurry—first of all on a question so delicate and *ridiculous*, I place no great confidence in my own judgment—of course I don't commend it as matter of popery to anybody else. Secondly, my faith and confidence in the *'everlasting distinction'* which has become the parent of another distinction between the bifurcated male galligaskin and the monopetalons tunic of the female, is so strong of itself that it hardly permits me to engage in any *conservative* measures. Truly I am a *conservative* in a certain sense,—I think the tom turkeys ought to do the gobbling. I am opposed to hens crowing, and surely as a general rule, to female preaching—but I think practically, there is as little need of my conservatism in the one case as the other. I am, therefore, disposed to give the *women people* all the rope they have a mind to take. Do they want to try the man's part? Let them try it as many of them and as long as they please. I have no sympathy with the terror of certain *male women* who quote Paul at the top of their lungs, as if our friend Theodore's wife or Abby Kelly were about to wrench from them their diploma of manhood forever and aye—but I have just no doubt at all that Paul and propriety are both on their side in the *argument*. Paul, if I understand him, however, did no less than hint that his instructions for the regulation of women might without much danger have been left to *nature herself*. And whatever was the confidence of the Apostle in the correctness of his views of propriety, I think he must have been too much of a gentleman to choke a woman with authority, as well as *too wise a man*. After giving his opinion (do his original words mean more?) I fancy he would have left it to nature and the women themselves whether they should exercise their gift in public. There certainly have been cases in which women have done the work of men nobly and well. If nature were called to account for this I imagine she would cry out *Exceptio probat* &c. That this question should be brought up by some of our friends as though it were a twin sister of Anti-Slavery, is mortifying the extreme. It belittles us—it is tying a tin kettle to the tail of our enterprise. But I don't see what we can do better than to let it take its course. Let the women take as much as they please of the liberty which the terms of our constitution give them—only the few exceptions of '*the female brethren*' will avail themselves of it and experience will in due time teach *them* the needful lesson. As to the terrors of their counterparts of our own gender, they will calm away in time, like all other terrors.

To Henry B. Stanton
October 12, 1839

Saw only the streak of you as you passed here. So I must say a word in scrawl which I should have said vocally. It is this—as you are a man and no

mouse, urge the Am. Soc. at Cleveland to take a decided step toward *Presidential Candidates*. Our labor will be more than half lost without them. It is a step which we have always contemplated as one which Providence *might* force upon us. Has not the time come? What else can we do except to *back out*? The South can outbid us, and hence she will buy up both political parties as to national politics, *ad infinitum*. We must have a free northern nucleus—a standard flung to the breeze—some thing around which to rally. While we are about it let's have *good stuff*. I am satisfied the best we have will do. Let a candidate take well in his own State (1.) and *he* can be made *popular* anywhere else. . . . There are men enough, if they will only stand, and they must be made to. If the thing is done judiciously and deliberately there will be no difficulty. Provided we get *good stuff*, not much will depend upon the previous fame of our candidates—we can manufacture their notoriety as we go along. Perhaps the Society can be got to pass a resolution asserting the propriety of an anti-slavery nomination in case Clay, Van Buren, &c., pro-slavery men, are nominated by the parties, and authorizing the Ex. Com., or a Committee to call a convention expressly to nominate Presidential candidates, when there is no longer any possibility of a proper candidate being nominated by either party. This will give time for minds to *turn*, and get rid of their *repugnancies*. Just about as soon as we can be sure of *good stuff* to stand the racket, our candidates should be brought before the public. We shall certainly gain more than we lose.

Benefits

1. Something practical for every man to do.
2. Terror struck to the heart of the south from Clay downwards.
3. Concert of action—iron sharpening iron.
4. Leaving non resistance abolitionism *hors du combat*. (What will our "ninety-nine hundredths" do? vote for Clay, Van Buren,... or Scattering or Nobody?)
5. Politics enobled—glorious object—clean skirts.
6. Interest, discussion and liberality increased a hundred fold—the matter being carried *home* to everybody.
7. Consistency—the jewel—the everything of such a cause as ours.

If we gain these points, what can we lose? Have we not now thoroughly tried everything short of this?

Precedents are not to be quoted against us. Anti-Masonry had not such a *quarry*. Its object shrunk away from it. The enterprise was never half baked. Yet it died, not by nominating separate candidates so much as by amalgamating with existing parties. (2.) After all it died for want of *tangible work* more than anything else. Our cause is entirely different.

But you have thought of this more than I. So no more coals to Newcastle. I throw in my mite.

One thing I *know*. Unless you do take such a step, our New Organization [Massachusetts Abolitionist Society] here is a gone case. (3.) It has been, inter nos, shockingly mismanaged. Everything has been made to turn upon the *woman question*. The political has been left to fall out of sight. (4.) In our State politics the Temperance question is so fairly on the ground that we have not room to stand. (5.) I wont do for us to start the national politics. (6.) But if the *parent society* does so, and not by *our* move—then we can take hold with all our might, the non resistants will have to be Out upon us under a true flag—the *confounded* woman question will be forgotten—and we shall take a *living* position. You certainly *see* this. Take my solemn assurance that it is life and death with us. Make the move, and we will follow and live. How have I wished since this shattered right fist has failed me for *voice*, and brains to match! (7.) But *you* can do it. For the love of heaven and earth *do it*; and write me the earliest word.

A Call for Slave Revolution, 1843

Henry Highland Garnet

At the National Negro Convention held in Buffalo from August 21 to 24, 1843, Henry Highland Garnet (1815–1882), a twenty-seven-year-old Presbyterian minister from Troy, New York, set the standard for militancy in an open call for slave insurrection. His speech, "An Address to the Slaves of the United States," was rejected by a majority of only one vote (including that of Frederick Douglass) from representing an affirmation of the seventy participants. The delegates feared that the speech, which soon attracted national attention, would lead to further repression of free blacks in the South.

Garnet's oratory shocked many black and white abolitionists in its justification of violent means. Nonetheless the sentiments were in the African-American tradition of resistance as exemplified by Denmark Vesey, Nat Turner, Joseph Cinque, and David Walker's *Appeal* with which the "Address" was jointly published in 1848. The grandson of a Mandingo leader, Garnet fled slavery in Maryland as a youth, suffered the separation of his family by slave catchers in New York City, and, at school in Canaan, New Hampshire, stood off white vigilantes with a shotgun. His "Address" proved prophetic of impending national violence over slavery, including "Bleeding Kansas," the Harpers Ferry raid, and the Civil War itself.

✳ ✳ ✳ ✳ ✳

Fellow-men! patient sufferers! behold your dearest rights crushed to the earth! See your sons murdered, and your wives, mothers, and sisters, doomed to prostitution! In the name of the merciful God and by all that life is worth, let it no longer be a debateable question, whether it is better to choose LIBERTY or DEATH!

In 1822, Denmark Veazie, of South Carolina, formed a plan for the liberation of his fellow men. In the whole history of human efforts to overthrow slavery, a more complicated and tremendous plan was never formed. He was betrayed by the treachery of his own people, and died a martyr to freedom. Many a brave hero fell, but History, faithful to her high trust, will transcribe his name on the same monument with Moses, Hampden, Tell, Bruce, and Wallace, Touissaint L'Overteur, Lafayette and Washington. That tremendous movement shook the whole empire of slavery. The guilty soul thieves were overwhelmed with fear. It is a matter of fact, that at that time, and in consequence of the threatened revolution, the slave states talked strongly of emancipation. But they blew but one blast of the trumpet of freedom, and then laid it aside. As these men became quiet, the slaveholders ceased to talk about emancipation: and now, behold your condition to-day! Angels sigh over it, and humanity has long since exhausted her tears in weeping on your account!

The patriotic Nathaniel Turner followed Denmark Veazie. He was goaded to desperation by wrong and injustice. By Despotism, his name has been recorded on the list of infamy, but future generations will number him among the noble and brave.

Next arose the immortal Joseph Cinque, the hero of the Amistad. He was a native African, and by the help of God he emancipated a whole ship-load of his fellow men on the high seas. And he now sings of liberty on the sunny hills of Africa, and beneath his native palm trees, where he hears the lion roar, and feels himself as free as that king of the forest.

Next arose Madison Washington, that bright star of freedom, and took his station in the constellation of freedom. He was a slave on board the brig Creole, of Richmond, bound to New Orleans, that great slave mart, with a hundred and four others. Nineteen struck for liberty or death. But one life was taken, and the whole were emancipated, and the vessel was carried into Nassau, New Providence. Noble men! Those who have fallen in freedom's conflict, their memories will be cherished by the true hearted, and the God-fearing, in all future generations; those who are living, their names are surrounded by a halo of glory.

We do not advise you to attempt a revolution with the sword, because it would be inexpedient. Your numbers are too small, and moreover the rising spirit of the age, and the spirit of the gospel, are opposed to war and bloodshed. But from this moment cease to labor for tyrants who will not remunerate you. Let every slave throughout the land do this, and the days of slavery are numbered. You cannot be more oppressed than you have been—you cannot suffer greater cruelties than you have already. RATHER DIE FREEMEN, THAN LIVE TO BE SLAVES. Remember that you are THREE MILLIONS.

It is in your power so to torment the God-cursed slaveholders, that they will be glad to let you go free.

If the scale was turned, and black men were the masters, and white men the slaves, every destructive agent and element would be employed to lay the oppressor low. Danger and death would hang over their heads day and night. Yes, the tyrants would meet with plagues more terrible than those of Pharaoh. But you are a patient people. You act as though you were made for the special use of these devils. You act as though your daughters were born to pamper the lusts of your masters and overseers. And worse than all, you tamely submit, while your lords tear your wives from your embraces, and defile them before your eyes. In the name of God we ask, are you men? Where is the blood of your fathers? Has it all run out of your veins? Awake, awake; millions of voices are calling you! Your dead fathers speak to you from their graves. Heaven, as with a voice of thunder, calls on you to arise from the dust.

Let your motto be RESISTANCE! REISTANCE! RESISTANCE! No oppressed people have ever secured their liberty without resistance. What kind of resistance you had better make, you must decide by the circumstances that surround you, and according to the suggestion of expediency. Brethren, adieu. Trust in the living God. Labor for the peace of the human race, and remember that you are three millions.

The Confession of Nat Turner

Nat Turner

Agreeable to his own appointment, on the evening he was committed to prison, with permission of the jailer, I visited NAT on Tuesday the 1st November, when, without being questioned at all, he commenced his narrative in the following words:—

✳ ✳ ✳ ✳ ✳

Sir,—You have asked me to give a history of the motives which induced me to undertake the late insurrection, as you call it—To do so I must go back to the days of my infancy, and even before I was born. I was thirty-one years of age the 2d of October last, and born the property of Benj. Turner, of this county. In my childhood a circumstance occurred which made an indelible impression on my mind, and laid the ground work of that enthusiasm, which has terminated so fatally to many, both white and black, and for which I am about to atone at the gallows. It is here necessary to relate this circumstance—trifling as it may seem, it was the commencement of that belief which has grown with time, and even now, sir, in this dungeon, helpless and forsaken as I am, I cannot divest myself of. Being at play with other children, when three or four years old, I was telling them something, which my mother overhearing, said it had happened before I was born—I stuck to my story, however, and related somethings which went, in her opinion, to confirm it—others being called on were greatly astonished, knowing that these things had happened, and caused them to say in my hearing, I surely would be a prophet, as the Lord had shewn me things that had happened before my birth. And my father and mother strengthened me in this my first impression, saying in my presence, I was intended for some great purpose, which they had always thought from certain marks on my head and breast—[a parcel of excrescences which I believe are not at all uncommon, particularly among negroes, as I have seen several with the same. In this case he has either cut them off or they have nearly disappeared]—My grandmother, who was very religious, and to whom I was much attached—my master, who belonged to the church, and other religious persons who visited the house, and whom I often saw at prayers, noticing the singularity of my manners, I suppose, and my uncommon intelligence for a child, remarked I had too much sense to be raised, and if I was, I would never be of any service to any one as a slave—To a mind like mine, restless, inquisitive and observant of every thing that was passing, it is easy to suppose that religion was the subject to which it would be directed, and although this subject principally occupied my thoughts—was nothing that I saw or heard of to which my attention was not directed—The manner in which I learned to read and write, not only had great influence on my own mind, as I acquired it with the most perfect ease, so much so, that I have no recollection whatever of learning the alphabet—but to the astonishment of the family, one day, when a book was shewn me to keep me from crying, I began spelling the names of different objects—this was a source of wonder to all in the neighborhood, particularly the blacks—and this learning was constantly improved at all opportunities—when I got large enough to go to work, while employed, I was reflecting on many things that would present themselves to my imagination, and whenever an opportunity occurred of looking at a book, when the school children were getting their lessons, I would find many things that the fertility of my own imagination had depicted to me before; all my time, not devoted to my master's service, was spent either in prayer, or in making experiments in casting different things in moulds made of earth, in attempting to make paper, gunpowder, and many other experiments, that although I could not perfect, yet convinced me of its practicability if I had the means.* I was not addicted to stealing in my youth, nor have ever been—Yet such was the confidence of the negroes in the neighborhood, even at this early period of my life, in my superior judgment, that they would often carry me with them when they were going on any roguery, to plan for them. Growing up among them, with this confidence in my superior judgment, and when this, in their opinions, was perfected by Divine inspiration, from the circumstances already alluded to in my infancy, and which belief was ever afterwards zealously inculcated by the austerity of my life and manners, which became the subject of remark by white and black.—Having soon discovered to be great, I must appear so, and therefore studiously avoided mixing in society, and wrapped myself in mystery, devoting my time to fasting and prayer—By this time, having arrived to man's estate, and hearing the scriptures commented on at meetings, I was struck with that particular passage which says: "Seek ye the kingdom of Heaven and all things shall be added unto you." I reflected much on this passage, and prayed daily for light on this subject—As I was praying one day at my plough, the spirit spoke to me, saying "Seek ye the kingdom of Heaven and all things shall be added unto you."

Question—what do you mean by the Spirit.

Ans. The Spirit that spoke to the prophets in former days—and I was greatly astonished, and for two years prayed continually, whenever my duty would permit—and then again I had the same revelation, which fully confirmed me in the impression that I was ordained for some great purpose in the hands of the Almighty. Several years rolled round, in which many events occurred to strengthen me in this my belief. At this time I reverted in my mind to the remarks made of me in my childhood, and the things that had been shewn me—and as it had been said of me in my childhood by those by whom I had been taught to pray, both white and black, and in whom I had the greatest confidence, that I had too much sense to be raised, and if I was, I would never be of any use to any one as a slave. Now finding I had arrived to man's estate, and was a slave, and these revelations being made known to me, I began to direct my attention to this great

object, to fulfil the purpose for which, by this time, I felt assured I was intended. Knowing the influence I had obtained over the minds of my fellow servants, (not by the means of conjuring and such like tricks—for to them I always spoke of such things with contempt) but by the communion of the Spirit whose revelations I often communicated to them, and they believed and said my wisdom came from God. I now began to prepare them for my purpose, by telling them something was about to happen that would terminate in fulfilling the great promise that had been made to me—About this time I was placed under an overseer, from whom I ran away—and after remaining in the woods thirty days, I returned, to the astonishment of the negroes on the plantation, who thought I had made my escape to some other part of the country, as my father had done before. But the reason of my return was, that the Spirit appeared to me and said I had my wishes directed to the things of this world, and not to the kingdom of Heaven, and that I should return to the service of my earthly master—"For he who knoweth his Master's will, and doeth it not, shall be beaten with many stripes, and thus have I chastened you." And the negroes found fault, and murmured against me, saying that if they had my sense they would not serve any master in the world. And about this time I had a vision—and I saw white spirits and black spirits engaged in battle, and the sun was darkened—the thunder rolled in the Heavens, and blood flowed in streams—and I heard a voice saying, "Such is your luck, such you are called to see, and let it come rough or smooth, you must surely bare it." I now withdrew myself as much as my situation would permit, from the intercourse of my fellow servants, for the avowed purpose of serving the Spirit more fully—and it appeared to me, and reminded me of the things it had already shown me, and that it would then reveal to me the knowledge of the elements, the revolution of the planets, the operation of tides, and changes of the seasons. After this revelation in the year 1825, and the knowledge of the elements being made known to me, I sought more than ever to obtain true holiness before the great day of judgment should appear, and then I began to receive the true knowledge of faith. And from the first steps of righteousness until the last, was I made perfect; and the Holy Ghost was with me, and said, "Behold me as I stand in the Heavens"—and I looked and saw the forms of men in different attitudes—and there were lights in the sky to which the children of darkness gave other names than what they really were—for they were the lights of the Saviour's hands, stretched forth from east to west, even as they were extended on the cross on Calvary for the redemption of sinners. And I wondered greatly at these miracles, and prayed to be informed of a certainty of the meaning thereof—and shortly afterwards, while laboring in the field, I discovered drops of blood on the corn as though it were dew from heaven—and I communicated it to many, both white and black, in the neighborhood—and I then found on the leaves in the woods hieroglyphic characters, and numbers, with the forms of men in different attitudes, portrayed in blood, and representing the figures I had seen before in the heavens. And now the Holy Ghost had revealed itself to me, and made plain the miracles it had shown me—For as the blood of Christ had been shed on this earth, and had ascended to heaven for the salvation of sinners, and was now returning to earth again in the form of dew—and as the leaves on the trees bore the impression of the figures I had seen in the heavens, it was plain to me that the Saviour was about to lay down the yoke he had borne for the sins of men, and the great day of judgment was at hand. About this time I told these things to a white man, (Etheldred T. Brantley) on whom it had a wonderful effect—and he ceased from his wickedness, and was attacked immediately with a cutaneous eruption, and blood ozed from the pores of his skin, and after praying and fasting nine days, he was healed, and the Spirit appeared to me again, and said, as the Saviour had been baptised so should we be also—and when the white people would not let us be baptised by the church, we went down into the water together, in the sight of many who reviled us, and were baptised by the Spirit —After this I rejoiced greatly, and gave thanks to God. And on the 12th of May, 1828, I heard a loud noise in the heavens, and the Spirit instantly appeared to me and said the Serpent was loosened, and Christ had laid down the yoke he had borne for the sins of men, and that I should take it on and fight against the Serpent, for the time was fast approaching when the first should be last and the last should be first.

Ques. Do you not find yourself mistaken now?

Ans. Was not Christ crucified. And by signs in the heavens that it would make known to me when I should commence the great work—and until the first sign appeared, I should conceal it from the knowledge of men—And on the appearance of the sign, (the eclipse of the sun last February) I should arise and prepare myself, and slay my enemies with their own weapons. And immediately on the sign appearing in the heavens, the seal was removed from my lips, and I communicated the great work laid out for me to do, to four in whom I had the greatest confidence. (Henry, Hark, Nelson, and Sam)—It was intended by us to have begun the work of death on the 4th July last—Many were the plans formed and rejected by us, and it affected my mind to such a degree, that I fell sick, and the time passed without our coming to any determination how to commence—Still forming new schemes and rejecting them, when the sign appeared again, which determined me not to wait longer.

Since the commencement of 1830, I had been living with Mr. Joseph Travis, who was to me a kind master, and placed the greatest confidence in me; in fact I had no cause to complain of his treatment to me. On Saturday evening, the 20th of August, it was agreed between Henry, Hark and myself, to prepare a dinner the next day for the men we expected, and then to concert a plan, as we had not yet determined on any. Hark, on the following morning, brought a pig, and Henry brandy, and being joined by Sam, Nelson, Will and Jack, they prepared in the woods a dinner, where, about three o'clock, I joined them.

Q. Why were you so backward in joining them.

A. The same reason that had caused me not to mix with them for years before.

I saluted them on coming up, and asked Will how came he there, he answered, his life was worth no more than others, and his liberty as dear to him. I asked him if he thought to obtain it? He said he would, or loose his life. This was enough to put him in full confidence. Jack, I knew, was only a tool in the hands of Hark, it was quickly agreed we should commence at home (Mr. J. Travis') on that night, and until we had armed and equipped ourselves, and gathered sufficient force, neither age nor sex was to be spared, (which was invariably adhered to.) We remained at the feast, until about two hours in the night, when we went to the house and found Austin; they all went to the cider press and drank, except myself. On returning to the house, Hark went to the door with an axe, for the purpose of breaking it open, as we knew we were strong enough to murder the family, if they were awaked by the noise; but reflecting that it might create an alarm in the neighborhood, we determined to enter the house secretly, and murder them whilst sleeping. Hark got a ladder and set it against the chimney, on which I ascended, and hoisting a window, entered and came down stairs, unbarred the door, and removed the guns from their places. It was then observed that I must spill the first blood. On which, armed with a hatchet, and accompanied by Will, I entered my master's chamber, it being dark, I could not give a death blow, the hatchet glanced from his head, he sprang from the bed and called his wife, it was his last word, Will laid him dead, with a blow of his axe, and Mrs. Travis shared the same fate, as she lay in bed. The murder of this family, five in number, was the work of a moment, not one of them awoke; there was a little infant sleeping in a cradle, that was forgotten, until we had left the house and gone some distance, when Henry and Will returned and killed it; we got here, four guns that would shoot, and several old muskets, with a pound or two of powder. We remained some time at the barn, where we paraded; I formed them in a line as soldiers, and after carrying them through all the manoevres I was master of, marched them off to Mr. Salathul Francis', about six hundred yards distant. Sam and Will went to the door and knocked. Mr. Francis asked who was there, Sam replied it was him, and he had a letter for him, on which he got up and came to the door; they immediately seized him, and dragging him out a little from the door, he was dispatched by repeated blows on the head; there was no other white person in the family. We started from there for Mrs. Reese's, maintaining the most perfect silence on our march, where finding the door unlocked, we entered, and murdured Mrs. Reese in her bed, while sleeping; her son awoke, but it was only to sleep the sleep of death, he had only time to say who is that, and he was no more. From Mrs. Reese's we went to Mrs. Turner's, a mile distant, which we reached about sunrise, on Monday morning. Henry, Austin, and Sam, went to the still, where, finding Mr. Peebles, Austin shot him, and the rest of us went to the house; as we approached, the family discovered us, and shut the door. Vain hope! Will, with one stroke of his axe, opened it, and we entered and found Mrs. Turner and Mrs. Newsome in the middle of a room, almost frightened to death. Will immediately killed Mrs. Turner, with one blow of his axe. I took Mrs. Newsome by the hand, and with the sword I had when I was apprehended, I struck her several blows over the head, but not being able to kill her, as

the sword was dull. Will turning around and discovering it, despatched her also. A general destruction of property and search for money and ammunition, always succeeded the murders. By this time my company amounted to fifteen, and nine men mounted, who started for Mrs. Whitehead's, (the other six were to go through a by way to Mr. Bryant's, and rejoin us at Mrs. Whitehead's) as we approached the house we discovered Mr. Richard Whitehead standing in the cotton patch, near the lane fence; we called him over into the lane, and Will, the executioner, was near at hand, with his fatal axe, to send him to an untimely grave. As we pushed on to the house, I discovered some one run round the garden, and thinking it was some of the white family, I pursued them, but finding it was a servant girl belonging to the house, I returned to commence the work of death, but they whom I left, had not been idle; all the family were already murdered, but Mrs. Whitehead and her daughter Margaret. As I came round to the door I saw Will pulling Mrs. Whitehead out of the house, and at the step he nearly severed her head from her body, with his broad axe. Miss Margaret, when I discovered her, had concealed herself in the comer, formed by the projection of the cellar cap from the house; on my approach she fled, but was soon overtaken, and after repeated blows with a sword, I killed her by a blow on the head, with a fence rail. By this time, the six who had gone by Mr. Bryant's, rejoined us, and informed me they had done the work of death assigned them. We again divided, part going to Mr. Richard Porter's, and from thence to Nathaniel Francis', the others to Mr. Howell Harris', and Mr. T. Doyles. On my reaching Mr. Porter's, he had escaped with his family. I understood there, that the alarm had already spread, and I immediately returned to bring up those sent to Mr. Doyles', and Mr. Howell Harris'; the party I left going on to Mr. Francis', having told them I would join them in that neighborhood. I met these sent to Mr. Doyles' and Mr. Harris' returning, having met Mr. Doyle on the road and killed him; and learning from some who joined them, that Mr. Harris was from home, I immediately pursued the course taken by the party gone on before; but knowing they would complete the work of death and pillage, at Mr. Francis' before I could get there, I went to Mr. Peter Edwards', expecting to find them there, but they had been here also. I then went to Mr. John T. Barrows, they had been here and murdered him. I pursued on their track to Capt. Newit Harris', where I found the greater part mounted, and ready to start; the men now amounting to about forty, shouted and hurraed as I rode up, some were in the yard, loading their guns, others drinking. They said Captain Harris and his family had escaped, the property in the house they destroyed, robbing him of money and other valuables. I ordered them to mount and march instantly, this was about nine or ten o'clock, Monday morning. I proceeded to Mr. Levi Waller's, two or three miles distant. I took my station in the rear, and as it 'twas my object to carry terror and devastation wherever we went, I placed fifteen or twenty of the best armed and most to be relied on, in front, who generally approached the house as fast as their horses could run; this was for two purposes, to prevent their escape and strike terror to the inhabitants—on this account I never got to the houses, after leaving Mrs. Whitehead's, until the murders were committed, except in one case. I sometimes got in sight in time to see the work of death completed, viewed the mangled bodies as they lay, in silent satisfaction, and immediately started in quest of other victims—Having murdered Mrs. Waller and ten children, we started for Mr. William Williams'—having killed him and two little boys that were there; while engaged in this, Mrs. Williams fled and got some distance from the house, but she was pursued, overtaken, and compelled to get up behind one of the company, who brought her back, and after showing her the mangled body of her lifeless husband, she was told to get down and lay by his side, where she was shot dead. I then started for Mr. Jacob Williams, where the family were murdered—Here we found a young man named Drury, who had come on business with Mr. Williams—he was pursued, overtaken and shot. Mrs. Vaughan was the next place we visited—and after murdering the family here, determined on starting for Jerusalem—Our number amounted now to fifty or sixty, all mounted and armed with guns, axes, swords and clubs—On reaching Mr. James W. Parkers' gate, immediately on the road leading to Jerusalem, and about three miles distant, it was proposed to me to call there, but I objected, as I knew he was gone to Jerusalem, and my object was to reach there as soon as possible; but some of the men having relations at Mr. Parker's it was agreed that they might call and get his people. I remained at the gate on the road, with seven or eight; the others going across the field to the house, about half a mile off. After waiting some time for

them, I became impatient, and started to the house for them, and on our return we were met by a party of white men, who had pursued our blood-stained track, and who had fired on those at the gate, and dispersed them, which I new nothing of, not having been at that time rejoined by any of them—Immediately on discovering the whites, I ordered my men to halt and form, as they appeared to be alarmed—white men, eighteen in number, approached us in about one hundred yards, when one of them fired, (this was against the positive orders of Captain Alexander P. Peete, who commanded, and who had directed the men to reserve their fire until within thirty paces). And I discovered about half of them retreating, I then ordered my men to fire and rush on them; the few remaining stood their ground until we approached within fifty yards, when they fired and retreated. We pursued and overtook some of them who we thought we left dead; (they were not killed) after pursuing them about two hundred yards, and rising a little hill, I discovered they were met by another party, and had haulted, and were re-loading their guns, (this was a small party from Jerusalem who knew the negroes were in the field, and had just tied their horses to await their return to the road, knowing that Mr. Parker and family were in Jerusalem, but knew nothing of the party that had gone in with Captain Peete; on hearing the firing they immediately rushed to the spot and arrived just in time to arrest the progress of these barbarous villains, and save the lives of their friends and fellow citizens.) Thinking that those who retreated first, and the party who fired on us at fifty or sixty yards distant, had all only fallen back to meet others with ammunition. As I saw them re-loading their guns, and more coming up than I saw at first, and several of my bravest men being wounded, the others became panick struck and squandered over the field; the white men pursued and fired on us several times. Hark had his horse shot under him, and I caught another for him as it was running by me; five or six of my men were wounded, but none left on the field; finding myself defeated here I instantly determined to go through a private way, and cross the Nottoway river at the Cypress Bridge, three miles below Jerusalem, and attack that place in the rear, as I expected they would look for me on the other road, and I had a great desire to get there to procure arms and amunition. After going a short distance in this private way, accompanied by about twenty men, I overtook two or three who told me the others were dispersed in every direction. After trying [sic) in vain to collect a sufficient force to proceed to Jerusalem, I determined to return, as I was sure they would make back to their old neighborhood, where they would rejoin me, make new recruits, and come down again. On my way back, I called at Mrs. Thomas's, Mrs. Spencer's, and several other places, the white families having fled, we found no more victims to gratify our thirst for blood, we stopped at Majr. Ridley's quarter for the night, and being joined by four of his men, with the recruits made since my defeat, we mustered now about forty strong. After placing out sentinels, I laid down to sleep, but was quickly roused by a great racket; starting up, I found some mounted, and others in great confusion; one of the sentinels having given the alarm that we were about to be attacked, I ordered some to ride round and reconnoitre, and on their return the others being more alarmed, not knowing who they were, fled in different ways, so that I was reduced to about twenty again; with this I determined to attempt to recruit, and proceed on to rally in the neighborhood, I had left. Dr. Blunt's was the nearest house, which we reached just before day; on riding up the yard, Hark fired a gun. We expected Dr. Blunt and his family were at Maj. Ridley's, as I knew there was a company of men there; the gun was fired to ascertain if any of the family were at home; we were immediately fired upon and retreated, leaving several of my men. I do not know what became of them, as I never saw them afterwards. Pursuing our course back and coming in sight of Captain Harris', where we had been the day before, we discovered a party of white men at the house, on which all deserted me but two, (Jacob and Nat) we concealed ourselves in the woods until near night, when I sent them in search of Henry, Sam, Nelson, and Hark, and directed them to rally all they could, at the place we had had our dinner the Sunday before, where they would find me, and I accordingly returned there as soon as it was dark and remained until Wednesday evening, when discovering white men riding around the place as though they were looking for some one, and none of my men joining me, I concluded Jacob and Nat had been taken, and compelled to betray me. On this I gave up all hope for the present; and on Thursday night after having supplied myself with provisions from Mr. Travis's, I scratched a hole under a pile of fence rails in a field, where I concealed myself for six weeks, never leaving my hiding place but for a few minutes in the dead of night to get water which was very near; thinking by this time I could venture out, I began to go about in the night and eaves drop the houses in the neighborhood; pursuing this course for about a fortnight and gathering little or no intelligence, afraid of speaking to any human being, and returning every morning to my cave before the dawn of day. I know not how long I might have led this life, if accident had not betrayed me, a dog in the neighborhood passing by my hiding place one night while I was out, was attracted by some meat I had in my cave, and crawled in and stole it, and was coming out just as I returned. A few nights after, two negroes having started to go hunting with the same dog, and passed that way, the dog came again to the place, and having just gone out to walk about, discovered me and barked, on which thinking myself discovered, I spoke to them to beg concealment. On making myself known they fled from me. Knowing then they would betray me, I immediately left my hiding place, and was pursued almost incessantly until I was taken a fortnight afterwards by Mr. Benjamin Phipps, in a little hole I had dug out with my sword, for the purpose of concealment, under the top of a fallen tree. On Mr. Phipps' discovering the place of my concealment, he cocked his gun and aimed at me. I requested him not to shoot and I would give up, upon which he demanded my sword. I delivered it to him, and he brought me to prison. During the time I was pursued, I had many hair breadth escapes, which your time will not permit you to relate. I am here loaded with chains, and willing to suffer the fate that awaits me.

I here proceeded to make some inquiries of him, after assuring him of the certain death that awaited him, and that concealment would only bring destruction on the innocent as well as guilty, of his own color, if he knew of any extensive or concerted plan, His answer was, I do not. When I questioned him as to the insurrection in North Carolina happening about the same time, he denied any knowledge of it; and when I looked him in the face as though I would search his inmost thoughts, he replied, "I see sir, you doubt my word; but can you not think the same ideas, and strange appearances about this time in the heaven's might prompt others, as well as myself, to this undertaking." I now had much conversation with and asked him many questions, having forborne to do so previously, except in the cases noted in parenthesis; but during his statement, I had, unnoticed by him, taken notes as to some particular circumstances, and having the advantage of his statement before me in writing, on the evening of the third day that I had been with him, I began a cross examination, and found his statement corroborated by every circumstance coming within my own knowledge or the confessions of others whom had been either killed or executed, and whom he had not seen nor had any knowledge since 22d of August last, he expressed himself fully satisfied as to the impracticability of his attempt. It has been said he was ignorant and cowardly, and that his object was to murder and rob for the purpose of obtaining money to make his escape. It is notorious, that he was never known to have a dollar in his life; to swear an oath, or drink a drop of spirits. As to his ignorance, he certainly never had the advantages of education, but he can read and write, (it was taught him by his parents,) and for natural intelligence and quickness of apprehension, is surpassed by few men I have ever seen. As to his being a coward, his reason as given for not resisting Mr. Phipps, shews the decision of his character. When he saw Mr. Phipps present his gun, he said he knew it was impossible for him to escape as the woods were full of men; he therefore thought it was better to surrender, and trust to fortune for his escape. He is a complete fanatic, or plays his part most admirably. On other subjects he possesses an uncommon share of intelligence, with a mind capable of attaining any thing; but warped and perverted by the influence of early impressions. He is below the ordinary stature, though strong and active, having the true negro face, every feature of which is strongly marked. I shall not attempt to describe the effect of his narrative, as told and commented on by himself, in the condemned hole of the prison. The calm, deliberate composure with which he spoke of his late deeds and intentions, the expression of his fiend-like face when excited by enthusiasm, still bearing the stains of the blood of helpless innocence about him; clothed with rags and covered with chains; yet daring to raise his manacled hands to heaven, with a spirit soaring above the attributes of man; I looked on him and my blood curdled in my veins.

I will not shock the feelings of humanity, nor wound afresh the bosoms of the disconsolate sufferers in this unparalleled and inhuman massacre, by detailing the deeds of their fiend-like barbarity. There were two or three who were in the power of these wretches, had they known it, and who escaped in the most providential manner. There were two whom they thought they left dead on the field at Mr. Parker's, but who were only stunned by the blows of their guns, as they did not take time to re-load when they charged on them. The escape of a little girl who went to school at Mr. Waller's, and where the children were collecting for that purpose, excited general sympathy. As their teacher had not arrived, they were at play in the yard, and seeing the negroes approach, she ran up on a dirt chimney, (such as are common to log houses,) and remained there unnoticed during the massacre of the eleven that were killed at this place. She remained on her hiding place till just before the arrival of a party, who were in pursuit of the murderers, when she came down and fled to a swamp, where, a mere child as she was, with the horrors of the late scene before her, she lay concealed until the next day, when seeing a party go up to the house, she came up, and on being asked how she escaped, replied with the utmost simplicity, "The Lord helped her." She was taken up behind a gentleman of the party, and returned to the arms of her weeping mother. Miss Whitehead concealed herself between the bed and the mat that supported it, while they murdered her sister in the same room, without discovering her. She was afterwards carried off, and concealed for protection by a slave of the family, who gave evidence against several of them on their trial. Mrs. Nathaniel Francis, while concealed in a closet heard their blows, and the shrieks of the victims of these ruthless savages; they then entered the closet where she was concealed, and went out without discovering her. While in this hiding place, she heard two of her women in a quarrel about the division of her clothes. Mr. John T. Baron, discovering them approaching his house, told his wife to make her escape, and scorning to fly, fell fighting on his own threshold. After firing his rifle, he discharged his gun at them, and then broke it over the villain who first approached him, but he was overpowered, and slain. His bravery, however, saved from the hands of these monsters, his lovely and amiable wife, who will long lament a husband so deserving of her love. As directed by him, she attempted to escape through the garden, when she was caught and held by one of her servant girls, but another coming to her rescue, she fled to the woods, and concealed herself. Few indeed, were those who escaped their work of death. But fortunate for society, the hand of retributive justice has overtaken them, and not one that was known to be concerned has escaped.

The Commonwealth, vs. Nat Turner

Charged with making insurrection, Nat Turner. and plotting to take away the lives of divers free white persons, &c. on the 22d of August, 1831.

The court composed of———, having met for the trial of Nat Turner, the prisoner was brought in and arraigned, and upon his arraignment pleaded *Not guilty*; saying to his counsel, that he did not feel so.

On the part of the Commonwealth, Levi Waller was introduced, who being sworn, deposed as follows: (*agreeably to Nat's own Confession.*) Col. Trezvant* was then introduced, who being sworn,

$$* * * * *$$

A LIST OF PERSONS MURDERED IN THE INSURRECTION, ON THE 21ST AND 22D OF AUGUST, 1831.

Joseph Travers and wife and three children, Mrs. Elizabeth Turner, Hartwell Prebles, Sarah Newsome, Mrs. P. Reese and son William, Trajan Doyle, Henry Bryant and wife and child, and wife's mother, Mrs. Catharine Whitehead, son Richard and four daughters and grand-child, Salathiel Francis, Nathaniel Francis' overseer and two children, John T. Barrow, George Vaughan, Mrs. Levi Waller and ten children, William Williams, wife and two boys, Mrs. Caswell Worrell and child, Mrs. Rebecca Vaughan, Ann Eliza Vaughan, and son Arthur, Mrs. John K. Williams and child, Mrs. Jacob Williams and three children, and Edwin Drury—amounting to fifty-five.

A LIST OF NEGROES BROUGHT BEFORE THE COURT OF SOUTHAMPTON, WITH THEIR OWNERS' NAMES, AND SENTENCE.

Name	Owner	Sentence
Daniel	Richard Porter,	Convicted.
Moses	J. T. Barrow,	Do.
Tom Caty	Whitehead,	Discharged.
Jack and Andrew	Caty Whitehead,	Con. and transported.
Jacob Geo.	H. Charlton,	Disch'd without trial.
Isaac	Ditto,	Convi. and transported.
Jack	Everett Bryant,	Discharged.
Nathan	Benj. Blunt's estate,	Convicted.
Nathan, Tom, and Davy, (boys,)	Nathaniel Francis,	Convi. and transported.
Davy	Elizabeth Turner,	Convicted.
Curtis	Thomas Ridley,	Do.
Stephen	Do.	Do.
Hardy and Isham	Benjamin Edwards,	Convicted and transp'd.
Sam	Nathaniel Francis,	Convicted.
Hark	Joseph Travis'estate.	Do.
Moses, (a boy,)	Do.	Do. and transported
Davy	Levi Waller,	Convicted.
Nelson	Jacob Williams,	Do.
Nat,	Edm'd Turner's estate,	Do.
Jack	Wm. Reese's estate,	Do.
Dred	Nathaniel Francis,	Do.
Arnold, Artist (free,)		Discharged.
Sam	J. W. Parker,	Acquitted.
Ferry and Archer	J. W. Parker,	Disch'd without trial.
Jim	William Vaughan,	Acquitted.
Bob	Temperance Parker,	Do.
Davy	Joseph Parker,	
Daniel	Solomon D. Parker,	Disch'd without trial.
Thomas Haithcock, (free,)		Sent on for further trial.

Joe	John C. Turner,	Convicted.
Lucy	John T. Barrow,	Do.
Matt	Thomas Ridley,	Acquitted,
Jim	Richard Porter,	Do.
Exurn Artes, (free,)		Sent on for further trial.
Joe Richard P. Briggs		Disch'd without trial.
Bury Newsome, (free,)		Sent on for further trial.
Stephen James Bell, Acquitted.		
Jim and Isaac	Samuel Champion,	Convicted and trans'd.
Proston	Hannah Williamson,	Acquitted.
Frank	Solomon D. Parker,	Convi'd and transp'd.
Jack and Shadrach	Nathaniel Simmons,	Acquitted.
Nelson	Benj. Blunt's estate,	Do.
Sam	Peter Edwards,	Convicted.
Archer	Arthur G. Reese,	Acquitted.
Isham Turner, (free,)		Sent on for further trial.
Nat Turner	Putnam Moore, dec'd	Convicted.

narrated Nat's Confession to him, as follows: (*his Confession as given to Mr. Gray*.) The prisoner introduced no evidence, and the case was submitted without argument to the court, who having found him guilty, Jeremiah Cobb, Esq. Chairman, pronounced the sentence of the court, in the following words: "Nat Turner! Stand up. Have you any thing to say why sentence of death should not be pronounced against you?

Ans. I have not. I have made a full confession to Mr. Gray, and I have nothing more to say.

Attend then to the sentence of the Court. You have been arraigned and tried before this court, and convicted of one of the highest crimes in our criminal code. You have been convicted of plotting in cold blood, the indiscriminate destruction of men, of helpless women, and of infant children. The evidence before us leaves not a shadow of doubt, but that your hands were often imbrued in the blood of the innocent; and your own confession tells us that they were stained with the blood of a master; in your own language, "too indulgent." Could I stop here, your crime would be sufficiently aggravated. But the original contriver of a plan, deep and deadly, one that never can be effected, you managed so far to put it

into execution, as to deprive us of many of our most valuable citizens; and this was done when they were asleep, and defenceless; under circumstances shocking to humanity. And while upon this part of the subject, I cannot but call your attention to the poor misguided wretches who have gone before you. They are not few in number—they were your bosom associates; and the blood of all cries aloud, and calls upon you, as the author of their misfortune. Yes! You forced them unprepared, from Time to Eternity. Borne down by this load of guilt, your only justification is, that you were led away by fanaticism. If this be true, from my soul I pity you; and while you have my sympathies, I am, nevertheless called upon to pass the sentence of the court. The time between this and your execution, will necessarily be very short; and your only hope must be in another world. The judgment of the court is, that you be taken hence to the jail from whence you came, thence to the place of execution, and on Friday next between the hours of 10 A.M. and 2 P. M. be hung by the neck until you are dead! dead! dead and may the Lord have mercy upon your soul.

Endnotes

*The committing Magistrate.

Running a Thousand Miles for Freedom or the Escape of William and Ellen Craft from Slavery

So many individual slaves ran away from their masters during the first half of the nineteenth century that a certain Dr. Samuel Cartwright of the University of Louisiana declared that the blacks suffered from a peculiar disease he called: *Drapetornania, or the Disease Causing Negroes to Run Away.* "The story of the runaways and those who aided them in both North and South is one of the most exciting chapters of American history.

William and Ellen Craft were a slave couple in Macon, Georgia. Their escape plan was made possible by the fact that Ellen was fair-skinned enough to pass for white. They decided to flee to the North by having William pose as the slave of Ellen, who would have to act as though she were his master. The dramatic story of their adventures on their way out of the South and bondage provides many insights into the oppression of the slave system.

After the passage of the new Fugitive Slave Act in 1850, the Crafts realized that the North no longer provided a significant margin of safety for fugitives, and they eventually made their way to England, where their freedom would be secure.

✳ ✳ ✳ ✳ ✳

My wife was torn from her mother's embrace in childhood, and taken to a distant part of the country. She had seen so many other children separated from their parents in this cruel manner, that the mere thought of her ever becoming the mother of a child, to linger out a miserable existence under the wretched system of American slavery, appeared to fill her very soul with horror; and as she had taken what I felt to be an important view of her condition, I did not, at first, press the marriage, but agreed to assist her in trying to devise some plan by which we might escape from our unhappy condition, and then be married.

We thought of plan after plan, but they all seemed crowded with insurmountable difficulties. We knew it was unlawful for any public conveyance to take us as passengers, without our master's consent. We were also perfectly aware of the startling fact, that had we left without this consent the professional slave-hunters would have soon had their ferocious bloodhounds baying on our track, and in a short time we should have been dragged back to slavery not to fill the more favourable situations which we had just left, but to be separated for life, and put to the very meanest and most laborious drudgery; or else have been tortured to death as examples, in order to strike terror into the hearts of others, and thereby prevent them from even attempting to escape from their cruel taskmasters. It is a fact worthy of remark, that nothing seems to give the slaveholders so much pleasure as the catching and torturing of fugitives. They had much rather take the keen and poisonous lash, and with it cut their poor trembling victims to atoms, than allow one of them to escape to a free country, and expose the infamous system from which he fled.

The greatest excitement prevails at a slave-hunt. The slaveholders and their hired ruffians appear to take more pleasure in this inhuman pursuit than English sportsmen do in chasing a fox or a stag. Therefore, knowing what we should have been compelled to suffer, if caught and taken back, we were more than anxious to hit upon a plan that would lead us safely to a land of liberty.

But after puzzling our brains for years, we were reluctantly driven to the sad conclusion, that it was almost impossible to escape from slavery in Georgia, and travel 1,000 miles across the slave States. We therefore resolved to get the consent of our owners, be married, settle down in slavery, and endeavour to make ourselves as comfortable as possible under that system; but at the same time ever to keep our

Source: *Running a Thousand Miles for Freedom or The Escape of William and Ellen Craft From Slavery* by William Craft.

dim eyes steadily fixed upon the glimmering hope of liberty, and earnestly pray God mercifully to assist us to escape from our unjust thraldom.

We were married, and prayed and toiled on till December, 1848, at which time (as I have stated) a plan suggested itself that proved quite successful, and in eight days after it was first thought of we were free from the horrible trammels of slavery, and glorifying God who had brought us safely out of a land of bondage.

Knowing that slaveholders have the privilege of taking their slaves to any part of the country they think proper, it occurred to me that, as my wife was nearly white, I might get her to disguise herself as an invalid gentleman, and assume to be my master, while I could attend as his slave, and that in this manner we might effect our escape. After I thought of the plan, I suggested it to my wife, but at first she shrank from the idea. She thought it was almost impossible for her to assume that disguise, and travel a distance of 1,000 miles across the slave States. However, on the other hand, she also thought of her condition. She saw that the laws under which we lived did not recognize her to be a woman, but a mere chattel, to be bought and sold, or otherwise dealt with as her owner might see fit. Therefore the more she contemplated her helpless condition, the more anxious she was to escape from it. So she said, "I think it is almost too much for us to undertake; however, I feel that God is on our side, and with his assistance, notwithstanding all the difficulties, we shall be able to succeed. Therefore, if you will purchase the disguise, I will try to carry out the plan."

But after I concluded to purchase the disguise, I was afraid to go to any one to ask him to sell me the articles. It is unlawful in Georgia for a white man to trade with slaves without the master's consent. But, notwithstanding this, many persons will sell a slave any article that he can get the money to buy. Not that they sympathize with the slave, but merely because his testimony is not admitted in court against a free white person.

Therefore, with little difficulty I went to different parts of the town, at odd times, and purchased things piece by piece. (except the trowsers which she found necessary to make,) and took them home to the house where my wife resided. She being a ladies' maid, and a favourite slave in the family, was allowed a little room to herself, and amongst other pieces of furniture which I had made in my overtime, was a chest of drawers; so when I took the articles home, she locked them up carefully in these drawers. No one about the premises knew that she had anything of the kind. So when we fancied we had everything ready the time was fixed for the flight. But we knew it would not do to start off without first getting our master's consent to be away for a few days. Had we left without this, they would soon have had us back into slavery and probably we should never have got another fair opportunity of even attempting to escape.

Some of the best slaveholders will sometimes give their favourite slaves a few days' holiday at Christmas time; so, after no little amount of perseverance on my wife's part, she obtained a pass from her mistress, allowing her to be away for a few days. The cabinet-maker with whom I worked gave me a similar paper, but said that he needed my services very much, and wished me to return as soon as the time granted was up. I thanked him kindly; but somehow I have not been able to make it convenient to return yet; and, as the free air of good old England agrees so well with my wife and our dear little ones, as well as with myself, it is not at all likely we shall return at present to the "peculiar institution" of chains and stripes.

On reaching my wife's cottage she handed me her pass, and I showed mine, but at that time neither of us were able to read them. It is not only unlawful for slaves to be taught to read, but in some of the States there are heavy penalties attached, such as fines and imprisonment, which will be vigorously enforced upon any one who is humane enough to violate the so-called law.

The following case will serve to show how persons are treated in the most enlightened slaveholding community.

Indictment

COMMONWEALTH OF VIRGINIA, Norfolk County, *ss.* } *In the Circuit Court*. The Grand jurors empannelled and sworn to inquire of offences committed in the body of the said County on their oath present, that Margaret Douglass, being an evil disposed person, not having the fear of God before her eyes, but moved and instigated by the devil, wickedly, maliciously, and feloniously, on the fourth day of July, in the year of our Lord one thousand eight, hundred and fifty-four, at Norfolk, in said Country, did teach a certain black girl named Kate to read in the Bible, to the great displeasure of Almighty God, to the pernicious example of others in like case offending, contrary to the form of the statute in such case made and provided, and against the peace and dignity of the Commonwealth of Virginia

"Victor Vagabond, *Prosecuting Attorney*."

"On this indictment Mrs. Douglass was arraigned as a necessary matter of form, tried, found guilty of course; and Judge Scalaway, before whom she was tried, having consulted with Dr. Adams, ordered the sheriff to place Mrs. Douglass in the prisoner's box, when he addressed her as follows: 'Margaret Douglass, stand up. You are guilty of one of the vilest crimes that ever disgraced society; and the jury have found you so. You have taught a slave girl to read in the Bible. No enlightened society can exist where such offences go unpunished. The Court, in your case, do not feel for you one solitary ray of sympathy, and they will inflict on you the utmost penalty of the law. In any other civilized country you would have paid the forfeit of your crime with your life, and the Court have only to regret that such is not the law in this country. The sentence for your offence is, that you be imprisoned one month in the county jail, and that you pay the costs of this prosecution. Sheriff, remove the prisoner to jail.' On the publication of these proceedings, the Doctors of Divinity preached each a sermon on the necessity of obeying the laws; the *New York Observer* noticed with much pious gladness a revival of religion on Dr. Smith's plantation in Georgia, among his slaves; while the *Journal of Commerce* commended this political preaching of the Doctors of Divinity because it favoured slavery Let us do nothing to offend our Southern brethren."

— — —

However, at first, we were highly delighted at the idea of having gained permission to be absent for a few days; but when the thought flashed across my wife's mind, that it was customary for travellers to register their names in the visitors' book at hotels, as well as in the clearance or Custom-house book at Charleston, South Carolina—it made our spirits droop within us.

So, while sitting in our little room upon the verge of despair, all at once my wife raised her head, and with a smile upon her face, which was a moment before bathed in tears, said, "I think I have it!" I asked what it was. She said, "I think I can make a poultice and bind up my right hand in a sling, and

with propriety ask the officers to register my name for me." I thought that would do.

It then occurred to her that the smoothness of her face might betray her; so she decided to make another poultice, and put it in a white handkerchief to be worn under the chin, up the cheeks, and to tie over the head. This nearly hid the expression of the countenance, as well as the beardless chin.

The poultice is left off in the engraving, because the likeness could not have been taken well with it on.

My wife, knowing that she would be thrown a good deal into the company of gentlemen, fancied that she could get on better if she had something to go over the eyes; so I went to a shop and bought a pair of green spectacles. This was in the evening.

We sat up all night discussing the plan, and making preparations. Just before the time arrived, in the morning, for us to leave, I cut off my wife's hair square at the back of the head, and got her to dress in the disguise and stand out on the floor. I found that she made a most respectable looking gentleman.

My wife had no ambition whatever to assume this disguise, and would not have done so had it been possible to have obtained our liberty by more simple means; but we knew it was not customary in the South for ladies to travel with male servants; and therefore, notwithstanding my wife's fair complexion, it would have been a very difficult task for her to have come off as a free white lady, with me as her slave; in fact, her not being able to write would have made this quite impossible. We knew that no public conveyance would take us, or any other slave, as a passenger, without our master's consent. This consent could never be obtained to pass into a free State. My wife's being muffled in the poultices, &c., furnished a plausible excuse for avoiding general conversation, of which most Yankee travellers are passionately fond.

There are a large number of free negroes residing in the southern States; but in Georgia (and I believe in all the slave States,) every coloured person's complexion is *primâ facie* evidence of his being a slave; and the lowest villain in the country, should he be a white man, has the legal power to arrest, and question, in the most inquisitorial and insulting manner, any coloured person, male or female, that he may find at large, particularly at night and on Sundays, without a written pass, signed by the master or some one in authority; or stamped free papers, certifying that the person is the rightful owner of himself.

If the coloured person refuses to answer questions put to him, he may be beaten, and his defending himself against this attack makes him an outlaw, and if he be killed on the spot, the murderer will be exempted from all blame; but after the coloured person has answered the questions put to him, in a most humble and pointed manner, he may then be taken to prison; and should it turn out, after further examination, that he was caught where he had no permission or legal right to be, and that he has not given what they term a satisfactory account of himself, the master will have to pay a fine. On his refusing to do this, the poor slave may be legally and severely flogged by public officers. Should the prisoner prove to be a free man, he is most likely to be both whipped and fined.

The great majority of slaveholders hate this class of persons with a hatred that can only be equalled by the condemned spirits of the infernal regions. They have no mercy upon, nor sympathy for, any negro whom they cannot enslave. They say that God made the black man to be a slave for the white, and act as though they really believed that all free persons of colour are in open rebellion to a direct command from heaven, and that they (the whites) are God's chosen agents to pour out upon them unlimited vengeance. For instance, a Bill has been introduced in the Tennessee Legislature to prevent free negroes from travelling on the railroads in that State. It has passed the first reading. The bill provides that the President who shall permit a free negro to travel on any road within the jurisdiction of the State under his supervision shall pay a fine of 500 dollars; any conductor permitting a violation of the Act shall pay 250 dollars; provided such free negro is not under the control of a free white citizen of Tennessee, who will vouch for the character of said free negro in a penal bond of one thousand dollars. The State of Arkansas has passed a law to banish all free negroes from its bounds, and it came into effect on the 1st day of January, 1860. Every free negro found there after that date will be liable to be sold into slavery, the crime of freedom being unpardonable. The Missouri Senate has before it a bill providing that all free negroes above the age of eighteen years who shall be found in the State after September, 1860, shall be sold into slavery; and that all such negroes as shall enter the State after September, 1861, and remain there twenty-four hours, shall also be sold into slavery for ever. Mississippi, Kentucky, and

Georgia, and in fact, I believe, all the slave States, are legislating in the same manner. Thus the slaveholders make it almost impossible for free persons of colour to get out of the slave States, in order that they may sell them into slavery if they don't go. If no white persons travelled upon railroads except those who could get some one to vouch for their character in a penal bond of one thousand dollars, the railroad companies would soon go to the "wall." Such mean legislation is too low for comment; therefore I leave the villainous acts to speak for themselves.

But the Dred Scott decision is the crowning act of infamous Yankee legislation. The Supreme Court, the highest tribunal of the Republic, composed of nine judge Jeffries's, chosen both from the free and slave States, has decided that no coloured person, or persons of African extraction, can ever become a citizen of the United States, or have any rights which white men are bound to respect. That is to say, in the opinion of this Court, robbery, rape, and murder are not crimes when committed by a white upon a coloured person.

Judges who will sneak from their high and honourable position down into the lowest depths of human depravity, and scrape up a decision like this, are wholly unworthy the confidence of any people. I believe such men would, if they had the power, and were it to their temporal interest, sell their country's independence, and barter away every man's birthright for a mess of pottage. Well may Thomas Campbell say

> United States, your banner wears,
> Two emblems,—one of fame,
> Alas, the other that it bears
> Reminds us of your shame!
> The white man's liberty in types
> Stands blazoned by your stars;
> But what's the meaning of your stripes?
> They mean your Negro-scars.

When the time had arrived for us to start, we blew out the lights, knelt down, and prayed to our Heavenly Father mercifully to assist us, as he did his people of old, to escape from cruel bondage; and we shall ever feel that God heard and answered our prayer. Had we not been sustained by a kind, and I sometimes think special, providence, we could never have overcome the mountainous difficulties which I am now about to describe.

After this we rose and stood for a few moments in breathless silence,—we were afraid that some one might have been about the cottage listening and watching our movements. So I took my wife by the hand, stepped softly to the door, raised the latch, drew it open, and peeped out. Though there were trees all around the house, yet the foliage scarcely moved; in fact, everything appeared to be as still as death. I then whispered to my wife, "Come my dear, let us make a desperate leap for liberty!" But poor thing, she shrank back, in a state of trepidation. I turned and asked what was the matter; she made no reply, but burst into violent sobs, and threw her head upon my breast. This appeared to touch my very heart, it caused me to enter into her feelings more fully than ever. We both saw the many mountainous difficulties that rose one after the other before our view, and knew far too well what our sad fate would have been, were we caught and forced back into our slavish den. Therefore on my wife's fully realizing the solemn fact that we had to take our lives, as it were, in our hands, and contest every inch of the thousand miles of slave territory over which we had to pass, it made her heart almost sink within her, and, had I known them at that time, I would have repeated the following encouraging lines, which may not be out of place here—

> "The hill, though high, I covet to ascend,
> The *difficulty will not me offend;*
> For I perceive the way to life lies here:
> Come, pluck up heart, let's neither faint nor fear;
> Better, though difficult, the right way to go,
> wrong, though easy, where the end is woe."

However, the sobbing was soon over, and after a few moments of silent prayer she recovered her self-possession, and said, "Come, William, it is getting late, so now let us venture upon our perilous journey."

We then opened the door, and stepped as softly out as "moonlight upon the water." I locked the door with my own key, which I now have before me, and tiptoed across the yard into the street. I say tiptoed, because we were like persons near a tottering avalanche, afraid to move, or even breathe freely, for fear the sleeping tyrants should be aroused, and come down upon us with double vengeance, for daring to attempt to escape in the manner which we contemplated.

We shook hands, said farewell, and started in different directions for the railway station. I took the nearest possible way to the train, for fear I should be recognized by some one, and got into the negro car in which I knew I should have to ride; but my *master* (as I will now call my wife) took a longer way round, and only arrived there with the bulk of the passengers. He obtained a ticket for himself and one for his slave to Savannah, the first port, which was about two hundred miles off. My master then had the luggage stowed away, and stepped into one of the best carriages.

But just before the train moved off I peeped through the window, and, to my great astonishment, I saw the cabinet-maker with whom I had worked so long, on the platform. He stepped up to the ticket-seller, and asked some question, and then commenced looking rapidly through the passengers, and into the carriages. Fully believing that we were caught, I shrank into a corner, turned my face from the door, and expected in a moment to be dragged out. The cabinetmaker looked into my master's carriage, but did not know him in his new attire, and, as God would have it, before he reached mine the bell rang, and the train moved off.

I have heard since that the cabinet-maker had a presentiment that we were about to "make tracks for parts unknown;" but, not seeing me, his suspicions vanished, until he received the startling intelligence that we had arrived safely in a free State.

As soon as the train had left the platform, my master looked round in the carriage, and was terror-stricken to find a Mr. Cray—an old friend of my wife's master, who dined with the family the day before, and knew my wife from childhood—sitting on the same seat.

The doors of the American railway carriages are at the ends. The passengers walk up the aisle, and take seats on either side; and as my master was engaged in looking out of the window, he did not see who came in.

My master's first impression, after seeing Mr. Cray, was, that he was there for the purpose of securing him. However, my master thought it was not wise to give any information respecting himself, and for fear that Mr. Cray might draw him into conversation and recognize his voice, my master resolved to feign deafness as the only means of self-defence.

After a little while, Mr. Cray said to my master, "It is a very fine morning, sir." The latter took no notice, but kept looking out of the window. Mr. Cray soon repeated this remark, in a little louder tone, but my master remained as before. This indifference attracted the attention of the passengers near, one of whom laughed out. This, I suppose, annoyed the old gentleman; so he said, "I will make him hear;" and in a loud tone of voice repeated, "It is a very fine morning, sir."

My master turned his head, and with a polite bow said, "Yes," and commenced looking out of the window again.

One of the gentlemen remarked that it was a very great deprivation to be deaf. "Yes," replied Mr. Cray, "and I shall not trouble that fellow any more." This enabled my master to breathe a little easier, and to feel that Mr. Cray was not his pursuer after all.

The gentlemen then turned the conversation upon the three great topics of discussion in first-class circles in Georgia, namely, Niggers, Cotton, and the Abolitionists.

My master had often heard of abolitionists, but in such a connection as to cause him to think that they were a fearful kind of wild animal. But he was highly delighted to learn, from the gentlemen's conversation, that the abolitionists were persons who were opposed to oppression; and therefore, in his opinion, not the lowest, but the very highest, of God's creatures.

Without the slightest objection on my master's part, the gentlemen left the carriage at Gordon, for Milledgeville (the capital of the State).

We arrived at Savannah early in the evening, and got into an omnibus, which stopped at the hotel for the passengers to take tea. I stepped into the house and brought my master something on a tray to the omnibus, which took us in due time to the steamer, which was bound for Charleston, South Carolina.

Soon after going on board, my master turned in; and as the captain and some of the passengers seemed to think this strange, and also questioned me respecting him, my master thought I had better get out the flannels and opodeldoc which we had prepared for the rheumatism, warm them quickly by the stove in the gentleman's saloon, and bring them to his berth. We did this as an excuse for my master's retiring to bed so early.

While at the stove one of the passengers said to me, "Buck, what have you got there?" "Opodeldoc,

sir," I replied. "I should think it's opo*devil*," said a lanky swell, who was leaning back in a chair with his heels upon the back of another, and chewing tobacco as if for a wager; "it stinks enough to kill or cure twenty men. Away with it, or I reckon I will throw it overboard!"

It was by this time warm enough, so I took it to my master's berth, remained there a little while, and then went on deck and asked the steward where I was to sleep. He said there was no place provided for coloured passengers, whether slave or free. So I paced the deck till a late hour, then mounted some cotton bags, in a warm place near the funnel, sat there till morning, and then went and assisted my master to get ready for breakfast.

He was seated at the right hand of the captain, who, together with all the passengers, inquired very kindly after his health. As my master had one hand in a sling, it was my duty to carve his food. But when I went out the captain said, "You have a very attentive boy, sir; but you had better watch him like a hawk when you get on to the North. He seems all very well here, but he may act quite there. I know several gentlemen who have lost their valuable niggers among them d—d cut-throat abolitionists."

Before my master could speak, a rough slave-dealer, who was sitting opposite, with both elbows on the table, and with a large piece of broiled fowl in his fingers, shook his head with emphasis, and in a deep Yankee tone, forced through his crowded mouth the words, "Sound doctrine, captain, very sound." He then dropped the chicken into the plate, leant back, placed his thumbs in the armholes of his fancy waistcoat, and continued, "I would not take a nigger to the North under no consideration. I have had a deal to do with niggers in my time, but I never saw one who ever had his heel upon free soil that was worth a d—n." "Now stranger," addressing my master, "if you have made up your mind to sell that ere nigger, I am your man; just mention your price, and if it isn't out of the way, I will pay for him on this board with hard silver dollars." This hard-featured, bristly-bearded, wire-headed, red-eyed monster, staring at my master as the serpent did at Eve, said, "What do you say, stranger?" He replied, "I don't wish to sell, sir; I cannot get on well without him."

"You will have to get on without him if you take him to the North," continued this man; "for I can tell ye, stranger, as a friend, I am an older cove than you, I have seen lots of this ere world, and I reckon I have had more dealings with niggers than any man living or dead. I was once employed by General Wade Hampton, for ten years, in doing nothing but breaking 'em in; and everybody knows that the General would not have a man that didn't understand his business. So I tell ye, stranger, again, you had better sell, and let me take him down to Orleans. He will do you no good if you take him across Mason's and Dixon's line; he is a keen nigger, and I can see from the cut of his eye that he is certain to run away." My master said," I think not, sir; I have great confidence in his fidelity." "Fi*devil*," indignantly said the dealer, as his fist came down upon the edge of the saucer and upset a cup of hot coffee in a gentleman's lap. (As the scalded man jumped up the trader quietly said, "Don't disturb yourself, neighbour; accidents will happen in the best of families.") "It always makes me mad to hear a man talking about fidelity in niggers. There isn't a d—d one on 'em who wouldn't cut sticks," if he had half a chance."

By this time we were near Charleston; my master thanked the captain for his advice, and they all withdrew and went on deck, where the trader fancied he became quite eloquent. He drew a crowd around him, and with emphasis said, "Cap'en, if I was the President of this mighty United States of America, the greatest and freest country under the whole univarse, I would never let no man, I don't care who he is, take a nigger into the North and bring him back here, filled to the brim, as he is sure to be, with d—d abolition vices, to taint all quiet niggers with the hellish spirit of running away. These air, cap'en, my flat-footed, every day, right up and down sentiments, and as this is a free country, cap'en, I don't care who hears 'em; for I am a Southern man, every inch on me to the backbone." "Good!" said an insignificant-looking individual of the slave-dealer stamp. "Three cheers for John C. Calhoun and the whole fair sunny South!" added the trader. So off went their hats, and out burst a terrific roar of irregular but continued cheering. My master took no more notice of the dealer. He merely said to the captain that the air on deck was too keen for him, and he would therefore return to the cabin.

While the trader was in the zenith of his eloquence, he might as well have said, as one of his kith did, at a great Filibustering meeting, that "When the great American Eagle gets one of his mighty claws upon Canada and the other into South America, and his glorious and starry wings of liberty extending from the Atlantic to the Pacific, oh! then, where will England be, ye gentlemen? I tell ye, she will only serve as a pocket-handkerchief for Jonathan to wipe his nose with."

On my master entering the cabin he found at the breakfast-table a young southern military officer, with whom he had travelled some distance the previous day.

After passing the usual compliments the conversation turned upon the old subject,—niggers.

The officer, who was also travelling with a man-servant, said to my master, "You will excuse me, Sir, for saying I think you are very likely to spoil your boy by saying 'thank you' to him. I assure you, sir, nothing spoils a slave so soon as saying, 'thank you' and 'if you please' to him. The only way to make a nigger toe the mark, and to keep him in his place, is to storm at him like thunder, and keep him trembling like a leaf. Don't you see, when I speak to my Ned, he darts like lightning; and if he didn't I'd skin him."

Just then the poor dejected slave came in, and the officer swore at him fearfully, merely to teach my master what he called the proper way to treat me.

After he had gone out to get his master's luggage ready, the officer said, "That is the way to speak to them. If every nigger was drilled in this manner, they would be as humble as dogs, and never dare to run away."

The gentleman urged my master not to go to the North for the restoration of his health, but to visit the Warm Springs in Arkansas.

My master said, he thought the air of Philadelphia would suit his complaint best; and, not only so, he thought he could get better advice there.

The boat had now reached the wharf. The officer wished my master a safe and pleasant journey, and left the saloon.

There were a large number of persons on the quay waiting the arrival of the steamer: but we were afraid to venture out for fear that some one might recognize me; or that they had heard that we were gone, and had telegraphed to have us stopped. However, after remaining in the cabin till all the other passengers were gone, we had our luggage placed on a fly, and I took my master by the arm, and with a little difficulty he hobbled on shore, got in and drove off to the best hotel, which John C. Calhoun, and all the other great southern fire-eating statesmen, made their head-quarters while in Charleston.

On arriving at the house the landlord ran out and opened the door: but judging, from the poultices and green glasses, that my master was an invalid, he took him very tenderly by one arm and ordered his man to take the other.

My master then eased himself out, and with their assistance found no trouble in getting up the steps into the hotel. The proprietor made me stand on one side, while he paid my master the attention and homage he thought a gentleman of his high position merited.

My master asked for a bed-room. The servant was ordered to show a good one, into which we helped him. The servant returned. My master then handed me the bandages, I took them downstairs in great haste, and told the landlord my master wanted two hot poultices as quickly as possible. He rang the bell, the servant came in, to whom he said, "Run to the kitchen and tell the cook to make two hot poultices right off, for there is a gentleman upstairs very badly off indeed!"

In a few minutes the smoking poultices were brought in. I placed them in white handkerchiefs, and hurried upstairs, went into my master's apartment, shut the door, and laid them on the mantelpiece. As he was alone for a little while, he thought he could rest a great deal better with the poultices off. However, it was necessary to have them to complete the remainder of the journey. I then ordered dinner, and took my master's boots out to polish them. While doing so I entered into conversation with one of the slaves. I may state here, that on the sea-coast of South Carolina and Georgia the slaves speak worse English than in any other part of the country. This is owing to the frequent importation, or smuggling in, of Africans, who mingle with the natives. Consequently the language cannot properly be called English or African, but a corruption of the two.

The shrewd son of African parents to whom I referred said to me, "Say, brudder, way you come from, and which side you goin day wid dat ar little don up buckra" (white man)?

I replied, "To Philadelphia."

"What!" he exclaimed, with astonishment, "to Philumadelphy?

"Yes," I said.

"By squash! I wish I was going wid you! I hears urn say dat dare's no slaves way over in dem parts; is um so?"

I quietly said, I have heard the same thing."

"Well," continued he, as he threw down the boot and brush, and, placing his hands in his pockets, strutted across the floor with an air of independence—"Gorra Mighty, dem is de parts for Pompey; and I hope when you get dare you will stay, and nebber follow dat buckra back to dis hot quarter no more, let him be eber so good."

I thanked him; and just as I took the boots up and started off, he caught my hand between his two, and gave it a hearty shake, and, with tears streaming down his cheeks, said:

"God bless you, broder, and may de Lord be wid you. When you gets de freedom, and sitin under your own wine and fig-tree, don't forget to pray for poor Pompey."

I was afraid to say much to him, but I shall never forget his earnest request, nor fail to do what little I can to release the millions of unhappy bondmen, of whom he was one.

At the proper time my master had the poultices placed on, came down, and seated himself at a table in a very brilliant dining-room, to have his dinner. I had to have something at the same time, in order to be ready for the boat; so they gave me my dinner in an old broken plate, with a rusty knife and fork, and said, "Here, boy, you go in the kitchen." I took it and went out, but did not stay more than a few minutes, because I was in a great hurry to get back to see how the invalid was getting on. On arriving I found two or three servants waiting on him; but as he did not feel able to make a very hearty dinner, he soon finished, paid the bill, and gave the servants each a trifle, which caused one of them to say to me, "Your massa is a big bug"—meaning a gentleman of distinction—"he is the greatest gentleman dat has been dis way for dis six months." I said, "Yes, he is some pumpkins," meaning the same as "big bug."

When we left Macon it was our intention to take a steamer at Charleston through to Philadelphia; but on arriving there we found that the vessels did not run during the winter, and I have no doubt it was well for us they did not; for on the very last voyage the steamer made that we intended to go by, a fugitive was discovered secreted on board, and sent back to slavery. However, as we had also heard of the Overland Mail Route, we were all right. So I ordered a fly to the door, had the luggage placed on; we got in, and drove down to the Customhouse Office, which was near the wharf where we had to obtain tickets, to take a steamer for Wilmington, North Carolina. When we reached the building,

I helped my master into the office, which was crowded with passengers. He asked for a ticket for himself and one for his slave to Philadelphia. This caused the principal officer—a very mean-looking, cheese-coloured fellow, who was sitting there—to look up at us very suspiciously, and in a fierce tone of voice he said to me, "Boy, do you belong to that gentleman?" I quickly replied, "Yes, sir" (which was quite correct). The tickets were handed out, and as my master was paying for them the chief man said to him, "I wish you to register your name here, sir, and also the name of your nigger, and pay a dollar duty on him."

My master paid the dollar, and pointing to the hand that was in the poultice, requested the officer to register his name for him. This seemed to offend the "high-bred" South Carolinian. He jumped up, shaking his head; and, cramming his hands almost through the bottom of his trousers pockets, with a slave-bullying air, said, "I shan't do it."

This attracted the attention of all the passengers. Just then the young military officer with whom my master travelled and conversed on the steamer from Savannah stepped in, somewhat the worse for brandy; he shook hands with my master, and pretended to know all about him. He said, "I know his kin (friends) like a book;" and as the officer was known in Charleston, and was going to stop there with friends, the recognition was very much in my master's favour.

The captain of the steamer, a good-looking jovial fellow, seeing that the gentleman appeared to know my master, and perhaps not wishing to lose us as passengers, said in an off-hand sailor-like manner, "I will register the gentleman's name, and take the responsibility upon myself." He asked my master's name. He said, "William Johnson." The names were put down, I think, "Mr. Johnson and slave." The captain said, "It's all right now, Mr. Johnson." He thanked him kindly, and the young officer begged my master to go with him, and have something to drink and a cigar; but as he had not acquired these accomplishments, he excused himself, and we went on board and came off to Wilmington, North Carolina. When the gentleman finds out his mistake, he will, I have no doubt, be careful in future not to pretend to have an intimate acquaintance with an entire stranger. During the voyage the captain said, "It was rather sharp shooting this morning, Mr. Johnson. It was not out of any disrespect to you, sir; but they make it a rule to be very strict at Charleston. I have known families to be detained there with their slaves till reliable information could be received respecting them. If they were not very careful, any d—d abolitionist might take off a lot of valuable niggers."

My master said, "I suppose so," and thanked him again for helping him over the difficulty.

We reached Wilmington the next morning, and took the train for Richmond, Virginia. I have stated that the American railway carriages (or cars, as they are called), are constructed differently to those in England. At one end of some of them, in the South, there is a little apartment with a couch on both sides for the convenience of families and invalids; and as they thought my master was very poorly, he was allowed to enter one of these apartments at Petersburg, Virginia, where an old gentleman and two handsome young ladies, his daughters, also got in, and took seats in the same carriage. But before the train started, the gentleman stepped into my car, and questioned me respecting my master. He wished to know what was the matter with him, where he was from, and where he was going. I told him where he came from, and said that he was suffering from a complication of complaints, and was going to Philadelphia, where he thought he could get more suitable advice than in Georgia.

The gentleman said my master could obtain the very best advice in Philadelphia. Which turned out to be quite correct, though he did not receive it from physicians, but from kind abolitionists who understood his case much better. The gentleman also said, "I reckon your master's father hasn't any more such faithful and smart boys as you." "O, yes, sir, he has," I replied, "lots on 'em." Which was literally true. This seemed all he wished to know. He thanked me, gave me a ten-cent piece, and requested me to be attentive to my good master. I promised that I would do so, and have ever since endeavoured to keep my pledge. During the gentleman's absence, the ladies and my master had a little cosy chat. But on his return, he said, "You seem to be very much afflicted, sir." "Yes, sir," replied the gentleman in the poultices. "What seems to be the matter with you, sir; may I be allowed to ask?" "Inflammatory rheumatism, sir." "Oh, that is very bad, sir," said the kind gentleman: "I can sympathise with you; for I know from bitter experience what the rheumatism is." If he did, he knew a good deal more than Mr. Johnson.

The gentleman thought my master would feel better if he would lie down and rest himself, and as he was anxious to avoid conversation, he at once acted upon this suggestion. The ladies politely rose, took their extra shawls, and made a nice pillow for the invalid's head. My master wore a fashionable cloth cloak, which they took and covered him comfortably on the couch. After he had been lying a little while the ladies, I suppose, thought he was asleep; so one of them gave a long sigh, and said, in a quiet fascinating tone, "Papa, he seems to be a very nice young gentleman." But before papa could speak, the other lady quickly said, "Oh! dear me, I never felt so much for a gentleman in my life!" To use an American expression, "they fell in love with the wrong chap."

After my master had been lying a little while he got up, the gentleman assisted him in getting on his cloak, the ladies took their shawls, and soon they were all seated. They then insisted upon Mr. Johnson taking some of their refreshments, which of course he did, out of courtesy to the ladies. All went on enjoying themselves until they reached Richmond, where the ladies and their father left the train. But, before doing so, the good old Virginian gentleman, who appeared to be much pleased with my master, presented him with a recipe, which he said was a perfect cure for the inflammatory rheumatism. But the invalid not being able to read it, and fearing he should hold it upside down in pretending to do so, thanked the donor kindly, and placed it in his waistcoat pocket. My master's new friend also gave him his card, and requested him the next time he travelled that way to do him the kindness to call; adding, "I shall be pleased to see you, and so will my daughters." Mr. Johnson expressed his gratitude for the proffered hospitality, and said he should feel glad to call on his return. I have not the slightest doubt that he will fulfil the promise whenever that return takes place. After changing trains we went on a little beyond Fredericksburg, and took a steamer to Washington.

At Richmond, a stout elderly lady, whose whole demeanour indicated that she belonged (as Mrs. Stowe's Aunt Chloe expresses it) to one of the "firstest families;" stepped into the carriage, and took a seat near my master. Seeing me passing quickly along the platform, she sprang up as if taken by a fit, and exclaimed, "Bless my soul! there goes my nigger, Ned!"

My master said, "No; that is my boy."

The lady paid no attention to this; she poked her head out of the window, and bawled to me, "You Ned, come to me, sir, you runaway rascal!"

On my looking round she drew her head in, and said to my master, "I beg your pardon, sir, I was sure it was my nigger; I never in my life saw two black pigs more alike than your boy and my Ned.".

After the disappointed lady had resumed her seat, and the train had moved off, she closed her eyes, slightly raising her hands, and in a sanctified tone said to my master, "Oh! I hope, sir, your boy will not turn out to be so worthless as my Ned has. Oh! I was as kind to him as if he had been my own son. Oh! sir, it grieves me very much to think that after all I did for him he should go off without having any cause whatever."

"When did he leave you?" asked Mr. Johnson.

"About eighteen months ago, and I have never seen hair or hide of him since."

"Did he have a wife?" enquired a very respectable-looking young gentleman, who was sitting near my master and opposite to the lady.

"No, sir; not when he left, though he did have one a little before that: She was very unlike him; she was as good and as faithful a nigger as any one need wish to have. But, poor thing! she became so ill, that she was unable to do much work; so I thought it would be best to sell her, to go to New Orleans, where the climate is nice and warm."

I suppose she was very glad to go South for the restoration of her health?" said the gentleman.

"No; she was not," replied the lady, "for niggers never know what is best for them. She took on a great deal about leaving Ned and the little nigger; but, as she was so weakly, I let her go."

Was she good-looking?" asked the young passenger, who was evidently not of the same opinion as the talkative lady, and therefore wished her to tell all she knew.

"Yes; she was very handsome, and much whiter than I am; and therefore will have no trouble in getting another husband. I am sure I wish her well. I asked the speculator who bought her to sell her to a good master. Poor thing! she has my prayers, and I know she prays for me. She was a good Christian, and always used to pray for my soul. It was through her earliest prayers," continued the lady, "that I was first led to seek forgiveness of my sins, before I was converted at the great camp-meeting."

This caused the lady to snuffle and to draw from her pocket a richly embroidered handkerchief, and apply it to the corner of her eyes. But my master could not see that it was at all soiled.

The silence which prevailed for a few moments was broken by the gentleman's saying, "As your 'July' was such a very good girl, and had served you so faithfully before she lost her health, don't you think it would have been better to have emancipated her?"

"No, indeed I do not!" scornfully exclaimed the lady, as she impatiently crammed the fine handkerchief into a little work-bag. "I have no patience with people who set niggers at liberty. It is the very worst thing you can do for them. My dear husband just before he died willed all his niggers free. But I and all our friends knew very well that he was too good a man to have ever thought of doing such an unkind and foolish thing, had he been in his right mind, and, therefore we had the will altered as it should have been in the first place."

"Did you mean, madam," asked my master, "that willing the slaves free was unjust to yourself, or unkind to them?"

"I mean that it was decidedly unkind to the servants themselves. It always seems to me such a cruel thing to turn niggers loose to shift for themselves, when there are so many good masters to take care of them. As for myself," continued the considerate lady, "I thank the Lord my dear husband left me and my son well provided for. Therefore I care nothing for the niggers, on my own account, for they are a great deal more trouble than they are worth, I sometimes wish that there was not one of them in the world: for the ungrateful wretches are always running away. I have lost no less than ten since my poor husband died. It's ruinous, sir!"

"But as you are well provided for, I suppose you do not feel the loss very much," said the passenger.

"I don't feel it at all," haughtily continued the good soul; "but that is no reason why property should be squandered. If my son and myself had the money for those valuable niggers, just see what a great deal of good we could do for the poor, and in sending missionaries abroad to the poor heathen, who have never heard the name of our blessed Redeemer. My dear son who is a good Christian minister has advised me not to worry and send my soul to hell for the sake of niggers; but to sell every blessed one of them for what they will fetch, and go and live in peace with him in New York. This I have concluded to do. I have just been to Richmond and made arrangements with my agent to make clean work of the forty that are left."

"Your son being a good Christian minister," said the gentleman," It's strange he did not advise you to let the poor negroes have their liberty and go North."

"It's not at all strange, sir; it's not at all strange. My son knows what's best for the niggers; he has always told me that they were much better off than the free niggers in the North. In fact, I don't believe there are any white labouring people in the world who are as well off as the slaves."

"You are quite mistaken, madam," said the young man. "For instance, my own widowed mother, before she died, emancipated all her slaves, and sent them to Ohio, where they are getting along well. I saw several of them last summer myself."

"Well," replied the lady, "freedom may do for your ma's niggers, but it will never do for mine; and, plague them, they shall never have it; that is the word, with the bark on it."

"If freedom will not do for your slaves:' replied the passenger, "I have no doubt your Ned and the other nine negroes will find out their mistake, and return to their old home."

"Blast them!" exclaimed the old lady, with great emphasis, "if I ever get them, I will cook their infernal hash, and tan their accursed black hides well for them! God forgive me," added the old soul, "the niggers will make me lose all my religion!"

By this time the lady had reached her destination. The gentleman got out at the next station beyond. As soon as she was gone, the young Southerner said to my master, "What a d—d shame it is for that old whining hypocritical humbug to cheat the poor negroes out of their liberty! If she has religion, may the devil prevent me from ever being converted!"

For the purpose of somewhat disguising myself, I bought and wore a very good second-hand white beaver, an article which I had never indulged in before. So just before we arrived at Washington, an uncouth planter, who had been watching me very closely, said to my master, "I reckon, stranger, you are '*spiling*' that ere nigger of yourn. by letting him wear such a devilish fine hat. Just look at the quality on it; the President couldn't wear a better. I should just like to go and kick it overboard." His friend touched him, and said, "Don't speak so to a gentleman." "Why not" exclaimed the fellow. He grated his short teeth, which appeared to be nearly worn away by the incessant chewing of tobacco, and said, "It always makes me itch all over, from head to toe, to get hold of every d—d nigger I see dressed like a white man. Washington is run away with *spiled* and free niggers. If I had my way I would sell every d—d rascal of 'em way down South, where the devil would be whipped out on 'em."

This man's fierce manner made my master feel rather nervous, and therefore he thought the less he said the better; so he walked off without making any reply. In a few minutes we were landed at Washington, where we took a conveyance and hurried off to the train for Baltimore.

We left our cottage on Wednesday morning, the 21st of December, 1848, and arrived at Baltimore, Saturday evening, the 24th (Christmas Eve). Baltimore was the last slave port of any note at which we stopped.

On arriving there we felt more anxious than ever, because we knew not what that last dark night would bring forth. It is true we were near the goal, but our poor hearts were still as if tossed at sea; and, as there was another great and dangerous bar to pass, we were afraid our liberties would be wrecked, and, like the ill-fated *Royal Charter*, go down for ever just off the place we longed to reach.

They are particularly watchful at Baltimore to prevent slaves from escaping into Pennsylvania, which is a free State. After I had seen my master into one of the best carriages, and was just about to step into mine, an officer, a full-blooded Yankee of the lower order, saw me. He came quickly up, and, tapping me on the shoulder, said in his unmistakable native twang, together with no little display of his authority, "Where are you going, boy?" "To Philadelphia, sir," I humbly replied. "Well, what are you going there for?" "I am travelling with my master, who is in the next carriage, sir." "Well, I calculate you had better get him out; and be mighty quick about it, because the train will soon be starting. It is against my rules to let any man take a slave past here, unless he can satisfy them in the office that he has a right to take him along."

The officer then passed on and left me standing upon the platform, with my anxious heart apparently palpitating in the throat. At first I scarcely knew which way to turn. But it soon occurred to me that the good God, who had been with us thus far, would not forsake us at the eleventh hour. So with renewed hope I stepped into my master's carriage, to inform him of the difficulty. I found him sitting at the farther end, quite alone. As soon as he looked up and saw me, he smiled. I also tried to wear a cheerful countenance, in order to break the shock of the sad news. I knew what made him smile. He was aware that if we were fortunate we should reach our destination at five o'clock the next morning, and this made it the more painful to communicate what the officer had said; but, as there was no time to lose, I went up to him and asked him how he felt. He said "Much better," and that he thanked God we were getting on so nicely. I then said we were not

getting on quite so well as we had anticipated. He anxiously and quickly asked what was the matter. I told him. He started as if struck by lightning, and exclaimed, "Good Heavens! William, is it possible that we are, after all, doomed to hopeless bondage?" I could say nothing, my heart was too full to speak, for at first I did not know what to do. However we knew it would never do to turn back to the "City of Destruction," like Bunyan's *Mistrust* and *Timorous*, because they saw lions in the narrow way after ascending the hill Difficulty; but press on, like noble *Christian* and *Hopeful*, to the great city in which dwelt a few "shining ones." So, after a few moments, I did all I could to encourage my companion, and we stepped out and made for the office: but how or where my master obtained sufficient courage to face the tyrants who had power to blast all we held dear, heaven only knows! Queen Elizabeth could not have been more terror-stricken, on being forced to land at the traitors' gate leading to the Tower, than we were on entering that office. We felt that our very existence was at stake, and that we must either sink or swim. But, as God was our present and mighty helper in this as well as in all former trials, we were able to keep our heads up and press forwards.

On entering the room we found the principal man, to whom my master said, "Do you wish to see me, sir?" "Yes," said this eagle-eyed officer; and he added, "It is against our rules, sir, to allow any person to take a slave out of Baltimore into Philadelphia, unless he can satisfy us that he has a right to take him along." "Why is that?" asked my master, with more firmness than could be expected. "Because, sir," continued he, in a voice and manner that almost chilled our blood, "if we should suffer any gentleman to take a slave past here into Philadelphia; and should the gentleman with whom the slave might be travelling turn out not to be his rightful owner; and should the proper master come and prove that his slave escaped on our road, we shall have him to pay for; and, therefore, we cannot let any slave pass here without receiving security to show, and to satisfy us, that it is all right."

This conversation attracted the attention of the large number of bustling passengers. After the officer had finished, a few of them said, "Chit, chit, chit;" not because they thought we were slaves endeavouring to escape, but merely because they thought my master was a slaveholder and invalid gentleman, and therefore it was wrong to detain him. The officer, observing that the passengers sympathised with my master, asked him if he was not acquainted with some gentleman in Baltimore that he could get to endorse for him, to show that I was his property, and that he had a right to take me off. He said, "No;" and added, "I bought tickets in Charleston to pass us through to Philadelphia, and therefore you have no right to detain us here." "Well, sir," said the man, indignantly, "right or no right, we shan't let you go." These sharp words fell upon our anxious hearts like the crack of doom, and made us feel that hope only smiles to deceive.

For a few moments perfect silence prevailed. My master looked at me, and I at him, but neither of us dared to speak a word, for fear of making some blunder that would tend to our detection. We knew that the officers had power to throw us into prison, and if they had done so we must have been detected and driven back, like the vilest felons, to a life of slavery, which we dreaded far more than sudden death.

We felt as though we had come into deep waters and were about being overwhelmed, and that the slightest mistake would clip asunder the last brittle thread of hope by which we were suspended, and let us down for ever into the dark and horrible pit of misery and degradation from which we were straining every nerve to escape. While our hearts were crying lustily unto Him who is ever ready and able to save, the conductor of the train that we had just left stepped in. The officer asked if we came by the train with him from Washington; he said we did, and left the room. Just then the bell rang for the train to leave; and had it been the sudden shock of an earthquake it could not have given us a greater thrill. The sound of the bell caused every eye to flash with apparent interest, and to be more steadily fixed upon us than before. But, as God would have it, the officer all at once thrust his fingers through his hair, and in a state of great agitation said, "I really don't know what to do; I calculate it is all right." He then told the clerk to run and tell the conductor to "let this gentleman and slave pass;" adding, "As he is not well, it is a pity to stop him here. We will let him go." My master thanked him, and stepped out and hobbled across the platform as quickly as possible. I tumbled him unceremoniously into one of the best carriages, and leaped into mine just as the train was gliding off towards our happy destination.

We thought of this plan about four days before we left Macon; and as we had our daily employment to attend to, we only saw each other at night. So we sat up the four long nights talking over the plan and making preparations.

We had also been four days on the journey; and as we travelled night and day, we got but very limited opportunities for sleeping. I believe nothing in the world could have kept us awake so long but the intense excitement, produced by the fear of being retaken on the one hand, and the bright anticipation of liberty on the other.

We left Baltimore about eight o'clock in the evening; and not being aware of a stopping-place of any consequence between there and Philadelphia, and also knowing that if we were fortunate we should be in the latter place early the next morning, I thought I might indulge in a few minutes' sleep in the car; but I, like Bunyan's Christian in the arbour, went to sleep at the wrong time, and took too long a nap. So, when the train reached Havre de Grace, all the first-class passengers had to get out of the carriages and into a ferry-boat, to be ferried across the Susquehanna river, and take the train on the opposite side.

The road was constructed so as to be raised or lowered to suit the tide. So they rolled the luggage-vans on to the boat, and off on the other side; and as I was in one of the apartments adjoining a baggage-car, they considered it unnecessary to awaken me, and tumbled me over with the luggage. But when my master was asked to leave his seat, he found it very dark, and cold, and raining. He missed me for the first time on the journey. On all previous occasions, as soon as the train stopped, I was at hand to assist him. This caused many slaveholders to praise me very much: they said they had never before seen a slave so attentive to his master: and therefore my absence filled him with terror and confusion; the children of Israel could not have felt more troubled on arriving at the Red Sea. So he asked the conductor if he had seen anything of his slave. The man being somewhat of an abolitionist, and believing that my master was really a slaveholder, thought he would tease him a little respecting me. So he said, "No, sir; I haven't seen anything of him for some time: I have no doubt he has run away, and is in Philadelphia, free, long before now." My master knew that there was nothing in this; so he asked the conductor if he would please to see if he could find me. The man indignantly replied, "I am no slave-hunter; and as far as I am concerned everybody must look after their own niggers." He went off and left the confused invalid to fancy whatever he felt inclined. My master at first thought I must have been kidnapped into slavery by some one, or left, or perhaps killed on the train. He also thought of stopping to see if he could hear anything of me, but he soon remembered that he had no money. That night all the money we had was consigned to my own pocket, because we thought, in case there were any pickpockets about, a slave's pocket would be the last one they would look for. However, hoping to meet me some day in a land of liberty, and as he had the tickets, he thought it best upon the whole to enter the boat and come off to Philadelphia, and endeavour to make his way alone in this cold and hollow world as best he could. The time was now up, so he went on board and came across with feelings that can be better imagined than described.

After the train had got fairly on the way to Philadelphia, the guard came into my car and gave me a violent shake, and bawled out at the same time, "Boy, wake up!" I started, almost frightened out of my wits. He said, "Your master is scared half to death about you." That frightened me still more I thought they had found him out; so I anxiously inquired what was the matter. The guard said, "He thinks you have run away from him." This made me feel quite at ease. I said, "No, sir; I am satisfied my good master doesn't think that." So off I started to see him. He had been fearfully nervous, but on seeing me he at once felt much better. He merely wished to know what had become of me.

On returning to my seat, I found the conductor and two or three other persons amusing themselves very much respecting my running away. So the guard said, "Boy, what did your master want?"[1] I replied, "He merely wished to know what had become of me." "No," said the man, "that was not it; he thought you had taken French leave, for parts unknown. I never saw a fellow so badly scared about losing his slave in my life. Now," continued the guard, "let me give you a little friendly advice. When you get to Philadelphia, run away and leave that cripple, and have your liberty." "No, sir," I indifferently replied, "I can't promise to do that." "Why not?" said the conductor, evidently much surprised; "don't you want your liberty?" "Yes, sir," I replied; "but I shall never run away from such a good master as I have at present."

One of the men said to the guard, "Let him alone; I guess he will open his eyes when he gets to Philadelphia, and see things in another light." After giving me a good deal of information, which I afterwards found to be very useful, they left me alone.

I also met with a coloured gentleman on this train, who recommended me to a boarding-house that was kept by an abolitionist, where he thought I would be quite safe, if I wished to run away from my master. I thanked him kindly, but of course did not let him know who we were. Late at night, or rather early in the morning, I heard a fearful whistling of the steam-engine; so I opened the window and looked out, and saw a large number of flickering lights in the distance, and heard a passenger in the next carriage—who also had his head out of the window—say to his companion, "Wake up, old horse, we are at Philadelphia!"

The sight of those lights and that announcement made me feel almost as happy as Bunyan's Christian must have felt when he first caught sight of the cross. I, like him, felt that the straps that bound the heavy burden to my back began to pop, and the load to roll off. I also looked, and looked again, for it appeared very wonderful to me how the mere sight of our first city of refuge should have all at once made my hitherto sad and heavy heart become so light and happy. As the train speeded on, I rejoiced and thanked God with all my heart and soul for his great kindness and tender mercy, in watching over us, and bringing us safely through.

As soon as the train had reached the platform, before it had fairly stopped, I hurried out of my carriage to my master, whom I got at once into a cab, placed the luggage on, jumped in myself, and we drove off to the boardinghouse which was so kindly recommended to me. On leaving the station, my master—or rather my wife, as I may now say—who had from the commencement of the journey borne up in a manner that much surprised us both, grasped me by the hand, and said, "Thank God, William, we are safe!" and then burst into tears, leant upon me, and wept like a child. The reaction was fearful. So when we reached the house, she was in reality so weak and faint that she could scarcely stand alone. However, I got her into the apartments that were pointed out, and there we knelt down, on this Sabbath, and Christmas-day, —a day that will ever be memorable to us, —and poured out our heartfelt gratitude to God, for his goodness in enabling us to overcome so many perilous difficulties, in escaping out of the jaws of the wicked.

Endnotes

1. I may state here that every man slave is called boy till he is very old, then the more respectable slaveholders call him uncle. The women are all girls till they are aged, then they are called aunts. This is the reason why Mrs. Stowe calls her characters Uncle Tom, Aunt Chloe, Uncle Tiff, &c.

"What to the Slave Is the Fourth of July?"

Frederick Douglass July 5, 1852

Mr. President, Friends and Fellow Citizens:

He who could address this audience without a quailing sensation, has stronger nerves than I have. I do not remember ever to have appeared as a speaker before any assembly more shrinkingly, nor with greater distrust of my ability, than I do this day. A feeling has crept over me, quite unfavorable to the exercise of my limited powers of speech. The task before me is one which requires much previous thought and study for its proper performance. I know that apologies of this sort are generally considered flat and unmeaning. I trust, however, that mine will not be so considered. Should I seem at ease, my appearance would much misrepresent me. The little experience I have had in addressing public meetings, in country schoolhouses, avails me nothing on the present occasion.

The papers and placards say, that I am to deliver a 4th [of] July oration. This certainly sounds large, and out of the common way, for it is true that I have often had the privilege to speak in this beautiful Hall, and to address many who now honor me with their presence. But neither their familiar faces, nor the perfect gage I think I have of Corinthian Hall, seems to free me from embarrassment.

The fact is, ladies and gentlemen, the distance between this platform and the slave plantation, from which I escaped, is considerable—and the difficulties to be overcome in getting from the latter to the former, are by no means slight. That I am here to-day is, to me, a matter of astonishment as well as of gratitude. You will not, therefore, be surprised, if in what I have to say I evince no elaborate preparation, nor grace my speech with any high sounding exordium. With little experience and with less learning, I have been able to throw my thoughts hastily and imperfectly together; and trusting to your patient and generous indulgence, I will proceed to lay them before you.

This, for the purpose of this celebration, is the 4th of July. It is the birthday of your National Independence, and of your political freedom. This, to you, is what the Passover was to the emancipated people of God. It carries your minds back to the day, and to the act of your great deliverance; and to the signs, and to the wonders, associated with that act, and that day. This celebration also marks the beginning of another year of your national life; and reminds you that the Republic of America is now 76 years old. I am glad, fellow-citizens, that your nation is so young. Seventy-six years, though a good old age for a man, is but a mere speck in the life of a nation. Three score years and ten is the allotted time for individual men; but nations number their years by thousands. According to this fact, you are, even now, only in the beginning of your national career, still lingering in the period of childhood. I repeat, I am glad this is so. There is hope in the thought, and hope is much needed, under the dark clouds which lower above the horizon. The eye of the reformer is met with angry flashes, portending disastrous times; but his heart may well beat lighter at the thought that America is young, and that she is still in the impressible stage of her existence. May he not hope that high lessons of wisdom, of justice and of truth, will yet give direction to her destiny? Were the nation older, the patriot's heart might be sadder, and the reformer's brow heavier. Its future might be shrouded in gloom, and the hope of its prophets go out in sorrow. There is consolation in the thought that America is young. Great streams are not easily turned from channels, worn deep in the course of ages. They may sometimes rise in quiet and stately majesty, and inundate the land, refreshing and fertilizing the earth with their mysterious properties. They may also rise in wrath and fury, and bear away, on their angry waves, the accumulated wealth of years of toil and hardship. They, however, gradually flow back to the same old channel, and flow on as serenely as ever. But, while the river may not be turned aside, it may dry up, and leave nothing behind but the withered branch, and the unsightly rock, to howl in the abyss-sweeping wind, the sad tale of departed glory. As with rivers so with nations.

Fellow-citizens, I shall not presume to dwell at length on the associations that cluster about this day. The simple story of it is that, 76 years ago, the people of this country were British subjects. The style and title of your "sovereign people" (in which you now glory) was not then born. You were under the British Crown. Your fathers esteemed the English Government as the home government; and England as the fatherland. This home government, you know, although a considerable distance from your home, did, in the exercise of its parental prerogatives, impose upon its colonial children, such restraints, burdens and limitations, as, in its mature judgment, it deemed wise, right and proper.

But, your fathers, who had not adopted the fashionable idea of this day, of the infallibility of government, and the absolute character of its acts, presumed to differ from the home government in respect to the wisdom and the justice of some of those burdens and restraints. They went so far in their excitement as to pronounce the measures of government unjust, unreasonable, and oppressive, and altogether such as ought not to be quietly submitted to. I scarcely need say, fellow-citizens, that my opinion of those measures fully accords with that of your fathers. Such a declaration of agreement on my part would not be worth much to anybody. It would, certainly, prove nothing, as to what part I might have taken, had I lived during the great controversy of 1776. To say now that America was right, and England wrong, is exceedingly easy. Everybody can say it; the dastard, not less than the noble brave, can flippantly discant on the tyranny of England towards the American Colonies. It is fashionable to do so; but there was a time when to pronounce against England, and in favor of the cause of the colonies, tried men's souls. They who did so were accounted in their day, plotters of mischief, agitators and rebels, dangerous men. To side with the right, against the wrong, with the weak against the strong, and with the oppressed against the oppressor! here lies the merit, and the one which, of all others, seems unfashionable in our day. The cause of liberty may be stabbed by the men who glory in the deeds of your fathers. But, to proceed.

Feeling themselves harshly and unjustly treated by the home government, your fathers, like men of honesty, and men of spirit, earnestly sought redress. They petitioned and remonstrated; they did so in a decorous, respectful, and loyal manner. Their conduct was wholly unexceptionable. This, however, did not answer the purpose. They saw themselves treated with sovereign indifference, coldness and scorn. Yet they persevered. They were not the men to look back.

As the sheet anchor takes a firmer hold, when the ship is tossed by the storm, so did the cause of your fathers grow stronger, as it breasted the chilling blasts of kingly displeasure. The greatest and best of British statesmen admitted its justice, and the loftiest eloquence of the British Senate came to its support. But, with that blindness which seems to be the unvarying characteristic of tyrants, since Pharaoh and his hosts were drowned in the Red Sea, the British Government persisted in the exactions complained of.

The madness of this course, we believe, is admitted now, even by England; but we fear the lesson is wholly lost on our present ruler.

Oppression makes a wise man mad. Your fathers were wise men, and if they did not go mad, they became restive under this treatment. They felt themselves the victims of grievous wrongs, wholly incurable in their colonial capacity. With brave men there is always a remedy for oppression. Just here, the idea of a total separation of the colonies from the crown was born! It was a startling idea, much more so, than we, at this distance of time, regard it. The timid and the prudent (as has been intimated) of that day, were, of course, shocked and alarmed by it.

Such people lived then, had lived before, and will, probably, ever have a place on this planet; and their course, in respect to any great change, (no matter how great the good to be attained, or the wrong to be redressed by it), may be calculated with as much precision as can be the course of the stars. They hate all changes, but silver, gold and copper change! Of this sort of change they are always strongly in favor.

These people were called Tories in the days of your fathers; and the appellation, probably, conveyed the same idea that is meant by a more modern, though a somewhat less euphonious term, which we often find in our papers, applied to some of our old politicians.

Their opposition to the then dangerous thought was earnest and powerful; but, amid all their terror and affrighted vociferations against it, the alarming and revolutionary idea moved on, and the country with it.

On the 2d of July, 1776, the old Continental Congress, to the dismay of the lovers of ease, and the worshipers of property, clothed that dreadful idea with all the authority of national sanction. They did so in the form of a resolution; and as we seldom hit upon resolutions, drawn up in our day whose transparency is at all equal to this, it may refresh your minds and help my story if I read it. "Resolved, That these united colonies are, and of right, ought to be free and Independent States; that they are absolved from all allegiance to the British Crown; and that all political connection between them and the State of Great Britain is, and ought to be, dissolved."

Citizens, your fathers made good that resolution. They succeeded; and to-day you reap the fruits of their success. The freedom gained is yours; and you, therefore, may properly celebrate this anniversary. The 4th of July is the first great fact in your nation's history—the very ring-bolt in the chain of your yet undeveloped destiny.

Pride and patriotism, not less than gratitude, prompt you to celebrate and to hold it in perpetual remembrance. I have said that the Declaration of Independence is the ring-bolt to the chain of your nation's destiny; so, indeed, I regard it. The principles contained in that instrument are saving principles. Stand by those principles, be true to them on all occasions, in all places, against all foes, and at whatever cost.

From the round top of your ship of state, dark and threatening clouds may be seen. Heavy billows, like mountains in the distance, disclose to the leeward huge forms of flinty rocks! That bolt drawn, that chain broken, and all is lost. Cling to this day—cling to it, and to its principles, with the grasp of a storm-tossed mariner to a spar at midnight.

The coming into being of a nation, in any circumstances, is an interesting event. But, besides general considerations, there were peculiar circumstances which make the advent of this republic an event of special attractiveness.

The whole scene, as I look back to it, was simple, dignified and sublime.

The population of the country, at the time, stood at the insignificant number of three millions. The country was poor in the munitions of war. The population was weak and scattered, and the country a wilderness unsubdued. There were then no means of concert and combination, such as exist now. Neither steam nor lightning had then been reduced to order and discipline. From the Potomac to the Delaware was a journey of many days. Under these, and innumerable other disadvantages, your fathers declared for liberty and independence and triumphed.

Fellow Citizens, I am not wanting in respect for the fathers of this republic. The signers of the Declaration of Independence were brave men. They were great men too—great enough to give fame to a great age. It does not often happen to a nation to raise, at one time, such a number of truly great men. The point from which I am compelled to view them is not, certainly, the most favorable; and yet I cannot contemplate their great deeds with less than admiration. They were statesmen, patriots and heroes, and for the good they did, and the principles they contended for, I will unite with you to honor their memory.

They loved their country better than their own private interests; and, though this is not the highest form of human excellence, all will concede that it is a rare virtue, and that when it is exhibited, it ought to command respect. He who will, intelligently, lay down his life for his country, is a man whom it is not in human nature to despise. Your fathers staked their lives, their fortunes, and their sacred honor, on the cause of their country. In their admiration of liberty, they lost sight of all other interests.

They were peace men; but they preferred revolution to peaceful submission to bondage. They were quiet men; but they did not shrink from agitating against oppression. They showed forbearance; but that they knew its limits. They believed in order; but not in the order of tyranny. With them, nothing was "settled" that was not right. With them, justice, liberty and humanity were "final;" not slavery and oppression. You may well cherish the memory of such men. They were great in their day and generation. Their solid manhood stands out the more as we contrast it with these degenerate times.

How circumspect, exact and proportionate were all their movements! How unlike the politicians of an hour! Their statesmanship looked beyond the passing moment, and stretched away in strength into the distant future. They seized upon eternal principles, and set a glorious example in their defense. Mark them!

Fully appreciating the hardship to be encountered, firmly believing in the right of their cause, honorably inviting the scrutiny of an on-looking world, reverently appealing to heaven to attest their sincerity, soundly comprehending the solemn responsibility they were about to assume, wisely measuring the terrible odds against them, your fathers, the fathers of this republic, did, most deliberately, under the inspiration of a glorious patriotism, and with a sublime faith in the great principles of justice and freedom, lay deep the corner-stone of the national superstructure, which has risen and still rises in grandeur around you.

Of this fundamental work, this day is the anniversary. Our eyes are met with demonstrations of joyous enthusiasm. Banners and pennants wave exultingly on the breeze. The din of business, too, is hushed. Even Mammon seems to have quitted his grasp on this day. The ear-piercing fife and the stirring drum unite their accents with the ascending peal of a thousand church bells. Prayers are made, hymns are sung, and sermons are preached in honor of this day; while the quick martial tramp of a great and multitudinous nation, echoed back by all the hills, valleys and mountains of a vast continent, bespeak the occasion one of thrilling and universal interest—a nation's jubilee.

Friends and citizens, I need not enter further into the causes which led to this anniversary. Many of you understand them better than I do. You could instruct me in regard to them. That is a branch of knowledge in which you feel, perhaps, a much deeper interest than your speaker. The causes which led to the separation of the colonies from the British crown have never lacked for a tongue. They have all been taught in your common schools, narrated at your firesides, unfolded from your pulpits, and thundered from your legislative halls, and are as familiar to you as household words. They form the staple of your national poetry and eloquence.

I remember, also, that, as a people, Americans are remarkably familiar with all facts which make in their own favor. This is esteemed by some as a national trait—perhaps a national weakness. It is a fact, that whatever makes for the wealth or for the reputation of Americans, and can be had cheap! will be found by Americans. I shall not be charged with slandering Americans, if I say I think the American side of any question may be safely left in American hands.

I leave, therefore, the great deeds of your fathers to other gentlemen whose claim to have been regularly descended will be less likely to be disputed than mine!

My business, if I have any here to-day, is with the present. The accepted time with God and his cause is the ever-living now.

> *Trust no future, however pleasant,*
> *Let the dead past bury its dead;*
> *Act, act in the living present,*
> *Heart within, and God overhead.*

We have to do with the past only as we can make it useful to the present and to the future. To all inspiring motives, to noble deeds which can be gained from the past, we are welcome. But now is the time, the important time. Your fathers have lived, died, and have done their work, and have done much of it well. You live and must die, and you must do your work. You have no right to enjoy a child's share in the labor of your fathers, unless your children are to be blest by your labors. You have no right to wear out and waste the hard-earned fame of your fathers to cover your indolence. Sydney Smith tells us that men seldom eulogize the wisdom and virtues of their fathers, but to excuse some folly or wickedness of their own. This truth is not a doubtful one. There are illustrations of it near and remote, ancient and modern. It was fashionable, hundreds of years ago, for the children of Jacob to boast, we have "Abraham to our father," when they had long lost Abraham's faith and spirit. That people contented themselves under the shadow of Abraham's great name, while they repudiated the deeds which made his name great. Need I remind you that a similar thing is being done all over this country to-day? Need I tell you that the Jews are not the only people who built the tombs of the prophets, and garnished the sepulchres of the righteous? Washington could not die till he had broken the chains of his slaves. Yet his monument is built up by the price of human blood, and the traders in the bodies and souls of men shout—"We have Washington to *our father*."— Alas! that it should be so; yet so it is.

The evil that men do, lives after them, The good is oft-interred with their bones.

Fellow-citizens, pardon me, allow me to ask, why am I called upon to speak here to-day? What have I, or those I represent, to do with your national independence? Are the great principles of political freedom and of natural justice, embodied in that Declaration of Independence, extended to us? and am I, therefore, called upon to bring our humble offering to the national altar, and to confess the benefits and express devout gratitude for the blessings resulting from your independence to us?

Would to God, both for your sakes and ours, that an affirmative answer could be truthfully returned to these questions! Then would my task be light, and my burden easy and delightful. For who is there so cold, that a nation's sympathy could not warm him? Who so obdurate and dead to the claims of gratitude, that would not thankfully acknowledge such priceless benefits? Who so stolid and selfish, that would not give his voice to swell the hallelujahs of a nation's jubilee, when the chains of servitude had been torn from his limbs? I am not that man. In a case like that, the dumb might eloquently speak, and the "lame man leap as an hart."

But, such is not the state of the case. I say it with a sad sense of the disparity between us. I am not included within the pale of this glorious anniversary! Your high independence only reveals the immeasurable distance between us. The blessings in which you, this day, rejoice, are not enjoyed in common.—The rich inheritance of justice, liberty, prosperity and independence, bequeathed by your fathers, is shared by you, not by me. The sunlight that brought life and healing to you, has brought stripes and death to me. This Fourth [of] July is *yours*, not *mine*. *You* may rejoice, *I* must mourn. To drag a man in fetters into the grand illuminated temple of liberty, and call upon him to join you in joyous anthems, were inhuman mockery and sacrilegious irony. Do you mean, citizens, to mock me, by asking me to speak to-day? If so, there is a parallel to your conduct. And let me warn you that it is dangerous to copy the example of a nation whose crimes, lowering up to heaven, were thrown down by the breath of the Almighty, burying that nation in irrecoverable ruin! I can to-day take up the plaintive lament of a peeled and woe-smitten people!

"By the rivers of Babylon, there we sat down. Yea! we wept when we remembered Zion. We hanged our harps upon the willows in the midst thereof. For there, they that carried us away captive, required of us a song; and they who wasted us required of us mirth, saying, Sing us one of the songs of Zion. How can we sing the Lord's song in a strange land? If I forget thee, O Jerusalem, let my right hand forget her cunning. If I do not remember thee, let my tongue cleave to the roof of my mouth."

Fellow-citizens; above your national, tumultuous joy, I hear the mournful wail of millions! whose chains, heavy and grievous yesterday, are, to-day, rendered more intolerable by the jubilee shouts that reach them. If I do forget, if I do not faithfully remember those bleeding children of sorrow this day, "may my right hand forget her cunning, and may my tongue cleave to the roof of my mouth!" To forget them, to pass lightly over their wrongs, and to chime in with the popular theme, would be treason most scandalous and shocking, and would make me a reproach before God and the world. My subject, then fellow-citizens, is AMERICAN SLAVERY. I shall see, this day, and its popular characteristics, from the slave's point of view. Standing, there, identified with the American bondman, making his wrongs mine, I do not hesitate to declare, with all my soul, that the character and conduct of this nation never looked blacker to me than on this 4th of July! Whether we turn to the declarations of the past, or to the professions of the present, the conduct of the nation seems equally hideous and revolting. America is false to the past, false to the present, and solemnly binds herself to be false to the future. Standing with God and the crushed and bleeding slave on this occasion, I will, in the name of humanity which is outraged, in the name of liberty which is fettered, in the name of the constitution and the Bible, which are disregarded and trampled upon, dare to call in question and to denounce, with all the emphasis I can command, everything that serves to perpetuate slavery—the great sin and shame of America! "I will not equivocate; I will not excuse;" I will use the severest language I can command; and yet not one word shall escape me that any man, whose judgment is not blinded by prejudice, or who is not at heart a slaveholder, shall not confess to be right and just.

But I fancy I hear some one of my audience say, it is just in this circumstance that you and your brother abolitionists fail to make a favorable impression on the public mind. Would you argue more, and denounce less, would you persuade more, and rebuke less, your cause would be much more likely to succeed. But, I submit, where all is plain there is nothing to be argued. What point in the anti-slavery creed would you have me argue? On what branch of the subject do the people of this country need light? Must I undertake to prove that the slave is a man? That point is conceded already. Nobody doubts it. The slaveholders themselves acknowledge it in the enactment of laws for their government. They acknowledge it when they punish disobedience on the part of the slave. There are seventy-two crimes in the State of Virginia, which, if committed by a black man, (no matter how ignorant he be), subject him to the punishment of death; while only two of the same crimes will subject a white man to the like punishment. What is this but the acknowledgement that the slave is a moral, intellectual and responsible being? The manhood of the slave is conceded. It is admitted in the fact that Southern statute books are covered with enactments forbidding, under severe fines and penalties, the teaching of the slave to read or to write. When you can point to any such laws, in reference to the beasts of the field, then I may consent to argue the manhood of the slave. When the dogs in your streets, when the fowls of the air, when the cattle on your hills, when the fish of the sea, and the reptiles that crawl, shall be unable to distinguish the slave from a brute, *then* will I argue with you that the slave is a man!

For the present, it is enough to affirm the equal manhood of the Negro race. Is it not astonishing that, while we are ploughing, planting and reaping, using all kinds of mechanical tools, erecting houses, constructing bridges, building ships, working in metals of brass, iron, copper, silver and gold; that, while we are reading, writing and cyphering, acting as clerks, merchants and secretaries, having among us lawyers, doctors, ministers, poets, authors, editors, orators and teachers; that, while we are engaged in all manner of enterprises common to other men, digging gold in California, capturing the whale in the Pacific, feeding sheep and cattle on the hill-side, living, moving, acting, thinking, planning, living in families as husbands, wives and children, and, above all, confessing and worshipping the Christian's God, and looking hopefully for life and immortality beyond the grave, we are called upon to prove that we are men!

Would you have me argue that man is entitled to liberty? that he is the rightful owner of his own body? You have already declared it. Must I argue the wrongfulness of slavery? Is that a question for Republicans? Is it to be settled by the rules of logic and argumentation, as a matter beset with great difficulty, involving a doubtful application of the principle of justice, hard to be understood? How should I look to-day, in the presence of Americans, dividing, and subdividing a discourse, to show that men have a natural right to freedom? speaking of it relatively, and positively, negatively, and affirmatively. To do so, would be to make myself ridiculous, and to offer an insult to your understanding.—There is not a man beneath the canopy of heaven, that does not know that slavery is wrong *for him.*

What, am I to argue that it is wrong to make men brutes, to rob them of their liberty, to work them without wages, to keep them ignorant of their relations to their fellow men, to beat them with sticks, to flay their flesh with the lash, to load their limbs with irons, to hunt them with dogs, to sell them at auction, to sunder their families, to knock out their teeth, to burn their flesh, to starve them into obedience and submission to their masters? Must I argue that a system thus marked with blood, and stained with pollution, is *wrong*? No! I will not. I have better employments for my time and strength than such arguments would imply.

What, then, remains to be argued? Is it that slavery is not divine; that God did not establish it; that our doctors of divinity are mistaken? There is blasphemy in the thought. That which is inhuman, cannot be divine! Who can reason on such a proposition? They that can, may; I cannot. The time for such argument is passed.

At a time like this, scorching irony, not convincing argument, is needed. O! had I the ability, and could I reach the nation's ear, I would, to-day, pour out a fiery stream of biting ridicule, blasting reproach, withering sarcasm, and stern rebuke. For it is not light that is needed, but fire; it is not the gentle shower, but thunder. We need the storm, the whirlwind, and the earthquake. The feeling of the nation must be quickened; the conscience of the nation must be roused; the propriety of the nation must be startled; the hypocrisy of the nation must be exposed; and its crimes against God and man must be proclaimed and denounced.

What, to the American slave, is your 4th of July? I answer: a day that reveals to him, more than all other days in the year, the gross injustice and cruelty to which he is the constant victim. To him, your celebration is a sham; your boasted liberty, an unholy license; your national greatness, swelling vanity; your sounds of rejoicing are empty and heartless; your denunciations of tyrants, brass fronted impudence; your shouts of liberty and equality, hollow mockery; your prayers and hymns, your sermons and thanksgivings, with all your religious parade, and solemnity, are, to him, mere bombast, fraud, deception, impiety, and hypocrisy—a thin veil to cover up crimes which would disgrace a nation of savages. There is not a nation on the earth guilty of practices, more shocking and bloody, than are the people of these United States, at this very hour.

Go where you may, search where you will, roam through all the monarchies and despotisms of the old world, travel through South America, search out every abuse, and when you have found the last, lay your facts by the side of the everyday practices of this nation, and you will say with me, that, for revolting barbarity and shameless hypocrisy, America reigns without a rival.

Take the American slave-trade, which, we are told by the papers, is especially prosperous just now. Ex-Senator Benton tells us that the price of men was never higher than now. He mentions the fact to show that slavery is in no danger. This trade is one of the peculiarities of American institutions. It is carried on in all the large towns and cities in one-half of this confederacy; and millions are pocketed every year, by dealers in this horrid traffic. In several states, this trade is a chief source of wealth. It is called (in contradistinction to the foreign slave-trade) "*the internal slave trade.*" It is, probably, called so, too, in order to divert from it the horror with which the foreign slave-trade is contemplated. That trade has long since been denounced by this government, as piracy. It has been denounced with burning words, from the high places of the nation, as an execrable traffic. To arrest it, to put an end to it, this nation keeps a squadron, at immense cost, on the coast of Africa. Everywhere, in this country, it is safe to speak of this foreign slave-trade, as a most inhuman traffic, opposed alike to the laws of God and of man. The duty to extirpate and destroy it, is admitted even by our DOCTORS OF DIVINITY. In order to put an end to it, some of these last have consented that their colored brethren (nominally free) should leave this country, and establish themselves on the western coast of Africa! It is, however, a notable fact that, while so much execration is poured out by Americans upon those engaged in the foreign slave-trade, the men engaged in the slave-trade between the states pass without condemnation, and their business is deemed honorable.

Behold the practical operation of this internal slave-trade, the American slave-trade, sustained by American politics and America religion. Here you will see men and women reared like swine for the market. You know what is a swine-drover? I will show you a man-drover. They inhabit all our Southern States. They perambulate the country, and crowd the highways of the nation, with droves of human stock. You will see one of these human flesh-jobbers, armed with pistol, whip and bowie-knife, driving a company of a hundred men, women, and children, from the Potomac to the slave market at New Orleans. These wretched people are to be sold singly, or in lots, to suit purchasers. They are food for the cotton-field, and the deadly sugar-mill. Mark the sad procession, as it moves wearily along, and the inhuman wretch who drives them. Hear his savage yells and his blood-chilling oaths, as he hurries on his affrighted captives! There, see the old man, with locks thinned and gray. Cast one glance, if you please, upon that young mother, whose shoulders are bare to the scorching sun, her briny tears falling on the brow of the babe in her arms. See, too, that girl of thirteen, weeping, *yes!* weeping, as she thinks of the mother from whom she has been torn! The drove moves tardily. Heat and sorrow have nearly consumed their strength; suddenly you hear a quick snap, like the discharge of a rifle; the fetters clank, and the chain rattles simultaneously; your ears are saluted with a scream, that seems to have torn its way to the center of your soul! The crack you heard, was the sound of the slave-whip; the scream you heard, was from the woman you saw with the babe. Her speed had faltered under the weight of her child and her chains! that gash on her shoulder tells her to move on. Follow the drove to New Orleans. Attend the auction; see men examined like horses; see the forms of women rudely and brutally exposed to the shocking gaze of American slave-buyers. See this drove sold and separated forever; and never forget the deep, sad sobs that arose from that scattered multitude. Tell me citizens, WHERE, under the sun, you can witness a spectacle more fiendish and shocking. Yet this is but a glance at the American slave-trade, as it exists, at this moment, in the ruling part of the United States.

I was born amid such sights and scenes. To me the American slave-trade is a terrible reality. When a child, my soul was often pierced with a sense of its horrors. I lived on Philpot Street, Fell's Point, Baltimore, and have watched from the wharves, the slave ships in the Basin, anchored from the shore, with their cargoes of human flesh, waiting for favorable winds to waft them down the Chesapeake. There was, at that time, a grand slave mart kept at the head of Pratt Street, by Austin Woldfolk. His agents were sent into every town and county in Maryland, announcing their arrival, through the papers, and on flaming "*hand-bills,*" headed CASH FOR NEGROES. These men were generally well dressed men, and very captivating in their manners. Ever ready to drink, to treat, and to gamble. The fate of many a slave has depended upon the turn of a single card; and many a child has been snatched from the arms of its mother by bargains arranged in a state of brutal drunkenness.

The flesh-mongers gather up their victims by dozens, and drive them, chained, to the general depot at Baltimore. When a sufficient number have been collected here, a ship is chartered, for the purpose of conveying the forlorn crew to Mobile, or to New Orleans. From the slave prison to the ship, they are usually driven in the darkness of night; for since the antislavery agitation, a certain caution is observed.

In the deep still darkness of midnight, I have been often aroused by the dead heavy footsteps, and the piteous cries of the chained gangs that passed our door. The anguish of my boyish heart was intense; and I was often consoled, when speaking to my mistress in the morning, to hear her say that the custom was very wicked; that she hated to hear the rattle of the chains, and the heart-rending cries. I was glad to find one who sympathized with me in my horror.

Fellow-citizens, this murderous traffic is, to-day, in active operation in this boasted republic. In the solitude of my spirit, I see clouds of dust raised on the highways of the South; I see the bleeding foot-steps; I hear the doleful wail of fettered humanity, on the way to the slave-markets, where the victims are to be sold like *horses*, *sheep*, and *swine*, knocked off to the highest bidder. There I see the tenderest ties ruthlessly broken, to gratify the lust, caprice and rapacity of the buyers and sellers of men. My soul sickens at the sight.

> Is this the land your Fathers loved,
> The freedom which they toiled to win?
> Is this the earth whereon they moved?
> Are these the graves they slumber in?

But a still more inhuman, disgraceful, and scandalous state of things remains to be presented. By an act of the American Congress, not yet two years old, slavery has been nationalized in its most horrible and revolting form. By that act, Mason and Dixon's line has been obliterated; New York has become as Virginia; and the power to hold, hunt, and sell men, women, and children as slaves remains no longer a mere state institution, but is now an institution of the whole United States. The power is co-extensive with the Star-Spangled Banner and American Christianity. Where these go, may also go the merciless slave-hunter. Where these are, man is not sacred. He is a bird for the sportsman's gun. By that most foul and fiendish of all human decrees, the liberty and person of every man are put in peril. Your broad republican domain is hunting ground for *men*. Not for thieves and robbers, enemies of society, merely, but for men guilty of no crime. Your lawmakers have commanded all good citizens to engage in this hellish sport. Your President, your Secretary of State, our *lords*, *nobles*, and ecclesiastics, enforce, as a duty you owe to your free and glorious country, and to your God, that you do this accursed thing. Not fewer than forty Americans have, within the past two years, been hunted down and, without a moment's warning, hurried away in chains, and consigned to slavery and excruciating torture. Some of these have had wives and children, dependent on them for bread; but of this, no account was made. The right of the hunter to his prey stands superior to the right of marriage, and to *all* rights in this republic, the rights of God included! For black men there are neither law, justice, humanity, not religion. The Fugitive Slave *Law* makes mercy to them a crime; and bribes the judge who tries them. An American judge gets ten dollars for every victim he consigns to slavery, and five, when he fails to do so. The oath of any two villains is sufficient, under this hell-black enactment, to send the most pious and exemplary black man into the remorseless jaws of slavery! His own testimony is nothing. He can bring no witnesses for himself. The minister of American justice is bound by the law to hear but *one* side; and *that* side, is the side of the oppressor. Let this damning fact be perpetually told. Let it be thundered around the world, that, in tyrant-killing, king-hating, people-loving, democratic, Christian America, the seats of justice are filled with judges, who hold their offices under an open and palpable *bribe*, and are bound, in deciding in the case of a man's liberty, *hear only his accusers!*

In glaring violation of justice, in shameless disregard of the forms of administering law, in cunning arrangement to entrap the defenseless, and in diabolical intent, this Fugitive Slave Law stands alone in the annals of tyrannical legislation. I doubt if there be another nation on the globe, having the brass and the baseness to put such a law on the statute-book. If any man in this assembly thinks differently from me in this matter, and feels able to disprove my statements, I will gladly confront him at any suitable time and place he may select.

I take this law to be one of the grossest infringements of Christian Liberty, and, if the churches and ministers of our country were not stupidly blind, or most wickedly indifferent, they, too, would so regard it.

At the very moment that they are thanking God for the enjoyment of civil and religious liberty, and for the right to worship God according to the dictates of their own consciences, they are utterly silent in respect to a law which robs religion of its chief significance, and makes it utterly worthless to a world lying in wickedness. Did this law concern the "*mint, anise, and cumin*"—abridge the right to sing psalms, to partake of the sacrament, or to engage in any of the ceremonies of religion, it would be smitten by the thunder of a thousand pulpits. A general shout would go up from the church, demanding *repeal, repeal, instant repeal!*—And it would go hard with that politician who presumed to solicit the votes of the people without inscribing this motto on his banner. Further, if this demand were not complied with, another Scotland would be added to the history of religious liberty, and the stern old Covenanters would be thrown into the shade. A John Knox would be seen at every church door, and heard from every pulpit, and Fillmore would have no more quarter than was shown by Knox, to the beautiful, but treacherous queen Mary of Scotland. The fact that the church of our country, (with fractional exceptions), does not esteem "the Fugitive Slave Law" as a declaration of war against religious liberty, implies that that church regards religion simply as a form of worship, an empty ceremony, and *not* a vital principle, requiring active benevolence, justice, love and good will towards man. It esteems sacrifice above mercy; psalm-singing above right doing; solemn meetings above practical righteousness. A worship that can be conducted by persons who refuse to give shelter to the houseless, to give bread to the hungry, clothing to the naked, and who enjoin obedience to a law forbidding these acts of mercy, is a curse, not a blessing to mankind. The Bible addresses all such persons as "scribes, Pharisees, hypocrites, who pay tithe of *mint*, *anise*, and *cumin*, and have omitted the weightier matters of the law, judgment, mercy and faith."

But the church of this country is not only indifferent to the wrongs of the slave, it actually takes sides with the oppressors. It has made itself the bulwark of American slavery, and the shield of American slave-hunters. Many of its most eloquent Divines. who stand as the very lights of the church, have shamelessly given the sanction of religion and the Bible to the whole slave system. They have taught that man may, properly, be a slave; that the relation of master and slave is ordained of God; that to send back an escaped bondman to his master is clearly the duty of all the followers of the Lord Jesus Christ; and this horrible blasphemy is palmed off upon the world for Christianity.

For my part, I would say, welcome infidelity! welcome atheism! welcome anything! in preference to the gospel, *as preached by those Divines!* They convert the very name of religion into an engine of tyranny, and barbarous cruelty, and serve to confirm more infidels, in this age, than all the infidel writings of Thomas Paine, Voltaire, and Bolingbroke,

put together, have done! These ministers make religion a cold and flinty-hearted thing, having neither principles of right action, nor bowels of compassion. They strip the love of God of its beauty, and leave the throng of religion a huge, horrible, repulsive form. It is a religion for oppressors, tyrants, man-stealers, and *thugs*. It is not that *"pure and undefiled religion"* which is from above, and which is *"first pure, then peaceable, easy to be entreated, full of mercy and good fruits, without partiality, and without hypocrisy."* But a religion which favors the rich against the poor; which exalts the proud above the humble; which divides mankind into two classes, tyrants and slaves; which says to the man in chains, *stay there*; and to the oppressor, *oppress on*; it is a religion which may be professed and enjoyed by all the robbers and enslavers of mankind; it makes God a respecter of persons, denies his fatherhood of the race, and tramples in the dust the great truth of the brotherhood of man. All this we affirm to be true of the popular church, and the popular worship of our land and nation—a religion, a church, and a worship which, on the authority of inspired wisdom, we pronounce to be an abomination in the sight of God. In the language of Isaiah, the American church might be well addressed, "Bring no more vain ablations; incense is an abomination unto me: the new moons and Sabbaths, the calling of assemblies, I cannot away with; it is iniquity even the solemn meeting. Your new moons and your appointed feasts my soul hateth. They are a trouble to me; I am weary to bear them; and when ye spread forth your hands I will hide mine eyes from you. Yea! when ye make many prayers, I will not hear. YOUR HANDS ARE FULL OF BLOOD; cease to do evil, learn to do well; seek judgment; relieve the oppressed; judge for the fatherless; plead for the widow."

The American church is guilty, when viewed in connection with what it is doing to uphold slavery; but it is superlatively guilty when viewed in connection with its ability to abolish slavery. The sin of which it is guilty is one of omission as well as of commission. Albert Barnes but uttered what the common sense of every man at all observant of the actual state of the case will receive as truth, when he declared that "There is no power out of the church that could sustain slavery an hour, if it were not sustained in it."

Let the religious press, the pulpit, the Sunday school, the conference meeting, the great ecclesiastical, missionary, Bible and tract associations of the land array their immense powers against slavery and slave-holding; and the whole system of crime and blood would be scattered to the winds; and that they do not do this involves them in the most awful responsibility of which the mind can conceive.

In prosecuting the anti-slavery enterprise, we have been asked to spare the church, to spare the ministry; but *how*, we ask, could such a thing be done? We are met on the threshold of our efforts for the redemption of the slave, by the church and ministry of the country, in battle arrayed against us; and we are compelled to fight or flee. From *what-* quarter, I beg to know, has proceeded a fire so deadly upon our ranks, during the last two years, as from the Northern pulpit? As the champions of oppressors, the chosen men of American theology have appeared—men, honored for their so-called piety, and their real learning. The Lords of Buffalo, the Springs of New York, the Lathrops of Auburn, the Coxes and Spencers of Brooklyn, the Gannets and Sharps of Boston, the Deweys of Washington, and other great religious lights of the land have, in utter denial of the authority of *Him* by whom they professed to be called to the ministry, deliberately taught us, against the example or the Hebrews and against the remonstrance of the Apostles, they teach *that we ought to obey man's law before the law of God.*

My spirit wearies of such blasphemy; and how such men can be supported, as the "standing types and representatives of Jesus Christ," is a mystery which I leave others to penetrate. In speaking of the American church, however, let it be distinctly understood that I mean the great mass of the religious organizations of our land. There are exceptions, and I thank God that there are. Noble men may be found, scattered all over these Northern States, of whom Henry Ward Beecher of Brooklyn, Samuel J. May of Syracuse, and my esteemed friend (Rev. R. R. Raymond) on the platform, are shining examples; and let me say further, that upon these men lies the duty to inspire our ranks with high religious faith and zeal, and to cheer us on in the great mission of the slave's redemption from his chains.

One is struck with the difference between the attitude of the American church towards the anti-slavery movement, and that occupied by the churches in England towards a similar movement in that country. There, the church, true to its mission of ameliorating, elevating, and improving the condition of mankind, came forward promptly, bound up the wounds of the West Indian slave, and restored him to his liberty. There, the question of emancipation was a high religious question. It was demanded, in the name of humanity, and according to the law of the living God. The Sharps, the Clarksons, the Wilberforces, the Buxtons, and Burchells and the Knibbs, were alike famous for their piety, and for their philanthropy. The anti-slavery movement *there* was not an anti-church movement, for the reason that the church took its full share in prosecuting that movement: and the anti-slavery movement in this country will cease to be an anti-church movement, when the church of this country shall assume a favorable, instead of a hostile position towards that movement. Americans! your republican politics, not less than your republican religion, are flagrantly inconsistent. You boast of your love of liberty, your superior civilization, and your pure Christianity, while the whole political power of the nation (as embodied in the two great political parties), is solemnly pledged to support and perpetuate the enslavement of three millions of your countrymen. You hurl your anathemas at the crowned headed tyrants of Russia and Austria, and pride yourselves on your Democratic institutions, while you yourselves consent to be the mere *tools* and *body-guards* of the tyrants of Virginia and Carolina. You invite to your shores fugitives of oppression from abroad, honor them with banquets, greet them with ovations, cheer them, toast them, salute them, protect them, and pour out your money to them like water; but the fugitives from your own land you advertise, hunt, arrest, shoot and kill. You glory in your refinement and your universal education yet you maintain a system as barbarous and dreadful as ever stained the character of a nation—a system begun in avarice, supported in pride, and perpetuated in cruelty. You shed tears over fallen Hungary, and make the sad story of her wrongs the theme of your poets, statesmen and orators, till your gallant sons are ready to fly to arms to vindicate her cause against her oppressors; but, in regard to the ten thousand wrongs of the American slave, you would enforce the strictest silence, and would hail him as an enemy of the nation who dares to make those wrongs the subject of public discourse! You are all on fire at the mention of liberty for France or for Ireland; but are as cold as an iceberg at the thought of liberty for the enslaved of America. You discourse eloquently on the dignity of labor; yet, you sustain a system which, in its very essence, casts a stigma upon labor. You can bare your bosom to the storm of British artillery to throw off a threepenny tax on tea; and yet wring the last hard-earned farthing from the grasp of the black laborers of your country. You profess to believe "that, of one blood, God made all nations of men to dwell on the face of all the earth," and hath commanded all men, everywhere to love one another; yet you notoriously hate, (and glory in your hatred), all men whose skins are not colored like your own. You declare, before the world, and are understood by the world to declare, that you "*hold these truths to be self evident, that all men are created equal; and are endowed by their Creator with certain inalienable rights; and that, among these are, life, liberty, and the pursuit of happiness;*" and yet, you hold securely, in a bondage which, according to your own Thomas Jefferson, "*is worse than ages of that which your fathers rose in rebellion to oppose,*" a *seventh part* of the inhabitants of your country.

Fellow-citizens! I will not enlarge further on your national inconsistencies. The existence of slavery in this country brands your republicanism as a sham, your humanity as a base pretence, and your Christianity as a lie. It destroys your moral power abroad; it corrupts your politicians at home. It saps the foundation of religion; it makes your name a hissing, and a bye-word to a mocking earth. It is the antagonistic force in your government, the only thing that seriously disturbs and endangers your *Union.* It fetters your progress; it is the enemy of improvement, the deadly foe of education; it fosters pride; it breeds insolence; it promotes vice; it shelters crime; it is a curse to the earth that supports it; and yet, you cling to it, as if it were the sheet anchor of all your hopes. Oh! be warned! be warned! a horrible reptile is coiled up in your nation's bosom; the venomous creature is nursing at the tender breast of your youthful republic; *for the love of God,* tear away, and fling from you the hideous monster, and *let the weight of twenty millions crush and destroy it forever*!

But it is answered in reply to all this, that precisely what I have now denounced is, in fact, guaranteed and sanctioned by the Constitution of the United States; that the right to hold and to hunt slaves is a part of that Constitution framed by the illustrious Fathers of this Republic.

Then, I dare to affirm, notwithstanding all I have said before, your fathers stooped, basely stooped

> *To palter with us in a double sense:*
> *And keep the word of promise to the ear,*
> *But break it to the heart.*

And instead of being the honest men I have before declared them to be, they were the veriest imposters that ever practiced on mankind. This is the inevitable conclusion, and from it there is no escape. But I differ from those who charge this baseness on the framers of the Constitution of the United States. It is a slander upon their memory, at least, so I believe. There is not time now to argue the constitutional question at length—nor have I the ability to discuss it as it ought to be discussed. The subject has been handled with masterly power by Lysander Spooner, Esq., by William Goodell, by Samuel E. Sewall, Esq., and last, though not least, by Gerrit Smith, Esq. These gentlemen have, as I think, fully and clearly vindicated the Constitution from any design to support slavery for an hour.

Fellow-citizens! there is no matter in respect to which, the people of the North have allowed themselves to be so ruinously imposed upon, as that of the pro-slavery character of the Constitution. In that instrument I hold there is neither warrant, license, nor sanction of the hateful thing; but, interpreted as it ought to be interpreted, the Constitution is a GLORIOUS LIBERTY DOCUMENT. Read its preamble, consider its purposes. Is slavery among them? Is it at the gateway? or is it in the temple? It is neither. While I do not intend to argue this question on the present occasion, let me ask, if it be not somewhat singular that, if the Constitution were intended to be, by its framers and adopters, a slave-holding instrument, why neither slavery, slaveholding, nor slave can anywhere be found in it. What would be thought of an instrument, drawn up, legally drawn up, for the purpose of entitling the city of Rochester to a track of land, in which no mention of land was made? Now, there are certain rules of interpretation, for the proper understanding of all legal instruments. These rules are well established. They are plain, common-sense rules, such as you and I, and all of us, can understand and apply, without having passed years in the study of law. I scout the idea that the question of the constitutionality or unconstitutionality of slavery is not a question for the people. I hold that every American citizen has a right to form an opinion of the constitution, and to propagate that opinion, and to use all honorable means to make his opinion the prevailing one. Without this right, the liberty of an American citizen would be as insecure as that of a Frenchman. Ex-Vice-President Dallas tells us that the Constitution is an object to which no American mind can be too attentive, and no American heart too devoted. He further says, the Constitution, in its words, is plain and intelligible, and is meant for the home-bred, unsophisticated understandings of our fellow-citizens. Senator Berrien tell us that the Constitution is the fundamental law, that which controls all others. The charter of our liberties, which every citizen has a personal interest in understanding thoroughly. The testimony of Senator Breese, Lewis Cass, and many others that might be named, who are everywhere esteemed as sound lawyers, so regard the constitution. I take it, therefore, that it is not presumption in a private citizen to form an opinion of that instrument.

Now, take the Constitution according to its plain reading, and I defy the presentation of a single pro-slavery clause in it. On the other hand it will be found to contain principles and purposes, entirely hostile to the existence of slavery.

I have detained my audience entirely too long already. At some future period I will gladly avail myself of an opportunity to give this subject a full and fair discussion.

Allow me to say, in conclusion, notwithstanding the dark picture I have this day presented of the state of the nation, I do not despair of this country. There are forces in operation, which must inevitably work the downfall of slavery. "The arm of the Lord is not shortened," and the doom of slavery is certain. I, therefore, leave off where I began, with hope. While drawing encouragement from the Declaration of Independence, the great principles it contains, and the genius of American Institutions, my spirit is also cheered by the obvious tendencies of the age. Nations do not now stand in the same relation to each other that they did ages ago. No nation can now shut itself up from the surrounding world, and trot round in the same old path of its fathers without interference. The time was when such could be done. Long established customs of hurtful character could formerly fence themselves in, and do their evil work with social impunity. Knowledge was then confined and enjoyed by the privileged few, and the multitude walked on in mental darkness. But a change has now come over the affairs of mankind. Walled cities and empires have become unfashionable. The arm of commerce has borne away the gates of the strong city. Intelligence is penetrating the darkest corners of the globe. It makes its pathway over and under the sea, as well as on the earth. Wind, steam, and lightning are its chartered agents. Oceans no longer divide, but link nations together. From Boston to London is now a holiday excursion. Space is comparatively annihilated. Thoughts expressed on one side of the Atlantic, are distinctly heard on the other. The far off and almost fabulous Pacific rolls in grandeur at our feet. The Celestial Empire, the mystery of ages, is being solved. The fiat of the Almighty, "Let there be Light," has not yet spent its force. No abuse, no outrage whether in taste, sport or avarice, can now hide itself from the all-pervading light. The iron shoe, and crippled foot of China must be seen, in contrast with nature. Africa must rise and put on her yet unwoven garment. "Ethiopia shall stretch out her hand unto God." In the fervent aspirations of William Lloyd Garrison, I say, and let every heart join in saying it:

> God speed the year of jubilee
> The wide world o'er
> When from their galling chains set free,
> Th' oppress'd shall vilely bend the knee,
>
> And wear the yoke of tyranny
> Like brutes no more.
> That year will come, and freedom's reign,
> To man his plundered fights again
> Restore.
>
> God speed the day when human blood
> Shall cease to flow!
> In every clime be understood,
> The claims of human brotherhood,
> And each return for evil, good,
> Not blow for blow;
> That day will come all feuds to end.
> And change into a faithful friend
> Each foe.
>
> God speed the hour, the glorious hour,
> When none on earth
> Shall exercise a lordly power,
> Nor in a tyrant's presence cower;
> But all to manhood's stature tower,
> By equal birth!
> That hour will come, to each, to all,
> And from his prison-house, the thrall
> Go forth.
>
> Until that year, day, hour, arrive,
> With head, and heart, and hand I'll strive,
> To break the rod, and rend the gyve,
> The spoiler of his prey deprive—
> So witness Heaven!
> And never from my chosen post,
> Whate'er the peril or the cost,
> Be driven.

Declaration of Sentiments, Seneca Falls, New York, 1848

Declaration of Sentiments

When, in the course of human events, it becomes necessary for one portion of the family of man to assume among the people of the earth a position different from that which they have hitherto occupied, but one to which the laws of nature and of nature's God entitle them, a decent respect to the opinions of mankind requires that they should declare the causes that impel them to such a course.

We hold these truths to be self-evident: that all men and women are created equal; that they are endowed by their Creator with certain inalienable rights; that among these are life, liberty, and the pursuit of happiness; that to secure these rights governments are instituted, deriving their just powers from the consent of the governed. Whenever any form of government becomes destructive of these ends, it is the right of those who suffer from it to refuse allegiance to it, and to insist upon the institution of a new government, laying its foundation on such principles, and organizing its powers in such form, as to them shall seem most likely to effect their safety and happiness.

Prudence, indeed, will dictate that governments long established should not be changed for light and transient causes; and, accordingly, all experience has shown that mankind are more disposed to suffer, while evils are sufferable, than to right themselves by abolishing the forms to which they were accustomed. But when a long train of abuses and usurpations, pursuing invariably the same object, evinces a design to reduce them under absolute despotism, it is their duty to throw off such government and to provide new guards for their future security. Such has been the patient sufferance of the women under this government, and such is now the necessity which constrains them to demand the equal station to which they are entitled.

The history of mankind is a history of repeated injuries and usurpations on the part of man toward woman, having in direct object the establishment of an absolute tyranny over her. To prove this, let facts be submitted to a candid world.

He has never permitted her to exercise her inalienable right to the elective franchise.

He has compelled her to submit to law in the formation of which she had no voice.

He has withheld from her rights which are given to the most ignorant and degraded men, both natives and foreigners.

Having deprived her of this first right as a citizen, the elective franchise, thereby leaving her without representation in the halls of legislation, he has oppressed her on all sides.

He has made her, if married, in the eye of the law, civilly dead.

He has taken from her all right in property, even to the wages she earns.

He has made her morally, an irresponsible being, as she can commit many crimes with impunity, provided they be done in the presence of her husband. In the covenant of marriage, she is compelled to promise obedience to her husband, he becoming, to all intents and purposes, her master—the law giving him power to deprive her of her liberty and to administer chastisement.

He has so framed the laws of divorce, as to what shall be the proper causes and, in case of separation, to whom the guardianship of the children shall be given, as to be wholly regardless of the happiness of the women—the law, in all cases, going upon a false supposition of the supremacy of man and giving all power into his hands.

After depriving her of all rights as a married woman, if single and the owner of property, he has taxed her to support a government which recognizes her only when her property can be made profitable to it.

He has monopolized nearly all the profitable employments, and from those she is permitted to follow, she receives but a scanty remuneration. He closes against her all the avenues to wealth and distinction which he considers most honorable to himself.

As a teacher of theology, medicine, or law, she is not known.

111

He has denied her the facilities for obtaining a thorough education, all colleges being closed against her.

He allows her in church, as well as state, but a subordinate position, claiming apostolic authority for her exclusion from the ministry, and, with some exceptions, from any public participation in the affairs of the church.

He has created a false public sentiment by giving to the world a different code of morals for men and women, by which moral delinquencies which exclude women from society are not only tolerated but deemed of little account in man.

He has usurped the prerogative of Jehovah himself, claiming it as his right to assign for her a sphere of action, when that belongs to her conscience and to her God.

He has endeavored, in every way that he could, to destroy her confidence in her own powers, to lessen her self-respect, and to make her willing to lead a dependent and abject life.

Now, in view of this entire disfranchisement of one-half the people of this country, their social and religious degradation, in view of the unjust laws above mentioned, and because women do feel themselves aggrieved, oppressed, and fraudulently deprived of their most sacred rights, we insist that they have immediate admission to all the rights and privileges which belong to them as citizens of the United States.

In entering upon the great work before us, we anticipate no small amount of misconception, misrepresentation, and ridicule; but we shall use every instrumentality within our power to effect our object. We shall employ agents, circulate tracts, petition the state and national legislatures, and endeavor to enlist the pulpit and the press in our behalf. We hope this Convention will be followed by a series of conventions embracing every part of the country.

Resolutions

Whereas, the great precept of nature is conceded to be that "man shall pursue his own true and substantial happiness." Blackstone in his *Commentaries* remarks that this law of nature, being coeval with mankind and dictated by God himself, is, of course, superior in obligation to any other. It is binding over all the globe, in all countries and at all times; no human laws are of any validity if contrary to this, and such of them as are valid derive all their force, and all their validity; and all their authority, mediately and immediately, from this original; therefore,

Resolved, That such laws as conflict, in any way, with the true and substantial happiness of woman, are contrary to the great precept of nature and of no validity, for this is "superior in obligation to any other."

Resolved, that all laws which prevent woman from occupying such a station in society as her conscience shall dictate, or which place her in a position inferior to that of man, are contrary to the great precept of nature and therefore of no force or authority.

Resolved, that woman is man's equal, was intended to be so by the Creator, and the highest good of the race demands that she should be recognized as such.

Resolved, that the women of this country ought to be enlightened in regard to the laws under which they live, that they may no longer publish their degradation by declaring themselves satisfied with their present position, nor their ignorance, by asserting that they have all the rights they want.

Resolved, that inasmuch as man, while claiming for himself intellectual superiority, does accord to woman moral superiority, it is preeminently his duty to encourage her to speak and teach, as she has an opportunity, in all religious assemblies.

Resolved that the same amount of virtue, delicacy, and refinement of behavior that is required of woman in the social state also be required of man, and the same transgressions should be visited with equal severity on both man and woman.

Resolved, that the objection of indelicacy and impropriety, which is so often brought against woman when she addresses a public audience, comes with a very ill grace from those who encourage, by their attendance, her appearance on the stage, in the concert, or in feats of the circus.

Resolved, that woman has too long rested satisfied in the circumscribed limits which corrupt customs and a perverted application of the Scriptures have marked out for her, and that it is time she should move in the enlarged sphere which her great Creator has assigned her.

Resolved, that it is the duty of the women of this country to secure to themselves their sacred right to the elective franchise.

Resolved, that the equality of human rights results necessarily from the fact of the identity of the race in capabilities and responsibilities.

Resolved, that the speedy success of our cause depends upon the zealous and untiring efforts of both men and women for the overthrow of the monopoly of the pulpit, and for the securing to woman an equal participation with men in the various trades, professions, and commerce

Resolved, therefore, that, being invested by the Creator with the same capabilities and same consciousness of responsibility for their exercise, it is demonstrably the right and duty of woman, equally with man, to promote every righteous cause by every righteous means; and especially in regard to the great subjects of morals and religion, it is self-evidently

her right to participate with her brother in teaching them, both in private and in public, by writing and by speaking, by any instrumentalities proper to be used, and in any assemblies proper to be held; and this being a self-evident truth growing out of the divinely implanted principles of human nature, any custom or authority adverse to it, whether modern or wearing the hoary sanction of antiquity, is to be regarded as a self-evident falsehood, and at war with mankind.

Signers of the Declaration of Sentiments

**Seneca Falls New York
July 19–20, 1848**

Barker, Caroline
Barker, Eunice
Barker, William G.
Bonnel, Rachel D. (Mitchell)
Bunker, Joel D.
Burroughs, William
Capron, E.W.
Chamberlain, Jacob P.
Conklin, Elizabeth
Conklin, Mary
Culvert, P.A.
Davis, Cynthia
Dell, Thomas
Dell, William S.
Doty, Elias J.
Doty, Susan R.
Douglass, Frederick
Drake, Julia Ann
Eaton, Harriet Cady
Foote, Elisha
Foote, Eunice Newton
Frink, Mary Ann
Fuller, Cynthia
Gibbs, Experience
Gilbert, Mary
Gild, Lydia
Hallowell, Sarah
Hallowell, Mary H.
Hatley, Henry
Hoffinan, Sarah
Hoskins, Charles L.
Hunt, Jane C.
Hunt, Richard P.
Jenkins, Margaret

Jones, John
Jones, Lucy
King, Phebe
Latham, Hannah J.
Latham, Lovina
Leslie, Elizabeth
Martin, Eliza
Martin, Nary
Mathews, Delia
Mathews, Dorothy
Mathews, Jacob
McClintock, Elizabeth W.
McClintock, Mary
McClintock, Mary Ann
McClintock, Thomas
Metcalf Jonathan
Milliken, Nathan J.
Mirror, Nary S.
Mosher, Pheobe
Mosher, Sarah A.
Mott, James
Mott, Lucretia
Mount, Lydia
Paine, Catharine G.
Palmer, Rhoda
Phillips, Saron
Pitcher, Sally
Plant, Hannah
Porter, Ann
Post, Amy
Pryor, George W.
Pryor, Margaret
Quinn, Susan
Race, Rebecca

Ridley, Martha
Schooley, Azaliah
Schooley, Margaret
Scott, Deborah
Segur, Antoinette E.
Seymour, Henry
Seymour, Henry W.
Seymour, Malvina,
Shaw, Catharine
Shear, Stephen
Sisson, Sarah
Smallbridge, Robert
Smith, Elizabeth D.
Smith, Sarah
Spalding, David
Spalding, Lucy
Stanton, Elizabeth Cady
Stebbins, Catharine F.
Taylor, Sophrouia
Tewksbury, Betsey
Tiliman, Samuel D.
Underhill, Edward F.
Underhill, Martha
Vail, Mary E.
Van Tassel, Isaac
Whitney, Sarah R.
Wilbur, Maria E.
Williams, Justin
Woods, Sarah R.
Woodward, Charlotte
Woodworth, S.E.
Wright, Martha C.

The Irish and the Unknown "Other": Blacks and the Irish in 19th Century San Francisco

Keith R. V. Heningburg

Not like the brazen giant of Greek fame,
With conquering limbs astride from land to land;
Here at our sea-washed, sunset gates shall stand
a mighty woman with a torch, where flame
is the imprisoned lightning, and her name
Mother of exiles. From her beacon-and
glows world-wide welcome; here mild eyes command
the air-bridged harbor that twin cities frame.
"Keep, ancient lands, your storied pomp!" cries she
with silent lips. "Give me your tired, your poor,
your huddled masses yearning to breathe free,
the wretched refuse of your teeming shore.
Send these, the homeless, tempest-tost to me.
I lift my lamp beside the golden door!"[1]

* * * * *

Emma Lazarus' sonnet expresses a theoretical hospitality toward all persons wanting entry into America. However, despite the beauty and promise of Lazarus' sonnet and the optimism of the emigres, the "welcome mat" has not always been set out for all immigrants. Over the years, America has excluded certain groups, like the Chinese or limited admission as with the Japanese. Our record toward indigenous populations—Native Americans—has not been "stellar" either. In relative terms, blacks and Mexicans have not fared well here either. In fact, the American record has not been exemplary toward immigrants of any stripe, unless they were white, Anglo-Saxon, and Protestant. Over the years, the tired, poor, and huddled masses have not always found respite in this "land of the free and home of the brave." This has resulted in heated, often deadly confrontations between the so-called dominant racial group and all "others."

Historians and Social Scientists have most often dichotomized discussions of race relations in the United States solely as the relationship between blacks and whites. However, this division does not account for intra minority group relations. On the surface, it does not acknowledge the existence of other minority groups. Such a division does not acknowledge a relationship, adversarial or not, between racialized and marginalized groups. Additionally, it does not venture to challenge the definition of "white," "black," or even the current catch phrase, "minority groups." How useful then is the current discussion on "black-white" relationships? It is useful as a model through which historians may study the relationship of white people and other disaffected groups. The relationship between blacks and whites in the United States is the template into which all other relationships between whites and "others," fit. Historian George M. Fredrickson argues that since 1830 whites considered blacks inherently inferior, temperamentally different, and intellectually deficient. If this were "fact," then whites must avoid any physical relationship between blacks and whites to retain racial purity.[2]

114

I argue that whites, in particular White Anglo-Saxon Protestants, used the same model on each group they encountered. As historians Bernard Baylin and Philip D. Morgan state, "English encounters with alien peoples had a number of common characteristics. One pervasive trait was English hostility to, or at least disdain for, the people they encountered and engendered. The English thought of the Gaelic Irish as barbarous and uncivilized ... and tended to extend these attributes to all inhabitants of the country. . . ." "Frontier antagonists of all stripes, . . . tended to look more or less alike to the English. 'Whether Irishmen or Pequots, Scots or Iroquois, they were enemies, they were ignorant, and they were animal-like.'" The most animal-like to English eyes were, of course, Africans and their descendants.[3] Thus, Protestant whites relegated Africans, Irishmen, Catholics, Native Americans, Asians, and other minorities, to "strangers status" and placed them at the edge of their cultural periphery. This method of categorization established a pattern for all future contact with "others." Consequently it is the manner by which whites viewed and subsequently responded to immigrants and other minority groups that comprise the body of United States history.

However, whites do not have a monopoly on the ill-treatment of minority groups. That would only be part of the story. A more comprehensive story must also include the responses and reactions that persons *within* the disaffected groups have toward one another. Take, for example the relationship of blacks and Native Americans. Historically, Native Americans have had an interesting relationship with black people that ranged from cautious bewilderment during the Lewis and Clark exploration of the newly acquired Louisiana Purchase, when the Mandan Indians tried to rub the black from York's skin to the so-called "Five Civilized Tribes"—the Cherokees, Chickasaws, Choctaws, Seminoles, and Creeks—emulation of white American slave holding. Historian Theda Perdue argues, these Native Americans accepted the Jeffersonian ideology that black people were inferior, beyond elevation and suitable only for service to a superior being. Perdue argues, "Southern society was becoming strictly biracial, and if given a choice between classification as black and white, Native peoples chose white."[4] Additionally, "Natives cast their lot with the dominant culture and strengthened the barrier separating them from blacks by adopting white racial

attitudes."[5] Thus, as we can see, racial antipathy was not the sole purview of white Americans, it is a hallmark of American race relations overall.

This paper is about the racial responses and reactions of two disaffected and racialized groups, the Irish and Black Americans in San Francisco during the nineteenth century. This relationship began on the eastern seaboard during the eighteenth century and migrated across the Great Plains, Rocky Mountains and the Sierra Nevada during the early part of the nineteenth century through the 1850s. Due to the intense labor competition between blacks and the Irish, overt and virulent racism characterized this relationship in the East. While on the West Coast, the relationship shifts to less overt racism and labor competition because of the unity and population of the Irish compared with the Negro population. As I will point out, Irish emigrants established themselves early in the racial hierarchy of a young California, whereas in New York, Philadelphia and Boston, they had not, at least to the same extent, done so. As a result, the Irish found themselves already defined as "white," having escaped the negative ascription of "blackness that hindered them in the east. Concurrently, Negroes, who also migrated to California, never escaped that negative appellation and thus, did not experience the social and political inclusion as did the Irish upon settling in California. This paper will briefly examine early American racial hierarchical development in the East and how this translated to the racial hierarchy in the West. Included in this discussion is Irish immigration to the United States, the notions of becoming "white" and black-Irish confrontation on the East coast then the West coast.

White American response took the form of a hierarchical system that resembled a pyramid with white folk at the top and Negroes at the bottom. As previously noted, this hierarchy developed from the pattern of English reaction to different ethnic groups. The greater the cultural, political, and social differences from white Europeans, the greater the ascription of "otherness." Thus, as white colonizers, in particular English colonizers, encountered the indigenous inhabitants of the American continent—Native Americans—they inserted them into the hierarchical pyramid above the blacks because they were, according to Jeffersonian ideology, "elevatable"—that is culturally inferior but capable of change. As ever more immigrants arrived on American shores, whites inserted them into the pyramid, always above the Negro. This pattern continued from the founding of the Republic until the 1840s when the Irish came to America *en masse.*

Irish immigration to America began in the eighteenth century and continued well into the nineteenth century with the coming of the Irish potato famine 1845–1851. As Noel Ignatiev has noted, "from 1815 to the Famine, between 800,000 and one million Irish—about twice the total for the two previous centuries—sailed for North America."[6] According to Ignatiev, not all Irish immigrants were poor and downtrodden and not all were Catholic. Ignatiev argues that from the beginning of the nineteenth century through 1832, Irish immigrants were primarily from Ulster and were Presbyterian and Anglicans. These Irish immigrants had similar characteristics as those who immigrated in the seventeenth century. According to Ignatiev, they were Presbyterian farmers, mechanics, tradesmen and professionals, and artisans. It was not until the early 1830s that many Irish Roman Catholics came, eventually overtaking the original Irish population.[7]

R. A. Burchell notes that, "the Irish arrived on the east coast of the United States and there a majority stayed, settling particularly as a result of their low level of skills and capital in ill-prepared urban areas. Even in 1870, when sufficient time had passed for Irish immigrants to join the westward movement, over half the Irish-born population of the country lived in the three states of New York, Pennsylvania, and Massachusetts, producing a very important Irish presence in the towns and cities of New York, Brooklyn, Albany, Buffalo, Troy, Philadelphia, Pittsburgh, Scranton, Boston, Fall River, Lawrence, and Lowell."[8]

By 1845, many poor, unskilled Irish Roman Catholic workers emigrated because of the crisis created by the potato famine. The Irish spoke a different language—many spoke Gaelic, English was their second language. Their poverty, mannerisms, and adherence to Roman Catholicism, separated them from Protestant white Americans who considered them, as had the British, uncivilized barbarians. As Clarence E. Walker has noted, "Having come to America in search of a better life, the Irish initially were treated in a white supremacist country almost as though they were—black: they became the white niggers of America."[9] The dominant White Anglo-Saxon Protestant considered the Irish as racially and culturally inferior. They held similar, if not identical, view of black Americans. It was,

therefore, no surprise that whites would relegate the Irish to a similar place in American society—the bottom. As Walker has argued, nineteenth century nomenclature placed "Americans"—White Anglo-Saxon Protestants—and "Irish" in two vastly different racial categories. Americans thought the Irish were so innately and physically different in their "intelligence, morality, religious inclination, political affiliation, social conduct and economic behavior" that they could never live in the same country.[10] White Anglo-Saxon Protestant Americans disliked the Irish because of their Catholicism and cultural strangeness and mistrust was a hallmark of their presence on the east coast.[11] Ultimately, Americans thought of the Irish as a cultural contamination and social pariahs.

The idea that the Irish were a social contamination was a common one for nineteenth century Protestant Americans. In an editorial in *The Massachusetts Teacher*, 1851, the author analogously called the Irish the "muddy Missouri river" in comparison to the "clear Mississippi." As the muddy Missouri river contaminated the Mississippi River yet making it stronger, so did the incorporation of the Irish immigrants contaminate yet strengthen America. Thus, it was the responsibility of the Americans to "purify these foreign people, enlighten their ignorance, and bring them up to our own level. . . ."[12] The notion of racial supremacy over these "white niggers" is evident in the river analogy—Americans were the "clear" Mississippi River whereas the Irish were the "muddy" Missouri River. (This becomes problematic when one considers the fact that original inhabitants of the land might also view "Americans" themselves as "contamination.")

Curative remedies included first, forcibly removing Irish immigrant children from their parents and placing them into Protestant schools. The *Teacher* argued that Irish parents were incorrigible and "unfit guardians of their children." The *Teacher* goes on, "nothing can operate effectually here but stringent legislation, thoroughly carried out by efficient police; children must be gathered up and forced into schools, and those who resist or impede this plan, whether parents or priests, must be held accountable and punished." They would take this action to forestall a second generation of vagrants, criminals and dissolute Irish persons. Second, White Protestants favored the restricting alcohol from adults because, stereotypically, "all Irish men were drunkards" and this led to intemperance, sloth, and improvident.

"Make it impossible for these people to obtain rum—compel them to be temperate, and the battle is more than half won; for with temperance come industry and frugality."[13] The *Teacher* argued for an increase in the police force to enforce the laws against intemperance. "A sufficient body of police should be employed to eradicate every grog hole and bring before the magistrates every drunkard.[14] If the laws were not sufficiently stringent, they should be made so and rigidly enforced. Finally, a third measure was the elimination of panhandlers and the incarceration of Irish beggars in the almshouse or give them employment. This, the *Teacher* argued, would eliminate their presence on the streets, reduce idleness and decrease the population of Irish paupers. By doing these things White Anglo-Saxon Protestant America could transform the Irish into productive citizens in society.[15] If these "remedies" have a familiar sound it is because they are similar to the ones used to transform Native Americans into "useful" citizens in the latter part of the nineteenth century.[16] If white Americans regarded the Irish in such negative terms, how did the blacks view these immigrants?

As most blacks of the nineteenth century were "Anglophiles," one can assume that blacks, particularly northern free blacks adopted the customary Anglo-Saxon derogatory attitude toward the Irish. In addition, because of labor competition between the two groups, blacks had no fond memories or feelings toward the Irish. Forced, because they lacked marketable skills, to take lower paying menial positions, Irish immigrants often competed with black Americans for the same low paying jobs that had been the purview of blacks alone.[17] Leon Litwack, quoting from a Negro author in the *Colored American*, July 28, 1838, illustrates this point. "These impoverished and destitute beings,—transported from the trans-Atlantic shores, are crowding themselves into every place of business and of labor, and driving the poor colored American citizen out. Along the wharves, where the colored man once done the whole business of shipping and un[-]shipping—in stores where his services were once rendered, and in families where the chief places were filled by him, in all these situations there are substituted foreigners or White Americans."[18]

Litwack goes on to note that the antipathy between the Irish and Northern free black workers worsened from 1842 through 1863 as violence often erupted with deadly results. In 1842, Pennsylvania Irish coal miners battled Negro competitors for employment; in 1853, Negro strike breakers replaced striking Irishmen on the Erie Railroad; Irish and free Negro workers clashed on New York's docks in 1855, and as the Civil War progressed, draft riots occurred in 1863.[19] Walker, quotes Frederick Douglass in 1853, as saying "the old avocations, by which colored men obtained a livelihood, are rapidly, increasingly, and inevitably passing into other hands."[20] As Litwack notes, the economic position of the Negro had been seriously compromised.[21] In 1830, free blacks occupied most service sector jobs—porters, house cleaners, laundry women, and general unskilled labor. By 1850, Irish immigrant workers outnumbered native black workers better than two-to-one. Negro workers found themselves displaced in service jobs by the Irish immigrant. By 1855, Douglass complained, "every hour sees us elbowed out of some employment to make room for some newly arrived immigrants, whose hunger and color are thought to give them title to especial favor. White men are becoming house-servants, cooks, and stewards, common laborers and flunkeys to our gentry and they adjust themselves to their stations with a becoming obsequiousness."[22]

Douglass arrived at this conclusion reluctantly. In 1846, in a letter to William Lloyd Garrison, Douglass expressed what may be considered a sentiment of commonality with the Irish. This commonality rested upon the degradation of both Irish and Negroes in white, Protestant, Americans' eyes. He believed that white Americans had no more regard toward the Irish than they had toward the "whipped, gagged, thumb-screwed slave." "Americans would willingly sell on the auction-block an Irishman, if it were popular to do so, as an African."[23] He went on to note the dire poverty of the Irish and compared it with the poverty of the American Negro slave. "I see much here to remind me of my former condition, and I confess I should be ashamed to lift up my voice against American slavery, but I know the cause of humanity is one the world over."[24] For him the degradation faced by the Irish emigrant was the same as that experienced by black Americans, thus resulting in a common history of oppression if not economic opportunity and liberty. By 1863, in a speech delivered in the "Church of the Puritans," Douglass, was forced to admit that the Irish were the Negro's worse enemy. "I am told that the Irish element on this country is exceedingly strong and that that element will never allow colored men to stand upon an equal footing with white men. I am pointed to the terrible outrages committed from time to time by Irishmen upon Negroes. The mobs at Detroit, Chicago, Cincinnati, and New York, are cited as proving the unconquerable aversion of the Irish towards the colored race. Well, my friends, I admit that the Irish people are among our bitterest persecutors."[25] Douglass explained the oppression by referring to the example of a black field hand that a slaveholder had elevated to the "status" of a driver. That slave, though yet a slave, became the fiercest overseer on the plantation. In the same manner, Douglass suggested that, because of the oppression the Irish had endured, they were as prone to engage in oppressive behavior as anyone else.

However, by late 1863, in a speech delivered to the American Anti-Slavery Society, Douglass employed common Irish stereotypes and made fun at their expense. This suggests that his stance had hardened since the speech in May. In calling for black suffrage, he remarked on how receptive the "body politic" was to ignorant and illiterate white men, while simultaneously denying the same privilege to black citizens. In this speech, Douglass alluded to the common stereotypes of Irish men—i.e., ignorant, pugilistic, and inebriated. "Next I saw a man stepping up to the body politic, casting his vote, having a black eye, and another one ready to be blacked, having been engaged in a street fight. I saw again, Pat, fresh from the Emerald Isle, with the delightful brogue particular to him, stepping up—not walking, but leaning upon the arms of two of his friends, unable to stand, passing into the body politic! I came to the conclusion that this body politic was, after all, not quite so pure a body as the representations of its friends would have us to believe."[26] His humorous appropriation of the stereotypical Irish man suggests a certain bitterness toward the Irish that we may ascribe to the nineteenth century free black community.

Using humor at the expense of the Irish was normal for Douglass and other blacks. Lawrence Levine argues in *Black Culture and Black Consciousness* that "jokes ridiculing the Irish became popular following the large-scale migrations from Ireland in the mid-nineteenth century. Negroes who had come into hostile contact with Irish immigrants both north and south learned these anecdotes and undoubtedly created many of their own."[27] The use of humor at the expense of the Irish allowed blacks to join with the white mainstream in ridiculing "the strange folkways of an alien group." It gave blacks a chance to look down on someone for the first time since arriving in America. As Levine says, "Irish jokes became a means to taking revenge upon these new-comers who had learned to hate Negroes so quickly and efficiently."[28] However, as Frederick Douglass' overall attitude suggests, "no matter how great the animosity between the two groups, they shared a lowly position in American society which created a certain empathy among Negroes for their Irish protagonists."[29]

Although Douglass used these negative ascriptions toward the Irish in a jovial, even, nonthreatening way, underneath one can sense a great disappointment that the Irish could shed their "blackness" and become "white." This whiteness became a door though which the Irish could enter the "body politic" and participate in the Herrenvolk democracy whereas the Negro's blackness prevented his entry until 1870 with the ratification of the Fifteenth Amendment. As I have suggested, the hostility of the northern free blacks was replicated in the south as well.

Arnold Shankman argues that blacks in the south generally held a negative view of immigrants from Europe and Asia and that the horrendous conditions of their lives facilitated this view, contributing to a hostility toward immigrants. In this, their attitude mirrored that of the white population.[30] According to the *Norfolk Journal and Guide*, "blacks had learned through bitter experiences that foreign labor, though it may be crude, illiterate, and hopelessly unsympathetic with American institutions and ideals, is used to press us farther down the economic ladder…in spite of our proved loyalty to America."[31] Shankman also argues that the xenophobic, ethnocentric, religiously biased, jealousy, and economic competition all contributed to blacks' unsympathetic view of immigrants. If, as Shankman argues, black attitudes mirrored white attitudes on the eastern seaboard, what was their response to the Irish on the west coast? Did the same types of hostilities exist in San Francisco as in New York, Boston or Philadelphia? What of the economic and political opportunities compared with the Irish in San Francisco? What was the nature of the relationship between the Irish and blacks in San Francisco?

In 1849, during the California Gold Rush, thousands of men—American white men, Europeans, South Americans, Asians—moved to California to seek their fortune in the gold fields. Sometimes, whole families made the perilous journey across the Great Plains to the Sierra Nevada and into the Sacramento Valley. Some of these men were slave owners and brought their slaves with them. Lillian Schlissel writes, "Sometimes whole [slave] families had come with their masters, traveling in their own wagons at the end of the long trains, secretly hoping to find a way to freedom in the territories."[32] A few came as result of "Gold Fever" and sought to make their fortune. The black men and women who made the journey were often enterprising if not always successful. Not all made their fortune in gold, some succeeded as entrepreneurs, establishing businesses, as was the case of Clara Brown. Upon her arrival in California, Brown took in washing at Horshoe Bar in Miner's Ravine and thus made her living.[33] Nevertheless, for the most part the black immigrants to San Francisco were highly literate, educated, overwhelmingly male with no familial attachments, fascinated with technology, and willing to forgo temporary pleasure in favor of long-term goal attainment.[34]

Rudolph M. Lapp notes that most of the black occupations in San Francisco involved, what twentieth century parlance would call the "service industry." That is, most blacks in San Francisco and Sacramento, held positions in the culinary arts, were barbers, or porters. According to Lapp, in 1852, out of 464 blacks in San Francisco sixty-seven were cooks. American blacks comprised the bulk of those at fifty-three while fourteen were West Indian blacks for a total of sixty-seven. For Sacramento, in 1852, forty-three of 388 were Americans while eight claimed West Indian heritage. Other occupations included, boot blacking, which garnered low social status but was quite remunerative. Some San Francisco blacks also owned boarding houses, secondhand stores, clothing stores and soap factories.[35] Nevertheless, as previously noted, the employment available to blacks was largely in the service sector. Most of the occupations were low paying and required long hours of tedious and sometimes torturous labor. The same jobs available to blacks back east with familiar patterns of racial discrimination. Although these positions are considered menial by today's standards, nineteenth century society deemed these same positions middle-class positions for the black community. Add to this, teachers, ministers, and newspaper editors and one can observe a class structure with black businessmen, newspaper editors, ministers, and teachers at the top, various

other occupations in the middle and agricultural workers at the bottom. Although excluded from white society, these occupations required education and "grit"—raw determination to succeed.

Far from being "utopian," however, San Francisco, although cosmopolitan for the nineteenth century, had its share of negative racial encounters. Delores McBroome argues that conditions in nineteenth century California were fraught with discriminatory practices against black Americans. According to McBroome, "African Americans migrating to California in the mid-nineteenth century experienced much of the discriminations which existed elsewhere in the Union; however, they soon developed both political and social strategies to eliminate the prejudice against them."[36] Ultimately, this led to the creation of separate communities in San Francisco and other areas where blacks resided. This community development task fell to the black leaders of the community. Black leaders such as Philip A. Bell, Peter Anderson, publisher/editors of San Francisco's two leading black newspapers, *The San Francisco Elevator* and the *Pacific Appeal* respectively, along with others, mounted editorial campaigns to grant black Californians the right to vote and for equal education for black children. Their demand was "equality before the law."[37]

On black inequality, Albert S. Broussard notes "the antipathy toward blacks could be found in virtually every major institution or organization. The press, legislature, churches, schools, unions, and political parties were all, at varying times, indifferent to the rights of Afro-Americans. Whites almost universally shared several beliefs and assumptions concerning blacks. As George Frederickson observed, this was "clearly indicative of a consensus in favor of white supremacy." California's white periodicals, public records, and secondary sources seem to confirm Frederickson's conclusions that whites believed blacks to be "physically, intellectually, and temperamentally different from whites, and inferior to whites in intelligence and in the temperamental basis of enterprise or initiative."[38] To illustrate the notion of supposed black inferiority and general antipathy toward the Negro further, Broussard quotes a state legislator who was not in favor of racial equality. "The African is not the equal of the European or the white man and no law can make him so. The European is the child of reason. The African is the child of passion."[39] The ruling of one's passion is what, ostensibly, distinguished White Anglo-Saxon

Protestant founders of the United States from the Native Americans and from blacks. It is this racialized view of the "other" that allowed social, political, economic, and cultural discrimination to exist both on the eastern seaboard and in the West.

As blacks on the east coast faced fierce labor competition, so also did blacks on the west coast. Whereas, on the east coast labor competition came primarily from the Irish, on the west coast, labor competition came from the Chinese. Broussard argues that black Americans in San Francisco faced stiff competition from Chinese immigrants for jobs because the Chinese undercut black wages by offering to do the same work for less pay. As the Chinese and black were at the bottom of the social and economic ladder, this caused intense competition between these two labor classes. The black press reacted by vilifying the Chinese in editorials and by ridiculing them in public employing common stereotypes—dirty, filthy, pagan, clannish, etc., generally mirroring white San Franciscans' attitude.[40] Black ire was not reserved for the Chinese alone. As noted previously, black San Franciscans were largely literate and middle-class blacks from the east. Having had hostile interactions with the Irish on labor issues in the east, one would expect such attitudes abounding in the west. This was the case in nineteenth century San Francisco. According to Bell, "the Irish came and a new element of labor was introduced."[41] This new labor force, the Irish, subsequently crowded out blacks from the laboring positions producing even more antagonisms. From 1865 through the end of the century, blacks wrote a barrage of editorials contesting the claims that they were inferior, while pointing out the strange ways of the Irish. Additionally, blacks tried to elevate themselves through thrift, education, and business. White San Franciscans made it twice as hard by excluding blacks from trade unions, and refusing black labor.

In 1869, a National labor convention convened to discuss the issue of labor in the United States. The stated purpose was to "elevate labor; to consolidate the interests of all who are opposed to the peonage, or semi-slavery of the Coolies, and to operate by organization against the ostracism of the labor leagues and trade unions of the whites."[42] One potential issue was labor, or better, the lack of free black labor in the south during Reconstruction. The vast amount of uncultivated arable land in the south and the exodus of black workers to the cities in the west and north, aggravated the need for

agricultural workers. The question was where would the labor come from? At the suggestion that Germans be employed as agricultural workers, San Francisco *Elevator* editor, Philip A. Bell, argued German immigrants, upon arriving in the United States, generally sought other independent occupations. Regarding the Irish, he felt that sufficient numbers had already immigrated such that they had depopulated Ireland. Moreover, the Irish were undesirable as laborers. According to Bell, the Irish sought to dominate other minorities since he could not dominate the American white man. Therefore, if large numbers of Irish came to the south, the editor predicted a race war would follow. Ultimately, he would rather have Chinese laborers than Irish.[43] This touched off a round of debate and a writer, W. H. Hall, a frequent correspondent to the *Elevator*, responded that although the Irish were ignorant, prejudiced, and Catholic, they—American Society—could train them. According to Hall, the Irish had a generosity and impulsiveness that Americans could train under the "influence of free schools, free press, and free constitutions."[44] Bell responded by saying "we have failed to see those 'traits of generosity' in the character of the ignorant Irish when their prejudices are excited. They are vindictive, revengeful, fiendish, and malicious. Witness the scenes in New York, and the outrages committed by the Irish in 1863 and then talk of the 'generosity' of the ignorant Irish."[45] The important point here is not the debate between W. H. Hall and Philip Bell. Instead, it is the idea of Irish depravity that both Hall and Bell expressed. The point is that these black men employed common stereotypes of the Irish, articulating the same epithets as white men.

Middle-class blacks disdained the Irish in the 19th century. Blacks viewed the Irish as politically ignorant, unable to distinguish between the Democratic Party and a democratic republic. Bell suggested that because the Irish "have been oppressed by a landlord and hereditary aristocracy, they immediately cast their allegiance with the Democratic Party and anyone not belonging to that party was part of the hated aristocracy."[46] Since most of the blacks belonged to the Republican Party, this was yet another point of contention between blacks and the Irish. This attitude also suggests that those in the middle-class felt a "social drain" from others in similar or lower class rankings. Bell suggested a strained relationship between blacks in the lower class and blacks in the middle-class. "These are not the only classes who use the term 'aristocrat' as an opprobrium. Among our own race, there are those who look upon everyone who aspires to decency or respectability, as aristocrats. The ignorant and vicious would bring everyone down to their level.[47]

If San Francisco blacks harbored such feelings, what of the Irish attitudes toward blacks? In a discussion of Irish antipathy toward Negroes, the *Elevator* reprinted an article from the *Christian Recorder* February 11, 1870. In it the author explained the hostility by noting that Irishmen were in the same position in Ireland as blacks were in the United States. Therefore, according to the *Recorder*, understanding how the oppressed became the oppressor was easy. It was a natural course of events in the human condition. He argued that the desire to oppress was not the major reason for antipathy toward Negroes but that this antipathy transcended race altogether. He likened it to the spirit of the Inquisition—unparalleled persecution. According to the author, the Irish persecuted blacks because they were Protestant and the "true democrats." "It is here that we find an explanation for the Negro, first and chiefly because he is a Protestant in religion, and a true democrat in politics! He hates him because the religion he professes hates the political bent of the Negro's mind, the religious inclination of the Negro's heart: and it was only possible for him to make manifest this hatred upon the lowly Negro."[48]

We have argued that general antipathy existed between the Irish and blacks and that this hostility increased because of being crowded out from jobs by the Irish. However, through all the examined documents—the black press and the Irish newspapers, an interesting item stands out amid the hostility. Whereas black newspapers spent a great deal of time decrying their political, economic and social encounters with the Irish and San Francisco society, the Irish ignored the blacks in San Francisco. Why was this so? Was it because racial prejudice toward blacks was so common nationwide and in San Francisco that it they did not merit editorial attention? Perhaps. However, I argue that a more plausible answer lies in the demography of San Francisco as compared with cities on the eastern seaboard. In addition, although a population comparison of San Francisco with Boston, New York, or Philadelphia alone does not account for the hostility between these two groups, it may explain the absence of any substantial press coverage.

In 1850, California's population, according to the Census takers, numbered 92,597. Whites made up 91,635 or 98.96%, while blacks made up the other 1.04%. White females numbered 6,927 and black females ninety. White males numbered 84,708 and blacks 872. By comparison, Massachusetts' population totaled 994,514, of these 985,450 or 98% were white, 9,094 or 91% were black. New York's population totaled 3,097,394 with 2,428,921 whites or 78%, 49,069 blacks or 1.6% of the population. Pennsylvania reported similar values. Ninety-seven percent of Pennsylvania's population of 2,311,786 was composed of 2,258,160 whites and 53,626 or 2.32% blacks.[49] As Table 1 indicates the black population was consistently small in comparison to the general white population. This pattern holds true for a black and Irish comparison also. Always, the black populations remained small in comparison to whites generally and Irish specifically.

By 1860, California's population had increased from 92,597 to 342,091. Again the population was largely white males owing in part to the California Gold Rush and the general westward migration. Blacks, totaling 4,086, made up 1.19% of the general population and continued to be an insignificant element compared with the population of California.

The population of San Francisco County in 1860 was 56,802, 98% of whom were white. Out of that 98% white population, 28,994 were foreign born. This made roughly half the white population in San Francisco foreigners. Just 2% of San Francisco's population was black. By comparison, the Irish made up 25% of Boston's population, 25% of New York's, 16.9% of Philadelphia, and 16.5% of San Francisco's. In the states of Massachusetts, New York, Pennsylvania, and California, the Irish show similar numbers statewide. Massachusetts had an Irish population of 15%, Pennsylvania, 7%, New York, 13% and California 11%.[50]

By 1870, in San Francisco County, the Irish comprised 17.3% of the general population and 19% of the aggregate white population of California, while blacks made up .85% of the population. The Chinese, at 12,022 or 8.04% however, outnumbered the blacks almost ten to one and were 8.5% of California's general population.[51] By the Tenth Census, 1880, the population of California had grown to 864,694. White people made up the bulk of the population with 767,181 or 88.7%, while black at 6,018, made up .7%–33% were foreign born. In San Francisco County, the aggregate population was 233,959, of

1850 Census

Black & Irish Compared to General Population

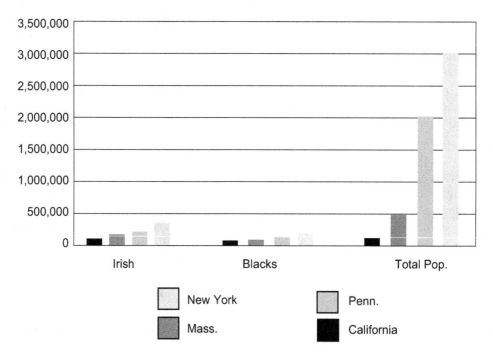

Whites and Blacks in 1850

California, New York, Massachusetts, & Pennsylvania

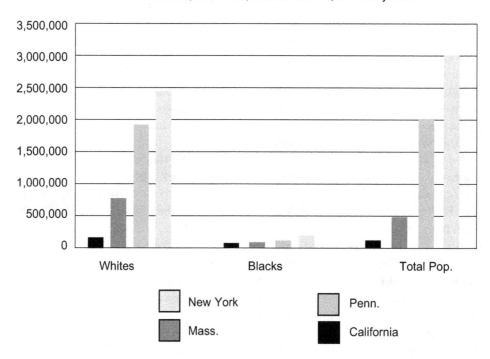

this number 210,496 or 89.97% were white, 1,628 or. 7% were black, 21,790 or 9.31% were Chinese. Out of the 210,496 white people in San Francisco County in 1880, 104,244 were foreign born, 30,721 of that number were Irish or 29.5%.

The point to be aware of is not the population number. For numbers do not necessarily suggest a predilection toward hostility, although it helps. As we have seen, the black population in these cities and states, Boston Massachusetts, New York,

New York, Philadelphia, Pennsylvania, and San Francisco, California, remained pitifully small. According to the records, the Irish/Black hostility was very much evident in these cities, except San Francisco. The fact that the black population was minuscule on the eastern seaboard did not hinder them from making their voices heard—concomitant results for example, the support of the Abolitionists, access to transportation, admittance to jury selection in Massachusetts.[52]

In California, however, in San Francisco in particular, the minuscule black population—largely eastern transplants with a history of media protest—was ineffective. Calls for black suffrage and admittance to jury selection fell upon deaf ears. California did not allow blacks to vote until 1870 and the ratification of the Fifteenth Amendment to the United States Constitution. Schools remained segregated. White men meant California for whites only. So what is significant about the population data in California. Why did the Irish not respond to editors' Philip A. Bell, Peter Anderson, et. al? The answer is found in labor.

During the Nineteenth century, the conflict between blacks and the Irish on the east coast involved labor. As noted above, the Irish immigrants summarily displaced blacks from the menial laboring positions they held. In doing so, the Irish undercut the black wage structure, causing unemployment, and hostility among the black community. However, as R. A. Burchell has noted, California was "an area where the eastern pattern of interaction between native stock and immigrant was missing, where local conditions produced idiosyncratic factors that distinguished the region even from the Middle West which also lack historical white communities."[53]

California lacked an established white hierarchy as was evident in the east. In San Francisco, the Irish could come in on the "bottom floor," so to speak, and become part of the foundation instead of the veneer on the "building." Once established, the Irish could then pave the way for future immigrants who would assume their place in the newly established white hierarchy.

Labor, an essential part of this hierarchy, was to be limited to workingmen—whites. Competition for jobs confined itself to white men. Blacks, because of their minuscule population, were no threat to the new hierarchy of which the Irish were now full members. The Chinese immigrant, sojourner, with their penchant for working for wages far less than either whites or blacks would settle for, represented the real threat in the eyes of the Irish and other whites. Therefore, the act of heaping racial epithets and cultural slights upon the Chinese in the news media and on the street became a means of defense.

The racial hostility between the Irish and blacks, so prevalent in the east, did not, I would argue, cease existence when confronted with the Sierra Nevada Mountains. Instead, it subsumed itself under general racial prejudice between blacks and whites. Blacks may have made much "noise" regarding their position and the Irish, but ultimately it was without success. They were just a voice in the vast wilderness of California politics and economics.

Endnotes

1. *The New Colossus*, By Emma Lazarus. Sonnet to the Statue of Liberty, 1903.
2. George M. Frederickson, *The Black Image in the White Mind: The Debate on Afro-American Character and Destiny, 1817-1914.* (New York: Harper and Row Pub., 1971). p. 321.
3. Bernard Bailyn and Philip D. Morgan, editors *Strangers within the Realm: Cultural Margins of the First British Empire.* (Chapel Hill: The University of North Carolina Press, 1991). p. 18.
4. Theda Perdue, "Indians in Southern History" in *Indians in American History: An Introduction,* ed. Frederick E. Hoxie and Peter Iverson (Wheeling, IL: Harlan Davidson, Inc, 1998), pp. 123–124.
5. *Ibid.*
6. Noel Ignatiev, *How the Irish Became White* (New York: Routledge, 1995), p. 38.
7. *Ibid.*
8. R. A. Burchell, *The San Francisco Irish, 1848-1880* (Berkeley: University of California Press, 1980), p. 1.
9. Clarence E. Walker, "How Many Niggers Did Karl Marx Know?" in *Deromanticizing Black History: Critical Essays and Reappraisals* (Knoxville: The University of Tennessee Press, 1991), p. 16.
10. *Ibid.*
11. Burchell, p. 2.
12. Editor, *The Massachusetts Teacher,* "Our chief difficulty is with the Irish," in Barbara M. Posadas & Robert McColley, eds. *Refracting America: Gender, Race, Ethnicity, and Environment in American History to 1877* (St. James, New York: Brandywine Press, 1993), p. 145.
13. *Ibid.* p. 146.
14. *Ibid.*
15. *Ibid.*

16. James S. Olsen and Raymond Wilson, *Native Americans in the Twentieth Century* (Urbana: University of Illinois Press, 1986), 53, 61. White American viewed the public inebriation of Native Americans as evidence of deficient character. Reformers, religious and otherwise, sought to alleviate the problem through severe restrictions in the sale of alcohol to Native Americans. This restriction was also part of the program of forced assimilation into white American culture. In the process of this assimilation, white men such as Richard Pratt, a Civil War veteran, argued that Native American adults were incorrigible and as such would not assimilate. Therefore, to facilitate assimilation on the Native Americans, it was necessary to forcibly remove Native American children from their homes and educate them in the ways of white American culture. This process was designed to "kill the Indian, but save the man" that is, break their ties to native culture. The ultimate goal was to create industrious citizens that would go back to the reservation and educate their elders. Thus, creating a ripple effect of acculturation and assimilation. However, the plan failed because the reformers failed to recognize the Native Americans' attachment to their land, families and culture.

17. Burchell, p. 2.

18. Leon Litwack, *North of Slavery: The Negro in the Free States, 1790–1860* (Chicago: The University of Chicago Press, 1961), p. 163.

19. *Ibid*, p. 165.

20. Walker, p. 14.

21. Litwack, p. 166.

22. *Ibid*. From Philip S. Foner, ed. *The Life and Writings of Frederick Douglass, Vol. II.* (New York: International Publishers, 1950), 249–50.

23. Philip S. Foner, ed, *"Letter to William Lloyd Garrison from Montrose Scotland, February 26, 1846,"* in, *The Life And Writings of Frederick Douglass, Vol. I* (New York: International Publishers, 1950), p. 139.

24. *Ibid*. p. 141.

25. Philip S. Foner, ed. "The Present and Future of the Colored Race in America," a Speech delivered in the Church of the Puritans, New York, in May, 1863: in *The Life and Writings of Frederick Douglass, Vol. III* (New York: International Publishers, 1952), p. 356.

26. *Ibid*. p. 382.

27. Lawrence W. Levine, *Black Culture and Black Consciousness: Afro-American Folk Thought from Slavery to Freedom*, (New York: Oxford University Press, 1977), p. 301.

28. *Ibid*. p. 302.

29. *Ibid*, p. 304.

30. Arnold Shankman, *Ambivalent Friends: Afro-Americans View the Immigrant*, Contributions in Afro-Americans Studies Number 67 (Westport, Ct.: Greenwood Press, 1982), p. 150.

31. San Francisco *Western Outlook and Norfolk Journal and Guide*, both March 17, 1928.

32. Lillian Schlissel, *Women's Diaries of the Westward Journey*, (New York, Schocken Books, 1982), p. 136.

33. *Ibid*. p. 138.

34. Douglas Henry Daniels, *Pioneer Urbanites: A Social and Cultural History of Black San Francisco*, (Berkeley: University of California Press, 1990), 12.

35. Rudolph M. Lapp, *Blacks in Gold Rush California* (New Haven: Yale University Press, 1977), pp. 96–98.

36. Delores McBroome, *Parallel Communities: African Americans in California's East Bay, 1850–1863*, (New York: Garland Publishing, Inc., 1993) pp. 3–31.

37. Philip A. Bell, editor, *San Francisco Elevator*, "Our Motto," April 6, 1865.

38. Albert S. Broussard, *The New Racial Frontier: San Francisco's Black Community, 1900–1940*, (Ph.D. Dissertation Duke University, 1977), p. 29.

39. *Ibid*. p. 30.

40. *Ibid*. pp. 15–17

41. Philip A. Bell, editor, *San Francisco Elevator*, "Antagonism of Labor," February 15, 1873.

42. Philip A. Bell, editor, *San Francisco Elevator*, "National Labor Convention," December 2, 1869.

43. *Ibid*.

44. W. H. Hall, letter to the editor, *San Francisco Elevator*, "Freedmen -vs- Chinamen," December 17, 1869.

45. Philip A. Bell, editor, *San Francisco Elevator*, "Freedmen and Chinamen," December 17, 1869.

46. *Ibid*. "The Irish," May, 27, 1870.

47. *Ibid*.

48. Reprint of "Irishmen -vs- Negroes," an article from the *Christian Recorder* in San Francisco *Elevator*, February 11, 1870.

49. J.D.B. DeBow, Superintendent of the United States Census, *The Seventh Census of the United States, 1850* (Washington, D. C.: Robert Armstrong, Public Printer, 1853).

50. Joseph O. G. Kennedy, Secretary of the Interior, *Population of the United States in 1860, Compiled from the Original Returns of the Eighth Census.* (Washington. D.C.: Government Publishing Office, 1864).

51. Francis A. Walker, Superintendent of Census, *A Compendium of the Ninth Census (June, 1, 1870) Compiled Pursuant to a Concurrent Resolution of the Secretary of the Interior* (Washington, D. C.: Government Publishing Office, 1872).

52. Litwack, *North Of Slavery*, p. 94.

53. Burchell, *The San Francisco Irish*, p. 3.

Bibliography

Primary Sources

Bell, Philip A. ed. *San Francisco Elevator*, April 6, 1865.

Bell, Philip A. ed. *San Francisco Elevator*, December 2, 1869.

Bell, Philip A. ed. *San Francisco Elevator*, December 17, 1869.

Bell, Philip A. ed. *San Francisco Elevator*, February 11, 1870.

Bell, Philip A. ed. *San Francisco Elevator*, May 27, 1870.

Bell, Philip A. ed. *San Francisco Elevator*, February 15, 1873.

Congress, House. *37th Congress 2nd Session. Ex. Doc no. 116. Preliminary Report on the Eighth Census, 1860*. Washington, D.C.: Government Printing House, 1862.

DeBow, J. D. B. Superintendent of the United States Census. *The Seventh Census Of the United States, 1850*. Washington, D.C.: Robert Armstrong, Public Printer, 1853.

Department of the Interior Census Office. *Statistics of Population of the United States at the 10th Census, June 1, 1880*. Washington, D.C.: Government Printing Office, 1883.

Foner, Philip S. ed. *The Life and Writings of Frederick Douglass, Vol. I* New York: International Publishers, 1950.

Foner, Philip S. ed. *The Life and Writings of Frederick Douglass, Vol. II*. New York: International Publishers, 1952.

Foner, Philip S. ed. *The Life and Writings of Frederick Douglass, Vol. III*. New York: International Publishers, 1952.

Hall, W. H. *San Francisco Elevator*, December, 17, 1869.

Kennedy, Joseph O. G. Superintendent of Census. *Population of the United States in 1860 Compiled from the Original Returns of the Eighth Census*. Washington, D.C.: Government Printing Office, 1864.

Posadas, Barbara M. and Robert McColley, eds. *Refracting America: Gender, Race, Ethnicity, and Environment in American History to 1877*. St. James, New York: Brandywine Press, 1993.

San Francisco *Western Outlook*, March 17, 1928.

Walker, Francis, A. *A Compendium of the Ninth Census (June 1, 1870) Compiled Pursuant to a Concurrent Resolution Under the Direction of the Secretary of the Interior*. Washington, D.C.: Government Printing Office, 1872.

Walker, Francis, A. *The Statistics of the Population of the United States etc., 1870, Under the Direction of the Secretary of the Interior*. Washington, D.C.: Government Printing Office, 1872.

Bibliography

Secondary Sources

Burchell, R.A. *The San Francisco Irish, 1848–1880*. Berkeley: University of California Press, 1980.

Broussard, Albert S. *The New Racial Frontier: San Francisco's Black Community, 1900–1940*. Ph.D. dissertation Duke University, 1977.

Daniels, Douglass Henry. *Pioneer Urbanites: A Social and Cultural History of Black San Francisco*. Berkeley: University of California Press, 1990.

Hellwig, David, Johns. *"The Afro-American and the Immigrant, 1880–1930: A Study of Black Social Thought"* Ph.D. Dissertation, Syracuse University, 1973.

Ignatiev, Noel. *How the Irish Became White*. New York: Routledge, 1995.

Lapp, Rudolph M. *Blacks in Gold Rush California*. New Haven: Yale University Press, 1977.

Lazarus, Emma. *The New Colossus. Sonnet to the Statue of Liberty*, 1903.

Levine, Lawrence. *Black Culture and Black Consciousness: Afro-American Folk Thought from Slavery to Freedom*. New York: Oxford University Press, 1977.

Litwack, Leon. *North of Slavery: The Negro in the Free States, 1790–1860*. Chicago: The University of Chicago Press, 1961.

McBroome, Delores. *Parallel Communities: African Americans in California's East Bay, 1850–1863*. New York: Garland Publishing Inc., 1993.

Schissel, Lilian. *Women's Diaries of the Westward Journey*. New York: Schocken Books, 1982.

Shankman, Arnold. *Ambivalent Friends: Afro-Americans View the Immigrant, Contributions in Afro-American Studies Number 67*. Westport, CT.: Greenwood Press, 1982.

Walker, Clarence E. *Deromanticizing Black History: Critical Essays and Reappraisals*. Knoxville: The University of Tennessee Press, 1991.

Anglo-Saxons and Mexicans

Reginald Horsman

The Anglo-Saxon blood could never be subdued
by anything that claimed Mexican origin.

James Buchanan, February 14, 1845

✳ ✳ ✳ ✳ ✳

The decisive years in the creation of a new Anglo-Saxon political ideology were from the mid-1830s to the mid-1840s. In these years American politicians and the American population were overwhelmed by a variety of influences, both practical and theoretical, which inspired a belief that the American Anglo-Saxons were destined to dominate or penetrate the American continents and large areas of the world. Americans had faith that they would increase in such numbers that they would personally shape the destiny of other areas.

The catalyst in the overt adoption of a racial Anglo-Saxonism was the meeting of Americans and Mexicans in the Southwest, the Texas Revolution, and the war with Mexico. In confronting the Mexicans the Americans clearly formulated the idea of themselves as an Anglo-Saxon race. The use of *Anglo-Saxon* in a racial sense, somewhat rare in the political arguments of the early 1830s, increased rapidly later in the decade and became commonplace by the mid-1840s. The manner in which the Anglo-Saxon race was being isolated from other peoples was stated with clarity by Senator Benjamin Leigh of Virginia in January 1836 when opposing the abolitionist petitions. After pointing out that his fellow Congressmen had only to remember how the mobs of Cincinnati, Philadelphia, and New York had dealt with the few free Negroes in their midst to appreciate what would follow general emancipation, he candidly sketched the problem: "It is peculiar to

the character of this Anglo-Saxon race of men to which we belong, that it has never been contented to live in the same country with any other distinct race, upon terms of equality; it has, invariably, when placed in that situation, proceeded to exterminate or enslave the other race in some form or other, or, failing in that, to abandon the country."[1]

The idea of the Anglo-Saxon race as a distinct, all-encompassing force was expressed with increasing frequency in the late 1830s. In February 1837 William Gilpin wrote to his father from New Orleans that while the town was still Gallic in character the "Anglo-Saxon is pushing aside the Frenchman and eating him up. The big steamers . . . are Anglo-Saxon, the huge stores and warehouses into which [goods] are piled have an Anglo-Saxon look and an Anglo-Saxon ship bears them hence. [Of] all the new part of the city, the only decent part is English."[2] When Horace Bushnell, in August 1837, delivered an oration on the principles of national greatness, he used old and familiar arguments concerning America as a land saved for events of world significance; however, he used a new precision in writing of the origin of the people for whom the New World had been preserved. "Out of all the inhabitants of the world," he said, ". . . a select stock, the Saxon, and out of this the British family, the noblest of the stock, was chosen to people our country." In contrast, the Mexican state, he said, had started with fundamental disadvantages in the character of its immigrants.

If the quality of the British people was changed into that of the Mexican, "five years would make their noble island a seat of poverty and desolation." For Bushnell, God had reserved America for a special people of Saxon blood.[3]

By the 1830s the Americans were eagerly grasping at reasons for their own success and for the failure of others. Although the white Americans of Jacksonian America wanted personal success and wealth, they also wanted a clear conscience. If the United States was to remain in the minds of its people a nation divinely ordained for great deeds, then the fault for the suffering inflicted in the rise to power and prosperity had to lie elsewhere. White Americans could rest easier if the sufferings of other races could be blamed on racial weakness rather than on the whites' relentless search for wealth and power. In the 1830s and 1840s, when it became obvious that American and Mexican interests were incompatible and that the Mexicans would suffer, innate weaknesses were found in the Mexicans. Americans, it was argued, were not to be blamed for forcibly taking the northern provinces of Mexico, for Mexicans, like Indians, were unable to make proper use of the land. The Mexicans had failed because they were a mixed, inferior race with considerable Indian and some black blood. The world would benefit if a superior race shaped the future of the Southwest.

By the time of the Mexican War, America had placed the Mexicans firmly within the rapidly emerging hierarchy of superior and inferior races. While the Anglo-Saxons were depicted as the purest of the pure—the finest Caucasians—the Mexicans who stood in the way of southwestern expansion were depicted as a mongrel race, adulterated by extensive intermarriage with an inferior Indian race. Travelers delighted in depicting the Mexicans as an unimprovable breed and were particularly scathing about the inhabitants of Mexico's northern provinces. T. J. Farnham in 1840 wrote of the Californians as "an imbecile, pusillanimous, race of men, and unfit to control the destinies of that beautiful country." No one who knew "the indolent, mixed race of California," he argued, could believe they would long populate much less govern, the region. The mixed white and Indian races of California and Mexico "must fade away; while the mingling of different branches of the Caucasian family in the States" would produce a race which would expand to cover all the northern provinces of Mexico. "The old Saxon blood must stride the continent," wrote Farnham, "must command all its northern shores . . . and . . . erect the altar of civil and religious freedom on the plains of the Californias."[4]

The Mexican Californians were constantly attacked as shiftless and ineffective. Richard Dana thought them "an idle, thriftless people" and asserted that nothing but the character of the population prevented Monterey from becoming a large town. "In the hands of an enterprising people," he said, "what a country this might be!"[5] Lansford Hastings, in his famous emigrants' guide of 1845, characterized the Mexican inhabitants of California as "scarcely a visible grade, in the scale of intelligence, above the barbarous tribes by whom they are surrounded." This was not surprising, said Hastings. There had been extensive intermarriage and "as most of the lower order of Mexicans, are Indians in fact, whatever is said in reference to the one, will also be applicable to the other." Stereotypes that were to persist in American thinking long after the 1840s were firmly fixed in Hastings's work. A Mexican, he said, "always pursues that method of doing things, which requires the least physical or mental exorcise [sic], unless it involves some danger, in which case, he always adopts some other method." Writing of soldiers who were brought into California in 1842, he commented that they were "mere Indians," and that it was "with these wild, shirtless, earless and heartless creatures, headed by a few timid, soulless, brainless officers, that these semi-barbarians, intend to hold this delightful region, as against the civilized world." The process of dehumanizing those who were to be misused or destroyed proceeded rapidly in the United States in the 1840s. To take lands from inferior barbarians was no crime; it was simply following God's injunctions to make the land fruitful.[6]

In the Southwest there was even a tendency for American travelers to praise the Pueblo Indians in order further to debase the "mongrel" Mexicans. George Kendall, who was on the Texas-Santa Fe expedition, commented in his account of that sorry affair that "the *pueblos*, or town Indians of New Mexico, are by far the better part of the population." Most Mexicans, he said, were content if they could satisfy their animal wants, "and so they will continue to be until the race becomes extinct or amalgamated with Anglo-Saxon stock."[7] Rufus Sage echoed, Kendall: "There are no people on the continent of America, whether civilized or uncivilized, with one or two exceptions, more miserable in condition or despicable in morals than the mongrel race inhabiting New Mexico."[8]

The scathing denunciations of the Mexican race encompassed the inhabitants of central Mexico as well as its outlying provinces, and these denunciations were not confined to writers from any one party or one region in the United States. Waddy Thompson of South Carolina, who went to Mexico in 1842 as minister for the Whig administration, advanced the familiar stereotype in his *Recollections,* which was published in 1847. While condemning aggressive expansionism and the rapacious spirit of acquisition which was developing in the United States, Thompson had no doubt at all of the ultimate result of the meeting of the Anglo-Saxon and the Mexican races. He objected to the means, not to the end. "That our language and laws are destined to pervade this continent," he wrote, "I regard as more certain than any other event which is in the future. Our race has never yet put its foot upon a soil which it has not only kept but has advanced. I mean not our English ancestors only, but that great Teuton race from which we have both descended."[9]

To Thompson an essential element in Mexican weakness was the mixed population. Of seven million inhabitants, he wrote, only one million were white Europeans or their descendants. Of the others there were some four to four and one-half million pure-blooded Indians, and the rest of mixed blood. Thompson, like many others at this time, was easily able to envisage a mysterious disappearance of millions of people. "That the Indian race of Mexico must recede before us," he wrote, "is quite as certain as that that is the destiny of our own Indians." Negroes in Mexico Thompson characterized as "the same lazy, filthy, and vicious creatures that they inevitably become where they are not held in bondage." The general Mexican population Thompson characterized as "lazy, ignorant, and, of course, vicious and dishonest."[10]

The American dismissal of the Mexicans as an inferior, largely Indian race did not pass unnoticed in Mexico. Mexican ministers in the United States warned their government that the Americans considered the Mexicans an inferior people. The Mexicans realized both that their neighbors to the north were likely to invade their northern provinces, and that they would claim that this was justified because they could make better use of the lands.

Mexicans who served as diplomatic representatives in the United States were shocked at the rabid anti-Mexican attitudes and at the manner in which Mexicans were lumped together with Indians and blacks as an inferior race.[11]

The Texas Revolution was from its beginnings interpreted in the United States and among Americans in Texas as a racial clash, not simply a revolt against unjust government or tyranny. Thomas Hart Benton said that the Texas revolt "has illustrated the Anglo-Saxon character, and given it new titles to the respect and admiration of the world. It shows that liberty, justice, valour—moral, physical, and intellectual power—discriminate that race wherever it goes." Benton asked "old England" to rejoice that distant Texas streams had seen the exploits of "a people sprung from their loins, and carrying their language, laws, and customs, their *magna charta* and all its glorious privileges, into new regions and far distant climes."[12]

In his two terms as president of Texas, Sam Houston consistently thought of the struggle in his region as one between a glorious Anglo-Saxon race and an inferior Mexican rabble. Victory for the Texans and the Americans in the Southwest would mean that larger areas of the world were to be brought under the rule of a race that could make best use of them. Houston was less imbued with the harsh scientific racial theories that carried most Americans before them in the 1840s than with the romantic exaltation of the Saxons given by Sir Walter Scott and his followers.

Houston's inaugural address in October 1836 contrasted the harsh, uncivilized warfare of the Mexicans with the more humane conduct of the Texans. He conjured up a vision of the civilized world proudly contemplating "conduct which reflected so much glory on the Anglo-Saxon race." The idea of the Anglo-Saxons as the living embodiment of the chivalric ideal always fascinated Houston; the Mexicans were "the base invader" fleeing from "Anglo-Saxon chivalry." In fighting Mexico the Texans were struggling to disarm tyranny, to overthrow oppression, and create representative government: "With these principles we will march across the Rio Grande, and . . . ere the banner of Mexico shall triumphantly float upon the banks of the Sabine, the Texian standard of the single star, borne by the Anglo-Saxon race, shall display its bright folds in Liberty's triumph, on the isthmus of Darien."[13]

While conceiving of the Texas Revolution as that of a freedom-loving Anglo-Saxon race rising up to throw off the bonds of tyranny imposed by a foreign despot, Houston was also fully convinced of the inevitability of general American Anglo-Saxon expansion. To him "the genius as well as the excitability" of the American people impelled them to war. "Their love of dominion," he said, "and the extension of their territorial limits, also, is equal to that of Rome in the last ages of the Commonwealth and the first of the Caesars." The people of the United States, he argued, were convinced that the North American continent had been bestowed on them, and if necessary they would take it by force.[14] He told one correspondent in 1844 that there was no need to be concerned about the population said to occupy the vast area from the 29th to the 46th latitude on the Pacific: "They will, like the Indian race yield to the advance of the North American population."[15]

For the most part Houston was content to exalt the Anglo-Saxons as a chivalric, freedom-loving, and expansionist race without launching bitter attacks on the capacities of other races. But the image he helped to create of a gallant band of Anglo-Saxon freemen struggling to throw off the yoke of Mexican oppression, and the more general image of the Mexicans that was present in the United States from the mid-1830s, helped breed a callousness toward the Mexicans as a people. The Alamo, the massacre at Goliad, and, later, the fate of the Texas-Santa Fe expedition received wide publicity in the United States and increased the venom with which the Mexican race was condemned. Hearing that those on the Texas-Santa Fe expedition had been captured and sent on a long march to Mexico City, the *Mobile Register and Journal* prophesied that a flame of resentment would sweep the United States which "will bring upon that feeble and treacherous race, a dreadful retribution for a long career of perfidy and cruelty."[16] Increasingly Mexicans were lumped with the blacks and the Indians. One man who had been on the Texas-Santa Fe expedition wrote of soon being able to have his turn "with the yellow skins" and said that though he did not think of himself as being much of a soldier he would risk his life in resisting "such beings as the Mexicans."[17] By the early 1840s few were willing to acknowledge that the Mexicans had anything to commend them as a race.

A notable exponent of the argument that Mexicans were worthless was Robert J. Walker,

the Pennsylvania-born senator from Mississippi. Walker made the Texas cause his own and for the next thirty years was to be one of the most rampant of expansionists, urging the extension of American power over all North and South America, Iceland, and Greenland, endlessly promoting trade ties to the Pacific, and arguing that ultimately the Anglo-Saxon race would reunite under the American federal system to bring a reign of peace throughout the world. In 1836 he was on the threshold of his career, having just been elected from Mississippi. When urging the recognition of Texas independence, he told the Senate that whether or not the United States extended its jurisdiction over Texas, as he wanted, it should rejoice that American institutions, language, "and our kindred race, predominated over that fair country, instead of the colored mongrel race, and barbarous tyranny, and superstitions of Mexico."[18]

Walker's virulence on racial matters increased with his prominence. By the mid-1840s he had become a leader in the Democratic party, and when in 1845 he became Polk's secretary of the treasury, some of his friends thought that the appointment showed an insufficient recognition of his talents and promise. His annual reports as secretary, in which he urged free trade, were praised in the Democratic press as the finest since Hamilton's.[19] He combined brilliance and an ebullient personality with extravagant racial theories. In 1844, when urging the annexation of Texas, he estimated that five-sixths of the Mexican population were "of the mixed races, speaking more than twenty different languages, composed of every poisonous compound of blood and color." He asked whether such a people could ever subdue and govern the American race in Texas. Even if it could, he argued, it would be folly for the United States to permit the establishment of "this ignorant and fanatical colored population" on the borders of the slave states. If the Mexicans succeeded in retaking Texas, the United States' instinct for self-preservation should force it to act rather than let the region fall again "into the hands of the semi-barbarous hordes of Mexico."[20]

To combat the abolitionists and Whigs who said that the annexation of Texas would mean the expansion of slave power, Walker developed the idea that such an action would both reduce slavery and the number of blacks in the United States. In doing so he increased the gulf between the "Anglo-Saxon" and the "Mexican" races by arguing for a close affinity between Latin Americans and the blacks of the United States. The Mexicans had already been debased in American eyes by being characterized as a race largely intermarried with the Indians; their debasement was now to be completed by the manner in which they were linked to the despised blacks.

In his *Letter on the Annexation of Texas*, which was distributed extensively throughout the country, Walker argued that the annexation of Texas would, by drawing off the slaves to the Southwest, help reduce the number of slaves in the slave states, free the northern states from "the evil" of free blacks, and help the slaves themselves by taking them to a warmer and more hospitable region. Texas would act as a safety valve for the whole union. Slaves siphoned off into Texas would eventually move still farther south into Mexico and Central and South America. Among whites in the United States free blacks would always be a degraded caste, because they were inferior, but blacks would happily move south of the Rio Grande to Mexico and South America where there were so many of their people. In this way the United States, in the course of time, could lose its blacks. With triumphant and specious reasoning Walker concluded that the only way to get rid of slavery was to annex Texas: "*it will certainly disappear if Texas is reannexed to the Union.*"[21]

Walker's theory of the mass movement of blacks southward was as obviously flawed as the theory that assumed that large populations of non-Anglo-Saxon races would simply recede and disappear before the advance of the Americans, but it immediately found enthusiastic adherents. "Who is there that will object," said Representative John W. Tibbatts of Kentucky, "if all of this unfortunate race shall thus gradually and peaceably finally be withdrawn from our republic?"[22] James Buchanan of Pennsylvania, who was to serve in Polk's cabinet as secretary of state, accepted Walker's contention that slaves would be drawn off into Texas and ultimately across the Rio Grande to mingle with the Mexicans—a nation "composed of Spaniards, Indians, and negroes, blended together in every variety." Texas should be taken, said Buchanan, because "only thus can we fulfill our high destinies, and run the race of greatness for which we are ordained." He thought it impossible that a nation such as Texas, composed chiefly of native-born Americans, could ever remain under the rule of Mexico—"our race of men can never be subjected to the imbecile and indolent Mexican race." Buchanan consistently maintained this position throughout the debates on the annexation of Texas. Texas was free from Mexican rule and could not be retaken: "The Anglo-Saxon blood could never be subdued by anything that claimed Mexican origin." The same blood ran in Texan as in American veins, and both drew course age from the parent stock.[23] As secretary of state under Polk, Buchanan had utter contempt for the Mexicans with whom he had to negotiate.

The racial affinity of Americans and Texans was constantly on the lips of those who favored the annexation of Texas. Levi Woodbury of New Hampshire stated that the Texans had "a body of intelligent and talented men of the true Saxon race. And if all these do not constitute a state, what does?" He thought it was much more the duty of the United States to receive these Saxons into the union than it had been to receive the French of Louisiana or the Spanish of Florida. To Woodbury the Texans had been decoyed to their country by liberal colonization laws, then their rights and privileges invaded, "and their Saxon blood humiliated, and enslaved to Moors, Indians, and mongrels."[24] David L. Seymour of New York saw annexation as "the easy and natural union of two contiguous nations, both founded by the Anglo-Saxon race, both organized upon the same basis of popular rights and republican equality." The Texans were a superior people. "They are of the Americo-Anglo-Saxon race," said Whig Alexander H. Stephens of Georgia. "They are from us, and of us; bone of our bone, and flesh of our flesh."[25]

Although many southern supporters of the annexation of Texas saw it as a means of protecting slavery and the interests of the slave states, there were supporters of annexation all over the country who saw the slavery question as irrelevant. They believed that the expansion of the Anglo-Americans into Texas was part of an inevitable movement of the American people, and that while the immediate effect might be the extension of slavery, the most important result would be the extension of the progressive power of the American race. As the blacks were more and more viewed as a race apart, whatever the fate of slavery, it was possible to conceive of an expansion which both extended slavery and the current boundaries of American settlement as being for the absolute good of the world. William J. Brown of Indiana was unwilling to accept the argument that the Rio Grande formed the natural boundary between races. To discuss whether or not the American advance should stop there was irrelevant, he argued, for "it *will not,* A half a century will not roll around before it will cover all Mexico; nor a century pass by before it will find its way to Patagonia's snow-invested wilds." He was uncertain how many republics would be carved from this area, but he had no doubt that their destinies "would be guided by Anglo-Saxon hands."[26]

The opponents of the annexation of Texas were unable to prevent it. The measure was firmly supported both in Congress and in the nation, and it was difficult to deny the argument that this was merely a reuniting of Americans who wished to be reunited. Although some objected to expansion that would mean the extension of slavery, practically all viewed the Southwest as an area that eventually would be transformed by Anglo-Saxons. It seemed that no human agency could stop the predestined outward thrust of the American people.

It was in commenting on the annexation of Texas that Democratic politician and publicist John L. O'Sullivan coined the phrase *Manifest Destiny* to describe the process of American expansion. In the early 1840s O'Sullivan, in editing the *Democratic Review,* had not accepted the most virulent of the new racial theories. Although he acknowledged black inferiority, he was generally reluctant to condemn all other races as being incapable of improvement. He had as much in common with the expansionists of the Jeffersonian generation as with those who seized on his phrases at mid-century, and he was more confident of general human improvement than most expansionists of the 1840s. Yet O'Sullivan was convinced that without violence America's population would expand outward in ever-increasing numbers, and though he had at first advised caution on the Texas issue, he was happy to accept the annexation of Texas. His qualms over methods were subsumed in his delight that his vision of American expansion was being realized.

O'Sullivan first used the phrase Manifest Destiny in criticizing other nations for attempting to interfere with a natural process: other nations had intruded, he said, "for the avowed object of thwarting our policy and hampering our power, limiting our greatness and checking the fulfillment of our manifest destiny to overspread the continent allotted by Providence for the free development of our yearly multiplying millions." Slavery had nothing to do with the annexation, he argued, for slaves would be drawn off to the South. Texas had been absorbed as part of the fulfillment of "the general law" which

was sending a rapidly increasing American population westward. California would probably soon follow Mexico within the American orbit: "The Anglo-Saxon foot is already on its borders. Already the advance guard of the irresistible army of Anglo-Saxon emigration has begun to pour down upon it, armed with the plough and the rifle, and marking its trail with schools and colleges, courts and representative halls, mills and meeting houses." There was to be no balance of power on the American continent: Spanish America had demonstrated no ability for growth; Canada would break away from England to be annexed by the United States; and no European power could contend "against the simple, solid weight of the two hundred and fifty, or three hundred millions—and American millions—destined to gather beneath the flutter of the stripes and stars in the fast hastening year of the Lord 1945!"[27] In his enthusiasm O'Sullivan had put a touch of Carlyle into his style.

The initial use of the phrase Manifest Destiny in the summer of 1845 attracted no particular attention, but in December of that year O'Sullivan used it again, this time in his newspaper, the *New York Morning News.* O'Sullivan was now concerned with the Oregon question. He maintained that although America's legal title to Oregon was perfect, its better claim was by "the right of our manifest destiny to overspread and to possess the whole of the continent which Providence has given us for the development of the great experiment of liberty and federated self-government entrusted to us." A week later Representative Robert C. Winthrop of Massachusetts referred to the phrase in Congress. It immediately became the subject of debate and inspired both praise and censure. In the following years it was referred to frequently both by advocates and opponents of expansion.[28]

O'Sullivan was able to meld the Texas and Oregon crises in his general assumptions of overriding American destiny, but in Congress discussions of the racial implications of the two controversies differed sharply. In discussing Texas and Mexican rule Congressmen drew few distinctions between Mexicans and their government. It was argued that the instability and ineffectiveness of the Mexican government stemmed from the inadequacies of an inferior population. In discussing Great Britain and Oregon even those Congressmen who were most critical of the British government usually made a clear distinction between the British government and the English race. The English were respected as fellow Anglo-Saxons who were not to be swept out of Oregon as an inferior breed; and those who opposed war with England frequently discussed the disastrous effects of a clash between the two great branches of the Anglo-Saxon race. The sense of Anglo-Saxon racial community, combined with a respect for British power and ability, helped mute the most strident demands for war. While the Texas issue had provided an opportunity for accentuating the differences between superior Americans and inferior Mexicans, the Oregon crisis stimulated a public avowal of the common roots of the American and English peoples.

When in the spring of 1861 the London *Times* correspondent William H. Russell visited Montgomery, Alabama, he said of Georgian Robert Toombs that "he is something of an Anglo-maniac, and an Anglo-phobist—a combination not unusual in America."[29] This duality of feeling toward England and the English was a persistent theme in the Oregon debates. In its simplest form it was expressed by Representative Samuel Gordon of New York. He admired the British people as "blood of our blood, bone of our bone, and flesh of our flesh," but he also announced that "I abhor and detest the British Government."[30] Robert J. Walker of Mississippi was able to draw the same distinction. In the 1850s he was to write in grandiloquent terms of plans for a world union of the Anglo-Saxon people, but in the 1840s he attacked British interference on the North American continent and America's abject dependence on the moneyed power of Great Britain: "let us draw nearer and nearer to that happy hour," he said in 1840, "that even our eyes may behold the glorious spectacle when not an acre of American soil shall be polluted by British dominion, or degraded by imperial or despotic power."[31]

Some in the Oregon debates had been so influenced by the surge of Saxonism that they justified a hard line on Oregon with the argument that American Anglo-Saxons were more than a match for English Anglo-Saxons still under an aristocratic government. Representative James B. Bowlin of Missouri argued in January 1845 that destiny had arranged for Americans to check in Oregon England's drive for universal dominion: "she meets those who sprung from a common stock—the same Anglo-Saxon race, and as little accustomed to witness a triumphal march over the ruins of their country, as are the would-be conquerors of

the earth." The English were in trouble in Oregon, he believed, because they were meeting free representatives of the same Anglo-Saxon race.[32] Seaborn Jones of Georgia followed a similar line of thought by arguing that the Revolution had "showed that the Anglo-Saxon blood was improved by the spirit of liberty." He then revealed that he had perhaps imbibed a little too much Scott in his youth: "I love a 'foeman worthy of our steel,'" he announced, "and would sooner throw the gage of battle to proud, and haughty, and powerful England, than to bullying, and blustering, and impotent Mexico."[33] Congress generally did not endorse this arrogance of choosing the most difficult opponent.

Although some members of Congress in the mid-1840s were willing, even happy, to talk of a future war with England, most seemed satisfied to believe that a firm American stance would persuade England to yield Oregon to the United States. Most did not want war against a formidable opponent. Representative John S. Pendleton of Virginia thought that though the United States could take Canada the cost would be too heavy. The United States would not have to take it from "the mongrels and hybrids" ("Canadian French and half-breed Indians") that might compose a Canadian army: "we should meet men of our own mettle; it would be Saxon against Saxon; and there is no child's play there."[34]

The desire for firmness, no war, and ultimate American Anglo-Saxon triumph was expressed well in an article in the *Merchants' Magazine* in the spring of 1846. The author asserted that Oregon was the rightful property of the United States, and that English efforts to stop the advance of American pioneers were futile. Yet war should be avoided; it was unnecessary and it would be destructive to commerce. "No power on earth, nor all the powers of the earth, can check the swelling tide of the American population," it was argued, ". . . Every portion of this continent, from the sunny south to the frozen north, will be, in a very few years, filled with industrious and thriving Anglo-Saxons." There need be no war—all could be won by the weight of numbers: "The Oregon country must, all of it, not only up to 54° 40', but beyond it, far up into what is now exclusively Russian, become peopled by the Anglo-Saxon race . . . This is the irresistible flow of our people."[35]

The Oregon debates, while stimulating attacks on British power, also brought out the degree to which many Americans could disregard any immediate differences on the North American continent and see an ultimate compatibility of interests between England and the United States—a compatibility based on the Anglo-Saxon race and on the heritage of democratic institutions that derived from the special abilities of this race. New Englander Caleb Cushing had no doubt about the expansionist destiny of the United States. He believed its destiny was "to people, cultivate, and civilize this Continent."[36] The United States, he thought, should assert its rights to the Oregon country, for this deeply involved the fur trade, the whale fisheries, and trade with Asia. The region would become American if the United States "temperately but firmly" pressed her rights. "The world is wide enough for England and for us," he said. "We have much to gain by a cordial intercourse, conducted as becomes nations of the same blood, and the same tongue, each at the head of civilization in its proper hemisphere . . . Off-shoots of that dominant race, which, starting from the mountains of Caucasus, has proceeded in opposite directions, east and west, encircling the globe."[37] Theodore Parker said that war with England over Oregon would retard the progress of man for half a century.[38]

In an unusual display of agreement, both Daniel Webster and John C. Calhoun opposed any steps that might lead to war and emphasized what they thought to be the underlying compatibility of interests between Great Britain and the United States. Webster said that the likelihood of conflict over Oregon was being overemphasized, and that there could and would be a peaceful solution. Oregon, he added, would be settled mainly by Americans, although with some settlers from England, "but all *Anglo-Saxons*; all men educated in notions of independent government and all self-dependent."[39] This settlement would eventually lead to a great independent power on the Pacific, a republican power of English and American descent. John C. Calhoun told the Senate in March 1846 that he was opposed to war between the United States and Great Britain: "They are the two countries the furthest in advance in this great career of improvement and amelioration of the condition of our race. They are, besides, the two most commercial, and are diffusing, by their widely extended commerce, their blessings over the whole globe. We have been raised up by Providence for these great and noble purposes, and I trust we shall not fail to fulfil our

high destiny."[40] In this context "our race" was undoubtedly the white race.

Most members of Congress were content neither to lambast the British government, nor analyze the possibilities of war, but simply to view the American advance to Oregon, for whatever commercial or agrarian reasons, as simply part of America's inevitable western and expansionist destiny. They were confident that this westward movement was one stage in the advance of the American Anglo-Saxons to world power. Senator David R. Atchison of Missouri said there was no way of dissuading the American people from occupying Oregon. Settlers were ready to move in an unbroken column west—" 'like the Goths and Huns of old; a nation will emigrate, not for the purpose of destroying, but of building up empires!'" He said nothing could check the westward march of empire. Atchison's predecessor, Lewis F. Linn, had stressed that Americans from the time they had first arrived in Massachusetts had "but obeyed the instinct of our peculiar race—that invincible longing for liberty and space which impels those of Anglo-Saxon descent to trace the rudest tracts, the wildest seas, range the Atlantic and the Indian waste of waters, explore the vast Pacific, and break through the icy barriers of the polar oceans." Rufus Choate of Massachusetts denied that the intense American feeling of nationality involved any deep-seated hatred of England. What it really involved, he said, was a feeling that Americans had "a transcendent destiny to fulfil . . . a career to run, up which we hope to ascend till we stand on the steadfast and glittering summits of the world."[41]

That the Oregon question was settled peacefully and the southwestern problem resulted in war with Mexico stemmed partially from the differences in strength between Great Britain and Mexico. But it also arose from the obvious fact that many American politicians were reluctant to clash with their Anglo-Saxon brethren, whereas they thought as little of clashing with the Mexicans as they did of clashing with the Indians. The Oregon debates revealed the extent to which the British government was hated by some Americans and the extent to which British imperial ambition was feared; but they also revealed a basic admiration for the English people and a pride in belonging to a common Anglo-Saxon stock.

The enthusiasm with which American politicians and publicists sang the praises of the Anglo-Saxon stock was heightened in these years of the mid-1840s by a growing concern about the rapid increase in Irish Catholic and in German immigration. As yet the concern was not general because most Americans had faith that the multiplying Anglo-Saxons could easily absorb other European stocks, particularly those of Teutonic origin; but already some were indicating a desire to preserve their own status and economic interests through a strong emphasis on racial exclusiveness. The prospect of increasing disruptions to society through large-scale immigration, added to the already rapid social and economic change of the 1830s and 1840s, helped encourage many to find security in racial solidarity. The extensive growth in the decades since 1815 had brought widespread opportunities for wealth; yet it had also brought widespread disruption and disappointments. The depression of the late 1830s and early 1840s had increased fears of competition from alien elements. In an age of constant change many were to find security in the certainty of a racial heritage that stretched back into the distant past.[42]

The 1844 election saw the flowering of a vigorous anti-immigrant movement, a movement which hoped to make it more difficult for foreigners (and they were thinking primarily of new non-English immigrants) to achieve the political rights of native-born Americans. In June a large meeting of nativists in Philadelphia praised their congressional supporters as "possessed of some slight recollections of those principles for which our fathers bled—the good old principles of Saxon liberty—the principles which cost to John, his power—to James, his throne—to Charles, his head—to George, his provinces."[43] The Whigs of New York were bitterly disappointed at Clay's loss of the state in 1844. Philip Hone told Clay that though the good, hard-working New York Whigs voted for Clay, "alas! the numerical strength lies not in those classes. Foreigners who have no lot or inheritance in the matter, have robbed us of our birthright, the 'scepter has departed from Israel.' Ireland has reconquered the country which England lost."[44] Although the nativist movement ostensibly supported the native-born against all aliens, in reality nativists were mostly interested in supporting American "Anglo-Saxons" against the rest. Those who thought of the existing American race as "Anglo-Saxon" were able to ignore their own particular origin in assuming that the basic stock should be preserved.

Even those who did not seek to preserve an intact Anglo-American race through specific political action had become convinced by the late 1830s and 1840s that American achievement depended upon more than fortunate institutions and a happy environment; it was a matter of blood. The United States had developed in its own unique manner because it had been settled by members of a particular, superior race, a race with innate attributes making possible the creation of a free, ever-growing government. Robert C. Winthrop of Massachusetts, who opposed militant Manifest Destiny, said in 1839 that "I cannot regard it . . . as a mere lucky accident, that this Atlantic seaboard was settled by colonies of the Anglo-Saxon race!" Providence had arranged for the colonization and civilization of the American continent by *"Englishmen."* One had only to compare American political institutions to the "loathsome and abhorrent" political condition of the French on the North American continent to realize that the superiority sprang from "the comparative capacities for self-improvement of the Races by which they were planted."[45] It was becoming just as important that the Americans were born Anglo-Saxons as that they were bred Americans.

Those who earlier had expressed hope for general human improvement were not immune to the new sense of Anglo-Saxon racial exclusiveness. Edward Everett, speaking in England in 1843, told an audience that "history warrants us in believing in races of men, as well as of inferior animals," and that "the Anglo-Saxon race, from which we Americans trace our descent, is surpassed by none other that ever existed."[46] Daniel Webster, in responding to a toast in 1843, emphasized that even with the separation of New England from Old England, both were proceeding on a mighty career of progress and power; he added that in explaining this, he would not dwell with any particular emphasis on the sentiment "which I nevertheless entertain, with respect to the great diversity in the races of men." Webster went on to point out that "on this continent *all* is to be *Anglo-American* from Plymouth Rock to the Pacific seas, from the north pole to California," and in the eastern world English settlements were everywhere. Webster mused that if there was anything in the idea of the supremacy of races "the experiment now in progress will develop it. If there be any truth in the idea, that those who issued from the great Caucasian fountain, and spread over Europe, are to act on India and on Asia, and to act on the whole Western world, it may not be for us, nor our children, nor our grandchildren to see it, but it will be for our descendants of some generation to see the extent of that progress and dominion of the favored races."[47] The tone of Webster's speech left no doubt as to what he believed, as there was no doubt that the German accounts of the Germanic tribes spreading westward from central Asia to regenerate the world were beginning to gain wide currency in the United States.

Even British imperial power could be viewed in a different light when it involved not resistance to American desires but a general triumph of the Anglo-Saxon race. England's attack on China in the Opium War was celebrated by John Gordon Bennett of the *New York Herald* as "another movement of the Anglo-Saxon spirit in the remotest east, against the barriers of semi-barbarians and a half-civilized race, who have been stationary for twenty centuries or more."[48] This was not a victory for British imperialism, but a triumph for the Anglo-Saxons.

By 1845 many were finding it difficult to believe that free institutions could flourish in any area that did not have a substantial Anglo-Saxon population. Representative Alexander Duncan of Ohio suggested that there "seems to be something in our laws and institutions peculiarly adapted to our Anglo-Saxon American race, under which they will thrive and prosper, but under which all others wilt and die." Even the French and Spanish whose land had been taken over were not moving away, Duncan said; they were gradually disappearing, Representative James E. Belser of Alabama stated it quite simply when he said it was impossible to limit "the area of freedom—the area of the Anglo-Saxon race."[49]

Along with the exaltation of a particular race came a new sense of urgency and ultimately a willingness to admit the necessity of force—when the ends were so sublime, could one continually quibble about the means? Anglo-Saxons, through the expansion of England and the United States, were visibly taking over the world, and by the 1840s only a few in the United States were prepared to suggest that this was not for the good of the world. Some even began to welcome force rather than regret its necessity, George O. Sanders of Kentucky, later a leader of the political Young America group, wrote in 1844 in regard to the Texas question that "the Americans are everywhere awake. They are booted and spurred, and are panting for the contest."[50] Representative Charles G. Ferris of New York noted that America's "march is *onward, onward*." The United States was springing forward "to greatness and empire." The imagery of American expansion no longer simply emphasized "spreading"; it stressed "marching." John Reynolds of Illinois thought that the Americans by 1890 would extend through Canada and would have large cities on the Pacific and extensive commerce across that ocean: this was the "onward march of the United States to her high destiny, which no foreign nation can arrest."[51] In this mood the Americans were ready to take what the Mexicans would not sell. Many had convinced themselves that what they wanted was for the good of the world as well as themselves.

Endnotes

1. *Register of Debates*, 24th Cong., 1st sess., p. 201, Jan. 19, 1836.
2. Quoted in Thomas L. Karnes, *William Gilpin: Western Nationalist* (Austin: Universtiy of Texas Press, 1970), p. 39.
3. Horace Bushnell, *An Oration, Pronounced before the Society of Phi Beta Kappa at New Haven, on the Principles of National Greatness*, (August 15, 1837), pp. 5, 9, 11, 16.
4. Quoted in Robert F. Heizer and Alan M. Almquist, *The Other Californians: Prejudice and Discrimination under Spain, Mexico, and the United States to 1920* (Berkeley and Los Angeles: University of California Press, 1971), p. 140.
5. Richard Henry Dana, *Two Years before the Mast*, intro. Charles Warren Stoddard (1840; New York, 1899), chaps. 13 and 21.
6. Lansford Hastings, *The Emigrants' Guide to Oregon and California* (1845; reprint ed., New York, Da Capo, 1969), chaps 13 and 21.
7. George Wilkins Kendall, *Narrative of the Texan Santa Fé Expedition*, intro. Milo M. Quaife (Chicago: R. R. Donnelley & Sons, 1929), p. 512.
8. David J. Weber, ed., *Foreigners in Their Native Land: Historical Roots of the Mexican Americans* (Albuquerque: University of New Mexico Press, 1973), p. 72.
9. Waddy Thompson, *Recollections of Mexico* (New York, 1847), pp. 204, 239.
10. Ibid., pp. 6, 23, 187, 239.
11. See Gene M. Brack, *Mexico Views Manifest Destiny, 1821–1846: An Essay on the Origins of the Mexican War* (Albuquerque: University of New Mexico Press, 1975), pp. 46, 104, 120, 169–181; Glenn W. Price, *Origins of the War with Mexico: The Polk-Stockton Intrigue* (Austin: University of Texas Press, 1967), p. 17; Weber, ed., *Foreigners in Their Native Land*, pp. 59–60.
12. *Congressional Globe*, 24th Cong., 1st sess., appendix, p. 512, July 1, 1836.

13. Inaugural, Oct. 22, 1836, Houston to Anna Raguet, New Year 1837, Houston to Santa Anna, March 21, 1842, in Amelia W. Williams and Eugene C. Barker, eds., *The Writings of Sam Houston, 1813–1863*, 8 vols. (Austin: University of Texas Press, 1928–1943), I, 450, II, 31, 526–527.

14. Houston to Capt. Charles Elliot, May 13, 1843, ibid., III, 386.

15. Houston to William S. Murphy, May 6, 1844, ibid., IV, 324, 403.

16. *Mobile Register and Journal*, Jan. 4, 1842.

17. S. P. Griswold to R. W. Griswold, Sept. 29, 1842, in *Passages from the Correspondence and Other Papers of Rufus W. Griswold* (Cambridge, Mass., 1898), pp. 124–125.

18. *Congressional Globe*, 24th Cong., 1st sess., p. 394, May 23, 1836.

19. See James P. Shenton, *Robert John Walker: A Politician from Jackson to Lincoln* (New York: Columbia University Press, 1961). Also "Memoirs of Robert J. Walker by Mrs. M. W. Cook (1873)," Robert J. Walker Papers, Library of Congress, Washington, D.C.: "Robert J. Walker," *Democratic Review*, 16 (Feb. 1845): 157–164.

20. *Congressional Globe*, 28th Cong., 1st sess., appendix, p. 557, May 20 and 21, 1844.

21. *Letter of Mr. Walker, of Mississippi, Relative to the Reannexation of Texas: In Reply to the Call of the People of Carroll County, Kentucky to Communicate His Views on That Subject* (Philadelphia 1844), pp. 13–15. See also Frederick Merk, *Fruits of Propaganda in the Tyler Administration* (Cambridge, Mass.: Harvard University Press, 1971), pp. 21–26. Walker's general argument, without the racial overtones regarding Latin Americans, had been used as early as the first decade of the nineteenth century by those who maintained that the Louisiana Purchase would encourage the wide dispersal of slaves and the eventual eradication of slavery; see MacLeod, *Slavery, Race, and the American Revolution*, pp. 57–58.

22. *Congressional Globe*, 28th Cong., 1st sess., appendix p. 450, May 7, 1844. See also *Democratic Review*, 15 (July 1844): 3–16; *Southern Quarterly Review*, 6 (Oct. 1844): 483–520; *Southern Literary Messenger*, 10 (May 1844): 315–326.

23. Buchanan, speeches, June 8, 1844, Feb. 14, 1845, in Moore, ed., *Works of Buchanan*, V, 11–12, 15–16, 40–41, 100, 106.

24. *Congressional Globe*, 28th Cong., 1st sess., appendix, pp. 764, 766, 771, June 4, 1844.

25. Ibid., 28th Cong., 2nd sess., appendix, pp. 212, 313, Jan 23, 25, 1845.

26. Ibid., appendix, pp. 96–97, Jan. 14, 1845. See also ibid., appendix p. 43, Jan. 3, 1845 (James Belser of Alabama).

27. *Democratic Review*, 17 (July-Aug. 1845): 5–10.

28. See Julius W. Pratt, "The Origin of Manifest Destiny," *American Historical Review*, 32 (July 1927): 795–798, 796 (quotation); Pratt, "John L. O'Sullivan and Manifest Destiny," *New York History*, 14 (July 1933): 213–234.

29. William Howard Russell, *My Diary North and South*, ed. Fletcher Pratt (New York: Harper, 1954), p. 101.

30. *Congressional Globe*, 29th Cong., 1st sess., appendix, p. 116, Jan. 14, 1846.

31. *Speech of Mr. Walker, of Mississippi, on the Bill to Provide for Collection, Safe-Keeping and Disbursement of the Public Monies.* Senate, Jan. 21, 1849 (Baltimore, 1840).

32. *Congressional Globe*, 28th Cong., 2nd sess., appendix, p. 163, Jan. 29, 1845.

33. Ibid., 29th Cong., 1st sess., appendix, p. 177, Jan. 15, 1846.

34. Ibid., appendix, p. 143, Jan. 26, 1846.

35. *Merchants' Magazine and Commercial Review*, 14 (May 1846): 435–439.

36. Speech of July 4, 1839, quoted in Fred Somkin, *Unquiet Eagle: Memory and Desire in the Idea of American Freedom, 1815–1860* (Ithaca, N.Y.: Cornell University Press, 1967), p. 64.

37. *Congressional Globe*, 25th Cong., 2nd sess., appendix, pp. 569–570, May 17 and 22, 1838.

38. See Parker to George Bancroft, Nov. 18, 1845, in Frothingham, *Theodore Parker*, p. 382. The *Casket* (Cincinnati), April 22, 1846, said that war between England and American would be "the most direful catastrophe that could befall humanity." (p. 11)

39. Speech on the Oregon question at Faneuil Hall, Boston, Nov. 7, 1845, in *Writings and Speeches of Daniel Webster*, XVI, 314–315.

40. *Congressional Globe*, 29th Cong., 1st sess., appendix, p. 475, March 16, 1846.

41. Ibid., 28th Cong., 1st sess., appendix, pp. 239–240 (Atchison, Feb. 22, 1844); ibid., 27th Cong., 3rd sess., appendix, pp. 152, 154 (Linn, Jan. 26, 1843); ibid., 28th Cong., 1st sess., appendix, pp. 585, 588 (Choate, March 21, 1844).

42. See Sam Bass Warner, Jr., *The Private City: Philadelphia in Three periods of Its Growth* (Philadelphia: University of Pennsylvania Press, 1968), pp. 125–157; David Brion Davis, *The Slave Power Conspiracy and the Paranoid Style* (Baton Rouge: Louisiana State University Press, 1969), pp. 26–28; Seymour Martin Lipset and Earl Raab, *The Politics of Unreason: Right Wing Extremism in America, 1790–1877*, 2nd ed. (Chicago: University of Chicago Press, 1978), pp. 47–67; Ray A. Billington *The Protestant Crusade, 1800–1860: A Study of the Origins of American Nativism* (New York: Macmillan, 1938).

43. Quoted in Billington, *Protestant Crusade*, p. 205.

44. Hone to Clay, Nov. 28, 1855, in *Works of Clay*, V, 509.

45. Winthrop, "Address to the New England Society of New York, 1839," in Brainerd and Brainerd, *New England Society Orations*, I, 240, 244, 248–250.

46. Everett, reply to a toast at Derby, July 13, 1842, in Everett, *Orations and Speeches*, II, 466.

47. Webster, reply to a toast, 1843, in Brainerd and Brainerd, eds., *New England Society Orations*, I, 364–370.

48. *New York Herald*, Nov. 24, 1840, quoted in Stuart Creighton Miller, *The Unwelcome Immigrant: The American Image of the Chinese, 1785–1882* (Berkeley and Los Angeles: University of California Press, 1969), p. 96; also ibid., pp. 104–106.

49. *Congressional Globe*, 28th Cong., 2nd sess., p. 88 (Belser, Jan. 3, 1845), appendix, p. 178 (Duncan, Jan. 29, 1845).

50. Sanders to R. J. Walker, March 17, 1844, in Robert J. Walker Papers, Library of Congress.

51. *Congressional Globe*, 27th Cong., 1st sess., appendix, p. 227 (Ferris, July 17, 1841); ibid., 27th Cong., 3rd sess., appendix, p. 111 (Reynolds, Jan. 30, 1843).

Race, Expansion, and the Mexican War

Reginald Horsman

> Though the barbarians fall thick as hail, still, as their
> disposition is warlike and as the slaughter of their armies
> by the superiority of scientific warfare and the unflinching
> bravery of men disposed to peace, would teach them
> helpful lessons, the loss of a few thousand of them would
> not be so deplorable. The Mexicans will be led by this war
> to think of their weakness and inferiority.

The *Casket* (Cincinnati), June 10, 1846

✳ ✳ ✳ ✳ ✳

The contradictions which had long been implicit in America's sense of mission became explicit at the time of the Mexican War. It became obvious in these years that the United States had now rejected the idea that most other peoples of the world could share in the free government, power, and prosperity of the United States. To sow the seeds of freedom and republicanism over an ever-widening area was not enough to secure world progress, because Americans now believed that these seeds were falling on barren ground. Most peoples, they believed, lacked the innate abilities to take advantage of free institutions. Some races were doomed to permanent inferiority, some to extinction.

While faith in general human improvability was often lost, faith in the expansive power of the American branch of the Anglo-Saxon race increased. The Americans were destined to continue to increase rapidly in numbers and to spread far and wide. But if other peoples could not be instructed in the establishment of free republican states, what would happen to the population in the areas into which the American Anglo-Saxons were expanding? The Americans had two immediate racial models—the Indians and the blacks. Wherever the whites had moved in large numbers the Indians had disappeared, and it was assumed that as the American population expanded its settlements to the Pacific the Indians would be eliminated. The blacks were not disappearing but were increasing in numbers. They were surviving, argued the advocates of slavery, because they had been totally subordinated to a superior race. Even many of those who opposed slavery believed that free blacks could not survive and prosper in close proximity to the white race.

The most irrational American expansionists in the 1840s appeared to believe that the Anglo-Saxons would actually replace numerous world peoples in the course of progress. The practical realities embodied in the idea of "the survival of the fittest" were made use of in America well before they were embodied in a statement of general principle. Some Americans believed that their problems would be solved by having other races, like the Indians, melt away before the American advance. The American Anglo-Saxons would not teach or rule other peoples—they would replace them.

For some, southern slavery taught that another route to a free, prosperous society was the total subordination of the inferior to the superior race. Perhaps this could be the future pattern of the American advance. Mexicans and others might not be enslaved, but they would be subordinated to the rule of a superior people. Military success in Mexico led some Americans to argue that the United States should enforce a military, colonial-style government. They asserted that this would bring prosperity to Mexico, more power and wealth to the United States, and would hasten the time when the whole world would become progressive. The United States would become a colonial power.

This last suggestion brought a crisis in American thinking on expansion. There were many in the United States who believed that the trappings of colonialism would ruin the republic. But they did not want to bring large numbers of non-Anglo-Saxon peoples as equal citizens within the American union. They thought such inferior peoples would also ruin the republic. This dilemma quickly produced strong opposition to immediate expansion. If Americans believed that other peoples would not disappear before the American advance, if they also thought that colonialism would corrupt the nation, and if they believed that other races were incapable of participating in a free government, then opposition to a further extension of territory became their only hope of preserving a free American Anglo-Saxon republic. It meant resisting those who were now convinced that the United States should rapidly assume political control over vast new areas. Yet the expansionists were to be resisted not because this would mean the degradation of other peoples, but because the presence of other races would ruin the society created in the United States.

The general low regard in which the people of Mexico were held by the government and people of the United States helped to precipitate the outbreak of war. Since the time of the Texas Revolution the Mexicans had been repeatedly attacked in the United States as a degenerate, largely Indian race unable to control or improve the territories they owned. Only a minority of Americans felt a sense of guilt in waging war on such a people. Indeed, faced by a people considered so feeble and lacking in self-respect, Polk's administration hoped to achieve the annexation of Texas and the purchase of California without resorting to overt force.

The American minister in Mexico, Wilson Shannon, commented to Calhoun in October 1844 that "I see it is predicted in some of the papers in the U.S. that Mexico will declare war against the U.S.; there is as much probability that the Emperor of China will do so."[1] Because the Mexicans were held in contempt, it was assumed that firmness would force them to yield to American wishes. Unlike the English in Oregon, the Mexicans were neither praised as fellow members of a special race, nor respected as a potentially formidable foe. Before going to Mexico in the fall of 1845 envoy John Slidell told Secretary of State James Buchanan that he did not believe that the Mexicans would go to war: "The truth is that although I have no very exalted idea of Mexican intellect, yet I cannot imagine that any one who could by possibility be elected president, could have so small a modicum of sense as to think seriously of going to war with [the] United States."[2] Secretary of War William L. Marcy as late as July 1845 expressed the opinion that he had at no time felt that war with Mexico was probable "and do not now believe it is."[3] Secretary of State James Buchanan had a particularly low opinion of Mexican character and talents and for much of the war balked at the idea of annexing territory that contained any large number of Mexicans. In his official instructions to Slidell he asked his envoy to be as conciliatory as possible and patiently to endure any unjust reproaches. "It would be difficult," he said, "to raise a point of honor between the United States and so feeble and degraded a Power as Mexico."[4]

The general assumption in the cabinet that Mexico would not fight the United States, or at worst could easily be defeated, was reflected in public opinion throughout the country. Although a few prominent individuals, including Senator Benton, warned that Mexico would fight valiantly to protect its lands, the general assumption was that a weak and degraded Mexico could offer no real resistance to the United States forces. It was even assumed at the beginning of the war that a Mexican population oppressed by the military, the clergy, and a corrupt government would welcome the invading armies. Throughout the conflict some argued that the United States was carrying freedom to the Mexicans, and that a true regeneration of the Mexicans was to take place. But it soon became apparent that most Americans believed that the Mexicans lacked the innate ability to benefit from the opportunity to be given them by liberating American armies.

The older idea of Americans actually carrying the seeds of free institutions to Mexicans who would throw off their bondage and create a sister republic was expressed most often at the beginning of the war in the writings of America's patriotic poets. Many obviously found their inspiration in the older tradition of the widening arc of free institutions. One poet envisioned the stars in America's flag increasing "Till the world shall have welcomed their mission sublime / And the nations of earth shall be one." Another, in leaden verse, sang that "The world is wide, our views are large / We're sailing on in Freedom's barge / Our God is good and we are brave / From tyranny the world well save." The sentiment that the United States' flag would be the flag of the world when tyranny had perished was a common one, and many united in conceiving of the invasion as a war of liberation. The inhabitants of Mexico were expected to welcome the Saxons with open arms. A New York poet in May 1846 conjured up an image of Mexicans joyously shouting "The Saxons are coming, our freedom is nigh."[5]

Yet while many poets wrote in an older, idealistic tradition, some reflected the prevailing racial stereotypes of the Mexicans and added sexual overtones to the image of the liberating drive into Mexico. A poem published in Boston in June 1846 and entitled "They Wait for us" foreshadowed the views of those expansionists who later in the war argued that the American Anglo-Saxons would simply absorb and eliminate what was left of the Mexican population. Neither this poet nor the later politicians had any doubt that extinguishing the remnants of the Mexican race was to be accomplished by a union of American men and Mexican women:

> The Spanish maid, with eye of fire,
> At balmy evening turns her lyre
> And, looking to the Eastern sky,
> Awaits our Yankee chivalry
> Whose purer blood and valiant arms,
> Are fit to clasp her budding charms.
>
> The man, her mate, is sunk in sloth
> To love, his senseless heart is loth:
> The pipe and glass and tinkling lute;
> A sofa, and a dish of fruit;
> A nap, some dozen times by day;
> Sombre and sad, and never gay.[6]

The image of lazy Mexican men and available Mexican women had already been established by the accounts of American travelers. Dana, in his *Two Years before the Mast*, had written of "thriftless,

proud, extravagant" California men and of women with "a good deal of beauty" whose morality was "none of the best." Kendall, who was on the Texas-Santa Fe expedition, dismissed Mexican men in the usual fashion, but was obviously fascinated by the women. The "Anglo-Saxon traveler" entering New Mexico, he said, "feels not a little astonished at the Eve-like and scanty garments of the females he meets." He went on to describe the beauty of Mexican women and was obviously delighted that "the forms of the gentler sex obtain a roundness, a fulness, which the divinity of tight lacing never allows her votaries." His general characterization of the women was in striking contrast to his dismissal of Mexican men: the women of northern Mexico "are joyous, sociable, kind-hearted creatures almost universally, liberal to a fault, easy and naturally graceful in their manners." Kendall's distinction between Mexican men and women was commonplace in the travel narratives. "The ladies," Rufus B. Sage wrote, "present a striking contrast to their countrymen in general character, other than morals."[7] The stereotype of exotic, receptive Mexican women and lazy, inept Mexican men was to sink deep into American racial mythology.

The old rhetoric of freeing oppressed peoples and providing for a widening arc of republican institutions, which inspired some of the patriotic poets, was never entirely lacking from more reasoned arguments in the era of the Mexican War. Even the southern *De Bow's Review* published an article explaining the trouble and turmoil of the Mexicans since independence in terms of the paucity of education, the lack of a middle class, and the domination of the people by the clergy and by militarists. "All these causes," it was argued, "must be removed before Mexico can be regenerated; and though difficult, there is no reason to despair of this, for the Mexicans are possessed of great natural capacities, which only require proper cultivation and a favorable field for their development, to enable them to obtain a high grade of intelligence." Although they were not yet ready for republican institutions, this was certainly possible in time.[8]

Expressions of optimism appeared sporadically throughout the war years. John Gordon Bennett's *New York Herald* suggested in the spring of 1847, when arguing that the United States should, if necessary, retain Mexico, that "the universal Yankee nation can regenerate and disenthrall the people of Mexico in a few years."[9] In Congress such sentiments were rare, but emerged in early 1848 among some of those willing to annex the whole of Mexico. Most who favored annexation thought of an Anglo-Saxon elite controlling the Mexicans and their affairs, but there was some sentiment in favor of an older view of regeneration. Senator Sidney Breese of Illinois acknowledged the prevailing view when he said "I have taken a different view of the people of that country, and I think I see in them attributes and elements quite susceptible, by proper appliances, of high improvement."[10]

Some, in the heat and emotion of the conflict, wavered between faith in the improvability of mankind and the new racial pride. Walt Whitman, then editor of the *Brooklyn Daily Eagle*, argued that American expansion was for the good of the whole world: "We pant to see our country and its rule far-reaching," he wrote, "only inasmuch as it will take off the shackles that prevent men the even chance of being happy and good." Yet while Whitman generally attacked the Mexican government rather than the Mexican people, he could not free himself from the prevailing racial interpretation of events. "What has miserable, inefficient Mexico . . . to do," he asked," with the great mission of peopling the New World with a noble race?" General Zachary Taylor's capture of Monterey in September 1846 was welcomed as "another clinging proof of the indomitable energy of the Anglo-Saxon character." Whitman now wanted peace and the cession of large areas by Mexico. This would be for the good of mankind.[11]

Wartime rhetoric more frequently involved the brutal language of dehumanization. The *Casket*, published in Cincinnati, argued at the beginning of the war that there was "a kind of charm in the thought of 'widening the area of freedom' that is difficult to resist," but discussed the war in terms that would have been completely unacceptable fifty years before. War was to be deplored, the editor argued, but it was sometimes a help to human progress. A war between enlightened nations would shock humanity, "but an occasional conflict with barbarians must be expected." The Mexicans were dismissed as beneath contempt: "Though the barbarians fall thick as hail, still, as their disposition is warlike and as the slaughter of their armies by the superiority of scientific warfare and the unflinching bravery of men disposed to peace, would teach them healthful lessons, the loss of a few thousand of them would not be so deplorable. The Mexicans will be led by this war to think of their weakness

and inferiority."[12] Journalists were inspired by the martial spirit of the times to excesses of bombastic pride. The rampantly expansionist *Illinois State Register* in June 1846 contained the comment that the Mexicans "are reptiles in the path of progressive democracy—who, with his bigboots on is bound to travel from Portland to Patagonia—and they must either crawl or be crushed."[13] At times the brutality of thought and language more clearly foreshadows the excesses of twentieth-century racism than it echoes the dreams of Jeffersonian America.

The bitter political dispute concerning the annexation of Mexican territory was primarily an argument not about territory but about Mexicans. Although abolitionists and some Whigs at first opposed any expansion because it involved extending slavery, and though some Southerners eventually opposed expansion because they feared free areas entering the union, most Americans expected and wanted the acquisition of Mexico's sparsely populated northern provinces. Also, many on both sides of the political argument believed that the rest of Mexico was eventually destined to be dominated by the American Anglo-Saxon race. When writing or talking of the indefinite future, rather than the immediate political destiny of Mexico, publicists and politicians argued in simplistic terms of supplanting inferior Mexicans by superior Anglo-Saxons. The antiwar *American Whig Review* summarized well the thinking it said had inspired Polk and impressed the American people: "Mexico was poor, distracted, in anarchy, and almost in ruins—what could she do to stay the hand of our power, to impede the march of our greatness? We are Anglo-Saxon Americans; it was our 'destiny' to possess and to rule this continent—we were *bound* to it! We were a chosen people, and this was our allotted inheritance, and we must drive out all other nations before us!"[14]

The simplistic rhetoric sketched by the *American Whig Review* was reiterated by American politicians throughout the war years. Ignoring the practical problems of the nature of American rule over adjacent areas, they argued that Providence was arranging for an American victory over Mexico in the same manner as she had provided for the vast increase in American power, the disappearance of the Indians, and earlier victories over England. Andrew Johnson of Tennessee both during and after the war argued that Mexico was doomed as a nation; it "had reached its acme, its apex of power under her present rulers." God intended to punish the "perfidious and half-civilized" Mexico, and "the Anglo-Saxon race has been selected as the rod of her retribution."[15]

Though God might be guiding the Americans to the conquest of Mexico, he had not provided a detailed plan for American rule over the Mexican people. American victories in the Mexican War meant that there had to be a practical discussion of the future relationship of the Mexicans to the American federal system. The prophesies of a Manifest Destiny sweeping Americans onward over ever greater areas appeared to be coming true with remarkable rapidity as American armies pressed on into Mexico. To some the northern provinces now seemed only the beginning. Mexico was there for the taking, and it was assumed that the American people, American energy, and American capital could quickly transform the whole region. The stumbling block was the Mexican people. From the very beginning of the war the Whigs had much support among the Democrats in resisting the acquisition of any heavily populated Mexican areas.

The Whigs were, of course, fearful that expansion in the Southwest would mean the extension of slavery, but even after the introduction of the Wilmot Proviso raised fears in the South of large additions of free territory, the Whigs continued to express a bitter opposition to expansion. To the Whig opposition Mexico presented a potential threat to American democratic institutions. They could not accept the idea of United States colonial rule in the area, for this would endanger the republican form of government; the power of the president would be enhanced, militarism would be rife, and corruption would sap the vitals of a free America. But the Whigs also felt that the American political system would be ruined by the participation of millions of "inferior" Mexican citizens. Education was no solution, for most Americans now firmly believed in innate, not simply environmental, inferiority.

Congressional opposition to the possibility of incorporating Mexican people into the union had been expressed even before the war started. Senator Jabez W. Huntington of Connecticut argued that the American constitution was not a constitution "for people of every color, and language, and habits."[16] Democrat William Wick of Indiana said "I do not want any mixed races in our Union, nor men of any color except white, unless they be slaves. Certainly not as voters or legislators." Wick, however, said he would annex any part of the world where American

people settled. Generally the Whigs wanted caution and gradualism in expansion, whereas many Democrats were ready for swift action; but neither party wanted other races to participate in the American government.[17]

After the outbreak of war, the Whig press constantly reiterated its fears of racial amalgamation. The *Charleston Mercury* asked if "we expect to melt into our population eight millions of men, at war with us by race, by language, by religion, manners and laws?" The *Richmond Whig* melded condemnation of the Mexican population with criticism of the change in the nature of America's mission, arguing that the United States had "a mission of peace, not of war." Contiguous territory would be annexed by purchase or cession as long as there was any left, but not by conquest. Republican institutions would be threatened by the forceful occupation of an immense territory "occupied by an ignorant, heterogeneous and bigoted population." The *Cincinnati Herald* also wanted no premature, forced extension of America's bounds. What would America do, the editor asked, with eight million Mexicans "with their idol worship, heathen superstition, and degraded mongrel races." They would provide America with more than twenty new senators and over one hundred representatives. The *Augusta Daily Chronicle*, whose editor balked at swallowing Mexico, went to the heart of the matter: "It would likely prove to be a sickening mixture, consisting of such a conglomeration of Negroes and Rancheros, Mestizoes and Indians, with but a few Castilians."[18] The Whig newspapers condemned the new militarism, but they accepted the new racial theories.

When in the late summer of 1846 the conquest of New Mexico was followed by Colonel Stephen W. Kearny's proclamation announcing America's intention to annex the region, there were immediate protests. "We have far more to dread from the acquisition of the debased population who have been so summarily manufactured into American citizens," said the *Richmond Whig*, "than to hope from the extension of our territorial limits." The *Chicago Daily Journal* expressed a similar objection and commented that these "barbarians will of course be Locofocos—so would an Esquimaux Indian."[19] Consistently, Whig newspapers pointed out that if Mexico, with its "wretched population," were kept, the future alternatives were equally bad: either inferior Mexicans would be incorporated into the union, or the United States would govern by force and weaken its own institutions. The Whigs saw no need for haste in American expansion. Americans were spreading relentlessly outward. Why should the national character be sullied by the use of force or the population diluted by alien ingredients?

Militarism, the extension of slavery, and the forcible addition of a mongrel race dominated the arguments of Whig orators in Congress. The plainest exposition of the problem was given by Representative James Pollock of Pennsylvania, who argued that "the public mind has become diseased" on the subject of territorial aggrandizement. Opposing the taking of any more territory, Pollock asserted that the "Mexican provinces are filled with a population, not only degraded, but of every possible shade and variety of color and complexion, from the deep black of the negro, to the sallow white of the Mexican Indian." Were these to become citizens, he asked, or were the Americans to enslave the colored? If the latter, then nine-tenths of the population of Mexico would have to be enslaved. The Spaniards had a peculiar obstinacy, he maintained, and would fight to the last inch of ground: "Extermination and acquisition must go together. Are we prepared for this? Are we prepared to make the war a war of races, and not stay our hand until every Mexican is driven from the land of his fathers, and the Anglo-Saxon race established in the Halls of the Montezumas?"[20] Antislavery Whig Columbus Delano of Ohio condemned the Mexicans as a "sad compound of Spanish, English, Indian, and negro bloods . . . resulting, it is said, in the production of a slothful, indolent, ignorant race of beings," and even Representative Thomas Corwin of Ohio, in his famous speech attacking American aggression, talked of the "half-savage, half-civilized race" of Mexico.[21] The Whigs regularly emphasized what aggression was doing to the United States, not what aggression was doing to Mexico.

The Democrats could agree neither on how much of Mexico should be taken nor on whether the United States should annex territory inhabited by large numbers of Mexicans. Nearly all could agree, however, that Mexicans could not be admitted as equal citizens within the American republic. At the beginning of the war the influential *Democratic Review* said that no period of tutelage would prepare the Mexicans for participation in a free republican system. "*Race*," wrote the author, "is the key to much that seems obscure in the history

of nations," and it explained Mexico's miseries. The largely Indian or half-breed Mexican population lacked the characteristics necessary for the creation and support of free institutions. Throughout the world it was the same—"the whiter race ruling the less white, through all the gradations of color, from the fairest European down to the darkest African." There was no hope for representative, democratic rule in Mexico.[22]

In the cabinet Secretary of State James Buchanan often expressed his fear of the admission of any large number of Mexicans to the union. He argued in the spring of 1847 that the United States should obtain Upper and Lower California, New Mexico, and a Rio Grande boundary, and that the safest way of extending the republic was by the acquisition of areas colonized almost exclusively by Americans. The acquisition of lands southward to the Sierra Madre mountains would raise the question of slavery, but more importantly it would raise basic questions about the nature of the population: "How should we govern the mongrel race which inhabits it? Could we admit them to seats in our Senate & House of Representatives? Are they capable of Self Government as States of this Confederacy?"[23] In the Senate John C. Calhoun strongly opposed expansion into Mexico: "Can we incorporate a people so dissimilar from us in every respect—so little qualified for free and popular government without certain destruction to our political institutions?"[24] Calhoun was supported by that old warhorse Lewis Cass of Michigan, who said, "We do not want the people of Mexico, either as citizens or subjects. All we want is a portion of territory, which, they nominally hold, generally uninhabited, or, where inhabited at all, sparsely so, and with a population, which would soon recede, or identify itself with ours."[25]

Within a year Cass was to modify his stance against expansion into Mexico, but Calhoun remained adamant. In a famous speech in January 1848 Calhoun defended the American government as a government of the white race. In his eagerness to exalt the Caucasians he was even prepared to acknowledge the major role of non-Anglo-Saxon white races. "We have never dreamt of incorporating into our Union any but the Caucasian race—the free white race." To incorporate Mexico would be to incorporate a race largely Indian. "Ours, sir, is the Government of a white race," thundered Calhoun. Although the largest portion of the human family was composed of colored races, he said, these races had never been "found equal to the establishment of free popular government." He admitted that the Mexicans had "Castilian blood in their veins—the old Gothic, quite equal to the Anglo-Saxon in many respects—in some respects superior," but most of the population were either completely or part Indian, "impure races, not as good as the Cherokees or Choctaws." Calhoun specifically rejected the idea that the United States had a mission to spread civil and religious liberty throughout the American continent and the world. Such a mission was impractical because most people lacked the ability to sustain free government.[26]

The fullest discussion of the racial dangers that would be created by Mexican annexation erupted during the late summer of 1847 as an increasing number of Democratic publications discussed the need to annex the whole of Mexico, and, if necessary, to rule it as a colonial possession. There were strong rumors that Polk and his cabinet were preparing at least to annex a considerable area south of the Rio Grande, in addition to New Mexico and California. Late in September Daniel Webster, while bitterly attacking the Mexican War as a Democratic war of aggression, expressed the same disillusionment with the concept of universal mission as Calhoun. Webster announced that he did not want more territory even if it were free territory. He pitied the people of Mexico, he said, but "I should pity them more if they appeared to me to have sense enough to understand the misery of their own condition." Further expansion ran the risk of despotic government in the United States, as it extended the country beyond the area peopled by inhabitants of similar character. Webster trusted that free institutions would eventually spread all over the world, but he said he was "by no means sure that all people are fit for them."[27]

Throughout the winter of 1847–48 the congressional Whigs pointed out the impossibility of integrating the Mexican population within the United States as citizens. Speaker after speaker attacked the Mexicans as unassimilable. In the Senate John M. Clayton of Delaware scoffed at the idea of incorporating eight million people "of a race totally different from ourselves." In the House Jacob Collamer of Vermont said "we should destroy our own nationality by such an act. We shall cease to be the people that we were; we cease to be the Saxon Americanized. . . . We shall take in seven or eight millions of people in no way homogenous, incapable of being

reduced to common feelings, common interests, common desires with us." Representative Edward C. Cabell of Florida pointed out that "if we annex the land, we must take the *population* along with it. And shall we, . . . by an act of Congress, convert the black, white, red, mongrel, miserable population of Mexico—the Mexicans, Indians, Mulattoes, Mestizos, Chinos, Zambos, Quinteros—into free and enlightened American citizens, entitled to all the privileges which we enjoy?"[28] Whatever the likelihood of replacing Mexicans by Anglo-Saxons in the future, most Americans realized that in practical terms the annexation of the whole of Mexico would mean either that eight million Mexicans would become American citizens or that they would be ruled as colonial subjects.

Even those who in 1847 and 1848 argued that all of Mexico should be annexed gave practically no support to the idea of allowing the Mexicans to enter the union as equal citizens. Some thought that education might ultimately make this possible, but most envisioned a military occupation of the country, an enthusiastic encouragement of commerce and trade with the United States, a rapid influx of American Anglo-Saxons attracted by an enlightened new order and increasing prosperity, a sharp reduction in the Mexican population, and the eventual absorption of a country that had been "Saxonized." The essential ingredients in this general scheme were that Mexico in the immediate future would be administered by the army as a colonial possession, and that the amalgamation of Mexico into the union would be made possible by reducing the Mexican population and gradually replacing Mexicans by Anglo-Saxons.

Most of the arguments claiming that large areas of Mexico could safely be annexed were based on the twin assumptions that the largely Indian Mexicans would fade away, and that the American Anglo-Saxons were destined to outbreed the whole world. "The Mexicans are no better than Indians," said Sam Houston in New York in 1848, "and I see no reason why we should not go in the same course now, and take their land."[29] Two New York senators found no difficulty in envisaging the disappearance of alien peoples before the advance of civilization. John A. Dix thought that the populations of California and New Mexico either would be overwhelmed and eliminated or they would be driven into ever narrower areas. As their usual sources of subsistence diminished, they would ultimately become extinct "by force of an invincible law." Daniel S. Dickinson said that a majority of the Mexican people belonged "to the fated aboriginal races, who can neither uphold government or be restrained by it; who flourish only amid the haunts of savage indolence, and perish under, if they do not recede before, the influences of civilization. Like their doomed brethren, who were once spread over the several States of the Union, they are destined, by laws above human agency, to give way to a stronger race from this continent or another."[30]

Articles in the *Democratic Review* sometimes contradicted each other on the question of just how much of Mexico could safely be taken, but they agreed on the gradual replacement of Mexicans by Anglo-Saxons. Mexico was eventually to be absorbed as part of that movement of the Germanic tribes which had thrust into the Roman Empire, "and which is destined to carry back to Asia the refinement of art and the influences of Christianity, gathered in a journey of two thousand years around the world, from east to west." Was this torrent, which had surged onward for two thousand years, to be "stopped by the theories of the Whig party, the voice of Daniel Webster or the frown of Santa Anna?" The Texas Revolution had been inevitable because the "very virtues of the Anglo-Saxon race made their political union with the degraded Mexican-Spanish impossible."[31] When in the fall of 1847 the magazine defended the occupation of Mexico by an American army, it suggested that the army would initially help instill the commercial principle by supporting free trade and the security of property, but it would eventually provide for a racial change. Soldiers, as they were discharged, would usually remain in Mexico "and gradually infusing vigor into the race, regenerate the whole nation."[32] Earlier the journal had suggested that simple military occupation might be too expensive, but that the Anglo-Saxons would solve the problem by colonization. It did not matter whether a treaty brought more or less territory—it would all be taken in time, "piece by piece."[33]

Although Polk disliked the peace treaty agreed to by Nicholas P. Trist in Mexico, his decision to submit it to Congress was a sensible one. Any attempt to continue the war to obtain substantial areas beyond the Rio Grande would have caused splits among the Democrats as well as incensed the Whig opposition. Polk admitted he would rather have settled for a boundary at the Sierra Madre mountains than at the Rio Grande, but also acknowledged that with Congress and the country reluctant to fight to obtain more territory from Mexico, Congress would probably not give him the men or the money to continue the war. Within the cabinet only Robert J. Walker actively wanted to continue the war to obtain large parts of Mexico, for he was the only member willing to accept a United States colonial domination over the whole area. Buchanan had softened enough to want a Sierra Madre rather than a Rio Grande boundary, but he did not want to annex the most populous areas of Mexico.[34] The Trist Treaty, with a Rio Grande boundary, New Mexico, and California was the most acceptable to the majority of Americans as it obtained the largest possible area from Mexico with the least number of Mexicans. It was not the problem of the extension of slavery but the Hobson's choice of racial amalgamation or imperial dominion that finally frustrated those who were prepared to take most or all of Mexico.

Press comment on the treaty itself echoed the racial arguments of the late stages of the war. The Whigs who wished to assail Polk attacked his militarism, as well as his bringing unsuitable people into the union by annexing the northern provinces of Mexico. The *Richmond Palladium* of Indiana criticized Polk for sacrificing more than twenty thousand lives and spending more than one hundred million dollars "to get hundreds of thousands of a mongrel and debased population upon which to found a representation in Congress."[35] The *American Whig Review* thought the acquisitions would prove to be "the bane and the curse of the country. We may, by these acquisitions of vast regions of territory beyond our lines, with the ignorant and degraded population that belongs to them, convert the Republic which our fathers created for us into an Empire, and our unpretending National Government into a great power bearing imperial sway over distant provinces and dependencies."[36]

While the Whigs attacked the treaty for the population it had brought into the union, many Democrats prided themselves on obtaining a great dominion comparatively unencumbered by inferior peoples. The *Louisville Democrat* supported the treaty because the United States had obtained "not the best boundary, but all the territory of value that we can get without taking the people. The people of the settled parts of Mexico are a negative quantity. We fear the land, minus the people, is not worth much. We think all Mexico will fall, piece by piece, into this government; but then it must first be settled by a different population, and the union effected by other means than the sword."[37] Some Americans persisted in the belief that seven or eight million Mexicans would somehow disappear or be completely overwhelmed by the all-encompassing American-Anglo-Saxon people.

The total Mexican defeat convinced the Americans that their original judgment of the Mexican race had been correct. The *Southern Quarterly Review* in surveying the causes of the war wrote of the discord that had long existed between the United States and Mexico because of Mexican hatred for their northern neighbor, a hatred "springing from our acknowledged superiority in every thing."[38] Several years later, in 1853, Senator John Clayton spoke of the difficulties this disparity created for further American expansion. He was quite willing to annex more land if, after filling what was available, the United States could honorably obtain contiguous territory (presumably Canada) inhabited by men of our own race and class; but he saw insuperable objections to the future acquisition of Mexico. He did not want imperialism, he did not want an extension of slavery, and he could not quite believe that the numerous Mexican population would simply fade away before Anglo-Saxon pressure. To take Mexico would be to take her people as citizens: "Yes! Aztecs, Creoles, Half-breeds, Quadroons, Samboes, and I know not what else—'ring-streaked and speckled'—all will come in, and, instead of our governing them, they, by their votes, will govern us."[39]

When, in the months after the conclusion of the Mexican War, the possibility arose of intervening in the Mexican province of Yucatan, opponents of intervention again cast their arguments in racial terms. The insurrection in that province brought fears in the American cabinet of English intervention in an area considered essential for future American communications from the Atlantic to the Pacific. Robert J. Walker, thinking primarily of its commercial importance, was in favor of the ultimate annexation of the region to the United States. President Polk was prepared to support him rather than have the area fall into the hands of England, and in April 1848 the president asked Congress to provide help to stop the area's becoming a European colony. This would also "rescue the white race from extermination or expulsion from their country."[40] Discussions of the question were cast in terms of

an uprising of barbarous Mexican Indians against a white ruling class. Representative Joseph R. Ingersoll of Pennsylvania, a Whig, defended intervention on the grounds that the United States would merely be providing aid against "barbarians," but this line of argument met resistance. Another Whig, Joseph M. Root of Ohio, reiterated what had so often been said in previous years—the Spanish-Mexican ruling class were themselves little better than Indians. He thought that the Spaniards in Yucatan "were about equal to the Mexicans; and if there was anything under the face of heaven meaner than a Mexican 'greaser' he should like to know it."[41] His general sympathies, he said, were in favor of the white race, but he would have to be shown better examples of the race than the Spaniards if his feelings were to be stirred.

The United States did not intervene in Yucatan, although the secretary of the navy pointed out in his annual report that American ships had helped white inhabitants fleeing from "a war of races."[42] *General* intervention in Yucatan, however desirable commercially, posed the same problems for the United States as annexation of large areas of Mexico south of the Rio Grande: there were too many nonwhite, non-Anglo-Saxon people.

After the Mexican War it was clear that if American expansion was to continue into populous areas it either had to be through colonial rule or economic penetration. The American republican government was not a government for all races and all colors—federalism had its limits. Yet Americans were determined to participate fully in shaping the economic future not only of the American continents but also of the world. A search for personal and national wealth was put in terms of world progress under the leadership of a supreme race. In thrusting into the Pacific, Americans revived arguments that the American advance would bring freedom and civilization to all peoples; but the reality of attitudes toward neighboring peoples in the years of the Mexican War made nonsense of the claims that the American penetration of Asia was intimately connected with the regeneration of other races.

Endnotes

1. Shannon to Calhoun, Oct. 29, 1844, "Correspondence of John C. Calhoun," ed. by Franklin Jameson, American Historical Association, Annual Report, 1899, II (Washington, D.C., 1900), 981.

2. Slidell to Buchanan, Sept. 25, 1845, in John B. Moore, ed., *The Works of James Buchanan*, 12 vols. (1908–1911; reprint ed., New York: Antiquarian Press, 1960), VI, 264.

3. Marcy to Prosper Wetmore, July 6, 1845, June 13, 1846, in William L. Marcy Papers, Library of Congress.

4. Buchanan to Slidell, Nov. 10, 1845, in Moore, ed., *Works of Buchanan*, VI, 305.

5. William M'Carty, comp., *National Songs, Ballads, and Other Patriotic Poetry, Chiefly Relating to the War of 1846* (Philadelphia, 1846), pp. 12, 22, 37.

6. Ibid., p. 45.

7. Dana, *Two Years before the Mast*, intro. Stoddard, chap. 21; Kendall, *Narrative of the Texan Santa Fé Expedition* (1929 ed.), pp. 428, 432–433; Weber, ed., *Foreigners in Their Native Land*, p. 174.

8. *De Bow's Review*, 1 (Feb. 1846): 130–131; also ibid., 2 (July 1846): 21–24.

9. *New York Herald*, May 15, 1847, quoted in John D. P. Fuller, *The Movement for the Acquisition of All Mexico, 1846–1848* (Baltimore: Johns Hopkins University Press, 1936), pp. 62–63.

10. *Congressional Globe*, 30th Cong., 1st sess., appendix, p. 349, Feb. 14, 1848.

11. *Brooklyn Daily Eagle*, June 6, July 7, Oct. 13, 1846, Dec. 2, 1847, in Walt Whitman, *The Gathering of the Forces*, ed. by Cleveland Rodgers and John Black, 2 vols. (New York: G. P. Putnam's Sons, 1920), I, 242–244, 246–248, 364–266. See also Kramer, *Prophetic Tradition in American Poetry*, pp. 60–62.

12. *Casket*, May 13, 1846, p. 37, June 10, 1846, p. 69.

13. *Illinois State Register*, July 17, 1846, quoted in Fuller, *Movement for the Acquisition of All Mexico*, p. 41.

14. *American Whig Review*, 4 (July 1846): 14.

15. LeRoy P. Graf and Ralph W. Haskins, eds., *The Papers of Andrew Johnson* (Knoxville: University of Tennessee Press, 1967–), I 312, 366, 456, May 29–30, 1846, Jan. 5, 1847, Aug. 2, 1848.

16. *Congressional Globe*, 28th Cong., 2nd sess., appendix p. 397, Feb. 21 and 22, 1845; see also ibid., pp. 353, 354.

17. Ibid., 29th Cong., 1st sess., appendix, p. 201, Jan. 30, 1846; also ibid., p. 184. There is an extensive discussion of Whig opposition to the war in John H. Schroeder, *Mr. Polk's War: American Opposition and Dissent, 1846–1848* (Madison: University of Wisconsin Press, 1973).

18. *Charleston Mercury*, May 25, 1846; *Richmond Whig*, June 10, 1846; *Cincinnati Herald and Philanthropist*, June 17, 1846; *Augusta Daily Chronicle and Sentinel*, July 31, 1846. I would like to thank Professor John H. Schroeder of the University of Wisconsin-Milwaukee for allowing me to use his extensive collection of extracts from Whig newspapers.

19. *Richmond Whig*, Oct. 9, 1846; *Chicago Daily Journal*, Oct. 30, 1846.

20. *Congressional Globe*, 29th Cong., 2nd sess., appendix, pp. 131, 133, Jan. 26, 1847; also ibid., p. 339.

21. Ibid., p. 281, Feb. 2, 1847; Joseph Morrow, *Life and Speeches of Thomas Corwin* (Cincinnati, 1896), p. 289, Feb. 11, 1847.

22. *Democratic Review*, 18 (June 1846): 434, 477.

23. Buchanan to General James Shields, April 23, 1847, in Moore, ed., *Works of Buchanan*, VII, 286–287.

24. *Congressional Globe*, 29th Cong., 2nd sess., appendix, p. 327, Feb. 9, 1847.

25. Ibid., p. 191, Feb. 10, 1847.

26. Ibid., 30th Cong., 1st sess., pp. 98–99, Jan. 4, 1848.

27. Webster, speech on the Mexican War, Springfield, Mass., Sept. 29, 1847, in *Writings and Speeches of Daniel Webster*, XVI, 351, 360.

28. *Congressional Globe*, 30th Cong., 1st sess. p. 162 (Clayton, Jan. 12, 1848); p. 283 (Collamer, Feb. 1, 1848); p. 299 (Bell, Feb. 34, 1848); p. 429 (Cabell, March 4, 1848).

29. Williams and Barker *Writings of Sam Houston*, V, 34–35.

30. *Congressional Globe*, 30th Cong., 1st sess., p. 256 (Dix, Jan. 26, 1848); p. 158 (Dickinson, Jan. 12, 1848).

31. *Democratic Review*, 20 (Feb. 1847): 99–100.

32. Ibid., 21 (Nov. 1847): 381–382, 388–390.

33. Ibid., 20 (June 1847): 484–485; 21 (Oct. 1847): 291.

34. James K. Polk, *The Diary of James K. Polk during His Presidency, 1845–1849*, ed. Milo M. Quaife, 4 vols. (Chicago: A. C. McClurg, 1910), II, 159–161, 162–165, 217, 276–277, 347–349.

35. *Richmond Palladium*, March 8, 1848.

36. *American Whig Review*, 7 (May 1848): 448.

37. *Louisville Democrat*, March 9, 1948, quoted in Merk, *Manifest Destiny and Mission*, pp. 151–152.

38. *Southern Quarterly Review*, 18 (Nov. 1850): 428.

39. *Congressional Globe*, 32nd Cong., 3rd sess., appendix, p. 270, March 15, 1853.

40. Polk to Senate and House of Representatives, April 29, 1848, in *Congressional Globe*, 30th Cong., 1st sess, p. 709; Quaife, ed., *Diary of Polk*, III, 444–445.

41. *Congressional Globe*, 30th Cong., 1st sess., p. 711 (Ingersoll, April 29, 1848); p. 712 (Root, April 29, 1848).

42. Report of the Secretary of the Navy, Dec. 4, 1848, ibid., 30th Cong., 2nd sess., appendix, p. 23.

SECTION FIVE

THE ROAD TO CIVIL WAR

CHAPTER 7

Speech on the Repeal of the Missouri Compromise

Abraham Lincoln
October 16, 1854

Peoria, Illinois

The repeal of the Missouri Compromise, and the propriety of its restoration, constitute the subject of what I am about to say.

As I desire to present my own connected view of this subject, my remarks will not be, specifically, an answer to Judge Douglas; yet, as I proceed, the main points he has presented will arise, and will receive such respectful attention as I may be able to give them.

I wish further to say, that I do not propose to question the patriotism, or to assail the motives of any man, or class of men; but rather to strictly confine myself to the naked merits of the question.

I also wish to be no less than National in all the positions I may take; and whenever I take ground which others have thought, or may think, narrow, sectional, and dangerous to the Union, I hope to give a reason, which will appear sufficient, at least to some, why I think differently.

And, as this subject is no other, than part and parcel of the larger general question of domestic-slavery, I wish to MAKE and to KEEP the distinction between the EXISTING institution, and the EXTENSION of it, so broad, and so clear, that no honest man can misunderstand me, and no dishonest one, successfully misrepresent me.

In order to [get?] a clear understanding of what the Missouri Compromise is, a short history of the preceding kindred subjects will perhaps be proper. When we established our independence, we did not own, or claim, the country to which this compromise applies. Indeed, strictly speaking, the confederacy then owned no country at all; the States respectively owned the country within their limits; and some of them owned territory beyond their strict State limits. Virginia thus owned the North-Western territory— the country out of which the principal part of Ohio, all Indiana, all Illinois, all Michigan and all Wisconsin, have since been formed. She also owned (perhaps within her then limits) what has since been formed into the State of Kentucky. North Carolina thus owned what is now the State of Tennessee; and South Carolina and Georgia, in separate parts, owned what are now Mississippi and Alabama. Connecticut, I think, owned the little remaining part of Ohio—being the same where they now send Giddings to Congress, and beat all creation at making cheese. These territories, together with the States themselves, constituted all the country over which the confederacy then claimed any sort of jurisdiction. We were then living under the Articles of Confederation, which were superceded by the Constitution several years afterwards. The question of ceding these territories to the general government was set on foot. Mr. Jefferson, the author of the Declaration of Independence, and otherwise a chief actor in the Revolution; then a delegate in Congress; afterwards twice President; who was, is, and perhaps will continue to be, the most distinguished politician of our history; a Virginian by birth and continued residence, and withal, a slave-holder; conceived the idea of taking that occasion, to prevent slavery ever going into the north-western territory. He prevailed on the Virginia legislature to adopt his views, and to cede the territory, making the prohibition of slavery therein, a condition of the deed. Congress accepted the cession, with the condition; and in the first Ordinance (which the acts of Congress were then called) for the government of the territory, provided that slavery should never be permitted therein. This is the famed ordinance of '87 so often spoken of. Thenceforward, for sixty-one years, and until in 1848, the last scrap of this territory came into the Union as the State of Wisconsin, all parties acted in quiet obedience to this ordinance. It is now what Jefferson foresaw and intended—the happy home of teeming millions of free, white, prosperous people, and no slave amongst them.

Thus, with the author of the Declaration of Independence, the policy of prohibiting slavery in new territory originated. Thus, away back of the Constitution, in the pure fresh, free breath of the revolution, the State of Virginia, and the National Congress put that policy in practice. —Thus, through sixty odd of the best years of the republic did that policy steadily work to its great and beneficent end. And thus, in those five states, and five millions of free, enterprising people, we have before us the rich fruits of this policy. But *now* new light breaks upon us. —Now Congress declares this ought never to have been; and the like of it, must never be again. —The sacred right of self-government is grossly violated by it! We even find some men, who drew their first breath, and every other breath of their lives, under this very restriction, now live in dread of absolute suffocation, if they should be restricted in the "sacred right" of taking slaves to Nebraska. That *perfect* liberty they sigh for—the liberty of making slaves of other people—Jefferson never thought of; their own father never thought of; they never thought of themselves, a year ago. How fortunate for them, they did not sooner become sensible of their great misery! Oh, how difficult it is to treat with respect, such assaults upon all we have ever really held sacred!

But to return to history. In 1803 we purchased what was then called Louisiana, of France. It included the now states of Louisiana, Arkansas, Missouri, and Iowa; also the territory of Minnesota, and the present bone of contention, Kansas and Nebraska. Slavery already existed among the French at New Orleans; and to some extent at St. Louis. In 1812 Louisiana came into the Union as a slave state, without controversy. In 1818 or '19, Missouri showed signs of a wish to come in with slavery. This was resisted by northern members of Congress;

and thus began the first great slavery agitation in the nation. This controversy lasted several months, and became very angry and exciting; the House of Representatives voting steadily for the prohibition of slavery in Missouri, and the Senate voting as steadily against it. Threats of breaking up the Union were freely made; and the ablest public men of the day became seriously alarmed. At length a compromise was made, in which, like all compromises, both sides yielded something. It was a law passed on the 6th day of March, 1820, providing that Missouri might come into the Union *with*slavery, but that in all the remaining part of the territory purchased of France, which lies north of 36 degrees and 30 minutes north latitude, slavery should never be permitted. This provision of law, *is the Missouri Compromise*. In excluding slavery north of the line, the same language is employed as in the Ordinance of '87. It directly applied to Iowa, Minnesota, and to the present bone of contention, Kansas and Nebraska. Whether there should or should not, be slavery south of that line, nothing was said in the law; but Arkansas constituted the principal remaining part, south of the line; and it has since been admitted as a slave state without serious controversy. More recently, Iowa, north of the line, came in as a free state without controversy. Still later, Minnesota, north of the line, had a territorial organization without controversy. Texas principally south of the line, and West of Arkansas; though originally within the purchase from France, had, in 1819, been traded off to Spain, in our treaty for the acquisition of Florida. It had thus become a part of Mexico. Mexico revolutionized and became independent of Spain. American citizens began settling rapidly, with their slaves in the southern part of Texas. Soon they revolutionized against Mexico, and established an independent government of their own, adopting a constitution, with slavery, strongly resembling the constitutions of our slave states. By still another rapid move, Texas, claiming a boundary much further West, than when we parted with her in 1819, was brought back to the United States, and admitted into the Union as a slave state. There then was little or no settlement in the northern part of Texas, a considerable portion of which lay north of the Missouri line; and in the resolutions admitting her into the Union, the Missouri restriction was expressly extended westward across her territory. This was in 1845, only nine years ago.

Thus originated the Missouri Compromise; and thus has it been respected down to 1845. —And even four years later, in 1849, our distinguished Senator, in a public address, held the following language in relation to it:

> "The Missouri Compromise had been in practical operation for about a quarter of a century, and had received the sanction and approbation of men of all parties in every section of the Union. It had allayed all sectional jealousies and irritations growing out of this vexed question, and harmonized and tranquilized the whole country. It had given to Henry Clay, as its prominent champion, the proud sobriquet of the *"Great Pacificator,"* and by that title and for that service, his political friends had repeatedly appealed to the people to rally under his standard, as a presidential candidate, as the man who had exhibited the patriotism and the power to suppress, an unholy and treasonable agitation, and preserve the Union. He was not aware that any man or any party from any section of the Union, had ever urged as an objection to Mr. Clay, that he was the great champion of the Missouri Compromise. On the contrary, the effort was made by the opponents of Mr. Clay, to prove that he was not entitled to the exclusive merit of that great patriotic measure, and that the honor was equally due to others as well as to him, for securing its adoption—that it had its origin in the hearts of all patriotic men, who desired to preserve and perpetuate the blessings of our glorious Union—an origin akin that of the Constitution of the United States, conceived in the same spirit of fraternal affection, and calculated to remove forever, the only danger, which seemed to threaten, at some distant day, to sever the social bond of union. All the evidences of public opinion at that day, seemed to indicate that this Compromise had been canonized in the hearts of the American people, as a sacred thing which no ruthless hand would ever be reckless enough to disturb."

I do not read this extract to involve Judge Douglas in an inconsistency—If he afterwards thought he had been wrong, it was right for him to change—I bring this forward merely to show the high estimate placed on the Missouri Compromise by all parties up to so late as the year 1849.

But, going back a little, in point of time, our war with Mexico broke out in 1846. When Congress was about adjourning that session, President Polk asked them to place two millions of dollars under his control, to be used by him in the recess, if found practicable and expedient, in negotiating a treaty of peace with Mexico, and acquiring some part of her territory. A bill was duly got up, for the purpose, and was progressing swimmingly, in the House of Representatives, when a member by the name of David Wilmot, a democrat from Pennsylvania, moved as an amendment "Provided that in any territory thus acquired, there shall never be slavery."

This is the origin of the far-famed "Wilmot Proviso." It created a great flutter; but it stuck like wax, was voted into the bill, and the bill passed with it through the House. The Senate, however, adjourned without final action on it and so both appropriation and proviso were lost, for the time. —The war continued, and at the next session, the President renewed his request for the appropriation, enlarging the amount, I think, to three million. Again came the proviso; and defeated the measure. Congress adjourned again, and the war went on. In Dec. 1847, the new congress assembled. —I was in the lower House that term. The "Wilmot Proviso" or the principle of it, was constantly coming up in some shape or other, and I think I may venture to say I voted for it at least forty times; during the short term I was there. The Senate, however, held it in check, and it never became law. In the spring of 1848 a treaty of peace was made with Mexico; by which we obtained that portion of her country which now constitutes the territories of New Mexico and Utah, and the now state of California. By this treaty the Wilmot Proviso was defeated, as so far as it was intended to be a condition of the acquisition of territory. Its friends, however, were still determined to find some way to restrain slavery from getting into the new country. This new acquisition lay directly West of our old purchase from France, and extended west to the Pacific Ocean—and was so situated that if the Missouri line should be extended straight west, the new country would be divided by such extended line, leaving some north and some south of it. On Judge Douglas' motion a bill, or provision of a bill, passed the Senate to so extend the Missouri line. The Proviso men in the House, including myself, voted it down, because by implication, it gave up the Southern part to slavery, while we were bent on having it *all* free.

In the fall of 1848 the gold mines were discovered in California. This attracted people to it with unprecedented rapidity, so that on, or soon after, the meeting of the new congress in Dec., 1849, she already had a population of nearly a hundred thousand, had called a convention, formed a state constitution, excluding slavery, and was knocking for admission into the Union. —The Proviso men, of course were for letting her in, but the Senate, always true to the other side would not consent to her admission. And there California stood, kept *out* of the Union, because she would not let slavery *into* her borders. Under all the circumstances perhaps this was not wrong. There were other points of dispute, connected with the general question of slavery, which equally needed adjustment. The South clamored for a more efficient fugitive slave law. The North clamored for the abolition of a peculiar species of slave trade in the District of Columbia, in connection with which, in view from the windows of the capitol, a sort of negro-livery stable, where droves of negroes were collected, temporarily kept, and finally taken to Southern markets, precisely like droves of horses, had been openly maintained for fifty years. Utah and New Mexico needed territorial governments; and whether slavery should or should not be prohibited within them, was another question. The indefinite Western boundary of Texas was to be settled. She was received a slave state; and consequently the farther West the slavery men could push her boundary, the more slave country they secured. And the farther East the slavery opponents could thrust the boundary back, the less slave ground was secured. Thus this was just as clearly a slavery question as any of the others.

These points all needed adjustment; and they were all held up, perhaps wisely, to make them help to adjust one another. The Union, now, as in 1820, was thought to be in danger; and devotion to the Union rightfully inclined men to yield somewhat, in points where nothing else could have so inclined them. A compromise was finally effected. The South got their new fugitive-slave law; and the North got California, (the far best part of our acquisition from Mexico,) as a free State. The south got a provision that New Mexico and Utah, *when admitted as States*, may come in *with* or *without* slavery as they may then choose; and the North got the slave-trade abolished in the District of Columbia. The North got the western boundary of Texas, thence further back eastward than the south desired; but, in turn, they gave Texas ten millions of dollars, with which to pay her old debts. This is the compromise of 1850.

Preceding the presidential election of 1852, each of the great political parties, democrats and whigs, met in convention, and adopted resolutions endorsing the compromise of '50; as a "finality," a final settlement, so far as these parties could make it so, of all slavery agitation. Previous to this, in 1851, the Illinois Legislature had indorsed it.

During this long period of time Nebraska had remained, substantially an uninhabited country, but now emigration to, and settlement within it began to take place. It is about one third as large as the present United States, and its importance so long overlooked, begins to come into view. The restriction of slavery by the Missouri Compromise directly applies to it; in fact, was first made, and has since been maintained, expressly for it. In 1853, a bill to give it a territorial government passed the House of Representatives, and, in the hands of Judge Douglas, failed of passing the Senate only for want of time. This bill contained no repeal of the Missouri Compromise. Indeed, when it was assailed because it did not contain such repeal, Judge Douglas defended it in its existing form. On January 4th, 1854, Judge Douglas introduces a new bill to give Nebraska territorial government. He accompanies this bill with a report, in which last, he expressly recommends that the Missouri Compromise shall neither be affirmed nor repealed.

Before long the bill is so modified as to make two territories instead of one; calling the southern one Kansas.

Also, about a month after the introduction of the bill, on the judge's own motion, it is so amended as to declare the Missouri Compromise inoperative and void; and, substantially, that the people who go and settle there may establish slavery, or exclude it, as they may see fit. In this shape the bill passed both branches of congress, and became a law.

This is the *repeal* of the Missouri Compromise. The foregoing history may not be precisely accurate in every particular; but I am sure it is sufficiently so, for all the uses I shall attempt to make of it, and in it, we have before us, the chief material enabling us to correctly judge whether the repeal of the Missouri Compromise is right or wrong.

I think, and shall try to show, that it is wrong; wrong in its direct effect, letting slavery into Kansas and Nebraska—and wrong in its prospective principle, allowing it to spread to every other part of the wide world, where men can be found inclined to take it.

This *declared* indifference, but as I must think, covert *real zeal* for the spread of slavery, I can not but hate. I hate it because of the monstrous injustice of slavery itself. I hate it because it deprives our republican example of its just influence in the world—enables the enemies of free institutions, with plausibility, to taunt us as hypocrites—causes the real friends of freedom to doubt our sincerity, and especially because it forces so many really good men amongst ourselves into an open war with the very fundamental principles of civil liberty—criticizing the Declaration of Independence, and insisting that there is no right principle of action but *self-interest.*

Before proceeding, let me say I think I have no prejudice against the Southern people. They are just what we would be in their situation. If slavery did not now exist amongst them, they would not introduce it. If it did now exist amongst us, we should not instantly give it up. —This I believe of the masses north and south. —Doubtless there are individuals on both sides, who would not hold slaves under any circumstances; and others who would gladly introduce slavery anew, if it were out of existence. We know that some southern men do free their slaves, go north, and become tip-top abolitionists; while some northern ones go south, and become most cruel slave-masters.

When southern people tell us they are no more responsible for the origin of slavery, than we; I acknowledge the fact. When it is said that the institution exists; and that it is very difficult to get rid of it, in any satisfactory way, I can understand and appreciate the saying. I surely will not blame them for not doing what I should not know how to do myself. If all earthly power were given me, I should not know what to do, as to the existing institution. My first impulse would be to free all the slaves, and send them to Liberia, —to their own native land. But a moment's reflection would convince me, that whatever of high hope, (as I think there is) there may be in this, in the long run, its sudden execution is impossible. If they were all landed there in a day, they would all perish in the next ten days; and there are not surplus shipping and surplus money enough in the world to carry them there in many times ten days. What then? Free them all, and keep them among us as underlings? Is it quite certain that this betters their condition? I think I would not hold one in slavery, at any rate; yet the point is not clear enough for me to denounce people upon. What next? Free them, and make them politically and socially, our equals? My own feelings will not admit of this; and if mine would, we well know that those of the great mass of white people will not. Whether this feeling accords with justice and sound judgment, is not the sole question, if indeed, it is any part of it. A universal feeling, whether well or ill-founded, can not be safely disregarded. We can

not, then, make them equals. It does seem to me that systems of gradual emancipation might be adopted; but for their tardiness in this, I will not undertake to judge our brethren of the south.

When they remind us of their constitutional rights, I acknowledge them, not grudgingly, but fully, and fairly; and I would give them any legislation for the reclaiming of their fugitives, which should not, in its stringency, be more likely to carry a free man into slavery, than our ordinary criminal laws are to hang an innocent one.

But all this, to my judgment, furnishes no more excuse for permitting slavery to go into our own free territory, than it would for reviving the African slave trade by law. The law which forbids the bringing of slaves *from* Africa; and that which has so long forbid the taking them *to* Nebraska, can hardly be distinguished on any moral principle; and the repeal of the former could find quite as plausible excuses as that of the latter.

The arguments by which the repeal of the Missouri Compromise is sought to be justified, are these:

> First, that the Nebraska country needed a territorial government.
>
> Second, that in various ways, the public had repudiated it, and demanded the repeal; and therefore should not now complain of it.
>
> And lastly, that the repeal establishes a principle, which is intrinsically right.

I will attempt an answer to each of them in its turn.

First, then, if that country was in need of a territorial organization, could it not have had it as well without as with the repeal? Iowa and Minnesota, to both of which the Missouri restriction applied, had, without its repeal, each in succession, territorial organizations. And even, the year before, a bill for Nebraska itself, was within an ace of passing, without the repealing clause; and this in the hands of the same men who are now the champions of repeal. Why no necessity then for the repeal? But still later, when this very bill was first brought in, it contained no repeal. But, say they, because the public had demanded, or rather commanded the repeal, the repeal was to accompany the organization, whenever that should occur.

Now I deny that the public ever demanded any such thing—ever repudiated the Missouri Compromise—ever commanded its repeal. I deny it, and call for the proof. It is not contended, I believe, that any such command has ever been given in express terms. It is only said that it was done *in principle*. The support of the Wilmot Proviso, is the first fact mentioned, to prove that the Missouri restriction was repudiated in *principle*, and the second is, the refusal to extend the Missouri line over the country acquired from Mexico. These are near enough alike to be treated together. The one was to exclude the chances of slavery from the *whole* new acquisition by the lump; and the other was to reject a division of it, by which one half was to be given up to those chances. Now whether this was a repudiation of the Missouri line, in *principle*, depends upon whether the Missouri law contained any principle requiring the line to be extended over the country acquired from Mexico. I contend it did not. I insist that it contained no general principle, but that it was, in every sense, specific. That its terms limit it to the country purchased from France, is undenied and undeniable. It could have no principle beyond the intention of those who made it. They did not intend to extend the line to country which they did not own. If they intended to extend it, in the event of acquiring additional territory, why did they not say so? It was just as easy to say, that "in all the country west of the Mississippi, which we now own, *or may hereafter acquire* there shall never be slavery," as to say, what they did say; and they would have said it if they had meant it. An intention to extend the law is not only not mentioned in the law, but is not mentioned in any contemporaneous history. Both the law itself, and the history of the times are a blank as to any *principle* of extension; and by neither the known rules for construing statutes and contracts, nor by common sense, can any such *principle* be inferred.

Another fact showing the *specific* character of the Missouri law—showing that it intended no more than it expressed—showing that the line was not intended as a universal dividing line between free and slave territory, present and prospective—north of which slavery could never go—is the fact that by that very law, Missouri came in as a slave state,*north* of the line. If that law contained any prospective *principle*, the whole law must be looked to in order to ascertain what the *principle* was. And by this rule, the South could fairly contend that inasmuch as they got one slave state north of the line at the inception of the law, they have the right to have another given them *north* of it occasionally—now and then

in the indefinite westward extension of the line. This demonstrates the absurdity of attempting to deduce a prospective *principle* from the Missouri Compromise line.

When we voted for the Wilmot Proviso, we were voting to keep slavery *out* of the whole Missouri [Mexican?] acquisition; and little did we think we were thereby voting, to let it *into* Nebraska, laying several hundred miles distant. When we voted against extending the Missouri line, little did we think we were voting to destroy the old line, then of near thirty years standing. To argue that we thus repudiated the Missouri Compromise is no less absurd than it would be to argue that because we have, so far, forborne to acquire Cuba, we have thereby, *in principle*, repudiated our former acquisitions, and determined to throw them out of the Union! No less absurd than it would be to say that because I may have refused to build an addition to my house, I thereby have decided to destroy the existing house! And if I catch you setting fire to my house, you will turn upon me and say I INSTRUCTED you to do it! The most conclusive argument, however, that, while voting for the Wilmot Proviso, and while voting against the EXTENSION of the Missouri line, we never thought of disturbing the original Missouri Compromise, is found in the facts that there was then, and still is, an unorganized tract of fine country, nearly as large as the state of Missouri, lying immediately west of Arkansas, and south of the Missouri Compromise line; and that we never attempted to prohibit slavery as to it. I wish particular attention to this. It adjoins the original Missouri Compromise line, by its northern boundary; and consequently is part of the country, into which, by implication, slavery was permitted to go, by that compromise. There it has lain open ever since, and there it still lies. And yet no effort has been made at any time to wrest it from the south. In all our struggles to prohibit slavery within our Mexican acquisitions, we never so much as lifted a finger to prohibit it, as to this tract. Is not this entirely conclusive that at all times, we have held the Missouri Compromise as a sacred thing; even when against ourselves, as well as when for us?

Senator Douglas sometimes says the Missouri line itself was, *in principle*, only an extension of the line of the ordinance of '87—that is to say, an extension of the Ohio river. I think this is weak enough on its face. I will remark, however, that, as a glance at the map will show, the Missouri line is a long way farther South than the Ohio; and that if our

Senator, in proposing his extension, had stuck to the *principle* of jogging southward, perhaps it might not have been voted down so readily.

But next it is said that the compromises of '50 and the ratification of them by both political parties, in '52, established a *new principle*, which required the repeal of the Missouri Compromise. This again I deny. I deny it, and demand the proof. I have already stated fully what the compromises of '50 are. The particular part of those measures, for which the virtual repeal of the Missouri compromise is sought to be inferred (for it is admitted they contain nothing about it, in express terms) is the provision in the Utah and New Mexico laws, which permits them when they seek admission into the Union as States, to come in with or without slavery as they shall then see fit. Now I insist this provision was made for Utah and New Mexico, and for no other place whatever. It had no more direct reference to Nebraska than it had to the territories of the moon. But, say they, it had reference to Nebraska, *in principle*. Let us see. The North consented to this provision, not because they considered it right in itself; but because they were compensated—paid for it. They, at the same time, got California into the Union as a free State. This was far the best part of all they had struggled for by the Wilmot Proviso. They also got the area of slavery somewhat narrowed in the settlement of the boundary of Texas. Also, they got the slave trade abolished in the District of Columbia. For all these desirable objects the North could afford to yield something; and they did yield to the South the Utah and New Mexico provision. I do not mean that the whole North, or even a majority, yielded, when the law passed; but enough yielded, when added to the vote of the South, to carry the measure. Now can it be pretended that the principle of this arrangement requires us to permit the same provision to be applied to Nebraska, *without any equivalent at all*? Give us another free State; press the boundary of Texas still further back, give us another step toward the destruction of slavery in the District, and you present us a similar case. But ask us not to repeat, for nothing, what you paid for in the first instance. If you wish the thing again, pay again. That is the *principle* of the compromises of '50, if indeed they had any principles beyond their specific terms—it was the system of equivalents.

Again, if Congress, at that time, intended that all future territories should, when admitted as States, come in with or without slavery, at their own option, why did it not say so? With such an universal provision, all know the bills could not have passed. Did they, then—could they—establish a principle contrary to their own intention? Still further, if they intended to establish the principle that wherever Congress had control, it should be left to the people to do as they thought fit with slavery, why did they not authorize the people of the District of Columbia at their adoption to abolish slavery within these limits? I personally know that this has not been left undone, because it was unthought of. It was frequently spoken of by members of Congress and by citizens of Washington six years ago; and I heard no one express a doubt that a system of gradual emancipation, with compensation to owners, would meet the approbation of a large majority of the white people of the District. But without the action of Congress they could say nothing; and Congress said "no." In the measures of 1850 Congress had the subject of slavery in the District expressly in hand. If they were then establishing the *principle* of allowing the people to do as they please with slavery, why did they not apply the *principle* to that people?

Again, it is claimed that by the Resolutions of the Illinois Legislature, passed in 1851, the repeal of the Missouri Compromise was demanded. This I deny also. Whatever may be worked out by a criticism of the language of those resolutions, the people have never understood them as being any more than an endorsement of the compromises of 1850; and a release of our Senators from voting for the Wilmot Proviso. The whole people are living witnesses, that this only, was their view. Finally, it is asked "If we did not mean to apply the Utah and New Mexico provision, to all future territories, what did we mean, when we, in 1852, endorsed the compromises of '50?"

For myself, I can answer this question most easily. I meant not to ask a repeal, or modification of the fugitive slave law. I meant not to ask for the abolition of slavery in the District of Columbia. I meant not to resist the admission of Utah and New Mexico, even should they ask to come in as slave States. I meant nothing about additional territories, because, as I understood, we then had no territory whose character as to slavery was not already settled. As to Nebraska, I regarded its character as being fixed, by the Missouri compromise, for thirty years—as unalterably fixed as that of my own home in Illinois. As to new acquisitions I said "sufficient unto the day is the evil thereof." When we make new acquaintances, [acquisitions?] we will, as heretofore, try to manage them some how. That is my answer. That is what I meant and said; and I appeal to the people to say, each for himself, whether that was not also the universal meaning of the free States.

And now, in turn, let me ask a few questions. If by any, or all these matters, the repeal of the Missouri Compromise was commanded, why was not the command sooner obeyed? Why was the repeal omitted in the Nebraska bill of 1853? Why was it omitted in the original bill of 1854? Why, in the accompanying report, was such a repeal characterized as a *departure* from the course pursued in 1850? and its continued omission recommended?

I am aware Judge Douglas now argues that the subsequent express repeal is no substantial alteration of the bill. This argument seems wonderful to me. It is as if one should argue that white and black are not different. He admits, however, that there is a literal change in the bill; and that he made the change in deference to other Senators, who would not support the bill without. This proves that those other Senators thought the change a substantial one; and that the Judge thought their opinions worth deferring to. His own opinions, therefore, seem not to rest on a very firm basis even in his own mind— and I suppose the world believes, and will continue to believe, that precisely on the substance of that change this whole agitation has arisen.

I conclude then, that the public never demanded the repeal of the Missouri compromise.

I now come to consider whether the repeal, with its avowed principle, is intrinsically right. I insist that it is not. Take the particular case. A controversy had arisen between the advocates and opponents of slavery, in relation to its establishment within the country we had purchased of France. The southern, and then best part of the purchase, was already in as a slave state. —The controversy was settled by also letting Missouri in as a slave State; but with the agreement that within all the remaining part of the purchase, north of a certain line, there should never be slavery. As to what was to be done with the remaining part south of the line, nothing was said; but perhaps the fair implication was, that it should come in with slavery if it should so choose. The southern part, except a portion heretofore mentioned, afterwards did come in with slavery, as the State of Arkansas. All these many years since 1820, the Northern part had remained a wilderness. At length settlements began in it also. In due course,

Iowa, came in as a free State, and Minnesota was given a territorial government, without removing the slavery restriction. Finally the sole remaining part, north of the line, Kansas and Nebraska, was to be organized; and it is proposed, and carried, to blot out the old dividing line of thirty-four years standing, and to open the whole of that country to the introduction of slavery. Now, this, to my mind, is manifestly unjust. After an angry and dangerous controversy, the parties made friends by dividing the bone of contention. The one party first appropriates her own share, beyond all power to be disturbed in the possession of it; and then seizes the share of the other party. It is as if two starving men had divided their only loaf; the one had hastily swallowed his half, and then grabbed the other half just as he was putting it to his mouth.

Let me here drop the main argument, to notice what I consider rather an inferior matter. It is argued that slavery will not go to Kansas and Nebraska, *in any event*. This is a *palliation*—a *lullaby*. I have some hope that it will not; but let us not be too confident. As to climate, a glance at the map shows that there are five slave States—Delaware, Maryland, Virginia, Kentucky, and Missouri—and also the District of Columbia, all north of the Missouri compromise line. The census returns of 1850 show that, within these, there are 867,276 slaves—being more than one-fourth of all the slaves in the nation.

It is not climate, then, that will keep slavery out of these territories. Is there any thing in the peculiar nature of the country? Missouri adjoins these territories, by her entire western boundary, and slavery is already within every one of her western counties. I have even heard it said that there are more slaves, in proportion to whites, in the north western county of Missouri, than within any county of the State. Slavery pressed entirely up to the old western boundary of the State, and when, rather recently, a part of that boundary, at the north-west was moved out a little farther west, slavery followed on quite up to the new line. Now, when the restriction is removed, what is to prevent it from going still further? Climate will not. —No peculiarity of the country will—nothing in *nature* will. Will the disposition of the people prevent it? Those nearest the scene, are all in favor of the extension. The yankees, who are opposed to it may be more numerous; but in military phrase, the battle-field is too far from *their* base of operations.

But it is said, there now is *no* law in Nebraska on the subject of slavery; and that, in such case, taking a slave there, operates his freedom. That is good book-law; but is not the rule of actual practice. Wherever slavery is, it has been first introduced without law. The oldest laws we find concerning it, are not laws introducing it; but regulating it, as an already existing thing. A white man takes his slave to Nebraska now; who will inform the negro that he is free? Who will take him before court to test the question of his freedom? In ignorance of his legal emancipation, he is kept chopping, splitting and plowing. Others are brought, and move on in the same track. At last, if ever the time for voting comes, on the question of slavery, the institution already in fact exists in the country, and cannot well be removed. The facts of its presence, and the difficulty of its removal will carry the vote in its favor. Keep it out until a vote is taken, and a vote in favor of it, cannot be got in any population of forty thousand, on earth, who have been drawn together by the ordinary motives of emigration and settlement. To get slaves into the country simultaneously with the whites, in the incipient stages of settlement, is the precise stake played for, and won in this Nebraska measure.

The question is asked us, "If slaves will go in, notwithstanding the general principle of law liberates them, why would they not equally go in against positive statute law?—go in, even if the Missouri restriction were maintained?" I answer, because it takes a much bolder man to venture in, with his property, in the latter case, than in the former—because the positive congressional enactment is known to, and respected by all, or nearly all; whereas the negative principle that *no* law is free law, is not much known except among lawyers. We have some experience of this practical difference. In spite of the Ordinance of '87, a few negroes were brought into Illinois, and held in a state of quasi slavery; not enough, however to carry a vote of the people in favor of the institution when they came to form a constitution. But in the adjoining Missouri country, where there was no ordinance of '87—was no restriction—they were carried ten times, nay a hundred times, as fast, and actually made a slave State. This is fact—naked fact.

Another LULLABY argument is, that taking slaves to new countries does not increase their number, does not make any one slave who otherwise would be free. There is some truth in this, and I am glad of it, but it is not WHOLLY true. The African slave trade is not yet effectually suppressed; and if we make a reasonable deduction for the

white people amongst us, who are foreigners, and the descendants of foreigners, arriving here since 1808, we shall find the increase of the black population out-running that of the white, to an extent unaccountable, except by supposing that some of them too, have been coming from Africa. If this be so, the opening of new countries to the institution, increases the demand for, and augments the price of slaves, and so does, in fact, make slaves of freemen by causing them to be brought from Africa, and sold into bondage.

But, however this may be, we know the opening of new countries to slavery, tends to the perpetuation of the institution, and so does KEEP men in slavery who otherwise would be free. This result we do not FEEL like favoring, and we are under no legal obligation to suppress our feelings in this respect.

Equal justice to the South, it is said, requires us to consent to the extending of slavery to new countries. That is to say, inasmuch as you do not object to my taking my hog to Nebraska, therefore I must not object to you taking your slave. Now, I admit this is perfectly logical, if there is no difference between hogs and negroes. But while you thus require me to deny the humanity of the negro, I wish to ask whether you of the south yourselves, have ever been willing to do as much? It is kindly provided that of all those who come into the world, only a small percentage are natural tyrants. That percentage is no larger in the slave States than in the free. The great majority, south as well as north, have human sympathies, of which they can no more divest themselves than they can of their sensibility to physical pain. These sympathies in the bosoms of the southern people, manifest in many ways, their sense of the wrong of slavery, and their consciousness that, after all, there is humanity in the negro. If they deny this, let me address them a few plain questions. In 1820 you joined the north, almost unanimously, in declaring the African slave trade piracy, and in annexing to it the punishment of death. Why did you do this? If you did not feel that it was wrong, why did you join in providing that men should be hung for it? The practice was no more than bringing wild negroes from Africa, to sell to such as would buy them. But you never thought of hanging men for catching and selling wild horses, wild buffaloes or wild bears.

Again, you have amongst you, a sneaking individual, of the class of native tyrants, known as the "SLAVE-DEALER." He watches your necessities, and crawls up to buy your slave, at a speculating price. If you cannot help it, you sell to him; but if you can help it, you drive him from your door. You despise him utterly. You do not recognize him as a friend, or even as an honest man. Your children must not play with his; they may rollick freely with the little negroes, but not with the "slave-dealers" children. If you are obliged to deal with him, you try to get through the job without so much as touching him. It is common with you to join hands with the men you meet; but with the slave dealer you avoid the ceremony—instinctively shrinking from the snaky contact. If he grows rich and retires from business, you still remember him, and still keep up the ban of non-intercourse upon him and his family. Now why is this? You do not so treat the man who deals in corn, cattle or tobacco.

And yet again; there are in the United States and territories, including the District of Columbia, 433,643 free blacks. At $500 per head they are worth over two hundred millions of dollars. How comes this vast amount of property to be running about without owners? We do not see free horses or free cattle running at large. How is this? All these free blacks are the descendants of slaves, or have been slaves themselves, and they would be slaves now, but for SOMETHING which has operated on their white owners, inducing them, at vast pecuniary sacrifices, to liberate them. What is that SOMETHING? Is there any mistaking it? In all these cases it is your sense of justice, and human sympathy, continually telling you, that the poor negro has some natural right to himself—that those who deny it, and make mere merchandise of him, deserve kickings, contempt and death.

And now, why will you ask us to deny the humanity of the slave and estimate him only as the equal of the hog? Why ask us to do what you will not do yourselves? Why ask us to do for *nothing*, what two hundred million of dollars could not induce you to do?

But one great argument in the support of the repeal of the Missouri Compromise, is still to come. That argument is "the sacred right of self government." It seems our distinguished Senator has found great difficulty in getting his antagonists, even in the Senate to meet him fairly on this argument. Some poet has said:

"Fools rush in where angels fear to tread."

At the hazzard of being thought one of the fools of this quotation, I meet that argument—I rush in, I take that bull by the horns.

I trust I understand, and truly estimate the right of self-government. My faith in the proposition that each man should do precisely as he pleases with all which is exclusively his own, lies at the foundation of the sense of justice there is in me. I extend the principles to communities of men, as well as to individuals. I so extend it, because it is politically wise, as well as naturally just; politically wise, in saving us from broils about matters which do not concern us. Here, or at Washington, I would not trouble myself with the oyster laws of Virginia, or the cranberry laws of Indiana.

The doctrine of self government is right—absolutely and eternally right—but it has no just application, as here attempted. Or perhaps I should rather say that whether it has such just application depends upon whether a negro is *not* or *is* a man. If he is *not* a man, why in that case, he who is a man may, as a matter of self-government, do just as he pleases with him. But if the negro *is* a man, is it not to that extent, a total destruction of self-government, to say that he too shall not govern *himself*? When the white man governs himself that is self-government; but when he governs himself, and also governs *another* man, that is *more* than self-government—that is despotism. If the negro is a *man*, why then my ancient faith teaches me that "all men are created equal;" and that there can be no moral right in connection with one man's making a slave of another.

Judge Douglas frequently, with bitter irony and sarcasm, paraphrases our argument by saying "The white people of Nebraska are good enough to govern themselves, *but they are not good enough to govern a few miserable negroes!!*"

Well I doubt not that the people of Nebraska are, and will continue to be as good as the average of people elsewhere. I do not say the contrary. What I do say is, that no man is good enough to govern another man, *without that other's consent.* I say this is the leading principle—the sheet anchor of American republicanism. Our Declaration of Independence says:

"We hold these truths to be self evident: that all men are created equal; that they are endowed by their Creator with certain inalienable rights; that among these are life, liberty and the pursuit of happiness. That to secure these rights, governments are instituted among men, DERIVING THEIR JUST POWERS FROM THE CONSENT OF THE GOVERNED."

I have quoted so much at this time merely to show that according to our ancient faith, the just powers of governments are derived from the consent of the governed. Now the relation of masters and slaves is, PRO TANTO, a total violation of this principle. The master not only governs the slave without his consent; but he governs him by a set of rules altogether different from those which he prescribes for himself. Allow ALL the governed an equal voice in the government, and that, and that only, is self government.

Let it not be said I am contending for the establishment of political and social equality between the whites and blacks. I have already said the contrary. I am not now combating the argument of NECESSITY, arising from the fact that the blacks are already amongst us; but I am combating what is set up as MORAL argument for allowing them to be taken where they have never yet been—arguing against the EXTENSION of a bad thing, which where it already exists we must of necessity, manage as we best can.

In support of his application of the doctrine of self-government, Senator Douglas has sought to bring to his aid the opinions and examples of our revolutionary fathers. I am glad he has done this. I love the sentiments of those old-time men; and shall be most happy to abide by their opinions. He shows us that when it was in contemplation for the colonies to break off from Great Britain, and set up a new government for themselves, several of the states instructed their delegates to go for the measure PROVIDED EACH STATE SHOULD BE ALLOWED TO REGULATE ITS DOMESTIC CONCERNS IN ITS OWN WAY. I do not quote; but this in substance. This was right. I see nothing objectionable in it. I also think it probable that it had some reference to the existence of slavery amongst them. I will not deny that it had. But had it, in any reference to the carrying of slavery into NEW COUNTRIES? That is the question; and we will let the fathers themselves answer it.

This same generation of men, and mostly the same individuals of the generation, who declared this principle—who declared independence—who fought the war of the revolution through—who afterwards made the constitution under which we still live—these same men passed the ordinance of '87, declaring that slavery should never go to the northwest territory. I have no doubt Judge Douglas thinks they were very inconsistent in this. It is a question of

discrimination between them and him. But there is not an inch of ground left for his claiming that their opinions—their example—their authority—are on his side in this controversy.

Again, is not Nebraska, while a territory, a part of us? Do we not own the country? And if we surrender the control of it, do we not surrender the right of self-government? It is part of ourselves. If you say we shall not control it because it is ONLY part, the same is true of every other part; and when all the parts are gone, what has become of the whole? What is then left of us? What use for the General Government, when there is nothing left for it [to] govern?

But you say this question should be left to the people of Nebraska, because they are more particularly interested. If this be the rule, you must leave it to each individual to say for himself whether he will have slaves. What better moral right have thirty-one citizens of Nebraska to say, that the thirty-second shall not hold slaves, than the people of the thirty-one States have to say that slavery shall not go into the thirty-second State at all?

But if it is a sacred right for the people of Nebraska to take and hold slaves there, it is equally their sacred right to buy them where they can buy them cheapest; and that undoubtedly will be on the coast of Africa; provided you will consent to not hang them for going there to buy them. You must remove this restriction too, from the sacred right of self-government. I am aware you say that taking slaves from the States of [to?] Nebraska, does not make slaves of freemen; but the African slave-trader can say just as much. He does not catch free negroes and bring them here. He finds them already slaves in the hands of their black captors, and he honestly buys them at the rate of about a red cotton handkerchief a head. This is very cheap, and it is a great abridgement of the sacred right of self-government to hang men for engaging in this profitable trade!

Another important objection to this application of the right of self-government, is that it enables the first FEW, to deprive the succeeding MANY, of a free exercise of the right of self-government. The first few may get slavery IN, and the subsequent many cannot easily get it OUT. How common is the remark now in the slave States—"If we were only clear of our slaves, how much better it would be for us." They are actually deprived of the privilege of governing themselves as they would, by the action of a very few, in the beginning. The same thing was true of the whole nation at the time our constitution was formed.

Whether slavery shall go into Nebraska, or other new territories, is not a matter of exclusive concern to the people who may go there. The whole nation is interested that the best use shall be made of these territories. We want them for the homes of free white people. This they cannot be, to any considerable extent, if slavery shall be planted within them. Slave States are places for poor white people to remove FROM; not to remove TO. New free States are the places for poor people to go to and better their condition. For this use, the nation needs these territories.

Still further; there are constitutional relations between the slave and free States, which are degrading to the latter. We are under legal obligations to catch and return their runaway slaves to them—a sort of dirty, disagreeable job, which I believe, as a general rule the slave-holders will not perform for one another. Then again, in the control of the government—the management of the partnership affairs—they have greatly the advantage of us. By the constitution, each State has two Senators—each has a number of Representatives, in proportion to the number of its people—and each has a number of presidential electors, equal to the whole number of its Senators and Representatives together. But in ascertaining the number of the people, for this purpose, five slaves are counted as being equal to three whites. The slaves do not vote; they are only counted and so used, as to swell the influence of the white people's votes. The practical effect of this is more aptly shown by a comparison of the States of South Carolina and Maine. South Carolina has six representatives, and so has Maine; South Carolina has eight presidential electors, and so has Maine. This is precise equality so far; and, of course they are equal in Senators, each having two. Thus in the control of the government, the two States are equals precisely. But how are they in the number of their white people? Maine has 581,813—while South Carolina has 274,567. Maine has twice as many as South Carolina, and 32,679 over. Thus each white man in South Carolina is more than the double of any man in Maine. This is all because South Carolina, besides her free people, has 384,984 slaves. The South Carolinian has precisely the same advantage over the white man in every other free State, as well as in Maine. He is more than the double of any one of us in this crowd. The same advantage, but not to the same extent, is held by all the citizens of the slave States, over those of the free; and it is an absolute truth, without an exception, that there is no voter in any slave State, but who has more legal power in the government, than any voter in any free State. There is no instance of exact equality; and the disadvantage is against us the whole chapter through. This principle, in the aggregate, gives the slave States, in the present Congress, twenty additional representatives—being seven more than the whole majority by which they passed the Nebraska bill.

Now all this is manifestly unfair; yet I do not mention it to complain of it, in so far as it is already settled. It is in the constitution; and I do not, for that cause, or any other cause, propose to destroy, or alter, or disregard the constitution. I stand to it, fairly, fully, and firmly.

But when I am told I must leave it altogether to OTHER PEOPLE to say whether new partners are to be bred up and brought into the firm, on the same degrading terms against me, I respectfully demur. I insist, that whether I shall be a whole man, or only, the half of one, in comparison with others, is a question in which I am somewhat concerned; and one which no other man can have a sacred right of deciding for me. If I am wrong in this—if it really be a sacred right of self-government, in the man who shall go to Nebraska, to decide whether he will be the EQUAL of me or the DOUBLE of me, then after he shall have exercised that right, and thereby shall have reduced me to a still smaller fraction of a man than I already am, I should like for some gentleman deeply skilled in the mysteries of sacred rights, to provide himself with a microscope, and peep about, and find out, if he can, what has become of my sacred rights! They will surely be too small for detection with the naked eye.

Finally, I insist that if there is ANY THING which it is the duty of the WHOLE PEOPLE to never entrust to any hands but their own, that thing is the preservation and perpetuity, of their own liberties, and institutions. And if they shall think, as I do, that the extension of slavery endangers them, more than any, or all other causes, how recreant to themselves, if they submit the question, and with it, the fate of their country, to a mere hand-full of men, bent only on temporary self-interest. If this question of slavery extension were an insignificant one—one having no power to do harm—it might be shuffled aside in this way. But being, as it is, the great Behemoth of danger, shall the strong gripe [grip?] of the nation be loosened upon him, to entrust him to the hands of such feeble keepers?

I have done with this mighty argument, of self-government. Go, sacred thing! Go in peace.

But Nebraska is urged as a great Union-saving measure. Well I too, go for saving the Union. Much as I hate slavery, I would consent to the extension of it rather than see the Union dissolved, just as I would consent to any GREAT evil, to avoid a GREATER one. But when I go to Union saving, I must believe, at least, that the means I employ has some adaptation to the end. To my mind, Nebraska has no such adaptation.

"It hath no relish of salvation in it."

It is an aggravation, rather, of the only one thing which ever endangers the Union. When it came upon us, all was peace and quiet. The nation was looking to the forming of new bonds of Union; and a long course of peace and prosperity seemed to lie before us. In the whole range of possibility, there scarcely appears to me to have been any thing, out of which the slavery agitation could have been revived, except the very project of repealing the Missouri compromise. —Every inch of territory we owned, already had a definite settlement of the slavery question, and by which, all parties were pledged to abide. Indeed, there was no uninhabited country on the continent, which we could acquire; if we except some extreme northern regions, which are wholly out of the question. In this state of case, the genius of Discord himself, could scarcely have invented a way of again getting [setting?] us by the ears, but by turning back and destroying the peace measures of the past. The councils of that genius seem to have prevailed, the Missouri compromise was repealed; and here we are, in the midst of a new slavery agitation, such, I think, as we have never seen before. Who is responsible for this? Is it those who resist the measure; or those who, causelessly, brought it forward, and pressed it through, having reason to know, and, in fact, knowing it must and would be so resisted? It could not but be expected by its author, that it would be looked upon as a measure for the extension of slavery, aggravated by a gross breach of faith. Argue as you will, and long as you will, this is the naked FRONT and ASPECT, of the measure. And in this aspect, it could not but produce agitation. Slavery is founded in the selfishness of man's nature—opposition to it, is his love of justice. These principles are an eternal antagonism; and when brought into collision so fiercely, as slavery extension brings them, shocks, and throes, and convulsions must ceaselessly follow. Repeal the Missouri compromise—repeal all compromises—repeal the declaration of independence—repeal all past history, you still can not repeal human nature. It still will be the abundance of man's heart, that slavery extension is wrong; and out of the abundance of his heart, his mouth will continue to speak.

The structure, too, of the Nebraska bill is very peculiar. The people are to decide the question of slavery for themselves; but WHEN they are to decide; or HOW they are to decide; or whether, when the question is once decided, it is to remain so, or is it to be subject to an indefinite succession of new trials, the law does not say, Is it to be decided by the first dozen settlers who arrive there? or is it to await the arrival of a hundred? Is it to be decided by a vote of the people? or a vote of the legislature? or, indeed by a vote of any sort? To these questions, the law gives no answer. There is a mystery about this; for when a member proposed to give the legislature express authority to exclude slavery, it was hooted down by the friends of the bill. This fact is worth remembering. Some Yankees, in the east, are sending emigrants to Nebraska to exclude slavery from it; and, so far as I can judge, they expect the question to be decided by voting, in some way or other. But the Missourians are awake too. They are within a stone's throw of the contested ground. They hold meetings, and pass resolutions, in which not the slightest allusion to voting is made. They resolve that slavery already exists in the territory; that more shall go there; that they, remaining in Missouri, will protect it; and that abolitionists shall be hung, or driven away. Through all this, bowie-knives and six-shooters are seen plainly enough; but never a glimpse of the ballot-box. And, really, what is to be the result of this? Each party WITHIN, having numerous and determined backers WITHOUT, is it not probable that the contest will come to blows, and bloodshed? Could there be a more apt invention to bring about collision and violence, on the slavery question, than this Nebraska project is? I do not charge, or believe, that such was intended by Congress; but if they had literally formed a ring, and placed champions within it to fight out the controversy, the fight could be no more likely to come off, than it is. And if this fight should begin, is it likely to take a very peaceful, Union-saving turn? Will not the first drop of blood so shed, be the real knell of the Union?

The Missouri Compromise ought to be restored. For the sake of the Union, it ought to be restored.

We ought to elect a House of Representatives which will vote its restoration. If by any means, we omit to do this, what follows!—Slavery may or may not be established in Nebraska. But whether it be or not, we shall have repudiated—discarded from the councils of the Nation—the SPIRIT OF COMPROMISE; for who after this will ever trust in a national compromise? The spirit of mutual concession—that spirit which first gave us the constitution, and which has thrice saved the Union—we shall have strangled and cast from us forever. And what shall we have in lieu of it? The South flushed with triumph and tempted to excesses; the North, betrayed, as they believe, brooding on wrong and burning for revenge. One side will provoke; the other resent. The one will taunt, the other defy; one agrees [aggresses?], the other retaliates. Already a few in the North, defy all constitutional restraints, resist the execution of the fugitive slave law, and even menace the institution of slavery in the states where it exists.

Already a few in the South, claim the constitutional right to take to and hold slaves in the free states—demand the revival of the slave trade; and demand a treaty with Great Britain by which fugitive slaves may be reclaimed from Canada. As yet they are but few on either side. It is a grave question for the lovers of the Union, whether the final destruction of the Missouri Compromise, and with it the spirit of all compromise will or will not embolden and embitter each of these, and fatally increase the numbers of both.

But restore the compromise, and what then? We thereby restore the national faith, the national confidence, the national feeling of brotherhood. We thereby reinstate the spirit of concession and compromise—that spirit which has never failed us in past perils, and which may be safely trusted for all the future. The south ought to join in doing this. The peace of the nation is as dear to them as to us. In memories of the past and hopes of the future, they share as largely as we. It would be on their part, a great act—great in its spirit, and great in its effect. It would be worth to the nation a hundred years' purchase of peace and prosperity. And what of sacrifice would they make? They only surrender to us, what they gave us for a consideration long, long ago; what they have not now, asked for, struggled or cared for; what has been thrust upon them, not less to their own astonishment than to ours.

But it is said we cannot restore it; that though we elect every member of the lower house, the Senate is still against us. It is quite true, that of the Senators who passed the Nebraska bill, a majority of the whole Senate will retain their seats in spite of the elections of this and the next year. But if at these elections, their several constituencies shall clearly express their will against Nebraska, will these senators disregard their will? Will they neither obey, nor make room for those who will?

But even if we fail to technically restore the compromise, it is still a great point to carry a popular vote in favor of the restoration. The moral weight of such a vote can not be estimated too highly. The authors of Nebraska are not at all satisfied with the destruction of the compromise—an endorsement of this PRINCIPLE they proclaim to be the great object. With them, Nebraska alone is a small matter—to establish a principle, for FUTURE USE, is what they particularly desire.

That future use is to be the planting of slavery wherever in the wide world, local and unorganized opposition can not prevent it. Now if you wish to give them this endorsement—if you wish to establish this principle—do so. I shall regret it; but it is your right. On the contrary if you are opposed to the principle—intend to give it no such endorsement—let no wheedling, no sophistry, divert you from throwing a direct vote against it.

Some men, mostly whigs, who condemn the repeal of the Missouri Compromise, nevertheless hesitate to go for its restoration, lest they be thrown in company with the abolitionist. Will they allow me as an old whig to tell them good humoredly, that I think this is very silly? Stand with anybody that stands RIGHT. Stand with him while he is right and PART with him when he goes wrong. Stand WITH the abolitionist in restoring the Missouri Compromise; and stand AGAINST him when he attempts to repeal the fugitive slave law. In the latter case you stand with the southern disunionist. What of that? you are still right. In both cases you are right. In both cases you oppose [expose?] the dangerous extremes. In both you stand on middle ground and hold the ship level and steady. In both you are national and nothing less than national. This is good old whig ground. To desert such ground, because of any company, is to be less than a whig—less than a man—less than an American.

I particularly object to the NEW position which the avowed principle of this Nebraska law gives to slavery in the body politic. I object to it because it assumes that there CAN be MORAL RIGHT in the enslaving of one man by another. I object to it as a dangerous dalliance for a few people—a sad evidence that, feeling prosperity we forget right—that liberty, as a principle, we have ceased to revere. I object to it because the fathers of the republic eschewed, and rejected it. The argument of "Necessity" was the only argument they ever admitted in favor of slavery; and so far, and so far only as it carried them, did they ever go. They found the institution existing among us, which they could not help; and they cast blame upon the British King for having permitted its introduction. BEFORE the constitution, they prohibited its introduction into the north-western Territory—the only country we owned, then free from it. AT the framing and adoption of the constitution, they forbore to so much as mention the word "slave" or "slavery" in the whole instrument. In the provision for the recovery of fugitives, the slave is spoken of as a "PERSON HELD TO SERVICE OR LABOR." In that prohibiting the abolition of the African slave trade for twenty years, that trade is spoken of as "The migration or importation of such persons as any of the States NOW EXISTING, shall think proper to admit," &c. These are the only provisions alluding to slavery. Thus, the thing is hid away, in the constitution, just as an afflicted man hides away a wen or a cancer, which he dares not cut out at once, lest he bleed to death; with the promise, nevertheless, that the cutting may begin at the end of a given time. Less than this our fathers COULD not do; and NOW [MORE?] they WOULD not do. Necessity drove them so far, and farther, they would not go. But this is not all. The earlier Congress, under the constitution, took the same view of slavery. They hedged and hemmed it in to the narrowest limits of necessity.

In 1794, they prohibited an out-going slave-trade—that is, the taking of slaves FROM the United States to sell. In 1798, they prohibited the bringing of slaves from Africa, INTO the Mississippi Territory—this territory then comprising what are now the States of Mississippi and Alabama. This was TEN YEARS before they had the authority to do the same thing as to the States existing at the adoption of the constitution.

In 1800 they prohibited AMERICAN CITIZENS from trading in slaves between foreign countries—as, for instance, from Africa to Brazil.

In 1803 they passed a law in aid of one or two State laws, in restraint of the internal slave trade.

In 1807, in apparent hot haste, they passed the law, nearly a year in advance to take effect the first day of 1808—the very first day the constitution would permit—prohibiting the African slave trade by heavy pecuniary and corporal penalties.

In 1820, finding these provisions ineffectual, they declared the trade piracy, and annexed to it, the extreme penalty of death. While all this was passing in the general government, five or six of the original slave States had adopted systems of gradual emancipation; and by which the institution was rapidly becoming extinct within these limits.

Thus we see, the plain unmistakable spirit of that age, towards slavery, was hostility to the PRINCIPLE, and toleration, ONLY BY NECESSITY.

But NOW it is to be transformed into a "sacred right." Nebraska brings it forth, places it on the high road to extension and perpetuity; and, with a pat on its back, says to it, "Go, and God speed you." Henceforth it is to be the chief jewel of the nation—the very figure-head of the ship of State. Little by little, but steadily as man's march to the grave, we have been giving up the OLD for the NEW faith. Near eighty years ago we began by declaring that all men are created equal; but now from that beginning we have run down to the other declaration, that for SOME men to enslave OTHERS is a "sacred right of self-government." These principles can not stand together. They are as opposite as God and mammon; and whoever holds to the one, must despise the other. When Pettit, in connection with his support of the Nebraska bill, called the Declaration of Independence "a self-evident lie" he only did what consistency and candor require all other Nebraska men to do. Of the forty odd Nebraska Senators who sat present and heard him, no one rebuked him. Nor am I apprized that any Nebraska newspaper, or any Nebraska orator, in the whole nation, has ever yet rebuked him. If this had been said among Marion's men, Southerners though they were, what would have become of the man who said it? If this had been said to the men who captured Andre, the man who said it, would probably have been hung sooner than Andre was. If it had been said in old Independence Hall, seventy-eight years ago, the very door-keeper would have throttled the man, and thrust him into the street.

Let no one be deceived. The spirit of seventy-six and the spirit of Nebraska, are utter antagonisms; and the former is being rapidly displaced by the latter.

Fellow countrymen—Americans south, as well as north, shall we make no effort to arrest this? Already the liberal party throughout the world, express the apprehension "that the one retrograde institution in America, is undermining the principles of progress, and fatally violating the noblest political system the world ever saw." This is not the taunt of enemies, but the warning of friends. Is it quite safe to disregard it—to despise it? Is there no danger to liberty itself, in discarding the earliest practice, and first precept of our ancient faith? In our greedy chase to make profit of the negro, let us beware, lest we "cancel and tear to pieces" even the white man's charter of freedom.

Our republican robe is soiled, and trailed in the dust. Let us repurify it. Let us turn and wash it white, in the spirit, if not the blood, of the Revolution. Let us turn slavery from its claims of "moral right," back upon its existing legal rights, and its arguments of "necessity." Let us return it to the position our fathers gave it; and there let it rest in peace. Let us re-adopt the Declaration of Independence, and with it, the practices, and policy, which harmonize with it. Let north and south—let all Americans—let all lovers of liberty everywhere—join in the great and good work. If we do this, we shall not only have saved the Union; but we shall have so saved it, as to make, and to keep it, forever worthy of the saving. We shall have so saved it, that the succeeding millions of free happy people, the world over, shall rise up, and call us blessed, to the latest generations.

At Springfield, twelve days ago, where I had spoken substantially as I have here, Judge Douglas replied to me—and as he is to reply to me here, I shall attempt to anticipate him, by noticing some of the points he made there. He commenced by stating I had assumed all the way through, that the principle of the Nebraska bill, would have the effect of extending slavery. He denied that this was INTENDED, or that this EFFECT would follow.

I will not re-open the argument upon this point. That such WAS the intention, the world believed at the start, and will continue to believe. This was the COUNTENANCE of the thing; and, both friends and enemies, instantly recognized it as such. That countenance can not now be changed by argument. You can as easily argue the color out of the negroes' skin. Like the "bloody hand" you may wash it, and wash it, the red witness of guilt still sticks, and stares horribly at you.

Next he says, congressional intervention never prevented slavery any where—that it did not prevent it in the north west territory, now [nor?] in Illinois—that in fact, Illinois came into the Union as a slave State—that the principle of the Nebraska bill expelled it from Illinois, from several old States, from every where.

Now this is mere quibbling all the way through. If the ordinance of '87 did not keep slavery out of the north west territory, how happens it that the north west shore of the Ohio river is entirely free from it; while the south east shore, less than a mile distant, along nearly the whole length of the river, is entirely covered with it?

If that ordinance did not keep it out of Illinois, what was it that made the difference between Illinois and Missouri? They lie side by side, the Mississippi river only dividing them; while their early settlements were within the same latitude. Between 1810 and 1820 the number of slaves in Missouri INCREASED 7,211; while in Illinois, in the same ten years, they DECREASED 51. This appears by the census returns. During nearly all of that ten years, both were territories—not States. During this time the ordinance forbid slavery to go into Illinois; and NOTHING forbid it to go into Missouri. It DID go into Missouri, and did NOT go into Illinois. That is the fact. Can any one doubt as to the reason of it?

But, he says, Illinois came into the Union as a slave State. Silence, perhaps, would be the best answer to this flat contradiction of the known history of the country. What are the facts upon which this bold assertion is based? When we first acquired the country, as far back as 1787, there were some slaves within it, held by the French inhabitants at Kaskaskia. The territorial legislation, admitted a few negroes, from the slave States, as indentured servants. One year after the adoption of the first State constitution the whole number of them was—what do you think? just 117—while the aggregate free population was 55,094—about 470 to one. Upon this state of facts, the people framed their constitution prohibiting the further introduction of slavery, with a sort of guaranty to the owners of the few indentured servants, giving freedom to their children to be born thereafter, and making no mention whatever, of any supposed slave for life. Out of this small matter, the Judge manufactures his argument that Illinois came into the Union as a slave State. Let the facts be the answer to the argument.

The principles of the Nebraska bill, he says, expelled slavery from Illinois. The principle of that bill first planted it here—that is, it first came, because there was no law to prevent it—first came before we owned the country; and finding it here, and having the ordinance of '87 to prevent its increasing, our people struggled along, and finally got rid of it as best they could.

But the principle of the Nebraska bill abolished slavery in several of the old States. Well, it is true that several of the old States, in the last quarter of the last century, did adopt systems of gradual emancipation, by which the institution has finally become extinct within their limits; but it MAY or MAY NOT be true that the principle of the Nebraska bill was the cause that led to the adoption of these measures. It is now more than fifty years, since the last of these States adopted its system of emancipation. If Nebraska bill is the real author of these benevolent works, it is rather deplorable, that he has, for so long a time, ceased working all together. Is there not some reason to suspect that it was the principle of the REVOLUTION, and not the principle of Nebraska bill, that led to emancipation in these old States? Leave it to the people of those old emancipating States, and I am quite sure they will decide, that neither that, nor any other good thing, ever did, or ever will come of Nebraska bill.

In the course of my main argument, Judge Douglas interrupted me to say, that the principle [of] the Nebraska bill was very old; that it originated when God made man and placed good and evil before him, allowing him to choose for himself, being responsible for the choice he should make. At the time I thought this was merely playful; and I answered it accordingly. But in his reply to me he renewed it, as a serious argument. In seriousness then, the facts of this proposition are not true as stated. God did not place good and evil before man, telling him to make his choice. On the contrary, he did tell him there was one tree, of the fruit of which, he should not eat, upon pain of certain death. I should scarcely wish so strong a prohibition against slavery in Nebraska.

But this argument strikes me as not a little remarkable in another particular—in its strong resemblance to the old argument for the "Divine right of Kings." By the latter, the King is to do just as he pleases with his white subjects, being responsible to God alone. By the former, the white man is to do just as he pleases with his black slaves, being responsible to God alone. The two things are precisely alike; and it is but natural that they should find similar arguments to sustain them.

I had argued, that the application of the principle of self-government, as contended for, would require the revival of the African slave trade—that no argument could be made in favor of a man's right to take slaves to Nebraska, which could not be equally well made in favor of his right to bring them from the coast of Africa. The Judge replied, that the Constitution requires the suppression of the foreign slave trade; but does not require the prohibition of slavery in the territories. That is a mistake, in point of fact. The Constitution does NOT require the action of Congress in either case; and it does AUTHORIZE it in both. And so, there is still no difference between the cases.

In regard to what I had said, the advantage the slave States have over the free, in the matter of representation, the Judge replied that we, in the free States, count five free negroes as five white people, while in the slave States, they count five slaves as three whites only; and that the advantage, at last, was on the side of the free States.

Now, in the slave States, they count free negroes just as we do; and it so happens that besides their slaves, they have as many free negroes as we have, and thirty-three thousand over. Thus their free negroes more than balance ours; and their advantage over us, in consequence of their slaves, still remains as I stated it.

In reply to my argument, that the compromise measures of 1850, were a system of equivalents; and that the provisions of no one of them could fairly be carried to other subjects, without its corresponding equivalent being carried with it, the Judge denied out-right, that these measures had any connection with, or dependence upon, each other. This is mere desperation. If they have no connection, why are they always spoken of in connection? Why has he so spoken of them, a thousand times? Why has he constantly called them a SERIES of measures? Why does everybody call them a compromise? Why was California kept out of the Union, six or seven months, if it was not because of its connection with the other measures? Webster's leading definition of the verb "to compromise" is "to adjust and settle a difference, by mutual agreement, with concessions of claims by the parties." This conveys precisely the popular understanding of the word "compromise." We knew, before the Judge told us, that these measures passed separately, and in distinct bills; and that no two of them were passed by the votes of precisely the same members. But we also know, and so does he know, that no one of them could have passed both branches of Congress but for the understanding that the others were to pass also. Upon this understanding each got votes, which it could have got in no other way. It is this fact, that gives to the measures their true character; and it is the universal knowledge of this fact, that has given them the name of compromise so expressive of that true character.

I had asked "If in carrying the provisions of the Utah and New Mexico laws to Nebraska, you could clear away other objection, how can you leave Nebraska "perfectly free" to introduce slavery BEFORE she forms a constitution—during her territorial government?—while the Utah and New Mexico laws only authorize it WHEN they form constitutions, and are admitted into the Union?" To this Judge Douglas answered that the Utah and New Mexico laws, also authorized it BEFORE; and to prove this, he read from one of their laws, as follows: "That the legislative power of said territory shall extend to all rightful subjects of legislation consistent with the constitution of the United States and the provisions of this act."

Now it is perceived from the reading of this, that there is nothing express upon the subject; but that the authority is sought to be implied merely, for the general provision of "all rightful subjects of legislation." In reply to this, I insist, as a legal rule of construction, as well as the plain popular view of the matter, that the EXPRESS provision for Utah and New Mexico coming in with slavery if they choose, when they shall form constitutions, is an EXCLUSION of all implied authority on the same subject—that Congress, having the subject distinctly in their minds, when they made the express provision, they therein expressed their WHOLE meaning on that subject.

The Judge rather insinuated that I had found it convenient to forget the Washington territorial law passed in 1853. This was a division of Oregon, organizing the northern part, as the territory of Washington. He asserted that, by this act, the ordinance of '87 theretofore existing in Oregon, was repealed; that nearly all the members of Congress voted for it, beginning in the H.R. [House of Representatives], with Charles Allen of Massachusetts, and ending with Richard Yates, of Illinois; and that he could not understand how those

who now oppose the Nebraska bill, so voted then, unless it was because it was then too soon after both the great political parties had ratified the compromises of 1850, and the ratification therefore too fresh, to be then repudiated.

Now I had seen the Washington act before; and I have carefully examined it since; and I aver that there is no repeal of the ordinance of '87, or of any prohibition of slavery, in it. In express terms, there is absolutely nothing in the whole law upon the subject—in fact, nothing to lead a reader to THINK of the subject. To my judgment, it is equally free from every thing from which such repeal can be legally implied; but however this may be, are men now to be entrapped by a legal implication, extracted from covert language, introduced perhaps, for the very purpose of entrapping them? I sincerely wish every man could read this law quite through, carefully watching every sentence, and every line, for a repeal of the ordinance of '87 or any thing equivalent to it.

Another point on the Washington act. If it was intended to be modeled after the Utah and New Mexico acts, as Judge Douglas, insists, why was it not inserted in it, as in them, that Washington was to come in with or without slavery as she may choose at the adoption of her constitution? It has no such provision in it; and I defy the ingenuity of man to give a reason for the omission, other than that it was not intended to follow the Utah and New Mexico laws in regard to the question of slavery.

The Washington act not only differs vitally from the Utah and New Mexico acts; but the Nebraska act differs vitally from both. By the latter act the people are left "perfectly free" to regulate their own domestic concerns, &c.; but in all the former, all their laws are to be submitted to Congress, and if disapproved are to be null. The Washington act goes even further; it absolutely prohibits the territorial legislation [legislature?], by very strong and guarded language, from establishing banks, or borrowing money on the faith of the territory. Is this the sacred right of self-government we hear vaunted so much? No sir, the Nebraska bill finds no model in the acts of '50 or the Washington act. It finds no model in any law from Adam till to-day. As Phillips says of Napoleon, the Nebraska act is grand, gloomy, and peculiar; wrapped in the solitude of its own originality; without a model, and without a shadow upon the earth.

In the course of his reply, Senator Douglas remarked, in substance, that he had always considered this government was made for the white people and not for the negroes. Why, in point of mere fact, I think so too. But in this remark of the Judge, there is a significance, which I think is the key to the great mistake (if there is any such mistake) which he has made in this Nebraska measure. It shows that the Judge has no very vivid impression that the negro is a human; and consequently has no idea that there can be any moral question in legislating about him. In his view, the question of whether a new country shall be slave or free, is a matter of as utter indifference, as it is whether his neighbor shall plant his farm with tobacco, or stock it with horned cattle. Now, whether this view is right or wrong, it is very certain that the great mass of mankind take a totally different view. They consider slavery a great moral wrong; and their feelings against it, is not evanescent, but eternal. It lies at the very foundation of their sense of justice; and it cannot be trifled with. It is a great and durable element of popular action, and, I think, no statesman can safely disregard it.

Our Senator also objects that those who oppose him in this measure do not entirely agree with one another. He reminds me that in my firm adherence to the constitutional rights of the slave States, I differ widely from others who are co-operating with me in opposing the Nebraska bill; and he says it is not quite fair to oppose him in this variety of ways. He should remember that he took us by surprise—astounded us—by this measure. We were thunderstruck and stunned; and we reeled and fell in utter confusion. But we rose each fighting, grasping whatever he could first reach—a scythe—a pitchfork—a chopping axe, or a butcher's cleaver. We struck in the direction of the sound, and we are rapidly closing in upon him. He must not think to divert us from our purpose, by showing us that our drill, our dress, and our weapons, are not entirely perfect and uniform. When the storm shall be past, he shall find us still Americans; no less devoted to the continued Union and prosperity of the country than heretofore.

Finally, the Judge invokes against me, the memory of Clay and of Webster. They were great men;

and men of great deeds. But where have I assailed them? For what is it, that their life-long enemy, shall now make profit, by assuming to defend them against me, their life-long friend? I go against the repeal of the Missouri compromise; did they ever go for it? They went for the compromise of 1850; did I ever go against them? They were greatly devoted to the Union; to the small measure of my ability, was I ever less so? Clay and Webster were dead before this question arose; by what authority shall our Senator say they would espouse his side of it, if alive? Mr. Clay was the leading spirit in making the Missouri compromise; is it very credible that if now alive, he would take the lead in the breaking of it? The truth is that some support from whigs is now a necessity with the Judge, and for thus it is, that the names of Clay and Webster are now invoked. His old friends have deserted him in such numbers as to leave too few to live by. He came to his own, and his own received him not, and Lo! he turns unto the Gentiles.

A word now as to the Judge's desperate assumption that the compromises of '50 had no connection with one another; that Illinois came into the Union as a slave state, and some other similar ones. This is no other than a bold denial of the history of the country. If we do not know that the Compromises of '50 were dependent on each other; if we do not know that Illinois came into the Union as a free State—we do not know any thing. If we do not know these things, we do not know that we ever had a revolutionary war, or such a chief as Washington. To deny these things is to deny our national axioms, or dogmas, at least; and it puts an end to all argument. If a man will stand up and assert, and repeat, and re-assert, that two and two do not make four, I know nothing in the power of argument that can stop him. I think I can answer the Judge so long as he sticks to the premises; but when he flies from them, I can not work an argument into the consistency of a maternal gag, and actually close his mouth with it. In such a case I can only commend him to the seventy thousand answers just in from Pennsylvania, Ohio and Indiana.

Dred Scott v. Sandford

Supreme Court of the United States (60 U.S. 393) March 6, 1857

[This is an abridged version of the document.]

Mr. Chief Justice TANEY delivered the opinion of the court. . . .

The question is simply this: can a negro whose ancestors were imported into this country and sold as slaves become a member of the political community formed and brought into existence by the Constitution of the United States, and as such become entitled to all the rights, and privileges, and immunities, guaranteed by that instrument to the citizen, one of which rights is the privilege of suing in a court of the United States in the cases specified in the Constitution?

It will be observed that the plea applies to that class of persons only whose ancestors were negroes of the African race, and imported into this country and sold and held as slaves. The only matter in issue before the court, therefore, is, whether the descendants of such slaves, when they shall be emancipated, or who are born of parents who had become free before their birth, are citizens of a State in the sense in which the word "citizen" is used in the Constitution of the United States. And this being the only matter in dispute on the pleadings, the court must be understood as speaking in this opinion of that class only, that is, of those persons who are the descendants of Africans who were imported into this country and sold as slaves. . . .

The words "people of the United States" and "citizens" are synonymous terms, and mean the same thing. They both describe the political body who, according to our republican institutions, form the sovereignty and who hold the power and conduct the Government through their representatives. They are what we familiarly call the "sovereign people," and every citizen is one of this people, and a constituent member of this sovereignty. The question before us is whether the class of persons described in the plea in abatement compose a portion of this people, and are constituent members of this sovereignty? We think they are not, and that they are not included, and

were not intended to be included, under the word "citizens" in the Constitution, and can therefore claim none of the rights and privileges which that instrument provides for and secures to citizens of the United States. On the contrary, they were at that time considered as a subordinate and inferior class of beings who had been subjugated by the dominant race, and, whether emancipated or not, yet remained subject to their authority, and had no rights or privileges but such as those who held the power and the Government might choose to grant them.

It is not the province of the court to decide upon the justice or injustice, the policy or impolicy, of these laws. The decision of that question belonged to the political or lawmaking power, to those who formed the sovereignty and framed the Constitution. The duty of the court is to interpret the instrument they have framed with the best lights we can obtain on the subject, and to administer it as we find it, according to its true intent and meaning when it was adopted. . . .

The question then arises, whether the provisions of the Constitution, in relation to the personal rights and privileges to which the citizen of a State should be entitled, embraced the negro African race, at that time in this country[,] or who might afterwards be imported, who had then or should afterwards be made free in any State, and to put it in the power of a single State to make him a citizen of the United States and endue him with the full rights of citizenship in every other State without their consent? Does the Constitution of the United States act upon him whenever he shall be made free under the laws of a State, and raised there to the rank of a citizen, and immediately clothe him with all the privileges of a citizen in every other State, and in its own courts?

The court think the affirmative of these propositions cannot be maintained. And if it cannot, the plaintiff in error could not be a citizen of the State of Missouri within the meaning of the Constitution of the United States, and, consequently, was not entitled to sue in its courts.

It is true, every person, and every class and description of persons who were, at the time of the adoption of the Constitution, recognised as citizens in the several States became also citizens of this new political body, but none other; it was formed by them, and for them and their posterity, but for no one else. And the personal rights and privileges guarantied to citizens of this new sovereignty were intended to embrace those only who were then members of the several State communities, or who should afterwards by birthright or otherwise become members according to the provisions of the Constitution and the principles on which it was founded. It was the union of those who were at that time members of distinct and separate political communities into one political family, whose power, for certain specified purposes, was to extend over the whole territory of the United States. And it gave to each citizen rights and privileges outside of his State which he did not before possess, and placed him in every other State upon a perfect equality with its own citizens as to rights of person and rights of property; it made him a citizen of the United States.

It becomes necessary, therefore, to determine who were citizens of the several States when the Constitution was adopted. And in order to do this, we must recur to the Governments and institutions of the thirteen colonies when they separated from Great Britain and formed new sovereignties, and took their places in the family of independent nations. We must inquire who, at that time, were recognised as the people or citizens of a State whose rights and liberties had been outraged by the English Government, and who declared their independence and assumed the powers of Government to defend their rights by force of arms.

In the opinion of the court, the legislation and histories of the times, and the language used in the Declaration of Independence, show that neither the class of persons who had been imported as slaves nor their descendants, whether they had become free or not, were then acknowledged as a part of the people, nor intended to be included in the general words used in that memorable instrument.

It is difficult at this day to realize the state of public opinion in relation to that unfortunate race which prevailed in the civilized and enlightened portions of the world at the time of the Declaration of Independence and when the Constitution of the United States was framed and adopted. But the public history of every European nation displays it in a manner too plain to be mistaken.

They had for more than a century before been regarded as beings of an inferior order, and altogether unfit to associate with the white race either in social or political relations, and so far inferior that they had no rights which the white man was bound to respect, and that the negro might justly and lawfully be reduced to slavery for his benefit. He was bought and sold, and treated as an ordinary article of merchandise and traffic whenever a profit could be made by it. This opinion was at that time fixed and universal in the civilized portion of the white race. It was regarded as an axiom in morals as well as in politics which no one thought of disputing or supposed to be open to dispute, and men in every grade and position in society daily and habitually acted upon it in their private pursuits, as well as in matters of public concern, without doubting for a moment the correctness of this opinion.

And in no nation was this opinion more firmly fixed or more uniformly acted upon than by the English Government and English people. They not only seized them on the coast of Africa and sold them or held them in slavery for their own use, but they took them as ordinary articles of merchandise to every country where they could make a profit on them, and were far more extensively engaged in this commerce than any other nation in the world.

The opinion thus entertained and acted upon in England was naturally impressed upon the colonies they founded on this side of the Atlantic. And, accordingly, a negro of the African race was regarded by them as an article of property, and held, and bought and sold as such, in every one of the thirteen colonies which united in the Declaration of Independence and afterwards formed the Constitution of the United States. The slaves were more or less numerous in the different colonies as slave labor was found more or less profitable. But no one seems to have doubted the correctness of the prevailing opinion of the time.

The legislation of the different colonies furnishes positive and indisputable proof of this fact.

It would be tedious, in this opinion, to enumerate the various laws they passed upon this subject. It will be sufficient, as a sample of the legislation which then generally prevailed throughout the British colonies, to give the laws of two of them, one being still a large slaveholding State and the other the first State in which slavery ceased to exist.

The province of Maryland, in 1717, ch. 13, s. 5, passed a law declaring "that if any free negro or mulatto intermarry with any white woman, or if any white man shall intermarry with any negro or mulatto woman, such negro or mulatto shall become a slave during life, excepting mulattoes born of white women, who, for such intermarriage, shall only become servants for seven years, to be disposed of as the justices of the county court where such marriage so happens shall think fit, to be applied by them towards the support of a public school within the said county. And any white man or white woman who shall intermarry as aforesaid with any negro or mulatto, such white man or white woman shall become servants during the term of seven years, and shall be disposed of by the justices as aforesaid, and be applied to the uses aforesaid."

The other colonial law to which we refer was passed by Massachusetts in 1705 (chap. 6). It is entitled "An act for the better preventing of a spurious and mixed issue," &c., and it provides, that "if any negro or mulatto shall presume to smite or strike any person of the English or other Christian nation, such negro or mulatto shall be severely whipped, at the discretion of the justices before whom the offender shall be convicted." And "that none of her Majesty's English or Scottish subjects, nor of any other Christian nation, within this province, shall contract matrimony with any negro or mulatto; nor shall any person, duly authorized to solemnize marriage, presume to join any such in marriage, on pain of forfeiting the sum of fifty pounds; one moiety thereof to her Majesty, for and towards the support of the Government within this province, and the other moiety to him or them that shall inform and sue for the same, in any of her Majesty's courts of record within the province, by bill, plaint, or information."

We give both of these laws in the words used by the respective legislative bodies because the language in which they are framed, as well as the provisions contained in them, show, too plainly to be misunderstood the degraded condition of this unhappy race. They were still in force when the Revolution began, and are a faithful index to the state of feeling towards the class of persons of whom they speak, and of the position they occupied throughout the thirteen colonies, in the eyes and thoughts of the men who framed the Declaration of Independence and established the State Constitutions and Governments. They show that a perpetual and impassable barrier was intended to be erected between the white race and the one which they had reduced to slavery, and governed as subjects with absolute and despotic power, and which they then looked upon as so far below them in the scale of created beings, that intermarriages between white persons and negroes or mulattoes were regarded as unnatural and immoral, and punished as crimes, not only in the parties, but in the person who joined them in marriage. And no distinction in this respect was made between the free negro or mulatto and the slave, but this stigma of the deepest degradation was fixed upon the whole race.

We refer to these historical facts for the purpose of showing the fixed opinions concerning that race upon which the statesmen of that day spoke and acted. It is necessary to do this in order to determine whether the general terms used in the Constitution of the United States as to the rights of man and the rights of the people was intended to include them, or to give to them or their posterity the benefit of any of its provisions.

The language of the Declaration of Independence is equally conclusive:

> It begins by declaring that, "[w]hen in the course of human events it becomes necessary for one people to dissolve the political bands which have connected them with another, and to assume among the powers of the earth the separate and equal station to which the laws of nature and nature's God entitle them, a decent respect for the opinions of mankind requires that they should declare the causes which impel them to the separation."

It then proceeds to say:

> "We hold these truths to be self-evident: that all men are created equal; that they are endowed by their Creator with certain unalienable rights; that among them is [sic] life, liberty, and the pursuit of happiness; that to secure these rights, Governments are instituted, deriving their just powers from the consent of the governed."

The general words above quoted would seem to embrace the whole human family, and if they were used in a similar instrument at this day would be so understood. But it is too clear for dispute that the enslaved African race were not intended to be included, and formed no part of the people who framed and adopted this declaration, for if the language, as understood in that day, would embrace them, the conduct of the distinguished men who framed the Declaration of Independence would have been utterly and flagrantly inconsistent with the principles they asserted, and instead of the sympathy of mankind to which they so confidently appealed, they would have deserved and received universal rebuke and reprobation.

Yet the men who framed this declaration were great men—high in literary acquirements, high in their sense of honor, and incapable of asserting principles inconsistent with those on which they were acting. They perfectly understood the meaning of the language they used, and how it would be understood by others, and they knew that it would not in any part of the civilized world be supposed to embrace the negro race, which, by common consent, had been excluded from civilized Governments and the family of nations, and doomed to slavery. They spoke and acted according to the then established doctrines and principles, and in the ordinary language of the day, and no one misunderstood them. The unhappy black race were separated from the white by indelible marks, and laws long before established, and were never thought of or spoken of except as property, and when the claims of the owner or the profit of the trader were supposed to need protection.

This state of public opinion had undergone no change when the Constitution was adopted, as is equally evident from its provisions and language.

The brief preamble sets forth by whom it was formed, for what purposes, and for whose benefit and protection. It declares that it is formed by the people of the United States—that is to say, by those who were members of the different political communities in the several States—and its great object is declared to be to secure the blessings of liberty to themselves and their posterity. It speaks in general terms of the people of the United States, and of citizens of the several States, when it is providing for the exercise of the powers granted or the privileges secured to the citizen. It does not define what description of persons are intended to be included under these terms, or who shall be regarded as a citizen and one of the people. It uses them as terms so well understood that no further description or definition was necessary.

But there are two clauses in the Constitution which point directly and specifically to the negro race as a separate class of persons, and show clearly that they were not regarded as a portion of the people or citizens of the Government then formed.

One of these clauses reserves to each of the thirteen States the right to import slaves until the year 1808 if it thinks proper. And the importation which it thus sanctions was unquestionably of persons of the race of which we are speaking, as the traffic in slaves in the United States had always been confined to them. And by the other provision the States pledge themselves to each other to maintain the right of property of the master by delivering up to him any slave who may have escaped from his service, and be found within their respective territories. By the first above-mentioned clause, therefore, the right to purchase and hold this property is directly sanctioned and authorized for twenty years by the people who framed the Constitution. And by the second, they pledge themselves to maintain and uphold the right of the master in the manner specified, as long as the Government they then formed should endure. And these two provisions show conclusively that neither the description of persons therein referred to nor their descendants were embraced in any of the other provisions of the Constitution, for certainly these two clauses were not intended to confer on them or their posterity the blessings of liberty, or any of the personal rights so carefully provided for the citizen.

No one of that race had ever migrated to the United States voluntarily; all of them had been brought here as articles of merchandise. The number that had been emancipated at that time were but few in comparison with those held in slavery, and they were identified in the public mind with the race to which they belonged, and regarded as a part of the slave population rather than the free. It is obvious that they were not even in the minds of the framers of the Constitution when they were conferring special rights and privileges upon the citizens of a State in every other part of the Union.

Indeed, when we look to the condition of this race in the several States at the time, it is impossible to believe that these rights and privileges were intended to be extended to them. . . .

The only two provisions which point to them and include them treat them as property and make it the duty of the Government to protect it; no other power, in relation to this race, is to be found in the Constitution; and as it is a Government of special, delegated, powers, no authority beyond these two provisions can be constitutionally exercised. The Government of the United States had no right to interfere for any other purpose but that of protecting the rights of the owner, leaving it altogether with the several States to deal with this race, whether emancipated or not, as each State may think justice, humanity, and the interests and safety of society, require. The States evidently intended to reserve this power exclusively to themselves.

No one, we presume, supposes that any change in public opinion or feeling, in relation to this unfortunate race, in the civilized nations of Europe or in this country, should induce the court to give to the words of the Constitution a more liberal construction in their favor than they were intended to bear when the instrument was framed and adopted. Such an argument would be altogether inadmissible in any tribunal called on to interpret it. If any of its provisions are deemed unjust, there is a mode prescribed in the instrument itself by which it may be amended; but while it remains unaltered, it must be construed now as it was understood at the time of its adoption. It is not only the same in words, but the same in meaning, and delegates the same powers to the Government, and reserves and secures the same rights and privileges to the citizen; and as long as it continues to exist in its present form, it speaks not only in the same words, but with the same meaning and intent with which it spoke when it came from the hands of its framers and was voted on and adopted by the people of the United States. Any other rule of construction would abrogate the judicial character of this court, and make it the mere reflex of the popular opinion or passion of the day. This court was not created by the Constitution for such purposes. Higher and graver trusts have been confided to it, and it must not falter in the path of duty.

What the construction was at that time we think can hardly admit of doubt. We have the language of the Declaration of Independence and of the Articles of Confederation, in addition to the plain words of the Constitution itself; we have the legislation of the different States, before, about the time, and since the Constitution was adopted; we have the legislation of Congress, from the time of its adoption to a recent period; and we have the constant and uniform action of the Executive Department, all concurring together, and leading to the same result. And if anything in relation to the construction of the Constitution can be regarded as settled, it is that which we now give to the word "citizen" and the word "people."

And, upon a full and careful consideration of the subject, the court is of opinion, that, upon the facts stated in the plea in abatement, Dred Scott was not a citizen of Missouri within the meaning of the Constitution of the United States, and not entitled as such to sue in its courts, and consequently that the Circuit Court had no jurisdiction of the case, and that the judgment on the plea in abatement is erroneous. . . .

We proceed, therefore, to inquire whether the facts relied on by the plaintiff entitled him to his freedom.

The case, as he himself states it, on the record brought here by his writ of error, is this:

> The plaintiff was a negro slave, belonging to Dr. Emerson, who was a surgeon in the army of the United States. In the year 1834, he took the plaintiff from the State of Missouri to the military post at Rock Island, in the State of Illinois, and held him there as a slave until the month of April or May, 1836. At the time last mentioned, said Dr. Emerson removed the plaintiff from said military post at Rock Island to the military post at Fort Snelling, situate on the west bank of the Mississippi river, in the Territory known as Upper Louisiana, acquired by the United States of France, and situate north of the latitude of thirty-six degrees thirty minutes north, and north of the State of Missouri. Said Dr. Emerson held the plaintiff in slavery at said Fort Snelling from said last-mentioned date until the year 1838. . . .

In the year 1838, said Dr. Emerson removed the plaintiff [*and wife Harriet and their daughter Eliza*] from said Fort Snelling to the State of Missouri, where they have ever since resided.

Before the commencement of this suit, said Dr. Emerson sold and conveyed the plaintiff, and Harriet, Eliza, and Lizzie, to the defendant, as slaves, and the defendant has ever since claimed to hold them, and each of them, as slaves.

In considering this part of the controversy, two questions arise: 1. Was he, together with his family, free in Missouri by reason of the stay in the territory of the United States hereinbefore mentioned? And 2. If they were not, is Scott himself free by reason of his removal to Rock Island, in the State of Illinois, as stated in the above admissions?

We proceed to examine the first question.

The act of Congress upon which the plaintiff relies declares that slavery and involuntary servitude, except as a punishment for crime, shall be forever prohibited in all that part of the territory ceded by France, under the name of Louisiana, which lies north of thirty-six degrees thirty minutes north latitude, and not included within the limits of Missouri.

And the difficulty which meets us at the threshold of this part of the inquiry is whether Congress was authorized to pass this law under any of the powers granted to it by the Constitution; for if the authority is not given by that instrument, it is the duty of this court to declare it void and inoperative, and incapable of conferring freedom upon anyone who is held as a slave under the laws of any one of the States.

The counsel for the plaintiff has laid much stress upon that article in the Constitution which confers on Congress the power "to dispose of and make all needful rules and regulations respecting the territory or other property belonging to the United States," but, in the judgment of the court, that provision has no bearing on the present controversy, and the power there given, whatever it may be, is confined, and was intended to be confined, to the territory which at that time belonged to, or was claimed by, the United States, and was within their boundaries as settled by the treaty with Great Britain, and can have no influence upon a territory afterwards acquired from a foreign Government. It was a special provision for a known and particular territory, and to meet a present emergency, and nothing more. . . .

We do not mean, however, to question the power of Congress in this respect. The power to expand the territory of the United States by the admission of new States is plainly given, and, in the construction of this power by all the departments of the Government, it has been held to authorize the acquisition of territory not fit for admission at the time, but to be admitted as soon as its population and situation would entitle it to admission. . . .

But, until that time arrives, it is undoubtedly necessary that some Government should be established in order to organize society and to protect the inhabitants in their persons and property, and as the people of the United States could act in this matter only through the Government which represented them and the through which they spoke and acted when the Territory was obtained, it was not only within the scope of its powers, but it was its duty, to pass such laws and establish such a Government as would enable those by whose authority they acted to reap the advantages anticipated from its acquisition and to gather there a population which would enable it to assume the position to which it was destined among the States of the Union. . . .

But the power of Congress over the person or property of a citizen can never be a mere discretionary power under our Constitution and form of Government. The powers of the Government and the rights and privileges of the citizen are regulated and plainly defined by the Constitution itself. And when the Territory becomes a part of the United States, the Federal Government enters into possession in the character impressed upon it by those who created it. It enters upon it with its powers over the citizen strictly defined, and limited by the Constitution, from which it derives its own existence and by virtue of which alone it continues to exist and act as a Government and sovereignty. It has no power of any kind beyond it, and it cannot, when it enters a Territory of the United States, put off its character and assume discretionary or despotic powers which the Constitution has denied to it. It cannot create for itself a new character separated from the citizens of the United States and the duties it owes them under the provisions of the Constitution. The Territory being a part of the United States, the Government and the citizen both enter it under the authority of the Constitution, with their respective rights defined and marked out, and the Federal Government can exercise no power over his person or property beyond what that instrument confers, nor lawfully deny any right which it has reserved. . . .

The powers over person and property of which we speak are not only not granted to Congress, but are in express terms denied, and they are forbidden to exercise them. And this prohibition is not confined to the States, but the words are general, and extend to the whole territory over which the Constitution gives it power to legislate, including those portions of it remaining under Territorial Government, as well as that covered by States. It is a total absence of power everywhere within the dominion of the United States, and places the citizens of a Territory, so far as these rights are concerned, on the same footing with citizens of the States, and guards them as firmly and plainly against any inroads which the General Government might attempt under the plea of implied or incidental powers. And if Congress itself cannot do this—if it is beyond the powers conferred on the Federal Government—it will be admitted, we presume, that it could not authorize a Territorial Government to exercise them. It could confer no power on any local Government established by its authority to violate the provisions of the Constitution.

It seems, however, to be supposed that there is a difference between property in a slave and other property and that different rules may be applied to it in expounding the Constitution of the United States. And the laws and usages of nations, and the writings of eminent jurists upon the relation of master and slave and their mutual rights and duties, and the powers which Governments may exercise over it have been dwelt upon in the argument.

But, in considering the question before us, it must be borne in mind that there is no law of nations standing between the people of the United States and their Government and interfering with their relation to each other. The powers of the Government and the rights of the citizen under it are positive and practical regulations plainly written down. The people of the United States have delegated to it certain enumerated powers and forbidden it to exercise others. It has no power over the person or property of a citizen but what the citizens of the United States have granted. And no laws or usages of other nations, or reasoning of statesmen or jurists upon the relations of master and slave, can enlarge the powers of the Government or take from the citizens the rights they have reserved. And if the Constitution recognises the right of property of the master in a slave, and makes no distinction between that description of property and other property owned by a citizen, no tribunal, acting under the authority of the United States, whether it be legislative, executive, or judicial, has a right to draw such a distinction or deny to it the benefit of the provisions and guarantees which have been provided for the protection of private property against the encroachments of the Government.

Now, as we have already said in an earlier part of this opinion upon a different point, the right of property in a slave is distinctly and expressly affirmed in the Constitution. The right to traffic in it, like an ordinary article of merchandise and property, was guarantied to the citizens of the United States in every State that might desire it for twenty years. And the Government in express terms is pledged to protect it in all future time if the slave escapes from his owner. This is done in plain words—too plain to be misunderstood. And no word can be found in the Constitution which gives Congress a greater power over slave property or which entitles property of that kind to less protection [than] property of any other description. The only power conferred is the power coupled with the duty of guarding and protecting the owner in his rights.

Upon these considerations, it is the opinion of the court that the act of Congress which prohibited a citizen from holding and owning property of this kind in the territory of the United States north of the line therein mentioned is not warranted by the Constitution, and is therefore void, and that neither Dred Scott himself nor any of his family were made free by being carried into this territory, even if they had been carried there by the owner with the intention of becoming a permanent resident. . . .

Upon the whole, therefore, it is the judgment of this court that it appears by the record before us that the plaintiff in error is not a citizen of Missouri in the sense in which that word is used in the Constitution, and that the Circuit Court of the United States, for that reason, had no jurisdiction in the case, and could give no judgment in it. Its judgment for the defendant must, consequently, be reversed, and a mandate issued directing the suit to be dismissed for want of jurisdiction.

House Divided Speech
Springfield, Illinois June 16, 1858

Abraham Lincoln

On June 16, 1858, more than 1,000 Republican delegates met in the Springfield, Illinois, statehouse for the Republican State Convention. At 5 p.m. they chose Abraham Lincoln as their candidate for the U.S. Senate, running against Democrat Stephen A. Douglas. At 8 p.m. Lincoln delivered this address to his Republican colleagues in the Hall of Representatives. The title comes from a sentence in the speech's introduction, "A house divided against itself cannot stand," which paraphrases a statement by Jesus in the New Testament.

Even Lincoln's friends believed the speech was too radical for the occasion. His law partner, William H. Herndon, thought that Lincoln was morally courageous but politically incorrect. Herndon said Lincoln told him he was looking for a universally know figure of speech that would rouse people to the peril of the times.

Another lawyer Leonard Swett, said the speech defeated Lincoln in the Senate campaign. In 1866 he wrote to Herndon complaining, "Nothing could have been more unfortunate or inappropriate; it was saying first the wrong thing, yet he saw it was an abstract truth, but standing by the speech would ultimately find him in the right place."

✳ ✳ ✳ ✳ ✳

Mr. President and Gentlemen of the Convention.

If we could first know *where* we are, and *whither* we are tending, we could then better judge *what* to do, and *how* to do it.

We are now far into the *fifth* year, since a policy was initiated, with the *avowed* object, and *confident* promise, of putting an end to slavery agitation.

Under the operation of that policy, that agitation has not only, *not ceased*, but has *constantly augmented*.

In *my* opinion, it *will* not cease, until a *crisis* shall have been reached, and passed.

"A house divided against itself cannot stand."

I believe this government cannot endure, permanently half *slave* and half *free*.

I do not expect the Union to be *dissolved*—I do not expect the house to *fall*—but I *do* expect it will cease to be divided.

It will become *all* one thing or *all* the other.

Either the *opponents* of slavery, will arrest the further spread of it, and place it where the public mind shall rest in the belief that it is in the course of ultimate extinction; or its *advocates* will push it forward, till it shall become alike lawful in *all* the States, *old* as well as *new*—*North* as well as *South*.

Have we no *tendency* to the latter condition?

Let any one who doubts, carefully contemplate that now almost complete legal combination—piece of *machinery* so to speak—compounded of the Nebraska doctrine, and the Dred Scott decision. Let him consider not only *what* work the machinery is adapted to do, and *how well* adapted; but also, let him study the *history* of its construction, and trace, if he can, or rather *fail*, if he can, to trace the evidence of design and concert of action, among its chief architects, from the beginning.

But, so far, *Congress* only, had acted; and an *indorsement* by the people, real or apparent, was indispensable, to save the point already gained, and give chance for more.

The new year of 1854 found slavery excluded from more than half the States by State Constitutions, and from most of the national territory by congressional prohibition.

Four days later, commenced the struggle, which ended in repealing that congressional prohibition.

This opened all the national territory to slavery, and was the first point gained.

This necessity had not been overlooked; but had been provided for, as well as might be, in the notable argument of "*squatter sovereignty*," otherwise called "*sacred right of self government*," which latter phrase, though expressive of the only rightful basis of any government, was so perverted in this attempted use of it as to amount to just this: That if any one man, choose to enslave *another*, no *third* man shall be allowed to object.

That argument was incorporated into the Nebraska bill itself, in the language which follows: "*It being the true intent and meaning of this act not to legislate slavery into any Territory or state, not to exclude it therefrom; but to leave the people thereof perfectly free to form and regulate their domestic institutions in their own way, subject only to the Constitution of the United States.*"

Then opened the roar of loose declamation in favor of "Squatter Sovereignty," and "Sacred right of self-government."

"But," said opposition members, "let us be more *specific* – let us *amend* the bill so as to expressly declare that the people of the territory may exclude slavery." "Not we," said the friends of the measure; and down they voted the amendment.

While the Nebraska Bill was passing through congress, a *law case* involving the question of a negroe's freedom, by reason of his owner having voluntarily taken him first into a free state and then a territory covered by the congressional prohibition, and held him as a slave, for a long time in each, was passing through the U. S. Circuit Court for the District of Missouri; and both Nebraska bill and law suit were brought to a decision in the same month of May, 1854. The negroe's name was "Dred Scott," which name now designates the decision finally made in the case.

Before the *then* next Presidential election, the law case came to, and was argued *in*, the Supreme Court of the United States; but the *decision* of it was deferred until *after* the election. Still, *before* the election, Senator Trumbull, on the floor of the Senate, requests the leading advocate of the Nebraska bill to state *his opinion* whether the people of a territory can constitutionally exclude slavery from their limits; and the latter answers: "That is a question for the Supreme Court."

The election came. Mr. Buchanan was elected, and the *indorsement*, such as it was, secured. That was the *second* point gained. The indorsement, however, fell short of a clear popular majority by nearly four hundred thousand votes, and so, perhaps, was not overwhelmingly reliable and satisfactory.

The *outgoing* President, in his last annual message, as impressively as possible, echoed back upon the people the weight and *authority* of the indorsement.

The Supreme Court met again; *did not* announce their decision, but ordered a re-argument.

The Presidential inauguration came, and still no decision of the court; but the *incoming* President, in his inaugural address, fervently exhorted the people to abide by the forthcoming decision, *whatever might be.*

Then, in a few days, came the decision.

The reputed author of the Nebraska Bill finds an early occasion to make a speech at this capital indorsing the Dred Scott Decision, and vehemently denouncing all opposition to it.

The new President, too, seizes the early occasion of the Silliman letter to *indorse* and strongly *construe* that decision, and to express his *astonishment* that any different view had ever been entertained.

At length a squabble springs up between the President and the author of the Nebraska Bill, on the *mere* question of *fact*, whether the Lecompton constitution was or was not, in any just sense, made by the people of Kansas; and in that squabble the latter declares that all he wants is a fair vote for the people, and that he cares not whether slavery be voted *down* or voted *up*. I do not understand his declaration that he cares not whether slavery be voted down or voted up, to be intended by him other than as an *apt definition* of the *policy* he would impress upon the public mind—the *principle* for which he declares he has suffered much, and is ready to suffer to the end.

And well may he cling to that principle. If he has any parental feeling, well may he cling to it. That principle, is the only *shred* left of his original Nebraska doctrine. Under the Dred Scott decision, "squatter sovereignty" squatted out of existence, tumbled down like temporary scaffolding—like the mould at the foundry served through one blast and fell back into loose sand—helped to carry an election, and then was kicked to the winds. His late *joint* struggle with the Republicans, against the Lecompton Constitution, involves nothing of the original Nebraska doctrine. That struggle was made on a point, the right of a people to make their own constitution, upon which he and the Republicans have never differed.

The several points of the Dred Scott decision, in connection with Senator Douglas's "care-not" policy, constitute the piece of machinery, in its present state of advancement. This was the third point gained. The working points of that machinery are:—

First, that no negro slave, imported as such from Africa, and no descendant of such slave, can ever be a citizen of any State, in the sense of that term as used in the Constitution of the United States. This point is made in order to deprive the negro, in every possible event, of the benefit of that provision of the United States Constitution, which declares that: "The citizens of each State shall be entitled to all privileges and immunities of citizens in the several States."

Second, that "subject to the Constitution of the United States," neither Congress nor a Territorial legislature can exclude slavery from any United States Territory. This point is made in order that individual men may fill up the Territories with slaves, without danger of losing them as property, and thus to enhance the chances of permanency to the institution through all the future.

Third, that whether the holding a negro in actual slavery in a free State makes him free, as against the holder, the United States courts will not decide, but will leave to be decided by the courts of any slave State the negro may be forced into by the master. This point is made, not to be pressed immediately; but, if acquiesced in for a while, and apparently indorsed by the people at an election, then to sustain the logical conclusion that what Dred Scott's master might lawfully do with Dred Scott, in the free State of Illinois, every other master may lawfully do with any other one, or one thousand slaves, in Illinois, or in any other free State.

Auxiliary to all this, and working hand in hand with it, the Nebraska doctrine, or what is left of it, is to educate and mold public opinion, at least Northern public opinion, not to care whether slavery is voted down or voted up. This shows exactly where we now are; and partially, also, whither we are tending.

It will throw additional light on the latter, to go back, and run the mind over the string of historical facts already stated. Several things will now appear less dark and mysterious than they did when they were transpiring. The people were to be left "perfectly free," subject only to the Constitution. What the Constitution had to do with it, outsiders could not then see. Plainly enough now, it was an exactly fitted niche, for the Dred Scott decision to afterward come in, and declare the perfect free freedom of the people to be just no freedom at all. Why was the amendment, expressly declaring the right of the people, voted down? Plainly enough now: the adoption of it would have spoiled the niche for the Dred Scott decision. Why was the court decision held up? Why even a Senator's individual opinion withheld, till after the presidential election? Plainly enough now—the speaking out then would have damaged the perfectly free argument upon which the election was to be carried. Why the outgoing President's felicitation on the indorsement? Why the delay of a re-argument? Why the incoming President's advance exhortation in favor of the decision? These things look like the cautious patting and petting of a spirited horse, preparatory to mounting him, when it is dreaded that he may give the rider a fall. And why the hasty after-indorsement of the decision by the President and others?

We cannot absolutely know that all these exact adaptations are the result of preconcert. But when we see a lot of framed timbers, different portions of which we know have been gotten out at different times and places, and by different workmen—Stephen, Franklin, Roger, and James, for instance—and when we see these timbers joined together, and see they exactly matte the frame of a house or a mill, all the tenons and mortices exactly fitting, and all the lengths and proportions of the different pieces exactly adapted to their respective places, and not a piece. too many or too few, —not omitting even scaffolding—or, if a single piece be lacking, we see the place in the frame exactly fitted and prepared yet to bring such piece in—in such a case we find it impossible not to believe that Stephen and Franklin and Roger and James all understood one another from the beginning and all worked upon a common plan or draft drawn up before the first blow was struck.

It should not be overlooked that, by the Nebraska Bill, the people of a State, as well as a Territory, were to be left "perfectly free," "subject only to the Constitution." Why mention a State? They were legislating for Territories, and not for or about States.

Certainly the people of a State are and ought to be subject to the Constitution of the United States; but why is mention of this lugged into this merely Territorial law? Why are the people of a Territory and the people of a State therein lumped together, and their relation to the Constitution therein treated as being precisely the same? While the opinion of the court, by Chief-Justice Taney, in the Dred Scott case and the separate opinions of all the concurring judges, expressly declare that the Constitution of the United States neither permits Congress nor a Territorial legislature to exclude slavery from any United States Territory, they all omit to declare whether or not the same Constitution permits a State, or the people of a State, to exclude it. Possibly this is a mere omission; but who can be quite sure, if McLean or Curtis had sought to get into the opinion a declaration of unlimited power in the people of a State to exclude slavery from their limits, just as Chase and Mace sought to get such declaration, in behalf of the people of a Territory, into the Nebraska Bill—I ask, who can be quite sure that it would not have been voted down in the one case as it ad been in the other? The nearest approach to the point of declaring the power of a State over slavery is made by Judge Nelson. He approaches it more than once, using the precise idea, and almost the language, too, of the Nebraska Act. On one occasion, his exact language is, "except in cases where the power is restrained by the Constitution of the United States the law of the State is supreme over the subject of slavery within its g jurisdiction." In what cases the power of the States is so restrained by the United States Constitution is left an open question, precisely as the same question, as to the restraint on the power of the Territories, was left open in the Nebraska Act Put this and that together, and we have another nice little niche which we may ere long see filled with another Supreme Court decisions declaring that the Constitution of the United States does not permit a State to exclude slavery from its limits. And this may especially be expected if the doctrine of "care not whether slavery be voted down or voted up," shall gain upon he public mind sufficiently to give promise that such a decision an be maintained when made.

Such a decision is all that slavery now lacks of being alike lawful in all the States. Welcome, or unwelcome, such decision is probably coming, and will soon be upon us, unless the power of the present political dynasty shall be met and overthrown.

We shall lie down pleasantly dreaming that the people of Missouri. are on the verge of making their State free, and we shall awake to the reality instead, that the Supreme Court has made Illinois a slave State. To meet and overthrow the power of that dynasty is the work now before all those who would prevent that consummation. This is what we have to do. How can we best do it? There are those who denounce us openly to their own friends and yet whisper us softly, that Senator Douglas is the aptest instrument there is with which to effect that object. They wish us to infer all from the fact that he now has a little quarrel with the present head of the dynasty; and that he has regularly voted with us on a single point, upon which he and we have never differed. They remind us that he is a great man, and that the largest of us are very small ones. Let this be granted. But "a living dog is better than a dead lion." Judge Douglas, if not a dead lion, for this work, is at least a caged and tooth. less one. How can he oppose the advances of slavery? He does not care anything about it. His avowed mission is impressing the "public heart" to care nothing about it. A leading Douglas Democratic newspaper thinks Douglas's superior talent will be needed to resist the revival of the African slave trade. Does Douglas believe an effort to revive that trade is approaching? He has not said so. Does he really think so? But if it is, how can he resist it? For years he has labored to prove it a sacred right of white men to take negro slaves into the new Territories. Can he possibly show that it is less a sacred right to buy them where they can be bought cheapest? And unquestionably they can be bought cheaper in Africa than in Virginia. He has done all in his power to reduce the whole question of slavery to one of a mere right of property; and as such, how can he oppose the foreign slave trade—how can he refuse that trade in that "property" shall be "perfectly free"—unless he does it as a protection to the home production? And as the home producers will probably not ask the protection, he will be wholly without a ground of opposition.

Senator Douglas holds, we know, that a man may rightfully be wiser today than he was yesterday—that he may rightfully change when he finds himself wrong. But can we, for that reason, run ahead, and infer that he will make any particular change, of which he, himself, has given no intimation? Can we safely base our action upon any such vague inference? Now, as ever, I wish not to misrepresent Judge Douglas's position, question his motives, or do aught that can be personally offensive to him. Whenever, if ever, he and we can come together on principle so that our cause may have assistance from his great ability, I hope to have interposed no adventitious obstacle. But clearly, he is not now with us—he does not pretend to be—he does not promise ever to be.

Our cause, then, must be intrusted to, and conducted by, its own undoubted friends—those whose hands are free, whose hearts are in the work—who do care for the result. Two years ago the Republicans of the nation mustered over thirteen hundred thousand strong. We did this under the single impulse of resistance to a common danger, with every external circumstance against us. Of strange, discordant, and even hostile elements, we gathered from the four winds, and formed and fought the battle through, under the constant hot fire of a disciplined, proud, and pampered enemy. Did we brave all them to falter now?—now, when that same enemy is wavering, dissevered, and belligerent? The result is not doubtful. We shall not fail—if we stand firm, we shall not fail. Wise counsels may accelerate, or mistakes delay it, but, sooner or later, the victory is sure to come.

The Lincoln-Douglas Debates

First Debate, August 21, 1858, Ottawa, Illinois

Douglas:

. . . I ask you, are you in favor of conferring upon the negro the rights and privileges of citizenship? Do you desire to strike out of our State constitution that clause which keeps slaves and free negroes out of the State, and allow the free negroes to flow in, and cover your prairies with black settlements? Do you desire to turn this beautiful State into a free negro colony, in order that when Missouri abolishes slavery she can send one hundred thousand emancipated slaves into Illinois, to become citizens and voters, on an equality with yourselves? If you desire negro citizenship, if you desire to allow them to come into the State and settle with the white man, if you desire them to vote on an equality with yourselves, and to make them eligible to office, to serve on juries, and to adjudge your rights, then support Mr. Lincoln and the Black Republican party, who are in favor of the citizenship of the negro. For one, I am opposed to negro citizenship in any and every form. I believe this government was made on the white basis. I believe it was made by white men, for the benefit of white men and their posterity forever, and I am in favor of confining citizenship to white men, men of European birth and descent, instead of conferring it upon negroes, Indians, and other inferior races. . . .

Lincoln:

. . . I have no purpose to introduce political and social equality between the white and the black races. There is a physical difference between the two, which, in my judgment, will probably forever forbid their living together upon the footing of perfect equality; and inasmuch as it becomes a necessity that there must be a difference, I, as well as Judge Douglas, am in favor of the race to which I belong having the superior position. I have never said anything to the contrary, but I hold that, notwithstanding all this, there is no reason in the world why the negro is not entitled to all the natural rights enumerated in the Declaration of Independence—the right to life, liberty, and the pursuit of happiness. I hold that he is as much entitled to these as the white man. I agree with Judge Douglas he is not my equal in many respects—certainly not in color, perhaps not in moral or intellectual endowment. But in the right to eat the bread, without the leave of anybody else, which his own hand earns, he is my equal and the equal of Judge Douglas, and the equal of every living man. . . .

Second Debate, August 27, 1858, Freeport, Illinois

Douglas:

. . . The last time I came here to make a speech, while talking from the stand to you, people of Freeport, as I am doing today, I saw a carriage, and a magnificent one it was, drive up and take a position on the outside of the crowd; a beautiful young lady was sitting on the box-seat, whilst Fred Douglass and her mother reclined inside, and the owner of the carriage acted as driver. I saw this in your own town. . . . All I have to say of it is this, that if you Black Republicans think that the negro ought to be on a social equality with your wives and daughters, and ride in a carriage with your wife, whilst you drive the team, you have perfect right to do so. I am told that one of Fred Douglass's kinsmen, another rich black negro, is now traveling in this part of the State making speeches for his friend Lincoln as the champion of black men. . . . All I have to say on that subject is, that those of you who believe that the negro is your equal and ought to be on an equality with you socially, politically, and legally, have a right to entertain those opinions, and of course will vote for Mr. Lincoln.

Fourth Debate, September 18, 1858, Charleston, Illinois

Lincoln:

. . . I am not, nor ever have been, in favor of making voters or jurors of negroes, nor of qualifying them to hold office, nor to intermarry with white people, and I will say in addition to this that there is a physical difference between the white and black races which I believe will forever forbid the two races living together on terms of social and political equality. And inasmuch as they cannot so live, while they do remain together there must be the position of superior and inferior, and I as much as any other man am in favor of having the superior position assigned to the white race. I say upon this occasion I do not perceive that because the white man is to have the superior position the negro should be denied everything. I do not understand that because I do not want a negro woman for a slave I must necessarily want her for a wife. My understanding is that I can just let her alone. I am now in my fiftieth year, and I certainly never have had a black woman for either a slave or a wife. So it seems to me quite possible for us to get along without making either slaves or wives of negroes. . . . I have never had the least apprehension that I or my friends would marry negroes if there was no law to keep them from it, but as Judge Douglas and his friends seem to be in great apprehension that they might, if there was no law to keep them from it, I give him the most solemn pledge that I will to the very last stand by the law of this State, which forbids the marrying of white people with negroes. . . .

Fifth Debate, October 7, 1858, Galesburg, Illinois

Douglas:

. . . The signers of the Declaration of Independence never dreamed of the negro when they were writing that document. They referred to white men, to men of European birth and European descent, when they declared the equality of all men. I see a gentleman there in the crowd shaking his head. Let me remind him that when Thomas Jefferson wrote that document he was the owner, and so continued until his death, of a large number of slaves. Did he intend to say in that Declaration that his negro slaves, which he held and treated as property, were created his equals by divine law, and that he was violating the law of God every day of his life by holding them as slaves? It must be borne in mind that when that Declaration was put forth, every one of the thirteen colonies were slave-holding colonies, and every man who signed that instrument represented a slaveholding constituency. Recollect, also, that no one of them emancipated his slaves, much less put them on an equality with himself, after he signed the Declaration. On the contrary, they all continued to hold their negroes as slaves during the Revolutionary War. Now, do you believe—are you willing to have it said—that every man who signed the Declaration of Independence declared the negro his equal, and then was hypocrite enough to hold him as a slave, in violation of what he believed to be the divine law? And yet when you say that the Declaration of Independence includes the negro, you charge the signers of it with hypocrisy.

I say to you frankly, that in my opinion this government was made by our fathers on the white basis. It was made by white men for the benefit of white men and their posterity forever, and was intended to be administered by white men in all time to come. But while I hold that under our Constitution and political system the negro is not a citizen, cannot be a citizen, and ought not to be a citizen, it does not follow by any means that he should be a slave. On the contrary, it does follow that the negro as an inferior race ought to possess every right, every privilege, every immunity which he can safely exercise consistent with the safety of the society in which he lives. Humanity requires, and Christianity commands, that you shall extend to every inferior being, and every dependent being, all the privileges, immunities, and advantages which can be granted to them consistent with the safety of society. If you ask me the nature and extent of these privileges, I answer that that is a question which the people of each State must decide for themselves. Illinois has decided that question for herself. We have said that in this State the negro shall not be a slave, nor shall he be a citizen. Kentucky holds a different doctrine. . . . Illinois had as much right to adopt the policy which we have on that subject as Kentucky had to adopt a different policy. The great principle of this government is that each State has the right to do as it pleases on all these questions, and no other State or power on earth has the right to interfere with us, or complain of us merely because our system differs from theirs. In the compromise measures of 1850, Mr. Clay declared that this great principle ought to exist in the Territories as well as in the States, and I reasserted his doctrine in the Kansas and Nebraska bill in 1854. . . .

Seventh Debate, October 15, 1858, Alton, Illinois

Lincoln:

. . . The real issue in this controversy—the one pressing upon every mind–is the sentiment on the part of one class that looks upon the institution of slavery as a wrong, and of another class that does not look upon it as a wrong. The sentiment that contemplates the institution of slavery in this country as a wrong is the sentiment of the Republican party. It is the sentiment around which all their actions, all their arguments, circle; from which all their propositions radiate. They look upon it as being a moral, social, and political wrong; and while they contemplate it as such, they nevertheless have due regard for its actual existence among us, and the difficulties of getting rid of it in any satisfactory way, and to all the constitutional obligations thrown about it. Yet having a due regard for these, they desire a policy in regard to it that looks to its not creating any more danger. . . .

[Douglas] contends that whatever community wants slaves has a right to have them. So they have if it is not a wrong. But if it is a wrong, he cannot say people have a right to do wrong. . . .

That is the real issue. That is the issue that will continue in this country when these poor tongues of Judge Douglas and myself shall be silent. It is the eternal struggle between these two principles—right and wrong–throughout the world. They are the two principles that have stood face to face from the beginning of time; and will ever continue to struggle. The one is the common right of humanity, and the other the divine right of kings. It is the same principle in whatever shape it develops itself. It is the same spirit that says, "You toil and work and earn bread, and I'll eat it." No matter in what shape it comes, whether from the mouth of a king who seeks to bestride the people of his own nation and live by the fruit of their labor, or from one race of men as an apology for enslaving another race, it is the same tyrannical principle.. . .

Declaration of the Immediate Causes Which Induce and Justify the Secession of South Carolina from the Federal Union

C. G. Memminger

The people of the State of South Carolina, in Convention assembled, on the 26th day of April, A.D., 1852, declared that the frequent violations of the Constitution of the United States, by the Federal Government, and its encroachments upon the reserved rights of the States, fully justified this State in then withdrawing from the Federal Union; but in deference to the opinions and wishes of the other slaveholding States, she forbore at that time to exercise this right. Since that time, these encroachments have continued to increase, and further forbearance ceases to be a virtue.

And now the State of South Carolina having resumed her separate and equal place among nations, deems it due to herself, to the remaining United States of America, and to the nations of the world, that she should declare the immediate causes which have led to this act.

In the year 1765, that portion of the British Empire embracing Great Britain, undertook to make laws for the government of that portion composed of the thirteen American Colonies. A struggle for the right of self-government ensued, which resulted, on the 4th of July, 1776, in a Declaration, by the Colonies, "that they are, and of right ought to be, FREE AND INDEPENDENT STATES; and that, as free and independent States, they have full power to levy war, conclude peace, contract alliances, establish commerce, and to do all other acts and things which independent States may of right do."

They further solemnly declared that whenever any "form of government becomes destructive of the ends for which it was established, it is the right of the people to alter or abolish it, and to institute a new government." Deeming the Government of Great Britain to have become destructive of these ends, they declared that the Colonies "are absolved from all allegiance to the British Crown, and that all political connection between them and the State of Great Britain is, and ought to be, totally dissolved."

In pursuance of this Declaration of Independence, each of the thirteen States proceeded to exercise its separate sovereignty; adopted for itself a Constitution, and appointed officers for the administration of government in all its departments—Legislative, Executive and Judicial. For purposes of defense, they united their arms and their counsels; and, in 1778, they entered into a League known as the Articles of Confederation, whereby they agreed to entrust the administration of their external relations to a common agent, known as the Congress of the United States, expressly declaring, in the first Article "that each State retains its sovereignty, freedom and independence, and every power, jurisdiction and right which is not, by this Confederation, expressly delegated to the United States in Congress assembled."

Under this Confederation the war of the Revolution was carried on, and on the 3rd of September, 1783, the contest ended, and a definite Treaty was signed by Great Britain, in which she acknowledged the independence of the Colonies in the following terms: "ARTICLE 1—His Britannic Majesty acknowledges the said United States, viz: New Hampshire, Massachusetts Bay, Rhode Island and Providence Plantations, Connecticut, New York, New Jersey, Pennsylvania, Delaware, Maryland, Virginia, North Carolina, South Carolina and Georgia, to be FREE, SOVEREIGN AND INDEPENDENT STATES; that he treats with them as such; and for himself, his heirs and successors, relinquishes all claims to the government, propriety and territorial rights of the same and every part thereof."

Thus were established the two great principles asserted by the Colonies, namely: the right of a State to govern itself; and the right of a people to abolish a Government when it becomes destructive of the ends for which it was instituted. And concurrent with the establishment of these principles, was the fact, that each Colony became and was recognized by the mother Country a FREE, SOVEREIGN AND INDEPENDENT STATE.

In 1787, Deputies were appointed by the States to revise the Articles of Confederation, and on 17th September, 1787, these Deputies recommended for the adoption of the States, the Articles of Union, known as the Constitution of the United States.

The parties to whom this Constitution was submitted, were the several sovereign States; they were to agree or disagree, and when nine of them agreed the compact was to take effect among those concurring; and the General Government, as the common agent, was then invested with their authority.

If only nine of the thirteen States had concurred, the other four would have remained as they then were—separate, sovereign States, independent of any of the provisions of the Constitution. In fact, two of the States did not accede to the Constitution until long after it had gone into operation among the other eleven; and during that interval, they each exercised the functions of an independent nation.

By this Constitution, certain duties were imposed upon the several States, and the exercise of certain of their powers was restrained, which necessarily implied their continued existence as sovereign States. But to remove all doubt, an amendment was added, which declared that the powers not delegated to the United States by the Constitution, nor prohibited by it to the States, are reserved to the States, respectively, or to the people. On the 23d May, 1788, South Carolina, by a Convention of her People, passed an Ordinance assenting to this Constitution, and afterwards altered her own Constitution, to conform herself to the obligations she had undertaken.

Thus was established, by compact between the States, a Government with definite objects and powers, limited to the express words of the grant. This limitation left the whole remaining mass of power subject to the clause reserving it to the States or to the people, and rendered unnecessary any specification of reserved rights.

We hold that the Government thus established is subject to the two great principles asserted in the Declaration of Independence; and we hold further, that the mode of its formation subjects it to a third fundamental principle, namely: the law of compact. We maintain that in every compact between two or more parties, the obligation is mutual; that the failure of one of the contracting parties to perform a material part of the agreement, entirely releases the obligation of the other; and that where no arbiter is provided, each party is remitted to his own judgment to determine the fact of failure, with all its consequences.

In the present case, that fact is established with certainty. We assert that fourteen of the States have deliberately refused, for years past, to fulfill their constitutional obligations, and we refer to their own Statutes for the proof.

The Constitution of the United States, in its fourth Article, provides as follows: "No person held to service or labor in one State, under the laws thereof, escaping into another, shall, in consequence of any law or regulation therein, be discharged from such service or labor, but shall be delivered up, on claim of the party to whom such service or labor may be due."

This stipulation was so material to the compact, that without it that compact would not have been made. The greater number of the contracting parties held slaves, and they had previously evinced their estimate of the value of such a stipulation by making it a condition in the Ordinance for the government of the territory ceded by Virginia, which now composes the States north of the Ohio River.

The same article of the Constitution stipulates also for rendition by the several States of fugitives from justice from the other States.

The General Government, as the common agent, passed laws to carry into effect these stipulations of the States. For many years these laws were executed. But an increasing hostility on the part of the non-slaveholding States to the institution of slavery, has led to a disregard of their obligations, and the laws of the General Government have ceased to effect the objects of the Constitution. The States of Maine, New Hampshire, Vermont, Massachusetts, Connecticut, Rhode Island, New York, Pennsylvania, Illinois, Indiana, Michigan, Wisconsin and Iowa, have enacted laws which either nullify the Acts of Congress or render useless any attempt to execute them. In many of these States the fugitive is discharged from service or labor claimed, and in none of them has the State

Government complied with the stipulation made in the Constitution. The State of New Jersey, at an early day, passed a law in conformity with her constitutional obligation; but the current of anti-slavery feeling has led her more recently to enact laws which render inoperative the remedies provided by her own law and by the laws of Congress. In the State of New York even the right of transit for a slave has been denied by her tribunals; and the States of Ohio and Iowa have refused to surrender to justice fugitives charged with murder, and with inciting servile insurrection in the State of Virginia. Thus the constituted compact has been deliberately broken and disregarded by the non-slaveholding States, and the consequence follows that South Carolina is released from her obligation.

The ends for which the Constitution was framed are declared by itself to be "to form a more perfect union, establish justice, insure domestic tranquility, provide for the common defence, promote the general welfare, and secure the blessings of liberty to ourselves and our posterity."

These ends it endeavored to accomplish by a Federal Government, in which each State was recognized as an equal, and had separate control over its own institutions. The right of property in slaves was recognized by giving to free persons distinct political rights, by giving them the right to represent, and burthening them with direct taxes for three-fifths of their slaves; by authorizing the importation of slaves for twenty years; and by stipulating for the rendition of fugitives from labor.

We affirm that these ends for which this Government was instituted have been defeated, and the Government itself has been made destructive of them by the action of the non-slaveholding States. Those States have assumed the right of deciding upon the propriety of our domestic institutions; and have denied the rights of property established in fifteen of the States and recognized by the Constitution; they have denounced as sinful the institution of slavery; they have permitted open establishment among them of societies, whose avowed object is to disturb the peace and to eloign the property of the citizens of other States. They have encouraged and assisted thousands of our slaves to leave their homes; and those who remain, have been incited by emissaries, books and pictures to servile insurrection.

For twenty-five years this agitation has been steadily increasing, until it has now secured to its aid the power of the common Government.

Observing the *forms* of the Constitution, a sectional party has found within that Article establishing the Executive Department, the means of subverting the Constitution itself. A geographical line has been drawn across the Union, and all the States north of that line have united in the election of a man to the high office of President of the United States, whose opinions and purposes are hostile to slavery. He is to be entrusted with the administration of the common Government, because he has declared that that "Government cannot endure permanently half slave, half free," and that the public mind must rest in the belief that slavery is in the course of ultimate extinction.

This sectional combination for the submersion of the Constitution, has been aided in some of the States by elevating to citizenship, persons who, by the supreme law of the land, are incapable of becoming citizens; and their votes have been used to inaugurate a new policy, hostile to the South, and destructive of its beliefs and safety.

On the 4th day of March next, this party will take possession of the Government. It has announced that the South shall be excluded from the common territory, that the judicial tribunals shall be made sectional, and that a war must be waged against slavery until it shall cease throughout the United States.

The guaranties of the Constitution will then no longer exist; the equal rights of the States will be lost. The slaveholding States will no longer have the power of self-government, or self-protection, and the Federal Government will have become their enemy.

Sectional interest and animosity will deepen the irritation, and all hope of remedy is rendered vain, by the fact that public opinion at the North has invested a great political error with the sanction of more erroneous religious belief.

We, therefore, the People of South Carolina, by our delegates in Convention assembled, appealing to the Supreme Judge of the world for the rectitude of our intentions, have solemnly declared that the Union heretofore existing between this State and the other States of North America, is dissolved, and that the State of South Carolina has resumed her position among the nations of the world, as a separate and independent State; with full power to levy war, conclude peace, contract alliances, establish commerce, and to do all other acts and things which independent States may of right do.

Adopted December 24, 1860

First Inaugural Speech

March 4 1861

Abraham Lincoln

Fellow-citizens of the United States:

In compliance with a custom as old as the government itself, I appear before you to address you briefly, and to take, in your presence, the oath prescribed by the Constitution of the United States, to be taken by the President "before he enters on the execution of this office."

I do not consider it necessary at present for me to discuss those matters of administration about which there is no special anxiety or excitement.

Apprehension seems to exist among the people of the Southern States, that by the accession of a Republican Administration, their property, and their peace, and personal security, are to be endangered. There has never been any reasonable cause for such apprehension. Indeed, the most ample evidence to the contrary has all the while existed, and been open to their inspection. It is found in nearly all the published speeches of him who now addresses you. I do but quote from one of those speeches when I declare that "I have no purpose, directly or indirectly, to interfere with the institution of slavery in the States where it exists. I believe I have no lawful right to do so, and I have no inclination to do so." Those who nominated and elected me did so with full knowledge that I had made this, and many similar declarations, and had never recanted them. And more than this, they placed in the platform, for my acceptance, and as a law to themselves, and to me, the clear and emphatic resolution which I now read:

Resolved, That the maintenance inviolate of the rights of the States, and especially the right of each State to order and control its own domestic institutions according to its own judgment exclusively, is essential to that balance of power on which the perfection and endurance of our political fabric depend; and we denounce the lawless invasion by armed force of the soil of any State or Territory, no matter what pretext, as among the gravest of crimes."

I now reiterate these sentiments; and in doing so, I only press upon the public attention the most conclusive evidence of which the case is susceptible, that the property, peace and security of no section are to be in any wise endangered by the now incoming Administration. I add too, that all the protection which, consistently with the Constitution and the laws, can be given, will be cheerfully given to all the States when lawfully demanded, for whatever cause—as cheerfully to one section as to another.

There is much controversy about the delivering up of fugitives from service or labor. The clause I now read is as plainly written in the Constitution as any other of its provisions:

"No person held to service or labor in one State, under the laws thereof, escaping into another, shall, in consequence of any law or regulation therein, be discharged from such service or labor, but shall be delivered up on claim of the party to whom such service or labor may be due."

It is scarcely questioned that this provision was intended by those who made it, for the reclaiming of what we call fugitive slaves; and the intention of the law-giver is the law. All members of Congress swear their support to the whole Constitution—to this provision as much as to any other. To the proposition, then, that slaves whose cases come within the terms of this clause, "shall be delivered," their oaths are unanimous. Now, if they would make the effort in good temper, could they not, with nearly equal unanimity, frame and pass a law, by means of which to keep good that unanimous oath?

There is some difference of opinion whether this clause should be enforced by national or by state authority; but surely that difference is not a very material one. If the slave is to be surrendered, it can be of but little consequence to him, or to others, by which authority it is done. And should any one, in any case, be content that his oath shall go unkept, on a merely unsubstantial controversy as to *how* it shall be kept?

Again, in any law upon this subject, ought not all the safeguards of liberty known in civilized and humane jurisprudence to be introduced, so that a free man be not, in any case, surrendered as a slave? And might it not be well, at the same time to provide by law for the enforcement of that clause in the Constitution which guarantees that "the citizens of each State shall be entitled to all privileges and immunities of citizens in the several States"?

I take the official oath to-day, with no mental reservations, and with no purpose to construe the Constitution or laws, by any hypercritical rules. And while I do not choose now to specify particular acts of Congress as proper to be enforced, I do suggest that it will be much safer for all, both in official and private stations, to conform to, and abide by, all those acts which stand unrepealed, than to violate any of them, trusting to find impunity in having them held to be unconstitutional.

It is seventy-two years since the first inauguration of a President under our national Constitution. During that period fifteen different and greatly distinguished citizens, have, in succession, administered the executive branch of the government. They have conducted it through many perils; and, generally, with great success. Yet, with all this scope for [of] precedent, I now enter upon the same task for the brief constitutional term of four years, under great and peculiar difficulty. A disruption of the Federal Union, heretofore only menaced, is now formidably attempted.

I hold, that in contemplation of universal law, and of the Constitution, the Union of these States is perpetual. Perpetuity is implied, if not expressed, in the fundamental law of all national governments. It is safe to assert that no government proper, ever had a provision in its organic law for its own termination. Continue to execute all the express provisions of our national Constitution, and the Union will endure forever—it being impossible to destroy it, except by some action not provided for in the instrument itself.

Again, if the United States be not a government proper, but an association of States in the nature of contract merely, can it, as a contract, be peaceably unmade, by less than all the parties who made it? One party to a contract may violate it—break it, so to speak; but does it not require all to lawfully rescind it?

Descending from these general principles, we find the proposition that, in legal contemplation, the Union is perpetual, confirmed by the history of the Union itself. The Union is much older than the Constitution. It was formed in fact, by the Articles of Association in 1774. It was matured and continued by the Declaration of Independence in 1776. It was further matured and the faith of all the then thirteen States expressly plighted and engaged that it should be perpetual, by the Articles of Confederation in 1778. And finally, in 1787, one of the declared objects for ordaining and establishing the Constitution, was *"to form a more perfect Union."* But if [the] destruction of the Union, by one, or by a part only, of the States, be lawfully possible, the Union is *less* perfect than before the Constitution, having lost the vital element of perpetuity.

It follows from these views that no State, upon its own mere motion, can lawfully get out of the Union, —that *resolves* and *ordinances* to that effect are legally void, and that acts of violence, within any State or States, against the authority of the United States, are insurrectionary or revolutionary, according to circumstances.

I therefore consider that in view of the Constitution and the laws, the Union is unbroken; and to the extent of my ability I shall take care, as the Constitution itself expressly enjoins upon me, that the laws of the Union be faithfully executed in all the States. Doing this I deem to be only a simple duty on my part; and I shall perform it, so far as practicable, unless my rightful masters, the American people, shall withhold the requisite means, or in some authoritative manner, direct the contrary. I trust this will not be regarded as a menace, but only as the declared purpose of the Union that will constitutionally defend and maintain itself.

In doing this there needs to be no bloodshed or violence; and there shall be none, unless it be forced upon the national authority. The power confided to me will be used to hold, occupy, and possess the property and places belonging to the government, and to collect the duties and imposts; but beyond what may be necessary for these objects, there will be no invasion—no using of force against or among the people anywhere. Where hostility to the United States in any interior locality, shall be so great and so universal, as to prevent competent resident citizens from holding the Federal offices, there will be no attempt to force obnoxious strangers among the people for that object. While the strict legal right may exist in the government to enforce the exercise of these offices, the attempt to do so would be so irritating, and so nearly impracticable with all, that I deem it better to forego, for the time, the uses of such offices.

The mails, unless repelled, will continue to be furnished in all parts of the Union. So far as possible, the people everywhere shall have that sense of perfect security which is most favorable to calm thought and reflection. The course here indicated will be followed, unless current events and experience shall show a modification or change to be proper; and in every case and exigency my best discretion will be exercised according to circumstances actually existing, and with a view and a hope of a peaceful solution of the national troubles, and the restoration of fraternal sympathies and affections.

That there are persons in one section or another who seek to destroy the Union at all events, and are glad of any pretext to do it, I will neither affirm nor deny; but if there be such, I need address no word to them. To those, however, who really love the Union may I not speak?

Before entering upon so grave a matter as the destruction of our national fabric, with all its benefits, its memories, and its hopes, would it not be wise to ascertain precisely why we do it? Will you hazard so desperate a step, while there is any possibility that any portion of the ills you fly from have no real existence? Will you, while the certain ills you fly to, are greater than all the real ones you fly from? Will you risk the commission of so fearful a mistake?

All profess to be content in the Union, if all constitutional rights can be maintained. Is it true, then, that any right, plainly written in the Constitution, has been denied? I think not. Happily the human mind is so constituted, that no party can reach to the audacity of doing this. Think, if you can, of a single instance in which a plainly written provision of the Constitution has ever been denied. If by the mere force of numbers, a majority should deprive a minority of any clearly written constitutional right, it might, in a moral point of view, justify revolution—certainly would, if such right were a vital one. But such is not our case. All the vital rights of minorities, and of individuals, are so plainly assured to them, by affirmations and negations, guaranties and prohibitions, in the Constitution, that controversies never arise concerning them. But no organic law can ever be framed with a provision specifically applicable to every question which may occur in practical administration. No foresight can anticipate, nor any document of reasonable length contain express provisions for all possible questions. Shall fugitives from labor be surrendered by national or by State authority? The Constitution does not expressly say. *May* Congress prohibit slavery in the territories? The Constitution does not expressly say. *Must* Congress protect slavery in the territories? The Constitution does not expressly say.

From questions of this class spring all our constitutional controversies, and we divide upon them into majorities and minorities. If the minority will not acquiesce, the majority must, or the government must cease. There is no other alternative; for continuing the government, is acquiescence on one side or the other. If a minority, in such case, will secede rather than acquiesce, they make a precedent which, in turn, will divide and ruin them; for a minority of their own will secede from them whenever a majority refuses to be controlled by such minority. For instance, why may not any portion of a new confederacy, a year or two hence, arbitrarily secede again, precisely as portions of the present Union now claim to secede from it? All who cherish disunion sentiments, are now being educated to the exact temper of doing this.

Is there such perfect identity of interests among the States to compose a new Union, as to produce harmony only, and prevent renewed secession?

Plainly, the central idea of secession, is the essence of anarchy. A majority, held in restraint by constitutional checks and limitations, and always changing easily with deliberate changes of popular opinions and sentiments, is the only true sovereign of a free people. Whoever rejects it, does, of necessity, fly to anarchy or to despotism. Unanimity is impossible; the rule of a minority, as a permanent arrangement, is wholly inadmissible; so that, rejecting the majority principle, anarchy or despotism in some form is all that is left.

I do not forget the position assumed by some, that constitutional questions are to be decided by the Supreme Court; nor do I deny that such decisions must be binding in any case, upon the parties to a suit; as to the object of that suit, while they are also entitled to very high respect and consideration in all parallel cases by all other departments of the government. And while it is obviously possible that such decision may be erroneous in any given case, still the evil effect following it, being limited to that particular case, with the chance that it may be over-ruled, and never become a precedent for other cases, can better be borne than could the evils of a different practice. At the same time, the candid citizen must confess that if the policy of the government upon vital questions, affecting the whole people, is to be irrevocably fixed by decisions of the Supreme Court, the instant they are made, in ordinary litigation between parties, in personal actions, the people will have ceased to be their own rulers, having to that extent practically resigned their government into the hands of that eminent tribunal. Nor is there in this view any assault upon the court or the judges. It is a duty from which they may not shrink, to decide cases properly brought before them; and it is no fault of theirs if others seek to turn their decisions to political purposes.

One section of our country believes slavery is *right*, and ought to be extended, while the other believes it is *wrong*, and ought not to be extended. This is the only substantial dispute. The fugitive slave clause of the Constitution, and the law for the suppression of the foreign slave trade, are each as well enforced, perhaps, as any law can ever be in a community where the moral sense of the people imperfectly supports the law itself. The great body of the people abide by the dry legal obligation in both cases, and a few break over in each. This, I think, cannot be perfectly cured, and it would be worse in both cases *after* the separation of the sections, than before. The foreign slave trade, now imperfectly suppressed, would be ultimately revived without restriction, in one section; while fugitive slaves, now only partially surrendered, would not be surrendered at all, by the other.

Physically speaking, we cannot separate. We can not remove our respective sections from each other, nor build an impassable wall between them. A husband and wife may be divorced, and go out of the presence, and beyond the reach of each other; but the different parts of our country cannot do this. They cannot but remain face to face; and intercourse, either amicable or hostile, must continue between them. Is it possible, then, to make that intercourse more advantageous or more satisfactory, *after* separation than *before*? Can aliens make treaties easier than friends can make laws? Can treaties be more faithfully enforced between aliens than laws can among friends? Suppose you go to war, you cannot fight always; and when, after much loss on both sides, and no gain on either, you cease fighting, the

identical old questions, as to terms of intercourse, are again upon you.

This country, with its institutions, belongs to the people who inhabit it. Whenever they shall grow weary of the existing Government, they can exercise their *constitutional* right of amending it, or their *revolutionary* right to dismember or overthrow it. I cannot be ignorant of the fact that many worthy and patriotic citizens are desirous of having the national Constitution amended. While I make no recommendation of amendments, I fully recognize the rightful authority of the people over the whole subject to be exercised in either of the modes prescribed in the instrument itself; and I should, under existing circumstances, favor rather than oppose a fair opportunity being afforded the people to act upon it.

I will venture to add that to me the Convention mode seems preferable, in that it allows amendments to originate with the people themselves, instead of only permitting them to take or reject propositions, originated by others, not especially chosen for the purpose, and which might not be precisely such as they would wish to either accept or refuse. I understand a proposed amendment to the Constitution, which amendment, however, I have not seen, has passed Congress, to the effect that the federal government shall never interfere with the domestic institutions of the States, including that of persons held to service. To avoid misconstruction of what I have said, I depart from my purpose not to speak of particular amendments, so far as to say that holding such a provision to now be implied constitutional law, I have no objection to its being made express and irrevocable.

The Chief Magistrate derives all his authority from the people, and they have referred none upon him to fix terms for the separation of the States. The people themselves can do this if also they choose; but the executive, as such, has nothing to do with it. His duty is to administer the present government, as it came to his hands, and to transmit it, unimpaired by him, to his successor.

Why should there not be a patient confidence in the ultimate justice of the people? Is there any better or equal hope, in the world? In our present differences, is either party without faith of being in the right? If the Almighty Ruler of nations, with his eternal truth and justice, be on your side of the North, or on yours of the South, that truth, and that justice, will surely prevail, by the judgment of this great tribunal of the American people.

By the frame of the government under which we live, this same people have wisely given their public servants but little power for mischief; and have, with equal wisdom, provided for the return of that little to their own hands at very short intervals.

While the people retain their virtue and vigilance, no administration, by any extreme of wickedness or folly, can very seriously injure the government in the short space of four years.

My countrymen, one and all, think calmly and *well*, upon this whole subject. Nothing valuable can be lost by taking time. If there be an object to *hurry* any of you, in hot haste, to a step which you would never take*deliberately,* that object will be frustrated by taking time; but no good object can be frustrated by it. Such of you as are now dissatisfied still have the old Constitution unimpaired, and, on the sensitive point, the laws of your own framing under it; while the new administration will have no immediate power, if it would, to change either. If it were admitted that you who are dissatisfied, hold the right side in the dispute, there still is no single good reason for precipitate action. Intelligence, patriotism, Christianity, and a firm reliance on Him, who has never yet forsaken this favored land, are still competent to adjust, in the best way, all our present difficulty.

In *your* hands, my dissatisfied fellow countrymen, and not in *mine,* is the momentous issue of civil war. The government will not assail *you.* You can have no conflict without being yourselves the aggressors. *You* have no oath registered in Heaven to destroy the government, while *I* shall have the most solemn one to "preserve, protect, and defend it."

I am loath to close. We are not enemies, but friends. We must not be enemies. Though passion may have strained, it must not break our bonds of affection. The mystic chords of memory, stretching from every battle-field, and patriot grave, to every living heart and hearth-stone, all over this broad land, will yet swell the chorus of the Union, when again touched, as surely they will be, by the better angels of our nature.

SECTION SIX

THE CIVIL WAR AND RECONSTRUCTION

CHAPTER 8

Provisional Congress of the Confederate States

First Session, February 4, 1861, to March 16, 1861
In the Capitol of the State of Alabama.

Open Session

Be it remembered that on the fourth day of February, in the year of our Lord one thousand eight hundred and sixty-one, and in the Capitol of the State of Alabama, in the city of Montgomery, at the hour of noon, there assembled certain deputies and delegates from the several independent Southern States of North America, to wit: Alabama, Florida, Georgia, Louisiana, Mississippi, and South Carolina; the said delegates and deputies being thus assembled and convened under and by virtue of divers ordinances and resolutions adopted by the several conventions of peoples of the independent States aforenamed; which said ordinances and resolutions are severally as follows:

An ordinance to dissolve the Union between the State of South Carolina and the other States united with her under the compact entitled "The Constitution of the United States of America."

We the people of the State of South Carolina in convention assembled do declare and ordain and it is hereby declared and ordained, That the ordinance adopted by us in convention, on the 23d day of May, in the year of our Lord 1788, whereby the Constitution of the United States of America was ratified, and also all acts and parts of acts of the general assembly of this State, ratifying amendments of the said Constitution, and hereby repealed, and that the Union now subsisting between South Carolina and other States under the name of the United States of America is hereby dissolved.

Unanimously adopted 20th day of December, A. D. 1860.

An ordinance to dissolve the Union between the State of Georgia and other States united with her under a compact of Government entitled "The Constitution of the United States of America," passed January 19, 1861.

We the people of the State of Georgia in convention assembled do declare and ordain and it is hereby declared and ordained, That the ordinance adopted by the people of the State of Georgia in convention on the 2d day of January, in the year of our Lord 1788, when the Constitution of the United States was assented to, ratified, and adopted, and also all acts and parts of acts of the general assembly of this State, ratifying and adopting amendments of the said Constitution, are hereby repealed, rescinded, and abrogated.

We do further declare and ordain, That the Union now subsisting between the State of Georgia and other States under the name of the United States of America is hereby dissolved, and that the State of Georgia is in the full possession and exercise of all those rights of sovereignty which belong and appertain to a free and independent State.

The ordinance of succession of the State of Florida.

We the people of the State of Florida in convention assembled do solemnly ordain, publish, and declare, That the State of Florida hereby withdraws herself from the Confederacy of States existing under the name of the United States of America and from the existing Government of said States, and that all political connection between her and the Government of the said States, ought to be, and the same is hereby, totally annulled and said Union of States dissolved, and the State of Florida is hereby declared a sovereign and independent nation, and that all ordinances heretofore adopted, in so far as they create or recognize said Union, are rescinded, and all laws or parts of laws in force in this State, in so far as they recognize or assent to said Union be, and they are hereby, repealed.

Adopted, January 11, A. D. 1861.

———

An ordinance to dissolve the Union between the State of Alabama and the other States under the compact and style of the United States of America.

Whereas the election of Abraham Lincoln and Hannibal Hamlin to the office of President and Vice-President of the United States of America by a sectional party avowedly hostile to the domestic institutions and peace and security of the people of the State of Alabama, following upon the heels of many and dangerous infractions of the Constitution of the United States by many of the States and people of the northern section, is a political wrong of so insulting and menacing a character as to justify the people of the State of Alabama in the adoption of prompt and decided measures for their future peace and security: Therefore,

Be it declared and ordained by the people of the State of Alabama in convention assembled, That the State of Alabama now withdraws from the Union known as the United States of America and henceforth ceases to be one of the said United States, and is, and of right ought to be, a sovereign independent State.

Sec. 2. *And be it further declared by the people of the State of Alabama in convention assembled,* That all powers over the territories of said State and over the people thereof heretofore delegated to the Government of the United States of America be, and they are hereby, withdrawn from the said Government and are hereby resumed and vested in the people of the State of Alabama.

And as it is the desire and purpose of the people of Alabama to meet the slaveholding States, who approve of such purpose, in order to frame a provisional or a permanent government, upon the principles of the Government of the United States;

Be it also resolved by the people of Alabama in convention assembled, That the people of the States of Delaware, Maryland, Virginia, North Carolina, South Carolina, Florida, Georgia, Mississippi, Louisiana, Texas, Arkansas, Tennessee, Kentucky, and Missouri be, and they are hereby, invited to meet the people of the State of Alabama by their delegates in convention, on the 4th day of February next, in Montgomery, in the State of Alabama, for the purpose of consultation with each other as to the most effectual mode of securing connected, harmonious action in whatever measure may be deemed most desirable for the common peace and security.

And be it further resolved, That the president of this convention be, and he is hereby, instructed to transmit forthwith a copy of the foregoing preamble, ordinance, and resolutions to the governors of the several States named in the said resolutions.

Done by the people of Alabama in convention assembled at Montgomery, this 11th day of January, 1861.

———

An ordinance to dissolve the Union between the State of Mississippi and other States united with her under the compact entitled "The Constitution of the United States of America."

The people of Mississippi in convention assembled do ordain and declare and it is hereby ordained and declared as follows, to wit:

Section 1. That all the laws and ordinances by which the said State of Mississippi became a member of the Federal Union of the United States of America be, and the same are hereby, repealed, and that all obligations on the part of said State, or the people thereof, to observe the same, be withdrawn, and that said State shall hereby resume the rights, functions, and powers which by any of said laws and ordinances were conveyed to the Government of the said United States, and is absolved from all the obligations, restraints, and duties incurred to the said Federal Union, and shall henceforth be a free, sovereign, and independent State.

Sec. 2. That so much of the first section of the seventh article of the constitution of this State as requires members of the legislature and all officers, legislative and judicial, to take an oath to support the Constitution of the United States be, and the same is hereby, abrogated and annulled.

Sec. 3. That all rights acquired and vested under the Constitution of the United States, or under any act of Congress passed in pursuance thereof, or under any law of this State and not incompatible with this ordinance, shall remain in force and have the same effect as if this ordinance had not been passed.

Sec. 4. That the people of the State of Mississippi hereby consent to form a federal union with such of the States as have seceded, or may secede, from the Union of the United States of America, upon the basis of the present Constitution of the said United States, except such parts thereof as embrace other portions than such seceding States.

Adopted, 11th day of January, A. D. 1861.

––––

An ordinance to dissolve the Union between the State of Louisiana and other States united with her under the compact entitled "The Constitution of the United States."

We the people of the State of Louisiana in convention assembled do declare and ordain and it is hereby declared and ordained, That the ordinance passed by us in convention on the 22d day of November, in the year 1811, whereby the Constitution of the United States of America and the amendments of said Constitution were adopted, and all laws and ordinances by which the State of Louisiana became a member of the Federal Union be, and the same are hereby, repealed and abrogated, and that the Union now subsisting between Louisiana and other States under the name of "The United States of America" is hereby dissolved.

We do further declare and ordain, That the State of Louisiana hereby resumes all rights and powers heretofore delegated to the Government of the United States of America; that her citizens are absolved from all allegiance to said Government, and that she is in full possession and exercise of all those rights of sovereignty which appertain to a free and independent State.

We do further declare and ordain, That all rights acquired and vested under the Constitution of the United States, or any act of Congress, or treaty, or under any law of this State, and not incompatible with this ordinance, shall remain in force and have the same effect as if this ordinance had not been passed.

Adopted in convention at Baton Rouge, this 26th day of January, 1861.

––––

Resolution of the convention of Louisiana in reference to the free navigation of the Mississippi River.

Resolved, That we the people of the State of Louisiana recognize the right of the free navigation of the Mississippi River and its tributaries by all friendly States bordering thereon, and we also recognize the right of egress and ingress of the mouths of the Mississippi River by all friendly States and powers, and we do hereby declare our willingness to enter into any stipulations to guarantee the exercise of said rights.

Adopted in convention at Baton Rouge, this 26th day of January, 1861.

––––

Resolutions adopted by the convention of South Carolina.

Resolved, First. That this convention do appoint a commissioner to proceed to each of the slaveholding States that may assemble in convention, for the purpose of laying our ordinance of secession before the same and respectfully inviting their cooperation in the formation of a southern confederacy.

Second. That our commissioners aforesaid be further authorized to submit, on our part, the Federal Constitution as a basis of a provisional government for such States as shall have withdrawn their connection with the Government of the United States of America: *Provided,* That the said provisional government and the tenure of all officers and appointments arising under it shall cease and determine in two years from the 1st day of July next, or when a permanent government shall have been organized.

Third. That the said commissioners be authorized to invite the seceding States to meet in convention, at such time and places as may be agreed upon, for the purpose of forming and putting in motion such provisional government, and so that the said provisional government shall be organized and go into effect at the earliest period previous to the 4th of March, 1861; and that the same convention of seceding States shall proceed forthwith to consider and propose a constitution and a plan for a permanent government for such States, which proposed plan shall be referred back to the several State conventions for their adoption or rejection.

Fourth. That eight deputies shall be elected by ballot by this convention, who shall be authorized to meet in convention such deputies as may be appointed by the other slaveholding States who may secede from the Federal Union, for the purpose of carrying into effect the foregoing resolutions; and that it be recommended to the said States that each State be entitled to one vote in the said convention upon all questions which may be voted upon therein, and that each State send as many deputies as are equal in number to the Senators and Representatives to which it was entitled in the Congress of the United States.

———

Resolutions adopted by the convention of Alabama, January 17, 1861.

Resolved, That this convention cordially approve of the suggestions of the convention of the people of South Carolina to meet them in convention at Montgomery, in the State of Alabama, on the 4th day of February, 1861, to frame a provisional government upon the principles of the Constitution of the United States, and also to prepare and consider upon a plan for the creation and establishment of a permanent government for the seceding States upon the same principles, which shall be submitted to conventions of such seceding States for adoption or rejection.

Resolved, That we approve of the suggestion that each State shall send to said convention as many deputies as it now has or has lately had Senators and Representatives in the Congress of the United States; and that each State shall have one vote upon all questions upon which a vote may be taken in said convention.

Resolved, That this convention will proceed to elect by ballot one deputy from each Congressional district in this State and two deputies from the State at large at 12 o'clock m. on Friday, the 18th day of January instant, who shall be authorized to meet in convention such deputies as may be appointed by the other slaveholding States who may secede from the Federal Union, for the purpose of carrying into effect the foregoing and the resolutions attached to the ordinance dissolving the Union; and that

deputies shall be elected separately, and each deputy shall receive a majority of the members voting.

———

An ordinance to provide for the appointment of delegates to a convention to form a southern confederacy.

We the people of Louisiana in convention assembled do declare and ordain and it is hereby declared and ordained:

First. That this convention will, on the 30th day of January instant, at the hour of 12 m., proceed to elect viva voce six delegates, two from the State at large and one from each Congressional district, to represent this State in the convention of seceding States proposed to be held at Montgomery, in the State of Alabama, on the 4th day of February, 1861, for the purpose of securing concerted and harmonious action, and also of forming a provisional government for those States which have seceded and which may secede and intend to form a southern confederacy.

Second. That the said delegates be instructed to aid in forming a provisional government on the basis of the Constitution of the United States for such States as have seceded, or may secede, to be established and put into operation before the 4th day of March, 1861, and that the same convention of seceding States shall proceed forthwith to consider and propose a constitution and plan for a permanent government for such States, which proposed plan shall be referred back to the several State conventions for their adoption or rejection.

Third. That this convention accepts the recommendation of the State of South Carolina, that each State be entitled to one vote in the said convention upon all questions which may be voted upon therein, and that each State send as many delegates as are equal in number to the number of Senators and Representatives to which it was entitled in the Congress of the United States.

Fourth. That if from any cause the said convention should not assemble at the time and place above mentioned, then and in that event the said delegates be, and they are hereby, accredited to any convention of seceding States which may meet at any other time and place, having for its object the formation of a government and the establishing of a confederacy, as hereinbefore prescribed, and which may adjourn to meet at any other time and place.

Adopted in convention at the city of New Orleans, this 29th day of January, 1861.

———

Resolutions by the convention of the State of Georgia.

Resolved, That the delegates sent from this State by this convention to the proposed congress to assemble at Montgomery, Ala., on the 4th day of February next, be fully authorized and empowered, upon free conference and consultation with delegates that may be sent from other seceding States to said congress, to unite with them in forming and putting into immediate operation a temporary or provisional government for the common safety and defense of all the States represented in said congress, such temporary or provisional government not to extend beyond the period of twelve months from the time it goes into operation, and to be modeled, as nearly as practicable, on the principles and basis of the late Government of the United States of America, the powers of the delegates so appointed by this convention in this particular being hereby declared full and plenary.

Be it further resolved, That said delegates be likewise authorized, upon like conference and consultation with the delegates from the other States in said congress, to agree upon a plan of permanent government for said States upon the principles and basis of the Constitution of the late United States of America, which said plan or constitution of permanent government shall not be binding or obligatory upon the people of Georgia until submitted to, approved, and ratified by this convention.

Mr. William P. Chilton of Alabama, called the Congress to order, and moved that Mr. Robert W. Barnwell, of South Carolina, be appointed to preside temporarily over the Congress and until its permanent organization; and said motion was unanimously concurred in.

Mr. Barnwell assumed the chair, and tendered his thanks to the Congress for the proof of their confidence and respect.

The Chairman then called on the Rev. Dr. Basil Manly, of Montgomery, who offered up an impressive prayer to Almighty God in behalf of the Congress and the States whose interests it represents.

On motion of Mr. John Gill Shorter, of Alabama, A. R. Lamar, esq., of Georgia, was appointed temporary secretary.

Mr. Robert B. Rhett, of South Carolina, suggested that the proper time had arrived for the presentation of their credential by the deputies of this Congress.

Mr. Christopher G. Memminger, of South Carolina, then moved that the deputies from the several independent Southern States now present their credentials to the secretary, in the alphabetical order of the several States, and that they also sign the roll of the Congress.

And thereupon the deputies whose names are underwritten appeared and signed said roll, to wit:

From the State of—

Alabama	R. W. Walker.
	R. H. Smith.
	J. L. M. Curry.
	William P. Chilton.
	S. F. Hale.
	Colin J. McRae.
	Jno. Gill Shorter.
Florida	Jas. B. Owens.
	J. Patton Anderson.
Georgia	Robert Toombs.
	Howell Cobb.
	Francis S. Bartow.
	Martin J. Crawford.
	Eugenius A. Nisbet.
	Benj. H. Hill.
	A. R. Wright.
	Thomas R. R. Cobb.
	Augustus H. Kenan.
	Alex. H. Stephens.
Louisiana	John Perkins, jr.
	Edward Sparrow.
	A. De Clouet.
	D. F. Kenner.
	Henry Marshall.
Mississippi	W. P. Harris.
	Walker Brooke.
	W. S. Wilson.
	W. S. Barry.
	J. T. Harrison.
South Carolina	R. B. Rhett, sr.
	R. W. Barnwell.
	L. M. Keitt.
	James Chesnut, jr.
	C. G. Memminger.
	W. Porcher Miles.
	Thomas J. Withers.
	W. W. Boyce.

"Corner Stone" Speech
Alexander H. Stephens

Savannah, Georgia March 21, 1861

When perfect quiet is restored, I shall proceed. I cannot speak so long as there is any noise or confusion. I shall take my time I feel quite prepared to spend the night with you if necessary. I very much regret that everyone who desires cannot hear what I have to say. Not that I have any display to make, or anything very entertaining to present, but such views as I have to give, I wish all, not only in this city, but in this State, and throughout our Confederate Republic, could hear, who have a desire to hear them.

I was remarking that we are passing through one of the greatest revolutions in the annals of the world. Seven States have within the last three months thrown off an old government and formed a new. This revolution has been signally marked, up to this time, by the fact of its having been accomplished without the loss of a single drop of blood.

This new constitution. or form of government, constitutes the subject to which your attention will be partly invited. In reference to it, I make this first general remark: it amply secures all our ancient rights, franchises, and liberties. All the great principles of Magna Charta are retained in it. No citizen is deprived of life, liberty, or property, but by the judgment of his peers under the laws of the land. The great principle of religious liberty, which was the honor and pride of the old constitution, is still maintained and secured. All the essentials of the old constitution, which have endeared it to the hearts of the American people, have been preserved and perpetuated. Some changes have been made. Some of these I should have preferred not to have seen made; but other important changes do meet my cordial approbation. They form great improvements upon the old constitution. So, taking the whole new constitution, I have no hesitancy in giving it as my judgment that it is decidedly better than the old.

Allow me briefly to allude to some of these improvements. The question of building up class interests, or fostering one branch of industry to the prejudice of another under the exercise of the revenue power, which gave us so much trouble under the old constitution, is put at rest forever under the new. We allow the imposition of no duty with a view of giving advantage to one class of persons, in any trade or business, over those of another. All, under our system, stand upon the same broad principles of perfect equality. Honest labor and enterprise are left free and unrestricted in whatever pursuit they may be engaged. This old thorn of the tariff, which was the cause of so much irritation in the old body politic, is removed forever from the new.

Again, the subject of internal improvements, under the power of Congress to regulate commerce, is put at rest under our system. The power, claimed by construction under the old constitution, was at least a doubtful one; it rested solely upon construction. We of the South, generally apart from considerations of constitutional principles, opposed its exercise upon grounds of its inexpediency and injustice. Notwithstanding this opposition, millions of money, from the common treasury had been drawn for such purposes. Our opposition sprang from no hostility to commerce, or to all necessary aids for facilitating it. With us it was simply a question upon whom the burden should fall. In Georgia, for instance, we have done as much for the cause of internal improvements as any other portion of the country, according to population and means. We have stretched out lines of railroads from the seaboard to the mountains; dug down the hills, and filled up the valleys at a cost of not less than $25,000,000. All this was done to open an outlet for our products of the interior, and those to the west of us, to reach the marts of the world. No State was in greater need of such facilities than Georgia, but we did not ask that these works should be made by appropriations out of the common treasury. The cost of the grading, the superstructure, and the equipment of our roads was borne by those who had entered into the enterprise. Nay, more not only the cost of the iron no small item in the aggregate cost was borne in the same way, but we were compelled to pay into the common treasury several millions of dollars for the privilege of importing the iron, after the price was paid for it abroad. What justice was there in taking this money, which our people paid into the common treasury on the importation of our iron, and applying it to the improvement of rivers and harbors elsewhere? The true principle is to subject the commerce of every locality, to whatever burdens may be necessary to facilitate it. If Charleston harbor needs improvement, let the commerce of Charleston bear the burden. If the mouth of the Savannah river has to be cleared out, let the sea-going navigation which is benefited by it, bear the burden. So with the mouths of the Alabama and Mississippi river. Just as the products of the interior, our cotton, wheat, corn, and other articles, have to bear the necessary rates of freight over our railroads to reach the seas. This is again the broad principle of perfect equality and justice, and it is especially set forth and established in our new constitution.

Another feature to which I will allude is that the new constitution provides that cabinet ministers and heads of departments may have the privilege of seats upon the floor of the Senate and House of Representatives and may have the right to participate in the debates and discussions upon the various subjects of administration. I should have preferred that this provision should have gone further, and required the President to select his constitutional advisers from the Senate and House of Representatives. That would have conformed entirely to the practice in the British Parliament, which, in my judgment, is one of the wisest provisions in the British constitution. It is the only feature that saves that government. It is that which gives it stability in its facility to change its administration. Ours, as it is, is a great approximation to the right principle.

Under the old constitution, a secretary of the treasury for instance, had no opportunity, save by his annual reports, of presenting any scheme or plan of finance or other matter. He had no opportunity of explaining, expounding, enforcing, or defending his views of policy; his only resort was through the medium of an organ. In the British parliament, the premier brings in his budget and stands before the nation responsible for its every item. If it is indefensible, he falls before the attacks upon it,

as he ought to. This will now be the case to a limited extent under our system. In the new constitution, provision has been made by which our heads of departments can speak for themselves and the administration, in behalf of its entire policy, without resorting to the indirect and highly objectionable medium of a newspaper. It is to be greatly hoped that under our system we shall never have what is known as a government organ.

Another change in the constitution relates to the length of the tenure of the presidential office. In the new constitution it is six years instead of four, and the President rendered ineligible for a re-election. This is certainly a decidedly conservative change. It will remove from the incumbent all temptation to use his office or exert the powers confided to him for any objects of personal ambition. The only incentive to that higher ambition which should move and actuate one holding such high trusts in his hands, will be the good of the people, the advancement, prosperity, happiness, safety, honor, and true glory of the confederacy.

But not to be tedious in enumerating the numerous changes for the better, allow me to allude to one other though last, not least. The new constitution has put at rest, forever, all the agitating questions relating to our peculiar institution African slavery as it exists amongst us the proper status of the negro in our form of civilization. This was the immediate cause of the late rupture and present revolution. Jefferson in his forecast, had anticipated this, as the "rock upon which the old Union would split." He was right. What was conjecture with him, is now a realized fact. But whether he fully comprehended the great truth upon which that rock stood and stands, may be doubted. The prevailing ideas entertained by him and most of the leading statesmen at the time of the formation of the old constitution, were that the enslavement of the African was in violation of the laws of nature; that it was wrong in principle, socially, morally, and politically. It was an evil they knew not well how to deal with, but the general opinion of the men of that day was that, somehow or other in the order of Providence, the institution would be evanescent and pass away. This idea, though not incorporated in the constitution, was the prevailing idea at that time. The constitution, it is true, secured every essential guarantee to the institution while it should last, and hence no argument can be justly urged against the constitutional guarantees thus secured, because of the common sentiment of the day. Those ideas, however, were fundamentally wrong. They rested upon the assumption of the equality of races. This was an error. It was a sandy foundation, and the government built upon it fell when the "storm came and the wind blew."

Our new government is founded upon exactly the opposite idea; its foundations are laid, its corner-stone rests, upon the great truth that the negro is not equal to the white man; that slavery subordination to the superior race is his natural and normal condition. This, our new government, is the first, in the history of the world, based upon this great physical, philosophical, and moral truth. This truth has been slow in the process of its development, like all other truths in the various departments of science. It has been so even amongst us. Many who hear me, perhaps, can recollect well, that this truth was not generally admitted, even within their day. The errors of the past generation still clung to many as late as twenty years ago. Those at the North, who still cling to these errors, with a zeal above knowledge, we justly denominate fanatics. All fanaticism springs from an aberration of the mind from a defect in reasoning. It is a species of insanity. One of the most striking characteristics of insanity, in many instances, is forming correct conclusions from fancied or erroneous premises; so with the anti-slavery fanatics. Their conclusions are right if their premises were. They assume that the negro is equal, and hence conclude that he is entitled to equal privileges and rights with the white man. If their premises were correct, their conclusions would be logical and just but their premise being wrong, their whole argument fails. I recollect once of having heard a gentleman from one of the northern States, of great power and ability, announce in the House of Representatives, with imposing effect, that we of the South would be compelled, ultimately, to yield upon this subject of slavery, that it was as impossible to war successfully against a principle in politics, as it was in physics or mechanics. That the principle would ultimately prevail. That we, in maintaining slavery as it exists with us, were warring against a principle, a principle founded in nature, the principle of the equality of men. The reply I made to him was, that upon his own grounds, we should, ultimately, succeed, and that he and his associates, in this crusade against our institutions, would ultimately fail. The truth announced, that it was as impossible to war successfully against a principle in politics as it was in physics and mechanics, I admitted; but told him

that it was he, and those acting with him, who were warring against a principle. They were attempting to make things equal which the Creator had made unequal.

In the conflict thus far, success has been on our side, complete throughout the length and breadth of the Confederate States. It is upon this, as I have stated, our social fabric is firmly planted; and I cannot permit myself to doubt the ultimate success of a full recognition of this principle throughout the civilized and enlightened world.

As I have stated, the truth of this principle may be slow in development, as all truths are and ever have been, in the various branches of science. It was so with the principles announced by Galileo it was so with Adam Smith and his principles of political economy. It was so with Harvey, and his theory of the circulation of the blood. It is stated that not a single one of the medical profession, living at the time of the announcement of the truths made by him, admitted them. Now, they are universally acknowledged. May we not, therefore, look with confidence to the ultimate universal acknowledgment of the truths upon which our system rests? It is the first government ever instituted upon the principles in strict conformity to nature, and the ordination of Providence, in furnishing the materials of human society. Many governments have been founded upon the principle of the subordination and serfdom of certain classes of the same race; such were and are in violation of the laws of nature. Our system commits no such violation of nature's laws. With us, all of the white race, however high or low, rich or poor, are equal in the eye of the law. Not so with the negro. Subordination is his place. He, by nature, or by the curse against Canaan, is fitted for that condition which he occupies in our system. The architect, in the construction of buildings, lays the foundation with the proper material-the granite; then comes the brick or the marble. The substratum of our society is made of the material fitted by nature for it, and by experience we know that it is best, not only for the superior, but for the inferior race, that it should be so. It is, indeed, in conformity with the ordinance of the Creator. It is not for us to inquire into the wisdom of His ordinances, or to question them. For His own purposes, He has made one race to differ from another, as He has made "one star to differ from another star in glory." The great objects of humanity are best attained when there is conformity to His laws and decrees, in the formation of governments as well as in all things else. Our confederacy is founded upon principles in strict conformity with these laws. This stone which was rejected by the first builders "is become the chief of the corner" the real "corner-stone" in our new edifice. I have been asked, what of the future? It has been apprehended by some that we would have arrayed against us the civilized world. I care not who or how many they may be against us, when we stand upon the eternal principles of truth, if we are true to ourselves and the principles for which we contend, we are obliged to, and must triumph.

Thousands of people who begin to understand these truths are not yet completely out of the shell; they do not see them in their length and breadth. We hear much of the civilization and Christianization of the barbarous tribes of Africa. In my judgment, those ends will never be attained, but by first teaching them the lesson taught to Adam, that "in the sweat of his brow he should eat his bread," and teaching them to work, and feed, and clothe themselves.

But to pass on: Some have propounded the inquiry whether it is practicable for us to go on with the confederacy without further accessions? Have we the means and ability to maintain nationality among the powers of the earth? On this point I would barely say, that as anxiously as we all have been, and are, for the border States, with institutions similar to ours, to join us, still we are abundantly able to maintain our position, even if they should ultimately make up their minds not to cast their destiny with us.

That they ultimately will join us be compelled to do it is my confident belief; but we can get on very well without them, even if they should not.

We have all the essential elements of a high national career. The idea has been given out at the North, and even in the border States, that we are too small and too weak to maintain a separate nationality. This is a great mistake. In extent of territory we embrace five hundred and sixty-four thousand square miles and upward. This is upward of two hundred thousand square miles more than was included within the limits of the original thirteen States. It is an area of country more than double the territory of France or the Austrian empire. France, in round numbers, has but two hundred and twelve thousand square miles. Austria, in round numbers, has two hundred and forty-eight thousand square miles. Ours is greater than both combined. It is greater than all France, Spain, Portugal, and Great

Britain, including England, Ireland, and Scotland, together. In population we have upward of five millions, according to the census of 1860; this includes white and black. The entire population, including white and black, of the original thirteen States, was less than four millions in 1790, and still less in 76, when the independence of our fathers was achieved. If they, with a less population, dared maintain their independence against the greatest power on earth, shall we have any apprehension of maintaining ours now?

In point of material wealth and resources, we are greatly in advance of them. The taxable property of the Confederate States cannot be less than twenty-two hundred millions of dollars! This, I think I venture but little in saying, may be considered as five times more than the colonies possessed at the time they achieved their independence. Georgia, alone, possessed last year, according to the report of our comptroller-general, six hundred and seventy-two millions of taxable property. The debts of the seven confederate States sum up in the aggregate less than eighteen millions, while the existing debts of the other of the late United States sum up in the aggregate the enormous amount of one hundred and seventy-four millions of dollars. This is without taking into account the heavy city debts, corporation debts, and railroad debts, which press, and will continue to press, as a heavy incubus upon the resources of those States. These debts, added to others, make a sum total not much under five hundred millions of dollars. With such an area of territory as we have- with such an amount of population-with a climate and soil unsurpassed by any on the face of the earth- with such resources already at our command-with productions which control the commerce of the world-who can entertain any apprehensions as to our ability to succeed, whether others join us or not?

It is true, I believe I state but the common sentiment, when I declare my earnest desire that the border States should join us. The differences of opinion that existed among us anterior to secession, related more to the policy in securing that result by co-operation than from any difference upon the ultimate security we all looked to in common.

These differences of opinion were more in reference to policy than principle, and as Mr. Jefferson said in his inaugural, in 1801, after the heated contest preceding his election, that there might be differences of opinion without differences on principle, and that all, to some extent, had been Federalists and all Republicans; so it may now be said of us, that whatever differences of opinion as to the best policy in having a co-operation with our border sister slave States, if the worst came to the worst, that as we were all co-operationists, we are now all for independence, whether they come or not.

In this connection I take this occasion to state, that I was not without grave and serious apprehensions, that if the worst came to the worst, and cutting loose from the old government should be the only remedy for our safety and security, it would be attended with much more serious ills than it has been as yet. Thus far we have seen none of those incidents which usually attend revolutions. No such material as such convulsions usually throw up has been seen. Wisdom, prudence, and patriotism, have marked every step of our progress thus far. This augurs well for the future, and it is a matter of sincere gratification to me, that I am enabled to make the declaration. Of the men I met in the Congress at Montgomery, I may be pardoned for saying this, an abler, wiser, a more conservative, deliberate, determined, resolute, and patriotic body of men, I never met in my life. Their works speak for them; the provisional government speaks for them; the constitution of the permanent government will be a lasting monument of their worth, merit, and statesmanship.

But to return to the question of the future. What is to be the result of this revolution?

Will every thing, commenced so well, continue as it has begun? In reply to this anxious inquiry, I can only say it all depends upon ourselves. A young man starting out in life on his majority, with health, talent, and ability, under a favoring Providence, may be said to be the architect of his own fortunes. His destinies are in his own hands. He may make for himself a name, of honor or dishonor, according to his own acts. If he plants himself upon truth, integrity, honor and uprightness, with industry, patience and energy, he cannot fail of success. So it is with us. We are a young republic, just entering upon the arena of nations; we will be the architects of our own fortunes. Our destiny, under Providence, is in our own hands. With wisdom, prudence, and statesmanship on the part of our public men, and intelligence, virtue and patriotism on the part of the people, success, to the full measures of our most sanguine hopes, may be looked for. But if unwise counsels prevail if we become divided if schisms arise if dissentions spring up if factions are engendered if party spirit, nourished by unholy personal ambition

shall rear its hydra head, I have no good to prophesy for you. Without intelligence, virtue, integrity, and patriotism on the part of the people, no republic or representative government can be durable or stable.

We have intelligence, and virtue, and patriotism. All that is required is to cultivate and perpetuate these. Intelligence will not do without virtue. France was a nation of philosophers. These philosophers become Jacobins. They lacked that virtue, that devotion to moral principle, and that patriotism which is essential to good government Organized upon principles of perfect justice and right-seeking amity and friendship with all other powers-I see no obstacle in the way of our upward and onward progress. Our growth, by accessions from other States, will depend greatly upon whether we present to the world, as I trust we shall, a better government than that to which neighboring States belong. If we do this, North Carolina, Tennessee, and Arkansas cannot hesitate long; neither can Virginia, Kentucky, and Missouri. They will necessarily gravitate to us by an imperious law. We made ample provision in our constitution for the admission of other States; it is more guarded, and wisely so, I think, than the old constitution on the same subject, but not too guarded to receive them as fast as it may be proper. Looking to the distant future, and, perhaps, not very far distant either, it is not beyond the range of possibility, and even probability, that all the great States of the north-west will gravitate this way, as well as Tennessee, Kentucky, Missouri, Arkansas, etc. Should they do so, our doors are wide enough to receive them, but not until they are ready to assimilate with us in principle.

The process of disintegration in the old Union may be expected to go on with almost absolute certainty if we pursue the right course. We are now the nucleus of a growing power which, if we are true to ourselves, our destiny, and high mission, will become the controlling power on this continent. To what extent accessions will go on in the process of time, or where it will end, the future will determine. So far as it concerns States of the old Union, this process will be upon no such principles of reconstruction as now spoken of, but upon reorganization and new assimilation. Such are some of the glimpses of the future as I catch them.

But at first we must necessarily meet with the inconveniences and difficulties and embarrassments incident to all changes of government. These will be felt in our postal affairs and changes in the channel of trade. These inconveniences, it is to be hoped, will be but temporary, and must be borne with patience and forbearance.

As to whether we shall have war with our late confederates, or whether all matters of differences between us shall be amicably settled, I can only say that the prospect for a peaceful adjustment is better, so far as I am informed, than it has been. The prospect of war is, at least, not so threatening as it has been. The idea of coercion, shadowed forth in President Lincoln's inaugural, seems not to be followed up thus far so vigorously as was expected. Fort Sumter, it is believed, will soon be evacuated. What course will be pursued toward Fort Pickens, and the other forts on the gulf, is not so well understood. It is to be greatly desired that all of them should be surrendered. Our object is peace, not only with the North, but with the world. All matters relating to the public property, public liabilities of the Union when we were members of it, we are ready and willing to adjust and settle upon the principles of right, equity, and good faith. War can be of no more benefit to the North than to us. Whether the intention of evacuating Fort Sumter is to be received as an evidence of a desire for a peaceful solution of our difficulties with the United States, or the result of necessity, I will not undertake to say. I would feign hope the former. Rumors are afloat, however, that it is the result of necessity. All I can say to you, therefore, on that point is, keep your armor bright and your powder dry.

The surest way to secure peace, is to show your ability to maintain your rights. The principles and position of the present administration of the United States the republican party present some puzzling questions. While it is a fixed principle with them never to allow the increase of a foot of slave territory, they seem to be equally determined not to part with an inch "of the accursed soil." Notwithstanding their clamor against the institution, they seemed to be equally opposed to getting more, or letting go what they have got. They were ready to fight on the accession of Texas, and are equally ready to fight now on her secession. Why is this? How can this strange paradox be accounted for? There seems to be but one rational solution and that is, notwithstanding their professions of humanity, they are disinclined to give up the benefits they derive from slave labor. Their philanthropy yields to their interest. The idea of enforcing the laws, has but one object, and that is a collection of the taxes, raised by slave labor to swell the fund necessary to meet their heavy appropriations. The spoils is what they are after though they come from the labor of the slave.

That as the admission of States by Congress under the constitution was an act of legislation, and in the nature of a contract or compact between the States admitted and the others admitting, why should not this contract or compact be regarded as of like character with all other civil contracts liable to be rescinded by mutual agreement of both parties? The seceding States have rescinded it on their part, they have resumed their sovereignty. Why cannot the whole question be settled, if the north desire peace, simply by the Congress, in both branches, with the concurrence of the President, giving their consent to the separation, and a recognition of our independence?

Source: Henry Cleveland, *Alexander H. Stephens, in Public and Private: With Letters and Speeches, Before, During, and Since the War* (Philadelphia, 1886), pp. 717–729.

Final Emancipation Proclamation

Abraham Lincoln January 1, 1863

By the President of the United States of America:
A Proclamation.

Whereas, on the twentysecond day of September, in the year of our Lord one thousand eight hundred and sixty two, a proclamation was issued by the President of the United States, containing, among other things, the following, to wit:

"That on the first day of January, in the year of our Lord one thousand eight hundred and sixty-three, all persons held as slaves within any State or designated part of a State, the people whereof shall then be in rebellion against the United States, shall be then, thenceforward, and forever free; and the Executive Government of the United States, including the military and naval authority thereof, will recognize and maintain the freedom of such persons, and will do no act or acts to repress such persons, or any of them, in any efforts they may make for their actual freedom.

"That the Executive will, on the first day of January aforesaid, by proclamation, designate the States and parts of States, if any, in which the people thereof, respectively, shall then be in rebellion against the United States; and the fact that any State, or the people thereof, shall on that day be, in good faith, represented in the Congress of the United States by members chosen thereto at elections wherein a majority of the qualified voters of such State shall have participated, shall, in the absence of strong countervailing testimony, be deemed conclusive evidence that such State, and the people thereof, are not then in rebellion against the United States."

Now, therefore I, Abraham Lincoln, President of the United States, by virtue of the power in me vested as Commander-in-Chief, of the Army and Navy of the United States in time of actual armed rebellion against authority and government of the United States, and as a fit and necessary war measure for suppressing said rebellion, do, on this first day of January, in the year of our Lord one thousand eight hundred and sixty three, and in accordance with my purpose so to do publicly proclaimed for the full period of one hundred days, from the day first above mentioned, order and designate as the States and parts of States wherein the people thereof respectively, are this day in rebellion against the United States, the following, to wit:

Arkansas, Texas, Louisiana, (except the Parishes of St. Bernard, Plaquemines, Jefferson, St. Johns, St. Charles, St. James, Ascension, Assumption, Terrebonne, Lafourche, St. Mary, St. Martin, and Orleans, including the City of New-Orleans) Mississippi, Alabama, Florida, Georgia, South-Carolina, North-Carolina, and Virginia, (except the forty-eight counties designated as West Virginia, and also the counties of Berkley, Accomac, Northampton, Elizabeth-City, York, Princess Ann, and Norfolk, including the cities of Norfolk & Portsmouth); and which excepted parts are, for the present, left precisely as if this proclamation were not issued.

And by virtue of the power, and for the purpose aforesaid, I do order and declare that all persons held as slaves within said designated States, and parts of States, are, and henceforward shall be free; and that the Executive government of the United States, including the military and naval authorities thereof, will recognize and maintain the freedom of said persons.

And I hereby enjoin upon the people so declared to be free to abstain from all violence, unless in necessary self-defence; and I recommend to them that, in all cases when allowed, they labor faithfully for reasonable wages.

And I further declare and make known, that such persons of suitable condition, will be received into the armed service of the United States to garrison forts, positions, stations, and other places, and to man vessels of all sorts in said service.

And upon this act, sincerely believed to be an act of justice, warranted by the Constitution, upon military necessity, I invoke the considerate judgment of mankind, and the gracious favor of Almighty God.

In witness whereof, I have hereunto set my hand and caused the seal of the United States to be affixed.

Done at the City of Washington, this first day of January, in the year of our Lord one thousand eight hundred and sixty three, and of the Independence of the United States of America the eighty-seventh.

By the President: ABRAHAM LINCOLN

WILLIAM H. SEWARD, Secretary of State.

Proclamation of Amnesty and Reconstruction, December 18, 1863

Abraham Lincoln,

Abraham Lincoln, Proclamation of Amnesty and Reconstruction [Draft][1] December 8, 1863

[Note 1 During his illness with varioloid (a mild form of smallpox), Lincoln was drafting both his annual message to Congress (See Abraham Lincoln to Congress, December 8, 1863 and *Collected Works*, VII, 36–53), and this document, which was announced by the president in that message. Though this proclamation was unanticipated, the annual message was anxiously awaited, for it was presumed that in it, Lincoln would address the issue of reconstruction. The president had received a variety of advice as he was in the process of composing the two documents. For a sampling, see Zachariah Chandler to Lincoln, November 15, 1863, Andrew Johnson to Montgomery Blair, November 24, 1863, Salmon P. Chase to Lincoln, November 25, 1863, and Isaac N. Arnold to Lincoln, December 4, 1863. The Proclamation of Amnesty and Reconstruction that follows embodies Lincoln's "ten per cent" plan of reconstructing the seceded states. The plan was based on the affirmations of future loyalty to the Union of at least one tenth of the 1860 voters in those states, which loyal voters would then be a core of electors involved in the re-establishment of new republican governments there. That Lincoln was willing to rely on a minority of previously-qualified voters for this task shows how far he had come from his earlier conviction of the underlying loyalty to the Union of the Southern masses. When announced, the plan given here had at least the temporary approval of a broad spectrum of Unionists, from war Democrats to radical Republicans. In the enthusiastic words of his secretary, John Hay: "Men acted as if the Milleniurn had come. Chandler was delighted, Sumner was beaming, while at the other political pole Dixon and Reverdy Johnson said it was highly satisfactory." See Michael Burlingame and John Turner Ettlinger, eds., *Inside Lincoln's White House: The Complete Civil War Diary of John Hay* (Carbondale: Southern Illinois University Press, 1997), 121–122. The manuscript carries the names of typesetters assigned various parts, indicating that this copy, which was likely the final handwritten draft, was set up in print.]

Abraham Lincoln Papers at the Library of Congress. Transcribed and Annotated by the Lincoln Studies Center, Knox College. Galesburg, Illinois.

Dec. 8, 1863

Proclamation.[2]

[Note 2 Both the date and the heading "Proclamation" appear to be in another hand, not Lincoln's.]

Whereas in and by the Constitution of the United States, it is provided that the President "shall have power to grant reprieves and pardons for offences against the United States, except in cases of impeachment, and

Whereas a rebellion now exists whereby the loyal State governments of several States have for a long time been subverted, and many persons have committed, and are now guilty of treason against the United States, and

Whereas, with reference to said rebellion and treason, laws have been enacted by Congress, declaring forfeitures, and confiscations of property, and liberation of slaves, all upon terms and conditions therein stated, and also declaring that the President was thereby authorized at any time thereafter, by proclamation, to extend to persons who may have participated in the existing rebellion, in any State or part thereof, pardon and amnesty, with such exceptions, and at such time, and on such conditions, as he may deem expedient for the public welfare, and

Whereas the Congressional declaration for limited and conditional pardon, accords with well established judicial exposition of the pardoning power, ~~under the British, and American Constitutions~~, and

Whereas, with reference to said rebellion, the President of the United States has issued several proclamations, with provisions in regard to the liberation of slaves, and

Whereas it is now desired by some persons heretofore engaged in said rebellion, to resume their allegiance to the United States, and to re-inaugurate loyal State governments within and for their respective States, therefore

I, Abraham Lincoln, President of the United States, do proclaim, declare, and make known, to all persons who have, directly or by implication, participated in the existing rebellion, except

[Space in Manuscript :][3]
[Note 3 In the official copy, the words "as hereinafter excepted," follow at this point.]

that a full pardon is hereby granted to them and each of them, with restoration of all rights of property, except as to slaves, and upon the condition that every such person shall take and subscribe an oath, and thenceforward keep and maintain said oath inviolate; and which oath shall be registered for permanent preservation and shall be of the tenor and effect following, towit:

"I . . . do solemnly swear in presence of Almighty God, that I will henceforth faithfully support, protect, and defend the Constitution of the United States, and the Union of the States thereunder; and that I will, in like manner, abide by, and faithfully support all Acts of Congress passed during the existing rebellion, with reference to slaves, so long, and so far, as not repealed, modified, or held void by Congress, or by decision of the Supreme Court; and that I will, in like manner, abide by and faithfully support, all proclamations of the President made during the existing rebellion, having reference to slaves, so long, and so far as not modified, or declared void by decision of the Supreme Court, so help me God."*[4]

[Note 4 The asterisk indicates the insertion point for a paragraph written out as an addition on a separate slip. The list of exceptions is based on War Department, Memoranda for Proclamation of Amnesty and Reconstruction, December, 1863 (*q. v.*), a document which was provided Lincoln to aid in preparing this proclamation.]

*The persons excepted from the benefits of the foregoing provisions are all who are, or shall have been civil or diplomatic officers or agents of the so-called Confederate government; all who have left judicial stations under the United States to aid the rebellion; all who are, or shall have been military or naval officers of said so-called confederate government, above the rank of Colonel in the Army, or of lieutenant in the Navy; all who left seats in the United States Congress to aid the rebellion; all who resigned commissions in the army or navy of the United States, and afterwards aided the rebellion; and all who have engaged in any way, in treating colored persons, or white persons in charge of such, otherwise than lawfully as prisoners of war, and which persons may have been found in the United States service as soldiers, seamen, or in any other capacity.

And I do further proclaim, declare, and make known that whenever, in any of the States of Arkansas, Texas, Louisiana, Mississippi, Tennessee,

Alabama, Georgia, Florida, South-Carolina, and North Carolina, a number of persons, not less than one tenth in number of the votes cast ~~at~~ in such state, at the Presidential election of the year of our Lord, one thousand eight hundred and sixty, each having taken the oath aforesaid, and not having since violated it, and being a qualified voter by the election law of the state, existing immediately before the so-called act of secession, and excluding all others, shall re-establish a State government, which shall be republican, and in no wise contravening said ~~said~~ oath, such shall be recognized as the true government of the State, and the State shall receive thereunder the benefits of the Constitutional provision which declares that "The United States shall guaranty to every State in the Union a republican form of government, and shall protect each of them against invasion, and on application of the legislature, or the executive (when the legislature can not be convened against domestic violence."

And I do further proclaim, declare, and make known that any provision which may be adopted by such State government in relation to the freed people of such State, which shall recognize and declare their permanent freedom, provide for their education, and which may yet be consistent, as a temporary arrangement, with their present condition as a laboring, landless, and homeless class, shall not be objected to by the national executive.*5

[Note 5 The asterisk indicates the insertion point for the addition to the text that follows. For preliminary drafts of this passage, see the memorandum on the reverse side of Lincoln's draft of a letter to George Opdyke, December 2, 1863.]

*And it is suggested as not improper that in constructing a loyal State government in any State, the name of the State, the boundary, the subdivisions, the Constitution, and the general code of laws, as before the rebellion, be maintained, subject only to the modifications made necessary by the conditions hereinbefore stated, and such others, if any, not contravening said conditions, and which may be deemed expedient by those framing the new State government.

To avoid misunderstanding it may be proper to say that this ~~paper~~ proclamation, so far as it relates to State governments, has no reference to States wherein loyal State governments have all the while been maintained. And for the same reason it may be proper to further say that whether members sent to Congress from any State shall be admitted to seats constitutionally rests exclusively with the respective Houses, and not to any extent with the executive.

And still further that this proclamation is intended to present the people of the States wherein the national authority has been suspended, and loyal State governments have been subverted, a mode in and by which the national authority and loyal States governments may be re-established within said States, or in any of them; and, while the mode presented is the best the executive can ~~present~~ suggest, with his present impressions, it must not be understood that no other possible mode would be acceptable.

Given under my hand at the City of Washington, the 8th of December, A. D. one thousand eight hundred and sixty three, and of the independence of the United States of America the eightyeighth.

Abraham Lincoln

Proclamation Concerning Reconstruction, 1864

Abraham Lincoln

Whereas, at the late Session, Congress passed a Bill, "To guarantee to certain States, whose governments have been usurped or overthrown, a republican form of Government," a copy of which is hereunto annexed:

And whereas, the said Bill was presented to the President of the United States, for his approval, less than one hour before the *sine die* adjournment of said Session, and was not signed by him:

And whereas, the said Bill contains, among other things, a plan for restoring the States in rebellion to their proper practical relation in the Union, which plan expresses the sense of Congress upon that subject, and which plan it is now thought fit to lay before the people for their consideration:

Now, therefore, I, Abraham Lincoln, President of the United States, do proclaim, declare, and make known, that, while I am, (as I was in December last, when by proclamation I propounded a plan for restoration) unprepared, by a formal approval of this Bill, to be inflexibly committed to any single plan of restoration; and, while I am also unprepared to declare, that the free-state constitutions and governments, already adopted and installed in Arkansas and Louisiana, shall be set aside and held for nought, thereby repelling and discouraging the loyal citizens who have set up the same, as to further effort; or to declare a constitutional competency in Congress to abolish slavery in States, but am at the same time sincerely hoping and expecting that a constitutional amendment, abolishing slavery throughout the nation, may be adopted, nevertheless, I am fully satisfied with the system for restoration contained in the Bill, as one very proper plan for the loyal people of any State choosing to adopt it; and that I am, and at all times shall be, prepared to give the Executive aid and assistance to any such people, so soon as the military resistance to the United States shall have been suppressed in any such State, and the people thereof shall have sufficiently returned to their obedience to the Constitution and the laws of the United States,—in which cases, military Governors will be appointed, with directions to proceed according to the Bill.

Source: R. Basler, ed., 7 *Collected Works of Abraham Lincoln* 433 (1953).

Wade-Davis Bill, 1864

Melvin I. Urofsky, ed.

Be it enacted, That in the states declared in rebellion against the United States, the President shall, by and with the advice and consent of the Senate, appoint for each a provisional governor, who shall be charged with the civil administration of such state until a state government therein shall be recognized as hereinafter provided.

Sec. 2. That so soon as the military resistance to the United States shall have been suppressed in any such state, and the people thereof shall have sufficiently returned to their obedience to the constitution and the laws of the United States, the provisional governor shall direct the marshal of the United States, as speedily as may be, to name a sufficient number of deputies, and to enroll all white male citizens of the United States, resident in the state in their respective counties, and to request each one to take the oath to support the constitution of the United States, and in his enrollment to designate those who take and those who refuse to take that oath, which rolls shall be forthwith returned to the provisional governor; and if the persons taking that oath shall amount to a majority of the persons enrolled in the state, he shall, by proclamation, invite the loyal people of the state to elect delegates to a convention charged to declare the will of the people of the state relative to the reëstablishment of a state government subject to, and in conformity with, the constitution of the United States.

Sec. 3. That the convention shall consist of as many members as both houses of the last constitutional state legislature, apportioned by the provisional governor among the counties, parishes, or districts of the state, in proportion to the white population, returned as electors, by the marshal, in compliance with the provisions of this act. The provisional governor shall, . . . provide an adequate force to keep the peace during the election.

Sec. 4. That the delegates shall be elected by the loyal white male citizens of the United States of the age of twenty-one years, and resident at the time in the county, parish, or district in which they shall offer to vote, and enrolled as aforesaid, or absent in the military service of the United States, and who shall take and subscribe the oath of allegiance to the United States in the form contained in the act of July 2, 1862; and all such citizens of the United States who are in the military service of the United States shall vote at the headquarters of their respective commands, under such regulations as may be prescribed by the provisional governor for the taking and return of their votes; but no person who has held or exercised any office, civil or military, state or confederate, under the rebel usurpation, or who has voluntarily borne arms against the United States, shall vote, or be eligible to be elected as delegate, at such election.

Sec. 5. That the said commissioners, . . . shall hold the election in conformity with this act and. . . . shall proceed in the manner used in the state prior to the rebellion. The oath of allegiance shall be taken and subscribed on the poll-book by every voter in the form above prescribed, but every person known by, or proved to, the commissioners to have held or exercised any office, civil or military, state or confederate, under the rebel usurpation, or to have voluntarily borne arms against the United States, shall be excluded, though he offer to take the oath; and in case any person who shall have borne arms against the United States shall offer to vote he shall be deemed to have borne arms voluntarily unless he shall prove the contrary by the testimony of a qualified voter. . . .

Sec. 6. That the provisional governor shall, by proclamation, convene the delegates elected as aforesaid, at the capital of the state, on a day not more than three months after the election, giving at least thirty days' notice of such day. In case the said capital shall in his judgment be unfit, he shall

Source: Richardson, ed., 6 *Messages and Papers of the Presidents* 223 (1897).

in his proclamation appoint another place. He shall preside over the deliberations of the convention, and administer to each delegate, before taking his scat in the convention, the oath of allegiance to the United States in the form above prescribed.

Sec. 7. That the convention shall declare, on behalf of the people of the state, their submission to the constitution and laws of the United States, and shall adopt the following provisions, hereby prescribed by the United States in the execution of the constitutional duty to guarantee a republican form of government to every state, and incorporate them in the constitution of the state, that is to say:

First. No person who has held or exercised any office, civil or military, except offices merely ministerial, and military offices below the grade of colonel, state or confederate, under the usurping power, shall vote for or be a member of the legislature, or governor.

Second. Involuntary servitude is forever prohibited, and the freedom of all persons is guaranteed in said state.

Third. No debt, state or confederate, created by or under the sanction of the usurping power, shall be recognized or paid by the state.

Sec. 8. That when the convention shall have adopted those provisions, it shall proceed to reëstablish a republican form of government, and ordain a constitution containing those provisions, which, when adopted, the convention shall by ordinance provide for submitting to the people of the state, entitled to vote under this law, at an election to be held in the manner prescribed by the act for the election of delegates; but at a time and place named by the convention, at which election the said electors, and none others, shall vote directly for or against such constitution and form of state government, and the returns of said election shall be made to the provisional governor, who shall canvass the same in the presence of the electors, and if a majority of the votes cast shall be for the constitution and form of government, he shall certify the same, with a copy thereof, to the President of the United States, who, after obtaining the assent of congress, shall, by proclamation, recognize the government so established, and none other, as the constitutional government of the state, and from the date of such recognition, and not before, Senators and Representatives, and electors for President and Vice-President may be elected in such state, according to the laws of the state and of the United States.

Sec. 9. That if the convention shall refuse to reestablish the state government on the conditions aforesaid, the provisional governor shall declare it dissolved; but it shall be the duty of the President, whenever he shall have reason to believe that a sufficient number of the people of the state entitled to vote under this act, in number not less than a majority of those enrolled, as aforesaid, are willing to reëstablish a state government on the conditions aforesaid, to direct the provisional governor to order another election of delegates to a convention for the purpose. . . .

Sec. 10. That, until the United States shall have recognized a republican form of state government, the provisional governor in each of said states shall see that this act, and the laws of the United States, and the laws of the state in force when the state government was overthrown by the rebellion, are faithfully executed within the state; but no law or usage whereby any person was heretofore held in involuntary servitude shall be recognized or enforced by any court or officer in such state, and the laws for the trial and punishment of white persons shall extend to all persons, and jurors shall have the qualifications of voters under this law for delegates to the convention. . . .

Sec. 11. That until the recognition of a state government as aforesaid, the provisional governor shall, under such regulations as he may prescribe, cause to be assessed, levied, and collected, for the year eighteen hundred and sixty-four, and every year thereafter, the taxes provided by the laws of such state to be levied during the fiscal year preceding the overthrow of the state government thereof, in the manner prescribed by the laws of the state, as nearly as may be; . . . The proceeds of such taxes shall be accounted for to the provisional governor, and be by him applied to the expenses of the administration of the laws in such state, subject to the direction of the President, and the surplus shall be deposited in the treasury of the United States to the credit of such state, to be paid to the state upon an appropriation therefor, to be made when a republican form of government shall be recognized therein by the United States.

Sec. 12. That all persons held to involuntary servitude or labor in the states aforesaid are hereby emancipated and discharged therefrom, and they and their posterity shall be forever free. And if any such persons or their posterity shall be restrained of liberty, under pretence of any claim to such service or labor, the courts of the United States shall, on habeas corpus, discharge them.

Sec. 13. That if any person declared free by this act, or any law of the United States, or any proclamation of the President, be restrained of liberty, with intent to be held in or reduced to involuntary servitude or labor, the person convicted before a court of competent jurisdiction of such act shall be punished by fine of not less than fifteen hundred dollars, and be imprisoned not less than five nor more than twenty years.

Sec. 14. That every person who shall hereafter hold or exercise any office, civil or military, except offices merely ministerial, and military offices below the grade of colonel, in the rebel service, state or confederate, is hereby declared not to be a citizen of the United States.

Wade-Davis Manifesto, 1864

Melvin I. Urofsky, ed.

We have read without surprise, but not without indignation, the Proclamation of the President of the 8th of July. . . .

The President, by preventing this bill from becoming a law, holds the electoral votes of the rebel States at the dictation of his personal ambition.

If those votes turn the balance in his favor, is it to be supposed that his competitor, defeated by such means, will acquiesce?

If the rebel majority assert their supremacy in those States, and send votes which elect an enemy of the Government, will we not repel his claims?

And is not that civil war for the Presidency inaugurated by the votes of rebel States?

Seriously impressed with these dangers, Congress, *"the proper constituted authority,"* formally declared that there are no State governments in the rebel States, and provided for their erection at a proper time; and both the Senate and the House of Representatives rejected the Senators and Representatives chosen under the authority of what the President calls the free constitution and government of Arkansas.

The President's proclamation *"holds for naught"* this judgment, and discards cards the authority of the Supreme Court, and strides headlong toward the anarchy his proclamation of the 8th of December inaugurated.

If electors for President be allowed to be chosen in either of those States, a sinister light will be cast on the motives which induced the President to "hold for naught" the will of Congress rather than his government in Louisiana and Arkansas.

That judgment of Congress which the President defies was the exercise of an authority exclusively vested in Congress by the Constitution to determine what is the established government in a State, and in its own nature and by the highest judicial authority binding on all other departments of the Government

A more studied outrage on the legislative authority of the people has never been perpetrated.

Congress passed a bill; the President refused to approve it, and then by proclamation puts as much of it in force as he sees fit, and proposes to execute those parts by officers unknown to the laws of the United States and not subject to the confirmation of the Senate!

The bill directed the appointment of Provisional Governors by and with the advice and consent of the Senate.

The President, after defeating the law, proposes to appoint without law, and without the advice and consent of the Senate, *Military Governors* for the rebel States!

He has already exercised this dictatorial usurpation in Louisiana, and he defeated the bill to prevent its limitation. . . .

The President has greatly presumed on the forbearance which the supporters of his Administration have so long practiced, in view of the arduous conflict in which we are engaged, and the reckless ferocity of our political opponents.

But he must understand that our support is of a cause and not of a man; that the authority of Congress is paramount and must be respected; that the whole body of the Union men of Congress will not submit to be impeached by him of rash and unconstitutional legislation; and if he wishes our support, he must confine himself to his executive duties—to obey and execute, not make the laws—to suppress by arms armed rebellion, and leave political reorganization to Congress.

If the supporters of the Government fail to insist on this, they become responsible for the usurpations which they fail to rebuke, and are justly liable to the indignation of the people whose rights and security, committed to their eeping, they sacrifice.

Let them consider the remedy for these usurpations, and, having found it, fearlessly execute it.

Source: *New York Tribune*, 5 August 1864.

Second Inaugural Address

Abraham Lincoln March 4, 1865

Fellow Countrymen:

At this second appearing to take the oath of the presidential office, there is less occasion for an extended address than there was at the first. Then a statement, somewhat in detail, of a course to be pursued, seemed fitting and proper. Now, at the expiration of four years, during which public declarations have been constantly called forth on every point and phase of the great contest which still absorbs the attention, and engrosses the energies of the nation, little that is new could be presented. The progress of our arms, upon which all else chiefly depends, is as well known to the public as to myself; and it is, I trust, reasonably satisfactory and encouraging to all. With high hope for the future, no prediction in regard to it is ventured.

On the occasion corresponding to this four years ago, all thoughts were anxiously directed to an impending civil war. All dreaded it, all sought to avert it. While the inaugural address was being delivered from this place, devoted altogether to *saving* the Union without war, insurgent agents were in the city seeking to *destroy* it without war—seeking to dissolve the Union, and divide effects, by negotiation. Both parties deprecated war; but one of them would *make* war rather than let the nation survive; and the other would *accept* war rather than let it perish. And the war came.

One eighth of the whole population were colored slaves, not distributed generally over the Union, but localized in the Southern part of it. These slaves constituted a peculiar and powerful interest. All knew that this interest was, somehow, the cause of the war. To strengthen, perpetuate, and extend this interest was the object for which the insurgents would rend the Union, even by war; while the government claimed no right to do more than to restrict the territorial enlargement of it. Neither party expected for the war, the magnitude, or the duration, which it has already attained. Neither anticipated that the *cause* of the conflict might cease with, or even before, the conflict itself should cease. Each looked for an easier triumph, and a result less fundamental and astounding. Both read the same Bible, and pray to the same God; and each invokes His aid against the other. It may seem strange that any men should dare to ask a just God's assistance in wringing their bread from the sweat of other men's faces; but let us judge not that we be not judged. The prayers of both could not be answered; that of neither has been answered fully. The Almighty has His own purposes. Woe unto the world because of offences! for it must needs be that offences come; but woe to that man by whom the offence cometh! If we shall suppose that American Slavery is one of those offences which, in the providence of God, must needs come, but which, having continued through His appointed time, He now wills to remove, and that He gives to both North and South, this terrible war, as the woe due to those by whom the offence came, shall we discern therein any departure from those divine attributes which the believers in a Living God always ascribe to Him? Fondly do we hope, fervently do we pray, that this mighty scourge of war may speedily pass away. Yet, if God wills that it continue, until all the wealth piled by the bond-man's two hundred and fifty years of unrequited toil shall be sunk, and until every drop of blood drawn with the lash, shall be paid by another drawn with the sword, as was said three thousand years ago, so still it must be said "the judgments of the Lord, are true and righteous altogether."

With malice toward none; with charity for all; with firmness in the right, as God gives us to see the right, let us strive on to finish the work we are in; to bind up the nation's wounds; to care for him who shall have borne the battle, and for his widow, and his orphan—to do all which may achieve and cherish a just and a lasting peace, among ourselves, and with all nations.

First Annual Address to Congress, December 4, 1865

Richard N. Current, ed.

[In his first annual message to Congress, December 4, 1865, Johnson undertook to justify the reconstruction policy he had put into practice during the summer. James D. Richardson, ed., *A Compilation of the Messages and Papers of the Presidents* (Washington, 1897), VIII, 3,554–58.]

✳ ✳ ✳ ✳ ✳

The Spirit of Mutual Conciliation

I found the States suffering from the effects of a civil war. Resistance to the General Government appeared to have exhausted itself. The United States had recovered possession of their forts and arsenals, and their armies were in the occupation of every State which had attempted to secede. Whether the territory within the limits of those States should be held as conquered territory, under military authority emanating from the President as the head of the Army, was the first question that presented itself for decision.

Now military governments, established for an indefinite period, would have offered no security for the early suppression of discontent, would have divided the people into the vanquishers and the vanquished, and would have envenomed hatred rather than have restored affection. Once established, no precise limit to their continuance was conceivable. They would have occasioned an incalculable and exhausting expense. Peaceful emigration to and from that portion of the country is one of the best means that can be thought of for the restoration of harmony, and that emigration would have been prevented; for what emigrant from abroad, what industrious citizen at home, would place himself willingly under military rule? The chief persons who would have followed in the train of the Army would have been dependents on the General Government or men who expected profit from the miseries of their erring fellow-citizens. The powers of patronage and rule which would have been exercised, under the President, over a vast and populous and naturally wealthy region are greater than, unless under extreme necessity, I should be willing to intrust to any one man. They are such as, for myself, I could never, unless on occasions of great emergency, consent to exercise. The willful use of such powers, if continued through a period of years, would have endangered the purity of the general administration and the liberties of the States which remained loyal.

Besides, the policy of military rule over a conquered territory would have implied that the States whose inhabitants may have taken part in the rebellion had by the act of those inhabitants ceased to exist. But the true theory is that all pretended acts of secession were from the beginning null and void. The States can not commit treason nor screen the individual citizens who may have committed treason any more than they can make valid treaties or engage in lawful commerce with any foreign power. The States attempting to secede placed themselves in a condition where their vitality was impaired, but not extinguished; their functions suspended, but not destroyed.

From *Reconstruction, 1865–1877* by Richard Current (Ed.). Reprinted by permission of the editor.

But if any State neglects or refuses to perform its offices there is the more need that the General Government should maintain all its authority and as soon as practicable resume the exercise of all its functions. On this principle I have acted, and have gradually and quietly, and by almost imperceptible steps, sought to restore the rightful energy of the General Government and of the States. To that end provisional governors have been appointed for the States, conventions called, governors elected, legislatures assembled, and Senators and Representatives chosen to the Congress of the United States. At the same time the courts of the United States, as far as could be done, have been reopened, so that the laws of the United States may be enforced through their agency. The blockade has been removed and the customhouses reestablished in ports of entry, so that the revenue of the United States may be collected. The Post-Office Department renews its ceaseless activity, and the General Government is thereby enabled to communicate promptly with its officers and agents. The courts bring security to persons and property; the opening of the ports invites the restoration of industry and commerce; the post-office renews the facilities of social intercourse and of business. And is it not happy for us all that the restoration of each one of these functions of the General Government brings with it a blessing to the States over which they are extended? Is it not a sure promise of harmony and renewed attachment to the Union that after all that has happened the return of the General Government is known only as a beneficence?

I know very well that this policy is attended with some risk; that for its success it requires at least the acquiescence of the States which it concerns; that it implies an invitation to those States, by renewing their allegiance to the United States, to resume their functions as States of the Union. But it is a risk that must be taken. In the choice of difficulties it is the smallest risk; and to diminish and if possible to remove all danger, I have felt it incumbent on me to assert one other power of the General Government—the power of pardon. As no State can throw a defense over the crime of treason, the power of pardon is exclusively vested in the executive government of the United States. In exercising that power I have taken every precaution to connect it with the clearest recognition of the binding force of the laws of the United States and an unqualified acknowledgment of the great social change of condition in regard to slavery which has grown out of the war.

The next step which I have taken to restore the constitutional relations of the States has been an invitation to them to participate in the high office of amending the Constitution. Every patriot must wish for a general amnesty at the earliest epoch consistent with public safety. For this great end there is need of a concurrence of all opinions and the spirit of mutual conciliation. All parties in the late terrible conflict must work together in harmony. It is not too much to ask, in the name of the whole people, that on the one side the plan of restoration shall proceed in conformity with a willingness to cast the disorders of the past into oblivion, and that on the other the evidence of sincerity in the future maintenance of the Union shall be put beyond any doubt by the ratification of the proposed amendment to the Constitution, which provides for the abolition of slavery forever within the limits of our country. So long as the adoption of this amendment is delayed, so long will doubt and jealousy and uncertainty prevail. This is the measure which will efface the sad memory of the past; this is the measure which will most certainly call population and capital and security to those parts of the Union that need them most. Indeed, it is not too much to ask of the States which are now resuming their places in the family of the Union to give this pledge of perpetual loyalty and peace. Until it is done the past, however much we may desire it, will not be forgotten. The adoption of the amendment reunites us beyond all power of disruption; it heals the wound that is still imperfectly closed; it removes slavery, the element which has so long perplexed and divided the country; it makes of us once more a united people, renewed and strengthened, bound more than ever to mutual affection and support.

The amendment to the Constitution being adopted, it would remain for the States whose powers have been so long in abeyance to resume their places in the two branches of the National Legislature, and thereby complete the work of restoration. Here it is for you, fellow-citizens of the Senate, and for you, fellow-citizens of the House of Representatives, to judge, each of you for yourselves, of the elections, returns, and qualifications of your own members. . . .

The relations of the General Government toward the 4,000,000 inhabitants whom the war has called into freedom have engaged my most serious consideration. On the propriety of attempting to make the freedmen electors by the proclamation of the

Executive I took for my counsel the Constitution itself, the interpretations of that instrument by its authors and their contemporaries, and recent legislation by Congress. When, at the first movement toward independence, the Congress of the United States instructed the several States to institute governments of their own, they left each State to decide for itself the conditions for the enjoyment of the elective franchise. During the period of the Confederacy there continued to exist a very great diversity in the qualifications of electors in the several States, and even within a State a distinction of qualifications prevailed with regard to the officers who were to be chosen. The Constitution of the United States recognizes these diversities when it enjoins that in the choice of members of the House of Representatives of the United States "the electors in each State shall have the qualifications requisite for electors of the most numerous branch of the State legislature." After the formation of the Constitution it remained, as before, the uniform usage for each State to enlarge the body of its electors according to its own judgment, and under this system one State after another has proceeded to increase the number of its electors, until now universal suffrage, or something very near it, is the general rule. So fixed was this reservation of power in the habits of the people and so unquestioned has been the interpretation of the Constitution that during the civil war the late President never harbored the purpose—certainly never avowed the purpose—of disregarding it; and

in the acts of Congress during that period nothing can be found which, during the continuance of hostilities much less after their close, would have sanctioned any departure by the Executive from a policy which has so uniformly obtained. Moreover, a concession of the elective franchise to the freedmen by act of the President of the United States must have been extended to all colored men, wherever found, and so must have established a change of suffrage in the Northern, Middle, and Western States, not less than in the Southern and Southwestern. Such an act would have created a new class of voters, and would have been an assumption of power by the President which nothing in the Constitution or laws of the United States would have warranted.

On the other hand, every danger of conflict is avoided when the settlement of the question is referred to the several States. They can, each for itself, decide on the measure, and whether it is to be adopted at once and absolutely or introduced gradually and with conditions. In my judgment the freedmen, if they show patience and manly virtues, will sooner obtain a participation in the elective franchise through the States than through the General Government, even if it had power to intervene. When the tumult of emotions that have been raised by the suddenness of the social change shall have subsided, it may prove that they will receive the kindest usage from some of those on whom they have heretofore most closely depended.

Black Codes, 1865
Aims of the Ex-Confederates

Richard N. Current, ed.

A prompt "restoration" of the Southern states would seemingly be justified if the former rebels were no longer rebellious but, instead, were quite willing to accept the consequences of the war. A sterner reconstruction policy would seem to be indicated, however, if most of the Southern whites persisted in refusing to give federal authorities their loyal obedience or to recognize the Negroes as truly free.

Hence both President Johnson and the congressional Radicals were interested in ascertaining the predominant Southern attitudes. During the summer and fall of 1865 Johnson sent one personal representative after another to visit the South, talk with the people, and report back to him. During the winter of 1865–66 the Radicals brought witnesses from the South to Washington and examined them before the joint Committee on Reconstruction. Meanwhile, a number of journalists and other travelers toured the South on their own and wrote accounts that were published in newspapers, magazines, and books.

The reports differed in emphasis and detail. Those of two of Johnson's emissaries for example, seemed mutually contradictory. On the one hand, General U. S. Grant concluded: "I am satisfied that the mass of thinking men of the South accept the present situation of affairs in good faith. The questions which have heretofore divided the sentiments of the people of the two sections—slavery and States' rights, or the right of a State to secede from the Union—they regard as having been settled forever by the highest tribunal—arms—that man can resort to. I was pleased to learn from the leading men whom I met that they not only accepted the decision arrived at as final, but, now that the smoke of battle has cleared away and time has been given for reflection, [they feel] that this decision has been a fortunate one for the whole country, they receiving like benefits from it with those who opposed them in the field and in council." On the other hand, the German-born Republican soldier and politician Carl Schurz stated: "Treason does, under existing circumstances, not appear odious in the South. The people are not impressed with any sense of its criminality. And . . . there is as yet among the Southern people *an utter absence of national feeling.*" Schurz added: "Although the freedman is no longer considered the property of the individual master, he is considered the slave of society, and all independent state legislation will share the tendency to make him so."

It would have been surprising if the ex-Confederates, facing the ashes of defeat, had immediately given loyal devotion to the authority they had fought four years to overthrow. It would have been surprising if many of these people, brought up on the proslavery argument with its doctrine of Negro inferiority, had suddenly welcomed the former slave as a person completely free and equal. Within those limits there was undoubtedly a wide range of Southern opinion. In the absence of scientific polls (which were not invented until the 1930s) the shades of opinion and their distribution can only be estimated. A sampling of statements of ex-Confederates themselves will at least suggest the prevailing points of view.

From *Reconstruction, 1865–1877* by Richard Current (Ed.). Reprinted by permission of the editor.

"Slavery . . . the Best System of Labor"

A Georgia Leader on Reconstruction, 1865

[Howell Cobb, a leading Georgian, had had a distinguished career before the war as governor, congressman, and Secretary of the Treasury. During the war he served as a member of the Confederate Congress and then as a general in the Confederate army. On June 14, 1865, he expressed his views on reconstruction in a letter he wrote to a Union general, J. H. Wilson, to be forwarded to President Johnson. The original of the letter is in the Andrew Johnson Papers in the Library of Congress.]

It is due to candor to say that I was a secessionist, and counselled the people of Georgia to secede. When the adoption of that policy resulted in War, I felt it my duty to share in the privations of the struggle, and accordingly at the commencement of the contest, I entered the army. . . . I was an earnest supporter of the cause throughout the struggle. Upon the surrender of General Johnston I regarded the contest at an end, and have since that time conformed my action to that conviction. . . .

The contest has ended in the subjugation of the South. The parties stand towards each other in the relative positions of conqueror and conquered; and the question for statesmen to decide is the policy and duty of the respective parties. . . .

The whole country [South] has been more or less devastated. Their physical condition in the loss of property, and the deprivation of the comforts of life . . . is as bad, as their worst enemy could desire. If left to employ all their resources . . . it would require much time to recover from the effects of a devastating war. The abolition of slavery not only deprives them of a large property, but revolutionizes the whole system of agricultural labor; and must necessarily retard the restoration of former prosperity. So completely has this institution been interwoven with the whole frame work of society, that its abolition involves a revision and modification of almost every page of the Statute books of the States, where it has existed. It is with a people thus depressed in mind, seriously injured in estate, and surrounded by embarrassing questions of the greatest magnitude, that the Government has to deal. . . . The avowed object of the Government was to restore the Union. The successful termination of the war has effected that result, so far as further resistance on the part of the South is concerned. The people of the South, being prepared to conform to that result, all else for the restoration of the Union is in the hands of the Government.

Looking to the future interests not only of the southern people, but of the whole country, it is desirable that the bitter animosities . . . should be softened, as much as possible; and a devastated country restored . . . to comparative prosperity. To effect these results requires the exercise of virtues, which the history of the World shows, are not often, if ever found, in the hearts of the conquerors, magnanimity and generosity. The World is sadly in need of such an example. Let the United States furnish it. There never was a more fitting opportunity. It will never be followed by more satisfactory results. . . .

Giving to these general principles the form of practical recommendation, I would say that all prosecutions and penalties should cease against those who stand charged alone with the offense of being parties to and supporters of the southern cause. . . . The time for the exercise of this power of general amnesty, with which the President is clothed, will arrive when he is satisfied that the people of the South have abandoned the contest, and have in good faith returned to their allegiance to the United States. . . . In such a policy there would be exhibited a spirit of magnanimity, which would find its reward in the happiest results.

If my voice could be heard in the councils of the Government . . . I should seek to restore concord and good feeling by extending it to those from whom I asked it in return, and by a course of generous confidence to win the willing and cheerful support of those whose loyalty and allegiance, when thus won, could be relied upon. No man will doubt that the man who is received back into the Union, and feels that he has been subjected to no severe penalty and been required to submit to no humiliating test, will make a truer and better citizen than the one who feels that his citizenship has been obtained by submitting to harsh and degrading terms, which he was compelled to yield to, to secure the rights he has acquired. . . . Secure the honest loyalty of the people, by extending to them a generous confidence, but do not ask them to win your confidence, by losing their own self respect. . . .

By the abolition of slavery . . . a state of things has been produced, well calculated to excite the most serious apprehensions with the people of the South. I regard the result as unfortunate both for the white and black. The institution of slavery, in my judgment, provided the best system of labor that could be devised for the negro race. But that has passed away, and it will tax the abilities of the best and wisest statesmen to provide a substitute for it. It is due both to the white population and the negroes that the present state of things should not remain. You will find that our people are fully prepared to conform to the new state of things; and . . . will be disposed to pursue towards the negroes a course dictated by humanity and kindness. I take it for granted that the future relations between the negroes and their former owners, like all other questions of domestic policy, will be under the control and direction of the State Governments.

———

"Any Freedman . . . May Be Imprisoned"

———

The Mississippi Black Code, 1865

[Many Southerners, feeling sure that Negroes would work only under compulsion, agreed with Howell Cobb that some substitute for slavery must be devised. Accordingly, at the sessions of 1865–66 the new state legislatures which Johnson had sponsored passed laws regulating the life and labor of the Negro. These laws were commonly known as *black codes*. The Mississippi Black Code, one of the most comprehensive and most severe, even prohibited Negroes from owning their own farms. It consisted of a series of laws dealing with segregation, apprenticeship, vagrancy, legal rights, and disorderly conduct. W. L. Flerning, ed., *Documentary History of Reconstruction*, 2 vols. (Cleveland, 1906), 1, 281–90.]

Segregation

It shall be unlawful for any officer, station agent, collector, or employee on any railroad in this State, to allow any freedman, negro, or mulatto, to ride in any first class passenger cars, set apart, or used by, and for white persons; and any person offending against the provisions of this section, shall be deemed guilty of a misdemeanor; and on conviction thereof before the circuit court of the county in which said offence was committed, shall be fined not less than fifty dollars, nor more than five hundred dollars; and shall be imprisoned in the county jail, until such fine, and costs of prosecution are paid: *Provided,* That this section of this act, shall not apply, in the case of negroes or mulattoes, travelling with their mistress, in the capacity of maids.

Apprenticeship

It shall be the duty of all sheriffs, justices of the peace, and other civil officers of the several counties in this State, to report to the probate courts of their respective counties semi-annually, at the January and July terms of said courts, all freedmen, free negroes, and mulattoes, under the age of eighteen, in their respective counties, beats, or districts, who are orphans, or whose parent or parents have not the means or who refuse to provide and support said minors; and thereupon it shall be the duty of said probate court to order the clerk of said court to apprentice said minors to some competent and suitable person, on such terms as the court may direct, having a particular care to the interest of said minor: *Provided,* that the former owner of said minors shall have the preference when, in the opinion or she shall be a suitable person for that purpose. . . .

If any person entice away any apprentice from his or her master or mistress, or shall knowingly employ an apprentice, or furnish him or her food or clothing without the written consent of his or her master or mistress, or shall sell or give said apprentice ardent spirits without such consent, said person so offending shall be deemed guilty of a high misdemeanor, and shall, upon conviction thereof before the county court, be punished as provided for the punishment of persons enticing from their employer hired freedmen, free negroes or mulattoes.

Black Codes of Mississippi, 1865

An Act to Confer Civil Rights on Freedmen, and for Other Purposes

Section 1. All freedmen, free negroes and mulattoes may sue and be sued, implead and be impleaded, in all the courts of law and equity of this State, and may acquire personal property, and chooses in action, by descent or purchase, and may dispose of the same in the same manner and to the same extent that white persons may: Provided, That the provisions of this section shall not be so construed as to allow any freedman, free negro or mulatto to rent or lease any lands or tenements except in incorporated cities or towns, in which places the corporate authorities shall control the same.

Section 2. All freedmen, free negroes and mulattoes may intermarry with each other, in the same manner and under the same regulations that are provided by law for white persons: Provided, that the clerk of probate shall keep separate records of the same.

Section 3. All freedmen, free negroes or mullatoes who do now and have herebefore lived and cohabited together as husband and wife shall be taken and held in law as legally married, and the issue shall be taken and held as legitimate for all purposes; and it shall not be lawful for any freedman, free negro or mulatto to intermarry with any white person; nor for any person to intermarry with any freedman, free negro or mulatto; and any person who shall so intermarry shall be deemed guilty of felony, and on conviction thereof shall be confined in the State penitentiary for life; and those shall be deemed freedmen, free negroes and mulattoes who are of pure negro blood, and those descended from a negro to the third generation, inclusive, though one ancestor in each generation may have been a white person.

Section 4. In addition to cases in which freedmen, free negroes and mulattoes are now by law competent witnesses, freedmen, free negroes or mulattoes shall be competent in civil cases, when a party or parties to the suit, either plaintiff or plaintiffs, defendant or defendants; also in cases where freedmen, free negroes and mulattoes is or are either plaintiff or plaintiffs, defendant or defendants. They shall also be competent witnesses in all criminal prosecutions where the crime charged is alleged to have been committed by a white person upon or against the person or property of a freedman, free negro or mulatto: Provided, that in all cases said witnesses shall be examined in open court, on the stand; except, however, they may be examined before the grand jury, and shall in all cases be subject to the rules and tests of the common law as to competency and credibility.

Section 5. Every freedman, free negro and mulatto shall, on the seconhundred and sixty-six, and annually thereafter, have a lawful home or employment, and shall have written evidence thereof as follows, to wit: if living in any incorporated city, town, or village, a license from that mayor thereof; and if living outside of an incorporated city, town, or village, from the member of the board of police of his beat, authorizing him or her to do irregular and job work; or a written contract, as provided in Section 6 in this act; which license may be revoked for cause at any time by the authority granting the same.

Section 6. All contracts for labor made with freedmen, free negroes and mulattoes for a longer period than one month shall be in writing, and a duplicate, attested and read to said freedman, free negro or mulatto by a beat, city or county officer, or two disinterested white persons of the county in which the labor is to performed, of which each party shall have one: and said contracts shall be taken and held as entire contracts, and if the laborer shall quit the service of the employer before the expiration of his term of service, without good cause, he shall forfeit his wages for that year up to the time of quitting.

Section 7. Every civil officer shall, and every person may, arrest and carry back to his or her legal employer any freedman, free negro, or mulatto who shall have quit the service of his or her employer before the expiration of his or her

222

term of service without good cause; and said officer and person shall be entitled to receive for arresting and carrying back every deserting employee aforesaid the sum of five dollars, and ten cents per mile from the place of arrest to the place of delivery; and the same shall be paid by the employer, and held as a set off for so much against the wages of said deserting employee: Provided, that said arrested party, after being so returned, may appeal to the justice of the peace or member of the board of police of the county, who, on notice to the alleged employer, shall try summarily whether said appellant is legally employed by the alleged employer, and has good cause to quit said employer. Either party shall have the right of appeal to the county court, pending which the alleged deserter shall be remanded to the alleged employer or otherwise disposed of, as shall be right and just; and the decision of the county court shall be final.

Section 8. Upon affidavit made by the employer of any freedman, free negro or mulatto, or other credible person, before any justice of the peace or member of the board of police, that any freedman, free negro or mulatto legally employed by said employer has illegally deserted said employment, such justice of the peace or member of the board of police issue his warrant or warrants, returnable before himself or other such officer, to any sheriff, constable or special deputy, commanding him to arrest said deserter, and return him or her to said employer, and the like proceedings shall be had as provided in the preceding section; and it shall be lawful for any officer to whom such warrant shall be directed to execute said warrant in any county in this State; and that said warrant may be transmitted without endorsement to any like officer of another county, to be executed and returned as aforesaid; and the said employer shall pay the costs of said warrants and arrest and return, which shall be set off for so much against the wages of said deserter.

Section 9. If any person shall persuade or attempt to persuade, entice, or cause any freedman, free negro or mulatto to desert from the legal employment of any person before the expiration of his or her term of service, or shall knowingly employ any such deserting freedman, free negro or mullato, or shall knowingly give or sell

to any such deserting freedman, free negro or mulatto, any food, raiment, or other thing, he or she shall be guilty of a misdemeanor, and, upon conviction, shall be fined not less than twenty-five dollars and not more than two hundred dollars and costs; and if the said fine and costs shall not be immediately paid, the court shall sentence said convict to not exceeding two months imprisonment in the county jail, and he or she shall moreover be liable to the party injured in damages: Provided, if any person shall, or shall attempt to, persuade, entice, or cause any freedman, free negro or mullatto to desert from any legal employment of any person, with the view to employ said freedman, free negro or mullato without the limits of this State, such costs; and if said fine and costs shall not be immediately paid, the court shall sentence said convict to not exceeding six months imprisonment in the county jail.

Section 10. It shall be lawful for any freedman, free negro, or mulatto, to charge any white person, freedman, free negro or mulatto by affidavit, with any criminal offense against his or her person or property, and upon such affidavit the proper process shall be issued and executed as if said affidavit was made by a white person, and it shall be lawful for any freedman, free negro, or mulatto, in any action, suit or controversy pending, or about to be instituted in any court of law equity in this State, to make all needful and lawful affidavits as shall be necessary for the institution, prosecution or defense of such suit or controversy.

Section 11. The penal laws of this state, in all cases not otherwise specially provided for, shall apply and extend to all freedman, free negroes and mulattoes . . .

An Act to Regulate the Relation of Master and Apprentice, as Relates to Freedmen, Free Negroes, and Mulattoes

Section 1. It shall be the duty of all sheriffs, justices of the peace, and other civil officers of the several counties in this State, to report to the probate courts of their respective counties semiannually, at the January and July terms of said courts, all freedmen, free negroes, and mulattoes, under the age of eighteen, in their respective counties, beats, or districts, who are orphans, or whose parent or parents have not the means or who refuse to provide for and support said minors; and thereupon it shall be the duty of said probate court to order the clerk of said court to apprentice said minors to some competent and suitable person on such terms as the court may direct, having a particular care to the interest of said minor: Provided, that the former owner of said minors shall have the preference when, in the opinion of the court, he or she shall be a suitable person for that purpose.

Section 2. The said court shall be fully satisfied that the person or persons to whom said minor shall be apprenticed shall be a suitable person to have the charge and care of said minor, and fully to protect the interest of said minor. The said court shall require the said master or mistress to execute bond and security, payable to the State of Mississippi, conditioned that he or she shall furnish said minor with sufficient food and clothing; to treat said minor humanely; furnish medical attention in case of sickness; teach, or cause to be taught, him or her to read and write, if under fifteen years old, and will conform to any law that may be hereafter passed for the regulation of the duties and relation of master and apprentice: Provided, that said apprentice shall be bound by indenture, in case of males, until they are twenty-one years old, and in case of females until they are eighteen years old.

Section 3. In the management and control of said apprentices, said master or mistress shall have the power to inflict such moderate corporeal chastisement as a father or guardian is allowed to infliction on his or her child or ward at common law: Provided, that in no case shall cruel or inhuman punishment be inflicted.

Section 4. If any apprentice shall leave the employment of his or her master or mistress, without his or her consent, said master or mistress may pursue and recapture said apprentice, and bring him or her before any justice of the peace of the county, whose duty it shall be to remand said apprentice to the service of his or her master or mistress; and in the event of a refusal on the part of said apprentice so to return, then said justice shall commit said apprentice to the jail of said county, on failure to give bond, to the next term of the county court; and it shall be the duty of said court at the first term thereafter to investigate said case, and if the court shall be of opinion that said apprentice left the employment of his or her master or mistress without good cause, to order him or her to be punished, as provided for the punishment of hired freedmen, as may be from time to time provided for by law for desertion, until he or she shall agree to return to the service of his or her master or mistress: Provided, that the court may grant continuances as in other cases: And provided further, that if the court shall believe that said apprentice had good cause to quit his said master or mistress, the court shall discharge said apprentice from said indenture, and also enter a judgment against the master or mistress for not more than one hundred dollars, from the use and benefit of said apprentice, to be collected on execution as in other cases.

Section 5. If any person entice away any apprentice from his or her master or mistress, or shall knowingly employ an apprentice, or furnish him or her food or clothing without the written consent of his or her master or mistress, or shall sell or give said apprentice spirits without such consent, said person so offending shall be guilty of a misdemeanor, and shall, upon conviction there of before the county court, be punished as provided for the punishment of person enticing from their employer hired freedmen, free negroes or mulattoes.

Section 6. It shall be the duty of all civil officers of their respective counties to report any minors within their respective counties to said probate court who are subject to be apprenticed under the provisions of this act, from time to time as the facts may come to their knowledge, and it shall be the duty of said court from time to time as said minors shall be reported to them, or otherwise come to their knowledge, to apprentice said minors as hereinbefore provided.

Section 9. It shall be lawful for any freedman, free negro, or mulatto, having a minor child or children, as provided for by this act.

Section 10. In all cases where the age of the freedman, free negro, or mulatto cannot be ascertained by record testimony, the judge of the county court shall fix the age. . . .

An Act to Amend the Vagrant Laws of the State

Section 1. All rogues and vagabonds, idle and dissipated persons, beggars, jugglers, or persons practicing unlawful games or plays, runaways, common drunkards, common night-walkers, pilferers, lewd, wanton, or lascivious persons, in speech or behavior, common railers and brawlers, persons who neglect their calling or employment, misspend what they earn, or do not provide for the support of themselves or their families, or dependents, and all other idle and disorderly persons, including all who neglect all lawful business, habitually misspend their time by frequenting houses of ill-fame, gaming-houses, or tippling shops, shall be deemed and considered vagrants, under the provisions of this act, and upon conviction thereof shall be fined not exceeding one hundred dollars, with all accruing costs, and be imprisoned, at the discretion of the court, not exceeding ten days.

Section 2. All freedmen, free negroes and mulattoes in this State, over the age of eighteen years, found on the second Monday in January, 1866, or thereafter, with no lawful employment or business, or found unlawful assembling themselves together, either in the day or night time, and all white persons assembling themselves with freedmen, Free negroes or mulattoes, or usually associating with freedmen, free negroes or mulattoes, on terms of equality, or living in adultery or fornication with a freed woman, freed negro or mulatto, shall be deemed vagrants, and on conviction thereof shall be fined in a sum not exceeding, in the case of a freedman, free negro or mulatto, fifty dollars, and a white man two hundred dollars, and imprisonment at the discretion of the court, the free negro not exceeding ten days, and the white man not exceeding six months.

Section 3. All justices of the peace, mayors, and aldermen of incorporated towns, counties, and cities of the several counties in this State shall have jurisdiction to try all questions of vagrancy in their respective towns, counties, and cities, and it is hereby made their duty, whenever they shall ascertain that any person or persons in their respective towns, and counties and cities are violating any of the provisions of this act, to have said party or parties arrested, and brought before them, and immediately investigate said charge, and, on conviction, punish said party or parties, as provided for herein. And it is hereby made the duty of all sheriffs, constables, town constables, and all such like officers, and city marshals, to report to some officer having jurisdiction all violations of any of the provisions of this act, and in case any officer shall fail or neglect any duty herein it shall be the duty of the county court to fine said officer, upon conviction, not exceeding one hundred dollars, to be paid into the county treasury for county purposes.

Section 4. Keepers of gaming houses, houses of prostitution, prostitutes, public or private, and all persons who derive their chief support in the employment's that militate against good morals, or against law, shall be deemed and held to be vagrants.

Section 5. All fines and forfeitures collected by the provisions of this act shall be paid into the county treasury of general county purposes, and in case of any freedman, free negro or mulatto shall fail for five days after the imposition of any or forfeiture upon him or her for violation of any of the provisions of this act to pay the same, that it shall be, and is hereby, made the duty of the sheriff of the proper county to hire out said freedman, free negro or mulatto, to any person who will, for the shortest period of service, pay said fine and forfeiture and all costs: Provided, a preference shall be given to the employer, if there be one, in which case the employer shall be entitled to deduct and retain the amount so paid from the wages of such freedman, free negro or mulatto, then due or to become due; and in case freedman, free negro or mulatto cannot hire out, he or she may be dealt with as a pauper.

Section 6. The same duties and liabilities existing among white persons of this State shall attach to freedmen, free negroes or mulattoes, to support their indigent families and all colored paupers; and that in order to secure a support for such indigent freedmen, free negroes, or mulattoes, it shall be lawful, and is hereby made the duty of the county police of each county in this State, to levy a poll or capitation tax on each and every freedman, free negro, or mulatto, between the ages of eighteen and sixty years, not to exceed the sum of one dollar annually to each person so taxed, which tax, when collected, shall be paid into the county treasurer's hands, and constitute a fund to be called the Freedman's Pauper Fund, which shall be applied by the commissioners of the poor for the maintenance of the poor of the freedmen, free negroes and mulattoes of this State, under such regulations as may be established by the boards of county police in the respective counties of this State.

Section 7. If any freedman, free negro, or mulatto shall fail or refuse to pay any tax levied according to the provisions of the sixth section of this act, it shall be *prima facie* evidence of vagrancy, and it shall be the duty of the sheriff to arrest such freedman, free negro, or mulatto, or such person refusing or neglecting to pay such tax, and proceed at once to hire for the shortest time such delinquent taxpayer to any one who will pay the said tax, with accruing costs, giving preference to the employer, if there be one.

Section 8. Any person feeling himself or herself aggrieved by judgment of any justice of the peace, mayor, or alderman in cases arising under this act, may within five days appeal to the next term of the county court of the proper county, upon giving bond and security in a sum not less than twenty-five dollars nor more than one hundred and fifty dollars, conditioned to appear and prosecute said appeal, and abide by the judgment of the county court; and said appeal shall be tried *de novo* in the county court, and the decision of the said court shall be final.

Louisana Black Codes, 1865

An Act Relative to Apprentices and Indentured Servants

Section 1. Be it enacted by the Senate and House of Representatives of the State of Louisiana, in General Assembly convened, That it shall be the duty of Sheriffs, Justices of the Peace and other civil officers of this State, to report to the Clerks of the District Courts of their respective Parishes, and in the Parish of Orleans (left bank) to the Mayor of the City of New Orleans, and on the right bank to the President of the Police Jury, on the first Monday of each month, for each and every year, all persons under the age of eighteen years, if females, and twenty-one, if males, who are orphans, or whose parent, parents, or tutor, have not the means, or who refuse to provide for and maintain said minors; and, thereupon, it shall be the duty of the Clerks of the District Courts, Mayor and President of the Police Jury aforesaid, to examine whether the party or parties, so reported from time to time, come within the purview and meaning of this Act, and if so, to apprentice said minor or minors, in manner and form as prescribed by the Civil Code of the State of Louisiana; provided, that orphans coming under the provisions of this Act shall be authorized to select said employers when they have arrived at the age of puberty, unless they shall have been previously apprenticed; provided, that any indenture of apprentice or indented servant, made before a Justice of the Peace and two disinterested witnesses, and the original deposited with and recorded by the recorder of Mortgages for the Parish, in a book provided for that purpose, shall be valid and binding on the parties, and when made by the clerk, shall be also deposited with the Recorder of Mortgages, and all expenses for passing said acts of indenture shall be paid by the employer.

Sec. 2. Be it further enacted, &c., That persons who have attained the age of majority, whether in this State or any other State of the United States, or in a foreign country, may bind themselves to services to be performed in this country, for the term of five years, on such terms as they may stipulate, as domestic servants and to work on farms, plantations or in manufacturing establishments, which contracts shall be valid and binding on the parties to the same.

See. 3. Be it further enacted, &c., That in all cases, when the age of the minor cannot be ascertained by record testimony, the Clerks of the District Courts, Mayor and President of the Police Jury, or Justices of the Peace aforesaid, shall fix the age, according to the best evidence before them.

Sec. 4. Be it further enacted, &c., That all laws or parts of laws conflicting with the provisions of this Act, be, and the same are hereby repealed, and that this Act take effect from and after its passage.

DUNCAN S. CAGE,
Speaker of the House of Representatives.

ALBERT VOORHIES, Lieutenant Governor and President of the Senate.

Approved December 21, 1865.

J. MADISON WELLS
Governor of the State of Louisiana

Radical Reconstruction, 1867–1877

The Radical Program

Richard N. Current, ed.

Maintaining that Southern Negroes needed additional protection, the Republicans early in 1866 carried through Congress a bill to lengthen the life and broaden the powers of the Freedmen's Bureau. President Johnson vetoed it. Later Congress passed a bill to guarantee civil rights to Negroes. Johnson vetoed this one also. Not only to the Radicals but also to moderate Republicans, the Freedmen's Bureau Bill and still more the Civil Rights Bill seemed like just and necessary measures. Finally breaking with the President, the moderates joined with the Radicals to repass both bills over the presidential veto.

In June, 1866, the joint Committee presented its reconstruction plan, the Fourteenth Amendment. This contained four main provisions: All persons born in the United States were declared citizens of the United States and of the state in which they happened to reside. States were forbidden to deprive any person of life, liberty, or property without due process of law and were required to give to all persons the equal protection of the laws. If a state kept Negroes from voting, the congressional representation of that state was to be reduced in proportion to the number of Negroes in the state. All persons who once had taken an oath of loyalty to the Constitution (congressmen, government officials, or army officers) and then had violated that oath by willingly supporting the Confederate cause were forbidden to hold any state or federal office until Congress, by a two-thirds vote, should remove the disability.

One Southern state—Johnson's home state of Tennessee—ratified the Fourteenth Amendment and was readmitted to the Union in the summer of 1866. The other ten states of the late Confederacy refused to ratify. Johnson himself advised them to refuse.

In the congressional elections of 1866 the Republicans greatly increased their majority in Congress, and they interpreted the returns as a popular repudiation of Johnson and his views. Now the Radical leaders were determined to require much more from the Southern states than ratification of the Fourteenth Amendment. Easily overriding Johnson's vetoes they passed in 1867 a series of Reconstruction Acts. These divided the Southern states (except Tennessee) into five military districts, with an army officer in command of each district. The officers were to supervise the formation of new constitutions and the election of new governments. In the process, Negroes were to take part as voters and officeholders. Those white leaders who were disqualified from officeholding by the Fourteenth Amendment were to be excluded from the state-making process. The states, once refashioned, would have to ratify the Fourteenth Amendment.

In 1868 six of the states completed the requirements and were admitted to the Union, Congress accepting their Senators and Representatives. The four other states delayed, and before they were admitted, in 1870, they were faced with an additional requirement—ratification of the Fifteenth Amendment, which forbade the states to deprive any person of the vote on account of "race, color, or previous condition of servitude."

The launching of the Radical program was accompanied by a hectic and wordy debate, both in Congress and throughout the country.

From *Reconstruction, 1865–1877* by Richard Current (Ed.). Reprinted by permission of the editor.

Stevens on Negro Suffrage, 1867

[At first, in 1865 and 1866, Thaddeus Stevens had hesitated to give Negroes the vote. There was the danger that this vote might be controlled by the former master class and used to strengthen the Democrats in the South. Besides, there was the risk of antagonizing Republican voters in Stevens' own state of Pennsylvania, where Negro suffrage was not popular. At that time Negroes could not vote in Pennsylvania nor in most of the Northern states (only in six of them: New York and all of New England except Connecticut). Nevertheless, by 1867 Stevens had decided that Congress must include suffrage in its reconstruction plan. He gave reasons for this in a House speech on January 3, 1867. *Congressional Globe*, 39th Congress, 2nd session, p. 252.]

Unless the rebel States, before admission, should be made republican in, spirit, and placed under the guardianship of loyal men, all our blood and treasure will have been spent in vain. I waive now the question of punishment which, if we are wise, will still be inflicted by moderate confiscations. . . . Having these States . . . entirely within the power of Congress, it is our duty to take care that no injustice shall remain in their organic laws. Holding them "like clay in the hands of the potter," we must see that no vessel is made for destruction. Having now no governments, they must have enabling acts. The law of last session with regard to Territories settled the principles of such acts. Impartial suffrage, both in electing the delegates and ratifying their proceedings, is now the fixed rule. There is more reason why colored voters should be admitted in the rebel States than in the Territories. In the States they form the great mass of the loyal men. Possibly with their aid loyal governments may be established in most of States. Without it all are sure to be ruled by traitors; and loyal men, black and white, will be oppressed, exiled, or murdered. There are several good reasons for the passage of this bill. In the first place, it is just. I am now confirming my argument to negro suffrage in the rebel States. Have not loyal blacks quite as good a right to choose rulers and make laws as rebel whites? In the second place, it is a necessity in order to protect the loyal white men in the seceded States. The white Union men are in a great minority in each of those States. With them the blacks would act in a body; and it is believed that in each of said States, except one, the two united would form a majority, control the States, and protect themselves. Now they are the victims of daily murder. They must suffer constant persecution or be exiled. . . .

Another good reason is, it would insure the ascendency of the Union party. . . . I believe . . . that on the continued ascendency of that party depends the safety of this great nation. If impartial suffrage is excluded in the rebel States, then every one of them is sure to send a solid rebel representative delegation to Congress, and cast a solid rebel electoral vote. They, with their kindred Copperheads of the North, would always elect the President and control Congress. While slavery sat upon her defiant throne, and insulted and intimidated the trembling North, the South frequently divided on questions of policy between Whigs and Democrats, and gave victory alternately to the sections. Now, you must divide them between loyalists, without regard to color, and disloyalists, or you will be the perpetual vassals of the free-trade, irritated, revengeful South. . . . I am for negro suffrage in every rebel State. If it be just, it should not be denied; if it be necessary, it should be adopted; if it be a punishment to traitors, they deserve it.

Senate Discussion of Negro Sufferage, 1867

[In the Senate in February, 1867, a conservative Republican, James Doolittle, and a Democrat, Reverdy Johnson, disagreed with a Radical, Henry Wilson, on the question of requiring Negro suffrage in the South. M. M. Miller, ed., *Great Debates in American History*, 14 vols. (New York, VIII, 57.1

JAMES DOLITTLE (Wisconsin)—I ask, if that is the true language of a statesman to say to a people who have been educated in the largest liberty, a people in whose veins the Anglo-Saxon blood is flowing, which, for a thousand years, has been fighting against despotism of every form: "You must accept this position at the point of the bayonet or forever live with the bayonet at your throats"? Is that the way to make peace?

HENRY WILSON (Massachusetts)—I think it is statesmanship to settle this question of reconstruction upon the solid basis of the perfect equality of rights and privileges among citizens of the United States. Colored men are citizens, and they have just as much right as this race whose blood has been fighting against oppression for a thousand years, as he says, and any settlement of this civil war upon any other basis than perfect equality rights and privileges among citizens of the United States is not statesmanship; it is mere trifling; only keeping open questions for future controversy. Nothing is settled unless it is settled upon the basis of justice.

REVERDY JOHNSON (Maryland)—The amendment is objectionable to me only upon the ground that it denies to those States the right of coming into the Union entitled to representation until they extend the suffrage, because I believe the right of suffrage is a matter with which the Congress of the United States has no concern.

"The End Itself Is Evil"

Johnson's Third Annual Message, 1867

[In his annual message of December 3, 1867, President Johnson called for the repeal of the Reconstruction Acts, the first of which had been passed the previous March. In this message he repeated and elaborated upon the objections he had already given in his veto messages. James D. Richardson, ed., *A Compilation of the Messages and Papers of the Presidents* (New York, 1897), VIII, 3,760–64.]

The acts of Congress in question are not only objectionable for their assumption of ungranted power, but many of their provisions are in conflict with the direct prohibitions of the Constitution. The Constitution commands that a republican form of government shall be guaranteed to all the States; that no person shall be deprived of life, liberty, or property without due process of law, arrested without a judicial warrant, or punished without a fair trial before an impartial jury; that the privilege of *habeas corpus* shall not be denied in time of peace, and that no bill of attainder shall be passed even against a single individual. Yet the system of measures established by these acts of Congress does totally subvert and destroy the form as well as the substance of republican government in the ten States to which they apply. It binds them hand and foot in absolute slavery, and subjects them to a strange and hostile power, more unlimited and more likely to be abused than any other now known among civilized men. It tramples down all those rights in which the essence of liberty consists, and which a free government is always most careful to protect. It denies the *habeas corpus* and the trial by jury. Personal freedom, property, and life, if assailed by the passion, the prejudice, or the rapacity of the ruler, have no security whatever. It has the effect of a bill of attainder or bill of pains and penalties, not upon a few individuals, but upon whole masses, including the millions who inhabit the subject States, and even their unborn children. These wrongs, being expressly forbidden, can not be constitutionally inflicted upon any portion of our people, no matter how they may have come within our jurisdiction, and no matter whether they live in States, Territories, or districts.

I have no desire to save from the proper and just consequences of their great crime those who engaged in rebellion against the Government, but as a mode of punishment the measures under consideration are the most unreasonable that could be invented. Many of those people are perfectly innocent; many kept their fidelity to the Union untainted to the last; many were incapable of any legal offense; a large proportion even of the persons able to bear arms were forced into rebellion against their will, and of those who are guilty with their own consent the degrees of guilt are as various as the shades of their character and temper. But these acts of Congress confound them all together in one common doom. Indiscriminate vengeance upon classes, sects, and parties, or upon whole communities, for offenses committed by a portion of them against the governments to which they owed obedience was common in the barbarous ages of the world; but Christianity and civilization have made such progress that recourse to a punishment so cruel and unjust would meet with the condemnation of all unprejudiced and right-minded men. The punitive justice of this age, and especially of this country, does not consist in stripping whole States of their liberties and reducing all their people, without distinction, to the condition of slavery. It deals separately with each individual, confines itself to the forms of law, and vindicates its own purity by an impartial examination of every case before a competent judicial tribunal. If this does not satisfy all our desires with regard to Southern rebels, let us console ourselves by reflecting that a free Constitution, triumphant in war and unbroken in peace, is worth far more to us and our children than the gratification of any present feeling.

I am aware it is assumed that this system of government for the Southern States is not to be perpetual. It is true this military government is to be only provisional, but it is through this temporary evil that a greater evil is to be made perpetual. If the guaranties of the Constitution can be broken provisionally to serve a temporary purpose, and in a part only of the country, we can destroy them everywhere and for all time. Arbitrary measures often change, but they generally change for the worse. It is the curse of despotism that it has no halting place. The intermitted exercise of its power brings no sense of security to its subjects, for they can never know what more they will be called to endure when its red right hand is armed to plague them again. Nor is it possible to conjecture how or where power, unrestrained by law, may seek its next victims. The States that are still free may be enslaved at any moment; for if the Constitution does not protect all, it protects none.

It is manifestly and avowedly the object of these laws to confer upon negroes the privilege of voting and to disfranchise such a number of white citizens as will give the former a clear majority at all elections in the Southern States. This, to the minds of some persons, is so important that a violation of the Constitution is justified as a means of bringing it about. The morality is always false which excuses a wrong because it proposes to accomplish a desirable end. We are not permitted to do evil that good may come. But in this case the end itself is evil, as well as the means. The subjugation of the States to negro domination would be worse than the military despotism under which they are now suffering. It was believed beforehand that the people would endure any amount of military oppression for any length of time rather than degrade themselves by subjection to the negro race. Therefore they have been left without a choice. Negro suffrage was established by act of Congress, and the military officers were commanded to superintend the process of clothing the negro race with the political privileges torn from white men.

The blacks in the South are entitled to be well and humanely governed, and to have the protection of just laws for all their rights of person and property. If it were practicable at this time to give them a Government exclusively their own, under which they might manage their own affairs in their own way, it would become a grave question whether we ought to do so, or whether common humanity would not require us to save them from themselves. But under the circumstances this is only a speculative point. It not proposed merely that they shall govern themselves, but that they shall rule the white race, make and administer State laws, elect Presidents and members of Congress, and shape to a greater or less extent the future destiny of the whole country. Would such a trust and power be safe in such hands?

The peculiar qualities which should characterize any people who are fit to decide upon the management of public affairs for a great state have seldom been combined. It is the glory of white men to know that they have had these qualities in sufficient measure to build upon this continent a great political fabric and to preserve its stability for more than ninety years, while in every other part of the world all similar experiments have failed. But if anything can be proved by known facts, if all reasoning upon evidence is not abandoned, it must be acknowledged that in the progress of nations negroes have shown less capacity for government than any other race of people. No independent government of any form has ever been successful in their hands. On the contrary, wherever they have been left to their own devices they have shown a constant tendency to relapse into barbarism. . . .

The plan of putting the Southern States wholly and the General Government partially into the hands of negroes is proposed at a time peculiarly unpropitious. The foundations of society have been broken up by civil war. Industry must be reorganized, justice reestablished, public credit maintained, and order brought out of confusion. To accomplish these ends would require all the wisdom and virtue of the great men who formed our institutions originally. I confidently believe that their descendants will be equal to the arduous task before them, but it is worse than madness to expect that negroes will perform it for us. Certainly we ought not to ask their assistance till we despair of our own competency.

The great difference between the two races in physical, mental, and moral characteristics will prevent an amalgamation or fusion of them together in one homogeneous mass. If the inferior obtains the ascendency over the other, it will govern with reference only to its own interests—for it will recognize no common interest—and create such a tyranny as this continent has never yet witnessed. Already the negroes are influenced by promises of confiscation and plunder. They are taught to regard as an enemy every white man who has any respect for the rights of his own race. If this continues it must become worse and worse, until all order will be subverted, all industry cease, and the fertile fields of the South grow up; into a wilderness. Of all the dangers which our nation has yet encountered, none are equal to those which must result from the success of the effort now making to Africanize the half of our country.

———

"The Worst Prejudices of Those Rebels"

———

Senatorial Comment on the President's Message, 1867

[The Presidents message of December 3, 1867, provoked a discussion in the Senate the next day. M. M. Miller, ed., *Great Debates in American History*, 14 vols. (New York, 1913), VIII, 80–81.]

SIMON CAMERON (Pennsylvania)—Mr. President, there was one part of the President's message which we heard read yesterday which I approved; it was the suggestion recommending economy in our expenses. We cannot begin at a better time than now, and, therefore, I oppose the printing of these extra numbers.

CHARLES SUMNER (Massachusetts)—There is really a reason, independent of economy, why we should not circulate extra copies of the President's message. It has already been characterized as a libel; unquestionably it is a libel; it is an incendiary document, calculated to stimulate the rebellion once more and to provoke civil war. It is a direct appeal to the worst passions and the worst prejudices of those rebels who, being subdued on the battlefield, still resist through the aid of the President of the United States. It is the evidence of a direct coalition between the President and the former rebels. If Jefferson Davis were President of the United States he could not send to this chamber a message different

in character. I have often said that Andrew Johnson was the successor of Jefferson Davis, and this message is a complete confirmation of all that I have heretofore said. I move to strike out the words relating to the President's message.

CHARLES R. BUCKALEW (Pennsylvania)—As to the amendment which the Senator from Massachusetts has proposed, it would be giving undue or untimely prominence to the differences of opinion which exist concerning the message to adopt his motion. Be it remembered, sir, that this message proposes to Congress the repeal of certain laws which were enacted in the month of March and in the month of July last. The President, under his clear constitutional power to recommend to Congress such measures as he may think important to the public interest, recommends the repeal of those laws, and, as a reason for that repeal, he goes on at length to submit an argument against their constitutionality. Now, sir, all that is perfectly legitimate; and to describe that argument of his as a libel on Congress or as a libel on those laws is an abuse of terms. There is certainly no impropriety in the fact that he denounces those laws as unconstitutional when he appeals to us to repeal them, because it is in the legitimate course of the argument which arises upon his recommendation. If we disagree with him in opinion we shall meet him in debate; we shall be heard by the country, and the people to whom we are both responsible will judge between us.

HENRY WILSON (Massachusetts)—Mr. President, nothing, I am sure, is to be gained by refusing to print the President's message according to the usual custom of the Senate. I go quite as far as any one in condemnation of the tone, temper, and doctrines of the message, but I think we are not justified in departing from the ordinary practice of this body. The message is an assault of the President of the United States upon the Congress of the United States for attempting by legislation to take the governments of the rebel States out of the control of traitors into whose keeping he had placed these governments. The writer of this message seems to have forgotten that we ever had any rebellion at all. The message remembers to forget that President Johnson, in the summer and autumn of 1865, assumed and exercised constitutional powers for the exercise of which he now condemns the legislative branch of the Government. If the President's reconstruction policy was within the provisions of the Constitution surely the reconstruction policy of Congress is within the provisions of the Constitution. If the President without the authority of law could fix the terms and conditions for the reconstruction of the rebel States surely Congress, the law-making power of the Government could determine the terms and conditions of reconstruction.

From those once conquered States, restored by Andrew Johnson to the control of rebels, there came to us a cry of agony, a voice of supplication, demanding the interposition of Congress and the protection of the national Government. Congress heard that cry; the country heard it; the world heard it; the God of the Universe heard it; but President Johnson could not hear it. Congress, after giving the President's policy a trial of nearly two years, adopted the policy of reconstruction against which the President now hurls his denunciations. This reconstruction policy of Congress immediately carried peace and comparative law and order into and through the rebellious States. The President's policy has failed, has been abandoned, and will not be revived. The policy of Congress is progressing, will be inflexibly adhered to, and will be consummated.

———

*"Anything for Human Rights
Is Constitutional"*

———

Senate Debate on the Fifteenth Amendment, 1869

[Two years after the debate leading to the Reconstruction Acts, which provided for Negro suffrage in the South, the Congress engaged in a debate on the proposed Fifteenth Amendment, which would provide for Negro suffrage throughout the country, North as well as South. Among those taking part in the Senate discussion, on January 28 and 29 and February 4, 1869, were the Republicans Samuel Shellabarger and Charles Sumner and the Democrats Thomas A. Hendricks and George Vickers. M.M. Miller, ed., *Great Debates in American History*, 14 vols. (New York, 1913), VIII, 100, 116, 122–30.]

THOMAS A. HENDRICKS (Indiana)—I call your attention to the election of last fall, honorable Senators, and I ask you now to stand upon the pledge of honor that your party made to the people in the election last fall.

The position of the Democratic party last summer, I presume, is not a question of doubt or of uncertainty. That the Democratic party, in casting its vote for Seymour and Blair, did not vote for negro suffrage is plain enough. That the Republican party last fall in voting for Grant and Colfax cast a vote against universal suffrage is as plain. You took the question away from the people. You said that they should not consider it last summer; and now I understand it to be proposed to submit it to legislatures that are not again responsible to the people, but that were elected before this question is submitted. The second section of the Chicago platform, not yet a year old, declared the doctrine of the Republican party, and I simply ask honorable Senators now to make the pledged and plighted faith of their party to the country good and true, and not in the face of the nation and of humanity to give it the lie. . . .

Not yet a year old is this political faith, declared by the grand council of your party, upon which Grant and Colfax stood before the people; and now you propose, without giving the people a voice or a hearing upon the question, to say that the right to control suffrage in the Northern States does not belong to the people of those States.

SAMUEL SHELLABARGER (Ohio)—By our reconstruction laws—now accepted by the country as permanent—we have required the reconstructed States to submit to equal suffrage. We have done this mainly, I admit, because it was absolutely impossible to organize or guarantee republican governments down there at all unless we enabled the only loyal race there was there to vote. This fact, distinguishing the Northern from the Southern States, might, perhaps, justify us in requiring temporarily of them what we did not accept for ourselves. But, if this be so, it can only be temporarily so; if, indeed, as we all devoutly hope, general loyalty is ultimately to come back to the South. We must, therefore, speedily either let the South disfranchise its colored races if they will, or else enfranchise our own, or else compel a submission by sister States to a rule of elective franchise pronounced by ourselves dangerous and ruinous to us. To so compel them permanently to submit to what we refuse ourselves to accept is dishonor—a dishonor which will soon become revolting to the sense of fair play for which the American people are not undistinguished, and will shock the moral sense of mankind. This consideration has exceeding force in impelling us to at once make the law of enfranchisement national, universal. . . .

CHARLES SUMNER (Massachusetts)— . . . It was in the name of State rights that slavery, with all its brood of wrong, was upheld; and it is now in the name of State rights that caste, fruitful also in wrong, is upheld. The old champions reappear, under other names, and from other States, each crying out that, under the national Constitution, notwithstanding even its supplementary amendments, a State may, if it pleases, deny political rights on account of race or color and thus establish that vilest institution, a caste and an oligarchy of the skin.

This perversity is easily understood when it is considered that the present generation grew up under an interpretation of the national Constitution supplied by the upholders of slavery. State rights were exalted and the nation was humbled, because in this way slavery might be protected. Anything for slavery was constitutional. Vain are all our victories, if this terrible rule is not reversed, so that State rights shall yield to human rights, and the nation be exalted as the bulwark of all. This will be the crowning victory of the war. Beyond all question the true rule under the national Constitution, especially since its additional amendments, is that *anything for human rights is constitutional*. Yes, sir; against the old rule, anything for slavery, I put the new rule, *anything for human rights*. . . .

It is under the National Constitution that the champions set up their pretension; therefore, to the National Constitution I go. And I begin by appealing to the letter, which from beginning to end does not contain one word recognizing "color." Its letter is blameless and its spirit is not less so. Surely a power to disfranchise for color must find some sanction in the Constitution. There must be some word of clear intent under which this terrible prerogative can be exercised. This conclusion of reason is reinforced by the positive text of our Magna Charta, the Declaration of Independence, where it is expressly announced that all men are equal in rights, and that just government stands only on the consent of the governed. In the face of the National Constitution interpreted, first, by itself, and then by the Declaration of Independence, how can this pretension prevail?

But there are positive texts of the National Constitution, refulgent as the Capitol itself, which forbid it with sovereign irresistible power, and invest Congress with all needful authority to maintain the prohibition.

There is that key-stone clause, by which it is expressly declared that "the United States shall guarantee to every State in this Union a republican form of Government," and Congress is empowered to enforce this guaranty. The definition of a republican government was solemnly announced by our fathers, first, in that great battle-cry which preceded the Revolution, "taxation without representation is tyranny," and, secondly, in the great Declaration at the birth of the Republic, that all men are equal in rights and that just government stands only on the consent of the governed. A republic is where taxation and representation go hand in hand; where all are equal in rights and no man is excluded from participation in the government. Such is the definition of a republican government, which it is the duty of Congress to maintain. Here is a bountiful source of power, which cannot be called in question. In the execution of the guaranty Congress may—nay, must—require that there shall be no caste or oligarchy of the skin.

If in the original text of the Constitution there could be any doubt, it was all relieved by the amendment abolishing slavery and empowering Congress to enforce this provision. Already Congress, in the exercise of this power, has passed a *civil rights act*. It only remains that it should now a *political rights act*, which, like the former, shall help consummate the abolition of slavery. According to a familiar rule of interpretation, expounded by Chief Justice Marshall in his most masterly judgment, Congress, when intrusted with any power, is at liberty to select the "means" for its execution. The civil rights act came under the head of "means" selected by Congress, and a political rights act will have the same authority. You may as well deny the constitutionality of the one as the other.

The amendment abolishing slavery has been reënforced by another, known as Article XIV, which declares peremptorily that "no State shall make or enforce any law which shall abridge the privileges and immunities of citizens of the United States," and again Congress is empowered to enforce this provision. What can be broader? Colored persons are citizens of the United States, and no State can abridge their privileges and immunities. It is a mockery to say that, under these explicit words, Congress is powerless to forbid any discrimination of color at the ballot-box. Why, then, were they inscribed in the Constitution? To what end? There they stand, supplying an additional and supernumerary power, ample for safeguard against caste or oligarchy of the skin, no matter how strongly sanctioned by any State government.

But the champions anxious for State rights against human rights strive to parry this positive text by insisting that, in another provision of this same amendment, the power over the right to vote is conceded to the States. Mark, now, the audacity and fragility of this pretext. It is true that "where the right to vote is denied to the male inhabitants of a State, or in any way abridged, except for participation in rebellion or crime," the basis of representation is reduced in corresponding proportion. Such is the penalty imposed by the Constitution on a State which denies the right to vote, except in a specific case. But this penalty on the State does not in any way, by the most distant implication, impair the plenary powers of Congress to enforce the guaranty of a republican government, the abolition of slavery, and that final clause guarding the rights of citizens, three specific powers which are left undisturbed, unless the old spirit of slavery is once more revived and Congress is compelled again to wear those degrading chains which for so long a time rendered it powerless for human rights.

I am now brought directly to the proposed amendment of the Constitution. Of course, the question stares us in the face, why amend what is already sufficient ? Why erect a supernumerary column?

So far as I know, two reasons are assigned. The first is that the power of Congress is doubtful. It is natural that those who do not sympathize strongly with the equal rights of all should doubt. Men ordinarily find in the Constitution what is in themselves, so that the Constitution in its meaning is little more than a reflection of their own inner nature.

Another reason assigned for a constitutional amendment is its permanent character in comparison with an act of Congress which may be repealed. On this head I have no anxiety. Let this beneficent prohibition once find a place in our statute-book, and it will be as lasting as the National Constitution itself, to which it will be only a legitimate corollary. In harmony with the Declaration of Independence and in harmony with the National Constitution, it will become of equal significance, and no profane hand will touch its sacred text. It will never be repealed. The elective franchise once recognized can never be denied; once conferred can never be resumed. The rule of equal rights once applied by

Congress under the National Constitution will be a permanent institution as long as the Republic endures; for it will be a vital part of that republican government to which the nation is pledged.

GEORGE VICKERS (Maryland)—I would ask the Senator from Massachusetts if the color of the hair added to the disqualification of the voter intellectually is not a power resident in the legislature? I would ask the honorable Senator if public virtue and public intelligence are not the very foundations of our Republic?

SENATOR SUMNER—The point is not whether public intelligence and public virtue are essential to a republic, for there we are agreed; not whether they may not be recognized as qualifications, but the point is whether any inherent quality under Providence planted in the human form by God can be made by any vote of man a qualification for an elector?

SENATOR VICKERS—There are five races of men, the red man, the yellow man, the white man, the black man, and the brown man. Now, I ask if it is not competent for a legislature to disfranchise or to withhold the elective franchise from any one of these races? Is not color the distinctive mark of the race? And because here is a distinct race, an inferior race, and, because this race has color, the race is disqualified. It is not altogether on account of the color of the skin. That is only one of the indications and marks by which you distinguish the race. Have we not a right to withhold the elective franchise from the Chinese, who are of a different color from us and from the negro? Would the Senator say that because the Chinese have a certain complexion therefore we have no right to disfranchise them because of that complexion? If they are a different race, if they are pagans, according to the speech of the Senator from Oregon have we not a right to disqualify them and withhold from them the elective franchise?

SENATOR SUMNER—That is not the question. I do not say that they may not be disqualified for their paganism. That is a question of character. A man may cease to be a pagan; he may change; he may become a Christian; but a man cannot cease to be a colored man if he is so made by Providence. The Ethiopian cannot change his skin.

SENATOR VICKERS—If the color of the skin, the color of the hair, or the color of the eye distinguishes one race from another, then I say color of skin, of hair, or of eye can make the disqualification, and the legislature has a right so to decree.

SENATOR SUMNER—I see my honorable friend does not flinch from the conclusion.

SENATOR VICKERS—Mr. President, I had never heard, until the honorable Senator from Massachusetts asserted it to-day, that when human rights and the Constitution came into conflict the Constitution was to yield to human rights. Why, sir, if that doctrine is to prevail, how many differences of opinion are there in reference to human rights ? We should have no Constitution; it would be undefined, and there would be nothing tangible in reference to the fundamental law. But if the doctrine of the Senator from Massachusetts prevails, if human rights are to override the Constitution of the country, then does not the doctrine of human rights asserted by the Senator apply as well to females as to males? The Senator from Kansas would say it did; and I ask if human rights are not as applicable to woman as to man? And, if the doctrine of human rights is to be the rule by which the Constitution is to be construed, then it must be so construed as to admit female suffrage; and yet I suppose the Senator from Massachusetts would not support a measure of this kind. It is not unusual for Senators to lay down a general principle and argue upon that principle, and then in the practical application of it to come short of its results. It has been beautifully said that "we go to man for philosophy and to woman for consolation"; and, although I am no advocate for woman suffrage, I believe that if the Congress of the United States had been composed exclusively of women we should have had no civil war. We might have had a war of words, but that would have been all. [Laughter.]

I would rather concede the ascendency of any party for twenty years or more if the country could thereby be shielded from any infraction or change of the Constitution, and its wonted prestige be preserved and continued. The success of party is a paltry consideration when weighed against the principles of the Constitution, of public tranquillity, and happiness. Parties are changing; they have changed. Mutability is stamped upon human productions, and disappointment to human plans and hopes; new generations are to succeed us, and the passions and prejudices of to-day cannot impress their minds and regulate their conduct. It is only by adhering to constitutional rules; to the principles of our fathers, whose purposes were single and patriotism undoubted; by a conformity to right, to

justice, and by doing to others as we would have others do unto us that we can expect to establish a party which shall "stand the test of human scrutiny, of talents, and of time." No legislation of Congress can elevate or improve the physical, moral, or intellectual condition of the negro; we cannot legislate into them any fitness or qualification which they do not now possess. We may descend from the high position in which the framers of the Constitution left us and place ourselves upon the common and degrading platform of negro suffrage and political equality.

Public virtue and intelligence are the foundations of a republic. It is a government of opinion, of principle; its officers and agents must be wise, capable, and patriotic. The people who select them must, to a great extent, possess the same elements; they must have some knowledge of statesmanship, of political economy, of trade, commerce, manufactures, agriculture, and mechanic arts, and of the resources and wealth of the country, and withal a fund of experience and common sense. Will the introduction of the negro into our political affairs add to the intelligence, statesmanship, wisdom, and judgment of the country? Will it not weaken our institutions and the confidence we have had in their stability and lay another and different foundation than that which was laid by our fathers? The negro as a class, as a race, is unfortunately ignorant and superstitious; with some exceptions, he cannot read nor understand your Constitution, is unacquainted with our laws, institutions, history, and policy; he at present lacks independence and that high sense of honor and integrity which every voter should possess to shield him from sinister or unworthy influences. If you had a house to build would you procure ignorant and unskillful hands to erect it? And yet, in so grave a matter as legislation, statesmanship, and the affairs, internal and external, of a great country, and in choosing Representatives and officers to discharge the most difficult and momentous duties, we are to call to our aid the power of numbers only, which possess not the moral or intellectual strength to render the slightest assistance. They may be made the dupes and instruments of interested persons, but it should be recollected that, like the elephants in battle, they will be as likely to trample upon friends as upon foes. No one political organization can long hold them, and they will become a *tertium quid* which will enervate rather than strengthen the body-politic.

SECTION SEVEN

THE RECONSTRUCTION AMENDMENTS AND CIVIL RIGHTS ACTS

CHAPTER 9

13th Amendment to the U.S. Constitution

Section 1. Neither slavery nor involuntary servitude, except as a punishment for crime whereof the party shall have been duly convicted, shall exist within the United States, or any place subject to their jurisdiction.

Section 2. Congress shall have power to enforce this article by appropriate legislation.

***** *****

Proposal and Ratification

The thirteenth amendment to the Constitution of the United States was proposed to the legislatures of the several States by the Thirty-eighth Congress, on the 31st day of January, 1865, and was declared, in a proclamation of the Secretary of State, dated the 18th of December, 1865, to have been ratified by the legislatures of twenty-seven of the thirty-six States. The dates of ratification were: Illinois, February 1, 1865; Rhode Island, February 2, 1865; Michigan, February 2, 1865; Maryland, February 3, 1865; New York, February 3, 1865; Pennsylvania, February 3, 1865; West Virginia, February 3, 1865; Missouri, February 6, 1865; Maine, February 7, 1865; Kansas, February 7, 1865; Massachusetts, February 7, 1865; Virginia, February 9, 1865; Ohio, February 10, 1865; Indiana, February 13, 1865; Nevada, February 16, 1865; Louisiana, February 17, 1865; Minnesota, February 23, 1865; Wisconsin, February 24, 1865; Vermont, March 9, 1865; Tennessee, April 7, 1865; Arkansas, April 14, 1865; Connecticut, May 4, 1865; New Hampshire, July 1, 1865; South Carolina, November 13, 1865; Alabama, December 2, 1865; North Carolina, December 4, 1865; Georgia, December 6, 1865.

Ratification was completed on December 6, 1865.

The amendment was subsequently ratified by Oregon, December 8, 1865; California, December 19, 1865; Florida, December 28, 1865 (Florida again ratified on June 9, 1868, upon its adoption of a new constitution); Iowa, January 15, 1866; New Jersey, January 23, 1866 (after having rejected the amendment on March 16, 1865); Texas, February 18, 1870; Delaware, February 12, 1901 (after having rejected the amendment on February 8, 1865); Kentucky, March 18, 1976 (after having rejected it on February 24, 1865).

The amendment was rejected (and not subsequently ratified) by Mississippi, December 4, 1865.

14th Amendment to the U.S. Constitution

July 28, 1868

Section 1. All persons born or naturalized in the United States, and subject to the jurisdiction thereof, are citizens of the United States and of the State wherein they reside. No State shall make or enforce any law which shall abridge the privileges or immunities of citizens of the United States; nor shall any State deprive any person of life, liberty, or property, without due process of law; nor deny to any person within its jurisdiction the equal protection of the laws.

Section 2. Representatives shall be apportioned among the several States according to their respective numbers, counting the whole number of persons in each State, excluding Indians not taxed. But when the right to vote at any election for the choice of electors for President and Vice-President of the United States, Representatives in Congress, the Executive and Judicial officers of a State, or the members of the Legislature thereof, is denied to any of the male inhabitants of such State, being twenty-one years of age, and citizens of the United States, or in any way abridged, except for participation in rebellion, or other crime, the basis of representation therein shall be reduced in the proportion which the number of such male citizens shall bear to the whole number of male citizens twenty-one years of age in such State.

Section 3. No person shall be a Senator or Representative in Congress, or elector of President and Vice-President, or hold any office, civil or military, under the United States, or under any State, who, having previously taken an oath, as a member of Congress, or as an officer of the United States, or as a member of any State legislature, or as an executive or judicial officer of any State, to support the Constitution of the United States, shall have engaged in insurrection or rebellion against the same, or given aid or comfort to the enemies thereof. But Congress may by a vote of two thirds of each House, remove such disability.

Section 4. The validity of the public debt of the United States, authorized by law, including debts incurred for payment of pensions and bounties for services in suppressing insurrection or rebellion, shall not be questioned. But neither the United States nor any State shall assume or pay any debt or obligation incurred in aid of insurrection or rebellion against the United States, or any claim for the loss or emancipation of any slave; but all such debts, obligations and claims shall be held illegal and void.

Section 5. The Congress shall have power to enforce, by appropriate legislation, the provisions of this article.

✳ ✳ ✳ ✳ ✳

Abolishment of Slavery

The word "slavery" does not appear in the U.S. Constitution, but the document gave indirect sanction to the institution. The delegates to the Continental Congress provided that three-fifths of "all other Persons" would be counted in determining the number of congressmen each state could elect to the House of Representatives. The Constitution then required the return to their owners of fugitive slaves ("persons held to Service or Labour") crossing state lines. And it set the date for ending the slave trade ("the Migration or Importation of such Persons as any of the States now existing shall think proper to admit") at 1808, 20 years after ratification.

Each of these provisions was hotly debated at the Convention, and each was finally accepted in a spirit of compromise. Even members of Northern antislavery societies, such as Alexander Hamilton, opposed pursuing the issue, arguing that such an effort would irrevocably divide the states and endanger the more urgent goal of a strong national government. Compromise was urged also by such prominent Southerners as George Washington and James Madison, who detested slavery but believed it would disappear once the Union was confirmed.

The moral issue, however, was raised passionately at the Convention on several occasions. Gouverneur Morris of Pennsylvania denounced slavery as a "nefarious institution, the curse of heaven on the states where it prevailed." He contrasted the prosperity and human dignity of free regions with "the misery and poverty" of slave states. Ironically, the most eloquent attack on slavery at the Convention was voiced by Virginian George Mason, whom Jefferson called "the wisest man of his generation."

Slavery, Mason said, "produces the most pernicious effect on manners. Every master of slaves is born a petty tyrant. . . . Slavery discourages arts and manufactures. The poor despise labor when they see it performed by slaves. . . . I hold it essential . . . that the general government should have the power to prevent the increase of slavery." In the coming years, the abolitionist movement would use the same arguments and bring to bear the same sense of moral outrage; but for the moment the issue of slavery was evaded, both as a word and as a moral challenge. It would ultimately take the tragic conflagration of the Civil War (1861–1865) to end human bondage in the United States and start the country along the difficult path to full racial equality.

15th Amendment to The United States Constitution

March 30, 1870

Section 1. The right of citizens of the United States to vote shall not be denied or abridged by the United States or by any State on account of race, color, or previous condition of servitude—

Section 2. The Congress shall have power to enforce this article by appropriate legislation.

The 14th and 15th Amendments were passed in 1868 and 1870, respectively. Initially meant to preserve personal freedoms of African Americans, they now stand, in large part, for the idea that the Constitution implies, but does not enumerate, certain fundamental rights for all citizens.

Civil Rights Acts: 1866, 1870, 1871, and 1875

Civil Rights Act of 1866, 14 Stat. 27 (1866)

Be it enacted by the Senate and House of Representatives of the United States of America in Congress assembled, That all persons born in the United States and not subject to any foreign power, excluding Indians not taxed, are hereby declared to be citizens of the United States; and such citizens, of every race and color, without regard to any previous condition of slavery or involuntary servitude, except as a punishment for crime whereof the party shall have been duly convicted, shall have the same right, in every State and Territory in the United States, to make and enforce contracts, to sue, be parties, and give evidence, to inherit, purchase, lease, sell, hold, and convey real and personal property, and to full and equal benefit of all laws and proceedings for the security of person and property, as is enjoyed by white citizens, and shall be subject to like punishment, pains, and penalties, and to none other, any law, statute, ordinance, regulation, or custom, to the contrary notwithstanding.

SEC. 2. And be it further enacted, That any person who, under color of any law, statute, ordinance, regulation, or custom, shall subject, or cause to be subjected, any inhabitant of any State or Territory to the deprivation of any right secured or protected by this act, or to different punishment, pains, or penalties on account of such person having at any time been held in a condition of slavery or involuntary servitude, except as a punishment for crime whereof the party shall have been duly convicted, or by reason of his color or race, than is prescribed for the punishment of white persons, shall be deemed guilty of a misdemeanor, and, on conviction, shall be punished by fine not exceeding one thousand dollars, or imprisonment not exceeding one year, or both, in the discretion of the court.

SEC. 6. And be it further enacted, That any person who shall knowingly and wilfully obstruct, hinder, or prevent any officer, or other person charged with the execution of any warrant or process issued under the provisions of this act . . . [shall] be subject to a fine not exceeding one thousand dollars, and imprisonment not exceeding six months. . . .

————

Civil Rights Act of 1870 (The Enforcement Act), 16 Stat. 140 (1870)

Be it enacted by the Senate and House of Representatives of the United States of America in Congress assembled, That all citizens of the United States who are or shall be otherwise qualified by law to vote at any election . . . shall be entitled and allowed to vote at all such elections, without distinction of race, color, or previous condition of servitude. . . .

SEC. 2. And be it further enacted, That it shall be the duty of every person and officer to give to all citizens of the United States the same and equal opportunity to perform [any] prerequisite, and to become qualified to vote without distinction of race, color, or previous condition of servitude; and if any person or officer shall refuse or knowingly omit to give full effect to this section, he shall . . . be deemed guilty of a misdemeanor, and shall, on conviction thereof, be fined not less than five hundred dollars, or be imprisoned not less than one month and not more than one year, or both, at the discretion of the court.

SEC. 6. And be it further enacted, That if two or more persons shall band or conspire together, or go in disguise upon the public highway, or upon the premises of another, with intent to violate any provision of this act, or to injure, oppress, threaten, or intimidate any citizen with intent to prevent or hinder his free exercise and enjoyment of any right or privilege granted or secured to him by the Constitution or laws of the United States, or because of his having exercised the same, such persons shall be held guilty of felony, and, on conviction thereof, shall be fined or imprisoned, or both, at the discretion of the court,—the fine not to exceed five thousand dollars, and the imprisonment not to exceed ten years,—and shall, moreover, be thereafter ineligible to, and disabled from holding, any office or place of honor, profit, or trust created by the Constitution or laws of the United States.

SEC. 17. And be it further enacted, That any person who, under color of any law, statute, ordinance, regulation, or custom, shall subject, or cause to be subjected, any inhabitant of any State or Territory to the deprivation of any right secured or protected by the last preceding section [giving all persons the same rights as white citizens] of this act, or to different punishment, pains, or penalties on account of such person being an alien, or by reason of his color or race, than is prescribed for the punishment of citizens, shall be deemed guilty of a misdemeanor, and, on conviction, shall be punished by fine not exceeding one thousand dollars, or imprisonment not exceeding one year, or both, in the discretion of the court.

———

Civil Rights Act of 1871, 17 Stat. 13 (1871)

SEC. 2. That if two or more persons within any State or Territory of the United States shall conspire together to overthrow, or to put down, or to destroy by force the government of the United States, or to levy war against the United States, or to oppose by force the authority of the government of the United States, or by force, intimidation, or threat to prevent, hinder, or delay the execution of any law of the United States, or by force to seize, take, or possess any property of the United States contrary to the authority thereof, or by force, intimidation, or threat to prevent any person from accepting or holding any office or trust or place of confidence under the United States, or from discharging the duties thereof, or by force, intimidation, or threat to induce any officer of the United States to leave any State, district, or place where his duties as such officer might lawfully be performed, or to injure him in his person or property on account of his lawful discharge of the duties of his office, or to injure his person while engaged in the lawful discharge of the duties of his office, or to injure his property so as to molest, interrupt, hinder, or impede him in the discharge of his official duty, or by force, intimidation, or threat to deter any party or witness in any court of the United States from attending such court, or from testifying in any matter pending in such court fully, freely, and truthfully, or to injure any such party or witness in his person or property on account of his having so attended or testified, or by force, intimidation, or threat to influence the verdict, presentment, or indictment, of any juror or grand juror in any court of the United States, or to injure such juror in his person or property on account of any verdict, presentment, or indictment lawfully assented to by him, or on account of his being or having been such juror, or shall conspire together, or go in disguise upon the public highway or upon the premises of another for the purpose, either directly or indirectly, of depriving any person or any class of persons of the equal protection of the laws, or of equal privileges or immunities under the laws, or for the purpose of preventing or hindering the constituted authorities of any State from giving or securing to all persons within such State the equal protection of the laws, or shall conspire together for the purpose of in any manner impeding, hindering, obstructing, or defeating the due course of justice in any State or Territory, with intent to deny to any citizen of the United States the due and equal protection of the laws, or to injure any person in his person or his property for lawfully enforcing the right of any person or class of persons to the equal protection of the laws, or by force, intimidation, or threat to prevent any citizen of the United States lawfully entitled to vote from giving his support or advocacy in a lawful manner towards or in favor of the election of any lawfully qualified person as an elector of President or Vice-President of the United States, or as a member of the Congress of the United States, or to injure any such citizen in his person or property on account of such support or advocacy, each and every person so offending shall be deemed guilty of a high crime, and, upon conviction thereof in any district or circuit court of the United States or district or supreme court of any Territory of the United States having jurisdiction of similar offences, shall be punished by a fine not less than five hundred nor more than five thousand dollars, or by imprisonment, with or without hard labor, as the court may determine, for a period of not less than six months nor more than six years, as the court may determine, or by both such fine and imprisonment as the court shall determine. . . .

———

Civil Rights Act of 1875, 18 Stat. 335 (1875)

Whereas, it is essential to just government we recognize the equality of all men before the law, and hold that it is the duty of government in its dealings with the people to mete out equal and exact justice to all, of whatever nativity, race, color, or persuasion, religious or political; and it being the appropriate object of legislation to enact great fundamental principles into law: Therefore,

Be it enacted by the Senate and House of Representatives of the United States of America in Congress assembled, That all persons within the jurisdiction of the United States shall be entitled to the full and equal enjoyment of the accommodations, advantages, facilities, and privileges of inns, public conveyances on land or water, theaters, and other places of public amusement; subject only to the conditions and limitations established by law, and applicable alike to citizens of every race and color, regardless of any previous condition of servitude.

SEC. 2. That any person who shall violate the foregoing section by denying to any citizen, except for reasons by law applicable to citizens of every race and color, and regardless of any previous condition of servitude, the full enjoyment of any of the accommodations, advantages, facilities, or privileges in said section enumerated, or by aiding or inciting such denial, shall, for every such offense, forfeit and pay the sum of five hundred dollars to the person aggrieved thereby, to be recovered in an action of debt, with full costs; and shall also, for every such offense, be deemed guilty of a misdemeanor and, upon conviction thereof, shall be fined not less than five hundred nor more than one thousand dollars, or shall be imprisoned not less than thirty days nor more than one year. . . .

SEC. 4. That no citizen possessing all other qualifications which are or may be prescribed by law shall be disqualified for service as a grand or petit juror in any court of the United States, or of any State, on account of race, color, or previous condition of servitude; and any officer or other person charged with any duty in the selection or summoning of jurors who shall exclude or fail to summon any citizen for the cause aforesaid shall, on conviction thereof, be deemed guilty of a misdemeanor and be fined not more than five thousand dollars.

Section Eight

Negro Uplift-v-Jim Crow

CHAPTER 10

Buffalo Soldiers: Reconstruction and the Indian Wars

Lt. Col. (Ret.) Michael Lee Lanning

Col. Thomas Morgan commanded the Fourteenth U.S. Colored Troops (USGT) from their first action at Dalton, Georgia, on August 15, 1864, until the end of the war. In his memoirs, published in 1885, Morgan wrote about his men's performance at the battle of Nashville, where more than three thousand Union and six thousand Confederate soldiers were killed, wounded, missing, or captured:

> Colored soldiers had fought side by side with white troops. They had mingled together in the charge. They had supported each other. They had assisted each other from the field when wounded, and they lay side by side in death. The survivors rejoiced together over a hard-fought field, won by common valor. All who witnessed their conduct gave them equal praise. . . . A new chapter in the history of liberty had been written. It had been shown that marching under the flag of freedom, animated by a love of liberty, even the slave becomes a man and a hero.

Because of such valor displayed and casualties taken at Nashville and other Civil War battlefields, the black soldier had earned a permanent place in the military. For the first time in U.S. history, African-American soldiers did not disappear from the ranks with the coming of peace, even when the million-man U.S. Army decreased to an authorized strength of only 54,641 officers and men. In fact, during the postwar reductions, black regiments were some of the last disbanded because they had been the last to join.

The retention of blacks in the army garnered supporters and opponents both within and outside the military. General Benjamin Butler became a vocal advocate, stating that the black soldier had "with bayonet . . . unlocked the iron barred gates of prejudice and opened new fields of freedom, liberty, and the equality of right."

Others, such as Sen. Willard Saulsbury of Delaware, did not share Butler's sentiments. To his fellow U.S. senators, Sanlsbury questioned, "What would be the effect if you were to send Negro regiments into the community in which I live to brandish their swords and exhibit their pistols and their guns?"

After much debate, an assignment process evolved that generally met the desires of both sides. Black soldiers remained in the army but received postings to remote areas west of the Mississippi where they would have limited contact with white Americans.

The only exception to the frontier assignments for black soldiers was duty as part of the occupation forces in the former Confederate states. Some Northern politicians and military officers relished the punitive impact of stationing blacks in the Deep South, where the two colors that could inflict the most pain and anguish were the blue uniform tunics of the Union army and the black skin of former slaves now soldiers wearing those uniforms. As a result, African Americans served as part of the occupation forces in several Southern states immediately after the war.

Reconstruction administrators from the North, known as carpetbaggers for their hastily packed luggage, made of carpet material, controlled most southern state and municipal governments and militia positions during the period. While evidence indicates that many of these officials were far more concerned with acquiring personal wealth and status than with ensuring proper conduct of their office, their tenure did allow limited opportunities for some blacks to flourish in both politics and in the state militias. Robert Smalls, the former captain of the *Planter,* gained promotion to major general in the South Carolina militia, and several other former slaves and freemen secured militia commissions and political office.

White-robed members of the Ku Klux Klan and similar organizations waged a reign of "bullet and the noose" terror to put their former chattel into "their place" by excluding or limiting their access to voting, education, and every other aspect of equality. Throughout the South and indeed the North as well, the United States reverted back to a segregated society in which whites denied blacks equal rights in the country they had fought to preserve. Even Smalls, who remained in politics, became much better known to white South Carolinians as "the boat thief" for his delivery of the *Planter* to the Union navy rather than a war hero or militia officer.

Some, however, did not waver. The "liberal Republicans" in Congress demanded that blacks be a part of the postwar Regular Army when Congress began debate about the future of the military in March 1866. A compromise on retaining African Americans in the army was ultimately won by the Republicans, who believed that blacks had earned the right to serve, and by pragmatic representatives, who knew that the hardships and danger of the Western plains would limit the number of volunteers.

On July 28, 1866, a congressional act authorized sixty-seven regiments—five artillery, twelve cavalry, and fifty infantry—to make up the Regular U.S. Army. Early drafts of the act called for six of the infantry regiments to be manned by blacks, but lobbying by Benjamin F. Wade of Ohio produced authorization for two of the six black regiments to be cavalry. Although African-American soldiers had successfully manned artillery units in the Civil War, advocates lost their bid to open that branch of the service to blacks because too many congressmen believed that African Americans did not possess the intelligence to be artillerymen. They led the vote to restrict the black regiments to the cavalry and infantry.

During the organizational and training phase for the Ninth and Tenth Cavalry Regiments and the Thirty-eighth, Thirty-ninth, Fortieth, and Forty-first Infantry Regiments, Congress further reduced the number of regiments, black and white, throughout the army. While the Ninth and Tenth Cavalry remained intact, the four infantry regiments merged into two. The Thirty-eighth and Forty-first consolidated into the Twenty-fourth Infantry Regiment and the Thirty-ninth and Fortieth became the Twenty-fifth Infantry Regiment. The U.S. revised statutes of 1869 designated all four regiments as "colored."

Despite their distinguished service in the Civil War and the professionalism of enlisted men reporting to the new black regiments, African Americans in uniform suffered the same discrimination and racism as their civilian brothers. Along with prejudice against the color of their skin, African American soldiers also experienced the disdain that their white countrymen felt toward soldiers in general. While lauded as saviors during the Civil War, all soldiers in the postconflict years—regardless of color—were viewed as a burden on the economy and as men who could not find other employment.

The black man in uniform found himself at the bottom of the despised military group. White Americans in both the North and the South generally condemned the black soldiers as shiftless, lazy, undisciplined, and ignorant. As they had proved in the Civil War and would continue to display in the long decades of the Indian Wars, African-American soldiers were guilty of none of these stereotypical accusations. The only description remotely accurate was "ignorant," in the literal sense, because most black enlistees of the period could neither read nor write. This, however, was not a matter of intelligence but the result of prewar restrictions in the South against educating African Americans.

Despite the lack of social esteem afforded soldiers in the postwar years, African Americans found many advantages in the military. The opportunity for education was one. Exposed to the classroom, usually headed by the regimental chaplain, blacks displayed a yearning for education and an ability to learn equal to their white counterparts. Another appeal was that since the prosperity of the postwar years did not otherwise extend to blacks, the military provided one of the few semblances of equality. In addition to food, clothing, and shelter, each recruit—regardless of race—received the same thirteen dollars per month salary, with an annual increase of one dollar per month and a reenlistment bonus at the end of five years.

While white regiments had difficulty in finding and retaining volunteers, black regiments had more applicants than positions available. Whereas white recruits believed that joining the army represented a step down in social position, black volunteers viewed military service as an elevation in status and an opportunity to improve themselves.

Both races shared rather simple enlistment requirements. Recruiters required volunteers to be physically healthy, unmarried, and between the ages of eighteen and thirty-five. Literacy was not a prerequisite. The army kept no statistics at the time, but the study of regimental records reveals that the typical black volunteer was about twenty-three years of age, either a farmer or laborer, and illiterate.

Filling the ranks of the four postwar black regiments proved to be no difficulty, but finding white officers to lead them created problems. Military personnel and civilians viewed officers assigned to black regiments as inferior to those serving with white units. As a result, officers often turned down commands as captains in the black regiments and accepted positions as lieutenants in white regiments. Few graduates of the U.S. Military Academy sought service in black regiments, making the artillery, which did not accept black enlistees, the most popular branch among West Point graduates. A young officer at Fort Monroe, Virginia, in 1883 perhaps best summed up the feelings of many of his contemporaries when he said that he would "rather be a second lieutenant of artillery than a captain of niggers."

While few desired to serve in black regiments, most white officers firmly believed that African Americans were incapable of leading themselves. Authorization of the four black regiments neither required whites in command positions nor excluded black officers from serving in any position. There were, however, no black officers available to seek positions in the regiments. The few African Americans who had gained commissions during the Civil war had been discharged after Appomattox. In the postwar era, blacks could apply for commissions, but in every instance their applications were denied.

With no commissions available from the ranks or by direct appointment from civilian life, the only other avenue for a black man to become an officer was the U.S. Military Academy. However, West Point, since its establishment in 1802, had never accepted an African American into its corps of cadets. In 1870, South Carolina congressman Solomon L. Hoge appointed James Webster Smith, a student at Howard University, as the academy's first black cadet. Smith passed the mental and physical entrance requirements but never gained the acceptance of his white classmates.

For the next four years, Smith experienced both official and unofficial harassment. Twice court-martialed, once for an altercation with a white cadet and a second time for "conduct unbecoming a gentleman," Smith endured being sentenced to repeating his plebe year. During his entire stay at West Point, Smith experienced ostracism by the white cadets; they "silenced" him, refusing to speak to him except in the line of duty. Smith remained resilient for four years before the academic department declared him deficient in a philosophy course and dismissed him from the academy in June 1874.

In 1873, a year prior to Smith's dismissal, a second black cadet, Henry O. Flipper of Georgia, entered the academy. Although he suffered the same "silence" treatment for four years, Flipper endured and in 1877 became the 2,690th graduate of the U.S. Military Academy and its first African-American alumnus.

Flipper's treatment improved little after he jointed the Tenth Cavalry, where he became the sole black officer not only in the regiment but in the entire U.S. Army. From all evidence, Flipper performed well for four years before being court-martialed for the alleged embezzlement of two thousand dollars from commissary funds. Although acquitted of the primary charge, the board convicted him of "conduct unbecoming an officer" and discharged him. Flipper maintained at his trial and for the rest of his life that his fellow officers had conspired against him first because of his race, and second, because of attentions he had paid to a white woman at Fort Concho, Texas.

Despite his later success a civilian engineer, Flipper carried the stigma of the army's charges. Not until nearly a century later did the U.S. Army Board for the Correction of Military Records review the circumstances of Flipper's discharge. The result was to clear his name and award him an honorable discharge. On the hundredth anniversary of his graduation from West Point in 1977, the academy dedicated a memorial bust in the cadet library to Lieutenant Flipper.

From the end of the Civil War until the turn of the century, only twenty-five black men received appointments to West Point. Of this number twelve passed the entrance examination. In addition to Flipper, only two others, John Alexander of Ohio, in the class of 1887, and Charles Young of Ohio, in the class of 1889, graduated and received commissions as second lieutenants in the Regular Army.

Discrimination against blacks in the military was by no means limited to black West Point cadets and graduates. The black regiments received no better welcome from the army. The Fortieth Infantry Regiment, soon to be redesignated the Twenty-fifth, assembled at the Goldsboro, North Carolina, railway station on March 31, 1869, only to find freight and cattle cars rather than passenger trains for their ten-day trip to Louisiana. When the Tenth Cavalry Regiment assembled at Fort Leavenworth, Kansas, in 1867, the post commander assigned them a swampy area for their camp, did not allow them to march in reviews, and ordered that no black cavalryman come within ten yards of a white soldier.

The Tenth Cavalry, as well as the other three black regiments, also suffered discrimination in the issuance of arms, horses, and supplies. In evaluating the first fifty horses assigned to the Tenth Cavalry, white commander Col. Benjamin Grierson reported that not a single animal was suitable for service. Included in the herd were cripples and worn-out horses more than a dozen years old that were veterans of the Civil War. The black regiments also received the lowest priority in the issue of saddles, harnesses, weapons, and uniforms.

The horse and equipment situation did not improve with time. In a letter to Colonel Grierson on May 22, 1870, the commander of the Company H, Tenth Cavalry, Capt. Louis H. Carpenter complained that his unit was "getting mean and worn out horses form the 7th Cavalry. Since our first mount in 1867 this regiment has received nothing but broken down horses and repaired equipment."

Perhaps the most pronounced indicator of the War Department's neglect of the black regiments was the lack of symbols for the units themselves. Historically, every regiment in the U.S. Army, as well as most military units around the world, has always carried a unit flag, usually an ornately embroidered silk, known as "the colors." These standards symbolize the identity of a regiment. They have been the impetus for some of the most remarkable examples of bravery in battle when soldiers fought to defend their colors from capture.

Yet the army did not issue the professionally manufactured regimental flags to the black units. So black soldiers secured cloth, thread, and needles to sew their own. Although not as "pretty" as the flags of the white regiments, the black soldiers served proudly under colors they created in their own barracks until the official flags finally arrived.

In addition to suffering the lowest priority for everything within the army, black regiments had to contend with hostile attitudes toward them in the towns and territories to which they were assigned. Even in the far reaches of the frontier, white pioneers refused to accept black soldiers as equals. The only places they found a welcome were "hog ranches," the separate areas just outside of town where saloons and brothels provided entertainment to the black soldiers on payday as long as their meager wages lasted.

Although they were protecting the settlements, black soldiers could not depend on equal justice form white sheriffs in the towns adjacent to their forts. On August 25, 1885, whites broke into the Sturgis City Jail in Dakota Territory and lynched a soldier of the Twenty-fifth Regiment charged with murdering a white man. At Sun River, Montana Territory, on June 10, 1885, vigilantes removed another member of the regiment from the local jail and lynched him. None of those responsible for either lynching was ever brought to justice.

Even when apprehended, whites seldom faced punishment for murdering black soldiers. On January 31, 1881, white sheep rancher Tom McCarthy shot and killed an unarmed private, William Watkins of Company E, Tenth Cavalry, in a San Angelo, Texas, saloon. Members of the Tenth Cavalry at nearby Fort Concho captured McCarthy and turned him over to the San Angelo sheriff, who released the rancher pending an investigation.

The African-American soldiers of the Tenth Cavalry did not take kindly to the murder of one of their comrades and the release of his killer. A hand-bill dated February 3, 1881, and signed by "U.S. Soldiers" appeared throughout the town: "We, the soldiers of the U.S. Army, do hereby warn the first and last time all citizens and cowboys, etc., of San Angelo and vicinity to recognize our right of way as just and peaceful men. If we do not receive justice and fair play, which we must have, some one will suffer—if not the guilty, the innocent. It has gone too far. Justice of death."

Some of the black soldiers followed the announcement by riding into San Angelo and firing warning shots into several buildings before Grierson confined the regiment to the post. Ultimately, a grand jury indicted McCarthy for first-degree murder, but a jury in Austin, Texas, took only minutes to find him not guilty.

Beyond the problems with supplies and the poor treatment by the civilian population they protected, black soldiers also faced unrelenting natural hardship in the vast western frontier. The white regiments, which shared frontier duties, rotated back East to relatively easy assignments in fairly pleasant surroundings every several years. The four black regiments, however, in what apparently was an "out of sight, out of mind" policy, remained on continuous duty in the West for more than two decades.

The black infantry and cavalry regiments served at remote outposts in extremely harsh conditions. An 1872 inspector general's report described Fort Clark, Texas: "The quarters are wretched and therefore nothing beyond shelter and ordinary police can reasonably be looked for. All except two companies of cavalry are in huts. . . . There is no place for divine service or instruction. . . . The public stores are imperfectly covered with paulins [sic] or put in insecure huts, improvised at great expense."

When the Twenty-fifth Infantry Regiment moved from Texas to Fort Randall, Dakota Territory, they found conditions improved, but a report in 1881 noted that the barracks were overcrowded, short of furniture and lighting, and generally in need of repairs. At nearby Fort Hale, black soldiers fared no better. An inspection report of the black regiment made by Capt. R. P. Hughes of the white Third Infantry Regiment in October 1883 noted: "The post commander has his post in excellent condition as to cleanliness and order, but he cannot make a tumble down log hut look either beautiful or inviting. I respectfully submit to the Department Commander that these two companies

are so much more badly off than any of the other troops in this geographical department that I think some strong measures should be adopted for their relief. . . . The troops are good, but their accommodations are wretched."

As if it were not enough that they suffered a low priority in receiving materiel, general discrimination by the white settlers, and wretched living conditions on their posts, African-American soldiers also faced one more major complication. The black regiments reported to the western frontier at the height of the Indian Wars, which reached their bloodiest period in the post-Civil War years.

It was, however, from the Indian enemy that the black regiments gained their most enduring label. While whites, whom they protected, referred to the black soldiers as "coloreds," "brunettes," "Africans," and much more commonly as "niggers." Indians, who faced them on the battlefield, had a more complimentary name for them—Buffalo Soldiers. Whether the name began as a form of respect or simply an acknowledgment of the similarity between the curly black hair of African Americans and that of the buffalo is unknown. Whatever the source, black soldiers, appreciating the comparison to the stoic animals the Indians considered sacred, adopted the name. The Tenth Cavalry even added a buffalo to their unit crest.

During the Civil War, Native American tribes on the Plains and in the Southwest had reclaimed much of their lands after army units withdrew east to fight the rebellious Confederates. When the war ended, veterans of both sides headed west in search of new opportunities, only to find the Indians prepared to fight to retain their way of life. For the next quarter century, much of the protection for white expansion westward came from the black infantry and cavalry.

For their first eight years, the Tenth Cavalry served in the Central Plains and then transferred to Texas in 1875, replacing the Ninth Cavalry, which moved to the New Mexico and Arizona Territories. The Twenty-fourth and Twenty-fifth Infantry Regiments also served in Texas. In 1880 the Twenty-fourth moved to the Oklahoma Territory and then, eight years later, on to the New Mexico and Arizona Territories.

During their service in Texas, the Twenty-fifth recruited yet another group of blacks to assist them—the only other black unit to participate in the Indian Wars besides the original four regiments. These new recruits were descendants of African

Americans and Seminole Indians who had migrated to Mexico at the end of the Second Seminole War in Florida and settled near the Texas border.

Because neither soldiers nor officers of the Twenty-fifth had experience in the southwestern terrain when the unit arrived in Texas, the regiment recognized its need for assistance from someone familiar with the territory. In 1870, Maj. Zenas R. Bliss crossed the border and convinced about fifty of the racially mixed black Seminoles to serve as scouts in return for land and food in Texas. The Seminole Negro Indian Scouts, under command of white lieutenant John Bullis, served for nine years with the Twenty-fifth Regiment and occasionally assisted other black regiments. The scouts participated in twenty-six major expeditions, including several raids into Mexico in pursuit of renegade Indians and bandit gangs.

Although these raids proved successful in halting the incursions from Mexico into Texas, they also engendered political difficulties and racial prejudice. After the Seminole Negro Indian Scouts assisted the Twenty-fifth Regiment in the summer of 1876, Gen. E. O. C. Ord, the commander of the Department of Texas, wrote to his superiors: "I must remark, however, that the use of colored soldiers to cross the river after raiding Indians, is in my opinion, impolitic, not because they have shown any want of bravery, but because their employment is much more offensive to Mexican inhabitants than white soldiers."

Despite the criticism, Seminole Negro Indian Scouts provided a needed service and, from all accounts, they performed well; four of them received the Medal of Honor. While the scouts more than met their end of the agreement by assisting black regiments in Texas, neither the army nor the U.S. government kept the promise of food and land grants. A *New York Times* reporter noted on September 1, 1875, that the scouts "are now living in great destitution, bordering on starvation."

Bliss, Bullis, and other officers lobbied for better treatment of the Scouts to no avail. When the border area became peaceful in 1881, the Seminole Negro Indian Scouts were disbanded and melted into oblivion.

The Twenty-fifth Regiment left Texas in 1880 without its Seminole Negro Indian Scouts for the Dakota and Montana Territories, but only after much debate on whether the black soldier could perform in a cold climate. Many officers, especially those in Washington, D.C., who had never served in African-American regiments, thought that because blacks had originated in the African tropics and then lived mostly in the American South, they would not be able to endure the harsh winters of Montana and the Dakotas. The army's quartermaster general expressed concern, stating, "Colored men will not enlist with the prospects of going to that rigorous climate . . . the effect of the cold will be very injurious to those men whose terms of enlistment do not soon expire."

As usual, the Buffalo Soldiers proved their critics and doubters wrong. The infantrymen of the Twenty-fifth Regiment found the northern Rockies a welcome relief from Texas and enjoyed an improvement in barracks and facilities. As for the cold, blacks showed that they could soldier under any condition. In the spring of 1881, after an extremely severe winter, black soldiers performed relief operations, rescuing stranded white homesteaders and their animals and delivering supplies to remote villages and camps. The regiment's Company F alone assisted more than eight hundred settlers in Dakota Territory, and when government supplies ran low, they contributed their own pay to provide additional relief supplies.

Despite their many missions, the primary purpose in assigning black regiments to the West was to suppress hostile Indians. African-American soldiers participated in some of the earliest fights against the Native Americans in the post-Civil War period and continued their campaigns until the concluding battles of the Indian Wars. The first skirmish occurred only a few months after the establishment of the Tenth Cavalry Regiment. On August 2, 1867, thirty-four members of the regiment's F Company rode in pursuit of a Cheyenne war party that had raided a camp of railway workers near Fort Hays, Kansas.

Capt. George Armes, in command of the F Company troopers, followed the Indians' trail, only to be attacked and surrounded by a group of seventy-five to eighty warriors. After a six-hour fight in which they killed six Indians, the cavalrymen broke through the encirclement. During the withdrawal, the Tenth Cavalry suffered its first fatality of the Indian Wars when Sgt. William Christy of Pennsylvania fell from a gunshot to the head.

A year later, the Tenth Cavalry rescued a detachment of scouts under the command of Maj. George A. Forsyth from a siege by Cheyenne, Sioux, and

Arapahos on an island in the Republican River in eastern Colorado. Moving day and night by alternating riding and walking to rest their horses, the soldiers of H Company rescued the white scouts after an eight-day journey.

Over the next twenty-five years, the Ninth and Tenth Cavalry and the Twenty-fourth and Twenty-fifth Infantry Regiments served throughout the West and Southwest, their assignments based on wherever the most significant Native American threat loomed at the time. During that period, the regiments engaged in more than two hundred battles and skirmishes, and their soldiers received eighteen Medals of Honor for bravery under fire.

The first Medal of Honor earned by an African American in the Indian Wars typified both the personal bravery and style of operations of the black regiments. On the morning of May 20, 1870, a ten-man patrol under the leadership of Sgt. Emanuel Stance from Company F, Ninth Cavalry Regiment, departed Fort McKavett in southwest Texas to scout twenty miles north to Kickapoo Springs. About halfway there, they spotted a half-dozen Indians driving a herd of horses suspected to be stolen. Stance, a native of Charleston, South Carolina, and barely five feet tall, ordered a charge that resulted in a running fight for eight miles that dispersed the Indians and captured nine horses.

Stance and his patrol rode on to Kickapoo Springs, where they camped for the night. On their way back to Fort McKavett, the cavalrymen surprised twenty Indians stalking a herd of horses and its small guard detail. Stance and his men again charged, dispersed the Indians, and captured five more horses. Minutes later, the Indians counterattacked, but Stance personally flanked the Indians and forced their retreat. Stance modestly reported on May 26 that when the fight began, he had "turned my little command loose on them . . . and after a few volleys they left me to continue my march in peace." His superiors recognized his bravery with the Medal of Honor.

The Native Americans rarely assembled numbers large enough to challenge Regular Army units and only on a few occasions showed any inclination to do so. Most of the Indian attacks focused on isolated ranches or on small parties moving cross-country. Guerrilla warfare—hit-and-run raids and small skirmishes of short duration—characterized the Indian Wars.

As a result, U.S. Army regiments on the frontier spent much of their time attempting to find Indian camps or pursuing raiders who had attacked farmers, miners, or other workers. Because of its mobility, the cavalry spent more time than the infantry in the field, covering vast distances looking for the hostiles.

After a month-long campaign by two companies of the Ninth Cavalry across West Texas in April–May 1870, the operation's commander, Maj. Albert P. Morrow, wrote in his official report, dated June 1, 1870, that his black cavalrymen had

> marched about 1,000 miles, over two hundred of which was through country never explored by troops, drove the Indians from every rancheria . . . destroyed immense amounts of . . . food, robes, skins, utensils and material, and captured 40 horses and mules. I cannot speak too highly of the conduct of the officers and men under my command, always cheerful and ready, braving the severest hardships with short rations and no water without a murmur. The Negro troops are peculiarly adapted to hunting Indians, knowing no fear and capable of great endurance.

The infantry regiments drew guard duty at the fort and at key points along the various communications routes, where they also on occasion became engaged with hostile Indians, who attacked work parties, mail stages, or supply trains. Besides pursuing their adversaries and guarding areas such as railway and telegraph construction sites, black regiments also performed routine garrison duties, which often included the building of their own forts and quarters and the care of their equipment and animals.

Despite all the hard work, the harsh weather, and the dangers from hostiles, boredom proved to be the enemy most difficult to combat. The remoteness of the camps and forts, combined with a lack of recreational facilities, frequently led to trouble. The African-American cavalrymen and infantrymen in the West proved that soldiers will be soldiers regardless of color. They will perform brave deeds when called upon; they will also get into trouble when left idle.

The ranks of the Buffalo Soldiers included deserters, malingerers, drunks, thieves, and even the occasional murderer. They were far from perfect, yet in every statistical category their meritorious performance exceeded that of the white regiments. In 1889, Secretary of War Redfield Proctor noted in his annual report to Congress that the desertion rate in the black regiments was only 2 percent, compared to 12 percent in the white units. Black regiments also had fewer alcohol-related incidents and enjoyed higher reenlistment rates.

Many direct and indirect factors influenced the superior morale and performance of the black regiments. Positive attributes—unit pride, a sense of belonging, and feelings of accomplishment—all contributed to the low desertion rate, as did the knowledge that each black soldier represented his entire race and determined its future treatment both in and outside the military. At the same time, negative alternatives also played a role in preventing black soldiers from deserting. Despite the hardships of their life, the army offered far more opportunity than did the civilian world for African Americans. Moreover, a black soldier on the run stood out anywhere he went in the predominantly white western territories.

By the end of the 1880s white farmers and ranchers occupied much of the West, and the various renegade Indians were either dead or restricted to reservations. However, black regiments continued to perform escort duty along the various stage and supply routes and to combat the final Indian uprisings. Their performance remained as dedicated in the final days as it had been during their more than two decades of service on the frontier.

On March 7, 1890, only ten days before the formal end of the campaigns against the Apaches, Sgt. William McBryar of Elizabethtown, North Carolina, earned the Medal of Honor near Fort Thomas, Arizona. The Tenth Cavalry soldier exposed himself to return fire against an Apache ambush that saved his comrades. In an understated nomination for the award, 1st Lt. J. W. Watson wrote, "Sergeant McBryar demonstrated coolness, bravery, and good marksmanship under circumstances very different from those on the target range."

On May 11, 1889, an eleven-man escort, composed of soldiers form the Twenty-fourth Infantry, engaged in their last major fight in the Southwest, on the road between Cedar Springs and Fort Thomas, Arizona, against bandits attempting to rob an army paymaster wagon. Two of the black soldiers, Sgt. Benjamin Brown of Spotsylvania, Virginia, and Cpl. Isaiah Mays of Carters Bridge, Virginia, received the Medal of Honor, and seven others were awarded Certificates of Merit for their valor.

In his official account, Maj. J. W. Wham, paymaster and commander of the detail, reported, "I served in the infantry during the entire Civil War and served in 16 major battles, but I never witnessed better courage, or better fighting than shown by those colored soldiers."

The final Medal of Honor awarded to an African American during the Indian Wars came in the conflict's last campaign. During the Sioux "Ghost Dance" uprising in late 1890, the Ninth Cavalry supported the white Seventh Cavalry in pursuing and returning Big Foot and his followers to their reservation. On December 13, near Pine Ridge, South Dakota, a patrol of I Company, Ninth Cavalry, found themselves surrounded by a large Sioux force. Cpl. William O. Wilson fought his way through the encirclement to bring help which rescued his fellow troopers.

During their more than two decades of service, generally in the most adverse terrain and against the most hostile Indians, the four regiments of black soldiers earned the respect of their Native American adversaries, the white regiments with whom they campaigned, and finally, Washington officials.

In recognition of their long and faithful service, the War Department retained all four black regiments on active duty after the conclusion of the Indian Wars. The battalions of the Ninth and Tenth Cavalry and the Twenty-fourth and Twenty-fifth Infantry were spread across the West, performing garrison duties and maintaining combat readiness. As an additional reward for their Indian War service, Secretary of War Redfield Proctor ordered the transfer of K Troop, Ninth Cavalry, from Fort Robinson, Nebraska, to Fort Myer, on the edge of Washington, D.C. They arrived on May 25, 1891, and for the first time since Reconstruction, black soldiers were serving east of the Mississippi River.

The Ninth Cavalry troopers remained for three years in Washington, where they gave riding demonstrations and performed ceremonial duties, including acting as a special escort for President Cleveland during a parade in 1893. Although their performance both on and off duty was exemplary, some white residents of Washington as well as Southern members of Congress complained abut the proximity of the black cavalrymen. On October 3, 1894, K Troop returned to Fort Robinson and rejoined their regiment.

During their tour in Washington, all of K Troops facilities—billets, dining halls, the post exchange, and the barbershop—were segregated. General discrimination remained a fact of life for the black regiments no matter where they served.

Shortly before K Troop rejoined the Ninth Cavalry at Fort Robinson, a reporter from a black Ohio newspaper visited the Nebraska camp. His report in the July 14, 1894, edition of the *Cleveland Gazette* declared:

> There is considerable discrimination going on at Fort Robinson, Neb. There are three white clerks in the commissary department, two in the post exchange, two in the post bakery, two in the post adjutant's office, two in the officers' club and mess room, the post librarian is a white soldier, two white soldiers at the post pump house, a white non-commissioned officer in charge of the post saw mills, five white men in the post quarter-master's department. All these places are filled by enlisted men of the Eighth Infantry of which there are only two companies at the post, while there are six cavalry companies, all colored.

Although all African Americans had gained their freedom in 1865 and the black regiments had performed well for more than two decades during the Indian Wars, the overall treatment of blacks had deteriorated by the close of the nineteenth century. Racial segregation, as established by what became known as Jim Crow laws, named after a popular contemporary minstrel song, separated black and white Americans in every way. Poll taxes, literacy tests, and other similar measures kept the right to vote form most blacks in the Southern states.

Various local and state segregation laws received federal support from the May 18, 1896, Supreme Court decision in the case of *Plessy v. Ferguson*. Although the issue focused on segregated public transportation in Louisiana, the court's majority opinion stated that both races benefited from segregation: "Legislation is powerless to eradicate racial instincts or to abolish distinctions based upon physical differences, and the attempt to do so can only result in accentuating the difficulties of the present situation."

At the end of the nineteenth century, Jim Crow laws in the South barred or restricted African Americans from white schools, churches, hotels, restaurants, theaters, and most every other public facility. Whites often enforced these laws by the hangman's rope or by fire. In both 1892 and 1893 white Americans either lynched or burned alive more than 150 black Americans.

Within the army, the four black regiments continued to be commanded almost exclusively by white officers and to face the same segregation as did their civilian brothers. Despite these conditions, the U.S. Army did provide equal pay and a semblance of equal, albeit separate facilities. At the close of the nineteenth century, the army continued to be one of the few U.S. institutions to afford African Americans the opportunity of service, advancement, and accomplishment.

Likewise, black sailors were afforded these opportunities but had to endure the same discrimination as those of the black army regiments and the black civilian population. Despite the reduction in ships and sailors in the post-Civil War period, the navy continued to enlist African Americans because it was still difficult to fill crews. During the first thirty years after the Civil War, the U.S. Navy averaged five thousand to six thousand men on duty at any given time, of whom 10–14 percent, or five hundred to eight hundred, were black. Because of the limited space aboard ships, both sleeping and eating areas were integrated.

Naval regulations did not restrict blacks from becoming regular seamen or gunners. In 1870 only 29 percent of black sailors served in the "domestic" positions of cooks and stewards, but this number increased to 49 percent by 1890. No official policy change prompted this movement, but some naval leaders believed that African Americans did not have the intelligence to adapt to the intricacies of the steam boilers and mechanization that replaced most of the old sailing ships in the 1880s. Since they had the latitude to transfer crew members wherever they wished, many captains chose to place the blacks in kitchens and dining rooms.

Despite mounting discrimination, black enlisted men served the navy bravely. Seaman Joseph B, Noil, who was born in Nova Scotia and enlisted in New York City, was the first African American to receive a post-Civil War Medal of Honor, by saving the life of a fellow sailor who fell overboard from the USS *Powhatan* on December 26, 1879. Five other black sailors received the medal before the end of the century for similar rescue efforts. One, Seaman Robert Sweeney, received the award twice for saving drowning sailors while aboard the USS *Kearsarge*, on October 26, 1881, and the USS *Jamestown*, on December 20, 1883.

Racism rather than recognition, however remained the norm. When abolitionist leader Frederick Douglass was appointed U.S. minister to

Haiti in 1889, the navy was ordered to transport him to his new port. The first captain given the assignment resigned, the second claimed his ship unseaworthy for the voyage, and the third requested a transfer to a new command.

Discrimination against African Americans was also blatant in the selection of officers. Between the Civil War and the end of the century, no African American gained commission in the U.S. Navy. The navy continued to limit the number of black naval volunteers and barred them from direct commissions. The only other avenue for commissions was the U.S. Naval Academy at Annapolis, Maryland, which proved to be just as inequitable as West Point—in fact, more so.

John Conyers of South Carolina received the first nomination of an African American to the U.S. Naval Academy in 1872, three decades after the school's establishment in 1842. Conyers found himself welcomed by neither faculty nor fellow cadets and suffered the same "silence" treatment that West Point cadets inflicted on black students. After a year of enduring ostracism and hazing, Conyers resigned when declared deficient in his mathematics and French classes.

A second black cadet, Alonzo McClennan, reported to Annapolis September 1873, followed a year later by Henry E. Baker Jr. Both encountered the same treatment that had greeted Conyers. McClennan resigned after six months; Baker stayed only ten weeks. No other African American received an appointment to the U.S. Naval Academy until 1936—more than seventy years after the end of the Civil War and sixty years after the resignations of the first three black cadets. It would be another thirteen years before the first black graduated and received his commission from the academy in 1949.

The more than a quarter century following the Civil War proved that segregated black cavalry and infantry units could perform as well as, or better than, white regiments. Sailors, integrated into ships throughout the navy, displayed their ability to contribute as efficient crew members. Soldiers and sailors alike set the example as patriotic black Americans who could and would serve loyally and bravely, if only given the chance. They were soon to receive even more opportunities to fight for their country and to continue to display their value to the American military.

Atlanta Compromise Speech, 1895

Booker T. Washington

On September 18, 1895, African-American spokesman and leader Booker T. Washington spoke before a predominantly white audience at the Cotton States and International Exposition in Atlanta. His "Atlanta Compromise" address, as it came to be called, was one of the most important and influential speeches in American history. Although the organizers of the exposition worried that "public sentiment was not prepared for such an advanced step," they decided that inviting a black speaker would impress Northern visitors with the evidence of racial progress in the South. Washington soothed his listeners' concerns about "uppity" blacks by claiming that his race would content itself with living "by the productions of our hands."

* * * * *

Mr. President and Gentlemen of the Board of Directors and Citizens:

One-third of the population of the South is of the Negro race. No enterprise seeking the material, civil, or moral welfare of this section can disregard this element of our population and reach the highest success. I but convey to you, Mr. President and Directors, the sentiment of the masses of my race when I say that in no way have the value and manhood of the American Negro been more fittingly and generously recognized than by the managers of this magnificent Exposition at every stage of its progress. It is a recognition that will do more to cement the friendship of the two races than any occurrence since the dawn of our freedom.

Not only this, but the opportunity here afforded will awaken among us a new era of industrial progress. Ignorant and inexperienced, it is not strange that in the first years of our new life we began at the top instead of at the bottom; that a seat in Congress or the state legislature was more sought than real estate or industrial skill; that the political convention or stump speaking had more attractions than starting a dairy farm or truck garden.

A ship lost at sea for many days suddenly sighted a friendly vessel. From the mast of the unfortunate vessel was seen a signal, "Water, water; we die of thirst!" The answer from the friendly vessel at once came back, "Cast down your bucket where you are." A second time the signal, "Water, water; send us water!" ran up from the distressed vessel, and was answered, "Cast down your bucket where you are." And a third and fourth signal for water was answered, "Cast down your bucket where you are. "The captain of the distressed vessel, at last heeding the injunction, cast down his bucket, and it came up full of fresh, sparkling water from the mouth of the Amazon River. To those of my race who depend on bettering their condition in a foreign land or who underestimate the importance of cultivating friendly relations with the Southern white man, who is their next-door neighbor, I would say: "Cast down your bucket where you are"—cast it down in making friends in every manly way of the people of all races by whom we are surrounded.

Cast it down in agriculture, mechanics, in commerce, in domestic service, and in the professions. And in this connection it is well to bear in mind that whatever other sins the South may be called to bear, when it comes to business, pure and simple, it is in the South that the Negro is given a man's chance in the commercial world, and in nothing is this Exposition more eloquent than in emphasizing this chance. Our greatest danger is that in the great

Source: Louis R. Harlan, ed., *The Booker T. Washington Papers*, Vol. 3, (Urbana: University of Illinois Press, 1974), 583–587.

leap from slavery to freedom we may overlook the fact that the masses of us are to live by the productions of our hands, and fail to keep in mind that we shall prosper in proportion as we learn to dignify and glorify common labour, and put brains and skill into the common occupations of life; shall prosper in proportion as we learn to draw the line between the superficial and the substantial, the ornamental gewgaws of life and the useful. No race can prosper till it learns that there is as much dignity in tilling a field as in writing a poem. It is at the bottom of life we must begin, and not at the top. Nor should we permit our grievances to overshadow our opportunities.

To those of the white race who look to the incoming of those of foreign birth and strange tongue and habits for the prosperity of the South, were I permitted I would repeat what I say to my, own race, "Cast down your bucket where you are." Cast it down among the eight millions of Negroes whose habits you know, whose fidelity and love you have tested in days when to have proved treacherous meant the ruin of your firesides. Cast down your bucket among these people who have, without strikes and labour wars, tilled your fields, cleared your forests, builded your railroads and cities, and brought forth treasures from the bowels of the earth, and helped make possible this magnificent representation of the progress of the South. Casting down your bucket among my people, helping and encouraging them as you are doing on these grounds, and to education of head, hand, and heart, you will find that they will buy your surplus land, make blossom the waste places in your fields, and run your factories. While doing this, you can be sure in the future, as in the past, that you and your families will be surrounded by the most patient, faithful, law-abiding, and unresentful people that the world has seen. As we have proved our loyalty to you in the past, in nursing your children, watching by the sick-bed of your mothers and fathers, and often following them with tear-dimmed eyes to their graves, so in the future, in our humble way, we shall stand by you with a devotion that no foreigner can approach, ready to lay down our lives, if need be, in defense of yours, interlacing our industrial, commercial, civil, and religious life with yours in a way that shall make the interests of both races one. In all things that are purely social we can be as separate as the fingers, yet one as the hand in all things essential to mutual progress.

There is no defense or security for any of us except in the highest intelligence and development of all. If anywhere there are efforts tending to curtail the fullest growth of the Negro, let these efforts be turned into stimulating, encouraging, and making him the most useful and intelligent citizen. Effort or means so invested will pay a thousand per cent interest. These efforts will be twice blessed—blessing him that gives and him that takes. There is no escape through law of man or God from the inevitable:

The laws of changeless justice bind Oppressor with oppressed;

And close as sin and suffering joined We march to fate abreast.

Nearly sixteen millions of hands will aid you in pulling the load upward, or they will pull against you the load downward. We shall constitute one-third and more of the ignorance and crime of the South, or one-third [of] its intelligence and progress; we shall contribute one-third to the business and industrial prosperity of the South, or we shall prove a veritable body of death, stagnating, depressing, retarding every effort to advance the body politic.

Gentlemen of the Exposition, as we present to you our humble effort at an exhibition of our progress, you must not expect overmuch. Starting thirty years ago with ownership here and there in a few quilts and pumpkins and chickens (gathered from miscellaneous sources), remember the path that has led from these to the inventions and production of agricultural implements, buggies, steam-engines, newspapers, books, statuary, carving, paintings, the management of drug stores and banks, has not been trodden without contact with thorns and thistles. While we take pride in what we exhibit as a result of our independent efforts, we do not for a moment forget that our part in this exhibition would fall far short of your expectations but for the constant help that has come to our educational life, not only from the Southern states, but especially from Northern philanthropists, who have made their gifts a constant stream of blessing and encouragement.

The wisest among my race understand that the agitation of questions of social equality is the extremest folly, and that progress in the enjoyment of all the privileges that will come to us must be the result of severe and constant struggle rather than of artificial forcing. No race that has anything to contribute to the markets of the world is long in any degree ostracized. It is important and right that all privileges of the law be ours, but it is vastly more important that we be prepared for the exercise of these privileges. The opportunity to earn a dollar in a factory just now is worth infinitely more than the opportunity to spend a dollar in an opera-house.

In conclusion, may I repeat that nothing in thirty years has given us more hope and encouragement, and drawn us so near to you of the white race, as this opportunity offered by the Exposition; and here bending, as it were, over the altar that represents the results of the struggles of your race and mine, both starting practically empty-handed three decades ago, I pledge that in your effort to work out the great and intricate problem which God has laid at the doors of the South, you shall have at all times the patient, sympathetic help of my race; only let this be constantly in mind, that, while from representations in these buildings of the product of field, of forest, of mine, of factory, letters, and art, much good will come, yet far above and beyond material benefits will be that higher good, that, let us pray God, will come, in a blotting out of sectional differences and racial animosities and suspicions, in a determination to administer absolute justice, in a willing obedience among all classes to the mandates of law. This, coupled with our material prosperity, will bring into our beloved South a new heaven and a new earth.

Plessy v. Ferguson

Supreme Court of the United States
(163 U.S. 537)

May 18, 1896

[*This is an abridged version of the document.*]

The statute of Louisiana, acts of 1890, c. 111, requiring railway companies carrying passengers in their coaches in that State, to provide equal, but separate, accommodations for the white and colored races, by providing two or more passenger coaches for each passenger train, or by dividing the passenger coaches by a partition so as to secure separate accommodations; and providing that no person shall be permitted to occupy seats in coaches other than the ones assigned to them, on account of the race they belong to; and requiring the officer of the passenger train to assign each passenger to the coach or compartment assigned for the race to which he or she belong; and imposing fines or imprisonment upon passengers insisting on going into a coach or compartment other than the one set aside for the race to which he or she belongs; and conferring upon officers of the train power to refuse to carry on the train passengers refusing to occupy the coach or compartment assigned to them, and exempting the railway company from liability for such refusal, are not in conflict with the provisions either of the Thirteenth Amendment or of the Fourteenth Amendment to the Constitution of the United States.

This was a petition for writs of prohibition and certiorari, originally filed in the Supreme Court of the State by Plessy, the plaintiff in error, against the Hon. John H. Ferguson, judge of the criminal District Court for the parish of Orleans, and setting forth in substance the following facts:

That petitioner was a citizen of the United States and a resident of the State of Louisiana, of mixed descent, in the proportion of seven eighths Caucasian and one eighth African blood; that the mixture of colored blood was not discernible in him, and that he was entitled to every recognition, right, privilege and immunity secured to the citizens of the United States of the white race by its Constitution and laws; that,

on June 7, 1892, he engaged and paid for a first class passage on the East Louisiana Railway from New Orleans to Covington, in the same State, and thereupon entered a passenger train, and took possession of a vacant seat in a coach where passengers of the white race were accommodated; that such railroad company was incorporated by the laws of Louisiana as a common carrier, and was not authorized to distinguish between citizens according to their race. But, notwithstanding this, petitioner was required by the conductor, under penalty of ejection from said train and imprisonment, to vacate said coach and occupy another seat in a coach assigned by said company for persons not of the white race, and for no other reason than that petitioner was of the colored race; that, upon petitioner's refusal to comply with such order, he was, with the aid of a police officer, forcibly ejected from said coach and hurried off to and imprisoned in the parish jail of New Orleans, and there held to answer a charge made by such officer to the effect that he was guilty of having criminally violated an act of the General Assembly of the State, approved July 10, 1890, in such case made and provided.

That petitioner was subsequently brought before the recorder of the city for preliminary examination and committed for trial to the criminal District Court for the parish of Orleans, where an information was filed against him in the matter above set forth, for a violation of the above act, which act the petitioner affirmed to be null and void, because in conflict with the Constitution of the United States. . . .

MR. JUSTICE BROWN, after stating the case, delivered the opinion of the court.

This case turns upon the constitutionality of an act of the General Assembly of the State of Louisiana, passed in 1890, providing for separate railway carriages for the white and colored races. . . .

The constitutionality of this act is attacked upon the ground that it conflicts both with the Thirteenth Amendment of the Constitution, abolishing slavery, and the Fourteenth Amendment, which prohibits certain restrictive legislation on the part of the States.

1. That it does not conflict with the Thirteenth Amendment, which abolished slavery and involuntary servitude, except as a punishment for crime, is too clear for argument. Slavery implies involuntary servitude—a state of bondage; the ownership of mankind as a chattel, or at least the control of the labor and services of one man for the benefit of another, and the absence of a legal right to the disposal of his own person, property and services. . . .

A statute which implies merely a legal distinction between the white and colored races—a distinction which is founded in the color of the two races and which must always exist so long as white men are distinguished from the other race by color—has no tendency to destroy the legal equality of the two races, or reestablish a state of involuntary servitude. Indeed, we do not understand that the Thirteenth Amendment is strenuously relied upon by the plaintiff in error in this connection.

2. By the Fourteenth Amendment, all persons born or naturalized in the United States and subject to the jurisdiction thereof are made citizens of the United States and of the State wherein they reside, and the States are forbidden from making or enforcing any law which shall abridge the privileges or immunities of citizens of the United States, or shall deprive any person of life, liberty, or property without due process of law, or deny to any person within their jurisdiction the equal protection of the laws. . . .

The object of the amendment was undoubtedly to enforce the absolute equality of the two races before the law, but, in the nature of things, it could not have been intended to abolish distinctions based upon color, or to enforce social, as distinguished from political, equality, or a commingling of the two races upon terms unsatisfactory to either. Laws permitting, and even requiring, their separation in places where they are liable to be brought into contact do not necessarily imply the inferiority of either race to the other, and have been generally, if not universally, recognized as within the competency of the state legislatures in the exercise of their police power. The most common instance of this is connected with the establishment of separate schools for white and colored children, which has been held to be a valid exercise of the legislative power even by courts of States where the political rights of the colored race have been longest and most earnestly enforced. . . .

We think the enforced separation of the races, as applied to the internal commerce of the State, neither abridges the privileges or immunities of the colored man, deprives him of his property without due process of law, nor denies him the equal protection of the laws within the meaning of the Fourteenth Amendment. . . .

We consider the underlying fallacy of the plaintiff's argument to consist in the assumption that the enforced separation of the two races stamps the colored race with a badge of inferiority. If this be so, it is not by reason of anything found in the act, but solely because the colored race chooses to put that construction upon it. The argument necessarily assumes that if, as has been more than once the case and is not unlikely to be so again, the colored race should become the dominant power in the state legislature, and should enact a law in precisely similar terms, it would thereby relegate the white race to an inferior position. We imagine that the white race, at least, would not acquiesce in this assumption. The argument also assumes that social prejudices may be overcome by legislation, and that equal rights cannot be secured to the negro except by an enforced commingling of the two races. We cannot accept this proposition. If the two races are to meet upon terms of social equality, it must be the result of natural affinities, a mutual appreciation of each other's merits, and a voluntary consent of individuals. As was said by the Court of Appeals of New York in *People v. Gallagher*, 93 N. Y. 438, 448, "this end can neither be accomplished nor promoted by laws which conflict with the general sentiment of the community upon whom they are designed to operate. When the government, therefore, has secured to each of its citizens equal rights before the law and equal opportunities for improvement and progress, it has accomplished the end for which it was organized, and performed all of the functions respecting social advantages with which it is endowed."

Legislation is powerless to eradicate racial instincts or to abolish distinctions based upon physical differences, and the attempt to do so can only result in accentuating the difficulties of the present situation. If the civil and political rights of both races be equal, one cannot be inferior to the other civilly or politically. If one race be inferior to the other socially, the Constitution of the United States cannot put them upon the same plane. . . .

The judgment of the court below is, therefore, Affirmed.

MR. JUSTICE HARLAN, dissenting.

We have before us a state enactment that compels, under penalties, the separation of the two races in railroad passenger coaches, and makes it a crime for a citizen of either race to enter a coach that has been assigned to citizens of the other race.

Thus, the State regulates the use of a public highway by citizens of the United States solely upon the basis of race.

However apparent the injustice of such legislation may be, we have only to consider whether it is consistent with the Constitution of the United States. . . .

In respect of civil rights common to all citizens, the Constitution of the United States does not, I think, permit any public authority to know the race of those entitled to be protected in the enjoyment of such rights. Every true man has pride of race, and, under appropriate circumstances, when the rights of others, his equals before the law, are not to be affected, it is his privilege to express such pride and to take such action based upon it as to him seems proper. But I deny that any legislative body or judicial tribunal may have regard to the race of citizens when the civil rights of those citizens are involved. Indeed, such legislation as that here in question is inconsistent not only with that equality of rights which pertains to citizenship, National and State, but with the personal liberty enjoyed by everyone within the United States.

The Thirteenth Amendment does not permit the withholding or the deprivation of any right necessarily inhering in freedom. It not only struck down the institution of slavery as previously existing in the United States, but it prevents the imposition of any burdens or disabilities that constitute badges of slavery or servitude. It decreed universal civil freedom in this country. This court has so adjudged. But that amendment having been found inadequate to the protection of the rights of those who had been in slavery, it was followed by the Fourteenth

Amendment, which added greatly to the dignity and glory of American citizenship and to the security of personal liberty by declaring that "all persons born or naturalized in the United States, and subject to the jurisdiction thereof, are citizens of the United States and of the State wherein they reside," and that "no State shall make or enforce any law which shall abridge the privileges or immunities of citizens of the United States; nor shall any State deprive any person of life, liberty or property without due process of law, nor deny to any person within its jurisdiction the equal protection of the laws."

These two amendments, if enforced according to their true intent and meaning, will protect all the civil rights that pertain to freedom and citizenship. Finally, and to the end that no citizen should be denied, on account of his race, the privilege of participating in the political control of his country, it was declared by the Fifteenth Amendment that "the right of citizens of the United States to vote shall not be denied or abridged by the United States or by any State on account of race, color or previous condition of servitude."

These notable additions to the fundamental law were welcomed by the friends of liberty throughout the world. They removed the race line from our governmental systems. They had, as this court has said, a common purpose, namely to secure "to a race recently emancipated, a race that through many generations have been held in slavery, all the civil rights that the superior race enjoy."

They declared, in legal effect, this court has further said, "that the law in the States shall be the same for the black as for the white; that all persons, whether colored or white, shall stand equal before the laws of the States, and, in regard to the colored race, for whose protection the amendment was primarily designed, that no discrimination shall be made against them by law because of their color." . . .

It was said in argument that the statute of Louisiana does not discriminate against either race, but prescribes a rule applicable alike to white and colored citizens. But this argument does not meet the difficulty. Everyone knows that the statute in question had its origin in the purpose not so much to exclude white persons from railroad cars occupied by blacks as to exclude colored people from coaches occupied by or assigned to white persons. Railroad corporations of Louisiana did not make discrimination among whites in the matter of accommodation for travelers. The thing to accomplish was, under the guise of giving equal accommodation for whites and blacks, to compel the latter to keep to themselves while traveling in railroad passenger coaches. No one would be so wanting in candor as to assert the contrary. The fundamental objection, therefore, to the statute is that it interferes with the personal freedom of citizens. . . .

It is one thing for railroad carriers to furnish, or to be required by law to furnish, equal accommodations for all whom they are under a legal duty to carry. It is quite another thing for government to forbid citizens of the white and black races from traveling in the same public conveyance, and to punish officers of railroad companies for permitting persons of the two races to occupy the same passenger coach. If a State can prescribe, as a rule of civil conduct, that whites and blacks shall not travel as passengers in the same railroad coach, why may it not so regulate the use of the streets of its cities and towns as to compel white citizens to keep on one side of a street and black citizens to keep on the other? Why may it not, upon like grounds, punish whites and blacks who ride together in streetcars or in open vehicles on a public road or street? Why may it not require sheriffs to assign whites to one side of a courtroom and blacks to the other? And why may it not also prohibit the commingling of the two races in the galleries of legislative halls or in public assemblages convened for the consideration of the political questions of the day? Further, if this statute of Louisiana is consistent with the personal liberty of citizens, why may not the State require the separation in railroad coaches of native and naturalized citizens of the United States, or of Protestants and Roman Catholics? . . .

The white race deems itself to be the dominant race in this country. And so it is in prestige, in achievements, in education, in wealth and in power. So, I doubt not, it will continue to be for all time if it remains true to its great heritage and holds fast to the principles of constitutional liberty. But in view of the Constitution, in the eye of the law, there is in this country no superior, dominant, ruling class of citizens. There is no caste here. Our Constitution is color-blind, and neither knows nor tolerates classes among citizens. In respect of civil rights, all citizens are equal before the law. The humblest is the peer of the most powerful. The law regards man as man, and takes no account of his surroundings or of his color when his civil rights as guaranteed by the supreme law of the land are involved. It is therefore to be regretted that this high tribunal, the final expositor of the fundamental law of the land, has reached the conclusion that it is competent for a State to regulate the enjoyment by citizens of their civil rights solely upon the basis of race.

In my opinion, the judgment this day rendered will, in time, prove to be quite as pernicious as the decision made by this tribunal in the *Dred Scott Case*. It was adjudged in that case that the descendants of Africans who were imported into this country and sold as slaves were not included nor intended to be included under the word "citizens" in the Constitution, and could not claim any of the rights and privileges which that instrument provided for and secured to citizens of the United States; that, at the time of the adoption of the Constitution, they were "considered as a subordinate and inferior class of beings, who had been subjugated by the dominant race, and, whether emancipated or not, yet remained subject to their authority, and had no rights or privileges but such as those who held the power and the government might choose to grant them."

The recent amendments of the Constitution, it was supposed, had eradicated these principles from our institutions. But it seems that we have yet, in some of the States, a dominant race—a superior class of citizens, which assumes to regulate the enjoyment of civil rights, common to all citizens, upon the basis of race. The present decision, it may well be apprehended, will not only stimulate aggressions, more or less brutal and irritating, upon the admitted rights of colored citizens, but will encourage the belief that it is possible, by means of state enactments, to defeat the beneficent purposes which the people of the United States had in view when they adopted the recent amendments of the Constitution, by one of which the blacks of this country were made citizens of the United States and of the States in which they respectively reside, and whose privileges and immunities, as citizens, the States are forbidden to abridge. Sixty millions of whites are in no danger from the presence here of eight millions of blacks. The destinies of the two races in this country are indissolubly linked together, and the interests of both require that the common government of all shall not permit the seeds of race hate to be planted under the sanction of law. What can more certainly arouse race hate, what more certainly create and perpetuate a feeling of distrust between these races, than state enactments which, in fact, proceed on the ground that colored citizens are so inferior and degraded that they cannot be allowed to sit in public coaches occupied by white citizens. That, as all will admit, is the real meaning of such legislation as was enacted in Louisiana.

The sure guarantee of the peace and security of each race is the clear, distinct, unconditional recognition by our governments, National and State, of every right that inheres in civil freedom, and of the equality before the law of all citizens of the United States, without regard to race. State enactments regulating the enjoyment of civil rights upon the basis of race, and cunningly devised to defeat legitimate results of the war under the pretence of recognizing equality of rights, can have no other result than to render permanent peace impossible and to keep alive a conflict of races the continuance of which must do harm to all concerned. This question is not met by the suggestion that social equality cannot exist between the white and black races in this country. That argument, if it can be properly regarded as one, is scarcely worthy of consideration, for social equality no more exists between two races when traveling in a passenger coach or a public highway than when members of the same races sit by each other in a street car or in the jury box, or stand or sit with each other in a political assembly, or when they use in common the street of a city or town, or when they are in the same room for the purpose of having their names placed on the registry of voters, or when they approach the ballot box in order to exercise the high privilege of voting.

There is a race so different from our own that we do not permit those belonging to it to become citizens of the United States. Persons belonging to it are, with few exceptions, absolutely excluded from our country. I allude to the Chinese race. But, by the statute in question, a Chinaman can ride in the same passenger coach with white citizens of the United States, while citizens of the black race in Louisiana, many of whom, perhaps, risked their lives for the preservation of the Union, who are entitled, by law, to participate in the political control of the State and

nation, who are not excluded, by law or by reason of their race, from public stations of any kind, and who have all the legal rights that belong to white citizens, are yet declared to be criminals, liable to imprisonment, if they ride in a public coach occupied by citizens of the white race. It is scarcely just to say that a colored citizen should not object to occupying a public coach assigned to his own race. He does not object, nor, perhaps, would he object to separate coaches for his race if his rights under the law were recognized. But he objecting, and ought never to cease objecting, to the proposition that citizens of the white and black race can be adjudged criminals because they sit, or claim the right to sit, in the same public coach on a public highway.

The arbitrary separation of citizens on the basis of race while they are on a public highway is a badge of servitude wholly inconsistent with the civil freedom and the equality before the law established by the Constitution. It cannot be justified upon any legal grounds.

If evils will result from the commingling of the two races upon public highways established for the benefit of all, they will be infinitely less than those that will surely come from state legislation regulating the enjoyment of civil rights upon the basis of race. We boast of the freedom enjoyed by our people above all other peoples. But it is difficult to reconcile that boast with a state of the law which, practically, puts the brand of servitude and degradation upon a large class of our fellow citizens, our equals before the law. The thin disguise of "equal" accommodations for passengers in railroad coaches will not mislead anyone, nor atone for the wrong this day done. . . .

I am of opinion that the statute of Louisiana is inconsistent with the personal liberty of citizens, white and black, in that State, and hostile to both the spirit and letter of the Constitution of the United States. If laws of like character should be enacted in the several States of the Union, the effect would be in the highest degree mischievous. Slavery, as an institution tolerated by law would, it is true, have disappeared from our country, but there would remain a power in the States, by sinister legislation, to interfere with the full enjoyment of the blessings of freedom to regulate civil rights, common to all citizens, upon the basis of race, and to place in a condition of legal inferiority a large body of American citizens now constituting a part of the political community called the People of the United States, for whom and by whom, through representatives, our government is administered. Such a system is inconsistent with the guarantee given by the Constitution to each State of a republican form of government, and may be stricken down by Congressional action, or by the courts in the discharge of their solemn duty to maintain the supreme law of the land, anything in the constitution or laws of any State to the contrary notwithstanding.

For the reasons stated, I am constrained to withhold my assent from the opinion and judgment of the majority.

Who Is Permanently Hurt?

June 1896

Booker T. Washington

The United States Supreme Court has recently handed down a decision declaring the separate coach law, or "Jim Crow" car law constitutional. What does this mean? Simply that the separation of colored and white passengers as now practiced in certain Southern States, is lawful and constitutional.

This separation may be good law, but it is not good common sense. The difference in the color of the skin is a matter for which nature is responsible. If the Supreme Court can say that it is lawful to compel all persons with black skins to ride in one car, and all with white skins to ride in another, why may it not say that it is lawful to put all yellow people in one car and all white people, whose skin is sun burnt, in another car. Nature has given both their color; or why cannot the courts go further and decide that all men with bald heads must ride in one car and all with red hair still in another. Nature is responsible for all these conditions.

But the colored people do not complain so much of the separation, as of the fact that the accommodations, with almost no exceptions, are not equal, still the same price is charged the colored passengers as is charged the white people.

Now the point of all this article is not to make a complaint against the white man or the "Jim Crow Car" law, but it is simply to say that such an unjust law injures the white man, and inconveniences the negro. No race can wrong another race simply because it has the power to do so, without being permanently injured in morals, and its ideas of justice. The negro can endure the temporary inconvenience, but the injury to the white man is permanent. It is the one who inflicts the wrong that is hurt, rather than the one on whom the wrong is inflicted. It is for the white man to save himself from this degradation that I plead.

If a white man steals a negro's ballot, it is the white man who is permanently injured. Physical death comes to the negro lynched—death of the morals—death of the soul—comes to the white man who perpetrates the lynching.

Souls of Black Folk, Chapters 3, 4, 6

3. Of Mr. Booker T. Washington and Others

W. E. B. Du Bois

From birth till death enslaved; in word, in deed, unmanned!

. . . .

Hereditary bondsmen! Know ye not
Who would be free themselves must strike the blow?

Byron

* * * * *

Easily the most striking thing in the history of the American Negro since 1876 is the ascendancy of Mr. Booker T. Washington. It began at the time when war memories and ideals were rapidly passing; a day of astonishing commercial development was dawning; a sense of doubt and hesitation overtook the freedmen's sons,—then it was that his leading began. Mr. Washington came, with a simple definite programme, at the psychological moment when the nation was a little ashamed of having bestowed so much sentiment on Negroes, and was concentrating its energies on Dollars. His programme of industrial education, conciliation of the South, and submission and silence as to civil and political rights, was not wholly original; the Free Negroes from 1830 up to wartime had striven to build industrial schools, and the American Missionary Association had from the first taught various trades; and Price and others had sought a way of honorable alliance with the best of the Southerners. But Mr. Washington first indissolubly linked these things; he put enthusiasm, unlimited energy, and perfect faith into this programme, and changed it from a by-path into a veritable Way of Life. And the tale of the methods by which lie did this is a fascinating study of human life.

It startled the nation to hear a Negro advocating such a programme after many decades of bitter complaint; it startled and won the applause of the South, it interested and won the admiration of the North; and after a confused murmur of protest, it silenced if it did not convert the Negroes themselves.

To gain the sympathy and cooperation of the various elements comprising the white South was Mr. Washington's first task; and this, at the time Tuskegee was founded, seemed, for a black man, well-nigh impossible. And yet ten years later it was done in the word spoken at Atlanta: "In all things purely social we can be as separate as the five fingers, and yet one as the hand in all things essential to mutual progress." This "Atlanta Compromise" is by all odds the most notable thing in Mr. Washington's career. The South interpreted it in different ways: the radicals received it as a complete surrender of the demand for civil and political equality; the conservatives, as a generously conceived working basis for mutual understanding. So both approved it, and to-day its author is certainly the most distinguished Southerner since Jefferson Davis, and the one with the largest personal following.

Next to this achievement comes Mr. Washington's work in gaining place and consideration in the North. Others less shrewd and tactful had formerly essayed to sit on these two stools and had fallen between them; but as Mr. Washington knew the heart of the South from birth and training, so by singular insight he intuitively grasped the spirit of the age which was dominating the North. And so thoroughly did he learn the speech and thought of triumphant commercialism, and the ideals of material prosperity, that the picture of a lone black boy poring over a French grammar amid the weeds and dirt of a neglected home soon seemed to him the acme of absurdities. One wonders what Socrates and St. Francis of Assisi would say to this.

And yet this very singleness of vision and thorough oneness with his age is a mark of the successful man. It is as though Nature must needs make men narrow in order to give them force. So Mr. Washington's cult has gained unquestioning followers, his work has wonderfully prospered, his friends are legion, and his enemies are confounded. To-day he stands as the one recognized spokesman of his ten million fellows, and one of the most notable figures in a nation of seventy millions. One hesitates, therefore, to criticise a life which, beginning with so little, has done so much. And yet the time is come when one may speak in all sincerity and utter courtesy of the mistakes and shortcomings of Mr. Washington's career, as well as of his triumphs, without being thought captious or envious, and without forgetting that it is easier to do ill than well in the world.

The criticism that has hitherto met Mr. Washington has not always been of this broad character. In the South especially has he had to walk warily to avoid the harshest judgments,—and naturally so, for he is dealing with the one subject of deepest sensitiveness to that section. Twice—once when at the Chicago celebration of the Spanish-American War he alluded to the color-prejudice that is "eating away the vitals of the South," and once when he dined with President Roosevelt—has the resulting Southern criticism been violent enough to threaten seriously his popularity. In the North the feeling has several times forced itself into words, that Mr. Washington's counsels of submission overlooked certain elements of true manhood, and that his educational programme was unnecessarily narrow. Usually, however, such criticism has not found

open expression, although, too, the spiritual sons of the Abolitionists have not been prepared to acknowledge that the schools founded before Tuskegee, by men of broad ideals and self-sacrificing spirit, were wholly failures or worthy of ridicule. While, then, criticism has not failed to follow Mr. Washington, yet the prevailing public opinion of the land has been but too willing to deliver the solution of a wearisome problem into his hands, and say, "If that is all you and your race ask, take it."

Among his own people, however, Mr. Washington has encountered the strongest and most lasting opposition, amounting at times to bitterness, and even to-day continuing strong and insistent even though largely silenced in outward expression by the public opinion of the nation. Some of this opposition is, of course, mere envy; the disappointment of displaced demagogues and the spite of narrow minds. But aside from this, there is among educated and thoughtful colored men in all parts of the land a feeling of deep regret, sorrow, and apprehension at the wide currency and ascendancy which some of Mr. Washington's theories have gained. These same men admire his sincerity of purpose, and are willing to forgive much to honest endeavor which is doing something worth the doing. They cooperate with Mr. Washington as far as they conscientiously can; and, indeed, it is no ordinary tribute to this man's tact and power that, steering as he must between so many diverse interests and opinions, he so largely retains the respect of all.

But the hushing of the criticism of honest opponents is a dangerous thing. It leads some of the best of the critics to unfortunate silence and paralysis of effort, and others to burst into speech so passionately and intemperately as to lose listeners. Honest and earnest criticism from those whose interests are most nearly touched,—criticism of writers by readers, of government by those governed, of leaders by those led,—this is the soul of democracy and the safeguard of modern society. If the best of the American Negroes receive by outer pressure a leader whom they had not recognized before, manifestly there is here a certain palpable gain. Yet there is also irreparable loss,—a loss of that peculiarly valuable education which a group receives when by search and criticism it finds and commissions its own leaders. The way in which this is done is at once the most elementary and the nicest problem of social growth. History is but the record of such group-leadership; and yet how infinitely changeful is its type and character! And of all types and kinds, what can be more instructive than the leadership of a group within a group?—that curious double movement where real progress may be negative and actual advance be relative retrogression. All this is the social student's inspiration and despair.

Now in the past the American Negro has had instructive experience in the choosing of group leaders, founding thus a peculiar dynasty which in the light of present conditions is worth while studying. When sticks and stones and beasts form the sole environment of a people, their attitude is largely one of determined opposition to and conquest of natural forces. But when to earth and brute is added an environment of men and ideas, then the attitude of the imprisoned group may take three main forms,—a feeling of revolt and revenge; an attempt to adjust all thought and action to the will of the greater group; or, finally, a determined effort at self-realization and self-development despite environing opinion. The influence of all of these attitudes at various times can be traced in the history of the American Negro, and in the evolution of his successive leaders.

Before 1750, while the fire of African freedom still burned in the veins of the slaves, there was in all leadership or attempted leadership but the one motive of revolt and revenge,—typified in the terrible Maroons, the Danish blacks, and Cato of Stono, and veiling all the Americas in fear of insurrection. The liberalizing tendencies of the latter half of the eighteenth century brought, along with kindlier relations between black and white, thoughts of ultimate adjustment and assimilation. Such aspiration was especially voiced in the earnest songs of Phyllis, in the martyrdom of Attucks, the fighting of Salem and Poor, the intellectual accomplishments of Banneker and Derham, and the political demands of the Cuffes.

Stern financial and social stress after the war cooled much of the previous humanitarian ardor. The disappointment and impatience of the Negroes at the persistence of slavery and serfdom voiced itself in two movements. The slaves in the South, aroused undoubtedly by vague rumors of the Haytian revolt, made three fierce attempts at insurrection,—in 1800 under Gabriel in Virginia, in 1822 under Vesey in Carolina, and in 1831 again in Virginia under the terrible Nat Turner. In the Free States, on the other hand, a new and curious attempt at self-development was made. In Philadelphia and New York color-prescription led to a withdrawal of Negro communicants from white churches and the formation of a peculiar socio-religious institution among the Negroes known as the African Church,—an organization still living and controlling in its various branches over a million of men.

Walker's wild appeal against the trend of the times showed how the world was changing after the coming of the cotton-gin. By 1830 slavery seemed hopelessly fastened on the South, and the slaves thoroughly cowed into submission. The free Negroes of the North, inspired by the mulatto immigrants from the West Indies, began to change the basis of their demands; they recognized the slavery of slaves, but insisted that they themselves were freemen, and sought assimilation and amalgamation with the nation on the same terms with other men. Thus, Forten and Purvis of Philadelphia, Shad of Wilmington, Du Bois of New Haven, Barbadoes of Boston, and others, strove singly and together as men, they said, not as slaves; as "people of color," not as "Negroes." The trend of the times, however, refused them recognition save in individual and exceptional cases, considered them as one with all the despised blacks, and they soon found themselves striving to keep even the rights they formerly had of voting and working and moving as freemen. Schemes of migration and colonization arose among them; but these they refused to entertain, and they eventually turned to the Abolition movement as a final refuge.

Here, led by Remond, Nell, Wells-Brown, and Douglass, a new period of self-assertion and self-development dawned. To be sure, ultimate freedom and assimilation was the ideal before the leaders, but the assertion of the manhood rights of the Negro by himself was the main reliance, and John Brown's raid was the extreme of its logic. After the war and emancipation, the great form of Frederick Douglass, the greatest of American Negro leaders, still led the host. Self-assertion, especially in political lines, was the main programme, and behind Douglass came Elliot, Bruce, and Langston, and the Reconstruction politicians, and, less conspicuous but of greater social significance, Alexander Crummell and Bishop Daniel Payne.

Then came the Revolution of 1876, the suppression of the Negro votes, the changing and shifting of ideals, and the seeking of new lights in the great night. Douglass, in his old age, still bravely stood for the ideals of his early manhood,—ultimate assimilation *through* self-assertion, on no other terms. For a time Price arose as a new leader, destined, it seemed, not to give up, but to re-state the old ideals in a form less repugnant to the white South. But he passed away in his prime. Then came the new leader. Nearly all the former ones had become leaders by the silent suffrage of their fellows, had sought to lead their own people alone, and were usually, save Douglass, little known outside their race. But Booker T. Washington arose as essentially the leader not of one race but of two,—a compromiser between the South, the North, and the Negro. Naturally the Negroes resented, at first bitterly, signs of compromise which surrendered their civil and political rights, even though this was to be exchanged for larger chances of economic development. The rich and dominating North, however, was not only weary of the race problem, but was investing largely in Southern enterprises, and welcomed any method of peaceful cooperation. Thus, by national opinion, the Negroes began to recognize Mr. Washington's leadership; and the voice of criticism was hushed.

Mr. Washington represents in Negro thought the old attitude of adjustment and submission; but adjustment at such a peculiar time as to make his programme unique. This is an age of unusual economic development, and Mr. Washington's programme naturally takes an economic cast, becoming a gospel of Work and Money to such an extent as apparently almost completely to overshadow the higher aims of life. Moreover, this is an age when the more advanced races are coming in closer contact with the less developed races, and the race-feeling is therefore intensified; and Mr. Washington's programme practically accepts the alleged inferiority of the Negro races. Again, in our own land, the reaction from the sentiment of war time has given impetus to race-prejudice against Negroes, and Mr. Washington withdraws many of the high demands of Negroes as men and American citizens. In other periods of intensified prejudice all the Negro's tendency to self-assertion has been called forth; at this period a policy of submission is advocated. In the history of nearly all other races and peoples the doctrine preached at such crises has been that manly self-respect is worth more than lands and houses, and that a people who voluntarily surrender such respect, or cease striving for it, are not worth civilizing.

In answer to this, it has been claimed that the Negro can survive only through submission. Mr. Washington distinctly asks that black people give up, at least for the present, three things,—

First, political power,

Second, insistence on civil rights,

Third, higher education of Negro youth,—and concentrate all their energies on industrial education, the accumulation of wealth, and the conciliation of the South. This policy has been courageously and insistently advocated for over fifteen years, and has been triumphant for perhaps ten years. As a result of this tender of the palm-branch, what has been the return? In these years there have occurred:

1. The disfranchisement of the Negro.
2. The legal creation of a distinct status of civil inferiority for the Negro.
3. The steady withdrawal of aid from institutions for the higher training of the Negro.

These movements are not, to be sure, direct results of Mr. Washington's teachings; but his propaganda has, without a shadow of doubt, helped their speedier accomplishment. The question then comes: Is it possible, and probable, that nine millions of men can make effective progress in economic lines if they are deprived of political rights, made a servile caste, and allowed only the most meagre chance for developing their exceptional men? If history and reason give any distinct answer to these questions, it is an emphatic *No.* And Mr. Washington thus faces the triple paradox of his career:

1. He is striving nobly to make Negro artisans business men and property-owners; but it is utterly impossible, under modern competitive methods, for workingmen and property-owners to defend their rights and exist without the right of suffrage.
2. He insists on thrift and self-respect, but at the same time counsels a silent submission to civic inferiority such as is bound to sap the manhood of any race in the long run.
3. He advocates common-school and industrial training, and depreciates institutions of higher learning; but neither the Negro common schools, nor Tuskegee itself, could remain open a day were it not for teachers trained in Negro colleges, or trained by their graduates.

This triple paradox in Mr. Washington's position is the object of criticism by two classes of colored Americans. One class is spiritually descended from Toussaint the Savior, through Gabriel, Vesey, and Turner, and they represent the attitude of revolt and revenge; they hate the white South blindly and distrust the white race generally, and so far as they agree on definite action, think that the Negro's only hope lies in emigration beyond the borders of the United States. And yet, by the irony of fate, nothing has more effectually made this programme seem hopeless than the recent course of the United States toward weaker and darker peoples in the West Indies, Hawaii, and the Philippines,—for where in the world may we go and be safe from lying and brute force?

The other class of Negroes who cannot agree with Mr. Washington has hitherto said little aloud. They deprecate the sight of scattered counsels, of internal disagreement; and especially they dislike making their just criticism of a useful and earnest man an excuse for a general discharge of venom from small-minded opponents. Nevertheless, the questions involved are so fundamental and serious that it is difficult to see how men like the Grimkes, Kelly Miller, J. W. E. Bowen, and other representatives of this group, can much longer be silent. Such men feel in conscience bound to ask of this nation three things:

1. The right to vote.
2. Civic equality.
3. The education of youth according to ability.

They acknowledge Mr. Washington's invaluable service in counselling patience and courtesy in such demands; they do not ask that ignorant black men vote when ignorant whites are debarred, or that any reasonable restrictions in the suffrage should not be applied; they know that the low social level of the mass of the race is responsible for much discrimination against it, but they also know, and the nation knows, that relentless color-prejudice is more often a cause than a result of the Negro's degradation; they seek the abatement of this relic of barbarism, and not its systematic encouragement and pampering by all agencies of social power from the Associated Press to the Church of Christ. They advocate, with Mr. Washington, a broad system of Negro common schools supplemented by thorough industrial training; but they are surprised that a man of Mr. Washington s insight cannot see that no such educational system ever has rested or can rest on any other basis than that of the well-equipped college and university, and they insist that there is a demand for a few such institutions throughout the south to train the best of the Negro youth as teachers, professional men, and leaders.

This group of men honor Mr. Washington for his attitude of conciliation toward the white South;

they accept the "Atlanta Compromise" in its broadest interpretation; they recognize, with him, many signs of promise, many men of high purpose and fair judgment, in this section; they know that no easy task has been laid upon a region already tottering under heavy burdens. But, nevertheless, they insist that the way to truth and right lies in straightforward honesty, not in indiscriminate flattery; in praising those of the South who do well and criticising uncompromisingly those who do ill; in taking advantage of the opportunities at hand and urging their fellows to do the same, but at the same time in remembering that only a firm adherence to their higher ideals and aspirations will ever keep those ideals within the realm of possibility. They do not expect that the free right to vote, to enjoy civic rights, and to be educated, will come in a moment; they do not expect to see the bias and prejudices of years disappear at the blast of a trumpet; but they are absolutely certain that the way for a people to gain their reasonable rights is not by voluntarily throwing them away and insisting that they do not want them; that the way for a people to gain respect is not by continually belittling and ridiculing themselves; that, on the contrary, Negroes must insist continually, in season and out of season, that voting is necessary to modern manhood, that color discrimination is barbarism, and that black boys need education as well as white boys.

In failing thus to state plainly and unequivocally the legitimate demands of their people, even at the cost of opposing an honored leader, the thinking classes of American Negroes would shirk a heavy responsibility,—a responsibility to themselves, a responsibility to the struggling masses, a responsibility to the darker races of men whose future depends so largely on this American experiment, but especially a responsibility to this nation,—this common Fatherland. It is wrong to encourage a man or a people in evil-doing; it is wrong to aid and abet a national crime simply because it is unpopular not to do so. The growing spirit of kindliness and reconciliation between the North and South after the frightful differences of a generation ago ought to be a source of deep congratulation to all, and especially to those whose mistreatment caused the war; but if that reconciliation is to be marked by the industrial slavery and civic death of those same black men, with permanent legislation into a position of inferiority, then those black men, if they are really men, are called upon by every consideration of patriotism and loyalty to oppose such a course by all civilized methods, even though such opposition involves disagreement with Mr. Booker T. Washington. We have no right to sit silently by while the inevitable seeds are sown for a harvest of disaster to our children, black and white.

First, it is the duty of black men to judge the South discriminatingly. The present generation of Southerners are not responsible for the past, and they should not be blindly hated or blamed for it. Furthermore, to no class is the indiscriminate endorsement of the recent course of the South toward Negroes more nauseating than to the best thought of the South. The South is not "solid"; it is a land in the ferment of social change, wherein forces of all kinds are fighting for supremacy; and to praise the ill the South is to-day perpetrating is just as wrong as to condemn the good. Discriminating and broad-minded criticism is what the South needs,—needs it for the sake of her own white sons and daughters, and for the insurance of robust, healthy mental and moral development.

To-day even the attitude of the Southern whites toward the blacks is not, as so many assume, in all cases the same; the ignorant Southerner hates the Negro, the workingmen fear his competition, the moneymakers wish to use him as a laborer, some of the educated see a menace in his upward development, while others—usually the sons of the masters—wish to help him to rise. National opinion has enabled this last class to maintain the Negro common schools, and to protect the Negro partially in property, life, and limb. Through the pressure of the moneymakers, the Negro is in danger of being reduced to semi-slavery, especially in the country districts; the workingmen, and those of the educated who fear the Negro, have united to disfranchise him, and some have urged his deportation; while the passions of the ignorant are easily aroused to lynch and abuse any black man. To praise this intricate whirl of thought and prejudice is nonsense; to inveigh indiscriminately against "the South" is unjust; but to use the same breath in praising Governor Aycock, exposing Senator Morgan, arguing with Mr. Thomas Nelson Page, and denouncing Senator Ben Tillman, is not only sane, but the imperative duty of thinking black men.

It would be unjust to Mr. Washington not to acknowledge that in several instances he has opposed movements in the South which were unjust to the Negro; he sent memorials to the Louisiana and Alabama constitutional conventions, he has spoken against lynching, and in other ways has openly or silently set his influence against sinister schemes and unfortunate happenings. Notwithstanding this, it is equally true to assert that on the whole the distinct impression left by Mr. Washington's propaganda is, first, that the South is justified in its present attitude toward the Negro because of the Negro's degradation; secondly, that the prime cause of the Negro's failure to rise more quickly is his wrong education in the past; and, thirdly, that his future rise depends primarily on his own efforts. Each of these propositions is a dangerous half-truth. The supplementary truths must never be lost sight of: first, slavery and race-prejudice are potent if not sufficient causes of the Negro's position; second, industrial and common-school training were necessarily slow in planting because they had to await the black teachers trained by higher institutions,—it being extremely doubtful if any essentially different development was possible, and certainly a Tuskegee was unthinkable before 1880; and, third, while it is a great truth to say that the Negro must strive and strive mightily to help himself, it is equally true that unless his striving be not simply seconded, but rather aroused and encouraged, by the initiative of the richer and wiser environing group, he cannot hope for great success.

In his failure to realize and impress this last point, Mr. Washington is especially to be criticised. His doctrine has tended to make the whites, North and South, shift the burden of the Negro problem to the Negro's shoulders and stand aside as critical and rather pessimistic spectators; when in fact the burden belongs to the nation, and the hands of none of us are clean if we bend not our energies to righting these great wrongs.

The South ought to be led, by candid and honest criticism, to assert her better self and do her full duty to the race she has cruelly wronged and is still wronging. The North—her co-partner in guilt—cannot salve her conscience by plastering it with gold. We cannot settle this problem by diplomacy and suaveness, by "policy" alone. If worse come to worst, can the moral fibre of this country survive the slow throttling and murder of nine millions of men?

The black men of America have a duty to perform, a duty stern and delicate,—a forward movement to oppose a part of the work of their greatest leader. So far as Mr. Washington preaches Thrift, Patience, and Industrial Training for the masses, we must hold up his hands and strive with him, rejoicing in his honors and glorying in the strength of this Joshua called of God and of man to lead the headless host. But so far as Mr. Washington apologizes for injustice, North or South, does not rightly value the privilege and duty of voting, belittles the emasculating effects of caste distinctions, and opposes the higher training and ambition of our brighter minds,—so far as he, the South, or the Nation, does this,—we must unceasingly and firmly oppose them. By every civilized and peaceful method we must strive for the rights which the world accords to men, clinging unwaveringly to those great words which the sons of the Fathers would fain forget: "We hold these truths to be self-evident: That all men are created equal; that they are endowed by their Creator with certain unalienable rights; that among these are life, liberty, and the pursuit of happiness."

4. Of the Meaning of Progress

Willst Du Deine Macht verkünden,
Wahle sie die frei von Sunden,
Steh'n in Deinem ew'gen Haus!
Deine Geister sende aus!
Die Unsterblichen, die Reinen,
Die nicht fühlen, die nicht weinen!
Nicht die zarte jungfrau wähle,
Nicht der Hirtin weiche Seele!

Schiller

* * * * *

Once upon a time I taught school in the hills of Tennessee, where the broad dark vale of the Mississippi begins to roll and crumple to greet the Alleghanies. I was a Fisk student then, and all Fisk men thought that Tennessee—beyond the Veil—was theirs alone, and in vacation time they sallied forth in lusty bands to meet the county school-commissioners. Young and happy, I too went, and I shall not soon forget that summer, seventeen years ago.

First, there was a Teachers' Institute at the county-seat; and there distinguished guests of the superintendent taught the teachers fractions and spelling and other mysteries,—white teachers in the morning, Negroes at night. A picnic now and then, and a supper, and the rough world was softened by laughter and song. I remember how—But I wander.

There came a day when all the teachers left the Institute and began schools. I learn from hearsay (for my mother was mortally afraid of fire-arms) that the hunting of ducks and bears and men is wonderfully interesting, but I am sure that the man who has never hunted a country school has something to learn of the pleasures of the chase. I see now the white, hot roads lazily rise and fall and wind before me under the burning July sun; I feel the deep weariness of heart and limb as ten, eight, six miles stretch relentlessly ahead; I feel my heart sink heavily as I hear again and again, "Got a teacher? Yes." So I walked on and on—horses were too expensive—until I had wandered beyond railways, beyond stage lines, to a land of "varmints" and rattlesnakes, where the coming of a stranger was an event, and men lived and died in the shadow of one blue hill.

Sprinkled over hill and dale lay cabins and farmhouses, shut out from the world by the forests and the rolling hills toward the east. There I found at last a little school. Josie told me of it; she was a thin, homely girl of twenty, with a dark-brown face and thick, hard hair. I had crossed the stream at Watertown, and rested under the great willows; then I had gone to the little cabin in the lot where Josie was resting on her way to town. The gaunt farmer made me welcome, and Josie, hearing my errand, told me anxiously that they wanted a school over the hill; that but once since the war had a teacher been there; that she herself longed to learn,—and thus she ran on, talking fast and loud, with much earnestness and energy.

Next morning I crossed the tall round hill, lingered to look at the blue and yellow mountains stretching toward the Carolinas, then plunged into the wood, and came out at Josie's home. It was a dull frame cottage with four rooms, perched just below the brow of the hill, amid peach-trees. The father was a quiet, simple soul, calmly ignorant, with no touch of vulgarity. The mother was different,—strong, bustling, and energetic, with a quick, restless tongue, and an ambition to live "like folks." There was a crowd of children. Two boys had gone away. There remained two growing girls; a shy midget of eight; John, tall, awkward, and eighteen; Jim, younger, quicker, and better looking; and two babies of indefinite age. Then there was Josie herself. She seemed to be the centre of the family: always busy at service, or at home, or berry-picking; a little nervous and inclined to scold, like her mother, yet faithful, too, like her father. She had about her a certain fineness, the shadow of an unconscious moral heroism that would willingly give all of life to make life broader, deeper, and fuller for her and hers. I saw much of this family afterwards, and grew to love them for their honest efforts to be decent and comfortable, and for their knowledge of their own ignorance. There was with them no affectation. The mother would scold the father for being so "easy"; Josie would roundly berate the boys for carelessness; and all knew that it was a hard thing to dig a living out of a rocky side-hill.

I secured the school. I remember the day I rode horseback out to the commissioner's house with a pleasant young white fellow who wanted the white school. The road ran down the bed of a stream; the sun laughed and the water jingled, and we rode on. "Come in," said the commissioner,—"come in. Have a seat. Yes, that certificate will do. Stay to dinner. What do you want a month?" "Oh," thought I, "this is lucky"; but even then fell the awful shadow of the Veil, for they ate first, then I—alone.

The schoolhouse was a log hut, where Colonel Wheeler used to shelter his corn. It sat in a lot behind a rail fence and thorn bushes, near the sweetest of springs. There was an entrance where a door once was, and within, a massive rickety fireplace; great chinks between the logs served as windows. Furniture was scarce. A pale blackboard crouched in the corner. My desk was made of three boards, reinforced at critical points, and my chair, borrowed from the landlady, had to be returned every night. Seats for the children—these puzzled me much. I was haunted by a New England vision of neat little desks and chairs, but, alas! the reality was rough plank benches without backs, and at times without legs. They had the one virtue of making naps dangerous,—possibly fatal, for the floor was not to be trusted.

It was a hot morning late in July when the school opened. I trembled when I heard the patter of little feet down the dusty road, and saw the growing row of dark solemn faces and bright eager eyes facing me. First came Josie and her brothers and sisters. The longing to know, to be a student in the great school at Nashville, hovered like a star above this child-woman amid her work and worry, and she studied doggedly. There were the Dowells from their farm over toward Alexandria,—Fanny, with her smooth black face and wondering eyes; Martha, brown and dull; the pretty girl-wife of a brother, and the younger brood.

There were the Burkes,—two brown and yellow lads, and a tiny haughty-eyed girl. Fat Reuben's little chubby girl came, with golden face and old-gold hair, faithful and solemn. 'Thenie was on hand early,—a jolly, ugly, good-hearted girl, who slyly dipped snuff and looked after her little bow-legged brother. When her mother could spare her, Tildy came,—a midnight beauty, with starry eyes and tapering limbs; and her brother, correspondingly homely. And then the big boys,—the hulking Lawrences; the lazy Neills, unfathered sons of mother and daughter; Hickman, with a stoop in his shoulders; and the rest.

There they sat, nearly thirty of them, on the rough benches, their faces shading from a pale cream to a deep brown, the little feet bare and swinging, the eyes full of expectation, with here and there a twinkle of mischief, and the hands grasping Webster's blue-back spelling-book. I loved my school, and the fine faith the children had in the wisdom of their teacher was truly marvellous. We read and spelled together, wrote a little, picked flowers, sang, and listened to stories of the world beyond the hill. At times the school would dwindle away, and I would start out. I would visit Mun Eddings, who lived in two very dirty rooms, and ask why little Lugene, whose flaming face seemed ever ablaze with the dark-red hair uncombed, was absent all last week, or why I missed so often the inimitable rags of Mack and Ed. Then the father, who worked Colonel Wheeler's farm on shares, would tell me how the crops needed the boys; and the thin, slovenly mother, whose face was pretty when washed, assured me that Lugene must mind the baby. "But we'll start them again next week." When the Lawrences stopped, I knew that the doubts of the old folks about book-learning had conquered again, and so, toiling up the hill, and getting as far into the cabin as possible, I put Cicero "pro Archia Poeta" into the simplest English with local applications, and usually convinced them—for a week or so.

On Friday nights I often went home with some of the children, sometimes to Doc Burke's farm. He was a great, loud, thin Black, ever working, and trying to buy the seventy-five acres of hill and dale where he lived; but people said that he would surely fail, and the "white folks would get it all." His wife was a magnificent Amazon, with saffron face and shining hair, uncorseted and barefooted, and the children were strong and beautiful. They lived in a one-and-a-half-room cabin in the hollow of the farm, near the spring. The front room was full of great fat white beds, scrupulously neat; and there were bad chromos on the walls, and a tired centre-table. In the tiny back kitchen I was often invited to "take out and help" myself to fried chicken and wheat biscuit, "meat" and corn pone, string-beans and berries. At first I used to be a little alarmed at the approach of bedtime in the one lone bedroom, but embarrassment was very deftly avoided. First, all the children nodded and slept, and were stowed away in one great pile of goose feathers; next, the mother and the father discreetly slipped away to the kitchen while I went to bed; then, blowing out the dim light, they retired in the dark. In the morning all were up and away before I thought of awaking. Across the road, where fat Reuben lived, they all went outdoors while the teacher retired, because they did not boast the luxury of a kitchen.

I liked to stay with the Dowells, for they had four rooms and plenty of good country fare. Uncle Bird had a small, rough farm, all woods and hills, miles from the big road; but he was full of tales,—he preached now and then,—and with his children, berries, horses, and wheat he was happy and prosperous. Often, to keep the peace, I must go where life was less lovely; for instance, 'Tildy's mother was incorrigibly dirty, Reuben's larder was limited seriously, and herds of untamed insects wandered over the Eddingses' beds. Best of all I loved to go to Josie's, and sit on the porch, eating peaches, while the mother bustled and talked: how Josie had bought the sewing-machine; how Josie worked at service in winter, but that four dollars a month was "mighty little" wages; how Josie longed to go away to school, but that it "looked like" they never could get far enough ahead to let her; how the crops failed and the well was yet unfinished; and, finally, how "mean" some of the white folks were.

For two summers I lived in this little world; it was dull and humdrum. The girls looked at the hill in wistful longing, and the boys fretted and haunted Alexandria. Alexandria was "town,"—a straggling, lazy village of houses, churches, and shops, and an aristocracy of Toms, Dicks, and Captains. Cuddled on the hill to the north was the village of the colored folks, who lived in three- or four-room unpainted cottages, some neat and homelike, and some dirty. The dwellings were scattered rather aimlessly, but they centred about the twin temples of the hamlet, the Methodist, and the Hard-Shell Baptist churches. These, in turn, leaned gingerly on a sad colored schoolhouse. Hither my little world wended its crooked way on Sunday to meet other worlds, and gossip, and wonder, and make the weekly sacrifice with frenzied priest at the altar of the "old-time religion." Then the soft melody and mighty cadences of Negro song fluttered and thundered.

I have called my tiny community a world, and so its isolation made it; and yet there was among us but a half-awakened common consciousness, sprung from common joy and grief, at burial, birth, or wedding; from a common hardship in poverty, poor land, and low wages; and, above all, from the sight of the Veil that hung between us and Opportunity. All this caused us to think some thoughts together; but these, when ripe for speech, were spoken in various languages. Those whose eyes twenty-five and more years before had seen "the glory of the coming of the Lord," saw in every present hindrance or help a dark fatalism bound to bring all things right in His own good time. The mass of those to whom slavery was a dim recollection of childhood found the world a puzzling thing: it asked little of them, and they answered with little, and yet it ridiculed their offering. Such a paradox they could not understand, and therefore sank into listless indifference, or shiftlessness, or reckless bravado. There were, however, some—such as Josie, Jim, and Ben—to whom War, Hell, and Slavery were but childhood tales, whose young appetites had been whetted to an edge by school and story and half-awakened thought. Ill could they be content, born without and beyond the World. And their weak wings beat against their barriers,—barriers of caste, of youth, of life; at last, in dangerous moments, against everything that opposed even a whim.

The ten years that follow youth, the years when first the realization comes that life is leading somewhere—these were the years that passed after I left my little school. When they were past, I came by chance once more to the walls of Fisk University, to the halls of the chapel of melody. As I lingered there in the joy and pain of meeting old school-friends, there swept over me a sudden longing to pass again beyond the blue hill, and to see the homes and the school of other days, and to learn how life had gone with my school-children; and I went.

Josie was dead, and the gray-haired mother said simply, "We've had a heap of trouble since you've been away." I had feared for Jim. With a cultured parentage and a social caste to uphold him, he might have made a venturesome merchant or a West Point cadet. But here he was, angry with life and reckless; and when Farmer Durham charged him with stealing wheat, the old man had to ride fast to escape the stones which the furious fool hurled after him. They told Jim to run away; but he would not run, and the constable came that afternoon. It grieved Josie, and great awkward John walked nine miles every day to see his little brother through the bars of Lebanon jail. At last the two came back together in the dark night. The mother cooked supper, and Josie emptied her purse, and the boys stole away. Josie grew thin and silent, yet worked the more. The hill became steep for the quiet old father, and with the boys away there was little to do in the valley. Josie helped them to sell the old farm, and they moved nearer town. Brother Dennis, the carpenter, built a new house with six rooms; Josie toiled a year in Nashville, and brought back ninety dollars to furnish the house and change it to a home.

When the spring came, and the birds twittered, and the stream ran proud and full, little sister Lizzie, bold and thoughtless, flushed with the passion of youth, bestowed herself on the tempter, and brought home a nameless child, Josie shivered and worked on, with the vision of schooldays all fled, with a face wan and tired,—worked until, on a summer's day, some one married another; then Josie crept to her mother like a hurt child, and slept—and sleeps.

I paused to scent the breeze as I entered the valley. The Lawrences have gone,—father and son forever,—and the other son lazily digs in the earth to live. A new young widow rents out their cabin to fat Reuben. Reuben is a Baptist preacher now, but I fear as lazy as ever, though his cabin has three rooms; and little Ella has grown into a bouncing woman, and is ploughing corn on the hot hillside. There are babies a-plenty, and one half-witted girl. Across the valley is a house I did not know before, and there I found, rocking one baby and expecting another, one of my schoolgirls, a daughter of Uncle Bird Dowell. She looked somewhat worried with her new duties, but soon bristled into pride over her neat cabin and the tale of her thrifty husband, the horse and cow, and the farm they were planning to buy.

My log schoolhouse was gone. In its place stood Progress, and Progress, I understand, is necessarily ugly. The crazy foundation stones still marked the former site of my poor little cabin, and not far away, on six weary boulders, perched a jaunty board house, perhaps twenty by thirty feet, with three windows and a door that locked. Some of the window-glass was broken, and part of an old iron stove lay mournfully under the house. I peeped through the window half reverently, and found things that were more familiar. The blackboard had grown by about two feet, and the seats were still without backs. The county owns the lot now, I hear, and every year there is a session of school. As I sat by the spring and looked on the Old and the New I felt glad, very glad, and yet—

After two long drinks I started on. There was the great double log-house on the corner. I remembered the broken, blighted family that used to live there. The strong, hard face of the mother, with its wilderness of hair, rose before me. She had driven her husband away, and while I taught school a strange man lived there, big and jovial, and people talked. I felt sure that Ben and 'Tildy would come to naught from such a home. But this is an odd world; for Ben is a busy farmer in Smith County, "doing well, too," they say, and he had cared for little 'Tildy until last spring, when a lover married her. A hard life the lad had led, toiling for meat, and laughed at because he was homely and crooked. There was Sam Carlon, an impudent old skinflint, who had definite notions about "niggers," and hired Ben a summer and would not pay him. Then the hungry boy gathered his sacks together, and in broad daylight went into Carlon's corn; and when the hard-fisted farmer set upon him, the angry boy flew at him like a beast. Doc Burke saved a murder and a lynching that day.

The story reminded me again of the Burkes, and an impatience seized me to know who won in the battle, Doc or the seventy-five acres. For it is a hard thing to make a farm out of nothing, even in fifteen years.

So I hurried on, thinking of the Burkes. They used to have a certain magnificent barbarism about them that I liked. They were never vulgar, never immoral, but rather rough and primitive, with an unconventionality that spent itself in loud guffaws, slaps on the back, and naps in the corner. I hurried by the cottage of the misborn Neill boys. It was empty, and they were grown into fat, lazy farm-hands. I saw the home of the Hickmans, but Albert, with his stooping shoulders, had passed from the world. Then I came to the Burkes' gate and peered through; the inclosure looked rough and untrimmed, and yet there were the same fences around the old farm save to the left, where lay twenty-five other acres. And lo! the cabin in the hollow had climbed the hill and swollen to a half-finished six-room cottage.

The Burkes held a hundred acres, but they were still in debt. Indeed, the gaunt father who toiled night and day would scarcely be happy out of debt, being so used to it. Some day he must stop, for his massive frame is showing decline. The mother wore shoes, but the lion-like physique of other days was broken. The children had grown up. Rob, the image of his father, was loud and rough with laughter. Birdie, my school baby of six, had grown to a picture of maiden beauty, tall and tawny. "Edgar is gone," said the mother, with head half bowed,—"gone to work in Nashville; he and his father couldn't agree."

Little Doc, the boy born since the time of my school, took me horseback down the creek next morning toward Farmer Dowell's. The road and the stream were battling for mastery, and the stream had the better of it. We splashed and waded, and the merry boy, perched behind me, chattered and laughed. He showed me where Simon Thompson had bought a bit of ground and a home; but his daughter Lana, a plump, brown, slow girl, was not there. She had married a man and a farm twenty miles away. We wound on down the stream till we came to a gate that I did not recognize, but the boy insisted that it was "Uncle Bird's. The farm was fat with the growing crop. In that little valley was a strange stillness as I rode up; for death and marriage had stolen youth and left age and childhood there. We sat and talked that night after the chores were done. Uncle Bird was grayer, and his eyes did not see so well, but he was still jovial. We talked of the acres bought,—one hundred and twenty-five, the new guest-chamber added, of Martha's marrying. Then we talked of death: Fanny and Fred were gone; a shadow hung over the other daughter, and when it lifted she was to go to Nashville to school. At last we spoke of the neighbors, and as night fell, Uncle Bird told me how, on a night like that, 'Thenie came wandering back to her home over yonder, to escape the blows of her husband. And next morning she died in the home that her little bow-legged brother, working and saving, had bought for their widowed mother.

My journey was done, and behind me lay hill and dale, and Life and Death. How shall man measure Progress there where the dark-faced Josie lies? How many heartfuls of sorrow shall balance a bushel of wheat? How hard a thing is life to the lowly, and yet how human and real! And all this life and love and strife and failure,—is it the twilight of nightfall or the flush of some faint-dawning day?

Thus sadly musing, I rode to Nashville in the Jim Crow car.

6. Of the Training of Black Men

Why, if the Soul can fling the Dust aside,
And naked on the Air of Heaven ride,
  Were't not a Shame—were't not a Shame for him
In this clay carcase crippled to abide?

OMAR KHAYYAM (FITZGERALD)

* * * * *

From the shimmering swirl of waters where many, many thoughts ago the slave ship first saw the square tower of Jamestown, have flowed down to our day three streams of thinking: one swollen from the larger world here and overseas, saying, the multiplying of human wants in culture-lands calls for the world-wide cooperation of men in satisfying them. Hence arises a new human unity, pulling the ends of earth nearer, and all men, black, yellow, and white. The larger humanity strives to feel in this contact of living Nations and sleeping hordes a thrill of new life in the world, crying, "If the contact of Life and Sleep be Death, shame on such Life." To be sure, behind this thought lurks the afterthought of force and dominion,—the making of brown men to delve when the temptation of beads and red calico cloys.

The second thought streaming from the death-ship and the curving river is the thought of the older South,—the sincere and passionate belief that somewhere between men and cattle, God created a *tertium quid*, and called it a Negro,—a clownish, simple creature, at times even lovable within its limitations, but straitly foreordained to walk within the Veil. To be sure, behind the thought lurks the afterthought,—some of them with favoring chance might become men, but in sheer self-defence we dare not let them, and we build about them walls so high, and hang between them and the light a veil so thick, that they shall not even think of breaking through.

And last of all there trickles down that third and darker thought,—the thought of the things themselves, the confused, half-conscious mutter of men who are black and whitened, crying "Liberty, Freedom, Opportunity—vouchsafe to us, O boastful World, the chance of living men!" To be sure, behind the thought lurks the afterthought,—suppose, after all, the World is right and we are less than men? Suppose this mad impulse within is all wrong, some mock mirage from the untrue?

So here we stand among thoughts of human unity, even through conquest and slavery; the inferiority of black men, even if forced by fraud; a shriek in the night for the freedom of men who themselves are not yet sure of their right to demand it. This is the tangle of thought and afterthought wherein we are called to solve the problem of training men for life.

Behind all its curiousness, so attractive alike to sage and *dilettante,* lie its dim dangers, throwing across us shadows at once grotesque and awful. Plain it is to us that what the world seeks through desert and wild we have within our threshold,—a stalwart laboring force, suited to the semi-tropics; if, deaf to the voice of the Zeitgeist, we refuse to use and develop these men, we risk poverty and loss. If, on the other hand, seized by the brutal afterthought, we debauch the race thus caught in our talons, selfishly sucking their blood and brains in the future as in the past, what shall save us from national decadence? Only that saner selfishness, which Education teaches men, can find the rights of all in the whirl of work.

Again, we may decry the color-prejudice of the South, yet it remains a heavy fact. Such curious kinks of the human mind exist and must be reckoned with soberly. They cannot be laughed away, nor always successfully stormed at, nor easily abolished by act of legislature. And yet they must not be encouraged by being let alone. They must be recognized as facts, but unpleasant facts; things that stand in the way of civilization and religion and common decency. They can be met in but one way,—the breadth and broadening of human reason, by catholicity of taste and culture. And so, too, the native ambition and aspiration of men, even though they be black, backward, and ungraceful, must not lightly be dealt with. To stimulate wildly weak and untrained minds is to play with mighty fires; to flout their striving idly is to welcome a harvest of brutish crime and shameless lethargy in our very laps. The guiding of thought and the deft coordination of deed is at once the path of honor and humanity.

And so, in this great question of reconciling three vast and partially contradictory streams of thought, the one panacea of Education leaps to the lips of all:— such human training as will best use the labor of all men without enslaving or brutalizing; such training as will give us poise to encourage the prejudices that bulwark society, and to stamp out those that in sheer barbarity deafen us to the wail of prisoned souls within the Veil, and the mounting fury of shackled men.

But when we have vaguely said that Education will set this tangle straight, what have we uttered but a truism? Training for life teaches living; but what training for the profitable living together of black men and white? A hundred and fifty years ago our task would have seemed easier. Then Dr. Johnson blandly assured us that education was needful solely for the embellishments of life, and was useless for ordinary vermin. To-day we have climbed to heights where we would open at least the outer courts of knowledge to all, display its treasures to many, and select the few to whom its mystery of Truth is revealed, not wholly by birth or the accidents of the stock market, but at least in part according to deftness and aim, talent and character. This programme, however, we are sorely puzzled in carrying out through that part of the land where the blight of slavery fell hardest, and where we are dealing with two backward peoples. To make here in human education that ever necessary combination of the permanent and the contingent—of the ideal and the practical in workable equilibrium—has been there, as it ever must be in every age and place, a matter of infinite experiment and frequent mistakes.

In rough approximation we may point out four varying decades of work in Southern education since the Civil War. From the close of the war until 1876, was the period of uncertain groping and temporary relief. There were army schools, mission schools, and schools of the Freedman's Bureau in chaotic disarrangement seeking system and cooperation. Then followed ten years of constructive definite effort toward the building of complete school systems in the South. Normal schools and colleges were founded for the freedmen, and teachers trained there to man the public schools. There was the inevitable tendency of war to underestimate the prejudices of the master and the ignorance of the slave, and all seemed clear sailing out of the wreckage of the storm. Meantime, starting in this decade yet especially developing from 1885 to 1895, began the industrial revolution of the South. The land saw glimpses of a new destiny and the stirring of new ideals. The educational system striving to complete itself saw new obstacles and a field of work ever broader and deeper. The Negro colleges, hurriedly founded, were inadequately equipped, illogically distributed, and of varying efficiency and grade; the normal and high schools were doing little more than common school work, and the common schools were training but a third of the children who ought to be in them, and training these too often poorly. At the same time the white South, by reason of its sudden conversion from the slavery ideal, by so much the more became set and strengthened in its racial prejudice, and crystallized it into harsh law and harsher custom; while the marvellous pushing forward of the poor white daily threatened to take even bread and butter from the mouths of the heavily handicapped sons of the freedmen. In the midst, then, of the larger problem of Negro education sprang up the more practical question of work, the inevitable economic quandary that faces a people in the transition from slavery to freedom, and especially those who make that change amid hate and prejudice, lawlessness and ruthless competition.

The industrial school springing to notice in this decade, but coming to full recognition in the decade beginning with 1895, was the proffered answer to this combined educational and economic crisis, and an answer of singular wisdom and timeliness. From the very first in nearly all the schools some attention had been given to training in handiwork, but now was this training first raised to a dignity that brought it in direct touch with the South's magnificent industrial development, and given an emphasis which reminded black folk that before the Temple of Knowledge swing the Gates of Toil.

Yet after all they are but gates, and when turning our eyes from the temporary and the contingent in the Negro problem to the broader question of the permanent uplifting and civilization of black men in America, we have a right to inquire, as this enthusiasm for material advancement mounts to its height, if after all the industrial school is the final and sufficient answer in the training of the Negro race; and to ask gently, but in all sincerity, the ever-recurring query of the ages, Is not life more than meat, and the body more than raiment? And men ask this today all the more eagerly because of sinister signs in recent educational movements. The tendency is here, born of slavery and quickened to renewed life by the crazy imperialism of the day, to regard human beings as among the material resources of a land to be trained with an eye single to future dividends. Race-prejudices, which keep brown and black men in their "places," we are coming to regard as useful allies with such a theory, no matter how much they may dull the ambition and sicken the hearts of struggling human beings. And above all, we daily hear that an education that encourages aspiration, that sets the loftiest of ideals and seeks as an end culture and character rather than bread-winning, is the privilege of white men and the danger and delusion of black.

Especially has criticism been directed against the former educational efforts to aid the Negro. In the four periods I have mentioned, we find first, boundless, planless enthusiasm and sacrifice; then the preparation of teachers for a vast public-school system; then the launching and expansion of that school system amid increasing difficulties; and finally the training of workmen for the new and growing industries. This development has been sharply ridiculed as a logical anomaly and flat reversal of nature. Soothly we have been told that first industrial and manual training should have taught the Negro to work, then simple schools should have taught him to read and write, and finally, after years, high and normal schools could have completed the system, as intelligence and wealth demanded.

That a system logically so complete was historically impossible, it needs but a little thought to prove. Progress in human affairs is more often a pull than a push, surging forward of the exceptional man, and the lifting of his duller brethren slowly and painfully to his vantage-ground. Thus it was no accident that gave birth to universities centuries before the common schools, that made fair Harvard the first

flower of our wilderness. So in the South: the mass of the freedmen at the end of the war lacked the intelligence so necessary to modern workingmen. They must first have the common school to teach them to read, write, and cipher; and they must have higher schools to teach teachers for the common schools. The white teachers who flocked South went to establish such a common-school system. Few held the idea of founding colleges; most of them at first would have laughed at the idea. But they faced, as all men since them have faced, that central paradox of the South,—the social separation of the races. At that time it was the sudden volcanic rupture of nearly all relations between black and white, in work and government and family life. Since then a new adjustment of relations in economic and political affairs has grown up,—an adjustment subtle and difficult to grasp, yet singularly ingenious, which leaves still that frightful chasm at the color-line across which men pass at their peril. Thus, then and now, there stand in the South two separate worlds; and separate not simply in the higher realms of social intercourse, but also in church and school, on railway and streetcar, in hotels and theatres, in streets and city sections, in books and newspapers, in asylums and jails, in hospitals and graveyards. There is still enough of contact for large economic and group cooperation, but the separation is so thorough and deep that it absolutely precludes for the present between the races anything like that sympathetic and effective group-training and leadership of the one by the other, such as the American Negro and all backward peoples must have for effectual progress.

This the missionaries of '68 soon saw; and if effective industrial and trade schools were impracticable before the establishment of a common school system, just as certainly no adequate common schools could be founded until there were teachers to teach them. Southern whites would not teach them; Northern whites in sufficient numbers could not be had. If the Negro was to learn, he must teach himself, and the most effective help that could be given him was the establishment of schools to train Negro teachers. This conclusion was slowly but surely reached by every student of the situation until simultaneously, in widely separated regions, without consultation or systematic plan, there arose a series of institutions designed to furnish teachers for the untaught. Above the sneers of critics at the obvious defects of this procedure must ever stand its one crushing rejoinder: in a single generation they put thirty thousand black teachers in the South; they wiped out the illiteracy of the majority of the black people of the land, and they made Tuskegee possible.

Such higher training-schools tended naturally to deepen broader development: at first they were common and grammar schools, then some became high schools. And finally, by 1900, some thirty-four had one year or more of studies of college grade. This development was reached with different degrees of speed in different institutions: Hampton is still a high school, while Fisk University started her college in 1871, and Spelman Seminary about 1896. In all cases the aim was identical,—to maintain the standards of the lower training by giving teachers and leaders the best practicable training; and above all, to furnish the black world with adequate standards of human culture and lofty ideals of life. It was not enough that the teachers of teachers should be trained in technical normal methods; they must also, so far as possible, be broad-minded, cultured men and women, to scatter civilization among a people whose ignorance was not simply of letters, but of life itself.

It can thus be seen that the work of education in the South began with higher institutions of training, which threw off as their foliage common schools, and later industrial schools, and at the same time strove to shoot their roots ever deeper toward college and university training. That this was an inevitable and necessary development, sooner or later, goes without saying; but there has been, and still is, a question in many minds if the natural growth was not forced, and if the higher training was not either overdone or done with cheap and unsound methods. Among white Southerners this feeling is widespread and positive. A prominent Southern journal voiced this in a recent editorial.

> "The experiment that has been made to give the colored students classical training has not been satisfactory. Even though many were able to pursue the course, most of them did so in a parrot-like way, learning what was taught, but not seeming to appropriate the truth and import of their instruction, and graduating without sensible aim or valuable occupation for their future. The whole scheme has proved a waste of time, efforts, and the money of the state."

While most fair-minded men would recognize this as extreme and overdrawn, still without doubt many are asking, Are there a sufficient number of Negroes ready for college training to warrant the undertaking? Are not too many students prematurely forced into this work? Does it not have the effect of dissatisfying the young Negro with his environment? And do these graduates succeed in real life? Such natural questions cannot be evaded, nor on the other hand must a Nation naturally skeptical as to Negro ability assume an unfavorable answer without careful inquiry and patient openness to conviction. We must not forget that most Americans answer all queries regarding the Negro *a priori*, and that the least that human courtesy can do is to listen to evidence.

The advocates of the higher education of the Negro would be the last to deny the incompleteness and glaring defects of the present system: too many institutions have attempted to do college work, the work in some cases has not been thoroughly done, and quantity rather than quality has sometimes been sought. But all this can be said of higher education throughout the land; it is the almost inevitable incident of educational growth, and leaves the deeper question of the legitimate demand for the higher training of Negroes untouched. And this latter question can be settled in but one way,—by a first-hand study of the facts. If we leave out of view all institutions which have not actually graduated students from a course higher than that of a New England high school, even though they be called colleges; if then we take the thirty-four remaining institutions, we may clear up many misapprehensions by asking searchingly, What kind of institutions are they? what do they teach? and what sort of men do they graduate?

And first we may say that this type of college, including Atlanta, Fisk, and Howard, Wilberforce and Lincoln, Biddle, Shaw, and the rest, is peculiar, almost unique. Through the shining trees that whisper before me as I write, I catch glimpses of a boulder of New England granite, covering a grave, which graduates of Atlanta University have placed there, with this inscription:

> "IN GRATEFUL MEMORY OF THEIR
> FORMER TEACHER AND FRIEND
> AND OF THE UNSELFISH LIFE HE
> LIVED, AND THE NOBLE WORK HE
> WROUGHT; THAT THEY, THEIR
> CHILDREN, AND THEIR CHILDREN'S
> CHILDREN MIGHT BE
> BLESSED."

This was the gift of New England to the freed Negro: not alms, but a friend; not cash, but character. It was not and is not money these seething millions want, but love and sympathy, the pulse of hearts beating with red blood;—a gift which to-day only their own kindred and race can bring to the masses, but which once saintly souls brought to their favored children in the crusade of the sixties, that finest thing in American history, and one of the few things untainted by sordid greed and cheap vainglory. The teachers in these institutions came not to keep the Negroes in their place, but to raise them out of the defilement of the places where slavery had wallowed them. The colleges they founded were social settlements; homes where the best of the sons of the freedmen came in close and sympathetic touch with the best traditions of New England. They lived and ate together, studied and worked, hoped and harkened in the dawning light. In actual formal content their curriculum was doubtless old-fashioned, but in educational power it was supreme, for it was the contact of living souls.

From such schools about two thousand Negroes have gone forth with the bachelor's degree. The number in itself is enough to put at rest the argument that too large a proportion of Negroes are receiving higher training. If the ratio to population of all Negro students throughout the land, in both college and secondary training, be counted, Commissioner Harris assures us "it must be increased to five times its present average" to equal the average of the land.

Fifty years ago the ability of Negro students in any appreciable numbers to master a modern college course would have been difficult to prove. To-day it is proved by the fact that four hundred Negroes, many of whom have been reported as brilliant students, have received the bachelor's degree from Harvard, Yale, Oberlin, and seventy other leading colleges. Here we have, then, nearly twenty-five hundred Negro graduates, of whom the crucial query must be made, How far did their training fit them for life? It is of course extremely difficult to collect satisfactory data on such a point,—difficult to reach the men, to get trustworthy testimony, and to gauge that testimony by any generally acceptable criterion of success. In 1900, the Conference at Atlanta University undertook to study these graduates, and published the results. First they sought to know what these graduates were doing, and succeeded in getting answers from nearly two-thirds of the living. The direct testimony was in almost all cases corroborated by the reports of the colleges where they graduated, so that in the main the

reports were worthy of credence. Fifty-three per cent of these graduates were teachers,—presidents of institutions, heads of normal schools, principals of city school systems, and the like. Seventeen per cent were clergymen; another seventeen per cent were in the professions, chiefly as physicians. Over six per cent were merchants, farmers, and artisans, and four per cent were in the government civil-service. Granting even that a considerable proportion of the third unheard from are unsuccessful, this is a record of usefulness. Personally I know many hundreds of these graduates, and have corresponded with more than a thousand; through others I have followed carefully the life-work of scores; I have taught some of them and some of the pupils whom they have taught, lived in homes which they have builded, and looked at life through their eyes. Comparing them as a class with my fellow students in New England and in Europe, I cannot hesitate in saying that nowhere have I met men and women with a broader spirit of helpfulness, with deeper devotion to their life-work, or with more consecrated determination to succeed in the face of bitter difficulties than among Negro college-bred men. They have, to be sure, their proportion of ne'er-do-weels, their pedants and lettered fools, but they have a surprisingly small proportion of them; they have not that culture of manner which we instinctively associate with university men, forgetting that in reality it is the heritage from cultured homes, and that no people a generation removed from slavery can escape a certain unpleasant rawness and *gaucherie*, despite the best of training.

With all their larger vision and deeper sensibility, these men have usually been conservative, careful leaders. They have seldom been agitators, have withstood the temptation to head the mob, and have worked steadily and faithfully in a thousand communities in the South. As teachers, they have given the South a commendable system of city schools and large numbers of private normal-schools and academies. Colored college-bred men have worked side by side with white college graduates at Hampton; almost from the beginning the back-bone of Tuskegee's teaching force has been formed of graduates from Fisk and Atlanta. And to-day the institute is filled with college graduates, from the energetic wife of the principal down to the teacher of agriculture, including nearly half of the executive council and a majority of the heads of departments. In the professions, college men are slowly but surely leavening the Negro church, are healing and preventing the devastations of disease, and beginning to furnish legal protection for the liberty and property of the toiling masses. All this is needful work. Who would do it if Negroes did not? How could Negroes do it if they were not trained carefully for it? If white people need colleges to furnish teachers, ministers, lawyers, and doctors, do black people need nothing of the sort?

If it is true that there are an appreciable number of Negro youth in the land capable by character and talent to receive that higher training, the end of which is culture, and if the two and a half thousand who have had something of this training in the past have in the main proved themselves useful to their race and generation, the question then comes, What place in the future development of the South ought the Negro college and college-bred man to occupy? That the present social separation and acute race-sensitiveness must eventually yield to the influences of culture, as the South grows civilized, is clear. But such transformation calls for singular wisdom and patience. If, while the healing of this vast sore is progressing, the races are to live for many years side by side, united in economic effort, obeying a common government, sensitive to mutual thought and feeling, yet subtly and silently separate in many matters of deeper human intimacy,—if this unusual and dangerous development is to progress amid peace and order, mutual respect and growing intelligence, it will call for social surgery at once the delicatest and nicest in modern history. It will demand broad-minded, upright men, both white and black, and in its final accomplishment American civilization will triumph. So far as white men are concerned, this fact is to-day being recognized in the South, and a happy renaissance of university education seems imminent. But the very voices that cry hail to this good work are, strange to relate, largely silent or antagonistic to the higher education of the Negro.

Strange to relate! for this is certain, no secure civilization can be built in the South with the Negro as an ignorant, turbulent proletariat. Suppose we seek to remedy this by making them laborers and nothing more: they are not fools, they have tasted of the Tree of Life, and they will not cease to think, will not cease attempting to read the riddle of the world. By taking away their best equipped teachers and leaders, by slamming the door of opportunity in the faces of their bolder and brighter minds, will you make them satisfied with their lot? or will you not rather transfer their leading from the hands

of men taught to think to the hands of untrained demagogues? We ought not to forget that despite the pressure of poverty, and despite the active discouragement and even ridicule of friends, the demand for higher training steadily increases among Negro youth: there were, in the years from 1875 to 1880, 22 Negro graduates from Northern colleges; from 1885 to 1890 there were 43, and from 1895 to 1900, nearly 100 graduates. From Southern Negro colleges there were, in the same three periods, 143, 413, and over 500 graduates. Here, then, is the plain thirst for training; by refusing to give this Talented Tenth the key to knowledge, can any sane man imagine that they will tightly lay aside their yearning and contentedly become hewers of wood and drawers of water?

No. The dangerously clear logic of the Negro's position will more and more loudly assert itself in that day when increasing wealth and more intricate social organization preclude the South from being, as it so largely is, simply an armed camp for intimidating black folk. Such waste of energy cannot be spared if the South is to catch up with civilization. And as the black third of the land grows in thrift and skill, unless skillfully guided in its larger philosophy, it must more and more brood over the red past and the creeping, crooked present, until it grasps a gospel of revolt and revenge and throws its new-found energies athwart the current of advance. Even to-day the masses of the Negroes see all too clearly the anomalies of their position and the moral crookedness of yours. You may marshal strong indictments against them, but their counter-cries, lacking though they be in formal logic, have burning truths within them which you may not wholly ignore, O Southern Gentlemen! If you deplore their presence here, they ask, Who brought us? When you cry, Deliver us from the vision of intermarriage, they answer that legal marriage is infinitely better than systematic concubinage and prostitution. And if in just fury you accuse their vagabonds of violating women, they also in fury quite as just may reply: The wrong which your gentlemen have done against helpless black women in defiance of your own laws is written on the foreheads of two millions of mulattoes, and written in ineffaceable blood. And finally, when you fasten crime upon this race as its peculiar trait, they answer that slavery was the arch-crime, and lynching and lawlessness its twin abortion; that color and race are not crimes, and yet they it is which in this land receives most unceasing condemnation, North, East, South, and West.

I will not say such arguments are wholly justified,—I will not insist that there is no other side to the shield; but I do say that of the nine millions of Negroes in this nation, there is scarcely one out of the cradle to whom these arguments do not daily present themselves in the guise of terrible truth. I insist that the question of the future is how best to keep these millions from brooding over the wrongs of the past and the difficulties of the present, so that all their energies may be bent toward a cheerful striving and co-operation with their white neighbors toward a larger, juster, and fuller future. That one wise method of doing this lies in the closer knitting of the Negro to the great industrial possibilities of the South is a great truth. And this the common schools and the manual training and trade schools are working to accomplish. But these alone are not enough. The foundations of knowledge in this race, as in others, must be sunk deep in the college and university if we would build a solid, permanent structure. Internal problems of social advance must inevitably come,—problems of work and wages, of families and homes, of morals and the true valuing of the things of life; and all these and other inevitable problems of civilization the Negro must meet and solve largely for himself, by reason of his isolation; and can there be any possible solution other than by study and thought and an appeal to the rich experience of the past? Is there not, with such a group and in such a crisis, infinitely more danger to be apprehended from half-trained minds and shallow thinking than from over-education and over-refinement? Surely we have wit enough to found a Negro college so manned and equipped as to steer successfully between the *dilettante* and the fool. We shall hardly induce black men to believe that if their stomachs be full, it matters little about their brains. They already dimly perceive that the paths of peace winding between honest toil and dignified manhood call for the guidance of skilled thinkers, the loving, reverent comradeship between the black lowly and the black men emancipated by training and culture.

The function of the Negro college, then, is clear: it must maintain the standards of popular education, it must seek the social regeneration of the Negro, and it must help in the solution of problems of race contact and co-operation. And finally, beyond all this, it must develop men. Above our modern socialism, and out of the worship of the mass, must persist and evolve that higher individualism which the centres of culture protect; there must come a loftier respect for the sovereign human soul that seeks to know itself and the world about it; that seeks a freedom for expansion and self-development; that will love and hate and labor in its own way, untrammeled alike by old and new. Such souls aforetime have inspired and guided worlds, and if we be not wholly bewitched by our Rhinegold, they shall again. Herein the longing of black men must have respect: the rich and bitter depth of their experience, the unknown treasures of their inner life, the strange rendings of nature they have seen, may give the world new points of view and make their loving, living, and doing precious to all human hearts. And to themselves in these the days that try their souls, the chance to soar in the dim blue air above the smoke is to their finer spirits boon and guerdon for what they lose on earth by being black.

I sit with Shakespeare and he winces not. Across the color line I move arm in arm with Balzac and Dumas, where smiling men and welcoming women glide in gilded halls. From out the caves of evening that swing between the strong-limbed earth and the tracery of the stars, I summon Aristotle and Aurelius and what soul I will, and they come all graciously with no scorn nor condescension. So, wed with Truth, I dwell above the Veil. Is this the life you grudge us, O knightly America? Is this the life you long to change into the dull red hideousness of Georgia? Are you so afraid lest peering from this high Pisgah, between Philistine and Amalekite, we sight the Promised Land!

The Black Man in the Revolution of 1914–1918

W. E. B. Du Bois

From The Crisis, March 1919

America did not win the war by fighting only. Her fighting both of colored and white troops covered less than a year of a four years' war. America's great contribution was her preparations which frightened Germany; and her sailors, engineers and laborers who made food and material available. Among these the black stevedores have won a world record. They have been the best workers in France, as is acknowledged by everybody, and their efficiency has been due in part to no small numbers of colored officers and under-officers and to colored Y. M. C. A. workers.

But America did some fighting and the most critical time of America's fighting was in the terrible days of last fall when the exhausted French had to have re-inforcements or yield. It was here that among the first units sent to aid was the Ninety-third Division. The Ninety-third was not a division. It consisted of the Eighth Illinois, the Fifteenth New York, the Separate Battalions of Maryland, the District of Columbia, and Ohio, Company L of the Sixth Massachusetts and others. It was an aggregation nobody wanted. It could not under the draft law go with its state units, or, at least, the law was so interpreted. A whole division was planned to include Colonel Young—but dark forces intervened. Yet these units were ready for work, they were eager, and they were sent to the French and have become known as the 369th, 370th, 371st and 372nd Regiments of the Ninety-third Division. Their black officers were transferred and changed considerably, but they went into battle practically with a complete roster of black officers except Colonels, a few Majors and several Captains. But most of the officers were black—for instance, the old Eighth Illinois, even after Colonel Dennison left, had a colored Lieutenant-Colonel, two colored Majors, nineteen colored Captains and ninety-eight colored First and Second Lieutenants. Colonel Hayward, of the old New York Fifteenth, succeeded in removing a larger proportion of his colored officers.

So at the most critical period of the American participation in the war these men went into action.

What was the result?

The colored Lieutenant-Colonel of the 370th, a colored Major, eight colored Captains, seventeen colored Lieutenants, eight colored under-officers and twenty-six colored privates received the *Croix de Guerre* in November.

On November 11, General Vincenden, the French Commanding Officer, said of the 370th: *"Fired by a noble ardor, they go at times even beyond the objectives given them by the higher command; they have always wished to be in the front line."* The final order of General Vincenden, December 9, said: *"In the name of France, I thank you."* He mentioned the *"hard and brilliant battles of Chavigny, Leury and the Bois de Beaumont."* He commends their *"fine appearance under arms"* like *"silk unrolling in wavy folds." He especially* mentions the exploits of three battalions (two with all colored officers and one with a white Captain) at Val St. Pierre, Aubenton and Logny, where the colored Lieutenant-Colonel distinguished himself. *"You have given us of your best and you have given it out of the fullness of your hears. The blood of your comrades who fell on the soil of France, mixed with the blood of our soldiers, renders indissoluble the bonds of affection that unite us. We have, besides, the pride of having worked together at a magnificent task and the pride of bearing on our foreheads the ray of a common grandeur. A last time—Au Revior!"*

The 371st and 372d Infantries were brigaded with the 157th French Division under General Goybet. On the occasion of their leaving, December 15, the General in Order No. 245 said:

"For seven months we have lived as brothers-at-arms, partaking of the same activities, sharing the same hardships and the same dangers. Side by side we took part in the great Champagne Battle, which was

to be crowned by a tremendous victory. Never will the 157th Division forget the indomitable dash, the heroic rush of the American (Negro) regiments up the observatory ridge and into the Plain of Monthois. The most powerful defenses, the most strongly organized machine gun nests, the heaviest artillery barrages—nothing could stop them. These crack regiments overcame every obstacle with a most complete contempt for danger. Through their steady devotion the Red Hand Division (157th French) for nine whole days' of severe struggle was constantly leading the way for the victorious advance of the Fourth Army. Officers, non-commissioned officers and men, I respectfully salute our glorious comrades who have fallen, and I bow to your colors—side by side with this—the flag of the 333rd Regiment of Infantry (French). They have shown us the way to victory. Dear Friends from America, when you reach the other side of the ocean, do not forget the Red Hand Division. Our brotherhood has been cemented in the blood of the brave, and such bonds will never be destroyed."

The Distinguished Service Cross was given, December 16, to four colored officers, five colored privates and one colored corporal, of the 372d Regiment. On December 13, the following honors were given the 371st and 372d, *Croix de Guerre* to two colored corporals and to two colored privates. There were also seventy other citations.

On October 7, General Garnier Duplossis, of the Ninth French Army Corps *"salutes the brave American (Negro) regiments who have rivaled in intrepidity their French comrades."*

On October 8, General Goybet (General Order 234) in submitting the above transmits *"from the bottom of the heart of a chief and soldier the expression of the gratitude for the glory which you have sent to our good 157th Division."* The same day Colonel Quillet notes their *"finest qualities of bravery and daring"* in an order to the 372d Regiment. On the battlefield, October 1, General Goybet said: *"You must be proud of the courage of your officers and men and I consider it an honor to have them under my command."* The 372d Regiment was cited as a whole for bravery and four *Medailles Militaires* and four *Croix de Guerre* were given. Similar words of farewell as went to the 370th Regiment were sent to this regiment.

So much for the soldiers brigaded with the French, to whom will be added later the equally fine record of the 369th (Fifteenth New York). In fine, the universal testimony of the French army is that black officers and men did extraordinarily well.

Thus much for the Ninety-third Division.

The Ninety-second Division went through hell. It was torn and shaken in morale, seriously so by General Ballou's apparent anxiety to preserve a "Jim-Crow" regime for his officers and by the determination of men like Colonel Moss not to insist on respect to his colored officers. The Division seethed with bitterness and discontent, but it stuck to its work.

Meantime, anti-Negro prejudice was rampant in the American army and the officers particularly were subjected to all sorts of discrimination. Scandalous tales were spread in French towns and villages; some villages were posted "Niggers keep out!" Incidents like this continually recurred. A black chaplain with the rank of a Lieutenant reported for duty with colored stevedore regiments at Bordeaux. All the officers were white. He presented himself at the officers' mess and was refused admission. He asked for meals in his room. That was contrary to regulations. He tried the non-commissioned officers' mess. He was refused here because he was an officer. He asked them to send him meals. They refused. He tried to eat with the privates. Again regulations intervened. After a day of hunger and insult he was finally accommodated with a side table for himself in the officers' mess-room.

In the fighting units not one-third of the white soldiers saluted colored officers; they were refused at officers' clubs and in several cases openly disparaged before their men. In hospitals they were often refused admittance to officers' quarters and placed with the privates. Gossip disparaging to the black officers filled the whole American army and clashes of white and colored soldiers ended in blood-shed in a number of cases.

On top of this came subtle German propaganda.

The following was dropped from a German balloon, September 3, 1918, near St.-Dié and Raon-l-Etape:

To the Colored Soldiers of the United States Army

Hello, boys, what are you doing over here? Fighting the Germans? Why? Have they ever done you any harm? Of course some white folks and the lying English-American papers told you that the Germans ought to be wiped out for the sake of humanity and democracy. What is democracy? Personal freedom, all citizens enjoying the same rights socially and before the law. Do you enjoy the same rights as the white people do in America, the land of freedom and democracy, or are you not rather treated over there as second-class citizens? Can you go into a restaurant where white people dine? Can you get a seat in the theatre where white people sit? Can you get a seat or a berth in the railroad car, or can you even ride in the South in the same street car with white people? And how about the law? Is lynching and the most horrible crimes connected therewith, a lawful proceeding in a democratic country? Now, all this is entirely different in Germany, where they do like colored people, where they treat them as gentlemen and as white men and quite a number of colored people have fine positions in business in Berlin and other German cities. Why, then, fight the Germans only for the benefit of the Wall Street robbers and to protect the millions they have loaned to the English, French and Italians? You have been made the tool of the egotistic and rapacious rich in England and America and there is nothing in the whole game for you but broken bones, horrible wounds, spoiled health or death. No satisfaction whatever will you get out of this unjust war. You have never seen Germany. So you are fools if you allow people to make you hate us. Come over and see for yourself. Let those do the fighting who make the profit out of this war. Don't allow them to use you as cannon-fodder. To carry a gun in this service is not an honor, but a shame. Throw it away and come over to the German lines. You will find friends who will help you along.

The black men never wavered. Why?

Because side by side with this treatment on the part of their own countrymen came the courtesy, the kindness and the utter lack of prejudice among the French. The black soldiers by their sweet-tempered consideration gained friends everywhere. They saw the wretched suffering of the French and they toiled and fought willingly for them. French officers and civilians of high social position vied with each other in doing all they could to show consideration. A Negro officer entered a café. The American white officers resented his seat at their table and started to rise—the French officers at a neighboring table very quietly and courteously nodded to the landlady and the black officer found a welcome seat with them.

Several high white southern officers of General Ballou's staff blocked nearly everything that would help or encourage the black men—the Chief of Staff repeatedly refused permissions to the photographers, with the result that the Division has almost no photographic record of its work.

But it did work and fight.

The single colored artillery brigade, 167th Field Artillery, had a General from Massachusetts, Sherburne, who believed in them. He said in General Order 11 that he desired *"to record his appreciation of the high qualities displayed by officers and men during the recent operations in this sector. They have been zealous soldiers and skilful artillerymen. Their recompense lies in their knowledge of work well done and in the commendation of those well qualified to speak. By day and night, often under a hail of shrapnel, often through clouds of deadly gas, they have marched and fought, dragged their guns sometimes by hand into the line, kept open their lines of communication and brought up their supplies always with a cheerfulness that earned them the admiration of all."*

The Division was repeatedly under fire. It went forward in the last great drive and was preparing to take part in the great assault on Metz when the armistice came.

In one instance alone has the white soldier been able even to disparage the actual work of the colored troops. In that case a battalion of the 368th Regiment was put in as support and, quite contrary to plan, was suddenly rushed forward as storm troops without equipment. Caught between the two barrages they fell back, contrary to orders, but another battalion of colored men relieved them and went forward. Where was the fault? The white officer, found skulking in the rear, said it was the cowardice of Negro officers.

So the word to acknowledge the Negro stevedore and the fighting black private has gone forth, but the American army is going to return to America determined to disparage the black officer and eliminate him from the army despite his record. And the black officer and private? They return at once bitter and exalted! They will not submit to American caste and they will ever love France!

Returning Soldiers
From The Crisis, May 1919

We are returning from war! THE CRISIS and tens of thousands of black men were drafted into a great struggle. For bleeding France and what she means and has meant and will mean to us and humanity and against the threat of German race arrogance, we fought gladly and to the last drop of blood;

for America and her highest ideals, we fought in far-off hope; for the dominant southern oligarchy entrenched in Washington, we fought in bitter resignation. For the America that represents and gloats in lynching, disfranchisement, caste, brutality and devilish insult—for this, in the hateful upturning and mixing of things, we were forced by vindictive fate to fight, also.

But today we return! We return from the slavery of uniform which the world's madness demanded us to don to the freedom of civil garb. We stand again to look America squarely in the face and call a spade a spade. We sing: This country of ours, despite all its better souls have done and dreamed, is yet a shameful land.

It lynches.

And lynching is barbarism of a degree of contemptible nastiness unparalleled in human history. Yet for fifty years we have lynched two Negroes a week, and we have kept this up right through the war.

It *disfranchises* its own citizens.

Disfranchisement is the deliberate theft and robbery of the only protection of poor against rich and black against white. The land that disfranchises its citizens and calls itself a democracy lies and knows it lies.

It encourages *ignorance*.

It never really tried to educate the Negro. A dominant minority does not want Negroes educated. It wants servants, dogs, whores and monkeys. And when this land allows a reactionary group by its stolen political power to force as many black folk into these categories as it possibly can, it cries in contemptible hypocrisy: "They threaten us with degeneracy; they cannot be educated."

It *steals* from us.

It organizes industry to cheat us. It cheats us out of our land; it cheats us out of our labor. It confiscates our savings. It reduces our wages. It raises our rent. It steals our profit. It taxes us without representation. It keeps us consistently and universally poor, and then feeds us on charity and derides our poverty.

It *insults* us.

It has organized a nation-wide and latterly a world-wide propaganda of deliberate and continuous insult and defamation of black blood wherever found. It decrees that it shall not be possible in travel nor residence, work nor play, education nor instruction for a black man to exist without tacit or open acknowledgment of his inferiority to the dirtiest white dog. And it looks upon any attempt to question or even discuss this dogma as arrogance, unwarranted assumption and treason.

This is the country to which we Soldiers of Democracy return. This is the fatherland for which we fought! But it is *our* fatherland. It was right for us to fight. The faults of *our* country are *our* faults. Under similar circumstances, we would fight again. But by the God of Heaven, we are cowards and jackasses if now that the war is over, we do not marshal every ounce of our brain and brawn to fight a sterner, longer, more unbending battle against the forces of hell in our own land.

We *return*.

We return from *fighting*.

We return *fighting*.

Make way for Democracy! We saved it in France, and by the Great Jehovah, we will save it in the United States of America, or know the reason why.

The Boycott Movement against Jim Crow Streetcars in the South, 1900–1906

by August Meier and Elliott Rudwick

The prelude to the civil rights revolution of the mid-twentieth century was the dramatic eighteen-month bus boycott in Montgomery, Alabama, led by Martin Luther King, Jr. Unknown at the time was the fact that Montgomery had witnessed a two-year boycott by its Negro citizens over a half-century before, when the city council enacted a trolley-car segregation bill. Like the bus boycott of 1955–56, the streetcar boycott of 1900–1902 was part of a larger regional Negro protest against Jim Crow urban transit. The boycotts in *Montgomery*, Birmingham, and Tallahassee during the late 1950's had their counterparts in more than twenty-five southern cities between 1900 and 1906. This earlier, forgotten movement was especially remarkable, for, unlike the Montgomery boycott which occurred in a period of rising Negro militance and increasing nothern sympathy for the Negroes' cause, the boycotts at the turn of the century came at a time when southern white hostility and northern white indifference were reaching their peak and when, as a result, a philosophy of accommodation had achieved ascendancy in Negro thought and action.

These protests arose in response to the Jim Crow streetcar laws passed at the height of the wave of segregation legislation enacted in southern states two generations ago. Georgia passed the first such law in 1891,[1] but it required segregation only "as much as practicable"; thus, it left implementation to the erratic discretion of the traction companies. Then, beginning about 1900, a number of southern cities passed municipal segregation ordinances. In that year, Atlanta,[2] Rome,[3] and Augusta[4] supplemented the state law with measures requiring segregation. Montgomery in 1900,[5] Jacksonville in 1901, Mobile in 1902, Columbia, South Carolina, and Houston and San Antonio in 1903,[6] all passed such ordinances. Meanwhile, states had begun to enact Jim Crow streetcar laws applicable only in certain localities. Thus a Virginia law of 1902 required segregation in Alexandria and in Fairfax County. An act of Arkansas in 1903 applied only to cities "of the first class," and one in Tennessee of the same year only to counties of 150,000 or more. The latter statute, which affected only Memphis, was never enforced.[7]

The first state to pass a mandatory statewide statute was Louisiana in 1902. Mississippi followed in 1904; and in the same year, Virginia authorized, but did not require, segregation in all cities. Tennessee and Florida required statewide segregation in 1905. The Florida law was declared unconstitutional, and the state did not enact another until 1909; but in the interim, Pensacola and Jacksonville had passed municipal ordinances which the high court sustained.[8] In 1906, Virginia finally made Jim Crow streetcars a requirement in all its cities; and the following year, Texas, Oklahoma, and North Carolina Joined the list. In South Carolina and Alabama, city ordinances and streetcar company regulations provided a substitute for state action.[9]

Nearly everywhere, the streetcar companies opposed enactment of the Jim Crow laws by citing the expense and difficulty in enforcement, and the fear of losing Negro customers. Often the companies were able to defeat such bills or postpone their enactment. Sometimes, however, faced with an aroused public opinion, the companies endorsed the Jim Crow regulation—even at the cost of reversing their earlier position.[10]

August Meier and Elliott Rudwick, "The Boycott Movement Against Jim Crow Streetcars in the South, 1900–1906," *Journal of American History*, Organization of American History, 1969, 55(4), March 1969, PP 756–775, by permission of Oxford University Press.

Neither the streetcar segregation which emerged at the turn of the century nor the Negro boycotts against it were without precedent. There had been successful protests against Jim Crow horsecars during Reconstruction in Richmond, New Orleans, Charleston, and Louisville; but Savannah was evidently the only city of the period where a boycott was reported.[11] However, in every state and in many of the cities which passed segregation laws between 1891 and 1906, their enforcement precipitated Negro boycotts. There were at least three successful ones in Georgia during the 1890's, when attempts were made to implement the law of 1891: Atlanta in 1892–93,[12] Augusta in 1898,[13] and on the line from Savannah to the resort of Warsaw in 1899.[14] Thereafter, only five boycotts were even temporarily successful: Jacksonville in 1901, Montgomery and Mobile in 1902, and Jacksonville and Pensacola in 1905; and of these, the victory in the two Florida protests of 1905 was achieved by court action rather than by the boycott itself.

Boycotts have been identified in the following cities: Atlanta[15] and Rome,[16] Georgia, 1900; Augusta, Georgia, 1900–1903;[17] Montgomery, Alabama, 1900–1902;[18] Jacksonville, Florida, 1901;[19] Mobile, Alabama, 1902;[20] New Orleans[21] and Shreveport,[22] Louisiana, 1902–3; Little Rock, Arkansas,[23] and Columbia, South Carolina,[24] 1903; Houston, Texas, 1903–5;[25] Vicksburg and Natchez, Mississippi, 1904;[26] San Antonio, Texas,[27] and Richmond, Virginia,[28] 1904–5; Memphis,[29] Chattanooga,[30] and Knoxville,[31] Tennessee, and Pensacola[32] and Jacksonville,[33] Florida, 1905; Nashville,[34] Tennessee, 1905–6; Danville, Lynchburg, Portsmouth, and Norfolk, Virginia, 1906;[35] Newport News, Virginia,[36] and Savannah, Georgia,[37] 1906–7.

This listing is probably an underenumeration, for there are serious lacunae in the surviving evidence.[38] The limitations of the sources notwithstanding, it is evident that the boycott movement was an extensive one. Protests occurred in all the states of the former Confederacy. Most of the major cities in Georgia, and every major city in Virginia and Tennessee had one. As the Mobile *Daily Register* observed in 1905: "In every city where it has been found advisable to separate the races in the street cars the experience has been the same. The negroes . . . have invariably declared a boycott."[39]

Negro protests through mass meetings, petitions to city councils and legislatures, and even an occasional boycott, often began while the segregation

bills were being considered. In Savannah, for example, in 1901 a bill before the city council was defeated, by the overt opposition of the streetcar company and by the more covertly expressed "conservative feeling of the leading white citizens," whose aid the Negroes had marshaled. Five years later, however, sentiment for segregation was much stronger among whites, and the Savannah Electric Company's president reversed his position. A Negro mass meeting urged defeat of the bill. The mayor, however, termed this protest inflammatory; the city council refused even to hear the Negro delegation and enacted the ordinance unanimously. In San Antonio, where the city council did permit a Negro committee to speak, an ordinance was also passed unanimously. In Jackson-ville, after the city council in 1901 had passed a bill over the, articulated opposition of the Negro community and its two Negro councilmen, colored people angrily stayed off the cars in an attempt to pressure the mayor into vetoing the bill. This boycotting proved futile, as did a similar step by Pensacola Negroes four years later, when they tried to force the city's streetcar company to lobby against the Avery streetcar-segregation bill, then before the legislature.[40]

Negroes resented these laws as a humiliating disgrace. The Nashville *Clarion* editorially condemned this effort "to humiliate, degrade, and stigmatize the negro." Several Lynchburg Negroes circulated a call for a boycott and termed the law "a gratuitous insult . . . to every one with a drop of Negro blood. . . . Let us touch to the quick the white man's pocket. 'Tis there his conscience often lies." In 1905, after the Avery bill had passed the Florida legislature, Jacksonville Negro ministers urged a boycott of this "unjust, barbaric and . . . cowardly measure" "in order to retain our self-respect." As the Savannah *Tribune* said: "Do not trample on our pride by being 'jim crowed,' Walk!"[41]

For Negroes the new order was startling, even shocking. One report spoke of the "mingled disgust and bewilderment; among Memphis colored people arising from the "obloquy and shame" imposed after forty years of unrestricted travel.[42] To men like John Mitchell, Jr., editor of the Richmond *Planet*, former city councilman, president of the Mechanics Savings Bank, and grand chancellor of the Virginia Knights of Pythias, the whites who demanded streetcar segregation represented a new and different Richmond. Mitchell maintained that since the Civil War no act had aroused "a more bitter feeling of racial antagonism." He deplored the passing of the "traditional harmony" between the races, survivals of which still existed in such events as the recent funerals of an "old mammy" and a church sexton who were buried from the churches and homes of the white Richmond patricians they had long served.[43]

Beyond this desire to preserve a status quo that in retrospect appeared to belong to a golden age of "harmonious," if paternalistic, race relations, there was the fear of physical maltreatment at the hands of "poor white trash"—conductors and motormen. The *St. Luke Herald* of Richmond predicted that "the very dangerous [police] power placed in the hands of hot headed and domineering young white men," already universally hated for their overbearing and insulting conduct, would "certainly provoke trouble."[44] Jacksonville Negroes also vigorously objected to the provision giving police power to conductors as "bound to bring about a strife and possibly bloodshed."[45] In fact, one of the reasons urged for boycotting was the belief that by keeping off the cars Negroes would avoid occasions for friction and disorder.[46]

Although in some cities the white press either ignored or attempted to minimize the extent of the boycott, generally, where the daily newspaper reported the protests, the editors commented upon the boycott's singular effectiveness. Universally the effect was startling to the white population. In Augusta, where the streetcar company instituted segregation on Sunday, May 20, 1900, about two weeks before the city council enacted its ordinance, the *Chronicle* reported: "It was noticeable that the negroes did not take to the cars as usual on Sunday. On about every fourth car passing one or two *could* be seen. . . ." The Mobile and New Orleans laws both went into effect early in November, 1902. The Mobile *Daily Register* admitted that "Nearly all of them are walking." In New Orleans, with its vast distances, the boycott was necessarily less marked. But there were so many empty seats in the Negro compartment that the whites bitterly resented having to stand. Little Rock conductors observed that very few Negroes used the lines most patronized by the race, "less than five percent as compared with the usual 60 percent." The day after the boycott started in Columbia, a white paper reported that "the absence of negroes was noted by everyone." In San Antonio, their presence on the vehicles was pronounced "a rarity." The Savannah *Morning News* commented that the colored clergy had been most effective in organizing the people. For example, the paper reported that Thomas Gamble, secretary to

the mayor, had given his Negro maid carfare to carry his two heavy suitcases to City Hall. When she belatedly arrived, soaked with perspiration, Gamble discovered that she had walked to town because her minister had admonished everyone to keep off the trolley cars.[47]

The colored weeklies proudly carried similar reports. The Atlanta *Age* declared "that you can stand on the streets all day and never see a Negro riding . . . unless he is going to Decatur, Edgewood, or the River."[48] A Negro visitor in Houston was surprised at "the completeness" of the boycott,[49] while one in Montgomery, nine months after the local Negroes began walking, marvelled at this "universal boycott."[50]

The boycotts were easily sustained in their early stages because they were a natural reaction to the humiliation and fears associated with riding the Jim Crow cars. However, informal pressures were also used. In San Antonio, a few days after the movement began, six Negroes were arrested for pulling a youth off a trolley car. In Columbia, the few who rode "were 'guyed' when the cars passed groups of negroes on the streets." In Savannah, those who opposed the boycotts were publicly denounced at mass meetings as "demagogues and hypocrites." The city's police quickly took to arresting Negroes who stood on downtown street corners, heckled riders as they got off, and urged those ready to board the trolleys to take a hack instead.[51];

The traction companies were undeniably hard hit. In April, 1908, the president of the Savannah Electric Company in- formed the city council that the boycott had resulted in a 25 percent decline in business and had cost about $50,000. He estimated that in 1906, when the movement was at its height, the company's loss was over $32,000. The Houston Electric Company, about five months after the boycott began, decided, that it was no longer possible to disguise the fact that the protest was "crippling" its receipts.[52]

In three cases, the companies temporarily capitulated to the protesters. Jacksonville city officials, undoubtedly acting at the request of the traction company, ceased enforcing their ordinance after a few months and quietly asked the Negro ministers to inform their congregations.[53] In Montgomery, after two years, the company was so hard hit that it simply suspended enforcement of the law.[54] The president of the Mobile Light and Railroad Company, in the face of the Negroes' financially ruinous action, decided to test the ordinance in the courts; and he directed employees to permit passengers to sit anywhere. A conductor was convicted in city court for doing this, and the company announced that it would appeal.[55] There was no further mention of the case, however. Apparently, in both Mobile and Montgomery, Jim Crow arrangements were quietly reinstated after a brief period.

In addition to walking, Negroes pressed private carriages, drays, and hacks into service. It is doubtful that the boycotts could have occurred at all except for the Negro hackmen and draymen, who in that period still dominated these two occupations in a number of southern cities.[56] In Jacksonville[57] and Savannah,[58] and undoubtedly elsewhere, the hackmen reduced their fare for boycotters from twenty-five to ten cents. In Savannah, the authorities became so concerned that the police began to look for overworked horses and to arrest unlicensed hackmen.[59]

In Houston, Negro hackowners lowered the price to five cents.[60] A Negro visitor reported that the protesters had developed an informal transit system of passenger vans, wagons, and carriages.[61] As the boycott entered its eighth month in June, 1904, a streetcar strike forced Houston whites to walk for a few days. The Houston *Post* noted the amusement of the boycotters and the advantage they had by virtue of their "crude omnibus lines."

> [I]n some instances the whites were hurrahed good-naturedly by acquaintances among the blacks. One well known businessman tells this on himself: "I live away out in the South End and having neither a horse nor carriage was forced to foot it to town. A conveyance came along driven by a negro and I asked him for a lift. Looking at me and grinning, he said: 'Boss, Ise bliged ter fuse yer de favor. De city council won't let de white folks and de black folks ride together, and I ain't got my compartmint sign up yit,' and with that he drove on." The negroes seemed to enjoy the predicament of the whites hugely, and along toward noon many of their conveyances could be seen driving about the streets with a space in the rear some two feet in length blocked off by a piece of cardboard bearing the legend, "For Whites Only."[62]

The step from these arrangements to actual transportation companies was not a long one, particularly in view of the trends in Negro thinking of the period. Because of deteriorating conditions, there had been a shift in emphasis from agitation and politics to economic advancement, self-help, and racial solidarity, often coupled with a philosophy

of accommodation. The development of transportation companies, therefore, functioned in three ways: as a means of protesting against discrimination, as a fulfillment of the dream of creating substantial Negro businesses by an appeal to racial solidarity, and—hopefully—as a practical solution to the transportation problems faced by the masses of boycotting Negroes.

In several cities Negroes talked about forming a transit company, and in Savannah two were actually organized, though there is no evidence that either put vehicles on the streets.[63] Only the Virginia and Tennessee boycotts of 1905 and 1906 produced functioning transportation lines.[64] Portsmouth Negroes obtained a "double horse wagonette" which seated about thirty passengers and made regular trips. Inspired by this example, members of the race in Norfolk formed the Metropolitan Transfer Company, which placed a yellow herdic on the streets—the first of a fleet of eight scheduled to arrive. Soon afterwards, however, the white daily newspaper noted that few Negroes were patronizing the vehicle, since by then most had returned to the streetcars.[65] In Chattanooga, where the boycott started on July 5, 1905, some unnamed "enterprising negroes" formed a hack line by the end of the month. After creating a stock company, they leased three carriages which made a regular schedule between downtown and a Negro section known as Churchville. Apparently this line did well, for in late August it was reported that, with the boycott continuing in "full force" and with the colored hackmen having "more business than they can handle," some "well known negroes" of the city had applied for a charter for the Transfer Omnibus Motor Car Company. A week later, however, there was evidence of a crackdown on the hack line. Charging that the Negroes were "working old, worn-out animals from early morning until late at night and are only half-feeding them," the county humane officer announced that he would prosecute the operators of the company.[66] While further evidence is lacking, it appears that harassment by the public authorities forced the Negro entrepreneurs out of business.

The most impressive attempt to develop a Negro-owned alternative to the Jim Crow trolley cars occurred in Nashville. There the boycott began July 5, and by the end of the summer the leaders formed the Union Transportation Company. Its incorporators included the elite of Nashville's business and professional community: the president was Preston Taylor, an undertaker and the pastor of the Lea Avenue Christian Church; its treasurer was a Fisk University official, George W. Henderson; and its purchasing agent was the Reverend Richard Henry Boyd, general secretary of the National Baptist Publishing Board.[67] For the first few weeks, the company used horses and wagons. By September 21, $7,000 worth of stock had been sold, another $18,000 worth subscribed, and five motor buses purchased. The buses arrived on September 29, and during the day large numbers of race-proud Negroes eagerly inspected them. According to the Nashville *Banner*, "the cars are on the steam wagonette style, and have a large front seat with two long seats running backward, band wagon style. They have a capacity for fifteen persons."[68]

The line began operations early in October. For at least a brief time, it invigorated the boycott, but the buses never fulfilled their expectation. The few vehicles naturally kept infrequent schedules. To remedy this problem, the company's inexperienced officers overpaid for nine more buses. These lacked sufficient power for Nashville's hills. Arrangements for boosting power were made with the local electric company, but either the results were unsatisfactory or the company reneged on its promises; in any event, the bus operations were constantly hampered. Little improvement resulted from a new generator installed at the National Baptist Publishing Board, and battery trouble repeatedly incapacitated the vehicles. Passengers became tired of waiting and increasingly used the Jim Crow streetcars. Two years later, W. E. B. Du Bois described this enterprise as one that cost its shareholders $20,000 for a few months of service.[69]

Legal efforts proved as futile as the transportation companies and, though not entirely eschewed, played a distinctly minor role. In a few cities Negroes seriously discussed going to court, but only in Florida did they actually undertake a legal attack. This litigation was directed by city councilman and attorney J. Douglas Wetmore, who twice carried test cases to the state supreme court. Arguing that the state law of 1905 was "vague and uncertain," that it violated the equal protection clause of the Fourteenth Amendment, and even that it discriminated among classes of Negroes by providing that Negro nurses accompanying whites could sit in the white section, Wetmore persuaded the court to hold the law unconstitutional. The judges did so, however, on the narrow ground that to allow Negro servants to sit in the white section was class legislation.

Negro jubilation over the victory and the temporary end of segregation was shortlived. Jacksonville and Pensacola authorities quickly passed municipal ordinances. This time there was no general boycott. Negroes in both cities again resorted to the courts, but early in 1906 the high court upheld both city laws.[70]

The boycott leaders, where they can be identified, were uniformly an elite group which consisted of prominent business and professional men, with at times a sprinkling of federal employees or a rare politician. Jacksonville, Savannah, Nashville, and Richmond provide the most complete information. In Savannah, the leadership included the outstanding Baptist and African Methodist Episcopal ministers, two physicians, an attorney, an undertaker, a prosperous barber with white patronage, and an insurance executive. The pattern in Jacksonville was similar, except that it was unique in including the city's two Negro councilmen. In Nashville, the prime movers were the Reverend E. W. D. Isaac, editor of the Nashville *Clarion* and the *National Baptist Union*, and the Reverend R. H. Boyd, president of the One Cent Savings Bank, as well as secretary of the Baptist Publishing Board. Supporting them were prominent citizens like J. C. Napier, former city councilman, cashier of the One Cent Savings Bank, and later register of the treasury under William Howard Taft; Bishop Evans Tyree of the African Methodist Episcopal Church; the Reverend William D. Chapelle, secretary-treasurer of the African Methodist Episcopal Sunday School Union; and professors at Meharry Medical School and Fisk University. In Richmond, the most dynamic force behind the movement was John Mitchell, Jr. Working with him were two or three professors at Virginia Union University, most notably J. R. L. Diggs, who was later president of Kentucky State College; Benjamin Jackson, grocer and former city councilman; and most important of all, the officials of the leading benefit societies and fraternal orders and their affiliated banks. Besides Mitchell himself, these included Maggie L. Walker, head of the Independent Order of St. Luke; and the Reverend W. P. Burrell, president of the Richmond Baptist Sunday School Union and general secretary of the United Order of True Reformers—the outstanding non-secret mutual benefit order among Negroes of the period.[71]

Especially important was the role of the newspaper editors. Mitchell of the Richmond *Planet* and

Sol Johnson of the Savannah *Tribune* clearly played leading parts in initiating and sustaining the boycott. W. A. Pledger of the Atlanta *Age* and Isaac of the Nashville *Clarion* evidently played comparable roles, although copies of their papers are not extant. The Chattanooga *Daily Times* denounced the Negro press of the city, especially the Chattanooga *Blade*, for stirring up "heresy" and disturbing racial harmony.[72] All six of the Richmond Negro newspapers supported the boycott there. In Augusta, W. J. White of the Georgia *Baptist* was nearly lynched for his denunciation of the Jim Crow law.[73]

The role of the ministers, in contrast, is a complex subject. The relationship of religion to Negro protest has always been paradoxical. The Negro church has played mainly an accommodating role, and its ministers have preached sermons about rewards in heaven for the meek on this earth. Yet Christian ideology has also served as a wellspring of protest from anti-slavery days down to Martin Luther King, Jr.[74] Ministers often represented the Negro community in dealings with whites, especially in the South. Such clergymen were influential among Negroes because they could obtain small favors from the white community. They were influential not because Negroes chose them, but because they were selected by prominent whites who utilized the clergy to control the Negro community.[75] A common dilemma was faced by the Reverend C. R. Dinkins, a minister in the Colored Methodist Episcopal Church and the principal leader of the boycott in Columbia, South Carolina. One-third of the cost of his church had been contributed by white people of Columbia. He was a man "in whom we have much confidence," said the Columbia *State* when it advised Negroes to drop the boycott.[76]

Ironically, because of this pattern of using the ministers to influence the Negro community, southern whites assumed that whatever happened there was the work of the "preachers." Clergymen were, in fact, often pictured as the provocateurs of the boycotts. As the Mobile *Register* said, wherever segregated streetcars had been inaugurated, invariably the Negroes had initiated a boycott, "backed by the exhortations of their religious leaders."[77]

It is true that often ministers were among the chief supporters of the streetcar protests. They were prominent in Pensacola, Jacksonville, and Savannah; they were the principal leaders in Montgomery and Columbia; and elsewhere, as in Memphis and Nashville, individual ministers were named as key

figures. Yet the individuals who stood out most prominently among the opponents of the boycotts were certain African Methodist Episcopal and especially the Baptist ministers. The Natchez movement was in its third month when it was drastically undermined by a religious conference which was sponsored by the prominent African Methodist Episcopal minister, W. H. Jernagin. The delegates freely used the streetcars in getting to and from the sessions. The Reverend T. O. Fuller of Memphis, principal of the Howe Institute and later a chronicler of Baptist church history, wrote a letter to the *Commercial Appeal* and advised Negroes that "Law-abiding citizens can do nothing else but respect" the provisions of the state law and obey the conductors.[78] In Atlanta, African Methodist Episcopal Bishop Henry M. Turner helped to break the boycott by ostentatiously riding on the Jim Crow cars.[79] In Savannah, the ministers first actively supported the protest movement. But later, in the spring of 1907, the boycott began to break when influential men among the Baptist clergy and the faculty at Georgia Industrial College rode the streetcars.[80] In Richmond, the situation was the most extreme of all. There, even before the boycott began, an open split developed in the Negro leadership. The powerful Baptist Ministers Conference, consisting of the pastors of three-fourths of the Negro churches of Richmond,[81] opposed the movement and thereby seriously weakened it. United against the clergymen were the businessmen, the editors, the bankers, and the leaders of fraternal and insurance societies. Some of the most important individuals in this group were also Baptist ministers, but they did not serve churches and their identification was with the business community rather than with the religious leadership.[82] In Nashville, however, a comparable cleavage failed to develop. There, preacher-businessmen such as R. H. Boyd were able to obtain support from important clerics like Bishop Evans Tyree who were not businessmen. Thus, Boyd led a united community.

The elite leaders who headed the protest were known as impeccably respectable men, rather than as radicals or fire-brands. Some, indeed, were close friends of the noted accommodator Booker T, Washington, whom contemporaries described as "conservative" in contrast to the "radical" minority of intellectuals that led the opposition to him and his philosophy of accommodation. Moreover, it should be emphasized that this widespread boycott movement occurred in an era when accommodation was in the ascendancy. One wonders, in fact, how it was that this protest movement occurred at all, given the context of race relations in which it took place.

The trolley-car boycotts can best be described as a "conservative protest." First, this movement was conservative in the sense that it was seeking to preserve the status quo—to prevent a change from an older and well-established pattern. Second, it is also noteworthy that the boycotts avoided a direct confrontation with the laws, such as would have occurred if Negroes had insisted on sitting in the white section. There were instances of Negroes being arrested for occupying seats assigned to whites, but these were rare incidents and, except for the Florida test cases, not part of the organized protest movements.[83]

Third, the statements of the boycott leaders themselves were often remarkably moderate or "conservative." This was true even of the editors, who formed the most militant segment of the movements' spokesmen. The Nashville *Clarion* vigorously supported the boycotters, yet added: "Their protestations are mild and peaceable however. They exhibit no spirit of anarchy or revenge, neither do they make any threatening demonstrations."[84] Mitchell, one of the most militant southern editors, described a meeting called to plan the Richmond protest: "The discussion was conservative and it was the opinion of the body that the colored people should do all in their power to promote peace and avoid any clash or disorder on the streetcars." The Richmond *Times-Dispatch* took a similar view of Mitchell's activities. In reporting a mass rally, it stated: "There was no turbulence, no fierce denunciation and no fire-eating, as many had feared. On the contrary, conservatism was urged . . . The paper noted that Mitchell advised Negroes "to be conservative and law-abiding, but to walk." Sternly, he warned his listeners to refuse to be provoked into confrontations with conductors which would lead to a race riot: "Then you will see their guns, their Winchesters. But we don't want guns, we want peace, and the way to keep it is to let the white people have their cars." Mitchell repeatedly urged Negroes who did board the street-cars to obey the law and sit in the rear; he emphatically declared: "Do not get on the streetcars to assert your rights."[85] Similarly, in Little Rock, boycotters were advised to "be obedient to the law. Let no one get on the cars and attempt to undo what the legislature of the great state of Arkansas has

done. . . . Never mind about framing resolutions or arguing the merits or demerits of the affair with anyone. Simply stay off the cars." In Columbia, Dinkins told the press that the Negroes would do nothing intemperately and that they regretted hurting the Columbia Electric Street Railway Company, since its officials were among the Negroes' "safe and trusted friends." Dinkins justified the boycott because "there was no occasion for this ordinance. . . . Everything was going along pleasantly and preachers here have always avoided discussion of racial issues, preferring to try to inspire their congregations with faith in their own race and to encourage them to trust and to depend upon the southern white people."[86]

Perhaps the most conservative of the protest leaders were those associated with the National Negro Business League, which Washington had founded in 1900. Indeed, Washington organized the overwhelming majority of leading Negro clergymen and businessmen into what was widely recognized and publicly labeled as a "conservative" clique. Boyd, president of the Nashville Business League, in a letter to the evening newspaper, pointed out that it was at the request of traction officials that Negro leaders had decided not to protest against the bill in the state legislature. They had then vainly begged the company to attach separate trailers and hire colored fare collectors on the routes where there was the most Negro patronage. Since the company had "denied [them] even serious consideration," he continued, the colored people felt that actually it was the street-cars which had boycotted them. It was in view of this situation, Boyd concluded, that the Negroes of Nashville had decided that this would be a good time for "stimulating the cause of the automobile as a common carrier." As this letter suggests, a secondary motivation behind Boyd's actions was the vision of Negro enterprise built on the Negro market, of Negro "captains of industry," to use Washington's phrase. Men like Boyd may have been as much interested in the possibility of business enterprise as in protesting discrimination. As he said at the meeting of the National Negro Business League in 1903: "These discriminations are only blessings in disguise. They stimulate and encourage rather than cower and humiliate the true, ambitious, self-determined Negro."[87]

Another leading Nashville businessman who backed the boycott and the bus company and who, like Boyd, was given to accommodating utterances was J. C. Napier. He was a man of whom Washington once said, "I have never heard Mr. Napier express a narrow or bitter thought toward the white race." The two men were so close that Washington once offered Napier the presidency of the National Negro Business League.[88] In Richmond, also, prominent League people were active in the boycott movement. Attorney Giles Jackson, secretary of the Virginia League, proved to be an exception when he sided with the Baptist ministers who opposed the boycott. But others, most notably Dr. R. E: Jones, president of the Richmond League, were the movement's ardent advocates.[89]

Although Washington did not personally involve himself with the streetcar boycotts, he had publicly approved the first one in Atlanta in 1892–93.[90] In contrast, it is interesting to note that the anti-Washington "radical" Niagara Movement, founded by Du Bois when the boycotts were at their height, paid no attention to them and failed to recommend this type of protest, even though two of its prominent members—J. R. L. Diggs of Richmond and the Reverend J. Milton Waldron of Jacksonville—were connected with the boycotts in their home cities. Indeed, the only public reference to the boycotts that came from the prolific pen of Du Bois concerned the transportation companies, which he discussed as exemplifying business enterprise rather than protest.[91]

Clearly, then, the streetcar protests were almost entirely led by conservative business and professional men. Their weapon was the boycott, a multifaceted response to oppression that protested and yet avoided confrontation with the discriminating whites. As the social psychologist Thomas F. Pettigrew has written, boycotts as a protest tactic have "the distinct psychological advantage" of appealing to all "three major types of responses human beings can make to oppression. . . . Such campaigns move toward the oppressor by seeking to achieve desegregation; they move against the oppressor by encouraging group unity and aggressively upsetting the white-controlled economy; and they move away from the oppressor by requesting the participators merely to avoid the scene of conflict."[92] By attacking and yet withdrawing, the boycotters—like the founders of the Negro churches a century before—were both protesting against race prejudice and accommodating to it.

It should be emphasized that, although the boycott was a tactic adopted by many conservative leaders, partly because it avoided confrontation and overt racial friction, it was, nevertheless, a genuine protest weapon. It was so considered by the whites and by those accommodating ministers who opposed its use. But as the least aggressive kind of protest, the least militant variety of what today is called nonviolent direct action, it fitted the conservatism of Negro leaders in southern cities during a period of accommodation. Even in such a time, the boycotts were a natural and spontaneous response, for they sought to preserve dignity in the face of a humiliating social change.

The streetcar boycotts varied considerably in length. The nature of the evidence is such that in most instances it is not possible to give a definite date for the conclusion of a boycott. After the first few days or weeks, the white press usually ignored the movement. Exchanges and other items from distant cities in the Negro weeklies were not ordinarily dated; and, thus, even for the victories in Jacksonville in 1901 and Montgomery in 1902, the Negro press failed to note the precise date.[93]

In Savannah, where the evidence is the most complete, the boycott began on September 13, 1906, and continued through the winter. As spring approached, the *Tribune* and the Chatham County Emancipation Association were urging Negroes not only to keep off the cars but also to refrain from patronizing the suburban Lincoln Amusement Park, owned by the transit company. Yet, as the *Morning News* observed a month earlier, "there has been a gradual tendency on the part of the negroes to resume riding on the cars." The last notice of a mass meeting published in the *Tribune* was for one scheduled for March 24, 1907. *Actually*, the *boycott* began *to* break down as important clerics and professors openly rode the streetcars. Some continued to walk, even though the majority slowly returned to the streetcars. In April, 1908, the president of the streetcar company indicated that it was still suffering to some extent; he put the return of colored patrons at 80 percent. As late as the following September, a few, like Johnson, were still boycotting the cars. But by then even the *Tribune* editor conceded defeat.[94]

The boycotts ranged in length from a few weeks to as long as two or three years. The Mobile *Daily Register* generalized that it took "about two months" to convince Negroes that they might as well use the cars again.[95] Yet some clearly lasted a good deal longer. The Montgomery boycott was entering its third month when the Atlanta *Constitution* marveled at its "surprising persistency. . . . The company reports that the receipts of the line have fallen off fully 25%.

All efforts heretofore made in Alabama to organize strikes among the negro miners . . . have proved unsuccessful and it has been believed that no considerable number of negroes could be organized for any length of time . . . they have almost entirely refrained from riding."[96] The New Orleans and Nashville boycotts lasted at least eight months, the Atlanta boycott at least ten months, the Savannah boycott six to ten months, and the Newport News boycott fourteen months. The white press in San Antonio indicated the boycott there was going on three months after it began, and the daily paper in Houston reported the local boycott as still strong eight months after it started. A July, 1905, report in the Charleston *News and Courier* indicated that both were still in existence—making their length fifteen months and twenty-two months respectively. And in June, 1903, three years after the Augusta boycott began, the manager of the Columbia traction company reported that this movement was so effective that. Negroes arriving on excursion trains from Augusta refused to ride the trolley cars even in Columbia.[97]

In some cities, like Atlanta, Memphis, Natchez, Richmond, and Savannah, leadership cleavages undoubtedly hastened the demise of the protests. But more than anything else, what undoubtedly caused their decline was a feeling of discouragement—a realistic pessimism—that must in time have come over the demonstrators as they saw that their withdrawal of patronage produced no results. Some, like editors Johnson and Mitchell, might continue to walk, but gradually a sense of futility set in.

It is not surprising that, in the end, the boycott movements against Jim Crow trolleys failed in all of the cities where they were initiated. They occurred at a time when southern racism was reaching its crest and when the white South had gained a respectful hearing in the North. With the Supreme Court endorsing the separate-but-equal doctrine and with Negroes in most places virtually disfranchised, the boycotts were the only way of protesting realistically open to them. In retrospect, it is easy to see that their failure was inevitable. The remarkable thing is not that the boycotts failed, but that they happened in so many places and lasted as long as they often did.

Endnotes

1. *Acts of Georgia*, 1891, pp. 157–58.
2. Atlanta *Constitution*, Feb. 6, 1900.
3. New Orleans *Southwestern Christian Advocate*, July 5, 1900; Cleveland *Gazette*, July 7, 1900.
4. Augusta *Chronicle*, June 5, 1900.
5. Montgomery *Advertiser*, July 3, 10, 24, Aug. 7, 1900.
6. Jacksonville *Florida Times-Union and Citizen*, Nov. 14, 1901; Mobile *Daily Register*, Oct. 17. 1902; Columbia *State*, June 24, 1903; Houston *Daily Post*, Sept. 29, 1903; San Antonio *Express*, Oct. 13, 1903.
7. *Acts of Virginia*, 1.901-2, pp. 639–40; *Acts of Arkansas*, 1903. pp. 178–79; *Acts of Tennessee*, 1903, p. 75; Memphis *Commercial Appeal*, Mar. 27, Apr. 26, May 30. June 8, 1903; *Memphis Street Railway Co. v. State*, 110 Tenn. 602 (1903).
8. *Acts of Louisiana*, 1902, pp. 89–90; *Laws of Mississippi*, 1904, pp. 140–41; *Virginia Laws*, extra session of 1902-3-4. pp. 990–92; *Acts of Tennessee*, 1905, pp. 321–22; Acts of Florida, 1905, pp. 99–100; *ibid.*, 1909, pp. 339–40. On the Pensacola and Jacksonville municipal ordinances, see note 70.
9. Acts *of Virginia*, 1906, pp. 92–94; *General Laws of Texas*, 1907, pp. 58–60; *Public Laws of North Carolina*, 1907, pp. 1238–39; *Oklahoma Laws*, 1907-8, pp. 201–4; Gilbert Thomas Stephenson, *Race Distinctions* in *American Law* (New York, 1910), p. 229.
10. Savannah *Tribune*, Sept. 23, 1899; Augusta *Chronicle*, May 15, 17, 19, 20, 21. 1900; Richmond *Planet*, Mar. 15, 1902, May 7. June 18. 1904; Richmond *Times-Dispatch*, Apr. 17, 1904; Richmond *News-Leader*, May 9, 1904; Savannah *Morning News*, July 10. 1902. Aug. 31, 1906.
11. C. Vann Woodward, *The Strange Career of Jim Crow*, 2nd rev. ed. (New York. 1966), p. 27; Alrutheus A. Taylor, *The Negro in the Reconstruction of Virginia* (Washington, 1926), pp. 52, 214; Roger A. Fischer. "A Pioneer Protest: The New Orleans Street-Car Controversy of 1867," *Journal of Negro History*, 53 (July, 1968). 219–33; Williamson, *After Slavery: The Negro in South Carolina During Reconstruction, 1861-1877* (Chapel Hill, 1965), pp. 281-83; Marjorie M. Norris, "An Early Instance of Nonviolence: The Louisville Demonstrations of 1870–1871," *Journal of Southern History*, 32 (Nov., 1966), 487–504: Savannah *Tribune*, Aug. 27, Oct. 22, 1892, Sept. 16. 1899.
12. Savannah *Tribune*, Nov. 5, 1892; Booker T. Washington. "Taking Advantage of Our Disadvantages," *African Methodist Episcopal Church Review*, 10 (Apr., 1894), 480; Clarence A. Bacote, "The Negro in Georgia Politics, 1880–1908" (Ph.D. dissertation. University of Chicago, 1955), p. 18.
13. Augusta *Chronicle*, Aug. 31, Sept. 10, 13, 1898; Savannah *Tribune*, Sept. 23, 1899.
14. Savannah *Tribune*, Sept. 16, 30, Oct. 7, Nov. 18, 25, Dec. 2, 9, 1899; Savannah *Morning News*, Sept. 10, 11, 1899; Augusta *Chronicle*, Sept. 13, 1899.

15. Washington *Colored American,* Mar. 17, Nov. 10, 1900; Atlanta *Age,* n.d., quoted in Richmond Planet, Apr. 7, 1900; Savannah *Tribune,* Sept. 15, Dec. 8, 1900; New York *Age,* July 5, 1900, in Hampton Institute Clipping Collection, Hampton Institute. Whether because of the vagueness of the ordinance or the pressure of the Negro boycott, until 1906 the Atlanta streetcars exhibited a flexible system of segregation, with mixed smoking sections at the back of the cars, and some Negroes sitting with whites in the middle part. Agitation in 1906 led the company to institute a rigid system of segregation. Charles Crowe, "Racial Violence and Social Reform—Origins of the Atlanta Riot of 1906," *Journal of Negro History,* 53 (July, 1968), 245–46.

16. New Orleans *Southwestern Christian Advocate,* July 5, 1900.

17. Augusta *Chronicle,* May 21, 1900; Washington *Colored American,* Nov. 10, 1900: Columbia (S.C.) *State,* June 28, 1903.

18. Atlanta *Constitution.* Aug. 16. Sept. 20, 1900; Montgomery *Advertiser,* Aug. 18. 1900; Cleveland *Gazette,* Mar. 16, 1901; New Orleans *Southwestern Christian Advocate.* June 12, 1902, and Mobile *Weekly Press,* quoted *ibid.,* Sept. 4, 1902.

19. Jacksonville *Florida Times-Union and Citizen,* Nov. 11, 1901; Savannah *Tribune.* Nov. 16, 1901; New Orleans *Southwestern Christian Advocate,* Jan. 30, 1902.

20. Mobile *Daily Register,* Nov. 4, 5, 11, Dec. 2, 1902.

21. New Orleans *Times-Democrat,* Nov. 4, 6, g, Dec. 4, 1902: New Orleans *Southwestern Christian Advocate,* Nov. 6, 1902, Mar. 26, Apr. 23, June 12, Dec. 3, 24, 1903; New Orleans *Daily Picayune,* Nov. 4, 5, 9, 1902.

22. New Orleans *Southwestern Christian Advocate,* Dec. 3, 1903.

23. Little Rock *Daily Arkansas Democrat,* June 2, 1903; Little Rock *Arkansas Gazette,* May 28, 1903.

24. Columbia *State,* June 28, 29, 1903.

25. Houston *Daily Post,* Nov. 1, 2, 3, 23, 1903, Mar. 8, 15, June 3, 1904: Charleston *News and Courier,* July 4, 1905; *African Methodist Episcopal Church Review,* 20 (Apr., 1904), 409.

26. Vicksburg *Daily Herald,* June 2, 5, 1904; Vicksburg *Light,* July 4, 1904, quoted in St. Louis *Palladium,* July 30, 1904; Natchez *Daily Democrat.* Aug. 23, 25, 1904.

27. San Antonio *Express,* Mar. 16, 17, 20, June 16, 1904; Kansas City (Mo.) *Rising Son.* May 20, 1904; Charleston *News and Courier,* July 4, 1905.

28. Richmond *News-Leader,* Apr. 20, May 20, 1904; Richmond *Times-Dispatch,* Apr. 21. 1904; Richmond *Planet,* Apr. 23, 30, May 7, June 4, July 23, Aug. 20, Oct. 15, 1904, June 10, 1905; Baltimore *Afro-American Ledger,* June 11, 18. 1904; James H. Brewer, "The War Against Jim Crow in the Land of Goshen," *Negro History Bulletin,* 24 (Dec. 1960). 53–57.

29. Nashville *American,* July 31, 1905; Cleveland *Gazette,* July 29. 1905.

30. Chattanooga *Daily Times,* July 17, 25, 26. Aug. 13, 1905; Memphis *Commencal Appeal,* Sept. 7, 1905.

31. Knoxville *Journal and Tribune,* July 6, 7, 9, 1905.

32. Pensacola *Journal,* May 7, 14, July 2, Aug. 1, 2, 4, 1905.

33. Richmond *Planet,* June 10, 1905; Jacksonville *Florida Times-Union,* July 1, 3, 24, 1905.

34. Nashville *Banner,* July 6, Aug. 1, Sept. 22, Oct. 17, 1905. Mar. 16, 1906; "Fighting 'Jim-Crowism' in Nashville," *Literary Digest,* 31 (Oct. 7, 1905), 474–75; Richmond *Planet,* Aug. 12, 1905; Indianapolis *Freeman,* Oct. 7, 1905.

35. Danville *Register,* June 20, 1906; Lynchburg *News,* June 15, 1906; Norfolk *Ledger-Dispatch,* June 15, 26, 1906; Norfolk *Virginian-Pilot,* July 15, Aug. 24, 29, 1906.

36. Newport News *Daily Press,* June 15, 1906; New York *Age,* Aug. 1, 1907.

37. Savannah *Morning News,* Sept. 14, 15, 17, 23, 1906, Feb. 3, 1907; Savannah *Tribune,* Sept. 15, 22, 29, 1906, Jan. 12, Mar. 9, 23, May 18, June 1, 1907.

38. Since the boycotts were not illegal, court records are not helpful. The Booker T. Washington Papers contain a few references to boycotts. The W. E. B. Du Bois Papers contain nothing on the subject (interview with Herbert Aptheker. Nov. 22, 1968). Inevitably, one is compelled to depend upon contemporary newspapers. Local white papers had every reason to deemphasize—even ignore—the boycotts. Neither in Memphis nor in Atlanta did the daily press even mention the ones in their own cities. And where the local dailies reported the beginnings of a boycott, almost invariably the editors seem to have decided, after a certain point, that continuing discussion was no longer in the public interest. Unfortunately, of the cities in which boycotts occurred, only for Richmond, Savannah, and New Orleans are there extant copies of Negro newspapers. Since the Negro weeklies were marginal operations which lacked an efficient national network of communication until the rise of the Associated Negro Press in the 1920's, news of events in distant cities necessarily came irregularly through correspondence and "exchanges." Yet these "exchanges" and. more rarely, letters which travelers wrote to editors, provided helpful information about the boycotts in a number of cities. Moreover, the Richmond *Planet* and the Savannah *Tribune* published unusually complete accounts of the respective boycotts in which their editors played prominent roles. Also, in a few cases, most notably in Jacksonville and Pensacola, and—during the early part of the boycotts—in Nashville, Richmond,

and Savannah, the accounts in at least one of the local white newspapers are remarkably full.

All non-southern papers cited are Negro weeklies. In every case but three, when a Negro paper unequivocally reported a boycott in a major city, corroborating evidence was found in southern white newspapers and almost always in the local dailies of the cities where the various boycotts occurred. The boycotts in Atlanta and Rome, Georgia, and in Shreveport, Louisiana, were mentioned in the Negro press but not in any white newspapers consulted. In the Rome and Shreveport cases it was not possible to obtain copies of the local papers either on microfilm or at the Library of Congress. Both the Atlanta and Memphis papers carried news of boycotts in other cities, but failed to report such protests in their own.

This is a conservative enumeration. A boycott certainly occurred in Wilmington, North Carolina, but it has not been possible to ascertain its dates. (See references to it in Charlotte *Daily Observer* and Raleigh *News and Observer,* both Apr. 3, 1907.) There were hints in the Negro press of a boycott in Macon in 1899 and in Austin in 1906 and suggestions in the white press of boycotts in Asheville. North Carolina, in 1907 and in Galveston in 1906. These have not been included because of a lack of firm evidence.

39. Mobile *Daily Register,* May 17, 1905.
40. Savannah *Morning News,* July 10, 1902, Sept. 12, 13, 1906: Savannah *Tribune,* July 12, 1902, Sept. 8, 1906; San Antonio *Express,* Sept. 15, 29, Oct. 13, 1903; Jackson-ville *Florida Times-Union and Citizen,* Oct. 2, Nov. 6, 8, 9, 14, 1901; Pensacola *Journal,* May 7, 1905.
41. Nashville *Clarion,* n.d., quoted in "Fighting Jim-Crowism' in Nashville." p. 474; Lynchburg *News,* June 9, 1906; Jacksonville *Florida Times-Union,* July 26, 1905; Savannah *Tribune,* Sept. 15, 1906.
42. Cleveland *Gazette,* July 29, 1905.
43. Richmond *Planet,* Apr. 16. 1904.
44. Richmond *St. Luke Herald,* n.d., quoted in Washington *Colored American,* Apr. 16. 1904.
45. Jacksonville *Florida Times-Union and Citizen.* Nov. 6, 11, 1901.
46. Savannah *Tribune,* Sept. 15, 1906; Jacksonville *Florida Times-Union and Citizen,* Nov, 8, 1901; Richmond *Times-Dispatch,* Apr. 20. 1904.
47. Augusta *Chronicle,* May 21. 1900; Mobile *Daily Register,* Nov. 4, 11. 1902: New Orleans *Times-Democrat,* Nov. 4, 6, 1902, and New Orleans *Southwestern Christian Advocate.* Nov. 6, 1902; Little Rock *Arkansas Gazette,* May 28. 1903; Columbia *State,* June 29. 1903; San Antonio *Express,* Mar. 16, 1904; Savannah *Morning News,* Sept. 15, 1906.
48. Atlanta *Age,* n.d., quoted in Richmond *Planet,* Apr. 7, 1900.
49. New Orleans *Southwest Christian Advocate,* Dec. 17, 1903.
50. Cleveland *Gazette,* Mar, 16, 1901.
51. San Antonio *Express,* Mar. 20, 1904; Columbia *State,* June 29, 1903; Savannah *Morning News,* Sept. 14, 16, 17, 23, Oct. 1, 2, 1906.
52. Savannah *Morning News,* Apr. 29, 1908, and Savannah *Tribune,* May 2, 1908; Houston *Daily Post,* Mar. 8, 1904; Henry H. Proctor to Booker T. Washington, Apr. 18. 1900, Booker T. Washington Papers, Manuscript Division, Library of Congress; courtesy of Louis Harlan.
53. New Orleans *Southwestern Christian Advocate,* Jan. 30, 1902; Indianapolis *Freeman,* Mar. 22, 1902.
54. New Orleans *Southwestern Christian Advocate.* June 12, 1902; Mobile *Weekly Press.* n.d., quoted *ibid.,* Sept. 4, 1902; Cleveland *Gazette,* July 5, 1902.
55. Mobile *Daily Register,* Dec. 2, 12, 1902.
56. The role of the Negroes in the transportation system of southern cities in the late nineteenth century is illustrated by the fact that the drivers on the Savannah horsecars were Negroes until the system was electrified and white motormen were substituted in 1892. Savannah *Tribune,* Sept, 3, 1892.
57. Jacksonville *Florida Times-Union.* July 25, 1905.
58. Savannah *Morning News,* Sept. 14. 1906; Savannah *Tribune.* Sept. 22, 1906.
59. Savannah *Morning News,* Sept. 17, 18, 24, 1906.
60. Houston *Daily Post,* Nov. 1. 1903: *African Methodist Episcopal Church Review,* 20 (Apr., 1904), 409.
61. New Orleans *Southwestern Christian Advocate,* Dec. 17, 1903.
62. Houston *Daily Post,* June 3, 1904.
63. Savannah *Tribune,* Sept. 22, 29, Oct. 27, Nov. 3, 1906: Savannah *Morning News,* Dec. 13, 1906.
64. Contrary to a widely held view at the time, the most noted of the Negro transportation companies, the North Jacksonville Street Railway, was not really a Negro-owned enterprise, nor was it organized as part of the 1901 boycott. Actually, its founder was an accommodator who had opposed the boycott; and at all times, most of the stock was owned by whites.
65. *Norfolk Ledger-Dispatch, July* 26, 1906; Norfolk *Virginian-Pilot,* June 26, July 15, Aug. 24, 29. 1906.
66. Chattanooga *Daily Times,* July 26, 28, 1905; Nashville *American.* Aug. 30, 1905; Memphis *Commercial Appeal.* Sept. 7, 1905.
67. Nashville *Banner,* Aug, 29, 1905; Indianapolis *Freeman.* Oct. 7, 1905.
68. Chattanooga *Daily Times,* Sept. 18, 1905; "Fighting 'Jim-Crow-ism' in Nashville," p. 475; Nashville *Banner,* Sept. 22, 30, 1905.

69. Nashville *Banner,* Oct. 17, 1905, Mar. 16. 1906; W. E. B. Du Bois. ed., *Economic Co-Operation Among Negro Americans* (Atlanta, 1907), p. 164.

70. Jacksonville *Florida Times-Union,* July 20, 21, 26, 29, 30. Oct. 18, Nov. 15, 25, Dec. 6, 7, 8, 1905, Feb. 7, 1906; Pensacola journal, Aug. 1, 2, 4, Oct. 15, 17, Nov. 22, 25, Dec. 6, 1905, Jan. 11, Feb. 11, 1906; *Florida* v. *Andrew Patterson,* 50 Fla. 127 (1905); *Andrew Patterson* v. *Isham Taylor,* 51 Fla. 275 (1906); *L. B. Crooms* v. *Fred Schad,* 51 Fla. 168(1906).

71. In the few other instances in which specific individuals are named in the press, they are of the same type; Dr. Charles Shelby and attorney J. T. Settle of Memphis; Dr. W. E. Atkins of Hampton, the most prominent Negro physician in Virginia; William H. Thorogood, a politician in Norfolk; and attorney I. L. Purcell of Pensacola.

Occupational information was gleaned from a variety of sources: the newspaper reports of the boycotts; city directories; and, for the major figures, from earlier research in the period. See August Meier, *Negro Thought in America, 1880-1915: Racial Ideologies in the Age of Booker T. Washington* (Ann Arbor, 1963); Elliott Rudwick, *W. E. B. Du Bois: A Study in Minority Group Leadership* (Philadelphia, 1960). The role of the fraternal and mutual benefit orders in the development of Negro business is discussed in Abram L. Harris, *The Negro as Capitalist: A Study of Banking and Business Among American Negroes* (Philadelphia, 1936), pp. 20, 21, 47–48; W. J. Trent, Jr., "Development of Negro Life Insurance Enterprise" (Master's thesis. University of Pennsylvania, 1932). On True Reformers and their importance, see esp. W. P. Burrell, *Twenty-five Years History of the United Order of True Reformers* (Richmond, 1909); Harris, *Negro as Capitalist,* pp. 62–67; and editorial by W. E. B. Du Bois in *The Crisis,* 3 (Nov., 1911), 9.

72. Chattanooga *Daily Times,* July 25, 1905.

73. Augusta *Chronicle,* June 3, 1900; Washington *Bee,* June 9, 1900.

74. On accommodating role of ministers, see esp. Ralph J. Bunche. "Conceptions and Ideologies of the Negro Problem," unpublished memorandum prepared for the Carnegie-Myrdal Study of the Negro in America, 1940, pp. 135–36. 147, Schomburg Collection, New York Public Library; Benjamin Elijah Mays and Joseph William Nicholson, *The Negro's Church* (New York, 1933); Meier, *Negro Thought in America,* pp. 218–24. On the ambivalent relationship of religion to Negro protest, see Vincent Harding, "Religion and Resistance Among Ante-Bellum Negroes, 1800–1860" (Paper presented at the Organization of American Historians convention. Chicago, 1967); Gary T. Marx, "Religion: Opiate or Inspiration of Civil Rights Militancy among Negroes?" *American Sociological Review,* 32 (Feb., 1967), 64–72.

75. For numerous examples of this, see Ralph J. Bunche, "An Analysis of Negro Leadership," unpublished memorandum prepared for the Carnegie-Myrdal Study of the Negro in America, 1940, Schomburg Collection.

76. Columbia *State,* June 28, 29, 1903.

77. Mobile *Daily Register,* May 17, 1905.

78. Natchez *Daily Democrat,* Aug. 23, 24, 25, 26, 27, 1904; Memphis *Commercial Appeal,* July 4, 1905.

79. Bacote, "Negro in Georgia Politics." pp. 302–6: Savannah *Tribune,* Sept. 15, Dec. 8, 1900; Atlanta *Independent.* Jan. 23, Feb. 6, 1904. Bishop Henry M. Turner was known as a militant colonizationist who denounced American racism in colorful phrases (Edwin S. Redkey, "Bishop Turner's African Dream," *Journal of American History,* 54 [Sept., 1967], 271–90). Yet he was actually a highly complex personality, not easily classifiable as either a protester or an accommodator. Thus, he urged Negroes to vote for southern white Democrats and engaged in political deals with Hoke Smith, while his colonization efforts were supported by the white supremacist senator from Alabama, John Tyler Morgan. Moreover, Negroes generally—even many Negro colonizanonists—regarded the American Colonization Society, which Turner served as vice-president, as dominated by racists and as hostile to the welfare of the race. Finally, it should be pointed out that, as in the case of the more recent Marcus Garvey and Black Muslim movements, separatist nationalism, even when associated with militant rhetoric, actually is a form of escape that avoids a confrontation with the white society and thus really functions as a form of accommodation.

80. Savannah *Tribune,* May 16, 18, June 1, 1907.

81. *Hill's Directory of Richmond,* 1904, pp. 1084–85.

82. Richmond *News-Leader,* Apr. 9, 15, 20, 25, June 4, 1904; Richmond *Times- Dispatch,* Apr. 20, 21, 1904; Richmond *St. Luke Herald,* n.d., quoted in Baltimore *Afro-American Ledger, June.* 11, 1904; Richmond *Planet,* Apr. 23, 1904, June 10, 1905.

83. Memphis *Commercial Appeal,* July 16, Aug. 7. 1905; Chattanooga *Daily Times,* July 7, 1905; Richmond *News-Leader,* June 10, 1904. On Florida cases, see above.

84. Nashville *Clarion;* n.d., quoted in "Fighting Jim-Crowism' in Nashville," p. 475.

85. Richmond *Planet,* Apr. 16, 1904; Richmond *Times-Dispatch,* Apr. 20, 1905: Richmond Planet, Apr. 9, 1904.

86. Shorter College, Arkansas, *Voice of the Twentieth Century,* n.d., quoted in Little Rock *Arkansas Democrat,* June 23, 1903; Columbia *State,* June 28, 1903.

87. Nashville *Banner,* Sept. 27, 1905; *Report of the Fourth Annual Convention of the National Negro Business League* (Wilberforce, Ohio. 1903), p. 24.

88. Booker T. Washington, *My Larger Education, Being Chapters From My Experience* (New York, 1911), p. 65; Washington to J. C. Napier, July 7, 1903. Washington Papers.

89. Richmond *News-Leader,* Apr. 15, 1904. See also W. E. Mollison of Vicksburg in Memphis *Scimitar,* Sept. 9, 1904, clipping in Washington Papers; courtesy of Louis Harlan.

90. Washington, "Taking Advantage of Our Disadvantages," p. 480.

91. Du *Bois, Economic Co-Operation Among Negro Americans,* pp. 164–65. The Niagara Movement was steeped in the tradition of middle-class reform tactics and failed to see the boycott as a strategy for social reform.

92. Thomas F. Pettigrew, *A Profile of the Negro American* (Princeton. 1964), p. 200.

93. In Jacksonville, where the white press gave unusually full coverage to the protests, it carried no indication that the 1901 boycott had been successful until four years later when, during the election campaign of 1905, the mayor's opponent charged that the mayor had failed to enforce the 1901 Jim Crow law. *See Florida Times-Union.* May 3, 16, 20, 30, June 6, 7, 1905.

94. Savannah *Morning News,* Sept. 14, 1906. Feb. 3, 1907; Savannah *Tribune,* Mar. 9, 16, 23, May 18, 1907, May 2, Sept. 19, 1908.

95. Mobile *Daily Register,* May 17, 1905.

96. Atlanta *Constitution,* Sept. 20, 1900; Cleveland *Gazette,* Mar. 16, 1901.

97. For New Orleans, see note 21; for Nashville, see note 34; for Atlanta, see note 15; for Newport News, see note 36; for Houston and San Antonio, see notes 25 and 27: for Augusta, see note 17.

Denouncing Lynching and Racism, 1918

Herbert Aptheker

Imperialist wars abroad intensify repression in general at home and especially that form of repression called racism. As World War I staggered on in blood and especially after the Bolshevik Revolution of November, 1917, domestic repression intensified; hence, fierce discrimination aimed against Black people and lynchings and pogroms multiplied. Protest from the offended never ceased. Two examples, from the month of March, 1918, follow: [a] is the text of a petition adopted at a mass meeting of Black people in Atlanta on March 5. The meeting was chaired by P. J. Bryant and its secretary was L. H. King; the petition—carrying the signatures of 114 of the leading Black men of the city—was addressed to the President, his cabinet, the Congress, and the governors and legislatures of the states; [b] is the newspaper account, in the Savannah, Ga., *Tribune* of March 23, 1918 (p. 1), of the petition presented in person to President Wilson on March 14. This account speaks for itself and is reprinted in full below, including the paper's headlines. Finally, on July 23, 1918, *The New York Times* reported from Washington that "President Wilson has become concerned over . . . the rise in the mob spirit"; and on July 26 he issued a formal statement, summarized in the headlines of *The New York Times* the next day, in these words: PRESIDENT DEMANDS THAT LYNCHING END. DENOUNCES MOB SPIRIT AND MOB ACTION AS EMULATING GERMAN LAWLESSNESS. Despite these words, lynching of Black people (and some white radicals and labor organizers) and wholesale attacks in ghettoes continued thereafter.

✳ ✳ ✳ ✳ ✳

[a]

The Atlanta Appeal

During the past three decades nearly three thousand American colored men, women and children have suffered butchery and death in almost every conceivable form at the hands of the lynchers of America. Last year alone the number thus murdered was *two hundred twenty-two*. The reported causes for such appalling brutality ran the gamut from alleged violation of the honor of white women to disputing the word of white men. The fact however that only about five per cent of these murders are reputed to have been inflicted upon accused violators of womanhood argues almost conclusively that the desire to protect womanhood is almost negligible among the so-called causes of lynchings.

We accordingly regard lynching as worse than Prussianism, which we are at war to destroy. Lynching is not a cure for crime, either imaginary or real. It decreases faith in the boasted justice of our so-called democratic institutions. It widens the frightful chasm of unfriendly and suspicious feeling between the races and positively foments the spirit of antipathy and resentment. We are accused of concealing criminals. Who has concealed the many criminals that have mercilessly murdered these three thousand defenseless men, women and children of our race? That these murderers frequently ply their trade in broad day light and in plain view of the entire citizenry even, does not facilitate their punishment or detection. Within less than one year one state alone has tortured and burned at the stake three colored men without even the semblance of a trial or an effort to apprehend and punish the murderers. In the last instance an entire helpless colored population was marched around the fire amid fumes of a burning human being and put on notice that as that black man was suffering they too should fear to suffer. Thus the defiant lynching giant strides on apace. While we are sacrificing the best blood of our sons upon our Nation's altar to help destroy Prussianism beyond the seas, we call upon you to use your high offices to destroy the lynching institution at our doors.

We are the one group of American people, than whom there is none more loyal, which is marked out for discrimination, humiliation and abuse. In the great patriotic and humanitarian movements, in public carriers, in federal service, the treatment accorded us is humiliating, dehumanizing and reprehensible in the extreme. This persistent and unreasonable practice is but a thrust at the colored man's self-respect—the object being not merely to separate the races but to impress us with the idea of supposed natural inferiority. Such demoralizing discrimination is not only a violation of the fundamental rights of citizens of the United States, but the persistent segregation of any element of our country's population into a separate and distinct group on the sole basis of color is creating a condition under which this nation cannot long endure.

When we reflect upon these brutalities and indignities we remember they are due to the fact that in almost every Southern State we have systematically, by law or chicanery, been deprived of the right of that very manhood suffrage which genuine democracy would guarantee to every citizen in the republic. This propaganda of filching from colored Americans the ballot is but a supreme effort to re-enslave us and to force our assent to, and our impotence against, any legislation of our opponents. To this policy the black man does not, cannot and will not agree. Of it, our intolerance is cumulative. Against it, we shall exert our righteous efforts until not only every eligible black man but every eligible black woman shall be wielding the ballot proudly in defense of our liberties and our homes.

We are appealing to you neither as vassals nor as inferiors. Bull Run and Appomattox fixed our status in this nation. We are free men. We are sovereign American citizens—freemen who purchased with our own blood on every battle field from Bunker Hill to Carrizal full rights and immunities such as are freely granted to others but systematically refused us.

We are writing to you, gentlemen, that you may give us the assurance and guarantee which every American citizen ought to have without reference to color. We are loyal and will remain so, but we are not blind. We cannot help seeing that white soldiers who massacred our black brothers and sisters in East St. Louis have gone scot free. We cannot help seeing that our black brothers who massacred white citizens in Houston have paid the most ignominious penalty that can come in this country to a man in uniform. Do not these undemocratic conditions, these inhumanities, these brutalities and savageries provoke the Rulers of the nation to speak out of their sphinx-like silence and utter a voice of hope, a word of promise for the black man? Do the rulers of the nation also hate us, and will they, Pilate-like, forever give their assent to the crucifixion of the bodies, minds and souls of those in whom there has been found nothing worthy of the death we are dying, save that we are black? May not your silence be construed as tacit approval or active tolerance of these things? The effect on the morale of black men in the trenches, when they reflect that they are fighting on foreign fields in behalf of their nation for those very rights and privileges which are denied at home, might be discouraging.

We appeal to you in the name of Democracy!

We appeal to you in the name of our American citizenship!

We appeal to you in the name of God, and,
We would be heard!

From mimeographed copy of original, in editor's possession.

[b]

ASK LYNCHING BE MADE FEDERAL CRIME
PRESIDENT WILSON RECEIVES
A.M.E. REPRESENTATIVES
STRONG PROTEST AGAINST LYNCHING AND
JIM CROWISM IS PRESENTED

Washington, D.C., March 14—Words urging patriotic duties upon the Negroes while they are lynched and jim crowed has the appearance of insincerity" was a sentiment expressed to President Woodrow

Wilson by a commission appointed by the Bishops' Council of the African Methodist Episcopal Church to make representations against discrimination against the Negroes of this country.

The appointment with the President was arranged by Prof. John R. Hawkins, financial secretary of the A.M.E. church. The Commission was headed by Bishop W. D. Chapelle of South Carolina. The other members of the committee were Prof. John R. Hawkins of Washington; Dr. W. T. Vernon of Tennessee; Dr. W. H. H. Butler of Pennsylvania; Dr. J. G. Robinson of Tennessee; Dr. A. H. Hill of Arkansas and Dr. A. L. Gaines of Baltimore.

Bishop Chappelle made the representations to the President and left with him a written document setting forth the views of the commission. The response of the President, though guarded, was very gratifying.

The sentiment of the commission follows:

Washington, D.C., March 14, 1918

Hon Woodrow Wilson,
President of the United States.
Mr. President, Sir:

We, the undersigned citizens of the United States, and representatives of the African Methodist Episcopal church appointed by the Bishops' Council of said church, which met at Louisville, Ky., Feb. 14, 1918, beg to submit to you the following memorial or prayer.

With a due sense of appreciation of the great struggle in which we are now engaged, and the arduous task laid upon you as Chief Magistrate of our country we pledge to you our fidelity as loyal citizens of our Republic.

These are trying times, and we are passing through ordeals that try men's souls, and now more than ever before, our people need hope and encouragement.

We believe you have read with deep regret of the inhuman and unlawful treatment of our people in many sections of the country; and we come praying you for relief from mob-violence and other discriminations which are so prevalent.

We do not condone crime committed by our people; nor are we asking that you wink at crime committed by any people; we ask that each and every individual be given a fair and impartial trial by a jury of twelve men of their fellow citizens.

Since Congress has given you, as President, power to conscript citizens from and within all the states of the Union, to fight for the common cause of human liberty, and for protection of this country; we believe that it is equally within the power of Congress to authorize you to enter any state in this union with said power, to protect the life and liberty of the citizens therein.

Believing this as we do, we ask: First, that lynching be made a federal offense. Second, we ask that in all cases of lynching and mob-violence where citizens are guilty of participating in the same, they shall be punished by law and declared ineligible to hold office in our government either federal or state.

Third: We ask that any sheriff allowing his prisoner to be lynched or maimed while in his custody, be declared unfit for that high office and at once removed by the governor.

Mr. President, we make this appeal to you because our people have always been loyal to this government and are still loyal and faithful in this the most trying time of its history.

We are in the midst of a great world-wide war which will take as we see it, the united efforts of all the people to gain victory, and to secure this, we must find a way to suppress mob-violence and lynching.

To tell us that we are fighting for world democracy and that this is a form of that democracy for which we are to fight and for which many of our boys are already on the field of battle, is not to say the least very encouraging.

The Negroes of this country have rallied to your call in this crisis and are doing their bit according to their ability from every view point.

No people have followed so uncomplainingly as have our people, and we are beginning to realize now that we are a part of this government which we have served so faithfully both in war and in peace. Thus we come asking our government through its executive to protect us in the pursuits of life, liberty and happiness.

Mr. President, our treatment upon the railroads of this country is unfair, unjust, degrading and unchristian and we ask that something be done to change such conditions and make them such as will guarantee to us peace and comfort while traveling in the discharge of our several duties.

In the face of such treatment we are being told now that we are fighting for a common cause—freedom.

We compare what is told us with what is being done to us, it must of necessity create a suspicion as to the sincerity of some of those who speak to us. If these difficulties are removed, then you make it easier for the leaders of our people to control them as patriots; and too, to advise and direct their activities in such movements as the purchase of Liberty Bonds, Thrift Stamps and the cheerful enlistment in the United States Army and Navy.

Mr. President, we can ask no less and be men. So in the interest of all that is righteous, of all that is just and of all that is in keeping with true democracy of which you are the exponent, we beg you to act.

Respectfully yours,

W. D. Chappelle, chairman, Bishop 7th Epis. Dist., Columbia, S.C.

John R. Hawkins, Financial Secretary, A.M.E. Church, Washington, D.C.

J. G. Robinson, Sec., P. E., Knoxville Dist., Knoxville, Tenn.

W. T. Vernon, Pastor A.M.E. Church, Memphis, Tenn.

A. H. Hill, Pastor A.M.E. church, Pine Bluff, Ark.

A. L. Gaines, Pastor A.M.E church, Baltimore, Md.

W. H. H. Butler, P.E., Washington District, Washington, Pa.

SECTION NINE

THE GREAT DEPRESSION

CHAPTER 11

The Economic Crisis of the Negro

A. Philip Randolph

We are in the grip of an intensive and extensive economic crisis. It is severe. It is stubborn. It is baffling. It involves the business man, the worker, the doctor, the lawyer, the teacher, the preacher and the farmer, the buyer, the seller, the tenant, the landlord—all.

It is not local. It is not national. It is not racial. It is not creedal. It is worldwide in scope. Different from and worse than a scourge or pestilence such as the Black Death of the Middle Ages in Europe or an earthquake anywhere, it is a blight on all lands and afflicts all peoples.

In its devastating path, stalk the menacing and unsightly figures of hunger and want, crime and corruption, crashes and conflicts of labor and capital, increased bankruptcies, mergers, mob violence, lynching, racketeers, bribery, blackmail, political and intellectual hijacking, moral malaise, misery and suffering of men and women, aged and children.

Unemployment, the most serious aspect of this crisis is guessed at, in the absence of an index gauge in the United States of America, to range from 3 to 8 millions. In England where more accurate figures obtain, the jobless are estimated at some 2,500,000; in Germany about, 3,000,000; in Italy 800,000; in Japan 500,000; and now even France of a small estate, peasant class population, hitherto relatively free from unemployment is swinging into the vicious cycle.

Estimated bank failings, another aspect of the crisis, for 1930 up to December are 981 with deposits of $312,000,000; fifty-one closing their doors in the

South in one day, according to the Literary Digest of December 27th, 1930. The record year for bank suspensions was 1926 with 956 involving $270,000,000 in deposits. Nineteen thirty, when the smoke clears, is expected to record 1000 failures with well-nigh three quarters of a billion deposits. The collapse of the Bank of United States in December with some $200,000,000 deposits and 400,000 depositors with 59 branches, together with the Chelsea Exchange Bank with 7 branches in New York, involving $23,000,000 in deposits, will quite considerably swell the sum. In this financial debacle, Negro banks and their general business have been hit hard. Probably the strongest bank ever organized among Negroes, the Binga State Bank of Chicago and the First Standard Savings, the American Mutual Savings of Louisville and the Peoples Savings Banks in Nashville, closed their doors.

In the last decade, according to the Comptroller of Currency, 5640 banks failed with deposits of $1,721,000,000. And the mortality among wholesale and retail merchants, foreclosures on homes and farms, is frightful and staggering. Commercial failures exclusive of banks numbered 26,335 with total liabilities of $668,283,842. There is no way of estimating its tremendous extent, and the social and economic losses entailed.

Suppose we say that an average of 5 millions of workers have been unemployed during the year 1930 which is probably more nearly right than wrong and that the average wage-salary loss is $3.00 per worker per day, the total wage-salary income loss is five billion four hundred million dollars.

From *Opportunity*, 9 (May 1931) by A. Philip Randolph. Copyright © 1934 by A. Philip Randolph Educational Fund. Reprinted by permission.

Now, it is estimated that the Negro working class population, as of the U.S. Census of 1920, represents 11.6 per cent of the general working class population of the country. Thus, considering the fact that the Negro is regarded as the marginal worker, "first fired and last hired," there are surely not less than 500,000 unemployed. Says the National Urban League, in a recent survey of unemployment in 25 industrial centers among Negroes, by T. Arnold Hill and Ira De A. Reid: "Unemployment statistics of twenty-five cities for the period January 1st to September 30th, 1930, show a decrease of 34.5 per cent in number of available jobs for Negroes and an increase of 39.9 per cent in number of applicants over same period for 1929. But the average wage-salary income per Negro worker is not as high as the general average for the country. Let us say that it is roughly $2.00 per day per worker, this would represent a minimum wage-salary income loss for the race for 1930 of some 360 million dollars or about a million dollars a day.

This economic loss reflects itself in increased physical deterioration, sickness, moral degeneration, family difficulties, reduced patronage of doctors and nonpayment of bills, less and poorer food and clothing, lapses of insurance policies, longer bread lines and the giving of the "dole."

According to the survey of the National Urban League: "In almost every city Negroes constitute a larger part of the beneficiaries of charitable agencies than they do of the population. This is because they receive a smaller share of the work."

Such are the plight and ills of the Negro.

What of the remedy? This may be more obvious after we seek the causes that appear to be many and varied. It is quite possible, too, that there is no absolute cure for unemployment under the present competitive economic system. But some fundamental remedies are applicable when the behavior of phenomena making for unemployment is adequately known.

As to the nature of the types of unemployment, there are residual, seasonal, cyclical, and technological.

Residual unemployment, like the poor, is always with us. The Committee on Elimination of Waste in Industry of the Federated Engineering Societies in its report, "Waste in Industry," published in 1921, states: In the best years, even the phenomenal years of 1917 and 1918 at the climax of war-time industrial activities, when plants were working to capacity and when unemployment reached its lowest point in twenty years, there was a margin of unemployment amounting to more than a million men. This margin is fairly permanent; seemingly one or more wage earners out of every forty are always out of work" (Hearings before the Committee on Education and Labor, Unemployment in the U.S., p. 491). And it is difficult to visualize the non-existence of some lag of unemployment, though short, less vexatious and burdensome, to be sure, even under a socialized and more highly coordinated economy.

Seasonal Unemployment

Seasonal unemployment has long since beset the heels of the worker. It is probably putting it conservatively to say that practically every industry is in a measure seasonal. Hoover engineers showed that workers in the building trades were employed on the average but 63 per cent of the year. Investigation discloses that factories in the men's clothing industry are running on the average of about 69 per cent of the possible working time, according to Dr. Harry W. Laidler, Director of the League for Industrial Democracy. Here again, seasonal unemployment seems to be indigenous and chronic to our Manchester laissez faire economy.

But probably the type of unemployment which occasions greatest fear and hardship among the workers is cyclical in its character. In the last 120 years in America about fifteen periods of industrial depression and prosperity, appearing with a sort of rhythmic regularity, have given us pause.

Technological Unemployment

But cyclical unemployment is not the most baffling aspect of the depression, for its average duration, says the Cambridge Associates of Boston, is slightly over 18 months. Whereas, there is no apparent end to technological unemployment, that is, unemployment created by the machine, labor-saving devices, efficiency methods and industrial and commercial consolidations.

Note this picture. The automatic elevator in apartments and office buildings has eliminated men. "Seven men now do the work which formerly required 60 to perform in casting pig iron; 2 men do the work which formerly required 128 to perform in loading pig iron! One man replaces 42 in operating open-hearth furnaces. A brick-making machine in Chicago makes 40,000 bricks in one hour. It formerly took one man 8 hours to make 450. In New York from 1914 to 1925 the number of workers in the paper box industry decreased 32 per cent while the output per wage earner increased 121 per cent."

It is estimated that some 15,000 or 25,000 extras in the motion picture industry are unfavorably affected by the "talkies" and that "canned" music in the movie theatres has destroyed the skill and rendered jobless thousands of musicians. According to the Federal Reserve Board, the output per man in manufacturing is 45 per cent greater in 1929 than in 1919, although there was a decrease in workers in manufacturing of 10 per cent, even before the depression of 1929. In mining, the output per person increased from 40 to 45 per cent, but the numbers employed dropped approximately 7 per cent. In the last decade, the efficiency of the railroad workers measured in ton-miles greatly increased, and rail employees lost jobs to the extent of 300,000 more or less. As a result of tractors, corn huskers, binders in the wheat fields and other machinery, the output per farm worker increased 25 per cent, and, according to the Department of Agriculture, about 3,800,000 left the farms for the cities, white and colored. In mining, railroading, manufacturing and farming, workers decreased in the last 10 years by about 2,800,000, observes Prof. S.H. Schlicter of Cornell.

Former Secretary of Labor James J. Davis points out "that a puddler and one helper, in the old days could turn out from 2,500 to 3,000 pounds of puddled iron a day. With a machine and the new process, an engineer has produced 2,000 tons in ten hours. The corn husker does the work of 5 men. Binders in the wheat fields in Kansas with 10,000 men will do what 30,000 men formerly did. One hundred men in the Bureau of Labor Statistics with the adding machine can do the work of 500 brain workers. There is a machine in the Census Bureau that with 1,000 employees does the work of 10,000." "Wherever you turn," he continued, "drills, machinery, conveyors, processes and chemicals are doing the work—Track-layers and the railroad section hands find rails laid by mechanical devices, riveted by acetylene welders, and the dirt tramped around the ties with mechanical trampers. Longshoremen find ships loaded by mechanical devices and the freight laid upon conveyors that carry it from the ship's hold into the storage warehouse on the dock.

The hod carrier finds the brick and mortar dumped into boxes automatically pulled by a chain into an elevator and scooted up to the top of the building without his assistance. The concrete mixer finds the mix poured into a great cylinder which is a part of an automobile truck and is mixed by the same power that propels the car from the material yard to the place where the concrete is to be used."

This is but a glimpse into the amazing technological revolution going on around us. It touches the Negro worker, skilled and unskilled, as farm laborers, longshoremen, hod carrier, rail employee, etc. And whether Negro workers are employed in an industry directly affected by technological changes or not, they are hit indirectly, since when the skill of a group of white workers is liquidated by an invention, they fall into the category of unskilled workers or competitors of Negro workers, unless, they (the white workers) are vocationally restrained, which is not yet the rule. Already in the South, the influence of the mechanization of the farms and the march of mass production are creating a surplus of white workers who are becoming absorbed easily into menial forms of work formerly considered "Negro jobs," such as teamsters, ice delivery men, scavengers, street cleaners, ashcart drivers, road making, etc.

Domestic work, too, is rapidly becoming mechanized, thereby requiring less and less personal servants. Besides, there is going on a process of hotelization and apartmentalization which tend to make for the centralization of personal service work where it is being subjected to the process of mass production, which, in turn, will result in more work done with less workers. While this may not be an immediate exigency, it is a rather certain future contingency, according to our present industrial trends.

Some Remedies

The machine is a challenge to the nation, not only to black and white workers, and this challenge cannot be met by charity, unemployment surveys and temporary jobs, however, important they may be for the nonce. No amount of charity is a remedy. It's a palliative. To feed the hungry and shelter the homeless is necessary but this should not obscure the fundamental problem.

The fact is the workers have worked themselves out of work and will repeat the process in the next five or six years. They have produced more goods and services than they can buy back with the wages they receive. The depression is not so much the result of over production as of under consumption. The people have a physical desire for goods they have no economic power to command.

High Wages

Obviously if the wage earners, the large majority of the population, cannot buy back what they produce which results in piling up large inventories, one remedy will consist in increasing the purchasing power by raising the wage scale. A word about this problem. In the decade from 1919 to 1929, the numbers of workers engaged in manufacturing decreased 449,775. Wages paid in 1929 showed an increase of $809,229,749 over 1919. Whereas the increase in the total value added by manufacture was $6,286,762,484. Put in another way, the employer was able to add $7.70 to the value of his goods for every dollar he gave to his employees in increased wages. The increase in the cost of raw materials in 1929 amounted to only $124,928,718 above the figures for 1919. Thus the value added by manufacture increased $5,352,604,017 more than the increase in raw materials and wages combined.

In 1914, the average wage in American manufacturing establishments was $589, the value added by manufacture per worker was $1,407. Five years later, in 1919, owing largely to the World War, wages had gone up to $1,162, but the value added by manufacture had increased to $2,756. In other words, the workers had received $573 more for creating $1,349 of additional value. Eight years later, in 1927, the average wage was $1,299 and value added by manufacture had gone up to $3,303. The worker was receiving $137 more wages than in 1919 but his production had increased $547 in value. Finally in 1929, the average wage was $1,318, and the value added by manufacture was $3,636. Here we find the workers' wages had increased $19 in two years and the value of his output had gone up $333. Herein lies the basic cause of recurring depressions. The problem can only be solved by the most scientific industrial statesmanship and social visions.

High wages (real wages) are most significant as a remedy because wage earners are the most important and largest group of consumers in the country. Roughly, with their families, they represent 70 per cent of the population and receive an income of something more than 32 billion dollars a year or 36 per cent of the national income; with the earnings of the salaried workers, who represent about 13 per cent of the population, the two groups, while constituting 83 per cent or more of the population, receive only 57 per cent of the nation's income. And they purchase a great deal more than 57 per cent of the nation's consumer goods. On the other hand, the bond and share-holders and property owners, though representing 17 per cent or less of the population, receive about 43 per cent of the nation's income, and most of this income is reinvested in producers' capital, which is, in turn, a source of the production of more commodities the workers cannot buy, thereby, creating huge inventories and commodity congestion or industrial paralysis.

Shorter Work Day and Week

But high wages alone will not solve the problem of depressions. This fact is clearly recognized by the American Federation of Labor which is fighting for a 5-day week and by the Big Four Railroad Brotherhood Unions that have inaugurated a crusade for the 6-hour day. The 6-hour day may absorb nearly a quarter of a million idle rail workers. The progress of productive machinery, too, may eventually render the 4-hour day and the 4-day week practicable. How else will the surplus workers be employed?

Labor Unions

Obviously neither high wages nor the shorter work day or week will come without the struggle of those who will benefit from them. All history attests that every social, economic, political and religious reform has only been won through the utmost struggle, sacrifice and suffering. "Verily, there is no remission of sin except through blood."

Thus, labor organization is the primary and most effective factor in the solution of the problem of seasonal cyclical and technological unemployment, for it is only through the exercise of power, attainable through the organization of wage earners is it possible increasingly to exact higher wages and shorter hours of work. Labor alone will make the necessary struggle, sacrifice and undergo the suffering to stop its own exploitation, But the workers must be organized. Out of 41 million—only 5 million are organized and benefit from fairly high wages and shorter work hours.

Social Legislation

But labor may be helped. Old Age Pensions are essential to those who have paid their price to society in industry in blood, sweat, tears and toil and are no longer able to keep the pace. And while the aged should be pensioned, the deadline against the men of 45 in industry should be removed.

Employment could also be provided by raising the compulsory school age and the adoption of a Federal Child Labor Law which would affect over a million child laborers who are competitors of their fathers in the labor market.

Unemployment insurance, too, like sick, accident, death and fire insurance, should be formulated and enacted as a national measure by Congress. Private charities are far too inadequate. If unemployment, like sickness and death are unavoidable, insurance against it is indispensable.

Of course, free national employment exchanges and government works, planned over a long period, will help, but usually the political red tape incidental to developing public works, prevents the works from beginning until after the depression ends.

Twenty-five Year Plan

Beside the above-mentioned measures is the broad field of self-help by the people. In this field may be listed consumers and producers, cooperatives and workers' credit unions, to mobilize small units of capital into large volumes, for economic strength and protection.Among Negroes as among farmers and economically weak groups, the Appian Way of private capitalism is difficult if not impossible to trod, especially, in view of the increasing concentration and centralization of financial and industrial power into fewer and fewer hands.

Through a process of interlocking directorships, about 1,000 corporations dominate American business, and at the top of these stand J.P. Morgan and Co., the Bankers Trust and Guarantee Companies, the First National, the National City and Chase National Banks, who have under their control over

$74,000,000,000, of corporate assets, equal to more than one-quarter of all the corporate assets of the United States. They practically dominate the business life of the United States, Central and South Americas and exercise a tremendous control in all Europe, Asia and Africa. This amazing empire of capital is more powerful than any political empire or monarchy the world has even seen.

In this regime, the individual, black or white, is helpless. Negroes can only survive modern science and industrialism through consumers' and producers' cooperatives and labor organizations and through the support of labor and social legislation and political action in sympathy with the collective ownership, control and operation of the social productive and distributive instrumentalities in our industrial society. This, however, requires scientific intelligence and a new type of character which can only come through systematic and methodical planning to eventuate through a period of a quarter of a century, much of a piece in principle, with the Russian 5-Year Plan. Much time is needed for the tragedy of it all is that there are but few, either among the leadership or followship, who are aware of what is happening to our modern, industrial life.

Major factors in the plan should be workers' and adult education, and a leadership of courage, education and integrity and a will to sacrifice for the economic well-being of the masses.

To the development of such a plan the "best minds" of the race should be called to form a sort of Supreme Economic Council through which such a plan might be formulated and executed. No existing Negro organization can do it. It should embrace the "best brains" in all of the Negro movements, somewhat of the nature of Kelly Miller's Sanhedrin, but smaller. Probably more nearly like the League of Nations which assembles the world's greatest experts to grapple with world problems such as the Young Plan. No single Negro organization is now strong enough to withstand the economic stress and strain of the coming years. United, scientific, courageous, honest and sacrificial endeavor alone can save the race. Have the leaders of church, school, press, politics, social service and race movements, the will and the spirit and world vision to meet this challenge? Either we accept the challenge, unite and rise or remain as we are and go down and perish. For, forsooth the old order passeth.

A Worse Depression

Black Americans in the 1930s

Robert S. McElvaine

etters written by black Americans during the Depression show both the similarities and differences between their problems and those of their white countrymen. Like many whites, black letter writers wanted no one to know that they had written; but their reason was not, in most cases, the shame that whites attached to seeking assistance. Instead, it was fear of reprisals by local whites against complaining blacks. Blacks expected to be jailed, killed, beaten, or run out of their homes if their letters were discovered.

Remarkably, in spite of the requests for confidentiality, many of the letters blacks addressed to the Roosevelts were referred to local relief agencies: to precisely the people against whom the allegations of discrimination had been made.

A significant similarity between black and white Depression victims was their love for the president. Most of the letters written by blacks show the same reverence for Roosevelt that was common in letters from white workers. The writers thanked the president because, as one put it, "You has prepare Money enough to give every one a Decent living." Like whites, many blacks blamed lower officials, rather than Roosevelt, for the inadequacy of relief funds. Other letters from blacks indicate an adherence to the work ethic and a desire for loans rather than charity. Thus it appears that the so-called middle-class values discussed in chapter 2 were shared by some poor blacks, even in the South.

The bulk of the letters that can be clearly identified as having been written by blacks* seem to have come from the South. This in no way indicates that Roosevelt's popularity among blacks was confined to that region. The shift in black voting allegiances demonstrated that the admiration for FDR was widespread in black communities throughout other parts of the nation. One of the letters, written by a

black woman in Iowa just after the 1936 campaign, says that the author hoped that the president would give recognition to blacks by mentioning in a radio broadcast that their votes were valuable to him.

One reason why Roosevelt never made such a broadcast is apparent in the last two letters of the chapter which were written by southern whites. The final letter, from a poor Georgia woman, is a good example of the success upper-class whites in the South had achieved in splitting the poor along racial lines.

———

*37. These white people will kill all
the Negroes in Marion*

Marion Ark
Feb 3, 1935

Pres Roosevelt
of Washington DC

Dear sir if every eny body need you we poor peoples need you here at marion   we are all sufing mody bad the drauf [drought] come and cut off the corn and white peoples took all the cotton and wont give us a day work at in the marion cort House mrs miller and mrs nomen and mr mace ant doing nottien for the poor negores at all wont give them no work and just robing the Govement and mr abry Kooser is roobing all the negroes one the farm   he wont furnish the peoples untell the last of april and the wont furnish nothen but a little somtom to eat and dont car how large your family is he just you 2 sack of flour and one sack of meat and 8 lbs of lard for weeks if you got 13 in family that is what he give   dont even gave a rag of clothen and shoes. and all of his peoples that is got large family has made from 11 to 17 bales of cotton and come out in deat over 300 hirndraw dellers in dat. you aught send a man around one his farm just talk with his negores and see how they is suffen and that money all the otheres white men has pay thay negroes he did not gives his negroes but 5 dollers and mad them sine on the

313

second day of this month and told all that dident sine to give him his house and move   please send a man here one orbry Kooser plase at marion ark and dont send the letter back here he will have every negro on his place put in jail   please come here at marion ark and helpe the poor negrous and stop them peoples at the cort house frome Robing the govment dont send this back here do these white peoples will kill all the negroes in marion   some of us have been here one this man place fore 10 to 17 years and all over 3 hundrew dollars in deat yet

[Anonymous]

— — — —

38. Cant sign my name Mr President they will beat me up and run me away from here and this is my home

Reidsville. Ga Oct 19th 1935

Hon. Franklin D. Roosevelt.
President of U.S. Washington D.C.

Dear Mr. President

Would you please direct the people in charge of the releaf work in Georgia to issue the provisions + other supplies to our suffering colored people. I am sorry to worrie you with this Mr. President but hard as it is to believe the releaf officials here are using up most every thing that you send for them self + their friends. they give out the releaf supplies here on Wednesday of this week and give us black folks, each one, nothing but a few cans of pickle meet and to white folks they give blankets, bolts of cloth and things like that. I dont want to take to mutch of your time Mr president but will give you just one example of how the releaf is work down here   the witto Nancy Hendrics own lands, stock holder in the Bank in this town and she is being supplied with Blankets cloth and gets a supply of cans goods regular this is only one case but I could tell you many.

Please help us mr President because we cant help our self and we know you is the president and a good Christian man   we is praying for you. Yours truly cant sign my name Mr President   they will beat me up and run me away from here and this is my home

[Anonymous]

— — — —

39. Som gets a little and som gets none

March 9th 1936 Dry Branch, Ga.

Mr. Franklin D. rusevelt President of the united States of america

Dear President

I am writing you a few words abot the condishioned of the poor oled aged collard people how thear are sufring

they are on the county an onley gets 2.50 per month and 1. 50 out of that for house rent and sum of them cant hardley get about and when the govenment senes cars loads of food sorn gets a little and som gets none and thats the way it is about the clothes some gets some and some gets none and if you do have Ennie pensions sent to the poor oled aged colard people pleas send them checkes if you dont they will never get a pennie of it this From

[Anonymous]

— — — —

40. They give all the worke to white people and give us nothing

[Picayune, Mississippi
September 3, 1935]

Dear Sir I am ritening you a few Lines to Let you no how they are treating we colored people on this releaf   I went up to our home Vister and replied for some Thing to do an Some Thing to eat and She told me that she has nothing for me at all and to they give all the worke to White people and give us nothing an Sir I wont you to no how we are treated here

So please help us if you can

[Anonymous]

— — — —

41. I am to old to be turned out of doors

7/31/34
West Point Ga East 7th St

Dear Mr President I dont no Just How to rite to you But I want to ask Your Help   I am a old Citizen of West Point and I am about 75 or 6 years old and Have Labored Hard all My days until depression Came on and I Had No Job in three years and I Have a Little Home I Bought when times was good and I managed to Pay my state and County tax But they Claim I owe about 15 fifteen dol City tax and going to sell my Little Home for that and will you Please sir Help me out the government Can Have a Lean on the Little House until I Get some way to Pay Back Please Sir do what you Can for me I am to old to be turned out of doors   I tried to get a Job on the CWA But they wanted younger men   Ive Never gave the City any troube Have always stood in fear of god and ben Law abiding and Ben a Hard Worker all my days and Is able and Can work   Now if I get any thing to do its Just about a quarter of an ace [acre] and a 2 room House and it Need Fixing Bad aint No account Much But I toil so Hard to get it I dont want to Loose it so Please Sir Help me I am and old Colored Man'and seems like they Just want to take my Place I aint got Nothing and Cant get Nothing if ever a Poor Person Need Help I do   Pleas Sir Let Me Hear from you at once I Havent got but a few days to get the Money up they Supose to sell it some time in Aug I dont No the excat day

> Yours and oblige your
> Humble Servent
> D. A. [male]
> West Point Ga

——— ——— ———

42. All I want is a chance and I wen prove to the world that I can come up the hill in stead of goin down

> Buncombe County Jail—
> Asheville N. C
> Feb. 1. 19.34

President hoover Dear Sir

well you Pleas help Poor me i am a Colored woman 34 years old have 4 Children 3 Girls 1 Boy I have work awFuly hard Every Senice i 9 years old. Did not Get to Go to School But very little—But I have all ways held my Job never Ben turn off unless Sickness I was Born in a little town By the name of Laurens S.C. I Came to ashevill N C 10 years aGo and I had very good Luck For awhile My husband wasen So well but he work on Just the Same he Got hurt in the world War at the Camp /wheller Makon Ga he and I Done all that we Could to Rear our 4 Children up RiGht. well he took Real Sick and Died. Well i nely went Crazy when the Dr told me that they Could Not Save him and BeGain to Drink I tried to Drink it off and Got in Jail why I Drank Every thing aney one would give me I [illegible] I was Sick and worred nely to Deth I have tried and tried to Get a Job But they are Scarse the City Releaf takes Care of my Children at Present Dear President Pleas—give me a Job. and I well Do my Best all I want is a Chance and I well Prove to the world that I can Come up the hill in Stead of goin Down I Relize it was wrong to Drink and I am Sorry that I Ever tourch it But I was Cold and hunGry a menie Day that no one Knew But God and I is had Plenty of Friend when my husband was—livinG and we all ways help others as Mutch as we Could. now my health is not So Good my hart is Bad and I haven Got aney Job no whear harley to Stay I had to all most give furnitur a way Because I Could not Pay the house Rent I Pray that you well Give Me Some thing to Do I Dont Care what I sure well thank god and you then I well Get me Some Clouse an Shoes an go to Church Every Sunday I have made up in my mind to Stop DrinkinG and if god for Give me and you give me a Job I never. never. tourch it aGain Pleas answer Soon i well Get out on the 18 of Feb. and haven Got aney money an no home no Job So I Pray you well tell Poor me what to Do may god tourch your hart that you well underStand Every thinG and help me I Feel Just like the whole world

is aGainst Me Sometime I am not a Bad—woman Just worred Crazy Pleas Give me a trial—

> yours truly
> Mrs. M. R.
> Buncombe County jail
> Ashevill N C.

——— ——— ———

43. The government has probale enough money to feed all Negro and poor white

> [Camp Hill, Alabama
> April 22, 19351

Mr Roosevelt the President of the unite State I want to Explain the condition of the poor farmer and the unemployed people. Mr Roosevelt I know that the government has ProBale enough Money to Feed all Negro and Poor White and to Day they are suffering For Food and clothes We know that you has perpare Money enough to give every one a Decent living But to Day the relief offices and other who has a plenty to live on is getting this money and slaving the Poor People.

> [Anonymous]

——— ——— ———

44. I have not got any thing for security but my honor

> Tupelo. Miss
> Feb. 4th 1935

Mr President and Wife

Im about to ask you A Question that I hate to trouble you with. but Ive tried hard to get by With out any assistance but Ive Nearly got to road end, I Just Cant make my way as I will explain. Now Mr President I owe Several different people that are compeling me to pay them They are Sending Squires an colectors To me every Week I hate not to pay them but I Just can not Ive a Job. but owing from 8 to 12 different ones It make it difficult To pay be Sides the fuel food House rent That has to be paid each week an fuel each Time it is ordered then Mr prisident the food is a Necessity We have to have that to keep going on our Jobs. every thing is very high in Tupelo but Im thankful To have a Job. Making Something but not nearly enough To pay those Bills I owe. Im not Writing Just because I can write for I have tried to borrow from the white people here and they say they have not got any money So I cannot get help from them as I used to. Now I am asking you please to help Me. Ive a little child 4 years a mother 62 years an She has ben Sick for 15 or 18 years Ive got along all right till the middle of last year up till now. It has ben hard for 7 or 8 month doctor Bills Groceries coal Bill I do not ask for Money for foolish thing an I do not ask you to give it to me. I am only asking a loan   an I will pay you as you desire Me to by the week or by the month only as you say. but please mr president keep This confidential as I would loose my Job. you See Mr President I can pay one person easier Than a lots of people. These Bill has got a head of me when I didnt have any work an they are demanding their pay   please if It will not Trouble you to much help me   I will appreciste it More than Any Thing. My bill Totals $150.00 that is for The Thing That I have Necessaraly needed not one bit of foolishness for I Tries to put every cent to good use please help me in the Name of the lord an I will pay you back. I have not got any thing for Security but my honor if you will Trust me   Thank you

> A Colored Friend down in Tupelo Miss
> G. T. [female]
> General delivery

P. S. please answer direct to me

———

45. And treates the colored peoples so bad that they cant help from crying at times

> Washington D.C.
> Portsmouth Sep 26, 1935
> and Norflet V.A.

Mr Presentdent its Certainly a strange thing the way we colored peoples is treated here this government money was sent down here for these peoples where is in knead and the poor widows Where is here going from place to place trying to get work and cant get Nothing to do and hungry and what they does with the Money we cant tell some thimes

we makes as much as a quarter aday in the field and some thing will have to be done or else the peoples will perish and freeze this winter because when we cant make no money to pay the doctors bills far sickness and house rent they usually Just turn us out doors and we is pitiful Object here in this world of sorry trying to do the best we can every thing is so high we isnt able harly to get a good meal and pay for it and we knead clothes and shoes and and they have at the city a plenty clothes and quilts and the peoples certain kneads do kned those clothes shoes we is treat some bad and treates the colored peoples so bad that they cant help from crying at times when they go to them and ask for work and they turn we colored peoples of in such way   the object is these peoples that did have work like washing and irning these white peoples is doing there own work and there fore that knocks the colored out of work and it isnt enough work in the field to depend on and these peoples isnt going to let us stay here in their houses with not pay they promist to give grocers every week but they fail to do that by some means. we is just in a place we dont know what to do but I hope you will make it better for we poor

colored peoples   Some of we colored peoples is so ragged we is asham to get out among the peoples like some Folks and its getting cold no wood and cold and if we dont get something to do in order so we can have some money we will Freeze to death doing the winter some of these peoples here where we rents houses from if a person cant pay house rent some of them will take the window out and take the doors of so please do what you can for we peoples please

> [Anonymous]

———

46. Mississippi is made her own laws an dont treat her destuted as her pres. has laid the plans for us

> May 1936
> Hattiesburg Miss

Mr Presedent Sir We are starving in Hattiesburg we poor White's + Negros too i wish you could See the poor hungry an naket half clad's at the relief office an is turned away With tears in their eys Mississippi is made her own laws an dont treat her destuted as her Pres. has laid the plans for us to live if the legislators would do as our good Pres. has Said What few days we have here we could be happy in our last old days both old white + Colard

Cencerely looking for our old age pension's an will thank you they has made us Sighn for $ 3 00 a Month Cant live at that

> [Anonymous]

———

47. Do the government insist on Jim Crow on the W. P. A. projects?

> Chicago Illi
> Mar 9, 1936

Mr. Hopkins:
Dear Sir:

We Are law biding Citizens and legal Voter's of the United States. We would like to know do the government insist on Jim Crow on the W. P. A. projects? We are working at 56th And So parkway and Collored are working at 51th and So Parkway, and the white to their self in Washington park located at 57 And Cottage grove Ave. We Are all on the Same project Number 2262. The white Are to their Self and the Collored to their Self. the men Are Kicking About this very much. Will You take Care of this particular Matter at Once? (yours Truly)

> [Anonymous]

———

48. *The white + colored is haveing a hard time here*

Memphis Ten
Mar. 30, 36

To the President Roosevelt we Poor People here in Memphis are having a hard way to go No work to do   If our Invester gatters wood See to us getting Fuel Clothes + Food we wood be in a better shape than what we are in. what hand full of Food do get From the relief we have to go up to the auditorium + work For it so Our worker says that we wont get Nothin else to eat on the relief because She is going See that we will be Cut of this comming Wednesday April the I   The most of us did not get no Wood or Coal this Winter + no cloths eather + hard words if we ask for enny Please turn us a helping Hand even Salt meat they dont give it to us + that we do get it wont last a week   4 in a Faimly dont get enough to last 4 + 5 days Most of the times we dont have Nothing to eat   The White + Colored is haveing a hard time here it Ought to be Some to took after this it was a hard Winter here + they did give us wood or Coal. Please dont For get

Memphis Tenn.

not 1 Faimly cut of the relief But all of us.

---

49. *The way they are treating the darkies here is a shame*

Vicksburg Miss
9-22-35

President Theo. D. Rosevelt. U.S.A.

Gentlemen: I think you Should invistigate this matter your Self. The way they are treating the Darkies here is A Shame, They wont give them food nor Cloths nor Work to do When they Ask for Any thing they drive them away as they were dogs. They wont even let them talk to the head man here. you Aught to See that Some men get this job that will give this Relief to whom it was Sent here for. you can prevent all brutle treatment of the Darkies here if you will. And its more than 200 Darkies in groups Standing on the Road each day. begging for food and Cloths. And the Relief working women. They tell them there is no job for them to hunt. And the Head men of the Office will help them to drive the Poor darkies as they were dogs. And I gets in My care and Rides from one end of the County to the other to See how the Darkies are treated. All of the Darkies in the Flooded District are in a Suffering condition I know Personally. And please Invistigate The Matter at once. The Darkies in Flooded District are not able to pay they Taxes and they wont let them make enough to pay them. And I Judge the Relief Workers are taking all of the Poor Darkies Money and buying fine Cars.

(Anonymous]

---

50. *They are helping white but are not me poor colored man*

October 27, 1935.
Marietta. Ga

The President Roosevelt:

You honor sir and your royalty. Majesty. This is the one of the most honable Colored workers of America who has been faithful and true law abiding Citizens of this Cob County & the City of Marietta, Ga   Your honor sir I am down now is very feeble and isnt able to work for my living Ive been keep up by the releif but now have fail   They haven't help me any in a month I am very poor and needing Condition I am not able to support my self so dear sir you honor I begging you please sir for food and raimont dear sir. I am very much in need now   They are helping white but are not me poor Colored man my whife has been going there times after times but refused give her anything to eat. So I am hoping through your highness and good natured and kindness that I succeed. So dear sir I am Thanldng you in Advance and your benevolence will never be for gotten here after For I know have the power to Correct such matters if you will.

Those of the Community Ches't and the state of Releif and the food Administration and distributors.

Your honorable
President Roosevelt.
Colored
Cob Co. Marietta. Ga.

---

51. *We will have to face the winter naked, hungry*

Huntsville Ala.
November 12, 1935

Mr. Woodworth
Dear Sir:

I wont to know why it is we people in Huntsville are working and cant get any money or food. We white and colored people we are on a starvation. It is any way on earth you can help us we are really in need. We han't got but one check in three months. We will have to face the winter naked, hungry + nothing to go up on not even fuel to burn. we can't live + work off of nothing.

We can't get any credit to get any food or any thing families of six + seven can't get food for their kids. The kids are hungry.

I will close
From Huntsville

52. We hope all will get some, some get and the other dont

Selma Alabama
Sept. 1935

Dear Mr. President:

Please, please dont let our checks be stop they say that they have close up. We can't even get by now, what shall we do.

Please when they open Work for us the Women let us have a fire our legs are acking now where they work us all the cold Winter And we did not have a fire. please send us some more good meat. for we Cant get Any it is so high. School os open We haven't got Any clotheing for our chridren and our self. Some got dresses and some did not. what shall we do. it is getting cold And we havent got no Coal + no wood we just can get a little food. Please see about us and when you send Any cover to Any thing We hope all Will get Some, Some get and the other dont, some get a raise And some get a cut. We thank you for All you are doing. Thank you.

The Colored
Women.

———

53. Hope that sometime . . . you will mention what the value of the coloured votes has been to you if you think they are worth it

Burlington, Iowa
Nov. 4–36

President + Mrs. Roosevelt
Dear Ones: —

Congratulating you first on your success in staying in the "White House." for which I am well pleased.

I want to write just briefly about my work in the campaign. First let me say most everyone takes for granted "Coloured" voters are Republican   we owe that party a debt.

I worked day and night proving to the U.S.A. voters that phrase is not true. I think this election will convince all, because the Negro of today are more educated. Of course when there are more in one locality it is easier for them to prove their ability to fill worth while positions.

I wasn't working in this campaign to fill an office. I was working for the betterment of this community in which I live, and the men I worked so hard for I feel are real men that will back me up and show a few of my race folk here a little consideration.

I struggle here trying to educate my boy (19 yrs.) and girl (17 yrs.) and trying to keep this locality a haven for them so to speak.

I worked without pay so as to prove to the people here I wasn't working for a personal cause.

I'm not on relief. My husband is a Railroad chef, I worked at odd jobs since where I live my vocation isn't patronized very much. Would like to obtain Ia. licinse but do not feel I can afford spending that much right now right on the verge of winter.

Hope that sometime during your future talks over the radio you will mention what the value of the coloured votes has been to you if you think they are worth it.

Trust that this letter will reach your hands.

Happiness and Success to Both of You.

Sincerely
Mrs. I. H.

———

54. All we ask is that you please remove this Negro sewing-room from our midst at once

July 10, 1936

Mr. Harry L. Hopkins
Washington, D. C.
Dear Sir:

We, the residents of N. Spring Street, Concord, N. C. are all ardent supporters of President Roosevelt and the New Deal and have been loyal Democrats for a long time, and in behalf of this same White neighborhood on N. Spring Street, we are asking you to remove a negro sewing-room that was put in our midst this week.

This is supposed to be a Government project, and it is at least a mile from the negro settlement. It is being conducted in a negro woman's home, in which she occupies part of the house, and there are 39 negro women attending the school. This negro owns five houses and lots, her own car, and also teaches a negro school, which is a project also. The two adjacent homes she owns on this street both have sewing-rooms in them. To make one of the houses available she had the sheriff of Cabarrus County evict a White family from the house, BECAUSE she said she could get more money from the Government. Now we believe in these projects and think you've done a wonderful work, but do you think that she deserves this position she has and the rent she is receiving from our Government?

I wish to refer you to the Sheriff of Cabbarus County, Mr. Ray C. Hoover, and also to the Mayor of this city, Mr. W A. Wilkinson.

Before closing let me state this negro has no dependents at all, and we would certainly appreciate you looking into this matter and removing this thorn at once. It is needless to say that this is one thing that the Southern people do not approve. If she were needy and deserving it would be an endrely different matter, but she doesn't need this income from the Government. Mr. Hopkins, we don't care how much the Government gives her, although we have plenty of other deserving people that need help, ALL we ask is that you please remove this NEGRO sewing-room from our midst at once.

Respectfully and sincerely,
Citizens and Residents of
N. Spring St.,
Concord, N. C.
Cabarrus County

———— —— ——

*55. Negroes being worked ever where instead
of white men it dont look like that is rite*

[Canton, Georgia
July 22, 1935]

[President Franklin D. Roosevelt]

dear Sur as you are the president of our State it looks like you could do Something to help out the poor white people the negroes can get work where the poor white man canot and his family are one Starvation   The negroes are in post offices getting $1000 dollars a month and white families Suffering and it is not write just look at it your Self if it was your family in Canton Ga there is a negro working in the post office and white men cant get a job to feed his family and a white woman up holding for just Such as that and negroes being worked ever where instead of white men it dont look like that is rite and is not rite and lay off white men where there is a large family and keep men with big farms and just a man and wife and both at work unless there are something done the poor people will pursh to death   will you please help the poor people out this relief work is not helping the poor out just make $300 a week them that uses the pick and Shovel and the ofice men and woman gets the rest there is to many in office for the poor working man to get any pay. rote by a woman that has a large family and is on Sufference

[Anonymous]

SECTION TEN

BROWN-V-BOARD OF EDUCATION, TOPEKA, KANSAS AND BEYOND

CHAPTER 12

Nineteen Forty-Eight—The Opening of the Breach

Jack M. Bloom

Jack M. Bloom, author of *Class, Race, and the Civil Rights Movement*, is a professor of sociology at Indiana University/Northwest. He was a movement activist in the 1970s.

✳ ✳ ✳ ✳ ✳

On Tuesday, July 13, 1948, George Vaughan rose to speak to the nominating convention of the Democratic party. Vaughan, a black attorney from St. Louis, was a member of the convention credentials committee. He was delivering a minority report, urging that Mississippi be excluded from the convention because of her commitment not to support Truman if he was nominated and his proposed civil rights platform plank adopted. After making the case, he raised his fist and spoke angrily into the microphone: "Three million Negroes have left the South since the outbreak of World War II to escape this thing. I ask the convention to give consideration...." Vaughan's voice was drowned out in the shouts and screams coming from the Southern delegations. The chair called for a voice vote, and although several Northern delegations were demanding a roll call, they were ignored. The motion was declared defeated, and the session was quickly adjourned for the night.

This incident was remarkable in that it showed the Democratic party, the party of slavery and white supremacy, at war with itself over racial issues. The Northern and Southern Democratic parties were clearly bound in different directions. Tuesday was just a prelude to the tumultuous Wednesday session, when the platform was debated. After the party adopted a more militant plank than even President Truman wanted, the Mississippi delegation walked out, along with half of the Alabama delegation. They left calling for an all-Southern meeting of the "true Democratic Party" Within a few days they and others joined in a meeting in Birmingham to launch a new party, the States' Rights party, to run against Truman.

This party was the second split-off from the Democratic party that year. Earlier, Henry Wallace, Roosevelt's vice-president from 1940 to 1944, had announced that he would run against Truman on the new Progressive party ticket. Wallace's was a left-wing split. So, in 1948 the Democratic party split into three parties. Nothing like that had happened since the election of 1860—the prelude to Civil War.

The treatment of blacks emerged as a central issue for the first time ever in a presidential election in 1948. It did so for a variety of reasons, but most particularly because blacks perceived that they had an opportunity to exert political pressure and to reap some important political gains. Seeing that opportunity, they acted.

The experience of the Great Depression—the worst depression in history, and of World War II—the most destructive and expensive war in history, also had profound and lasting effects. These began to make themselves felt seriously in 1948.

This election was the first since 1928 in which Franklin Roosevelt had not headed the Democratic ticket. The 1928 election had split the Democratic party in the South, with many Southerners voting for Hoover and against the Catholic candidate, Al Smith. The Depression had ended that episode, and the South had flocked home to the Democrats, but Roosevelt's economic policies had met with bitter opposition from the Southern leadership. In 1944 the South had led the effort at the Democratic convention to ditch Henry Wallace as the vice-presidential candidate. Wallace had become identified with the New Deal liberal economic and racial policies and the left wing of the administration. Many felt Roosevelt's victories to be his *personal* victories and that once he was gone his policies would be repudiated by the voters. The New Deal and the changes it had made in politics and economics were being fought over in 1948. That was one of the reasons the nation was seriously divided.

The United States had emerged from the war deeply involved in international affairs. As the most powerful nation in the world, it was busily involved in the reconstruction of that world. That effort ranged from transferring control of much of the oil in the Middle East from Britain to America to refashioning the international monetary system to make the dollar the preeminent currency in the world, and to reforming the world trade system to greatly diminish trade barriers and therefore to give U.S. products access to all world markets. What became most significant was the competition with Russia—the **cold war**. This issue was central in the election.

Splits and dislocations as the nation and the world came to grips with reconstructing political, economic, and social life were only natural. Structural changes in the world and within the United States brought about these splits, which in their turn provided new opportunities for blacks to influence the federal government, and through it to affect the South.

Black Political Power

But these were opportunities that blacks could take advantage of only from a position of strength. In 1948 they had potential power such as they had never before had—voting power, power to determine the outcome of the presidential election and of many local offices. Moreover, blacks were conscious of their power, militant, and better organized than they ever had been.

The simple movement of population is part of what created this new black political power. If Vaughan exaggerated in his claim that 3 million blacks had fled the South during the war, the number was still huge. Between 1940 and 1950, 1.5 million blacks left the South in search of jobs. These numbers increased the Northern black population of 2.8 million by over half. Moreover, this population movement was focused: in 1940, 90 percent of the black population outside the South was concentrated in urban areas; 47 percent of these lived in New York, Chicago, Philadelphia, Detroit, Cleveland, and Pittsburgh. The new migration continued and then accentuated that trend. In the Portland-Vancouver area, the increase of blacks was 437 percent; in San Francisco it was 227 percent; in Detroit it was 60 percent.

The political division in 1948 gave blacks a potential importance in the election that their numbers alone could still not account for. In the 1944 election, with Roosevelt at the head of the ticket, four Northern industrial states were decided by less than a I percent vote: Wisconsin, Ohio, New Jersey, and Michigan. Another three were carried by less than 2 percent: Pennsylvania, Missouri, Illinois; and four more had less than a 3 percent margin: Indiana, Massachusetts, and New York. In virtually all of these states, blacks were a greater percentage of the electorate than was needed to shift the results. By 1940 blacks were 4 to 5 percent of the electorate in New York, New Jersey, Pennsylvania, Ohio, Michigan, and Illinois. However, in that year Roosevelt was a sure winner and had no opposition organized in the Democratic party. In 1948 blacks were in a better position to demand that the piper be paid. Estimates of voting strength in 1948 saw blacks holding the balance of power in sixteen states with a total of 278 electoral votes, compared to 127 electoral votes controlled by the South. This fact alone was sufficient to suggest an important shift in the American political structure.

It didn't take long for this political potential to begin to be translated into actuality. In 1942, Democrat William Dawson was elected to Congress from Chicago. He was joined by Adam Clayton Powell from Harlem in 1944. In 1946, black candidates ran credible campaigns in Los Angeles, Philadelphia, and the Bronx. In that same year, thirty blacks won seats in ten state legislatures. By 1947 there were black judges in Cleveland, Chicago, Los Angeles, Washington, D.C., and seven in New York City, some elected and some appointed. "An alert, well-organized Negro electorate can be an effective factor in at least seventy-five congressional districts in eighteen Northern and border states," argued an observer in 1948. Clearly, black political power was becoming something to contend with.

Blacks and the Cold War

But politics is more than just numbers and votes. Conscious action and organization helped to make blacks into a cohesive and important political force. This strengthening occurred at the same time that changes were taking place in world politics that gave increasing prominence to black concerns and added to the pressures on the American government to do something about black treatment. America's increasing importance in world politics provided new leverage, which blacks were quick to take advantage of.

In 1942, a brutal racial lynching was picked up immediately by Japanese propaganda. The Japanese broadcast the news to the Dutch East Indies and India. It was presented as evidence of how those nations could expect to be treated under United States dominion. As the cold war took shape, Russia naturally picked up where the Japanese left off. The State Department estimated that almost half of all Russian propaganda against the United States at that time concerned racism. Secretary of State James Byrnes told of how the Soviet foreign minister had countered his attacks on Russia's activities in Eastern Europe with stories about racism and racist treatment in the United States.

What gave this matter particular urgency was the emerging revolution against colonialism. The war had hastened the process of the disintegration of the vast colonial empires. Shortly after the war's conclusion, India and Pakistan attained independence, as did several colonies in Africa. By the late forties, the Communist forces in China were clearly approaching victory. The United States was about to be deprived of vast markets, natural resources, and opportunities for investment, not to mention an important element in the world struggle for power. This movement toward self-determination meant that a great deal of the American competition with the Soviet Union focused on gaining the allegiance of the former colonies. In these circumstances, American treatment of blacks in their own country could not help but be weighed by these emerging countries and create serious difficulties for the United States.

Truman openly admitted the problem. Clark Clifford, Truman's special campaign strategist and advisor, recalled the president's feeling that failure to assure equal rights to blacks was one of the nation's weakest points in the struggle with Communism. As Truman delicately phrased it when speaking to the Black Press in 1947:

> More and more we are learning how closely our democracy is under observation. We are learning what loud echoes both our successes and our failures have in every corner of the world. That is one of the pressing reasons why we cannot afford failures. When we fail to live together in peace the failure touches not us, as Americans alone, but the cause of democracy itself in the whole world. That we must never forget.

Blacks could not help but be aware of the changing circumstances and their growing political importance. The NAACP not only saw the changes going on around the organization but directly experienced rapid growth. The association went from a membership of 50,000 before the war to 350,000 after. This change, naturally, provided the organization with many more resources, both finances and personnel. By the middle of the decade, a new mood was clearly sweeping the black communities across the nation. It was fueled by an increasing sense of power that blacks now had and an increased indignation concerning treatment they felt they no longer had to endure. The growth and conscious use of the black vote in the forties was part of a larger process of motion in the black community

In the early forties, blacks received few of the jobs that were created in the first part of the war boom. They were hardly inclined to submerge their struggle for equality during the war. Instead, they called for "Victory at Home as well as Abroad." In 1941 A. Philip Randolph had upped the ante by organizing the March on Washington movement to pressure Roosevelt to establish a Fair Employment Practices Committee in order to provide jobs for blacks. Randolph's statement was militant:

> The Negro's stake in national defense is big. it consists of jobs, thousands of jobs. It may represent millions, yes hundreds of millions of dollars in wages. It consists of new industrial opportunities and hope. This is worth fighting for. Most important and vital of all, Negroes by the mobilization and coordination of their mass power, can cause PRESIDENT ROOSEVELT TO ISSUE AN EXECUTIVE ORDER ABOLISHING DISCRIMINATION IN ALL GOVERNMENT DEPARTMENTS, ARMY, NAVY, AIR CORPS AND NATIONAL DEFENSE JOBS. (emphasis in original)

Randolph threatened to bring thousands of blacks to march on the capital demanding action. In the midst of the war, the movement organized mass rallies of tens of thousands of blacks in New York, Chicago, and St. Louis. They won their committee.

Militancy continued after the war. Walter White, leader of the NAACP, testified before the Senate in 1945: "Throughout the Pacific I was told with grim pessimism by Negro troops that 'we know that our fight for democracy will really begin when we reach San Francisco on our way home.'" Black veterans in the South began to organize protests against their conditions. In January of 1946, over a hundred black veterans marched to the Birmingham courthouse to demand their right to register to vote. They were turned away, but their demonstration helped to unite black pressure on Truman. He responded by establishing the President's Committee on Civil Rights. The committee was told to prepare recommendations for government action to protect civil rights.

The NAACP submitted a petition of grievances to the United Nations Committee on Human Rights. "This protest," it read, "is to induce the nations of the world to persuade this nation to be just to its own people." Though the petition was rejected, it caused great embarrassment to the United States government, especially when the Soviet Union used it as an opportunity to score propaganda points against the United States. The Soviets proposed making a crime of the "advocacy of national, racial and religious hostility or of national exclusiveness or hatred and contempt as well as of any action establishing privilege or discrimination based on distinction of race, nationality or religion."

These acts were minor compared with the organization of the Committee against Jim Crow in Military Service and Training in late 1947, when, because of the developing cold war, the government was preparing to reintroduce the draft. A. Philip Randolph, once again in the lead, threatened to organize refusal among blacks to be drafted into a segregated army:

> I personally will advise Negroes to refuse to fight as slaves for a democracy they cannot possess and cannot enjoy...I personally pledge myself to openly counsel and abet youth, both white and Negro, to quarantine a Jim Crow conscription system.

When reminded during his testimony at a Senate hearing that such an act would be treason in time of war, Randolph responded that

> the Government now has time to change its policy on segregation and discrimination and if the government does not change its policy . . . in the interests of the very democracy it is fighting for, I would advocate that Negroes take no part in the army."

I am prepared," he said, "to oppose a Jim Crow army 'til I rot in jail." Randolph led a picket line outside the Democratic Convention in 1948 demanding an end to segregation in the military. A poll of black youth in Harlem found 71 percent favoring refusal to be drafted into a segregated army. *Newsweek* reported that among Negro college students "there were indications of strong sympathy and support for Randolph."

These were serious actions that indicated that blacks were ready and able to organize to pressure the government for equal rights. They were obviously aware of and willing to use the increased leverage provided by the pressures of the developing cold war. As Truman had indicated, with the United States trying to present itself as the leader of the free world as against the totalitarian Communists, the condition of blacks was the country's weak point. Henry Moon, voting analyst for the NAACP wryly observed:

> Culturally and economically he [the Southern Negro] today surpasses the masses of the Rumanians, Bulgars and Poles for whom, ironically, former Secretary of State James F. Byrnes of South Carolina demanded "free and unfettered elections" at a time when this right was being denied to millions of Americans.

The Wallace Threat

Truman, heading the Democratic ticket for the first time, was in trouble with liberals who had been discontent with him for some time. In 1944 he had been a conservative replacement for the enormously popular Henry Wallace, and he was then strongly supported by the South, whose leaders felt that Truman would be more sympathetic to their problems. Wallace's support had been from labor, blacks, liberals, and the left. It was not long after Truman succeeded Roosevelt that liberals began to be unhappy with his policies. The most crucial of these was the issue of relations with Russia. The two countries had enjoyed a close working relationship during the war. But six weeks after Roosevelt's death, when two leading liberals went to visit the new president, they were shocked to hear him say: "We have got to get tough with the Russians. They don't know how to behave. They're like bulls in a china shop. . . . We've got to teach them to behave." He replaced a number of liberal Roosevelt appointees, which upset many. He appeared sufficiently antilabor that the president of the Brotherhood of Railway Trainmen promised to spend the whole union treasury, if necessary, to defeat him for reelection after Truman urged the drafting of strikers during a railroad strike. Other labor leaders were unhappy enough with Truman that they tried to replace him as the Democratic party candidate. Blacks were so discontented with his policies that many voted Republican or simply did not vote in 1946. Many liberals saw Wallace as the rightful heir to Roosevelt. The 1946 election debacle, which brought about a Republican-dominated legislature for the first time since 1930, shook up the left and sent it casting in new directions. A third party was widely discussed.

At the time Wallace was considering running against Truman, he had reason to believe that he would get some substantial labor support. Many unions had indicated their interest. But by the time he declared, at the end of December 1947, that support had disappeared. In part, labor's desertion of Wallace was due to a left turn that Truman had made after the 1946 mid-term elections. That election had brought serious losses to the Democrats in Congress, and it illustrated how far the president was from prevailing attitudes. In particular, his veto of the Taft-Hartley antilabor law was important in helping Truman to regain labor's support. But more fundamental were the cold war and the domestic red-baiting that went with it, both of which had a big impact on American politics.

Truman was very conscious about his use of red-baiting to increase his popularity. His strategy was to use the antagonism with Russia that was growing as American and Soviet interests collided in order to create anti-Communist hysteria at home, and to use that hysteria against his opposition. This strategy was part of the overall election "game plan" developed for the president by Clark Clifford.

In 1947, Truman had already instituted a loyalty program for federal employees. While it was ostensibly for the purposes of national security, in the program's implementation the division between espionage and political radicalism was obliterated. The president called opposition to his foreign policy an effort to "sabotage the foreign policy of the United States [which] is just as bad in this Cold War as it would be to shoot our soldiers in the back in a hot war." Although this particular barb was aimed at congressional opposition, it helped to create a general atmosphere that labeled dissent as being disloyal. He even suggested that the Republican party was soft on Communism because Republicans had expressed differences on foreign policy.

Truman's rhetoric raised the level of hysteria. He rejected the support of "Wallace and his Communists." The Democratic National Committee labeled the Progressive party as "Communist-influenced." Jack Redding, Truman's publicity director, wrote concerning the 1948 campaign: "Wallace was smarting as we pinned red labels on him and his followers. Through every avenue we were pointing out that Wallace and his third party were following the Kremlin line slavishly" The formation of another liberal anti-Communist organization, the Americans for Democratic Action, was very helpful in the effort; these liberals served as frontmen for the president in the attack on Wallace. Indeed, as other support dropped away, virtually the only organized backing Wallace had was from the Communist party and the organizations it controlled.

But if Wallace's campaign was weakened by this activity, it was certainly not destroyed. Although Wallace had few hopes of winning now, his political base could still affect the issues. In November of 1947, a Wallacite had garnered 40 percent of the vote in a Chicago judicial election. On February 17, a special congressional election in New York City produced a victory for the American Labor party candidate, who was backed by Wallace. The candidate, Leo Isaacson, took 56 percent of the vote and defeated the Democratic candidate by about two to one. A *New York Times* survey found that after the election, Wallace had increased support in the crucial states of Michigan, Pennsylvania, Illinois, and California, The *Times* argued that Wallace was a sufficient threat that it would be hard for Truman to win any of these states now. Polls taken before the convention showed the same trend. In Pennsylvania, Truman got 41 percent, Dewey 49 percent, Wallace 7 percent; in Illinois, it was Truman 44 percent, Dewey 43 percent, Wallace 13 percent; in New York, results were similar.

Wallace's main issue was opposition to the **Truman Doctrine**, which defined Communism and Russia as America's main enemies—Wallace was for recognizing Russia's sphere of influence in Eastern Europe and maintaining a cooperative relationship with her. Nonetheless, he waged a hard-hitting campaign on other issues. He made serious efforts to woo labor and black support. Paul Robeson was made vice-chairman of the Progressive party; Joe Louis was a public contributor to the Wallace campaign fund; and W. E. B. DuBois and other blacks played a prominent role at the party convention in July.

Indeed, because of his previous record and his campaign, Wallace's most important single source of strength was in the black community. The Associated Negro Press reported that in Los Angeles, "thousands of Negro voters here began lining up behind Henry A. Wallace the day after he announced that he would run for the Presidency." Wallace deliberately went after the black vote. He and his vice-presidential candidate, Senator Glen Taylor, held election rallies in several cities in the South, including Little Rock, Memphis, Asheville, Greenville, Knoxville, and Chattanooga. At these rallies they verbally assaulted the segregation system and physically challenged it by refusing to hold segregated meetings. In doing so, they courted arrest and violence. Taylor was arrested in Birmingham by Eugene "Bull" Connor, who became nationally infamous in 1963 because of his treatment of civil rights demonstrators. Wallace and Taylor had to endure eggs, tomatoes, peach stones, and other sundries being hurled at them as they attempted to speak. Wallace was several times forced to cancel meetings.

These efforts paid off. Though Wallace failed to win the support of the national black leadership, he gained the endorsement of the president of the Indiana NAACP and of officials in many of the large cities, including San Francisco and Philadelphia. Ward leaders in Brooklyn and Harlem thought that Wallace might get as much as 75 percent of the vote in their wards. Even as late as October 2, a poll taken in Baltimore indicated that Wallace was drawing a substantial percentage of the black vote—perhaps enough to hand the election to Dewey. The Chicago *Defender* was the only important black newspaper to endorse Truman, a fact that made the situation more worrisome for the president.

The Liberals Respond

It was the very strength of the Wallace campaign that made the liberal opposition within the Democratic party important. Many liberals who refused to follow Wallace were still quite unhappy with Truman. They organized the Americans for Democratic Action early in 1947 with a double aim: to exclude Communists from the liberal movement ("a reconstruction of the liberal movement free of totalitarian influence from either the Left or the Right") and to strengthen their own position within the Democratic party ("All our efforts, all our own ingenuity must be thrown into the struggle to establish liberal control of the Democratic Party"). The content of liberalism came very largely to be shaped in the course of the campaign itself.

The ADA was solidly behind the anti-Communist direction of Truman's policies at home and abroad. It was locked in battle against the Communists and their supporters for liberal supremacy in America. Nonetheless, the ADA was very much in opposition to Truman, because they felt he was not really a liberal, because of his antilabor policy, and because they felt he was a sure loser and would take the Democratic party and labor and the liberals down to defeat with him. Until shortly before the convention, the organization was engaged in a serious effort to deny the nomination to Truman. It was forced to abandon the effort when its candidate, General Eisenhower, announced that he would not accept the nomination.

Responding to the pressure of the Wallace campaign, the ADA now sought to shore up the Democratic party's weakest flank by turning to civil rights, which blacks had made an issue before Wallace began his campaign. The Civil Rights Committee that blacks had pressured the president to appoint in 1946 had produced a report of its findings in 1947. Truman had delivered a civil rights message to Congress in early 1948 that was largely based on this report. This act caused the white South to respond in anger, and Truman soon backed off. He refrained from sending legislation to Congress and from issuing any executive orders concerning the matter.

But it was impossible simply to placate the white South and ignore blacks. Truman himself had created expectations with his civil rights address to Congress; he had even had it broadcast over the Voice of America to make sure it would be used as a weapon in the cold war. Blacks were not letting the matter rest—Randolph was in the midst of campaigning against the segregated armed forces. And the Wallace threat continued.

Truman tried to respond to both pressures by resurrecting for the platform a rewritten version of the civil rights plank from 1944, which was an innocuous statement that read:

> We believe that racial and religious minorities have the right to live, develop and vote equally with all citizens and share the rights that are guaranteed by our Constitution. Congress should exert its full constitutional powers to protect those rights.

Even the Republican party platform was stronger than this statement. It included a call for abolition of the poll tax and for ending segregation in the armed forces.

Truman's proposal pleased no one. It certainly did not please the South, which wanted its own plank assuring states' rights. Nor did it please blacks, who felt it insufficient. Walter White, head of the NAACP, appeared before the convention platform representing not only the association but twenty other black organizations as well, with a combined membership of over six million. White said the plank was totally unsatisfactory and reminded the committee of the voting power of blacks, who, he said, would vote on issues, not party labels. The Truman forces continued to press on with their planned position, hoping to keep support of the South with it.

But the ADA was unwilling to let things stand and determined to challenge the president on the civil rights plank, if necessary in order to strengthen it. They took their proposal, which included the following points, to the floor of the convention after they failed to get it through the platform committee:

> The right to full and equal political participation, the right to equal opportunity of employment, the right of security of persons [referring to lynchings in particular], and the right of equal treatment in the services and defense of our nation.

They were backed in their efforts by several big-city-machine bosses, including those from Chicago, Pittsburgh, the Bronx, San Francisco, and Minneapolis, who were concerned about losing not only the presidential election but the local elections in which Wallace was giving them a hard time in competition for black votes. Hubert Humphrey, who was facing a strong Republican opponent in his bid to be elected senator of Minnesota, and who was threatened by the Wallacites, was the public leader of the fight. He presented the case eloquently:

> There are those who say this issue of civil rights is an infringement on states' rights. The time has come for the Democratic Party to get out of the shadow of states' rights and walk forthrightly into the bright sunshine of human rights.

What was most instructive was his clear explanation of the issue in terms of world politics:

> Yes, this is far more than a party matter. Every citizen has a stake in the emergence of the United States as the leader of the free world. That world is being challenged by the world of slavery. For us to play our part effectively we must be in a morally sound position. We cannot use a double standard for measuring our own and other people's policies. Our demands for democratic practices in other lands will be no more effective than the guarantee of those practiced in our own country.

Humphrey made the point clearly He and his coworkers had set the liberal and the Democratic party agenda. In order to be able to wage the cold war effectively, they had to espouse civil rights at home. The pressures of international politics together with changes in domestic politics gave civil rights their day—at least in rhetoric.

The amendment carried, and the states' rights advocates walked out. The ADA and their allies had carried off a remarkable feat. They had challenged a sitting president and defeated him within the party. They, rather than he, had determined one of the principal issues on which the campaign would be run. But it was black organization, activity, and power that had made it imperative to do and possible to accomplish. "Never since 1932," said the

New York Times, "had there been such a material change in a party platform after it had reached the convention floor."

Campaign and Election

Truman had little choice but to run on the platform, especially after the loss of the right-wing Southerners. Less than two weeks after the convention, he issued two executive orders that he had been sitting on for six months or more. He barred discrimination in federal employment and established a review board in each government department. Employees who felt discriminated against could appeal to this board.

Truman further announced a policy of "equality of treatment and opportunity for all persons in the armed services without regard to race, color, religion or national origin." It was unclear, however, if that meant a policy of desegregation in the armed forces, especially when he further announced that he would appoint a committee to study the problem. Two days later, General Bradley, army chief of staff, announced that the army would not be a laboratory for social reforms and that it would change "when the Nation as a whole changes." The president responded at a press conference that the policy indeed was to integrate the armed forces. In mid-August, when the civil disobedience campaign against the new draft was to have begun, Randolph terminated it, satisfied that the point had been won.

In the end, Truman felt compelled to pursue the black vote openly. At the end of October, he toured the black ghetto in Philadelphia; and on October 29 he became the first president to speak in Harlem. On the anniversary of his receipt of the report of his Civil Rights Committee, he addressed some 65,000 people and affirmed his commitment to civil rights: "Our determination to attain the goal of equal rights and equal opportunity must be resolute and unwavering."

Truman, of course, won. "Labor did it," said Truman. And it was true that labor had played a crucial role in his victory. But it was a very close election. The president beat Dewey by 2,000,000 votes, but he won three crucial states—Ohio, California, and Illinois—by a total of only 58,584 votes. If he had lost those states, he would have lost the election;

if he had lost two of them, it would have been thrown into the House of Representatives. Blacks, who voted 69 percent for Truman overall, carried those states for him. The black vote in Los Angeles, Chicago and Cleveland and Akron provided the margin of victory in those key states.

Truman's strategy with regard to blacks was successful. He won their vote and appears to have gotten a better percentage of it than had Roosevelt. So was the black strategy a success. For the first time blacks forced the issue of race into the very center of national politics.

The election was very much focused around the developing cold war, and Truman's strategy called for intensifying the emphasis on the competition with Russia. The emerging colonial revolution put extraordinary new pressures on the United States to develop an acceptable racial policy, while at the same time blacks were beginning to gain some power. Their activity and muscle forced the issue to public attention, thus making it a matter of international concern. These pressures persisted after 1948. As more colonies became independent, their presence encouraged American blacks to oppose their own conditions. The 1948 election demonstrated the new power and position that blacks had attained after depression and war. In that sense, it was a reflection of change, as well as a turning point that quickened the pace of events.

The election struggle had opened a breach in the Democratic party and in the nation. The country was becoming divided again. The strength of blacks in the North was pitted against the racists in the South, and the latter lost. Truman's appeal to blacks was a success, despite the States' Rights party, which carried four Southern states. That was an important lesson. It showed that it was possible for a Democrat to win by ignoring Southern racism and courting blacks. It was a lesson that would figure significantly in Senator John F. Kennedy's bid for the presidency in 1960. It illustrated, furthermore, how isolated the South's racist culture and political structure had become from the prevailing sentiments and political trends in the nation. Both of these perceptions would have an impact on the black community and, as they were reinforced in the fifties, would encourage black activism.

Brown v. Board of Education of Topeka I and II

Supreme Court of the United States (347 U.S. 483) May 17, 1954

[This is an abridged version of the document.]

Brown v. Board of Education of Topeka I, May 17, 1954

Segregation of white and Negro children in the public schools of a State solely on the basis of race, pursuant to state laws permitting or requiring such segregation, denies to Negro children the equal protection of the laws guaranteed by the Fourteenth Amendment—even though the physical facilities and other "tangible" factors of white and Negro schools may be equal. (a) The history of the Fourteenth Amendment is inconclusive as to its intended effect on public education. (b) The question presented in these cases must be determined not on the basis of conditions existing when the Fourteenth Amendment was adopted, but in the light of the full development of public education and its present place in American life throughout the Nation. (c) Where a State has undertaken to provide an opportunity for an education in its public schools, such an opportunity is a right which must be made available to all on equal terms. (d) Segregation of children in public schools solely on the basis of race deprives children of the minority group of equal educational opportunities, even though the physical facilities and other "tangible" factors may be equal. (e) The "separate but equal" doctrine adopted in *Plessy v. Ferguson*, 163 U.S. 537, has no place in the field of public education. (f) The cases are restored to the docket for further argument on specified questions relating to the forms of the decrees.

MR. CHIEF JUSTICE WARREN delivered the opinion of the Court.

These cases come to us from the States of Kansas, South Carolina, Virginia, and Delaware. They are premised on different facts and different local conditions, but a common legal question justifies their consideration together in this consolidated opinion.

In each of the cases, minors of the Negro race, through their legal representatives, seek the aid of the courts in obtaining admission to the public schools of their community on a nonsegregated basis. In each instance, they had been denied admission to schools attended by white children under laws requiring or permitting segregation according to race. This segregation was alleged to deprive the plaintiffs of the equal protection of the laws under the Fourteenth Amendment. In each of the cases other than the Delaware case, a three-judge federal district court denied relief to the plaintiffs on the so-called "separate but equal" doctrine announced by this Court in *Plessy v. Fergson*, 163 U.S. 537. Under that doctrine, equality of treatment is accorded when the races are provided substantially equal facilities, even though these facilities be separate....

The plaintiffs contend that segregated public schools are not "equal" and cannot be made "equal," and that hence they are deprived of the equal protection of the laws. ...

In the instant cases ... there are findings below that the Negro and white schools involved have been equalized, or are being equalized, with respect to buildings, curricula, qualifications and salaries of teachers, and other "tangible" factors. Our decision, therefore, cannot turn on merely a comparison of these tangible factors in the Negro and white schools involved in each of the cases. We must look instead to the effect of segregation itself on public education.

In approaching this problem, we cannot turn the clock back to 1868, when the Amendment was adopted, or even to 1896, when *Plessy v. Ferguson* was written. We must consider public education in the light of its full development and its present place in American life throughout the Nation. Only in this way can it be determined if segregation in public schools deprives these plaintiffs of the equal protection of the laws.

Today, education is perhaps the most important function of state and local governments. Compulsory school attendance laws and the great expenditures for education both demonstrate our recognition of the importance of education to our democratic society. It is required in the performance of our most basic public responsibilities, even service in the armed forces. It is the very foundation of good citizenship. Today it is a principal instrument in awakening the child to cultural values, in preparing him for later professional training, and in helping him to adjust normally to his environment. In these days, it is doubtful that any child may reasonably be expected to succeed in life if he is denied the opportunity of an education. Such an opportunity, where the state has undertaken to provide it, is a right which must be made available to all on equal terms.

We come then to the question presented: Does segregation of children in public schools solely on the basis of race, even though the physical facilities and other "tangible" factors may be equal, deprive the children of the minority group of equal educational opportunities? We believe that it does.

In *Sweatt v. Painter*, supra, in finding that a segregated law school for Negroes could not provide them equal educational opportunities, this Court relied in large part on "those qualities which are incapable of objective measurement but which make for greatness in a law school." In *McLaurin v. Oklahoma State Regents, supra*, the Court, in requiring that a Negro admitted to a white graduate school be treated like all other students, again resorted to intangible considerations: " . . . his ability to study, to engage in discussions and exchange views with other students, and, in general, to learn his profession." Such considerations apply with added force to children in grade and high schools. To separate them from others of similar age and qualifications solely because of their race generates a feeling of inferiority as to their status in the community that may affect their hearts and minds in a way unlikely ever to be undone. The effect of this separation on their educational opportunities was well stated by a finding in the Kansas case by a court which nevertheless felt compelled to rule against the Negro plaintiffs: Segregation of white and colored children in public schools has a detrimental effect upon the colored children. The impact is greater when it has the sanction of the law, for the policy of separating the races is usually interpreted as denoting the inferiority of the negro group. A sense of inferiority affects the motivation of a child to learn. Segregation with the sanction of law, therefore, has a tendency to [retard] the educational and mental development of negro children and to deprive

them of some of the benefits they would receive in a racial[ly] integrated school system. Whatever may have been the extent of psychological knowledge at the time of *Plessy v. Ferguson*, this finding is amply supported by modern authority. Any language in *Plessy v. Ferguson* contrary to this finding is rejected.

We conclude that, in the field of public education, the doctrine of "separate but equal" has no place. Separate educational facilities are inherently unequal. Therefore, we hold that the plaintiffs and others similarly situated for whom the actions have been brought are, by reason of the segregation complained of, deprived of the equal protection of the laws guaranteed by the Fourteenth Amendment. This disposition makes unnecessary any discussion whether such segregation also violates the Due Process Clause of the Fourteenth Amendment.

Because these are class actions, because of the wide applicability of this decision, and because of the great variety of local conditions, the formulation of decrees in these cases presents problems of considerable complexity. On reargument, the consideration of appropriate relief was necessarily subordinated to the primary question—the constitutionality of segregation in public education. We have now announced that such segregation is a denial of the equal protection of the laws. In order that we may have the full assistance of the parties in formulating decrees, the cases will be restored to the docket. . . .

It is so ordered.

Brown v. Board of Education of Topeka II, May 31, 1955

MR. CHIEF JUSTICE WARREN delivered the opinion of the Court.

These cases were decided on May 17, 1954. The opinions of that date, declaring the fundamental principle that racial discrimination in public education is unconstitutional, are incorporated herein by reference. All provisions of federal, state, or local law requiring or permitting such discrimination must yield to this principle. There remains for consideration the manner in which relief is to be accorded. . . .

Full implementation of these constitutional principles may require solution of varied local school problems. School authorities have the primary responsibility for elucidating, assessing, and solving these problems; courts will have to consider whether the action of school authorities constitutes good faith implementation of the governing constitutional principles. Because of their proximity to local conditions and the possible need for further hearings, the courts which originally heard these cases can best perform this judicial appraisal. Accordingly, we believe it appropriate to remand the cases to those courts.

In fashioning and effectuating the decrees, the courts will be guided by equitable principles. Traditionally, equity has been characterized by a practical flexibility in shaping its remedies and by a facility for adjusting and reconciling public and private needs. These cases call for the exercise of these traditional attributes of equity power. At stake is the personal interest of the plaintiffs in admission to public schools as soon as practicable on a nondiscriminatory basis. To effectuate this interest may call for elimination of a variety of obstacles in making the transition to school systems operated in accordance with the constitutional principles set forth in our May 17, 1954, decision. Courts of equity may properly take into account the public interest in the elimination of such obstacles in a systematic and effective manner. But it should go without saying that the vitality of these constitutional principles cannot be allowed to yield simply because of disagreement with them.

While giving weight to these public and private considerations, the courts will require that the defendants make a prompt and reasonable start toward full compliance with our May 17, 1954, ruling. Once such a start has been made, the courts may find that additional time is necessary to carry out the ruling in an effective manner. The burden rests upon the defendants to establish that such time is necessary in the public interest and is consistent with good faith compliance at the earliest practicable date. To that end, the courts may consider problems related to administration, arising from the physical condition of the school plant, the school transportation system, personnel, revision of school districts and attendance areas into compact units to achieve a system of determining admission to the public schools on a nonracial basis, and revision of local laws and regulations which may be necessary in solving the foregoing problems. They will also consider the adequacy of any plans the defendants may propose to meet these problems and to effectuate a transition to a racially nondiscriminatory school system. During this period of transition, the courts will retain jurisdiction of these cases. …

It is so ordered.

The Impact of Brown on the Education of Latinos

A. Reynaldo Contreras and Leonard A. Valverde

Introduction

Brown v. Board of Education of Topeka, Kansas (1954) was the basis for a number of initiatives and strategies to improve the educational treatment of people of color. While it had a dramatic impact on the quality of education for African American youth in the United States, Brown also became a major force for improving the educational experience of other ethnic and racial groups as well, notably Latinos. The Court's decision in Brown created not just desegregation strategies such as busing and the changing of school funding allocations but also instructional approaches such as Title I programs, magnet schools, and bilingual and multicultural education.

As with any movement, an evolutionary development rather than a radical change occurred after Brown. This article reports the progress made to improve the educational experience of Latinos incident to Brown by describing the legal history of Latino desegregation. Accordingly, it focuses on bilingual education as a remedy for educational inequity, and on the rise of multicultural education, the latest instructional approach to emerge in the evolution of desegregation, as a step toward integrating society. The article concludes with a review of the trends shaping future desegregation efforts.

Legal Roots of Latino Education

Prior to Brown, the educational conditions and treatment of Latinos and African Americans were very much alike. Members of both groups were disenfranchised. Most Latino children, like their African American counterparts, were denied access to formal schooling. The few who received instruction attended segregated schools, commonly referred to in the Southwest as "Mexican schools," that were clearly not equal to schools for Whites.

Segregation, strictly speaking, refers to the setting apart and isolation of individuals or groups. In the United States, that practice resulted in the exclusion of non - White students from a fundamentally adequate education. The segregation of racial and ethnic minority children from White students in U.S. public schools has always been rooted in unfounded misconceptions, better known as racist attitudes. To condone this banal irrational practice, various excuses were constructed. For example, prior to Brown, segregation was defended against attack by the misleading notion that "separate-but-equal" facilities were provided for Blacks and Whites. A similar excuse, based upon "language deficiency," was fabricated to justify the isolation of students with Spanish surnames. However, supporting separate and unequal school conditions throughout the U.S. for Latinos was not sanctioned by any state law except in California, where a statute providing for separate schools for "Mongolians" (Asian Americans) and "Indians" (Native Americans) was interpreted to include Mexican Americans as being in the latter category (National Association for Intergroup Relations, 1963). Generally, the placement of Spanish-surnamed students into separate schools or classrooms was an arbitrary action that lacked due process. No appropriate or systematic language assessment was made of these students

Contreras, A. Reynaldo & Leonard A. Valverde, "The Impact of Brown on the Education of Latinos," *Journal of Negro Education*, Vol. 63, No. 3, pp. 470–481. Copyright © 1994 by Howard University. All rights reserved.

for the purpose of pedagogical placement. Children with Spanish surnames who did not have a "language problem"—that is, those who were English-proficient—were automatically assigned to schools and classrooms composed of students of like ancestry.

For Latinos, the legal challenge against school segregation historically has been spearheaded by Mexican Americans. Judicial opposition to segregation of Latinos goes back to a 1930 Texas case, *Independent School District v. Salvatierra*, wherein the Del Rio Independent School District was charged with separating Mexican American children merely because of their race. In Salvatierra, the district successfully contended that the students' language deficiency warranted their separate schooling. The first federal court decision on the segregation of Mexican American students was handed down in California in *Mendez v. Westminster School District* (1946). In that case, the trial court ruled that separate schools with the same technical facilities did not satisfy the equal protection provisions of the Constitution. The Ninth Circuit Court affirmed the decision, finding that segregation of Mexican Americans denied them due process and equal protection. Despite this ruling, however, de facto segregation continued throughout California.

In Texas, where discrimination was more blatant and segregation more intensive than other states having large numbers of Spanish-surnamed people, *Delago v. Bastrop Independent School District* (1948) followed *Mendez* by stating that the district's segregative acts violated the 14th Amendment. Further, where the segregation of Mexican Americans was more by separate schools, the court directed that separate classes for non-English-proficient students must be held on the same campus. It thus forbade school authorities from further rationalizing the practice of completely separating Mexican American students into different schools based on their alleged language deficiencies.

Despite the rulings in *Mendez, Delago,* and *Brown*, school officials continued segregating Latinos from White students. This evasion was based on the technicality that Mexicans and other Latinos were also classified as "White" for desegregation purposes. As a result, in tri-ethnic settings, the post-*Brown* generation saw the desegregation of predominantly African American school settings with Latino students while White students continued to be assigned to all-White schools. Therefore,

by pairing Black students with Brown ones and excluding Whites, the two largest minority school populations in the U.S. continued to be exposed to inferior facilities, and unequal education prevailed.

The initial challenge to this technical subterfuge was raised by parents in *California in Romero v. Weakley* (1955); however, this case was settled out of court. It was not until *Cisneros v. Corpus Christi Independent School District* (1970) that the technical loophole was sealed off. *Cisneros* is of fundamental significance because, for the first time, a court declared Mexican Americans to be an identifiable ethnic minority group for the purposes of public school desegregation. Further, it was the first circuit court case to hold that the principles enunciated in *Brown* apply to Latinos as well as African Americans.

Subsequently, in *Keyes v. School District No 1, Denver, Colorado* (1973) the Supreme Court held that African American and Latino students suffered identical discrimination in treatment when compared to White students. Although *Keyes* was brought by African Americans and no proof of de jure segregation of Latino students was found, discrimination against Latino students was introduced at a remedy stage by intervenors. In support of its holding, the Court cited a report published by the United States Commission on Civil Rights (1967), which noted that, in parts of the Southwest, students with Spanish surnames suffered from the same educational inequities as African Americans.

The Latino community has expressed concern over the impact on the community of certain remedies ordered by the courts once constitutional violations are established (Cisneros, 1970). Often, because most school desegregation litigation as instituted by Black plaintiffs, remedies were framed in that context. Much of the relief sought by African American and Latinos has been the same; however, the special concerns of the Latino community often were not raised until the remedial phase. That Latino students may require, as part of any desegregation decree, special remedies not sought by litigants in multiracial desegregation cases, is a principal that has only gradually gained judicial recognition.

Cases following *Keyes* have treated discrimination against Latinos in the same manner as they did discrimination against African Americans. In tri-ethnic settings, this has often meant that the degree of segregation in any given school depends on the ratio of Whites to the combined number of identified minorities. In *Cisneros*, the court had already expressed the view that placing "Negroes and Mexican Americans in the same school does not achieve a minority system as contemplated by law" (p. 616). Although the court was concerned with the nature of the remedy rather than the violation, the underlying premise was the same: proving that the isolation of Latino students constitutes a violation of the Equal Protection Clause requires a showing of de jure segregation attributable to the action of school officials. In cases involving Latino students, the nation's courts seem to have applied a standard that places a heavy burden upon the plaintiff to establish a prima facie case of segregation. In the absence of a statutory history of de jure segregation, as in the case of African Americans, Latinos must show that schools are, in fact, segregated and that this condition is attributable to an intentional act by school authorities or other state officials.

In *United States v. Texas Education Agency* (1972), the Fifth Circuit found intentional segregative action by the school district, particularly in its choice of school sites, construction, drawing of attendance zones, student assignment and transfer policies, and faculty and staff assignments. Maintaining that *Texas* was "no different from any other school desegregation case" (p. 873), the court concluded that de jure segregation was present, despite the absence of a state law requiring segregation of Latino students. It noted that the pattern of segregation was nonstatutory because school board policies did nothing to counteract the effect of existing patterns of residential segregation, in light of existing viable alternatives to integrate Latino students. Thus, once the necessary intentional segregative actions were found, coupled with a large concentration of Latino students in specific schools, a prima facie case of unlawful segregation was established.

In *Morales v. Shannon* (1975), the Fifth Circuit court found that systematic segregation of Mexican Americans was evident in discriminatory school construction and assignment policies in Texas. Similarly, in *United States v. Midland Independent School District* (1975), the Fifth Circuit court, based on statistical evidence, found an overriding intent to isolate and segregate Mexican Americans and Blacks. This segregation was accomplished through the historical maintenance of "Mexican American" and "Black" schools; segregated transportation, construction and transfer practices; and the drawing of an attendance area circumscribing "El Barrio" or "Mexican Town."

The Instructional Dimension of Desegregation

In the four decades since *Brown* took dead aim at equal educational opportunity, a number of instructional programs were created in an attempt to bring into existence quality educational experiences for African Americans. The desegregation movement led to the creation of magnet schools in large metropolitan school districts. It was maintained that these schools, whose curricula focus on particular specialties such as the performing arts and whose enrollments are drawn from all areas within a district's attendance boundaries, would help eradicate segregation because they are open to students of all races and ethnicities regardless of residence.

Additionally, the federal government enacted and funded legislation to desegregate public schools and remediate the poor instruction previously provided to African Americans. The most prominent of these was Title I, which addressed education at the elementary and secondary school levels. Latinos, though classified as "White," also participated in these federally sponsored instructional programs. While Title I programs were created with African American students as the main recipients, Title VII established bilingual programs for Latinos. Title VII programs were targeted to accomplish two goals: first, to aid non- or limited-English-proficient (LEP) students to learn English and to thus move into full English-speaking classrooms; second, to help LEP students maintain their native language so as to become bilingual. INS latter goal, that of an educated person knowing more than one language, was consistent with long-standing educational values and with the requirements of most of the nation's higher education institutions.

Bilingual Education for Desegregation

In 1968, President Lyndon B. Johnson signaled the nation's first commitment to addressing the English language skills of minority students by signing into law Title VII of the Elementary and Secondary Education Act: the Bilingual Education Act. Focusing primarily on children who were both poor and educationally disadvantaged due to their inability to speak English, Title VII authorized monetary resources to support educational programs and develop necessary instructional resources. Previously, many districts offered Latino students segregated bilingual education or integration without bilingual education (Cardenas, 1975). With this Act, the federal government established a two-track policy toward the education of Latino students comprised of financial support programs and civil rights efforts to ensure that LEP students get an equal chance to succeed. Although both tracks are aimed at enhancing educational opportunities for student English language development, they have not always run side by side. Funding for bilingual education programs received priority before attention was given to language discrimination in the schools.

After the Supreme Court's remand in *Keyes* in 1974, the district court heard testimony on proposed desegregation plans. Intervenors, most notably the Congress of Hispanic Educators (CHE), put forth a plan calling for the establishment of a bilingual educational program for Latino students. District court judges concurred with the intervenors, declaring the "bilingual-bicultural approach to the education of Mexican Americans to be a very sensible method," and concluding that "to the extent that [this approach] can be useful to building bridges between the Spanish and Anglo cultures, it is to be fully utilized" (p. 692). The Denver School District was ordered to develop a bilingual-bicultural education program in accordance with the CHE model.

Significantly, the court took cognizance of the desire of Latino students not to be desegregated if it meant giving up bilingual education. It also noted that representatives of Denver's Mexican American community had asked that the schools in which the pilot bilingual-bicultural programs were located not be desegregated during the early stages of the program's implementation. The court therefore held that desegregation was not in the best interest of the Mexican American community and declined to include some of these pilot schools in the overall desegregation plan. On appeal, the 10th Circuit reversed this part of the order, ruling that bilingual education is not a substitute for desegregation and that it is permissible as a means of reducing the isolation of minority students only if it is part of a desegregation plan. It further pointed out that the district court, in adopting what became known as the Cardenas Plan, was not merely removing obstacles to effective desegregation; rather, it was imposing a pervasive and detailed system for

the education of minority children. The Cardenas Plan was an instructional program based upon the theory of incompatibilities, a tested belief that the failure of Black, Mexican American, and economically disadvantaged children can be attributed to a lack of compatibility between characteristics of minority children and the typical instructional program developed for White, Anglo-Saxon, English-speaking, middle-class children (Cardenas, 1975; Cardenas & Cardenas, 1972). The 10th Circuit implied that had there been proof that the school district's existing curricular offerings or its methods of educating minority students constituted illegal segregative conduct or resulted from such conduct, the trial court might not have overstepped the limits of its remedial powers. However, by doing so, the court appeared to endorse the idea that a meaningful desegregation plan must help Hispanic school children to reach the proficiency in English necessary to learn other basic subjects.

While the 10th Circuit's action stood as law within its jurisdiction, other circuits grappled with framing remedies in the absence of any clearly articulated policies, although intervention at the remedy stage was liberally granted. For example, in *Morgan v. Hennigan* (1974), a case originating in Boston, a brief was filed on behalf of Latino children as interveners to protect the state and federal statutory rights to bilingual education (The Aspira Association, 1975). The district court did not announce any general principles, but stated that *Keyes* would be observed and consideration given to the treatment of non-Whites other than Blacks. Therefore, bilingual students would be assigned before others to prevent their dispersal.

Similar cases arose in the Fifth Circuit. In *Tasby v. Estes* (1976), the district court directly confronted the dispersal of Latino children within the context of desegregation. It ordered bilingual education to be made available to all who needed it by permitting majority-to-minority transfers—that is, the transfer of students from schools with low concentrations of minority students to schools with high concentrations of minorities wherever Mexican Americans constituted less than 5% of the originally assigned school. It further noted that Hispanic minorities are recognized as an ethnic group for the purposes of equal protection.

In an earlier case, *United States v. Texas* (1971, 1972), the courts deemed Mexican American students to be a recognizable ethnic group protected by the 14th Amendment. It held that because these students had been discriminated against by the school system and the state, a comprehensive remedial educational plan, including bilingual education and recruitment of minority staff, was justified. In *United States v. Texas Education Agency* (1972), the Fifth Circuit court recommended a bilingual education program because it held that no remedy for a dual system could be acceptable if it operated to deprive members of a third ethnic group of the benefits of equal educational opportunity. Similarly, in *Arvizu v. Waco Independent School District* (1973), the court noted that all too often the practical effect of the desegregation of tri-ethnic school systems has been that Black students are mixed with Mexican American students, thereby denying both groups the benefit of any meaningful desegregation. It therefore ordered the implementation and continual re-evaluation of bilingual programs. However, in *Morales v. Shannon* (1975), the court was reluctant to order a specific bilingual remedy, noting that the need for bilingual education is a matter reserved to educators.

In other cases, parents of Mexican American children sought to intervene in suits filed by African Americans. In the Fort Worth, Texas, case of *Flax v. Pott* (1972), they alleged that Latino, students were denied equal educational opportunities by their assignment to segregated schools, by the failure of the school system to place qualified Latinos in faculty and administrative positions, and by the absence of a plan for the education of Latino students, and asked the court to order the school system to establish a bilingual curriculum. In *Milliken v. Bradley* (1975), even without the intervention of Latino complainants, the court included a requirement for bilingual instruction among the series of educational components. The court ordered this remedy because state law which required districts to provide such programs. It should be noted, however, that although the requirement for bilingual programs was part of the remedy, the order for educational components was in response to a finding that the school authorities had deliberately discriminated against African American students. The court made no such finding of discrimination against Latino students.

Latino students also benefitted from litigation involving other language-minority students. A major decision on the language rights of minority students, and the only such ruling by the Supreme

Court, *Lau v. Nichols* (1974) was a class-action suit filed on behalf of Chinese-speaking youngsters in San Francisco. The plaintiffs in this case alleged that these students were being denied an education on equal terms, the standard in Brown, because of their limited English skills. In 1974, the Supreme Court unanimously ruled in favor of the plaintiffs, embracing the logic that equality of treatment consists of more than merely providing students with the same facilities, textbooks, teachers, and curriculum. Students who do not understand English are effectively foreclosed from any meaningful education, the Court noted. It subsequently ruled that, under Title VI of the Civil Rights Act of 1964, Chinese-speaking children were entitled to special assistance to enable them to participate equally in school programs.

In response to *Lau,* federal guidelines, called the Lau Remedies, were drawn up for "educational approaches which would constitute appropriate 'affirmative steps' to be taken by a school district 'to open up its instructional program… (Crawford, 1989, p. 37). The remedies required adequate proficiency in English as an essential element for access to equal educational opportunities.

Multicultural Education as a Means of Addressing Diversity: Latino Perspectives

While judicial initiatives and strategies were necessary to bring about equal educational opportunity for minority youngsters, it became apparent to many leaders and educators in the Latino community that pedagogical and curricular innovations were necessary if students of different Latino origins, as well as those of other races and ethnicities, were to understand and respect one another. The racial conflicts of the 1960s and the resulting consciousness of ethnic diversity accelerated by the Immigration Act of 1965 made the need to meet a broader spectrum of social and cultural needs of students more explicit. Voices of the civil rights movement sought transformation of the curriculum. They argued for a curriculum that provides equitable opportunities to benefit from educational experiences, one with a relevant social and cultural basis in the structure, process, and content of schooling for all students regardless of their racial and ethnic roots. Thus, the multicultural education began to emerge in the mid- to late 1970s.

Multicultural education has multiple purposes but, in the main, there are four. The first involves content—that is, if persons are to understand each other, they must know about one another. Multicultural education addresses this lack of knowledge by providing information about various cultures, their histories, their customs, their languages, and their traditions. The second purpose is psychological: if persons are to respect and accept others, they must learn about the values, beliefs, and religion of others. They will need to appreciate differences and be able to feel comfortable with individuals who do not look like themselves. The third purpose is pedagogical in that it recognizes that all students do not learn in similar ways. For example, Ramirez and Castaneda (1974) maintain that Mexican American students are more field-dependent learners while White students are more field-independent. The fourth purpose involves motivation: students will learn only if they believe in themselves and if teachers believe in their ability. For Latinos, a primary outgrowth of multicultural education has been the resulting development, enhancement, and reinforcement of a positive self-image among members of minority groups. Moreover, multicultural education has helped many teachers overcome the stereotypical view that Latino students are deficient.

The impetus for multicultural education as an alternative pedagogical approach to integration escalated in the 1980s with the publication of reports such as *One-Third of a Nation* (Commission on Minority Education and American Life, 1987) and *Workforce 2000* (Johnston, 1987). Both reports document the extent to which the United States is changing and how the demand for education that can effectively prepare the citizenry and workforce for the high-tech future is accelerating. Additionally, they highlight the nation's need to develop the ability to relate more intimately with the people and nations of Central and South America as well as the Pacific Rim.

The most significant contribution of *Brown* for Latinos was the promotion of multicultural education which assures that all ethnic and racial minority students are seen as wholesome and capable. Prior to Brown and during the first 30 years thereafter, African American, Latino, and Native American students were viewed as educationally and culturally disadvantaged. Presently, the concept of "disadvantagement" is viewed as being just as fallacious as

the premise of "separate but equal." It is only now, 40 years post-*Brown*, that research and practice are giving credence to the view of minority students as being able to respond intellectually to their environments and to environmental stimuli. This evolution is, in part, the direct result of Brown.

Post-Brown Prospects

The Increasing Segregation of Latinos

While the diversity of Latinos has increased over the past two decades, a striking observation is that Latino students face high and increasing levels of segregation in all parts of the United States (Orfield, 1993; Orfield, Monfort, & Aaron, 1989). Contemporary data indicate that Latinos are highly educationally disadvantaged and segregated. The very rapid growth of Latino enrollment in the U.S. public schools, the disproportionate concentration of Latino students in urban school districts with large minority enrollments, and lack of any significant initiatives for desegregation in schools when Latinos are the primary minority group all contribute to this pattern.

The trend in Latino education in the U.S. is increasingly negative. Latino students continue to be disadvantaged in schools. Their dropout rate continues to be high and achievement levels low (Espinosa & Ochoa, 1986). Additionally, Latino students of every major Latino ethnic group are becoming more highly segregated in virtually every part of the country. No recent judicial, legislative, or pedagogical initiative has been strong enough to overcome this negative trend, although Latino areas with mandatory desegregation plans are far less segregated than others.

The Shift in Focus from Race to Resources

The issue of resources for desegregation assumed a central role in the late 1970s and 1980s, especially within inner-city districts (Berg & Colton, 1982). The case of *Milliken v. Bradley* (1977) linked race and resources to create a second focus: resource acquisition and allocation. New fiscal issues, goals, and policy questions arose, along with new relationships among interest groups. District budgeting and management procedures were altered as large sums of funds for desegregation purposes were mediated by the courts. Desegregation policies changed from the single-issue politics of busing to multiple-issue politics involving freedom of choice, quality of education, and district management and control. The relationship between state and local educational authorities was altered as the issues of law became a convoluted mixture of race and resource questions.

In 1990, nearly four decades after *Brown*, the Supreme Court addressed the issue of resources by asking whether a court could require authorities in Kansas City, Missouri, to set aside state tax limitation statutes in order to levy taxes for new programs and facilities in a desegregation plan (*Missouri v. Jenkins*, 1990). By a narrow margin, the Court declined to review the Kansas City desegregation plan, holding that the district could be ordered to levy taxes to pay for the plan even if this approach bypassed tax limitation statutes. Jenkins represented a major shift in the focus of school desegregation efforts from attention to racial balances and techniques for achieving racial balance to the provision of adequate resources to do the same (Foster, 1973; Orfield, 1978).

The Development of a Multicultural Education "Critical Mass"

Those who have shaped the knowledge base, practices, and attitudes of multicultural education in the past decade have obtained wide agreement on the goal of multicultural education. That goal is generally viewed as the restructuring of schools in such a fashion that all students will acquire the knowledge, attitudes, and skills needed to function in an ethnically and racially diverse world. While debates over multicultural education will continue, they will now occur within the boundaries of democracy and diversity.

The pace at which multicultural education is being progressively institutionalized in the structure, process, and content of U.S. schools, colleges, and universities is increasing. Yet, despite its success, multicultural education continues to face serious challenges. Therefore reformers cannot rest on their laurels but must continue to forge ahead in seeking to ensure equal educational opportunities for all students.

Conclusion

While the educational unfolding of *Brown* and its progeny has produced progress for Latinos, its speed has been slowed. A recent study by Orfield (1993) reports that schools in the United States are becoming more segregated than before 1954. Civil rights enforcement by national and state governments has been almost nonexistent since the Reagan administration. Bilingual education has recently been challenged during hearings on the reauthorization of the Elementary and Secondary Education Act (Garcia, 1994; Office of Bilingual Education and Minority Language Affairs, 1994). Multicultural education is repeatedly assaulted in discussions of "political correctness." The source of this resistance is the same as the source of its energy: politics (Crawford, 1989).

Counteracting these negative elements are the positive forces within education such as enlightened superintendents, progressive university faculty, and advocacy by national educational organizations. As long as open-minded professionals work at providing the best education for all children, then the promise of equal educational opportunities enunciated in Brown remains alive. The struggle to improve the educational experience of Latino students, especially those enrolled in schools that remain unequal, continues.

References

1. Arvizu v. Waco Independent School District, 373 F. Supp. 1264 (W.D. Tex. 1973) aff'd in part, rev'd in part on other issues, 495 F.2d 499 (5th Cir. 1976).
2. Berg, W., & Colton, D. L. (1982). *Brown* and the distribution of school resources. In D. Monti (Ed.), *New directions for testing and measurement: Impact of desegregation* (pp. 157–168). San Francisco: Jossey-Bass.
3. Milliken v. Bradley, 402 F. Supp. 1096 (E.D. Mich. 1975).
4. Brown v. Board of Education of Topeka, Kansas, 347 U.S. 483 (1954).
5. Cardenas, B., & Cardenas, J. (1972, February). The theory of incompatibilties. *Today's Education*, pp. 42-45.
6. Cardenas, J. (1975). Bilingual education, segregation and a third alternative. *Inequality in Education*, 19(20), 19.
7. Cisneros v. Corpus Christi Independent School District, 324 F. Supp. 599 (S.D. Tex. 1970).

8. Commission on Minority Education and American Life. (1988*). One-third of a nation.* Washington DC: American Council on Education.

9. Crawford, J. (1989). *Bilingual education: History, politics, theory, and practice.* Trenton, NJ: Crane.

10. Delago v. Bastrop Independent School District, Civil Action No. 388 (W.D. Texas, 1948).

11. Espinosa, R., & Ochoa, A. (1986). Concentration of California Hispanic students in schools with low achievement: A research note. *American Journal of Education, 95,* 77–95.

12. Flax v. Pott, 464 F.2d 865 (5th Cir. 1972).

13. Foster, G. (1973). Desegregating urban schools: A review of techniques. *Harvard Education Review, 43,* 5-36.

14. Garcia, E. (1994, May 13). *Letter to the field.* Washington, DC: Office of Bilingual and Minority Language Affairs, U.S. Department of Education.

15. Independent School District v. Salvatierra, 33. SW.2d 790 (Texas Civ. App. 1930.

16. Johnston, W. (1987). *Workforce 2000: Work and workers in the twenty-first century.* Indianapolis, IN: Hudson Institute.

17. Keyes v. School District No. 1, 413 U.S. 189 (1973).

18. Keyes v. School District No. 1, 380 F. Supp. 673 (D. Colo. 1974).

19. Lau v. Nichols, 414 U.S. 563 (1974).

20. The Aspira Association. (1975, February 3). Memorandum of Hispanic parents. *Clearinghouse Review, 13,* 159.

21. Mendez v. Westminster School District, 64 F. Supp. 544 (S.D. Cal. 1946).

22. Milliken v. Bradley, 433 U.S. 267 (1977).

23. Missouri v. Jenkins, 495 U.S. 33 (1990).

24. Morales v. Shannon, 516 F.2d 411 (5th Cir. 1975), cert. denied 423 U.S. 1034 (1975).

25. Morgan v. Hennigan, 379 F. Supp. 410 (D. Mass. 1974).

26. National Association of Intergroup Relations (NAIR). (1963). *Public school segregation and integration in the North.* Washington, DC: NAIR.

27. Office of Bilingual Education and Minority Language Affairs, U.S. Department of Education. (1994, March 4). *Legislative summary.* Washington, DC: U.S. Department of Education.

28. Orfield, G. (1978). *Must we bus?* Washington, DC: Brookings Institution.

29. Orfield, G. (1993). *The growth of segregation in American schools: Changing patterns of segregation and poverty since 1968.* Washington, DC: National School Boards Association.

30. Orfield, G., Monfort, F., & Aaron, M. (1989). *Study of desegregation, 1968–1986: A report of the council of urban boards of education and national school desegregation research project.* Washington, DC: National School Boards Association.

31. Ramirez, M., 111, & Castaneda, A. (1974). *Cultural democracy, bicognitive development and education.* San Francisco: Academic Press.

32. Romero v. Weakley, 131 F. Supp. 818 (9th Cir. 1955).

33. Tasby v. Estes, 412 F. Supp 1192 (N.D. Tex. 1976), on remand, 517 F.2d 92 (5th Cir. 1975), cert. denied 423 U.S. 939 (1975).

34. United States v. Midland Independent School District, 519 F.2d 60 (5th Cir. 1975), cert. denied, 424 U.S. 910 (1976).

35. United States v. Texas, 342 F. Supp. 24 (E.D. Tex. 1971) aff'd, 466 F. 2d 518 (5th Cir. 1972).

36. United States v. Texas Education Agency, 467 F.2d 848 (5th Cir. 1972).

37. United States Civil Rights Commission. (1967). *Racial isolation in the public schools.* Washington, DC: U.S. Government Printing Office.

SECTION ELEVEN

THE MODERN CIVIL RIGHTS MOVEMENT, 1955–1965

CHAPTER 13

The Cradle Rocks

Harvard Sitkoff

I think people were fed up, they had reached the point that they knew there was no return. That they had to do it or die. And that's what kept it going. It was the sheer spirit for freedom, for the feeling of being a man or a woman.

Jo Ann Robinson

✷ ✷ ✷ ✷ ✷

Mrs. Rosa Parks said no. Her feet hurt. Politely yet firmly, the forty-two-year-old brown-skinned seamstress said no a second time. Some black passengers on the bus, fearful for Parks's safety, and their own, shook their heads; others exclaimed "Lawd, Lawds," expecting a violent reprisal. The driver sternly insisted again that she move back and give up her seat to a standing white man. That was the law. Parks held fast. Weary after her long hard day of holiday-season work at the men's alteration shop of the Montgomery Fair department store, she wanted to remain seated for the rest of her ride. On that fateful first of December 1955, Parks demurred again, defying the canons of white supremacy.

"Are you going to stand up?"

"No."

"Well, if you don't stand up, I'm going to have you arrested."

Parks paused. Although she considered herself in the vanguard of the struggle for racial justice—she served as secretary of the Alabama State Conference of NAACP Branches, secretary of the Montgomery NAACP, adult adviser to the local NAACP Youth Council, and had recently returned from an integrated workshop on desegregation held at the Highlander Folk School in Tennessee—she had no intention of challenging the Jim Crow laws. Yet Parks believed "that the only way to let them know I felt I was being mistreated was to do just what I did—resist the order."

"Go on," she replied softly, deliberately, "and have me arrested."

The Black Panther publicist Eldridge Cleaver would later write about that moment: "Somewhere in the universe a gear in the machinery had shifted." At the next stop, Court Square, where slaves had once been auctioned, the driver summoned police to arrest Rosa Parks for violating the municipal ordinance mandating segregation on publicly owned vehicles. Martin Luther King, Jr. would describe this as the moment when Parks had been "tracked down by the *Zeitgeist*—the spirit of the times. . . . She was anchored to that seat by the accumulated indignities of days gone by and the boundless aspirations of generations yet unborn." Parks recalled: "I felt it was just something I had to do."

So did other blacks. News of her defiance, circulated by the telephone network of Montgomery's black elite, transmitted a surge of determination through the community, a resolve to do *something*. Many looked to E. D. Nixon for leadership. President of the Alabama NAACP and a veteran member of the Brotherhood of Sleeping Car Porters, Nixon had long sought to arouse black Montgomery to a mass protest of their mistreatment. He hurried to the jail to post bond for his friend Rosa Parks. The former local head of the World War II March-on-Washington Movement, Nixon remained a disciple of A. Philip Randolph's tactics and strategy. He longed for an opportunity to organize black power and pressure through mass demonstrations. As Nixon drove Parks home, he searched for an appropriate form of direct action, maybe a strike, perhaps a boycott. He thought about what had happened in Baton Rouge, where African-Americans had boycotted that city's segregated bus system in 1953. He felt sure that the arrest of Parks was a cause blacks would rally around. "Mrs. Parks," he finally summoned the courage to blurt out, "this is the case we've been looking for. We can break this situation on the bus with your case." Both knew the risks: the possibility of violence to Parks, the certainty of losing her job. Yet both knew the time had come. "I'll go along with it," Parks answered. *Something* had to be done.

"This is what we've been waiting for!" Nixon shouted on the telephone later that night to Jo Ann Robinson, an English professor at all-black Alabama State College. Robinson, president of the Women's Political Council, the black counterpart to Montgomery's segregated League of Women Voters, agreed. Impatient with the deferential leadership of Montgomery's black ministers, Robinson's council that year had pressured white merchants into ending the segregation of public drinking fountains and the custom of not using the courtesy titles of Mrs. and Miss when billing black women. They had also forced the city to begin hiring black policemen and were demanding equal recreational facilities for black Montgomery. The council, moreover, earlier in the year, had been set to stage a boycott of the city's buses to protest the arrest of a woman who refused to give up her seat to a white. But the fact that the defendant was an unwed mother made the Women's Political Council draw back. Rosa Parks, however, was dignified, intelligent, respectable, and married. Nixon and Robinson agreed that she was the perfect symbol. They would attempt to organize a one-day bus boycott on the fifth of December to coincide with Mrs. Parks's trial.

Early the next morning, Nixon began calling Montgomery's black ministers, college professors, physicians, and civic spokesmen. "We have taken this type of thing too long already. I feel the time has come to boycott the buses," Nixon repeated to each. "Only through a boycott can we make it clear to the white folks that we will not accept this type of treatment any longer." To his surprise, many of the elite Nixon telephoned accepted his invitation to meet that evening to plan a bus boycott. Most had previously exhibited little inclination to act in concert, and even less desire to act militantly. The nearly fifty representatives of black Montgomery, mostly ministers, who gathered in the Dexter Avenue Baptist Church agreed even more unexpectedly to deliver sermons on the proposed boycott to their congregations on Sunday, to ask Negro taxicab companies to transport blacks at bus-fare cost, to cap the boycott with a city-wide meeting, and to distribute the mimeographed leaflets written by Robinson. Claiming "The next time it may be you, or your daughter, or mother," she urged African-American Montgomerians to stay off the buses in a daylong gesture of solidarity with Parks.

On Monday, December 5, in the city called the Cradle of the Confederacy, over 90 percent of the blacks who ordinarily rode the buses stayed off them. Blacks walked, joined car pools, drove wagons, rode mules. They did not ride the buses. The historic Montgomery bus boycott had begun. It would last 381 days. It would cost blacks nearly a quarter of a million dollars. Out of it would come a towering leader, a new kind of Southern black leadership, an effective strategy for social change, and a determined spirit that Jim Crow could be ended, that life could be better. Historians eventually would look back to Montgomery as the Cradle of the New Negro.

Nixon had pressing concerns that fifth of December. Following Mrs. Parks's brief trial, which expectedly resulted in a guilty verdict and a fine of ten dollars plus four dollars court costs, Nixon met on the courthouse steps with several black ministers. He feared that without active leadership, specific goals, and a committed organization the boycott would fizzle and the mass meeting would fail. Nixon suggested that an ad hoc group continue to lead the boycott until the city and bus company agreed to hire Negro bus drivers in black neighborhoods, insist that all bus drivers treat black patrons more courteously, and adopt a first-come, first-served seating system. Nixon initially had no intention of attacking the segregation ordinance confining blacks to the back of the bus. He merely proposed that those blacks seated in the rear be allowed to keep their seats. Nixon also thought the name for the new organization ought to be the Citizens' Committee. But the Reverend Ralph D. Abernathy, the young pugnacious minister of the First Baptist Church, objected. The name sounded too much like the White Citizens' Council. Abernathy suggested, instead, the Montgomery Improvement Association, adding: "Brother Nixon, now you gon' serve as president, ain'tchya?" "No," Nixon shot back, "not unless'n you all don't accept my man."

Nixon had his reasons for declining. His job as a Pullman porter frequently kept him out of town. His lack of formal education inhibited him, and he considered himself too old to be an active leader. Too many black ministers would not work with him, a legacy of old conflicts and rivalries. What we need, Nixon went on, was an intelligent, respected minister, a dynamic orator, someone who could easily find another job if the boycott failed and the white community retaliated. He further suggested that a man new in the community would be less likely to be identified with any faction of Montgomery's divided black leadership or to be a lackey of the white establishment. Nixon might also have added that his ideal candidate needed to be extraordinarily brave or naive to be identified publicly as the leader of such an uncertain, hazardous, quixotic venture. He recommended Martin Luther King, Jr. The others agreed.

At three in the afternoon, Montgomery's black leaders met again, to prepare for the evening's mass rally. The old fears surfaced. How, some asked, could their involvement in the boycott be kept secret from the white community? Could they ban white reporters from the evening meeting? Could they forgo public forums and circulate their plans by mimeographed pamphlets and word of mouth? Enraged, Nixon jumped from his seat. "What the hell you people talking 'bout? How you gonna have a mass meeting, gonna boycott a city bus line without the white folks knowing it?" We are acting like little boys, he continued, afraid to discuss our plans in the open, wanting to pass around papers secretly. "You oughta make up your mind right now that you gon' either admit you are a grown man or concede to the fact that you are a bunch of scared boys." Silenced, the leaders rapidly agreed to an organizing

committee, named the Montgomery Improvement Association (MIA), to lead a bus boycott until the city met the three demands proposed by Nixon.

Rufus Lewis nominated Martin Luther King, Jr., to the MIA presidency and in a moment the motion carried. Stunned by the speed of the maneuver, King did not decline, although he had recently turned down the presidency of the local NAACP because of the press of his pastoral duties and the new obligations of fatherhood. He could not afford the luxury of second-guessing his decision. King had less than an hour before the evening mass meeting to prepare "the most decisive speech of my life."

At first glance, neither King nor the blacks of Montgomery appeared ready for what would come. The black community seemed complacent or cowed, and King hardly fitted the mold of a fiery freedom fighter who could arouse and lead. The son and grandson of pastors of Atlanta's prestigious Ebenezer Baptist Church, "Mike" King grew up on prosperous "sweet" Auburn Avenue—the capital of the black bourgeoisie. An avid student, he skipped two grades of high school and at fifteen enrolled at Morehouse College, a branch of the Atlanta University system. He dreamed of being a lawyer or a teacher. But his father insisted that he be a minister. King obeyed, and following his graduation in 1948, he entered Crozer Theological Seminary in Pennsylvania for his Bachelor of Divinity Degree.

King, one of six blacks in a student body of one hundred, happily immersed himself in the world of ideas, particularly the philosophy of Kant, Hegel, the religious existentialists, and Walter Rauschenbusch's social gospel. He finished first in his graduating class, earning a fellowship to pursue a doctorate. In 1951 King began his course of study at Boston University's School of Theology. While in Boston, King met Coretta Scott, a graduate of Antioch College who was studying voice at the New England Conservatory of Music. They were married in 1953. Each reinforced the other's desire to remain in the North and for King to pursue a career of religious scholarship. But family ties and an attractive job offer proved too strong a lure. "Finally we agreed," wrote King in his autobiography, "that, in spite of the disadvantages and inevitable sacrifices, our greatest service could be rendered in our native South. We came to the conclusion that we had something of a moral obligation to return—at least for a few years."

King arrived in Montgomery in September 1954, aged twenty-six, to serve as pastor of the Dexter

Avenue Baptist Church, "the big people's church." Its influential congregation, largely professionals and faculty members of Alabama State College, emanated a respectability and an aura of intellectualism that King highly prized. He still found the emotionalism of the traditional Negro church distasteful, and still believed in moderate, middle-class politics as the best path for Negro advancement. Quite removed from the needs and spirit of the black rank-and-file, King served on the Alabama Human Relations Council, a genteel, paternalistic organization as elitist as it was ineffectual.

Montgomery's blatant white supremacy, however, jolted King. A virulent white racism enveloped the city. It dictated its laws and mores. It poisoned white minds and destroyed the bodies and souls of blacks. The shocking contrast with what King had earlier experienced in Atlanta and Boston produced in him both a desire to change the racial situation and a belief that change was possible. He reread Gandhi and Thoreau on civil disobedience. He pondered the speeches he had heard on the application of Gandhian tactics to the race problem by Howard Thurman, dean of the Howard University chapel, and by A. J. Muste of the Fellowship of Reconciliation. In December 1955, King had not yet arrived at a definitive philosophy or strategy for racial change. But his thoughts were in flux. At the least, as he told his wife on the eve of the boycott, the continued passive acceptance of evil could only perpetuate its existence.

Beneath the placid surface of the black community in Montgomery, many had quietly come to the same realization. For some, the moment of decision came with the coupling of the 1954 Supreme Court decision and the white vow to fight integration at any cost, or with the juxtaposition of the news of successful beginnings of school desegregation in various border cities and headlines telling of violent riots to thwart the law of the land. For others, it came in 1955 with the brazen appearance of White Citizens' Councils and the brutal murder of fourteen-year-old Emmett Till in Mississippi—purportedly for whistling at, or speaking to, a white woman. The absurdity of the fact that the days of the cotton South had ended while its racial practices continued aroused many. Blacks had become far more educated, industrialized, and urbanized than their parents' generation, yet they experienced the same racial indignities and horrors. The African-American who had seen service in an integrated unit

during the Korean War, or who had lived for a while without Jim Crow in the North, or who worked on the desegregated military bases just outside the city, still faced in Montgomery a near-total system of segregation and white supremacy. It was pervasive, cruel, and humiliating.

Twice daily, for most Montgomery blacks, the Jim Crow buses served as a constant reminder of how far toward freedom they still had to travel. Blacks had to pay the driver at the front of the bus and then enter through the door at the rear, however inclement the weather. They had to stand in the crowded back of the bus while seats were empty in the white-only front section. They could do little to constrain a vicious bus driver, no matter how abusive or violent he became. Then, in the last week of November 1955, the Interstate Commerce Commission banned racial segregation in all facilities and vehicles engaged in interstate transportation. On the first of December, Rosa Parks said no. Could they now do less? The trend of the law seemed unmistakable. The Parks incident had unified the black community, for a while at the least. Perhaps . . . Maybe . . . The time had come to force Montgomery to change.

When King returned for the evening rally, Montgomery blacks had filled every seat in the Holt Street Baptist Church and stood shoulder to shoulder in the blocks surrounding the church. More than four thousand stood outside to listen to the loudspeakers, demonstrating the commitment and solidarity they had shown by staying off the buses. Seemingly with one voice they sang "Onward Christian Soldiers." In unison they shouted that "like a mighty army" they would march against the citadel of Jim Crow. Unanimously they voted to boycott the buses until they gained their three demands. Then the crowd grew silent. Dr. King began to speak.

King quietly recounted the arrest of Rosa Parks. He reviewed the many injustices blacks had endured on Montgomery buses. The murmurs of "Amen" grew louder and King suddenly brought his audience to a fever pitch.

> There comes a time when people get tired. We are here this evening to say to those who have mistreated us so long that we are tired—tired of being segregated and humiliated, tired of being kicked about by the brutal feet of oppression. We have no alternative but to protest. For many years, we have shown amazing patience. We have sometimes given our white brothers the feeling that we liked the way we were being treated. But we come

here tonight to be saved from that patience that makes us patient with anything less than freedom and justice.

"We are impatient for justice"—King moderated his tone—"but we will protest with love. There will be no violence on our part." He preached persuasion, not coercion. He dwelt on the transforming power of love. "Love must be our regulating ideal. . . . If we fail to do this our protest will end up as a meaningless drama on the stage of history, and its memory will be shrouded with the ugly garments of shame. Let no man pull you so low as to make you hate him," he quoted Booker T. Washington. The "Amens" swelled again. "If you will protest courageously"—King built to a crescendo—"and yet with dignity and Christian love, when the history books are written in future generations, the historians will have to pause and say 'There lived a great people—a black people— who injected new meaning and dignity into the veins of civilization.' This is our challenge and our overwhelming responsibility." The thousands listening roared their approval. Again and again they shouted their joyful determination. King had crystallized their feelings. He had articulated their mood and exalted their vision. The time had come.

White Montgomery at first ridiculed the boycott. Disdainful whites thought the fractious Negro leadership would be unable to maintain unity, much less be competent to deal with the complicated day-to-day operations of a city-wide boycott. They scorned the black masses as too apathetic to stay to a course of sacrifice. A little stalling, a bit of pressure, a few threats would surely end this folly. "Our niggers," the contemptuous assumed, "will soon tire out and start climbing back on the buses." Secretly, some blacks also feared the collapse of the boycott. Memory made them doubt the perseverance of the troops and the fortitude of their leaders. They hoped for a speedy settlement. After all, the doubtful black Montgomerians sought to reassure themselves, none of their three moderate demands struck directly at segregation, and their fares accounted for 75 percent of the Montgomery City Line revenue.

After three days of almost total black boycott, King met with Mayor W. A. Gayle, his commissioners, and the attorneys for the bus company. Logic and reasonableness, King optimistically believed, would prevail. He could not have been more wrong. There would be no compromise. The whites spurned King's proposals. They would not accept anything

that might suggest a black victory for fear that it would stimulate additional demands. They drew the line. To underscore their adamancy, the city fathers threatened legal action unless the black cab companies again began to charge the prescribed minimum fares for taxis.

Disheartened, King returned to confer with the MIA. He now realized that the matter was one of power, not reason, that "no one gives up his privileges without strong resistance." Far more than courtesy and comfort were involved in the bus issue, moreover, for "the underlying purpose of segregation was to oppress and exploit the segregated, not simply to keep [people] apart." A chastened MIA turned to the organization of car pools to replace the black taxis. Over a hundred and fifty blacks volunteered their automobiles at a mass rally that evening. Within several days forty-eight dispatch and forty-two collection stations were operating with what the local White Citizens' Council groused was "military precision." The boycott continued. Black Montgomery stayed off the buses. As one elderly black woman expressed it: "My feets is tired, but my soul is rested." And another, when offered a ride so she would not have to walk: "I'm not walking for myself. I'm walking for my children and my grandchildren." The days of the boycott became weeks and then months.

The white community, no longer deriding the boycott, felt its impact. The downtown merchants claimed that they had lost a million dollars in sales due to the restricted travel of blacks. The boycott cut into the bus company's income some 65 percent, forcing it to raise fares and trim schedules. Its losses mounted daily. At the end of January, Mayor Gayle announced a "get-tough" policy. He went on television to denounce the boycott as a campaign to stir up racial strife and its leaders as "a group of Negro radicals who have split asunder the fine relationships which have existed between the Negro and white people for generations." He warned Montgomery that the blacks sought to end segregation, that "what they are after is the destruction of our social fabric." It is time to be honest and frank, Gayle concluded: "The white people are firm in their convictions that they do not care whether the Negroes ever ride a city bus again if it means that the social fabric of our community is to be destroyed so that Negroes will start riding the buses again."

An official policy of harassment began. The mayor and his commissioners ceremoniously took out memberships in the White Citizens' Council. Boycott leaders lost their jobs; others were threatened with dismissal. Car-pool drivers faced warnings that their licenses would be revoked and their insurance policies cancelled. Many were fined on trumped-up charges of speeding. Indiscriminate arrests for imaginary violations followed. The old fears resurfaced. The car pool lost many of its volunteers. Some blacks climbed back on the rear of the buses. Four days of retaliation by white Montgomery had brought the boycott to the brink of collapse. Then two policemen arrested King for speeding.

His jailing revitalized the movement. Hundreds rushed to the jail to protest, and the police gave in, releasing King on bond. Several days later, as King addressed an MIA rally, a dynamite bomb shattered the front of his house. Quickly he left the meeting to return home. When he arrived, several hundred angry African-Americans, brandishing guns, knives, rocks, and broken soda pop bottles, surrounded his house. After assuring himself that no harm had come to his wife and baby, King stepped out on his porch. Now a volatile crowd of more than a thousand blacks milled in front of the house. "Don't get panicky," King raised his arms. "Get rid of your weapons"—he quieted the crowd. "We are not advocating violence. We want to love our enemies. We must love our white brothers no matter what they do to us." He spoke of forgiveness and promise. "I did not start this boycott. I was asked by you to serve as your spokesman. I want it to be known the length and breadth of the land that if I am stopped, our work will not stop, for what we are doing is right. What we are doing is just and God is with us."

This moment—Lerone Bennett, Jr., a biographer of King and a historian of the movement, would write—"changed the course of the protest and made King a living symbol. He and other members of the boycott directorate had spoken before of love and forgiveness. But now, *seeing the idea in action*, fleshed out by pain, paid for by anguish, millions were touched, if not converted. The parable of the porch went out now over the wires of the news media and King's name became a token for almost all American Negroes."

On February 21, 1956, city officials obtained indictments against King and some one hundred other boycott participants on charges of violating a 1921 law forbidding hindrance to a business without "just cause or legal excuse." "In this state," the indictment read, "We are committed to segregation by custom and law; we intend to maintain it." Instead of seeking to avoid arrest, the black leaders of Montgomery hurried to the police station to surrender. E. D. Nixon arrived first. "You are looking for me? Here I am." Hundreds of blacks gathered outside the station to applaud the leaders as they entered. King, visiting his parents in Atlanta, declined their advice that he not jeopardize his life by returning, and rushed to the Montgomery jail. The photograph of him with a numbered plaque hanging from his neck captured national and international attention. Statements in support of the boycott, as well as cash contributions, poured in from all over the world.

At a mass meeting the next evening, the indicted leaders marched between thousands of cheering men, women, and children who overflowed the street outside the Dexter Avenue Baptist Church. Inside, hundreds more chanted, and prayed, and pledged themselves to "passive resistance," to shun the buses and "walk with God." They learned a new song, to the tune of "Give Me That Old-Time Religion," whose four stanzas proclaimed the essential elements of their struggle: protest, unity, nonviolence, and equality.

> *We are moving on to vict'ry*
> *With hope and dignity.*
>
> *We shall all stand together*
> *Till every one is free.*
>
> *We know love is the watchword*
> *For peace and liberty*
>
> *Black and white, all our brothers*
> *To live in harmony.*

They sang "O lift me up and let me stand on higher ground," and then grew quiet to listen to King.

"We are not struggling merely for the rights of Negroes," the Baptist minister began, "but for all the people of Montgomery, black and white. We are determined to make America a better place for all people." The protest, said King, was not against a single incident but over things that "go deep down into the archives of history."

We have known humiliation, we have known abusive language, we have been plunged into the abyss of oppression. And we decided to rise up only with the weapon of protest. It is one of the greatest glories of America that we have the right to protest.

There are those who would try to make of this a hate campaign. This is not a war between the white and the Negro but a conflict between justice and injustice. This is bigger than the Negro race revolting against the white. We are seeking to improve not the Negro of Montgomery but the whole of Montgomery.

If we are arrested every day, if we are exploited every day, if we are trampled over every day, don't ever let anyone pull you so low as to hate them. We must use the weapon of love. We must have compassion and understanding for those who hate us. We must realize so many people are taught to hate us that they are not totally responsible for their hate. But we stand in life at midnight, we are always on the threshold of a new dawn.

On June 4, a three-judge federal district court handed down its ruling in the case brought by four Montgomery black women to end bus segregation in the city. "We hold that the statutes requiring segregation of the white and colored races on a common carrier," the majority declared, "violate the due process and equal protection of the law clauses of the Fourteenth Amendment." The order enjoined the mayor from enforcing racial segregation on the buses, but stayed the effect of the decision until Montgomery officials appealed the case to the Supreme Court. Fearing the worst from the high court, white leaders in Alabama again fought the boycott with vengeance. The state outlawed the NAACP as a foreign corporation that had failed to register; accused it of "causing irreparable injury to the property and civil rights of residents," a reference to its role in handling the federal suit against Montgomery; and fined the association $100,000 for refusing to surrender its membership lists. Concurrently, Montgomery obtained an indictment against the MIA on charges of operating a business—the car pool—without a license.

"You know the people are getting tired," King confided to his wife. "If the city officials get this injunction against the car pools—and they will get it—I am afraid our people will go back to the buses." The blacks of Montgomery had become dependent on the MIA station wagons and the volunteer automobiles. Their loss would be incalculable; the boycott without them inconceivable. At his lowest ebb since the boycott began, King awaited the crushing injunction. Instead, as if providentially, he received word that the Supreme Court had affirmed the district court's ruling voiding segregation on the buses. It came, said King, "as a joyous daybreak to end the long night of enforced segregation in public transportation." The boycott had proved that local activism could compel intervention from the federal government.

The next night, nearly ten thousand blacks convened to end the boycott officially. The Reverend Robert Graetz, the sole white in the MIA hierarchy, rose to read the scripture according to Paul to the meeting: "When I was a child, I spoke as a child, I understood as a child, I thought as a child. . . ." He could not go on. "There was a vast uproar," reported Lerone Bennett. "All over the floor now, men and women were on their feet, waving handkerchiefs and weeping." Belatedly, haltingly, Graetz ended the sentence: "But when I became a man, I put away childish things." Not since the Civil War had the Southern black rank-and-file protested so visibly and volubly against Jim Crow, smashing the stereotype of an acquiescent Negro content with segregation. Their numbers and courage would point the way for countless other blacks to assert their rights militantly. That was the meaning of the 381-day struggle.

On this same night, the Ku Klux Klan, hooded and gowned, appeared in black Montgomery. A procession of forty vehicles drove slowly through the black neighborhoods. In the past, such demonstrations had petrified the black community. They had caused African-Americans to flee and hide. "Fearing death, they played dead," King explained. But on the evening of November 13, 1956, most of black Montgomery reacted as if the Klan were truly invisible. No one ran away or dimmed their lights. Some blacks followed the Klan procession, applauding, laughing, jeering. Dumbstruck, the KKK terminated its effort at intimidation and slunk away into the night. That, too, was the meaning of the Montgomery bus boycott. "A once fear-ridden people had been transformed," King would write of the blacks who openly defied Montgomery statutes used to try to destroy the protest campaign. "Those who had previously trembled before the law were now proud to be arrested for the cause of freedom."

Shortly before 6 a.m. on December 21, 1956, King and his aides boarded a Montgomery bus and sat in the front, black next to white. Droves of news reporters and cameramen recorded the historic event, proclaiming its significance throughout the world. "For the first time in this 'cradle of the Confederacy' all the Negroes entered buses through the front door," *The New York Times* reported. "They sat in the first empty seats they saw, in the front of buses and in the rear. They did not get up to give a white passenger a seat. And whites sat with Negroes." The 381-day struggle which began as a hope for simple courtesy and convenience ended as a triumph for desegregation. And, King added: "The skies did not fall when integrated buses finally traveled the streets of Montgomery."

In preparation for this day, King had schooled blacks in the techniques and philosophy of nonviolence. The Montgomery movement had been explicitly Christian. King had quoted Jesus, not Gandhi. The tactics of the MIA had been patterned on previous examples of black protest, not on Thoreau's "Civil Disobedience." The fervor with which the MIA practiced passive resistance sprang from the religion of the Black Belt. Its strategy flowed from the pragmatic recognition that black violence in the Deep South, where whites held a preponderance of force and power, would be self-defeating even suicidal. The heart and soul of the movement—noncooperation with evil, coupled with love and forgiveness—exemplified the Southern blacks' faith in their church and in their leaders' gospel of avoiding armed conflict.

Gradually, however, King began to construct a strategy based on Gandhian precepts. African-Americans saw films of Gandhi's nonviolent movement; songs and skits emphasized the success of passive resistance in India. A leaflet given out in every black church urged the bus protesters to "read, study and memorize" seventeen rules, among them: "Pray for guidance and commit yourself to complete nonviolence in word and action as you enter the bus. . . . Be loving enough to absorb evil and understanding enough to turn an enemy to a friend. . . . If cursed, do not curse back. If pushed, do not push back. If struck, do not strike back, but evidence love and goodwill at all times. . . . If another person is being molested, do not arise to go to his defense, but pray for the oppressor and use moral and spiritual force to carry on the struggle for justice. . . . Do not be afraid to experiment with new and creative techniques for achieving reconciliation and social change. . . . If you feel you cannot take it, walk for another week or two."

King's doctoral education in theology led him to articulate the thrust of the movement in sweeping biblical terms and grand transcendental ideas. He adapted the rhythms and rhetoric of the African-American church to discourses on the Gandhian distinctions between *agape, eros*, and *philia*. At the same time, he larded his sermons with references to the documents of American democracy, translating the African-American quest for justice into an idiom whites could understand and accept. His unique blending of traditions was accentuated by the tendency of the press to label King the new African-American leader or the leader of the New Negro. Mistakenly, yet repeatedly, the news media depicted King's Gandhian views as a wholly novel approach to racial protest. By ignoring earlier Gandhian civil-rights groups and African-American ministers, they made King and the Montgomery bus boycott even more of a watershed.

The influence of Bayard Rustin and Reverend Glenn E. Smiley furthered King's Gandhian approach. Both had come to Montgomery in February 1956 to assist the MIA. They stayed and became indispensable to King, prodding him to articulate the bus boycott in Gandhian terms and persuading him to form a regional network of African-American ministers. Rustin, the black executive secretary of the War Resisters' League, and Smiley, a white field secretary for the Fellowship of Reconciliation (FOR), were both pacifist disciples of the Mahatma and of A. J. Muste, and they took every opportunity to reinforce King's understanding of *Satyagraha*. Both, as well, were thoroughly familiar with the wartime experiences of the March-on-Washington Movement and the Congress of Racial Equality (CORE). They recalled A. Philip Randolph's insistence on the need for broad, organized, militant mass action, rather than polite pleading, to achieve racial equality, and CORE's adoption of Gandhian nonviolence to the race problem. With their assistance, King developed an ideology of disciplined, nonviolent direct action by the black masses.

King's neo-Gandhian persuasion fit the needs of the American South in the mid-twentieth century. It offered something to nearly all in an especially palatable way. King had learned in the crucible of the boycott that this form of black protest weakened the white community's resolve, unity, and readiness to retaliate with violence. It placed blame on the impersonal system of segregation, not on individual segregationists; it played on the whites' growing feeling of guilt; it forced whites to confront the plight of blacks, while assuaging the white fear of bloody reprisals. King also emphasized that the achievement of the movement's goals would result not in victory for blacks alone but in triumph for all Americans. He clothed the consequences of racial change in the garb of reconciliation and the creation of a beloved community. At the least, this disarming message from a man of God minimized virulent white opposition and made the inevitable appear a bit more acceptable.

Simultaneously, King's words energized the black community, dispelling its feelings of helplessness, insignificance, and powerlessness. He sensed the untapped wellsprings of black hostility. He understood how the resentment of white supremacy had been kept in check by a Christian tradition tabooing hatred and by an awesome fear of white violence. So King transformed the immoral into the moral: "To accept passively an unjust system is to cooperate with that system; thereby the oppressed become as evil as the oppressor. Noncooperation with evil is as much a moral obligation as is cooperation with good." He equated apathy, not protest, with sin. He bestowed legitimacy on aggression against racism, redefining it as Christian love. Moreover, by lessening the likelihood of white vengeance, by decreasing the dangers to black protesters, King increased the probability of black militancy. The possibility of violent reactions by whites remained, and King made a virtue of it by exalting black suffering as redemptive, the highest manifestation of Christianity and the surest path to triumph. Unearned suffering, he preached, amplified the self-esteem of blacks much as knowing that they were part of a larger movement, a mass movement, gave them a sense of strength they had not possessed individually.

Inspired by one woman's courage and the successful example of an African-American community challenging racism in the Deep South, the boycott accelerated the movement of the struggle from the courtroom to the streets. It proved the power of organized collective action as an effective agent of social change. It ushered in an age of open confrontation with white racism; it encouraged large numbers of African-Americans to march under King's banner and to court beatings, jailings, even death, certain in the faith that their martyrdom would hasten the victory of their cause, firm in their belief that "we shall overcome."

The bus boycott also led to the organizing of black clergymen throughout the South into a cadre of protest leaders. The Southern Christian Leadership Conference (SCLC) sprang directly out of the Montgomery movement. Indeed, even before the successful termination of the Montgomery crusade, black ministers in other cities began to plan similar campaigns of noncooperation. After visiting King in the winter of 1956, the Reverend Charles K. Steele returned home to Tallahassee, Florida, to organize a bus boycott and form an Inter-Civic Council, modeled on the MIA. In Alabama, clergymen Joseph E. Lowery of Mobile and Fred L. Shuttlesworth of Birmingham met with King to plan the bus boycotts in their respective cities. In Tuskegee, blacks led by C. G. Gomillion, who also regularly conferred with King, boycotted white merchants to fight disenfranchisement. In Georgia, the Montgomery experience produced bus boycotts in Atlanta and Savannah.

King recognized the need to capitalize on this momentum. With Steele and Shuttlesworth, he issued a call for civil-rights-minded clergymen to convene in Atlanta on January 10–11, 1957. Sixty blacks from ten states agreed on the necessity of a coordinating force for their various movements. They named themselves the Southern Conference on Transportation and Nonviolent Integration and urged African-Americans "to assert their human dignity" by refusing "further cooperation with evil." A month later, nearly a hundred black ministers attended the formal organization of the conference in New Orleans. They elected King president and Abernathy treasurer, and tried several different names before calling themselves the Southern Christian Leadership Conference. In its first official declaration, the SCLC called upon blacks "to understand that nonviolence is not a symbol of weakness or cowardice, but as Jesus demonstrated, nonviolent resistance transforms weakness into strength and breeds courage in the face of danger." Until the founding of the SCLC, the struggle for racial equality had been largely the domain of a Northern elite oriented primarily toward legal action. Now the Southern black church would become preeminent in leading black resistance to white oppression, and they would do so by preaching the virtues of massive nonviolent protest. This crucial transformation in the African-American struggle had momentous consequences. The black churches, the hub of communities in the South, provided the movement with a stable base of supporters, a leadership economically independent of white society, a national ministerial communications network, a source of financial assistance, and a place to meet, to plan, to gain faith and courage. In addition, they gave the movement a language understood by all, expressed in biblical oratory and hymns, to battle against racial oppression; and they bestowed religious sanction on that battle. They would make possible the key ingredients of the modern civil-rights movement: large masses of African-Americans engaged in disruptive protest activities and the utilization of nonviolent direct action to create the necessary pressures for social change.

But they would not do so in the next three years. The SCLC initially accomplished little and failed to spark the mass, direct-action movement needed to alter the South. Blacks scored few victories for desegregation. Indeed, momentum shifted to those in the white South who defiantly said *Never* to black calls and court orders for integration. The second half of the fifties was the high tide of white massive resistance, of white reaction and repression. Authorities in Alabama had Autherine Lucy permanently expelled after she had won a federal court admitting her to the University of Alabama in 1956. The university would remain segregated for seven more years. Governor Orval Faubus closed the schools in Little Rock, and Virginia officials disbanded the public educational system of Prince Edward County rather than comply with desegregation. The KKK waxed and the White Citizens' Councils flourished. Crosses were burned; black churches, homes, and schools were bombed. The Southern Regional Council tabulated over two hundred acts of violence against black protesters and their allies from 1955 to 1959. The NAACP struggled just to survive. It channeled its energies and resources primarily into the effort to thwart the scores of Southern laws passed to outlaw the association directly or to hamstring its ability to function effectively. The civil-rights offensive envisioned by King seemed to many in the late 1950s more like a retreat before the forces of racism.

Not surprisingly, King's strategy of nonviolent resistance struck many African-Americans as unproductive, unbearable, even suicidal. "Are you Gandhi?" King's father asked. "The British threw him in jail. The 'Bamians and Mississippians would shoot him Dead!" Some considered nonviolence debasing; others questioned what fundamental conditions it could change; many simply tired of turning the other cheek. In 1959, the dismissal of Robert Williams as head of the Monroe, North Carolina, NAACP rocked the association's fiftieth annual convention. Earlier in the year, Williams had organized some fifty blacks into a gun club.

Armed and drilled, they repelled with gunfire a group of Klansmen threatening the home of an NAACP official. Williams then publicly advocated defensive guerilla warfare by blacks and called for the formation of rifle clubs throughout the South. The NAACP hierarchy defended the dismissal of Williams, but the deep rumblings of discontent by delegates served notice that proponents of civil rights would not indefinitely adhere to nonviolence if it proved fruitless. Near the end of the year, a two-hour television documentary, "The Hate That Hate Produced," shocked the nation with its portrayal of the Black Muslims, nearly a hundred thousand strong, rejecting Christianity and integration. The program focused national attention on Malcolm X and his fiery denunciations of all white people and their Negro stooges in the civil-rights movement. Emerging from prison in 1952 to become the head of the Nation of Islam's mosque in Harlem, Malcolm X dismissed any chance of meaningful racial change in the United States. He insisted that true African-Americans did not want "to *integrate* into this corrupt society, but to separate, from it, to a land of our *own*, where we can reform ourselves, lift up our moral standards, and try to be godly."

Yet other blacks, mainly the young, demonstrated an impatient hopefulness. They took heart from the legal and legislative victories of the NAACP. The desegregation efforts of the federal government, however irresolute, buoyed them. They knew that national and international politics made it imperative for Washington to deal with the racial problem. They sensed that the economic, educational, and demographic changes swirling about them foretold the crumbling of the old racial order. Montgomery had made them proud and confident. They read and reread FOR's widely circulated comic book *Martin Luther King and the Montgomery Story* and King's *Stride Toward Freedom: The Montgomery Story*. They dreamed of their opportunity to act.

Returning from a nonviolent action workshop in 1958, Barbara Ann Posey decided to act. A member of the Oklahoma City NAACP Youth Council, Posey organized a sit-in which resulted in the desegregation of five stores. The idea spread to the Youth Councils in Tulsa and Stillwater, and then across the state line to NAACP youth in Wichita and Kansas City, Kansas. King and Rustin organized a Youth March for Integrated Schools that brought nearly nine thousand young blacks to Washington, D.C. The following year, the March drew twenty-five thousand. Two thousand attended a Pilgrimage of Prayer for Public Schools in Richmond, Virginia, the first such large demonstration in the Deep South to decry "massive resistance" to school desegregation. Black students in Charlotte, North Carolina, protested being barred from state ceremonies which welcomed whites, while their counterparts in Marion, South Carolina, desegregated an ice-cream stand after a successful boycott. Also in 1959, African-American students began a sit-in in Durham, North Carolina, and CORE members in Miami, Florida, sat-in at a W. T. Grant's lunch counter and started a drive to desegregate the beaches of that resort city. None of these actions attracted national press coverage. None led to new organizations or leaders. None sparked a nationwide movement.

Yet together they revealed a new mood of restiveness, compounded of hope and anger. The charismatic young preacher who imparted a more moral and militant quality to the movement and the nonviolent, direct action campaign by the mass of ordinary black Montgomerians that rocked the Cradle of the Confederacy had together made an extraordinary impression on African-Americans, especially black middle-class youth. Disappointed with the NAACP's inability to provide immediate relief from the yoke of discrimination and oppression, they yearned to take to the streets. They bitterly decried the lack of racial progress in the late 1950s, yet optimistically believed that by using the strategy fashioned by Martin Luther King in Montgomery they could topple Jim Crow, quickly and throughout the South. King's prediction to the annual conveantion of the Fellowship of Reconciliation in mid-1959 that the coming years would witness mounting black "direct action against injustice without waiting for other agencies to act" defined their propensity. His thundering peroration to the FOR—"We will not obey unjust laws or submit to unjust practices"—adumbrated their cause.

Inaugural Address of John F. Kennedy
Friday, January 20, 1961

Vice President Johnson, Mr. Speaker, Mr. Chief Justice, President Eisenhower, Vice President Nixon, President Truman, reverend clergy, fellow citizens, we observe today not a victory of party, but a celebration of freedom—symbolizing an end, as well as a beginning—signifying renewal, as well as change. For I have sworn before you and Almighty God the same solemn oath our forebears prescribed nearly a century and three quarters ago.

The world is very different now. For man holds in his mortal hands the power to abolish all forms of human poverty and all forms of human life. And yet the same revolutionary beliefs for which our forebears fought are still at issue around the globe—the belief that the rights of man come not from the generosity of the state, but from the hand of God.

We dare not forget today that we are the heirs of that first revolution. Let the word go forth from this time and place, to friend and foe alike, that the torch has been passed to a new generation of Americans—born in this century, tempered by war, disciplined by a hard and bitter peace, proud of our ancient heritage—and unwilling to witness or permit the slow undoing of those human rights to which this Nation has always been committed, and to which we are committed today at home and around the world.

Let every nation know, whether it wishes us well or ill, that we shall pay any price, bear any burden, meet any hardship, support any friend, oppose any foe, in order to assure the survival and the success of liberty.

This much we pledge—and more.

To those old allies whose cultural and spiritual origins we share, we pledge the loyalty of faithful friends. United, there is little we cannot do in a host of cooperative ventures.

Divided, there is little we can do—for we dare not meet a powerful challenge at odds and split asunder.

To those new States whom we welcome to the ranks of the free, we pledge our word that one form of colonial control shall not have passed away merely to be replaced by a far more iron tyranny. We shall not always expect to find them supporting our view. But we shall always hope to find them strongly supporting their own freedom—and to remember that, in the past, those who foolishly sought power by riding the back of the tiger ended up inside.

To those peoples in the huts and villages across the globe struggling to break the bonds of mass misery, we pledge our best efforts to help them help themselves, for whatever period is required—not because the Communists may be doing it, not because we seek their votes, but because it is right. If a free society cannot help the many who are poor, it cannot save the few who are rich.

To our sister republics south of our border, we offer a special pledge—to convert our good words into good deeds—in a new alliance for progress—to assist free men and free governments in casting off the chains of poverty. But this peaceful revolution of hope cannot become the prey of hostile powers. Let all our neighbors know that we shall join with them to oppose aggression or subversion anywhere in the Americas. And let every other power know that this Hemisphere intends to remain the master of its own house.

To that world assembly of sovereign states, the United Nations, our last best hope in an age where the instruments of war have far outpaced the instruments of peace, we renew our pledge of support—to prevent it from becoming merely a forum for invective—to strengthen its shield of the new and the weak—and to enlarge the area in which its writ may run.

Finally, to those nations who would make themselves our adversary, we offer not a pledge but a request: that both sides begin anew the quest for peace, before the dark powers of destruction unleashed by science engulf all humanity in planned or accidental self-destruction.

We dare not tempt them with weakness. For only when our arms are sufficient beyond doubt can we be certain beyond doubt that they will never be employed.

But neither can two great and powerful groups of nations take comfort from our present course—both sides overburdened by the cost of modern weapons, both rightly alarmed by the steady spread of the deadly atom, yet both racing to alter that uncertain balance of terror that stays the hand of mankind's final war.

So let us begin anew—remembering on both sides that civility is not a sign of weakness, and sincerity is always subject to proof. Let us never negotiate out of fear. But let us never fear to negotiate.

Let both sides explore what problems unite us instead of belaboring those problems which divide us.

Let both sides, for the first time, formulate serious and precise proposals for the inspection and control of arms—and bring the absolute power to destroy other nations under the absolute control of all nations.

Let both sides seek to invoke the wonders of science instead of its terrors. Together let us explore the stars, conquer the deserts, eradicate disease, tap the ocean depths, and encourage the arts and commerce.

Let both sides unite to heed in all corners of the earth the command of Isaiah—to "undo the heavy burdens. . .and to let the oppressed go free."

And if a beachhead of cooperation may push back the jungle of suspicion, let both sides join in creating a new endeavor, not a new balance of power, but a new world of law, where the strong are just and the weak secure and the peace preserved.

All this will not be finished in the first 100 days. Nor will it be finished in the first 1,000 days, nor in the life of this Administration, nor even perhaps in our lifetime on this planet. But let us begin.

In your hands, my fellow citizens, more than in mine, will rest the final success or failure of our course. Since this country was founded, each generation of Americans has been summoned to give testimony to its national loyalty. The graves of young Americans who answered the call to service surround the globe.

Now the trumpet summons us again—not as a call to bear arms, though arms we need; not as a call to battle, though embattled we are—but a call to bear the burden of a long twilight struggle, year in and year out, "rejoicing in hope, patient in tribulation"—a struggle against the common enemies of man: tyranny, poverty, disease, and war itself.

Can we forge against these enemies a grand and global alliance, North and South, East and West, that can assure a more fruitful life for all mankind? Will you join in that historic effort?

In the long history of the world, only a few generations have been granted the role of defending freedom in its hour of maximum danger. I do not shrink from this responsibility—I welcome it. I do not believe that any of us would exchange places with any other people or any other generation. The energy, the faith, the devotion which we bring to this endeavor will light our country and all who serve it—and the glow from that fire can truly light the world.

And so, my fellow Americans: ask not what your country can do for you—ask what you can do for your country.

My fellow citizens of the world: ask not what America will do for you, but what together we can do for the freedom of man.

Finally, whether you are citizens of America or citizens of the world, ask of us the same high standards of strength and sacrifice which we ask of you. With a good conscience our only sure reward, with history the final judge of our deeds, let us go forth to lead the land we love, asking His blessing and His help, but knowing that here on earth God's work must truly be our own.

Inaugural Address of Lyndon Baines Johnson
Wednesday, January 20, 1965

My fellow countrymen, on this occasion, the oath I have taken before you and before God is not mine alone, but ours together. We are one nation and one people. Our fate as a nation and our future as a people rest not upon one citizen, but upon all citizens.

This is the majesty and the meaning of this moment.

For every generation, there is a destiny. For some, history decides. For this generation, the choice must be our own.

Even now, a rocket moves toward Mars. It reminds us that the world will not be the same for our children, or even for ourselves in a short span of years. The next man to stand here will look out on a scene different from our own, because ours is a time of change—rapid and fantastic change bearing the secrets of nature, multiplying the nations, placing in uncertain hands new weapons for mastery and destruction, shaking old values, and uprooting old ways.

Our destiny in the midst of change will rest on the unchanged character of our people, and on their faith.

The American Covenant

They came here—the exile and the stranger, brave but frightened—to find a place where a man could be his own man. They made a covenant with this land. Conceived in justice, written in liberty, bound in union, it was meant one day to inspire the hopes of all mankind; and it binds us still. If we keep its terms, we shall flourish.

Justice and Change

First, justice was the promise that all who made the journey would share in the fruits of the land.

In a land of great wealth, families must not live in hopeless poverty. In a land rich in harvest, children just must not go hungry. In a land of healing miracles, neighbors must not suffer and die unattended.

In a great land of learning and scholars, young people must be taught to read and write.

For the more than 30 years that I have served this Nation, I have believed that this injustice to our people, this waste of our resources, was our real enemy. For 30 years or more, with the resources I have had, I have vigilantly fought against it. I have learned, and I know, that it will not surrender easily.

But change has given us new weapons. Before this generation of Americans is finished, this enemy will not only retreat—it will be conquered.

Justice requires us to remember that when any citizen denies his fellow, saying, "His color is not mine," or "His beliefs are strange and different," in that moment he betrays America, though his forebears created this Nation.

Liberty and Change

Liberty was the second article of our covenant. It was self-government. It was our Bill of Rights. But it was more. America would be a place where each man could be proud to be himself: stretching his talents, rejoicing in his work, important in the life of his neighbors and his nation.

This has become more difficult in a world where change and growth seem to tower beyond the control and even the judgment of men. We must work to provide the knowledge and the surroundings which can enlarge the possibilities of every citizen.

The American covenant called on us to help show the way for the liberation of man. And that is today our goal. Thus, if as a nation there is much outside our control, as a people no stranger is outside our hope.

Change has brought new meaning to that old mission. We can never again stand aside, prideful in isolation. Terrific dangers and troubles that we once called "foreign" now constantly live among us. If American lives must end, and American treasure be spilled, in countries we barely know, that is the price that change has demanded of conviction and of our enduring covenant.

Think of our world as it looks from the rocket that is heading toward Mars. It is like a child's globe, hanging in space, the continents stuck to its side like colored maps. We are all fellow passengers on a dot of earth. And each of us, in the span of time, has really only a moment among our companions.

How incredible it is that in this fragile existence, we should hate and destroy one another. There are possibilities enough for all who will abandon mastery over others to pursue mastery over nature. There is world enough for all to seek their happiness in their own way.

Our Nation's course is abundantly clear. We aspire to nothing that belongs to others. We seek no dominion over our fellow man but man's dominion over tyranny and misery.

But more is required. Men want to be a part of a common enterprise—a cause greater than themselves. Each of us must find a way to advance the purpose of the Nation, thus finding new purpose for ourselves. Without this, we shall become a nation of strangers.

Union and Change

The third article was union. To those who were small and few against the wilderness, the success of liberty demanded the strength of union. Two centuries of change have made this true again.

No longer need capitalist and worker, farmer and clerk, city and countryside, struggle to divide our bounty. By working shoulder to shoulder, together we can increase the bounty of all. We have discovered that every child who learns, every man who finds work, every sick body that is made whole—like a candle added to an altar—brightens the hope of all the faithful.

So let us reject any among us who seek to reopen old wounds and to rekindle old hatreds. They stand in the way of a seeking nation.

Let us now join reason to faith and action to experience, to transform our unity of interest into a unity of purpose. For the hour and the day and the time are here to achieve progress without strife, to achieve change without hatred—not without difference of opinion, but without the deep and abiding divisions which scar the union for generations.

The American Belief

Under this covenant of justice, liberty, and union we have become a nation—prosperous, great, and mighty. And we have kept our freedom. But we have no promise from God that our greatness will endure. We have been allowed by Him to seek greatness with the sweat of our hands and the strength of our spirit.

I do not believe that the Great Society is the ordered, changeless, and sterile battalion of the ants. It is the excitement of becoming—always becoming, trying, probing, falling, resting, and trying again—but always trying and always gaining.

In each generation, with toil and tears, we have had to earn our heritage again.

If we fail now, we shall have forgotten in abundance what we learned in hardship: that democracy rests on faith, that freedom asks more than it gives, and that the judgment of God is harshest on those who are most favored.

If we succeed, it will not be because of what we have, but it will be because of what we are; not because of what we own, but, rather because of what we believe.

For we are a nation of believers. Underneath the clamor of building and the rush of our day's pursuits, we are believers in justice and liberty and union, and in our own Union. We believe that every man must someday be free. And we believe in ourselves.

Our enemies have always made the same mistake. In my lifetime—in depression and in war—they have awaited our defeat. Each time, from the secret places of the American heart, came forth the faith they could not see or that they could not even imagine. It brought us victory. And it will again.

For this is what America is all about. It is the uncrossed desert and the unclimbed ridge. It is the star that is not reached and the harvest sleeping in the unplowed ground. Is our world gone? We say "Farewell." Is a new world coming? We welcome it—and we will bend it to the hopes of man.

To these trusted public servants and to my family and those close fiends of mine who have followed me down a long, winding road, and to all the people of this Union and the world, I will repeat today what I said on that sorrowful day in November 1963: "I will lead and I will do the best I can."

But you must look within your own hearts to the old promises and to the old dream. They will lead you best of all.

For myself, I ask only, in the words of an ancient leader: "Give me now wisdom and knowledge, that I may go out and come in before this people: for who can judge this thy people, that is so great?"

Opening a Curtain

The Metamorphosis of Lyndon B. Johnson

Joe B. Frantz

Two decades ago a young lawyer friend of mine wound up in Houston with one of those huge law corporations with multiple partners, all with acceptable Anglo-Saxon names except the one at the tag end of the letterhead. The firm's name was something like Fulbright, Crooker, Bates, Freeman, and Jaworski. As my friend observed to me, "Obviously, Jaworski made it on merit." (This was before Leon Jaworski became Public Enemy No. I on the Richard Milhous Nixon Enemies List.)

I bring this story up only because I have been looking over the list of past presidents of the Southern Historical Association, and I can only surmise that most of them made it on merit. I don't make that claim for myself.

While I cannot identify the brand that the nominations committee was imbibing the night it chose me, I do accept its shaky judgment and say merely, "Here I am, undoubtedly the least southern of your presidents in the otherwise long and honorable history of this Association." My only claim to merit is genuine service on most of the SHA committees, especially the one once named to find a successor to Bennett H. Wall. After an exhaustive search we reported that there is no successor to—or substitute for—our reed of an executive secretary. That recommendation represents one of my rare right decisions, as well as a refusal to fly in the face of facts.

But I do have some credentials for what I am going to discuss with you tonight. For six years I pursued the trail of former President Lyndon Baines Johnson, tape recorder ready, seeing friend and foe alike, until my staff and I had some 1,200 interviews in hand. To date, no other President has been captured from as many aspects as was President Johnson by his contemporaries. Whether those interviewees were objective is beside the point. What matters is that we examined hundreds of witnesses who revealed facets of a man who served in Washington under one-sixth of all the Presidents, including himself, whose service was frequently significant and high level, and whose impact on the nation, whether for good or ill, will last most or all of our lives.

Oral history, as you know, is one of the newer adjuncts of the historical profession, with obvious faults as a historical procedure and with just as obvious advantages. Oral history holds the advantage of effortlessness. Most people talk more easily than they write. They talk more freely, more naturally. They freeze when they write; they act as if their written prose is imperishable, and they become self-conscious. Even scholars, who presumably write as part of their profession, suffer from this malady, as witness the turgid prose issuing from so many semi-somnolent typewriters.

Consequently, we have in the Lyndon B. Johnson Presidential Library ten million or more words that would likely have never found their way into the record, words that represent a sort of stream-of-consciousness approach to history as seen by eyewitnesses, words and thoughts that were articulated in usually relaxed situations, words that illumine the frequently opaque hard facts with which our profession deals.

As I have pondered these millions of words, several insights have emerged. For our purposes here one idea that stands apart and that deserves examination is the generally consistent development of Lyndon B. Johnson from a young politician who mirrored the strengths and biases of his central

Texas homeland to a mature politician who upended for the nation the greatest cornucopia of social legislation in its history.

Where did Johnson's social concern stem from? Why did he become so nationally concerned that his base of strength, the South, turned against him, even to the point of refusing to place the Democratic party—its historic friend, Johnson's party—on the ballot in several states in the presidential election of 1968? Why, as in 1964, had he already taken such alleged antisouthern actions in his brief Presidency that in that campaign year he readily conceded that Barry Morris Goldwater's greatest strength lay in the South? Why was his wife's whistle-stop campaign through her native South met with such occasional hostility?

Before we start chasing answers to these questions in earnest, let us diverge for one more suggestion. The South is currently booming, generally the most rapidly advancing section of the nation under its booster title of the Sun Belt. Vitality seems to ooze from its black soil and its red clay and from its pine forests and even its sluggish streams. The stereotype of the lazy Southerner has disappeared from contemporary folklore, except as it may linger in the emotions of a few outside observers who have been Rip Van Winkling for the past twenty years or so. And in 1976, when we witnessed the election of a man from the Deep South, from a country town called Plains, no less, most pundits agreed that his election was made possible by overwhelming majorities from southern blacks. Yet only a dozen years before Johnson himself had confided to Walter Wilson Jenkins, as the President debated whether to run for a full term or retire, "I just don't think a white Southerner is a man to unite this nation. . . ."[1]

Nor was Johnson the only person who felt so strongly about his being shut out from the Presidency because of his birth in the old Confederacy. Robert Jackson, a Texan from Corpus Christi then in Washington, tells how thirty years earlier he and his wife invited a newly arrived Johnson to their apartment. Johnson kept the pair awake most of the night talking, which led Mrs. Jackson to remark to her weary husband that their guest would probably be President some day. "I told her how stupid she was," recalled Jackson, "and how little she knew about politics, because nobody from Texas would ever be President."[2]

But in the past two decades we have come a long way in uniting the South with the remainder of the nation. Similarly, we have advanced in convincing the remainder of the nation and the world that the South is made up of human beings instead of ghostly leftovers in crinoline and string ties who eat blacks for breakfast and genuflect every time the name of Robert Edward Lee is mentioned. And no one did more to engineer this change in attitudes than Lyndon B. Johnson, who by the very nature of his background should have been designated as the least likely person to pull off such a revolution.

To be a Southerner in politics was to invite a similar discrimination as practiced nationally against blacks and women. None of the three groups could aspire to the Presidency.

As far back as 1953, when Johnson was a fairly new minority leader of the United States Senate, he told a *Time* magazine reporter that he did not aspire to the Presidency, because, as he said, "I come from the wrong part of the country."[3] And in 1960 he persuaded Sam Rayburn and John Bowden Connally to shut down the presidential campaign headquarters they had opened in Washington without his permission on the plea that "a Southerner could not, and probably should not, be elected."[4]

But Johnson did become President, as we know. Although it took a murder in Dallas, he made it to the White House. And afterwards he was elected to a full term, paving the way for James Earl "Jimmy" Carter. And meanwhile the nation witnessed the 1964 phenomenon of Johnson *versus* Goldwater, neither candidate from a state that traditionally supplies candidates and both from almost contiguous states that are tucked away in the southwestern corner of the United States. And eight years later South Dakota, with an even smaller population base, gave us one of the major presidential candidates in George Stanley McGovern. Perhaps we have begun to become the "land of the free," where any mother's son or daughter can dream of becoming President with some hope of achieving that goal. And once we cross each color and sex line, the second attempt will follow as easily as nominating Catholic John Fitzgerald Kennedy after Catholic Alfred Emanuel Smith, or sending Henry B. Gonzalez back to Congress from San Antonio for term after term or Edward William Brooke to the Senate from Massachusetts or Barbara C. Jordan from Houston for as long as she chose to remain—or electing as President the Georgian after the Texan. Maybe we will become a land of people finally.

But that is not my focus here tonight. Let's look more specifically at Johnson.

As the 1960s approached nationally syndicated cartoonists had their usual field day with unannounced presidential candidate Lyndon B. Johnson, the majority leader of the United States Senate. They depicted him, stretching his long frame over at least nine feet of height, looking still taller in a high-crowned, wide-brimmed Stetson and high-heeled, hand-tooled cowboy boots. He was typical Texan, whatever that image conveys, and the words that issued from his ample mouth were pure Texanese, as western as John Wayne, except that each sentence invariably ended with the phrase "you all," a concession to his southernism. Sometimes one boot would be planted firmly in West Texas, the other in the spongy soil of the Deep South. All that was lacking were the Sons of the Pioneers singing "Cool Water" in one corner and blacks strumming mandolins as darkness gathered on the delta—any delta—in the opposite corner.

The cartoons showed Johnson's dilemma. Was he a western candidate or was he a southern one? Or was he, as most cartoonists hinted, trying to straddle both sections, utilizing his Texas background to illustrate his transitional position? Never mind. You could accept him as belonging to one section or the other, or to both; but you never suggested that he represented the nation.

Other cartoons showed Adlai Ewing Stevenson wrestling in his eloquent way with Middle East and Russian problems; William Stuart Symington represented military problems; John F. Kennedy, labor and management; Hubert Horatio Humphrey, the minorities and the dispossessed. Each had national concerns involving national constituencies. But Johnson represented only the South and the West, when he wasn't representing the petroleum industry. To politicians and voters he remained a regional candidate, despite his national position as Senate majority leader. And when he was placed on the ticket as vice-presidential running mate with John F. Kennedy, the press quite correctly still looked on his selection as a device to hold the South in the party. Meanwhile, loyal Democrats like Walter Philip Reuther, G. Mennen Williams, and Robert Francis Kennedy protested his selection because of his presumed narrowness.[5] He was a regional man, nothing he could do would release him from that straitjacket.

Actually, this attitude toward Johnson was erroneous, though it had emotional authenticity because of his style and the nation's attitude toward Texas and the South. Without attempting to equate Johnson with more distinguished antecedents, public reaction to the man and to many more of similar background reminds one of the Biblical question: "Can . . .any good thing come out of Nazareth?" Could any good come out of Texas?

But from the first Johnson had shown certain progressive and even liberal tendencies, so that his performance as President remains consistent with his actions of the past. His Great Society does not represent a break with his past and is not, as charged by many contemporary southern leaders, an aberration, an alleged sellout to the votes of blacks and northern liberals.

Take, for instance, Johnson's very first noticeability in Washington. The year is 1933, the first spring of the New Deal, and Johnson is a twenty-four-year-old secretary to a Texas congressman, Richard Mifflin Kleberg, Sr. In that year Johnson led an "open revolt against the conduct of 'the Little Congress' (the secretarial organization modeled after Congress) by an 'oligarchy' of veteran members." A majority of the other secretaries named Johnson as their new speaker. Throughout the five-paragraph story in the *Washington Star* the victory for Johnson was trumpeted as a triumph of liberals over "standpatters" in "the most lively" sessions held by the Little Congress to that time. And the new speaker, borrowing from the nation's new symbol, promised all the secretaries a "new deal for all Little Congresses."[6]

Even before then, as a college youngster dropping out to recoup his finances teaching at Cotulla, Texas, Johnson had adumbrated his future Head Start program, more than forty years down the road. With a student body that was heavily Mexican-American and correspondingly deprived, he had written his mother to send him two hundred packages of toothpaste for his student body of 250.[7] And as Congressman Kleberg's secretary Johnson evidently prevailed on his employer to support the World War I veterans' bonus, the proposed Agricultural Adjustment Administration, and the projected regulation of holding companies, bills toward which Kleberg apparently had little affirmative inclination.[8]

Robert Clifton Weaver, the first secretary of housing and urban development as well as the first black cabinet member ever, once told the present speaker that he first heard of Lyndon B. Johnson when Weaver, Ralph Johnson Bunche, and other young black intellectuals in Washington began to get word that down in Texas a state National Youth Administration director in his mid-twenties was spending money and dreaming up projects that benefited, in Weaver's words, "Negroes and poor white folks." Such a practice was unheard of in most states, where the NYA chiefly helped young people whose social and political clout was well known. Weaver said that though the name Lyndon Johnson meant nothing to him then, he decided that he should keep an eye on this unique person from this strange faraway land.

From Houston came a report from Beatrice Denmark, saying that in Texas she had "found what I have been hoping to find for colored girls. . . . The Texas Director is doing what many of us are talking."[9] Three months later, just after Johnson was elected to his first congressional term, that angel of the modern black movement, Mary McLeod Bethune, wrote Johnson

> that the same energy and vigorous imagination that characterized the outstanding success of your program with the National Youth Administration will write your name high in the annals of the House of Rep[resentatives].
>
> We are indeed happy that one who has proven himself so conscious of and sympathetic with the needs of all the people should take his place in a Congress that is so indelibly writing a more human and more Christian concept of American democracy.[10]

When Johnson announced for Congress in 1937 Aubrey Willis Williams, national director of the NYA, called on President Franklin Delano Roosevelt to dissuade the young Texan, saying that Johnson was more important as state NYA director than he could ever be as a Texas congressman. (He probably thought, as I sometimes do in consonance with the remainder of the nation, that there are too many Texas congressmen already.) But Roosevelt demurred because Johnson was running on a platform promising all-out support to the President, even though the Texas delegation, ranging from the Texas Vice-President John Nance Garner down to local Texas officials, were all making political hay out of damning the New Deal. Roosevelt was not going to discourage a potential congressman from Texas who evidently would follow him all the way to the well.[11]

When four years later Johnson made his first run at elective office, again he joined the liberal wing of his party. Whether his liberality stemmed from conviction or merely represented shrewd politics can be debated, but no question exists as to the astuteness and direction of his move. Running against a double handful of opponents for the unexpired congressional term of James Paul Buchanan of the Tenth District of Texas, Johnson endorsed the New Deal down the line, including the reorganization package of the United States Supreme Court, which had set Texans' political teeth on edge. Some of the other candidates opposed the "packing bill," as its foes dubbed it. Johnson reasoned correctly that his opponents would split the anti-New Deal vote among themselves, while he should receive most of the pro-Franklin D. Roosevelt votes. Since he needed only a plurality, if he could segregate the Rooseveltians into his camp, he should win. That is the way the script read, and that is the way he produced it. Although campaign money lay heavily with those disenchanted Texans who were beginning to view Roosevelt as some sort of anti-Christ, the beleaguered New Dealers in Texas stayed with Johnson and put him officially and electively in Washington for the next nearly 12,000 days.

Of course, when the Supreme Court reorganization went down to defeat, in large part because of the opposing leadership of the Texas congressional delegation, the spotlight shone on the twenty-eight-year-old maverick who had refused to run with the Texas herd. His stance guaranteed at least minimum name recognition in the nation's press for the new congressman, and it brought him to the attention of no less a person than Roosevelt himself, who was in a position to appreciate and reward party loyalty.

And Johnson soon proved to be more than a one-issue New Dealer. In that first session he helped forward to completion such progressive measures as the Lower Colorado River Authority ("Texas' little TVA," in the words of Benjamin Victor Cohen), the Pedernales rural-electrification cooperative, the Brazos River flood-control plan, a bill to reduce farm tenancy (all measures aimed at increasing farm income and farm relief), and crop-control legislation. And wonder of wonders—for a Texas representative—he supported the wages and hours bill, which he defended as helping to eliminate abuses existing in industry. To the charge that the bill would discourage industries from moving to the South, Johnson answered: "If an industry cannot pay decent wages, I do not want it in my district." At this statement the Austin Chamber of Commerce fathers must have aged perceptibly.

Meanwhile Johnson's concern for the plight of the black spilled over into his first term as congressman. As a freshman congressman he obtained an appointment with President Roosevelt himself, his purpose being to complain about Milo Randolph Perkins, head of the Agricultural Adjustment Administration, the old Triple A. Although Perkins was one of the administration's stalwarts, Johnson told Roosevelt that Perkins was not passing on AAA benefits to Negro farmers in Texas. According to Grace Tully, Roosevelt's "first automatic instinct was, 'Now this is a smart politician.' And then he realized . . . that this was the day of the lily-white primary in Texas; and that contrary to the idea of adding votes or adding to the political career of Congressman Johnson, this might even backfire on him."[12]

That record, those concerns could have represented the forthrightness of a young, new congressman who hadn't yet fallen under the spell of Sam Rayburn's famous dictum: "To get along, you've got to go along." After all, Johnson was just finishing out a dead man's term. The test would come when he ran for a full term. Then the voters could see who would vote conviction and who would vote constituency.

That test came rather quickly. Senate Bill 2475 came over to the House of Representatives in 1938 and was quickly bottled up in the Committee on Rules. The bill placed a floor of twenty-five cents an hour on the wages of certain workers. The outcry in opposition to the bill was almost deafening. To its enemies it represented a definite concession to socialism, if not communism. To them it meant the ruination of the United States as it was then understood. It guaranteed the end of free, private enterprise in this nation, the termination of the southern way of life, and the destruction of Christianity and motherhood. When in May 1938 House Resolution 478 was voted on to discharge the Committee on Rules from considering HR 478 by making the Senate bill a special order of business, Johnson joined with five others as the only six Texas congressmen with the courage to back the bill. In Texas they were told that their stances assured their defeat in the upcoming congressional elections.

Their critics proved one-third correct. When the next congressional elections were held Fontaine Maury Maverick and William Doddridge McFarlane were no longer members of Congress. But Johnson survived, and as he admitted years later, "I don't know what happened to me except I didn't have an opponent."[13] Johnson, who often told this story,

conveniently forgot three of the Texans who voted with him—Sam Rayburn, Albert Thomas, and Robert Ewing Thomason. The story sounds better if he is the only one surviving, and Johnson had the instincts of a good storyteller who doesn't permit details to damage his impact. Although eastern politicians, labor leaders, and much of the national press praised the Texas sextet, the risk politically was hardly worth the accolades.

With Roosevelt running for an unprecedented third term in 1940 the Democratic leadership feared that a backlash might develop against senators and representatives seeking reelection by those Democrats who opposed breaking the two-term tradition for Presidents. At one time the White House feared losing as many as twelve seats in Illinois, five in Indiana, and three in Missouri. The Middle West promised to develop into a congressional disaster area. When, on the advice of Sam Rayburn and James H. Rowe, Roosevelt designated Johnson, still chronologically young at thirty-two years, to head the committee to rescue the threatened Democratic congressmen, no one questioned whether he came from the South or from Texas but whether he could get the job done. As Robert Sharon Allen was to write at the end of the campaign, "Lyndon performed miracles," meanwhile complimenting the congressman for his "enlightened view."[14]

Again, at the conclusion of World War II Johnson warned Texas legislators in a special ceremony at the state capitol in Austin that the soldiers who have "tasted achievement will never again be content with the mild tea of generous promises." He added, "In a democracy the greatest cannot rise far above the most humble. Were those men alive today who formed Texas they would say to us '. . . Lead our people up . . . and up. Bring to them education . . . sound minds in sound bodies. For the progress of men is limited only by the backwardness of men.'"[15]

This was strong talk to a home constituency which still believed that the American way of life was superior to any other in the world because it provided its citizens with more bathtubs, more telephones, and more automobiles. Many legislators groused that Johnson had confused democracy with equality, a dangerous misconception in a state that dotes on its status quo.

By the next year Johnson was sounding even more dangerous. Along with lonely President Harry S. Truman, Johnson was espousing federal assistance to health care—" socialized medicine," as its fearful opponents labeled the proposal. Charged Johnson: ". . . all of the talk about socializing medicine is nonsense and should be laid on the table. . . ." What the nation needed, added Johnson, was more doctors and nurses—Texas, he pointed out, was 1,400 doctors short for its population. The people were exercised over the wrong concerns— they worried about the doctors, not the patients, he declared. Talking in those plain terms that his critics would later decry, but terms nonetheless that people can understand, Johnson turned specific in his advocacy: ". . . the fly which eats at the open privy of a slum area has no scruples about carrying polio to the child in the silk-stocking area. . . . The health of a community can be no better than the health of those least able to afford medical and hospital care."[16]

But the idea of federal assistance to proper health care was too far ahead of its time and would wait another two decades—until Johnson himself was President—before it would become a merciful fact. But again Johnson was being consistent.

Up to now in this narrative Johnson has looked good, a somewhat radical agrarian from a land of worn-out soil and poor crops in sequence who had transferred some of that radicalism to larger problems. But Johnson's good record has its flip side, and this other side does him scant credit.

The year was 1946, the boys had returned from the war, and American manufacturing and selling of consumer goods had resumed its upward trend. Organized labor, only a decade old in political acceptance, was resolved to obtain its share of the prospective wealth, while management was equally resolute in pursuing its desires. The nation was turning conservative, a turn that Texas did not need to make since it had disliked New Deal social and labor gains since good times, never very far away, had begun to return early in the Roosevelt era. The prevailing mood in Texas and the South was decidedly antilabor, though organized labor in Texas was not without its clout.

The big issue in 1946 was the Taft-Hartley Act, passed by a Congress determined to redress the alleged imbalance between labor and management. Labor denounced the act as slave-labor legislation, a bit of overreaction but not without a certain justification. Johnson voted for the Taft-Hartley Act, Truman vetoed it, and Congress promptly overrode the veto. Johnson again voted against his party's leadership and against labor.

Organized labor, hitherto somewhat in his camp, as promptly denounced Johnson, and labor's opposition very nearly cost him his first election as United States senator two years later in that famous eighty-seven-vote campaign. Why did Johnson take such a chance with annoying one of his chief supports? For one thing, the district he represented as well as the people he most nearly claimed as his political friends in Congress, were all against the steadily rising influence of labor since the Wagner Act—"Labor's Magna Carta"—had been passed in 1935. Good central Texas politics demanded a vote for Taft-Hartley. But organized labor had invariably supported him, and for him to turn his back on labor in this crucial instance is difficult to justify.

William S. White, an appreciative biographer of Johnson, says that Taft-Hartley does not represent a backward step for Johnson in his public thinking, but simply "a change in the realities which underlay . . . [the times]."[17]

The President's brother, less blindly devoted in his admiration, does not entirely concur. According to Sam Houston Johnson, then assisting his congressman brother, he had prepared a press release attacking the Taft-Hartley bill, when Congressman Johnson told his younger brother to scrub it. Sam Houston Johnson writes that he could hardly believe his ears. "You can't do that," he told his brother. "Damn it, Lyndon, that's an antilabor law. The unions will crucify you!"

"Have you read the bill, Sam Houston?" LBJ asked, adding that if he had not, which indeed Sam Houston had not, he had "better read it before . . . [going] off half-cocked . . . it isn't what labor says it is. It's a good law, and I'm voting for it."

Sam Houston remonstrated with his erring brother, telling him that his vote would cost him 300,000 labor votes and probably the upcoming senatorial race. Johnson replied that "The working people know better than that." In that case, the younger brother was wiser politically, and most historians would agree that he was also more judicious socially. But organized labor in Texas turned on Johnson, and in Sam Houston's terms, "went all-out against him" because of his Taft-Hartley vote.[18] The result was that in the primary Johnson ran more than 71,000 votes behind his principal opponent, Coke Robert Stevenson, and in the runoff he just barely sneaked in with the notorious eighty-seven-vote margin. The irony is that Stevenson had no concern whatsoever for labor, a fact that was well known, but as governor of Texas at the time that Taft-Hartley became an issue he did not have to declare himself on the measure. Johnson, in short, was punished for taking a stance which he probably could not avoid.

On the other hand, Allan Shivers, former governor of Texas, thinks that Johnson's more conservative approach to the election of 1948, including his vote for Taft-Hartley, brought him enough conservative votes to enable him to squeeze home by the narrow margin. "I think that one thing alone enabled Johnson to get close enough in votes to where the Jim Wells box could make the difference," says Shivers.[19]

As we Tex-Mex types shrug, "¿*Quien sabe?*" Who knows?

Later, as Senate minority leader Johnson atoned slightly for his earlier support of Taft-Hartley. When the Republicans under Dwight David Eisenhower decided to strengthen the act in the 1950s Johnson had every one of the Democrats sitting in his seat—just an unheard-of thing," according to Kenneth Milton Birkhead, who adds that "when the voted started . . . he had every one of them, including Harry Byrd of Virginia, and some real mavericks in the party ready to vote to hold back on these amendments. I think it was one of the most dramatic highlights of his career as leader of the Senate when they were not in the majority. This was, I know, not easy for him to get to this point because I know he went through a long, tortuous struggle . . ., but this was a significant vote. It meant a lot to labor. He was able to bring them all together. He had Paul Douglas and Harry Byrd sitting there waiting for the vote when the roll call started." Not in their offices waiting for the quorum call, not in the dining room, not in the cloakrooms, not somewhere in the chamber, but sitting there waiting to vote unanimously against the Republican majority. As Johnson told Birkhead, "If we have our forty-seven members well-organized, this is a Democratic Senate."[20]

Again Johnson seemed to knuckle under to Texas conservative thinking when he led the fight to reject the nomination of Leland Olds as head of the Federal Power Commission in 1949. While the Olds incident is minor and not likely to be noted in any textbooks about the period, Olds was a darling of the liberals in the nation, and his rebuff by Johnson stung them more deeply than more nearly fundamental issues would have. As a member of the Federal Power Commission Olds had offended the private power companies by his advocacy of strong

regulation. When President Truman reappointed Olds to the commission the private power companies reacted. So did Johnson.

> It was a pre-Joe McCarthy campaign,. . . really vicious [Joseph L. Rauh, Jr., recalls]. The power and oil and gas companies were spending a lot of money; it's a sad fact, but [Abe] Fortas' firm was in on this thing with Johnson, and they really went after him. They quoted stuff [Olds] said twenty-five years earlier, which was pretty terrible stuff . . . I'm not defending the crap he said . . ., but that's a different story than after he'd become a leading figure in power regulations. . . . So there was a real confrontation between the liberals and Johnson. . . .
>
> Paul Douglas . . . was . . . the floor leader for Leland Olds. He feels as I do [observed Rauh]— that was one of the dirtiest pieces of work ever done. And of course it killed Olds. I don't know how many years he lived after that, but he never really recovered himself.

Asked why Johnson took such a vindictive stand against the foremost public-power advocate in the United States, Rauh admits to being puzzled.

> But all one has to do is to look at the *Congressional Record* [he noted]. Johnson read into the *Record* some of the most ancient stuff that Olds had said. And, as I said, it wasn't very pretty stuff, but a lot of things were said in the Depression, a lot of things . . . that the people wouldn't want to say. God knows, I'll challenge anybody that . . . repeated everything he has ever said, because in a long and full life you say some pretty stupid things. I'm not saying that Olds didn't. I'm saying the using of that in the McCarthy way in which they used it to end the career of the number one public power advocate in America was a shocking thing, and it must be on Johnson's conscience.

Rauh felt that the Texas private power interests got to Johnson and that his stand against Olds did not represent a philosophical difference between the two men so much as a political necessity on Johnson's part. That makes Johnson's performance even less acceptable. Rauh cites the Johnson of the National Youth Administration and the Johnson of the early 1940s, adding that "Whatever anyone else says about Johnson, there's a certain Populism in Johnson's makeup that I would think would have [supported] public power . . . for the people. I mean, I can't believe that Johnson wouldn't ordinarily have the same exact reaction that all the rest of us would have, which would be [that] there's something good about public power."[21]

Johnson's role reminds one of some advice that Johnson received from one of his early Texas advisers. He was going to have to make up his mind, the man said, "whether . . . to be a Congressman or a gentleman."[22] In the Olds instance Johnson chose the role of politician.

Johnson's procedure in taming Senator Joseph Raymond McCarthy likewise remains questionable. His detractors—liberals mostly—damn him for his tardiness in putting down the Wisconsin senator. He dallied and delayed, they claim, while all about him good men were being blasted out of useful service because they had either dared to confront or had inadvertently blundered into McCarthy's headlong rush for headlines and revenge. In short, say the liberals, Johnson toyed with the nation's soul and intellectual safety while McCarthy single-handedly destroyed the validity of the Fifth Amendment and scared many Americans out of their historic right to read and write as they chose.

Joseph Rauh would disagree in part:

> I think maybe Johnson and Eisenhower were about the same on McCarthy, frightened by his bullying tactics. Bullies are always scared of other bullies, and I think that's what you had there.
>
> But we didn't get the slightest bit of help in the fight against McCarthy from Johnson, and to a degree we got hurt because he was always counseling, "Don't attack him, leave him alone," etc. That just isn't the way a democracy can work. It was a lot harder to call Johnson a communist for standing up to McCarthy than it was a lot of the people who did stand up to McCarthy, but Johnson wouldn't stand up to McCarthy.

Rauh unconsciously reveals the liberal's penchant for excusing John F. Kennedy while damning Johnson for similar behavior. He says:

> . . . of course when they finally put the censure thing through late in '54, the guy [McCarthy] was a drunken discredited bum. . . . And of course every Democrat voted that way except for John Kennedy, who was in the hospital and who had special political problems including the fact that his father was one of McCarthy's real backers, so I never got too angry about the Kennedy thing.
>
> I thought Johnson's position was really more despicable because there was no reason why he couldn't have helped us. In the end it came out all right, and I think the inoculation has been good for the country. I think we have less McCarthyism

today because of McCarthy than we might otherwise have.

Rauh sums up: "Johnson was from, say, in the '50s a conservative Texan."[23] Like the advertisement for Budweiser, when you say *that*—that Johnson was a conservative Texan—you've said it all!

On the other hand, Johnson has his claque of admirers who argue as vehemently and as convincingly that the Senate majority leader handled McCarthy the only way he could be handled—by letting the conscienceless senator extend his power until he became ensnarled in his own deviousness and then striking quickly and tellingly to destroy his influence once and for all. No question remained as to the sentiments of many of Johnson's Texas constituency. In the Texas view McCarthy was against communism, and any person against communism is all right, even if he is as deadly as Adolf Hitler.

Now, Rauh didn't particularly admire Johnson, though he worked with him periodically. To balance the account, let's look at one of Johnson's most perfervid though realistic admirers Thomas Gardiner Corcoran—Tommy the Cork—the Franklin D. Roosevelt Whiz Kid who grew into a Washington elder statesman, though still hyper-adrenalized. Despite his unabashed advocacy of Johnson, Corcoran sounds as vehement as Rauh on the Olds fight.

"I think he is ashamed of . . . [it] now," Corcoran told me in 1969. "I told him to his face one day . . . that I thought it was the rottenest thing he'd ever done and that he could take it or . . . leave it . . . I realize . . . what a crucifiable position Mr. Johnson was in between the troglodytic state of mind in . . . Texas related to oil and gas, and the needs of a nation as a whole." Summarizing, Corcoran observed, "The Interstate and Foreign Commerce Committee . . . did as dirty a job of trying to crucify this guy à la McCarthy as I have ever heard . . . Now that's the only row I ever had with Lyndon."[24]

During the McCarthy days Johnson walked a political tightrope. Whether it was necessary can be debated but with no assured answers. During the senator from Wisconsin's period William Smith White went to Johnson to say, "You really must do something about this damned fellow." Johnson replied as follows:

> Bill, that's a good point, but let me explain something to you. In the present atmosphere, if I commit the Democratic party to the destruction of McCarthy [destruction probably meaning

censure here], first of all we will lose and he will win in the present atmosphere of the Senate. He'll be more powerful than ever. At this juncture I'm not about to commit the Democratic party to a high school debate on the subject, Resolved: That Communism is good for the United States, with my party taking the affirmative.

Johnson felt, according to White, that McCarthy was in a position to bring the "whole Senate to its knees."

"Now later on," continues White, "Johnson did indeed go after him and got him—got him in the sense that he brought about the creation of the select committee that investigated and censured McCarthy. But he waited until the atmosphere was right because he was afraid."

Not that Johnson was afraid of McCarthy as an opponent but only because of the lasting mischief he could deal the Democratic party, White believes. "McCarthy never would have dared take him on directly," he avers, "any more than, let's say, he would have Taft. But this was an illustration. . . .—I think an important one—of the profound common sense of Johnson to national issues."

White notes, incidentally, that the McCarthy issue represents the only time he ever volunteered any advice to Johnson.[25] Smart man!

In fact, according to George Edward Reedy, Johnson's former press secretary:

Johnson even developed techniques for using McCarthy. I can recall one day when we had a terribly close vote on the Social Security issue, and every single vote counted. Boy, that was a rough one! Because the whole White House staff was up on the Senate floor, and we'd get a vote and lose two, and then we'd get a couple and lose one. They had "Slick" Persons up there and . . . a whole crew lobbying at one point.

Johnson looked at McCarthy, and he walked over to him, and he said: "Joe, would you really like to screw Eisenhower, and screw him good?" And of course Joe was real mad at the President at that point. By God, that was one of the two or three votes, maybe even the vote . . . that put the Democratic position over.[26]

Harry Cummings McPherson confirms White's view of Johnson's caution where professional patriots were concerned—not on screwing Eisenhower. "He never had anything but contempt for McCarthyism, for hollering after Communists and all that," says McPherson, who served five years in the Senate with the majority leader.

He knew too God-damned many of them for one thing back in the 1930s. . . . And he has what Sidney Zion of the New York Times has said is probably the most acute sense of civil liberties of any modern President. But from a purely political point of view, he didn't want to go back to the days when Truman and the Truman Administration were under attack by Joe McCarthy, and the Democratic Party looked pro-Communist or looked as if it was soft on Communism.

The Johnson approach was to be tough on Communism, at home and abroad, and then to be able to get your liberal program through. He thought the odium attached to being soft on Communism would kill any possibility for progressive legislation, from a hardheaded point of view he was right.[27]

McPherson watched Johnson through a similar fight on the loyalty oath that again placed the majority leader at odds with the liberals in his party. The script reads like a cloning of the McCarthy problem.

Jack Kennedy had authored a bill [recalls McPherson] that would have repealed the loyalty oath requirement in the National Defense Education Act. This had been the subject of great controversy and bitterness in the colleges. A lot of college presidents, on the motion of their faculties, had said, "If the loyalty oath is retained, we won't accept any assistance from the NDEA." The bill was reported out by the labor committee, of which Kennedy was a member—It was heavily stacked with liberals—so it got out. And for several weeks, I kept nudging him to take the bill up. And one day he turned to me and said, "I am not going to get the Democratic Party into a national debate: Resolved, That the Communist Party is good for the United States with the Democratic Party taking the affirmative."

He came finally, I think, to support that repeal [continues McPherson]. He didn't like the loyalty oath; it was a Karl Mundt operation and he had a sublime contempt for that frame of mind.[28]

Although many people believe that Johnson's successive civil rights bills as Senate majority leader and as President possibly represent President Johnson's most significant contribution to the progress of this nation, as well as his greatest shift in political position from a Texan with southern prejudices to a national force with liberal outlook, not too much need be said here about Johnson's work on civil rights. Monroe Lee Billington has already chronicled this change in a thoroughly researched and equally convincing article,[29] so that about all that can be added is window dressing.

No question exists that Johnson did shift somewhat as he changed constituencies. When he represented the reasonably moderate Tenth District of Texas he could probably be classified as a moderate on civil rights, though the issue was not as sharply drawn in his congressional days.

But as senator from Texas Johnson pulled in his liberal horns to reveal a less attractive side. He supported the foes of antilynching bills, and he likewise supported the poll tax—the same poll tax which he later helped shuck from the codes of several southern states. But then, as a garden-variety senator, he represented all of Texas, which faces life from a basically conservative stance.

As he wrote one of his intermittent employees back in Texas,. . . if 'States' Rights' is to be a valid and responsible belief which progressive men can defend, then opportunities such as this should be passed by or ignored." Further, he cautioned, "social progress [should be] measured in terms of what is done for the mind, the body, and communication interlocking diverse areas and communities. The Negro and the Latin-American in Texas profits from many things other than the legislation affecting his status of well-being directly. What applies in Texas also applies nationally, although many lose sight of this."[30]

When he became Senate majority leader after his reelection in 1954 Johnson could feel secure that he had the power to continue as senator from Texas, for he had assumed a mantle of power—and Texans respect power, regardless of its political source or stance. He could neutralize the ultraconservatives, who handle the money in Texas and therefore underwrite or withhold from aspiring candidates, simply because Johnson was now who he was. Consequently, he could again become progressive, perhaps even liberal.[31] And down the road as President, he represented all of the United States, with a few disgruntled exceptions, and he had the political intuition to realize that the death of John F. Kennedy would make the nation more receptive and more lenient toward social advances for the less fortunate.

And so he struck, sometimes in too much haste but always with an impatience that was infectious and compelling. Whether his Great Society will be deemed a social and political success by historians awaits the judgment of future generations, but we can look about us now and see already that certain fundamental advances have been made that evidently will endure.

On this plane Johnson was consistent through the years, apparently biding his time until he could strike a blow here and there "keep his options open," as he liked to say. William Homer Thornberry, who succeeded Johnson as congressman when the latter moved up to senator in 1948, tells about being taken to New York to see the sights by the new senator. On one of New York's buses, crowded as often, an elderly Negro woman boarded to find no seats. Johnson arose to give her his seat, an act of courtesy generally unknown to Manhattanites regardless of race, color, sex, or ethnic origin. After they left the bus Thornberry complimented Johnson for his consideration of the black woman.

"I never see any woman standing," said Johnson, "black or white, that I don't think of my own mother and hope that if she is ever forced to stand on a bus, some man will show her the same courtesy."[32] To Johnson equal rights was a personal thing, not a piece of legislation.

Clarence M. Mitchell, Jr., who lobbied for the National Association for the Advancement of Colored People, came to support this view. At first suspicious and even put off by Johnson's way of working, Mitchell, who admits to the fact that in their early association Johnson would often indulge in plain talk that would cause the lobbyist's "hackles to rise," also admits that Johnson "did a good job of teaching" him. "He was of great help to us [Negroes]," says Mitchell. "And that is, he said again and again that people should have the right to vote. This bill had in it a provision protecting the right to vote, so this made him for it as a matter of principle. And I found then as well as now, that if he was for something as a matter of principle, his ingenuity would take over and the seemingly impossible could be made possible."[33]

Johnson's concern for ethnic minorities often expressed itself in little things that men of high principle but less humanity might pass by. When an undertaker in a small Texas city refused to handle the remains of a dead soldier of Latin American descent, Johnson arranged to have the soldier's body shipped to Arlington Cemetery across the river from Washington, D. C., and to have the lad's family brought to Washington to meet President Truman. When Henry B. Gonzalez first ran for Congress from Texas, Johnson took time from being Vice-President to spend a day on the back of a sound truck touring most of the shopping centers of San Antonio, telling that city's Mexican Americans "what opportunities they had to elect their first Latin American from Texas" to Congress.[34] Johnson had no stake in the election: San Antonio was not in his district; Gonzalez was not a particularly close friend; the Vice-President simply thought that the time had come for Texas to start recognizing a segment of its multiethnic population by sending a Mexican-American delegate to Washington.

And when Johnson purchased "The Elms," the home in which he lived as Vice-President, he and Mrs. Johnson filed an affidavit asserting that they intended to pay no attention to a covenant which came with the land which forbade its sale to Negroes. When they sold "The Elms" Mrs. Johnson told Sheldon Stanley Cohen to show the house to whoever was interested, regardless of color or ethnic origin. The house was to go to whoever agreed to the price, and in Cohen's words, no prospect was turned away—black, brown, yellow, Jew; he could even show it to "diplomats."[35]

Johnson's lack of self-consciousness represents another facet of this ability to place himself alongside ordinary people instead of on some higher plane as President. Sol Myron Linowitz, who is not exactly ordinary, remembers being flown to the LBJ Ranch, arriving at midnight to be met by an obvious farmhand, wearing a stocking cap and driving a station wagon. Only after he was in the car did Linowitz realize that this "hand" was the President of the United States.[36] And the first time J. Roy White, a local architect hired to do some remodeling for the Johnson ranch property, met Johnson, the Senate majority leader, clad only in his jockey shorts, came up to where White and Mrs. Johnson were standing. "I believe he must have had slippers on or something, but he was in his jockey shorts and nothing else. I didn't know whether to laugh, run, cry, or what . . . Or look. But . . . [Mrs. Johnson] was just as much at ease as if he was there without jockey shorts, with pants on."[37] And George Eastland Christian recalls being told by the President that he was balding and ought to hide his thin spots. Whereupon the President of one of the world's two most powerful nations, with Viet Nam and demonstrators crowding him from all sides, sat Christian down on the toilet seat and combed his hair like a fond mother for a half hour before being satisfied with his latest attempt at coiffing.[38]

While women don't exactly represent a minority, they do constitute an identifiable group that has received less than its due from politics. Johnson, who leaned on his mother and his wife for considerable advice and direction, never had misgivings about the place of women in political life. At his very first cabinet meeting as President, he said that "The day is over when top jobs are reserved for men." And a few weeks later, after having appointed some fifty women to government posts, he told the Women's National Press Club: "I would like at this time to make a policy announcement. I am unabashedly in favor of women." He went on: "I am insisting that women play a larger role in this government's plans and programs. Women have a willingness of heart; moreover, they have an instinct for rightness that is as important to decision-making as numbers or logic."[39] That this wasn't simply political rhetoric is indicated by the enlarged role of women in his administration.

Johnson is also given credit for having reformed the system of committee memberships in the Senate, a progressive move of which not all politicians approve even yet. But Richard Walker Bolling, Democrat from Missouri, called the reform "quite a remarkable rule . . . which we have never been able to achieve in the House. . . . everybody gets a good committee regardless of how junior they are; and nobody gets to be chairman of two committees, regardless of how senior they are. Before Mr. Johnson, that was not the case; and these seniors would pile up good committee on good committee and they would take every . . . damned chairmanship they could lay their hands on."[40]

Back to the treatment of blacks, McPherson tells of being with Johnson in his vice-presidential days when Senator John Cornelius Stennis, whom Johnson admired enormously, came in to protest the projected acceleration of civil rights under President Kennedy. Johnson responded by telling of his long-time cook and her husband, who doubled as Johnson's driver, having taken his automobile from Washington back to Texas and of their being forced to buy their lunches at grocery stores on the edges of town and preparing them themselves, of having to sleep in the car most of the nights, and of having to take to the fields to relieve themselves. "These people are the employees of the Vice-President of the United States, John," Johnson had said. According to McPherson, as a completely defused Stennis left the office, the Vice

President gave McPherson a big wink, as if to say, "We've got him!"[41]

As President Johnson told the students on a sentimental visit to an elementary school back in Cotulla in 1966, he had taught there when the school had no lunch facilities, no school buses, no playground equipment ("I took my first month's salary and invested in . . . [volleyballs and softball bats] for my children" he recalled), and he had worked as principal of five teachers, while teaching three grades himself, doubling as playground supervisor, coaching the boys' baseball team, directing debate, acting as song leader (that should have been taped!), and between times serving as assistant janitor. Yet, "In that year," he said, "I think I learned far more than I taught. And the greatest lesson was this one: . . . Our greatest resource is the skill, the vision, and the wisdom of our people."

Then he told how in Cotulla he had learned "the high price we pay for poverty and prejudice." "How long," he asked, "can we pay that price?" His answer was forthright: "no longer." He summarized thus: "Until the day comes when we can no longer hear the hum of the motor before daylight hauling the kids off in a truck to a beet patch or a cotton patch in the middle of the school year . . . I say we will not be satisfied with those conditions."[42]

Where are we then? Invariably, we return to the fact that as his time in service passed Johnson's liberality seemed to increase, a direction not followed by all politicians. We must also admit that Johnson was not above playing politics with issues, for after all he was—except on Viet Nam, which defied politics—a consummate politician who studied and practiced the art full time. He played to his constituencies tunes where he thought he had to, and like Barry Manilow he wrote the songs for those constituencies where he thought he could, and he made them sing along, whether they felt comfortable with the tune or not.

Most of all, I see Johnson as a symbol of that New South that is now a century or so old. (I don't know when we stop being New and become simply the South.) But in all the crybaby era from 1865 through the 1940s and with all the racial travail, much of it unnecessary, of the 1950s and 1960s, the South grew and retained a nucleus of decent people who didn't desert but instead stayed and toughed it out, ashamed of and humiliated by the actions of their antediluvian confrères, outraged by being assigned red-neck designation simply because of an accident of geographical birth south of the Ohio River, and hooted at by national comedians and pundit-authors because they talked more slowly and more softly and sometimes even took time to be polite.

But underneath the visible meanness of the South and southerners rested a hard core of decency lodged in the hearts and activities of decent people who could find no forum for their liberality among their own people. A person's first duty is to survive, as did the blacks for more than three centuries in the South, and as did many companion whites for the past century, feeling forever closer to the Medgar Wiley and Charles Everses, the James Howard Merediths, the lads at the lunch counters in the Carolinas, and the black children at Central High School in Little Rock than they did to their white brethren, insulated behind the walls of their air-conditioned homes and the lushness of their manicured lawns, talking about how blood would flow in the streets if the blacks or the browns or the poor whites ever got their share of the American Dream.

And then came Lyndon Johnson, big and sometimes gauche, and sometimes assertive and contentious, but almost always a compassionate man toward people who seldom tasted compassion, and he turned around many southern negatives, gave the deprived people a better opportunity to improve themselves through education, and guaranteed them access to some of the rights originally guaranteed in 1776 and thereafter, and in the process partially accomplished the impossible. If he didn't exactly change people's hearts, he made them self-conscious about their prejudices, and he helped the South to join the United States, perhaps even to take charge again.

If the foregoing sounds like effusive praise, let me say merely that I am more pro-Johnson than when I began examining the evidence that has produced this paper. In short, I started out to watch Lyndon B. Johnson turn 180 degrees as he progressed down the road toward national importance. Along the way I discovered that he was moving in a remarkably straight line, a generally progressive line, with now and then an aberration that might be inexcusable but no more damnable than the aberrations that most of the remainder of us sometimes perpetrate.

William S. White, who spent almost a professional lifetime covering Johnson, confirms this attitude. Says White: ". . . as we all get older, there are changes. In a political sense, in the philosophic sense, I have not seen any great changes [in Johnson].

I think at the end his political philosophy was basically what it was at the beginning. Mind you, when he was in the House and in the Senate, he was from Texas. His constituency was different, and he wasn't as liberal as he was later, but that was because he couldn't be. I don't think his mind was changed. I think circumstances changed."[43]

And so the metamorphosis promised in tonight's title did not occur after all, at least not in the political philosophy of Lyndon B. Johnson. Times changed. All of us changed with time, and Johnson changed along with us and the times. He simply had more opportunity to affect those changes, and with his acute political perception he often led and directed and challenged us as we leaped over a barrier that had stood in our way for either short periods or, as in the case of civil rights, for centuries.

As Johnson told a news conference in the summer of 1965, "I am particularly sensitive to the problems of the Negro and the problems of the city and the problems which the shift in population has caused, the problems of education. . . . I want to do my best to solve them in the limited time that I am allowed.

"I did not have that responsibility in the years past, and I did not feel it to the extent that I do today . . . I am going to try to provide all the leadership that I can, notwithstanding the fact that someone may point to a mistake or 100 mistakes that I made in my past."[44]

That he made mistakes is undeniable. That he corrected many of them is equally undeniable. But through it all, his line of procedure is as consistent as the investigator is likely to encounter for a person whose constituency enlarges from one employer to a district of several hundred thousand voters to a nation of two hundred million. If tonight I have pulled no curtain to reveal a changing person, it is because no revelations were there to be found. To declare otherwise would be to maneuver the evidence and strain the conclusion.

In short, the jury verdict must be, insofar as Lyndon Johnson's metamorphosis is concerned, CASE NOT PROVED.

Endnotes

1. Johnson, *The Vantage Point: Perspectives of the Presidency, 1963–1969* (New York, 1971), 97.
2. Interview, David G. McComb with Robert Jackson, Corpus Christi, Texas, Oral History Project, University of Texas at Austin. Tape and transcript are in the Lyndon Baines Johnson Presidential Library, Austin, Texas. The interviews took place between September 1968 and August 1974. All interviews cited hereinafter are in the same repository and are from the Oral History Project. The library will hereinafter be cited as LBJL.
3. *Time*, LXI (June 22, 1953), 23.
4. Johnson, *The Vantage Point*, 90.
5. *Ibid.*, 92.
6. *Washington Evening Star*, April 28, 1933.
7. Johnson to Mrs. Sam E. Johnson, October 17, 1928, LBJL.
8. Interview, McComb with Jackson, Corpus Christi, Texas.
9. Denmark to Richard R. Brown, February 9, 1937, United States Government Records, NYA 1935–1938, Box 6, Administrative Reports, June-September 1936, LBJL.
10. Bethune to Johnson, May 3, 1937, House of Representatives Papers, Box 2, "B", LBJL.
11. Interview, Joe B. Frantz with Thomas G. Corcoran, Washington, D. C.
12. Interview, Thomas Harrison Baker with Ernest Goldstein, Washington, D. C.
13. Joe B. Frantz, *37 Years of Public Service. The Honorable Lyndon B. Johnson* (Austin, 1974), n.p.
14. Allen to Sam Rayburn, November 7, 1940 (copy), LBJL.
15. Untitled speech, Austin, December 28, 1945, typescript, UIX.
16. "Not That Men Shall Die, but That Men May Live," *Congressional Record*, 79 Cong., 2 Sess., Appendix, A2153–55 (April 13, 1946).
17. White, *The Professional: Lyndon B. Johnson* (Boston and Cambridge, 1964), 155.
18. Johnson, *My Brother Lyndon* (New York, 1970), 74–75.
19. Interview, Frantz with Shivers, Austin, Texas.
20. Interview, Baker with Birkhead, Washington, D.C.
21. Interview, McComb with Rauh, Washington, D.C.
22. Interview, McComb with Claude C. Wild, Sr., Austin, Texas.
23. Interview, McComb with Rauh, Washington, D.C.
24. Interview, Frantz with Corcoran, Washington, D.C.
25. Interview, Baker with White, Washington, D.C.
26. Interview, Frantz with Reedy, Washington, D.C. Wilton B. Persons was deputy assistant to Eisenhower.
27. Interview, McComb with McPherson, Washington, D. C.; used with permission.
28. *Ibid.*
29. Billington, "Lyndon B. Johnson and Blacks: The Early Years," *Journal of Negro History*, LXII (January 1977), 26–42.
30. Johnson to Paul Bolton, July 21, 1949 (copy), LBJL; listed under LBJ, Names: Bolton, Paul, Box 12.

31. Carl Albert believes that Johnson's increased liberality as majority leader resulted from Johnson's brush with death during his heart attack in the middle 1950s. "After that," says the former Speaker of the House, ". . . (Johnson] began moving ahead, not as fast as the liberals wanted him to, but he began moving ahead with the national issues then. That was the making of the President back then." Interview, McComb with Albert, Washington, D. C.

32. Private conversation, Frantz with Thomberry, Stonewall, Texas.

33. Interview, Baker with Mitchell, Washington, D.C.

34. Interview, Frantz with Charles Jahleal Boatner, Washington, D.C.

35. Interview, McComb with Cohen, Washington, D.C.; used with permission.

36. Interview, Frantz with Linowitz, Washington, D.C.

37. Interview, Frantz with Roy White, Austin, Texas.

38. Interview, Frantz with Christian, Austin, Texas.

39. Interview, McComb with Richard Walker Bolling, Washington, D. C.; used with permission.

40. *Ibid*.

41. Interview, McComb with McPherson, Washington, D.C.; used with permission.

42. *Public Papers of the Presidents: Lyndon B. Johnson . . . 1966* (2 vols., Washington, D. C., 1967), II 1347–50; first two quotations on p. 1348, third on p. 1349, and fourth on p. 1350.

43. Interview, McComb with White, Washington, D.C.

44. *Public Papers of the Presidents: Lyndon B. Johnson . . . 1965* (2 vols., Washington, D. C., 1966), 11, 742.

Lyndon B. Johnson and Blacks

The Early Years

Monroe Billington*

History will award President Lyndon B. Johnson a prominent role in the legal advancement of civil rights for blacks. Judicial decisions, presidential actions, and congressional legislation promoting those rights occurred during the presidencies of Roosevelt, Truman, Eisenhower, and Kennedy, but these were only a prelude to the Johnson administration. Even though much remained undone when Johnson left office, the years when he was President—1963–1968—constituted an important era in the progress of civil rights for blacks. Passed during the Eisenhower administration, the Civil Rights Acts of 1957 and 1960 inaugurated the post-Reconstruction legislation helpful to blacks.[1] Considerably more significant was the Johnson administration's Civil Rights Act of 1964, an omnibus bill whose most far-reaching provisions related to nondiscrimination in public accommodations.[2] Fast upon the heels of this measure came the Voting Rights Act of 1965, providing for elaborate and more effective federal machinery for registering voters and assuring the right to vote in certain areas of the nation.[3] In early 1968 Congress passed another comprehensive civil rights bill, whose major provisions dealt with the reduction of discrimination in housing.[4] While President, Johnson pressed for the passage of these three bills, and he willingly signed each of them into law.

In addition, Johnson took other public actions which helped identify his administration with black civil rights. In February 1965 he issued an Executive Order designed to coordinate the various agencies of the federal government involved in the elimination of discrimination and the promotion of equal opportunity. Also, Johnson appointed a number of blacks to high office.[5]

Johnson spoke many times in behalf of the civil rights of black Americans. During the years he was President, on at least 232 occasions he made public references to the subject.[6] The highpoint of the President's public remarks came on March 15, 1965, when he spoke on black civil rights before a joint session of Congress and a national television audience. Referring to black voting rights, equal economic opportunity, and adequate housing, Johnson issued an emotional appeal to the nation to put aside "the crippling legacy of bigotry and injustice."[7] No President had ever publicly identified himself so closely with the problems of the nation's largest racial minority.

Was President Johnson sincere when he pressed for civil rights legislation, issued Executive Orders, and spoke out publicly for black rights? Did he always hold such expressed views? Was he consistent throughout his career regarding civil rights for blacks? Or was he an expedient politician who desired only to advance his own career by yielding to current pressures? This essay, focusing on Johnson's early relationships with and attitudes toward blacks and their civil rights, is addressed to these questions.

Lyndon B. Johnson was born in 1908 on a farm in Blanco County in central Texas, and he grew up in the small town of Johnson City, Blanco's county seat. Of the country's 4,311 inhabitants in 1910, only 350 were black. By 1920 the population had declined to 4,063, with blacks totaling only 169; and in 1930 these two figures had further declined to 3,842 and 133.[8] With so few blacks residing in the county during his childhood years, young Johnson had hardly any occasion to know or have dealings with blacks. Sometimes a black family passed

* Professor of History, New Mexico State University, Los Cruces, New Mexico.

From *The Journal of Negro History*, Vol. 62, issue 1, January 1977 by Monroe BIllington. Copyright © 1977 by Association for the Study of African-American Life and History. Reprinted by permission.

through Johnson City on the way somewhere else; an occasional black migrant was hired to help the family harvest its crops; but that was about all. Young Johnson matured without strong color prejudice. He neither liked nor disliked blacks. Not being visible, blacks were not an issue in his life. Reflecting the southern attitudes of other whites in the county, Johnson assumed that blacks and whites should be separated; but Blanco County was not a part of the old Confederacy, and Johnson later confessed that he "never sat on my parents' or grandparents' knees listening to nostalgic tales of the antebellum South.[9] Southern traditions and blacks were on the margin of young Johnson's frame of reference. The Mexican-American minority in Blanco County was no greater than was the black,[10] although Johnson had a few Mexican-American playmates. The only minority of some significance was the German-Americans,[11] and distinctions between them and the Anglo-Americans were virtually nonexistent. Under these circumstances, Johnson had no reason to be prejudiced toward any minority group–nor to feel any sympathy for such groups if they were downtrodden. Johnson did not seethe with indignation in regard to class or race struggles. In the cultural isolation of the Pedernales valley, he took his own rights for granted and paid little attention to his fellow men who did not have the same rights.[12]

This situation was altered when Johnson became a young adult. After attending Southwest Texas State Teachers College for a year and a half, Johnson took a job as an elementary school teacher in Cotulla, Texas, a small LaSalle County community in south Texas. Cotulla had a large Mexican-American population, and because of the tradition of segregation only Mexican-American pupils attended the small school to which he was assigned. During the 1928–29 school year at Cotulla, Johnson had intimate contact with Mexican-Americans. He came to love the children. He spent money from his own pockets so his poverty-stricken pupils could have play equipment at their impoverished school. He spent hours outside the classroom with his pupils in extracurricular activities such as softball, volleyball, debating, and a literary society.[13] In his later years Johnson often made reference to his Cotulla experience and the deep impressions his young pupils made upon him.[14] Also, for the first time in his life he became conscious of the white society's discrimination toward the Mexican-American minority, and in later years this consciousness was extended

to include blacks. This consciousness evolved into a genuine caring for members of minority groups.[15]

This concern became apparent when Johnson was director of Texas' National Youth Administration (NYA) from July 1935 to February 1937. The youngest state administrator in the nation, Lyndon Johnson was eager to succeed as he directed the activities of the largest NYA state agency. Johnson wrote thorough reports, unceasingly strove to acquire more money for Texas youth, instituted programs which were copied by other states (the most notable being the construction of "pocket- sized" highway parks), and garnered more than his share of newspaper publicity. His generally good job as state administrator greatly impressed the national office of the NYA.[16]

Johnson's concern was to help the youth of Texas—regardless of color—during the gloomy days of the Great Depression, and his administration was generally nondiscriminatory. Soon after Johnson set up his statewide headquarters in Austin, he initiated a meeting with black leaders in the city. In the basement of a black Methodist Church, Johnson informed the blacks that he was eager to assist jobless black youths. Some blacks were surprised that he would make such an overture, and many were distrustful of his motives. One black contemporary has concluded that Johnson helped blacks not only because he desired to do a good job, but also because he "cared for people."[17]

In view of Texas' historical racial customs, NYA director Johnson decided to have two advisory committees, one white, one black. He appointed leading black citizens to the Negro Advisory Committee.[18] This committee met separately from its white counterpart, its primary function being to assist Johnson and his staff in planning and promoting NYA programs for black youth.[19] The Negro Advisory Committee worked diligently, and Johnson's superiors were impressed with the cooperation its members gave Johnson.[20] Throughout his nearly two years in office Johnson met on a number of occasions with the presidents of the Negro colleges in Texas to discuss plans for greater participation by Texas Negro youths in the state program. These college presidents gave Johnson their full cooperation.[21]

Blacks had good reason to cooperate with Johnson. His lengthy monthly reports to the national office carried details of projects designed to give work to black young people, as well as reports revealing how much money college students at Negro colleges had received. Students in numerous Negro high schools and thirteen colleges regularly received NYA aid. While the figures varied, nearly 1,000 black high school students and nearly 500 black college students regularly received NYA aid in Texas.[22] These figures jumped for a brief period in 1936 when Johnson requested and received an additional $10,000 to be used specifically for Negro colleges.[23] On one occasion Johnson travelled to Washington to plead successfully for increased funds for Negro colleges. He somehow always managed to wrangle more money than his normal quotas allowed, and he never turned money back.[24]

Besides the general monies made available to black students, Johnson's administration supported a number of specific projects for black youth. It established successful domestic training projects for girls at four black colleges, plus one in the city of Corsicana in cooperation with the WPA Emergency Division. Johnson himself made trips to the local campuses to further the progress of these projects. On one such occasion he was accompanied to Prairie View State College by Byron Mitchell, State Director of the National Reemployment Service, who was interested in making arrangements for the placement of these project-trained girls in private employment.[25] Johnson established a number of camps to provide vocational instruction for unemployed young women, one near Houston being for blacks only.[26] The NYA financed a constructive clean-up program employing black boys and girls in the town of Taylor, when a sanitation and health survey of the city revealed problems regarding community health and the spread of disease.[27] Johnson also showed interest in a "Negro research project" to be established in Houston, and in response to a letter from the President of Prairie View State College he used his influence to have established near that campus a Civilian Conservation Corps (CCC) camp for black young men.[28]

The most interesting of Johnson's projects was the Freshman College Center Program, an educational endeavor sponsored by the NYA in conjunction with colleges or universities, offering first-year-college work to students whose families were subject to work relief. He established a number of such centers in the state, fifteen of which served a total of 471 black college freshmen.[29] Because of the success of all these programs, Johnson received continued praise from his superiors. After visiting San Antonio, Austin, and Houston, a field representative from the national office wrote: "I believe I know the Negro condition in the Southern states, and no one would be more delighted to see them have the kind of training that Mr. Johnson is setting up in Texas. The Texas Director is doing what many of us are talking." The letter concluded with the statement that the Texas training program "is a credit to the National Youth Administration."[30]

The NYA files contain no information that Johnson discriminated against black youth; no comments of disparagement; nothing negative. To be sure, he operated a segregated administration, but that was to be expected in view of the national organization and the times. There are at least two hints that Johnson discriminated against blacks within his own administration. After conferring with Mrs. Mary McLeod Bethune (national director of the NYA's division of Negro activities), the national Deputy Executive Director of the NYA recommended to Johnson that he hire a Negro assistant to help with black youth programs. Such an appointment would contribute to "a more efficient and harmonious program."[31] Johnson apparently did not reply to this letter, and he certainly did not follow the suggestion. Even though the members of the Negro Advisory Committee cooperated with Johnson, they complained when so few blacks were placed in paid supervisory positions on Johnson's staff. They were unhappy that all the supervisors of the Freshman College Centers were white. After the Johnson administration established a Junior Employment Service in Fort Worth, it assigned white counselors to interview black youths, In a letter to Johnson a field supervisor remarked pointedly: "The fact that the Government is aiding and supporting various projects in the State, seems to me to allow leeway for liberal and tolerant groups and individuals in the community to try to make the social patterns more just and equitable for all the people in the community."[32]

Johnson did not consciously discriminate against black youths, but he did not appoint blacks to paid supervisory capacities, and he was interested only in helping black youths economically, not in altering traditional social patterns. In a special report to his superiors, Johnson wrote: "The racial question during the past one hundred years in Texas . . . has resolved itself to a definite system of customs which cannot be up-set over night. So long as these customs are observed, there is peace and harmony between the races in Texas, but it is exceedingly difficult to step over a line so long established, and to up-set a custom so deeply rooted, by any act which would be shockingly against precedence . . ."[33] Johnson's was a paternalistic administration committed to the status quo in regard to race relations.

Johnson retained this general attitude toward Texas blacks throughout his nearly twelve-year stint as a national congressman. Having resigned from his NYA job in March 1937 to run for the position vacated by the death of the incumbent congressman of Texas' Tenth District, Johnson won the special election and took his seat in July 1937. The Tenth District is composed of ten counties in central Texas, including Travis, in which the state capital is located. On the western edge of the state's black belt, the district's counties varied greatly in the percentages of blacks in their populations. In 1940 the eastern-most Washington County was highest in black percentages with 38.1, while Burnet, the northwestern-most county, had only 1.7 percent of its population black. The average for all ten counties was 20.7 percent blacks. During an era when blacks were generally disfranchised, Johnson felt no compulsion to appeal to them. Even though he campaigned on the basis of being a representative for all the people, he omitted blacks when he listed the people in the district who had problems which he hoped to help solve.[34] No evidence indicates that the subject of black rights or problems arose in Johnson's 1937 congressional campaign, nor that black rights were issues in the subsequent congressional elections. The same statement can be made for Johnson's successful attempt in 1941 to move up to the Senate.[35]

Congressman Johnson concerned himself with constituent requests of both whites and blacks. He tried to answer every letter on the day it was received, and he earned the reputation of having never failed to answer a letter from a constituent. He was not embarrassed to be called "the bell boy" for his district. At the end of his congressional career he stated that he had been happy to run errands for "the farmer, the veteran, the little businessman, and all the people."[36] While he did not specifically list blacks, he did not exclude them from his assistance.[37] When federal slum clearance money was first made available, Johnson persuaded Congress to earmark $500,000 for a public housing project to alleviate somewhat the horrible conditions in an Austin slum inhabited by blacks and Mexican-Americans. In addition to looking after his black constituents specifically, Johnson worked and voted for legislation which would help both white and

black Texans. He always favored more money for the Farm Security Administration, which provided relief for tenant farmers and sharecroppers, and in the late 1930's a bureaucrat in that agency observed that Johnson "was the first man in Congress from the South ever to go to bat for the Negro farmer."[38] He favored increased appropriations for the National Youth Administration and the Civilian Conservation Corps, and he worked to insure that blacks were included within the provisions of the Agricultural Adjustment Act of 1938.

Throughout his congressional years, Johnson made few public statements revealing his attitudes toward blacks. While he did not join his southern colleagues in their anti-black remarks in Congress, neither did he protest their rantings; indeed, viewed from the perspective of his voting record alone, Johnson was a traditional southern congressman on the subject of civil rights for blacks. He voted against an anti-lynching bill in 1940, as well as anti-poll tax bills in 1942, 1943, 1945, and 1947. During the Second World War, when the Congress desired to provide more convenient absentee ballots for overseas soldiers, he voted with southerners who favored a state (as opposed to a federal) ballot, so that the states could control the voting process (i.e. regulate the black vote). In 1946 when Congress was considering a federal school-lunch program, he voted "No" on an antidiscrimination amendment offered by Adam Clayton Powell of Harlem, and in that same year he voted with those southerners who successfully employed parliamentary tactics to kill a bill to create a permanent Fair Employment Practices Commission (FEPC).[39] Johnson justified these votes on the basis of states' rights. He believed that law enforcement, voting qualifications, and economic opportunity were the proper domains of the states, and he did not want the national government involved in these areas of American life. Whenever he made these statements, he sounded very much like his southern colleagues. He protested that he was not "against" blacks, but was rather "for" states' rights.

When Johnson spoke with black constituents in his congressional district, he often tediously explained that he did not actually vote against particular civil rights bills; rather he voted to recommit them for revision or study.[40] He hoped these technical explanations would make blacks less unhappy with his votes. At other times he frankly informed the blacks that he had to vote with the southern leaders in Congress so that he could obtain their support on other matters of importance. He reminded the blacks that the civil rights bills against which he had voted would not have passed anyway, and he preferred to wait and vote "Yes" when his vote would make a difference. Johnson said, "I must vote this way, but I'm for you and I will get what I can for you in the future." In reference to civil rights, over and over again Johnson said, "Timing is important." Black supporters knew they were taking chances by backing Johnson during those years, but they had faith that Johnson "would do something for them when he had a real opportunity."[41] But many Texas blacks were suspicious of Johnson. They did not believe that he sincerely wanted to help them, and they looked upon him as cynically opportunistic in regard to their civil rights. These blacks believed not only that Johnson's public stands were conservative, but also that his private views were conservative.[42] Johnson left no records revealing his private thoughts, but his public stance tended to undermine his protestations that he was a true friend of blacks.

Johnson continued to take anti-civil rights stands after his career in the House of Representatives ended. When he ran for the Senate in 1948, he opposed President Harry Truman's announced civil rights program. Opening his senatorial bid on May 22 before a large crowd in Austin and over a twenty-station radio hookup, Johnson said: "The Civil Rights Program is a farce and a sham—an effort to set up a police state in the guise of liberty. I am opposed to that program. I have voted AGAINST the so-called poll tax repeal bill; the poll tax should be repealed by those states which enacted them. I have voted AGAINST the so-called anti-lynching bill; the state can, and DOES, enforce the law against murder. I have voted AGAINST the FEPC; if a man can tell you whom you must hire, he can tell you whom you can't hire."[43] Despite these remarks, Johnson did not emphasize civil rights as a campaign issue; rather his major campaign themes were preparedness, peace, and progress. Furthermore, among Johnson's ten opponents in the Democratic primary, only two were serious contenders for the nomination, and both of them were more opposed to black civil rights than was Johnson.[44] The three major candidates devoted much attention to the nation's foreign policy toward Russia, inflation, taxes, government controls, and deficit spending. Other subjects were the Taft-Hartley Act, selective service, and universal military training. As a

campaign issue civil rights trailed far behind.[45] After his opening speech, Johnson made no references to civil rights in his canned speeches. In the eastern sections of the state where prejudices were stronger, he occasionally reiterated his anti-civil rights stand, but the issue remained secondary.[46] A survey of 147 Texas newspapers revealed that civil rights was hardly mentioned during the 1948 campaign.[47]

Black newspapers gave little more attention to the civil rights issue than did the candidates or the white-controlled Texas papers. During this era Texas black newspapers were almost without exception politically independent. They wrote about discrimination, bigotry, segregation, inequality, and injustices based on color, but they seldom became more specific. They advocated black voting rights, but they said little about specific elections and the 1948 campaign was no exception.[48] The Dallas *Express* gave no attention to Johnson as a candidate in 1948, until after the runoff primary had been held."[49] It carried editorials on the subjects of civil rights, Truman, the Dixiecrats, and the Wallaceites, but it made no comments upon the Texas senatorial contest. The Houston *Informer* editorially criticized politicians who favored states' rights and who refused to consider civil rights advances for blacks, but it mentioned no candidate specifically–including Johnson.[50] The *Informer* supported Johnson after the runoff primary ended.[51]

The results of the July 24 Texas primary showed Coke Stevenson with 477,077 votes, Lyndon Johnson with 405,617, and George E. B. Peddy with 237,195, The eight minor candidates won a total of 82,503.[52] While issues had been discussed somewhat during the first primary, the runoff primary between Stevenson and Johnson focused almost entirely on personalities. If the issue of civil rights was played down before July 24, after that date it was nonexistent. Truman's renomination at the Democratic national convention in Philadelphia on July 15, the adoption of strong civil rights plank and the Dixiecrat walkout did not inject the civil rights issue into the Texas runoff primary. Nor did a southern filibuster of an anti-poll tax bill in the summer of 1948 bring out the issue in Texas.[53]

The runoff primary, held on August 28, did not immediately settle the political dust. The totals were so close that it took weeks of counting and recounting, much political maneuvering, and a lengthy court battle before Johnson was certified as the 87-vote victor. In the meantime, political manipulation, lawsuits, and charges of fraud and corruption occurred, all of which meant that no issue existed after August 28 except who would be the Democratic nominee. The race against an unknown Republican in the November election was wholly anticlimactic. Here again civil rights was not an issue. When President Truman made a train tour through Texas late in the campaign, Johnson happily rode across the state with the President, even though Johnson had spoken against Truman's civil rights program.[54] Such actions must have created some confusion in the minds of Texas voters.

A poll conducted a few weeks prior to the first primary revealed that an appalling number of voters were ignorant of the candidates' views. To a question, "What do you think these candidates' stands are on Truman" (i.e. civil rights), the following resulted:[55]

	for	against	don't know
Stevenson	15%	31%	54%
Johnson	24	12	64
Peddy	7	13	80

The white voters in the cotton-growing, heavily black populated counties of eastern Texas had voted for Peddy in large numbers in the first primary, but they switched their votes to Johnson in the second. Perhaps Johnson's occasional references to his anti-civil rights stand, or at least his image, had something to do with this new votes.[56]

When rural blacks exercised their right to vote, an estimated 65 to 90 percent of them voted for Johnson in the runoff.[57] Since about one-half of Texas' blacks lived in urban areas in 1948 and since a higher percentage of these blacks were involved in politics, the black urban vote was more significant than the black rural vote. In heavily populated black urban precincts in Dallas and Houston, Johnson ran up large majorities.[58] Many black leaders in the major cities had campaigned actively throughout the race and had contributed substantial sums to Johnson "because we believed in him."[59] Why this loyalty? Blacks looked upon Johnson as the liberal candidate. They knew Stevenson had not helped them while he was governor, and they preferred Johnson even though the latter was by no means liberal on the race issue.[60] In the national presidential campaign, Texas blacks chose Truman over Henry Wallace. They believed that Wallace was too pro-Russia and they felt he was too idealistic about civil rights.[61] They rejected Wallace because his racial views were too liberal (*i.e.*, impractical), and they rejected Stevenson because his were too conservative (*i.e.*, discriminatory). Thus, Texas blacks voted overwhelmingly for Truman and Johnson; they looked upon both men as moderates even though the two candidates disagreed on civil rights.[62]

While in the House of Representatives, Johnson had earned the reputation as a politician who knew where political power lay and who unabashedly moved toward it. Because of the bitterness and questionable procedures surrounding his narrow primary victory, Johnson informed John Stennis, Mississippi Senator and member of the Senate Rules Committee, that his (Johnson's) victory might be contested when his name was presented to the Senate for acceptance. In his reply Stennis informed Johnson that he would not judge the case until the facts were in, but Stennis negated this impartiality when he continued, "As far as our personal relationships are concerned, I just have a feeling that we will have a lot in common, I came very near being a Texan myself, as my parents once lived there before I was born."[63] In his reply Johnson thanked Stennis for his letter and wrote, "Your friendship will always be remembered and reciprocated."[64] By making contact with the only southerner on the Rules Committee, Johnson was not only solidifying his relationship with a key man in the Senate, but also he was deepening his ties with the southern bloc which had had great power in the Senate for many years.

This became patently clear when Johnson publicly aligned himself with the southern bloc less than two months after he took the oath of office as a senator in January 1949. Even though the civil rights issue had been muted in the Texas senatorial race, it was one of the major issues in the national arena. Truman's victory in the presidential race encouraged the President to continue to press for civil rights legislation, setting the stage for yet another southern filibuster in the Senate. Richard Russell of Georgia, leader of the southerners, had begun to apply filibustering tactics to motions to take up bills he opposed. To prevent his maneuver, Truman's supporters attempted to extend Senate Rule XXII to motions as well as to actual bills. Rule XXII permitted an end to debate on a bill when two-thirds of the senators present voted to do so. For over two weeks of the early days of the Eighty-first

Congress, this procedural question dominated the Senate's attention. Lyndon Johnson early realized that Richard Russell was a powerful leader, and the new Senator already had begun to flatter and cultivate the slow-talking Georgian.[65] Eager to become involved, Johnson persuaded Russell to permit him to make his first Senate speech during the filibuster. On March 9, Johnson delivered his now-famous address. Referring to "we of the South," Johnson firmly tied himself to the southern bloc with this speech. He advanced all the traditional arguments about free speech (i.e., the right to filibuster) which southern senators had been repeating for many years. Admitting that the filibuster was in fact against civil rights, not just a matter of free speech, he attacked Harry Truman's program unmercifully. Reiterating his stand that states should outlaw the poll tax and punish lynchers, he deplored efforts to pass national legislation. He also spoke out against the FEPC. Advancing an old southern platitude, he said, "We cannot legislate love."[66]

Although Johnson rationalized that he was not speaking against blacks, reaction from the minority race in Texas was immediate. The executive secretary of the Houston branch of the NAACP telegraphed: "THE NEGROES WHO SENT YOU TO CONGRESS ARE ASHAMED TO KONW THAT YOU HAVE STOOD ON THE FLOOR AGAINST THEM TODAY. DO NOT FORGET THAT YOU WENT TO WASHINGTON BY A SMALL MAJORITY VOTE AND THAT WAS BECAUSE OF THE NEGRO VOTE. THERE WILL BE ANOTHER ELECTION AND WE WILL BE REMEMBERING WHAT YOU HAD TO SAY TODAY."[67] Johnson's reply,[68] which majored on the general principle of unlimited debate, was unacceptable, and a delegation of Houston blacks traveled to Washington to protest. The confrontation ended unsatisfactorily after heated words had been exchanged between the visitors and the new Senator.[69] Other NAACP chapters passed resolutions censoring Johnson for his remarks.

Black newspaperman Carter Wesley editorially criticized the filibusterers,[70] and in strongly worded letters the powerful black leader expressed to Johnson his disappointment in the March 1949 speech.[71] Other disapproving blacks wrote to Johnson, and the Senator did not satisfy them when he pointed out, "Too many people confused the cloture issue with civil rights. Actually they had no direct connection since there have been many filibusters in the Senate on other subjects."[72] He

seemed hurt when he was accused of political expediency and when blacks pointed out the implications of his speech.[73] He wrote, "It has been a matter of profound regret to me that many Negro citizens of Texas have viewed my speech in the Senate as an affront to them. I did not and would not make a speech in that spirit."[74] White supporters of civil rights expressed their objections too. When Johnson had 15,000 copies of his speech printed and distributed in Texas, one man mailed a copy back to Johnson with a note scribbled across the front. With an arrow pointing to the "B." in Lyndon B. Johnson, he wrote: "Does the 'B' stand for 'Bilbo'? Really, now—we Texans aren't as ignorant (or as proud of our traditions) as you give us credit for being. Have the courage to defend your own convictions, Mr. Johnson, and you'll gather more votes than you will by aligning yourself with the old die-hards of the South."[75] Another disgusted Texan returned a copy of the speech with the following typed across the front: "Dear Lyndon: The Post Office Dept goes into the red handling this kind of hot air. Why don't you fellows cut out the bull and get down to work. A supporter of yours."[76]

Johnson's arguments in his replies to his constituents centered on free speech as a principle. He believed that civil rights issues and free speech in the Senate were distinctly separate issues. He argued that if the last vestiges of free speech and free debate were stricken, the nation would be playing directly into the hands of the Communists. He stated that the right of unlimited debate was the last hope of protection for the laboring man, the Negro, and all other minority groups against ruthless majorities.[77] He believed that the civil rights bills as then drawn were "obviously unconstitutional and certainly unworkable, more likely to create chaos than goodwill."[78] He would like to see poll taxes eliminated in Texas but not by federal legislation.[79] He believed that "the crime of lynching should be punished promptly and effectively," but this was a matter of state enforcement.[80] He believed the United States had "made great strides toward our goal through conviction rather than the proposed method of compulsion which we are considering here now. "[81]

When one Texan accused Johnson of having changed his position, he replied, "I can assure you that my views regarding the nation's difficulties are exactly the same as they were when I came to Congress twelve years ago. I said in 1937 that I was opposed to the poll tax and have said it in every campaign since. The same is true of my feelings regarding lynching. I abhor all types of violence and feel that strict measures should be taken to curb it *by the proper forum.*"[82] To another he wrote, "The position that I took in my speech is the same that I took in six campaigns for Congress and two for the United States Senate . . ."[83] To a personal friend who had written him after the speech, he said that the anti-poll tax bill, the anti-lynching bill, and the FEPC were not germane to the subject of civil rights. "To secure these rights," he confided, "I think we must carry on the frontal assault on the 'ill-housed, ill-clad, ill-fed' problem facing part of our nation. Until this problem is met, all your other legislation is built upon sand. That is the end of the problem I hope I can grab hold of and do something about during my years in the Senate."[84] Johnson believed that he remained wholly consistent in regard to civil rights for blacks. On the basis of principle he had continually opposed certain federal legislation for them; at the same time he did what he could to help the economic conditions of blacks.

But one should not forget that Johnson was in touch with the sentiment of white Texans. He knew that his anti-civil rights stand in the 1948 campaign and in the Senate in the spring of 1949 reflected the attitudes of the great majority of the Texas voters. While blacks and liberal whites wrote letters of criticism, a much larger number of Texans who agreed with him expressed their approval. Johnson appreciated these constituents' words of support, and he reveled in the more laudatory letters.[85] In all likelihood his positive response to letters of praise was greater than it otherwise might have been because he was offended by rumors that he had agreed to take a stronger anti-civil rights stand in return for assurance that the recent disputed election would end in his favor.[86]

Throughout his first term in the Senate, Johnson continued to hold the same public stand in regard to civil rights for blacks which he had previously held. In May 1949 he voted "Yes" on a discriminatory public accommodations amendment proposed by Mississippi Senator James Eastland to the perennial District of Columbia home rule bill. In 1950 he voted to table an amendment to outlaw poll taxes; he voted down the line with his southern colleagues against an FEPC measure the Senate was considering; he voted to table an amendment to prohibit racial discrimination in unions; and he supported an unsuccessful amendment to a military draft law

providing that a young man have the right to choose to serve in a unit composed only of members of his own race.[87]

When the San Antonio branch of the NAACP approved a resolution demanding that Johnson support Civil Rights Legislation, since citizens were "being denied the rights of first-class citizenship,"[88] Johnson replied, "I cannot agree that the civil rights legislation as it is currently written would extend to any citizen 'the rights of first-class citizenship.' First-class citizenship begins at the meal table, in the schools, at the doctor's office, and many places other than in court . . . . In the future, as in the past, I shall work to equalize the opportunity and reward of all Americans through better housing, better schooling, better health, and all those things which are the true rights of first-class citizenship."[89] To those who protested his stand, Johnson reminded them that he had supported public housing, federal aid to education, and many other measures "which have raised the living standards of all our people and expanded the economic opportunity for all."[90] Even while opposing anti-lynching bills and the FEPC, he wrote, "I shall support those measures which will help make America a better place for men to live."[91] To another he wrote, "I should not like to see the people of Texas and the South undergo the wave of riots and stress which I believe would follow if we tried to force people to do what they are not ready to do of their own free will and accord."[92]

When the Supreme Court in 1954 handed down its famous decision requiring the desegregation of the nation's schools, southerners in Congress circulated a "Southern Manifesto" expressing their opposition. Every senator from the old Confederacy except Johnson signed the protest document. He was "firmly opposed to forced integration," and he believed that "the states should be allowed to work out their own solutions to problems coming within their proper jurisdiction,"[93] but he could not sign the document. To a constituent he wrote, "Now that the Supreme Court has ruled, . . . I can only hope that the problem will be worked out reasonably and with fairness to all concerned."[94] In the wake of the Supreme Court decision blacks and others more strongly pressured the Congress to pass civil rights legislation, and a second "Southern Manifesto" was circulated in March 1956. Johnson did not sign this statement either. Having been elected Minority Leader in 1953 and elevated to Majority Leader in 1954, Johnson refrained from signing the documents because he did not want to endanger his position of leadership in the Senate. He told reporters, "I am not a civil rights advocate."[95] A few months later when a well-known reporter entitled a nationally-syndicated column "Lyndon Pushes Civil Rights," Johnson protested that he was not involved in planning civil rights legislation.[96] Johnson was upset that a nationally-circulated newspaper column so clearly identified him with efforts on Capitol Hill to legislate in this area.

Despite these protests, for the first time in his life Johnson in 1956 began to give serious thought to the possibility of the passage of a civil rights bill and to his role in that action. In a three-page memorandum to the Senator, George Reedy addressed himself to the then current civil rights "uproar" in the Democratic party. Reddy relegated to failure any policy which would approach the civil fights issue from the standpoint of recovering lost votes for the Democratic party; "Nevertheless, some effort should be made to produce legislation along the civil rights lines—not to recover votes but simply because the issue has reached a point where some action is necessary."[97] Johnson had always believed that "timing is important." With the Democratic party on the verge of splitting over the civil fights issue, with black pressures mounting, with Johnson's leadership under fire because of inaction, and with the Senator beginning to have more than vague aspirations to be President, Johnson decided that the time had come for Congress to pass a mild civil rights bill. The result was the Civil Rights Act of 1957. Whatever the weaknesses of that measure, it inaugurated an era of civil rights legislation unparalleled in the nation's history. Lyndon Johnson had taken a public stand for civil lights, and as Congress passed each succeeding law, he became more firmly committed to civil rights for all Americans. His later senatorial career, his vice-presidential years, and his presidency attest to his public posture. No evidence exists to indicate that his private thoughts in those years differed from this public statements and actions.

Cynics say that Johnson moved from anti-civil rights stands in the 1930's and 1940's to pro-civil rights stands in the late 1950's because he was ambitious, expedient, oppportunistic, and politically motivated. Johnson saw himself as totally consistent, always the friend of blacks even when voting against civil rights bills. Johnson was too complex to be categorized simply as "consistent" or "expedient." The record shows that over three decades in public life Johnson was not consistent. But that record shows less expediency than the growth of an individual in public life. While he was a congressman from Texas' Tenth District, Johnson naturally reflected in his voting record the anti-civil rights views of the majority of his constituents, during an era when black pressures were not great and when publicity about the plight of minorities was limited. When he became a senator his early Senate voting record and speeches continued to reflect his now statewide constituency. Concurrent with his elevation to the leadership of the Democratic Party in the national Congress was an increased national consciousness of minority rights and Johnson's own thoughts about the presidency. The converging of these streams of consciousness pushed Johnson in the direction of public action for blacks and explains his dominant role in the passing of the first civil rights act since Reconstruction. As Vice-President and as President, Johnson had a nationwide constituency at a time when black frustrations often resulted in violence. His role as national leader compelled him to act for the interests not only of the oppressed minority but also for all the people of the country. The story of Johnson's public stance on civil rights is one of evolution, of maturation, of growth.

The same may be said of Johnson's attitudes toward blacks and their civil rights, although here the evolutionary process was less dramatic. Johnson's love for people, with him from his earliest years, compelled him to be concerned about minority groups—from the Mexican-American children in Cotulla in the 1920's to the bitter black rioters in the 1960's. Even though he did not support civil rights legislation in the 1930's and 1940's there is no reason to believe that he did not sincerely desire to help blacks. The practical situation tempered his private attitudes. He had often told blacks that he would help them when had the power and when the timing was right; when those two conditions were met he carried out his promises.

Endnotes

1. *United States Statutes at Large*, vol. 71, pp. 634–38; vol. 74, pp. 86–92.
2. *Ibid.*, vol. 78, pp. 241–68.
3. *Ibid.*, vol. 79, pp. 437–46.
4. *Ibid.*, vol. 82, pp. 73–92.

5. For a detailed study of the progress of black civil rights and the Johnson presidential years, see James C. Harvey, *Black Civil Rights During the Johnson Administration* (Jackson: University and College Press of Mississippi, 1973).

6. Civil Rights Index of Statements of Lyndon B. Johnson as President, Lyndon Baines Johnson Library. (Hereafter referred to as LBJL.)

7. Remarks, Joint Session of Congress, 3–15–65," Box 25, Statements of Lyndon Baines Johnson, *ibid.*

8. *Thirteenth Census of the United States Taken In The Year 1910. Vol. III. Population*, 1910 (Washington: Government Printing Office, 1913), pg. 806; *Fourteenth Census of the United States Taken In The Year 1920. Vol. III. Population*, 1920 (Washington: Government Printing Office, 1922), pg. 991; *Fifteenth Census of the United States: 1930. Vol. III. Population*, 1930 (Washington: Government hinting Office, 1932), p. 976.

9. Lyndon Baines Johnson, *The Vantage Point: Perspectives of the Presidency*, 1963–1969 (New York: Holt, Rinehart & Winston, 1971), p. 155.

10. The U.S. census data for 1910 and 1920 do not list Mexican-American numbers apart from the white majority, but the 1930 census shows only 123 Mexican-American residents in Blanco County. *Fifteenth Census of the United States: 1930. Vol. III. Population*, 1930 (Washington: Government Printing Office, 1932), pp. 1014–15.

11. *Ibid.*, p. 976.

12. LBJ to Walter Cronkite, C.B.S. television program, Feb. 1, 1973, typed copy of transcript in LBJL; Rowland Evans and Robert Novak, *Lyndon B. Johnson: The Exercise of Power* (New York: New American Library, 1966), pp. 7, 120.

13. Dorothy Nichols Interview, Sept. 24, 1968, Oral History Collection, LBJL.

14. *E.g.*, see the transcript of the C.B.S. television program, Feb. 1, 1973, in *ibid*; and his major television address on civil rights in 1965: "Remarks, Joint Session of Congress, 3–15–65," Box 25, Statements of Lyndon Baines Johnson, *ibid.*

15. William S. White Interview, March 5 and 10, 1969, Oral History Collection, *ibid.* This care was illustrated in 1949 when Johnson was on a cross-town bus in New York City. An elderly black woman boarded the bus, and since no vacant seat was available, Johnson rose and gave his seat to her. His companion later asked Johnson why he had done this and the reply was that he hoped that if his mother entered a crowded bus, some man, whether black or white, would offer her his seat. Personal letter from Homer Thornberry, April 17, 1975.

16. Richard R. Brown to LBJ, March 17 and 20, 1936; LBJ to Brown, March 12, 1936, Box 2, NYA Files.

(These and future references to NYA Files are from copies in the LBJL.)

17. Telephone interview with O.H. Elliott, March 4, 1975.

18. Brown to LBJ, Dec. 2 and 19, 1935; LBJ to Brown, Dec. 7, 1935; N.Y.A. Table I, Texas State Advisory Committee, Dec. 24, 1936, Box 4, NYA Files.

19. Special Report of Negro Activities of the National Youth Administration of Texas, Box 11, *ibid.* Some black youths worked on Texas NYA projects—particularly those handled by the State Highway Department—which were not specifically designated as "Negro projects." However, on such projects the two races were "somewhat segregated" as far as the actual work was concerned. *Ibid.*

20. Juanita J. Saddler to LBJ, April 9, 1936, Box 2; Mary E. Branch to LBJ, March 11, 1936, in Special Report of Negro Activities of the National Youth Administration of Texas, Box 11, *ibid.*

21. Texas Administrator Monthly Reports, Feb. 1936, Box 8; Nov. 1936, Box 10, *ibid.*

22. See various monthly reports of the Texas State Administrator, *ibid.*

23. LBJ to Brown, Feb. 26, March 9 and 11, 1936; Brown to LBJ, March 5, 1936, Box 2, *ibid.*

24. LBJ to J.C. Kellam, (undated telegram, Box 11; S.S. Tucker to LBJ, Dec. 21, 1936; LBJ to Brown, Sept. 21 and Dec. 22, 1936; Sam Gilstrap to LBJ, Jan. 8, 1937, Box 1; memo of telephone conversation between LBJ and Brown, Oct. 29, 1936, Box 2, *ibid.*; telephone interview with O.H. Elliott, March 4, 1975.

25. LBJ to Brown (telegram), March 4, 1936, Box 2; State Administrator Monthly Reports, Oct., Nov., and Dec. 1936; Jan. 1937, Box 10, NYA Files.

26. General Report of NYA District No. 2, Sept. 17–28, 1935, Box 7, *ibid.*

27. Texas State Administrator Monthly Report, April 1936, Box 9, *ibid.*

28. LBJ to Brown, Feb. 18, 1936; Mary H.S. Hayes to LBJ, March 3, 1936, Box 2; W.R. Banks to LBJ, Sept. 4, 1935; LBJ to Hugh H. Bennett, Sept. 8, 1935; LBJ to John J. Corson, Sept. 8, 1935; Corson to LBJ, Sept. 12, 1935, Box 3, *ibid.*

29. Texas Administrator Monthly Reports, Feb. 8, 1936, Box 8; April through June, 1936, Box 9; Brown to LBJ, Feb. 11, 1936; LBJ to Brown, Feb. 6, 1936, Box 2, *ibid.*

30. Beatrice Denmark to Brown, Feb. 9, 1937, Box 10, *ibid.*

31. Brown to LBJ, Aug. 3, 1936, Box 2, *ibid.*

32. Juanita J. Saddler to LBJ, April 9, 1936, Box 2, *ibid.*

33. Special Report of Negro Activities of the National Youth Administration of Texas, Box 11, *ibid.*

34. Austin *American*, March 12, 1937; unidentified newspaper clipping, Feb. 28, 1937, in Scrapbooks, LBJL.

35. James W. Partin, Jr., "The Texas Senatorial Election of 1941" (M.A. thesis, Texas Technological

College, 1941). In later years Johnson professed to have taken the unpopular stand in 1937 favoring the right of blacks to vote, and he once stated that he came out for black rights in all of his congressional campaigns. Texas newspapers and documents in the LBJ Library do not substantiate these statements. For Johnson's recollections, see Robert C. Rooney (ed.), *Equal Opportunity in the United States: A Symposium on Civil Rights, December 11–12, 1972* (Lyndon B. Johnson School of Public Affairs, University of Texas at Austin, 1973), p. 166.

36. Houston *Post*, Aug. 27, 1948.
37. Mary E. Branch to LBJ, April 20, 1943; LBJ to Branch, April 23, 1943, Box 1, Education, House of Representatives, 1937–1949, LBJL.
38. Quoted in Booth Mooney, *The Lyndon Johnson Story* (New York: Farrar, Straus, 1956), p. 35. Also see Robert C. Weaver Interview, Nov. 19, 1968, Oral History Collection, LBJL.
39. *Cong. Record*, 76 Cong. 3 Sess., p. 253; 77 Cong. 2 Sess., p. 8174; 78 Cong. 1 Sess., p. 4889; 79 Cong. 1 Sess., p. 6003; 80 Cong. 1 Sess., p. 9552 (Johnson did not actually cast a vote when the 1947 anti-poll tax bill was before the House, but he was "paired against" it, and would have done so had he been present.); 78 Cong. 2 Sess., pp. 1229, 2639; 79 Cong. 2 Sess., pp. 1541, 6351, 6353, 6354, 6356, 6357, 7161, 7589.
40. Personal letter from Ben Ramey, June 25, 1975.
41. Telephone interview with O.H. Elliott, March 4, 1975; personal interview with M.J. ("Andy") Anderson, March 5, 1975.
42. Telephone interview with J.H. Morton, March 4, 1975.
43. "May 22 Speech," pp. 9–10, in "Speeches of Lyndon B. Johnson, 1948," vol. 1, Statements of Lyndon Baines Johnson, LBJL.
44. Dallas *News*, Feb. 28 and March 7, 1948.
45. June R. Welch, "The Texas Senatorial Election of 1948" (M.A. thesis, Texas Technological College, 1953), pp. 28–32.
46. See "Speeches of Lyndon B. Johnson, 1948," vols. 1 and 2, in Box 1, Statements of Lyndon B. Johnson, LBJL.
47. The Houston *Chronicle*, June 7, 1948, carried the headline "JOHNSON WILL GIVE VIEWS ON RACE ISSUES," but the entire article was devoted to a radio speech in which the candidate opposed "all violations of states' rights." The Fort Worth *Star-Telegram*, May 26, 1948, indicated that Johnson "mentioned" his civil rights stand in Amarillo, but nothing else was reported. By contrast, examples of the candidates' speeches and replies on other campaign issues were plentiful. See Houston *Post*, June 22, 1948; Dallas *News*, July 31, Aug. 7 and 20, 1948; Austin *American*, June 20 and Aug. 5, 1948; Lubbock *Avalanche*,

June 26, 1948; Waco *Herald-Tribune*, July 21, 1948; Fort Worth *Star-Telegram*, June 23, 1948; San Antonio *Express*, Aug. 15, 1948.
48. Charles William Grose, "Black Newspapers in Texas, 1868–1970" (Ph.D. dissertation, University of Texas at Austin, 1972), pp. 166–67, 225–26, 265, 276.
49. Oct. 2, 1948.
50. June 19, 1948.
51. Sept. 18, 1948.
52. *Texas Almanac*, 1949–1950, p. 462.
53. New York *Times*, Aug. 8, 1948.
54. Tom C. Clark Interview, Oct. 7, 1969, Oral History Collection, LBJL.
55. Austin *American*, July 3, 1948.
56. Houston *Post*, Aug. 28, 1948.
57. Robert T. Sakowitz, "The 1948 Texas Senatorial Campaign and the Crisis in the Democratic Party" (B.A. Honors thesis, Harvard College, 1960), pg. 127.
58. Houston *Post*, Aug. 31, 1948; Dallas News, Sept. 1, 1948.
59. Hobart Taylor, Sr. Interview, Jan. 29, 1972, Oral History Collection, LBJL.
60. Telephone interviews with O.H. Elliott and J.H. Morton, March 4, 1975.
61. Houston *Informer*, Aug. 7, 1948.
62. Dallas *Express*, Nov. 13, 1948; personal interview with M.R. ("Andy") Anderson, March 5, 1975. National black leaders such as Robert C. Weaver and Mrs. Mary McLeod Bethune strongly favored Johnson's election. Clarence Mitchell Interview, April 30, 1969, Oral History Collection, LBJL.
63. John C. Stennis to LBJ, Oct. 21, 1948 Box 5, Senate Congressional File, *ibid*.
64. LBJ to John Stennis, Oct. 25, 1948, *ibid*.
65. Allen Ellender Interview, July 30, 1969, Oral History Collection, *ibid*.
66. *Cong. Record*, 81 Cong. 1 Sess., pp. 2042–49.
67. Lulu B. White to LBJ, March 9, 1949, Box 1, Pre-Presidential Papers, LBJL.
68. LBJ to White, March 10, 1949, *ibid*.
69. Personal interview with Mike Gillette, March 3, 1975.
70. Dallas *Express*, March 12, 1949.
71. Wesley to LBJ, March 12, April 5 and 6, 1949; LBJ to Wesley, March 16 and April 11, 1949, Box 1, Pre-Presidential Papers, LBJL.
72. LBJ to Eewil Fernandez, May 10, 1949, Box 2, *ibid*.
73. LBJ to W. H. Harrison, March 24, 1949, Box 1, *ibid*.
74. LBJ to A.E. Holland, March 24, 1949, *ibid*.
75. Hal E. Tindall to LBJ, April 1, 1949, *ibid*.
76. *Ibid*.
77. LBJ to Roscoe H. Collier, March 18, 1949, *ibid*.
78. LBJ to Rev. Father James J. O'Brien, March 25, 1949, *ibid*.
79. LBJ to E.J. Siegert, March 15, 1949, *ibid*.
80. LBJ to R.N. Jones, March 28, 1949, *ibid*.

81. LBJ to Frank Baldwin, March 10, 1949, ibid.
82. LBJ to *C.C.* Creighton, March 23, 1949, *ibid.* Italics added.
83. LBJ to Frank Baldwin, March 10, 1949, *ibid.*
84. LBJ to James H. Rowe, Jr., March 15, 1949, *ibid.*
85. See LBJ to H. H. Fenner, March 31, 1949; LBJ to S. C. Hobbs, March 15, 1949; LBJ to J. P. Price, March 11, 1949; LBJ to Ben E. Keith, March 11, 1949; LBJ to Leila A. Van Hyning, March 25, 1949; LBJ to Joseph Jones, March 21, 1949, *ibid.*
86. Personal letter from A. Maceo Smith, March 21, 1975.
87. *Cong. Record*, 81 Cong. 1 Sess., p. 7018; 81 Cong. 2 Sess., pp. 512, 550, 551, 7300, 8996, 9074, 9982, 16,378.
88. "Resolution on Civil Rights," San Antonio Branch, National Association for the Advancement of Colored People, Jan. 16, 1950, Box 2, Pre-Presidential Papers, LBJL.
89. LBJ to Harry V. Burns, Jan. 18, 1950, *ibid.*
90. LBJ to Charles H. Braxton, Jan. 27, 1950, *ibid.*
91. *Ibid.*
92. LBJ to Mary Tom Jackson, Jan. 24, 1950, *ibid.*
93. LBJ to E.K. Snider, Jan. 16, 1957, Box 15, Pre-Presidential Papers, *ibid.*
94. LBJ to Merle Lorentz, Jan. 16, 1956; see also LBJ to Mrs. A. P. Andrews, Oct. 8, 1956, and LBJ to Charles L. Hachher, May 18, 1956, Box 7, *ibid.*
95. Quoted in Alfred Steinberg, *Sam Johnson's Boy: A Close-Up of the President from Texas* (New York: Macmillan, 1968), p. 434.
96. LBJ to Robert S. Allen, Dec. 26, 1956, Box 7, Pre-Presidential Papers, LBJL.
97. Dec. 3, 1956, *ibid.*

I Got it from the New York Times

Lyndon Johnson and the Kennedy Civil Rights Program

Steven F. Lawson*

When Harry Truman sent civil rights legislation up to Capitol Hill in 1949, Lyndon Johnson, a freshman senator from Texas, berated it as "sadistic" and "designed more to humiliate the South than to help the black man."[1] Fourteen years later, propelled into the White House after the assassination of John Kennedy, Johnson ushered in a series of measures which earned him recognition as the civil rights president. Dr. Benjamin E. Mays, President of Morehouse College, expressed in 1967 what has become the historical consensus: "President Johnson caused to be passed more Civil Rights Legislation than any other president in American history. . . . If Johnson was not sincere in his Civil Rights battles, he would have done far less and still been ahead of all other presidents in the area of civil rights."[2] Indeed, this white grandson of a Confederate veteran joined blacks in toppling the most pernicious legal barriers blocking first class citizenship.

In climbing up the political ladder, Johnson grew from a Dixie obstructionist to a civil rights advocate. As a young congressman, the Texan initially followed the traditional southern line; however, he refrained from the rhetorical excesses of race baiting. His major opportunity to part company from other practitioners of gentlemanly racism came after the *Brown* decision and the subsequent rise of massive resistance. Not only did he refuse in 1956 to sign the Southern Manifesto denouncing the Supreme Court's landmark school opinion, but as senate majority leader, Johnson paved the way and voted for civil rights laws passed in 1957 and 1960. Nevertheless, Johnson did not immediately convince civil rights supporters that he was a true believer in their cause. Suspicions about him lingered because he had compromised these two measures by eliminating their strongest provisions.[3]

Although Johnson did not completely satisfy northern liberals, his desertion from the anti-civil rights bloc earned him national appeal. Nominated as vice-president in 1960, Johnson assisted in holding most of the South in the Democratic column without alienating the party's more moderate northern electorate. For this consummate politician accustomed to exercising power strenuously, the thousand days of the Kennedy Administration brought many unhappy moments.[4] The nature of the office and the coolness felt toward him by Kennedy confidants kept Johnson operating on the periphery of the inner policy making circle. Lee White, Kennedy's civil rights specialist who remained to serve under President Johnson, recalled that during the Birmingham crisis in the spring of 1963, he neglected to invite the vice president to several important meetings concerning the tense Alabama situation. "I clean forgot about the Vice President—just forgot," White reflected. "When you're awful busy and you've got a hell of a lot of things to do and you're dictating into the typewriter twenty minutes before a meeting, it's possible, just possible, to forget."[5]

Whatever slights and discomfort Johnson may have endured, he gained valuable experience on racial matters in the course of his term. Responding to civil rights demands, the Kennedy Administration chose a strategy that minimized congressional legislation and preferred the use of executive action in housing, employment, and the suffrage. Johnson played his role in chairing the President's Committee on Equal Employment

* Steven F Lawson is an Associate Professor at the University of South Florida. Tampa, Florida.

From *The Journal of Negro History,* Vol. 67, Issue 2, Summer 1982 by Stephen F. Lawson. Copyright © 1982 by Association for the Study of African-American Life and History. Reprinted by permission.

Opportunity, an agency which attempted through voluntary means to combat bigoted hiring practices. The results of this program were meager, but Johnson came to grasp more deeply than before the moral dimensions of the civil rights struggle. He displayed this sensitivity especially on May 30, 1963, speaking at the Gettysburg battlefield immortalized by Abraham Lincoln one hundred years earlier: "The Negro today asks justice. We do not answer, and we do not answer those who lie beneath this soil when we reply to the Negro by asking 'Patience'."[6]

Several weeks later on June 19, President Kennedy submitted to Congress an omnibus civil rights measure dealing chiefly with combating racial discrimination in schools, public accomodations, government employment, and voting. In shaping this proposal, the role played by the vice president, one of the legislative masters of modern times, has never been adequately explained. However, the leading historian of Kennedy and civil rights concluded that in June 1963 Johnson "believed that a civil rights fight would be a mistake."[7] While Johnson did lift his voice for caution, he did so for tactical rather than philosophical considerations. He found fault with the preparation of the bill and believed that the White House had picked a poor time for introducing it. More striking than any hesitancy Johnson articulated towards pushing this specific plan was the transformation that had occurred in his views on civil rights. Five months later upon Kennedy's death, the Baltimore *Afro-American* acknowledged that those "Americans understandably uneasy about President Johnson's Southern background, have but to examine the man's record for full assurance that his heart is right in the civil rights issue."[8]

The following document provides a fascinating glimpse into the private thoughts of Lyndon Johnson shortly before President Kennedy lectured a nation-wide television audience about the morality of racial equality. Transcribed from a telephone conversation on June 3 between Johnson and Theodore Sorenson, a top Kennedy aide, the discussion candidly conveys Johnson's assessment of the administration's impending civil rights program. The original recording made by Johnson and the transcript of it are located in the pre-presidential files of the LBJ Library, and until recently were

not known to exist. Unlike the customary memos found in presidential libraries which amply detail the thoughts of advisors, this exceptional document furnishes direct and extended comment from the soon-to-be chief executive himself.[9]

Endnotes

1. Lyndon B. Johnson to James H. Rowe, March 15, 1949 pre-presidential files (civil rights), Lyndon B. Johnson Library.

2. *New Pittsburgh Courier,* May 27, 1967. For more recent appraisals, see Doris Kearns, *Lyndon Johnson and the American Dream* (New York: Harper and Row, 1976), p. 391; David J. Garrow, *Protest at Selma: Martin Luther King, Jr., and the voting Rights Act of 1965* (New Haven: Yale University Press, 1978), p. 133; Carl Degler, Affluence and Anxiety: 1945—Present (Glenview, Illinois: Scott Foresman and Company, 1975), p. 113; Steven F. Lawson, "Civil Rights" in R.A Divine, ed., *Exploring the Johnson Years*, pp. 93–125.

3. On Johnson's early career, Monroe Billington, "Lyndon B. Johnson and Blacks: The Early Years," *Journal of Negro History,* LXII (January 1977): 26–42; Joe B. Frantz, "Opening a Curtain: the Metamorphosis of Lyndon B. Johnson, "Journal of Southern History, XLV (February 1979): 3–26, Steven F. Lawson and Mark I. Gelfand, "Consensus and Civil Rights: Lyndon B. Johnson and the Black Franchise," *Prologue*, VIII (Summer 1976): 65–76.

4. T. Harry Williams, Huey, Lyndon, and Southern Radicalism," *Journal of American History*, LX (September 1973): 284.

5. Lee White, oral history interview, tape 1, pp. 12–13, Lyndon B. Johnson Library.

6. Quoted in Leonard Baker, *The Johnson Eclipse: A President's Vice Presidency,* (New York: McMillan Co., 1966), p. 219.

7. Carl M. Brauer, *John F. Kennedy and the Second Reconstruction,* (New York: Columbia University Press, 1977), p. 245.

8. Baltimore *Afro-American*, December 7, 1963.

9. "Edison Dictaphone Recording, LBJ–Sorenson, June 3, 1963," Lyndon B. Johnson Library. Unlike this tape, the tapes which exist from Johnson's presidential term currently have a fifty year restriction on their access to researchers. The contrast between availability of the two classifications of tapes stems from differences in the manner by which the materials were donated. At present, other pre-presidential tapes have not surfaced.

Mississippi Blacks and the Voting Rights Act of 1965*

Paul E. Joubert and Ben M. Crouch

Since Reconstruction, an integral part of the Southern status quo has been the absence or very limited participation of Blacks in the political arena. The reason for this is the well documented history of the South and the attitudes of its white majority. Given this history and attendant white attitudes, it is not surprising that any civil rights activity, and particularly the Voting Rights Act of 1965, were adversely viewed by this majority. The Voting Rights Act, like the 15th Amendment, carried the mandate that Blacks be given entry to the political process; it differed, however, in that it also provided means of enforcing the mandate in the form of Federal examiners.[1] This Federal move then gave Blacks access to collective political power.

This paper is an analysis of the impact of the Voting Rights Act (VRA) on black voter registration in Mississippi and a brief review of subsequent political gains made by Blacks in that state. The focus is on registration because it constitutes the primary prerequisite to the ultimate goal of attaining political power via the ballot box. Actual political gains, in the form of getting Blacks elected to office, are also important to note because they indicate the degree to which potential power is transformed into actual power. Mississippi was selected because it contained the largest proportion of Blacks of all the states of the union; at the same time, it had the lowest proportion of eligible Blacks registered to vote prior to the VRA.

Methodology

This study is concerned with all potential and actual black registrants living in the state of Mississippi (21 years of age and older) through the 1960s and early 1970s. Data for this study were obtained from the following sources: the U.S. Justice Department, the U.S. Commission on Civil Rights, and the Southern Regional Council (Atlanta, Ga.). In depth examination of the data on black registration begins with the year 1962 because before that time black registration in the state was negligible; also, reliable data prior to 1962 were not available.

Analysis focuses on three variables in the period prior to the VRA. The first is the proportion of Blacks living in each county, a factor which Mathews and Prothro[2] have shown to be crucial to black voter registration in the South. The second variable is the presence of Voter Education Projects (VEP). These projects, always limited in number, existed both before and after the VRA. The VEP would provide funds to local black organizations in order that they might be able to carry on activities such as holding meetings to encourage Blacks to attempt to register. Other services covered would be transportation of Blacks to meetings and to registration points in the county. Finally, the activities of the county registrars dealing with black registration is examined. Each county in Mississippi has an official elected by popular vote who is charged with the duty of registering all eligible voter applicants.

For the period following the VRA, an attempt is made to reveal the unique contribution of each of the above variables. It is at this point, of course, that the impact of the Federal examiners may be assessed. Since the Federal examiners authorized by the VRA were not operating in all Mississippi

* The authors gratefully acknowledge the information and data provided by the following agencies: The Southern Regional Council, the Voting Education Project, The U.S. Dept. of Justice, and the U.S. Commission on Civil Rights.

counties, it is then possible to suggest the degree to which the passage of the law in general, and the presence of the Federal examiners in particular, facilitated increases in the registration activities of the VEP and local registrars.

Available data on the combinations of Federal examiners and VEP (along with local registrars who are always present) in the various counties are examined to see which combinations seem to have the greatest success in getting Blacks registered. Then, in order to see if there is interaction between these variables and the variable of percent Negro, a purposive sample is drawn. All counties that had at least 50 per cent of their eligible Blacks registered are included in the sample. The reason that this level was chosen is that until Blacks reach this level in a county, they have little chance of influencing local politics and are not truly representative of the views of Blacks in the county.

Before the Voting Rights Act

Prior to the VRA, many charges had been leveled at Mississippi regarding discrimination against Blacks who sought to register. In order to determine the extent of this discrimination, the U.S. Commission on Civil Rights held hearings in Jackson, the state capital, in February of 1965, roughly six months before the passage of the VRA.[3] The hearings revealed that threats of violence, economic reprisal, the poll tax, overly difficult literacy tests, and other means were used to prevent Blacks from registering to vote. The Commission concluded that the same patterns of discrimination would continue unless some sort of Federal action was taken.

That these techniques of disenfranchisement were effective is evident from the data in Table I. Since Federal examiners were not present prior to the signing of the VRA in August, 1965, all of the black registration can be attributed to local registrars. From 1962 to August 1, 1965, a period which included considerable civil rights activity on the national scene and the Civil Rights Act of 1964, there occurred only negligible changes in the proportion of eligible Blacks registered.

During the above-mentioned period, Voter Education Projects (VEP) were present in 34 counties of the state. Of the Mississippi counties with VEP, seventeen of them showed no gain in registrants, seven actually lost registrants and the remaining ten experienced negligible gains. This would agree with Watter's and Cleghorn's contention that the VEP's were successful in every state in which they operated, except in Mississippi. The failure of the projects demonstrated the need for Federal action in getting Blacks registered to vote.[4]

Mathews and Prothro maintain that as the concentration of Blacks in a county get above 30 per cent, Blacks experience considerable difficulty in registering to vote.[5] In order to determine whether the variable of per cent Black was influencing registration rates, all counties that were above 30 per cent Black in 1964 (in terms of their total populations) were grouped together and an overall proportion of eligible Blacks registered was computed. The data[6] revealed the following: of the 363,303 eligible Blacks, 19,933 were registered, giving a proportion of .06. The same was done for the counties that were less than 30 per cent Black. These counties had 58,953 eligible Blacks, with 5,515 of that number registered (a significantly higher proportion, .09, than the counties with over 30%). Computation yielded a z score of 6.0, significant at the .05 level. Thus, the notion of Mathews and Prothro is corroborated. But this relationship will be retested for the period following the VRA.

Table I Black Voter Registration in Mississippi, From June 1962 to August 1, 1965[a]

Year	Number of Eligible Blacks[b]	Number Registered	Proportion of Eligible Registered	Increase
1962 (June)	422,256	21,209	.05	
1964 (Nov.)	422,256	25,448	.06	.01
1965 (Aug. 1)	422,256	35,000	.08	.02

[a] Calculated from: *Voter Registration, Mississippi* (Atlanta: Southern Regional Council), p. 8 and U.S. Department of Justice, Voter Registration Statistics (Washington: U.S. Government Printing Office, 1967), p. 1.

[b] Based on the 1960 Census. If the later figures were available, it would have the effect of making the proportions slightly larger, therefore not altering the basic conclusions of the research.

After the Voting Rights Act

On August 6, 1965, President Lyndon Johnson signed the Voting Rights Act of 1965. This act specifically guaranteed the Negro the right to register to vote and outlawed literacy tests and all other measures serving as obstacles to that end.[7] The 15th Amendment (1870) clearly stated that neither the Federal Government nor the states could deny any citizen the right to vote on the basis of race or color. The Voting Rights Act, however, went further in that it provided for enforcement at the local level in the form of Federal examiners for counties that would not comply with the law.

If the Voting Rights Act really did end discriminatory practices with regard to Blacks registering to vote, it would be reasonable to assume that some immediate effect of the law could be noted. During the first month of the law, August 6 to September 3, 1965, black voter registration in Mississippi increased from 35,000 to 77,222 registrants, an increase of 120 per cent (see Table II). Large increases continued into the early 1970s but the rate of increases slowed down. By the end of 1970, 171 per cent of all eligible Blacks were registered to vote in the state of Mississippi.

The increase in black registration just noted, testifies to the apparent success of the VRA.

Table II Per Cent Change in Black Registration in Mississippi From August 1, 1965 Through 1970

	Number Registered	Per Cent Increase (Over Previous Period)
1965 (Aug. 1)	35,000[a]	
1965 (Sept. 3)	77,222[b]	120
1966 (Jan.)	112 114[c]	45
1967 (Feb.)	177,700[d]	58
1968 (Dec.)	251,000[e]	41
1970 (Dec.)	286,000[e]	14

[a] U.S. Dept. of Justice, *Voter Registration Statistics* (Washington: U.S. Government Printing Office, 1967), p. 1.

[b] U.S. Commission on Civil Rights, *The Voting Rights Act . . . The First Months* (Washington: U.S. Government Printing Office, 1965), p. 6.

[c] *Voter Registration, Mississippi*, (Atlanta: Southern Regional Council), p. 8.

[d] *Voter Registration Statistics,* (Washington: U.S. Government Printing Office, 1967), p. 1.

[e] Figures are rounded off to nearest thousand. Source: Voter Education Project, Inc., Atlanta, Ga. *Voter Registration in the South,* Summer, 1966.

Mississippi, which is the "blackest" state in the union (percentage wise),[8] became the state with not only the highest percentage of whites registered in the South (82 per cent)[9] but also the highest percentage of blacks registered. Clearly, in the five-year period, Mississippi Blacks moved from a position of political power proportionately comparable to that of the white majority.

It is now necessary to look inside these changes to see which forces seemed to bring them about, other than the VRA itself. Beginning with the local registrars, it should be recalled that they had registered about 8 per cent of black eligibles before the Voting Rights Act. By September 3, 1965 (one month after the VRA), they had registered about 14 per cent,[10] an increase which is significant statistically. But statistical significance does not mean that much here, considering that the black electorate still would not be large enough to influence much change. The increase is notable, however, in that it suggests that local registrars were apparently complying with the new law at least in a limited fashion.

During the first month of the VRA, four counties in Mississippi were assigned Federal examiners–Leflore, Madison, Jefferson Davis, and Jones.[11] The corresponding per cent increases in these counties in black registration were 1800%, 2300%, 750%, and 220%. So, during the first month, although there were noticeable registration increases in counties with local registrars only, these increases did not begin to approach those observed in counties where Federal examiners were present. Apparently Blacks were quite willing to register to vote if allowed to do so.

A more accurate picture of the registration patterns in counties with Federal examiners as opposed to counties without Federal examiners can be obtained by examining data for July, 1966, almost one year after the VRA was passed. At that time, there were twenty-one counties with Federal examiners. These counties were compared (in terms of proportion of eligible Blacks registered) to twenty-six counties without Federal examiners. The following results were obtained:

With examiner–number eligible = 114,659; number registered = 47,223; proportion registered = .41.

Without examiner–number eligible = 149,246; number registered = 36,190; proportion registered = .24.

(A z score of 3.33 was obtained, significant at the .05 level.)[12]

It is evident that in terms of black registration, counties without Federal examiners were lagging behind counties with examiners. Even one year after the VRA, local registrars in counties without Federal examiners still were not achieving levels of registration being reached in counties with Federal examiners. But local registrars were beginning to conform more closely to the law than previously, even when Federal examiners were not present in their counties. Only tentative explanations for this can be offered. One possible explanation is that the registrars underwent a change in feelings regarding black registration. A more plausible explanation is that the local registrars in counties without Federal examiners concluded that if they did not show some measurable gains, Federal examiners would enter their counties and usurp their power, thus causing them to "lose face." It would seem reasonable that the local registrars would want to avoid Federal intervention, if at all possible.

The question of the combined impact of the registration devices being considered here may now be taken up. The data indicate that the combination of Federal examiners and Voter Education Projects did result in the highest proportion of Blacks getting registered (see Table III). Counties with Federal examiners (and no VEP) were second, and so on. But there is a limitation here. Available data only show one county, Coahoma, with both Federal examiners and a Voter Education Project present. Other counties did have the VEP present following the VRA, but reliable data were not available on them. The differences between all proportions, in descending order, are statistically significant. It might tentatively be concluded that VEP's were more successful in influencing black registration in the state following the VRA than they were before

the VRA. The effect of Federal examiners, however, is quite evident. Wherever present, the Federal examiners did aid in enfranchising increasing numbers of eligible Blacks.

But the variable of per cent black (residing in each county) must also be considered, both as a single variable and in combination with the other variables, in terms of effects on black registration. First of all, a retest of the variable "per cent Black" was made by again dichotimizing the counties into those above 30 per cent Black and those below 30 per cent Black. The data revealed the following: counties above 30 per cent Black in 1966 registered 27 per cent of their eligible Blacks (number eligible—363,303; number registered—98,208), while counties that were less than 30 per cent Black registered 22 per cent of their eligible Blacks (number eligible—58,913; number registered—13,926). A z score of 1.69 was obtained, significant at the .05 level. Apparently the VRA, along with the Federal examiners, was able to reverse a trend initially noted by Mathews and Prothro and replicated earlier in this paper. That is, a heavy concentration of Blacks in a county (above 30%) no longer meant that Black registration in that county would necessarily be lagging behind registration in a "less Black" county (below 30%).

To get another view of the major registration devices in combination with one another, a purposive sample of Mississippi counties was drawn. The criterion for selection was that the county have at least 50 per cent of its eligible Blacks registered to vote. In July, 1966, seven Mississippi counties had met this criterion (see Table IV). It is noteworthy that six out of these seven counties had Black populations above 30 per cent. This would give further credence to the reversal of the Mathews and Prothro

Table III Combinations of the Major Variables[a]

Variables	Black Registration	Voting Age Population Registered	Propotion Registered	z Score
Both V. E. P & Fed. Exam.	7,583	14,604	.51	
Federal Examiners	47,223	114,659	.41	2.29[b]
V. E. P.	377	1,081	.34	4.28[b]
Local Registrars (only)	36,190	149,264	.24	5.00[b]

[a] Calculated from: *Voter Registration, Mississippi* (Atlanta: Southern Regional Council), p. 8 and U.S. Department of Justice, Voter Registration Statistics (Washington: U.S. Government Printing Office, 1967), p. 1.

Table IV Mississippi Counties Above .50 in Registration*

County	Proportion Registered[a]	% Negro[b]	Other Variables Present[c]
Coahoma	.81	45	Fed. Exam & VEP
Lawrence	.74	37	Neither Fed. Exam nor VEP
Benton	.62	46	Fed. Exam. (only)
Jefferson	.57	75	Fed. Exam. (only)
Jeff. Davis	.55	54	Fed. Exam. (only)
Jones	.54	25	Fed. Exam. (only)
Walthall	.50	45	Fed. Exam. (only)

*July 1966.

[a] *Voter Registration,*

[b] *Mississippi's Counties, Some Social and Economic Aspects* (Mississippi State University: Agricultural Experiment Station, 1966), p. 19.

[c] The *Effects of Federal Examiners and Organized Registration Campaigns on Negro Voter Registration*, by Marvin Wall (Atlanta: Southern Regional Council,Inc., 1966).

[d] July 1966.

finding reported above. It should also be noted that six of the seven counties had Federal examiners. Apparently, by concentrating Federal examiners in some of the "blackest" counties, Federal action was able to help overcome the earlier impediment to black registration—too many Blacks in the counties. Thus, large concentrations of Blacks in particular counties became a potential political advantage

After 1966, the activities of Federal examiners tapered off considerably. The examiners completed most of their work by the end of 1968, although spot visits to various counties did continue into the 1970s.[13] By 1970, 71 per cent of all the eligible Blacks were registered to vote in the state of Mississippi. Most of this new electorate were registered during the first two years of the law, 1965–1966. Thus, registration activities in the 1960s provided Blacks with a potential power base from which to launch political activity in the 1970s.

Blacks at the Polls

But, if Blacks were to become a potent force, politically, in Mississippi, they had to not only register but also vote in elections. The following discussion assumes that the number of black candidates actually elected represent a conservative estimate of the exercise of black political power.

During the year 1971, 50 Blacks were elected to various offices in the state of Mississippi, giving Mississippi more elected black officials than any other southern state.[14] The period 1970–72 saw 129 Blacks get elected to offices in the state.[15] Apparently, Blacks did turn out to vote in the early 1970s and were able to accomplish measurable gains–made possible by the VRA and registration activities in the 1960s.

However, it appears that whites in the state are taking a dim view of the newly found black political strength. The Voting Rights Act of 1965 (along with 1970 amendments to it) prevented counties from changing local elections laws without first consulting with the office of the Attorney General of the United States. But some Mississippi counties are instituting reregistration laws, thus purging sizable parts of the black electorate without the consent of the Attorney General.[16]

Other means have also been employed by whites to curb black voting. In some instances, Blacks have been denied poll watchers, and black candidates have not had the privilege of being listed on sample ballots.[17] Threats of economic reprisal and racial killings can also be linked to attempts by Blacks to vote.[18] Therefore, the future of black politics is highly uncertain in Mississippi. If the movement on the part of whites to disenfranchise Blacks succeeds, and intimidation at the polls continues, advances made in the early 1970s could be seriously undermined.

Summary and Implications

Before the passage of the Voting Rights Act, one could hardly speak of a black electorate in Mississippi, and no significant gains in registration could be noted. There can be no doubt that the VRA brought about drastic changes in black registration in that state. The law was made especially effective due to its enforcibility at the local level. Even if one were to concede the fact that changes in black registration may have occurred anyway over time, it is highly unlikely that they would have occurred as rapidly as they did without Federal examiners to enforce the law. The law itself and its enforcibility are the important factors in determining whether Blacks can register to vote in Mississippi, such things as VEP and per cent Negro in the counties no longer seem to have a great deal of influence as they presumably did before the VRA.

Substantial increases in black registration, mostly during the late 1960s allowed black officials to get elected in the early 1970s. Paradoxically, this new found political strength may be short lived. It seems that Federal influence will continue to be necessary in the state in order that Blacks be assured of voting rights. Ironically, a "liberal goal" i.e., black voting, may require considerable Federal intervention to become a reality.

But there is one problem which no amount of Federal activity will be able to overcome in the foreseeable future. This is the fact that Blacks are still economically dependent on whites and, unless this situation changes, Blacks will have to live with threats of reprisals whenever they engage in political activity.[19] It must be remembered that politics is intimately tied in with the prevailing economic and social milieu.

Finally, it is possible to extend the findings reported here to the question of the legislation of moral norms. Since the passage of the Voting Rights Act it seems clear that no real change in attitude has taken place on the part of whites in Mississippi with regard to black participation in the political processes. Apparently, whites complied with the law up to a certain point largely because of Federal pressure. But when Blacks began to get elected to office, the white power structure was able to find means of circumventing the law. This suggests support for the classic position of Sumner that moral norms can not be legislated.[20] While legislation has been shown to positively affect moral norms in some institutional spheres[21] the results of the present study lead to the conclusion that when the present extension of the Voting Rights Act expires in 1975, black enfranchisement will still be very problematic in Mississippi. (*Editor's Note*: The Voting Rights Act of 1965 expired on August 6, 1975, but was extended for another 10 years. This paper was accepted in 1974.)

Endnotes

1. U.S. Commission on Civil Rights, "The Voting Rights Act . . . The First Months" (Washington, 1965), 1–6. For a complete description of the Voting Rights Act of 1965 and 1970 Amendments, see also the following Civil Rights Publications: The Voting Rights of 1965, August, 1965; and Summary and Text of the Voting Rights Act, Sept., 1971. See also, Paul E. Joubert, The Effects of the Voting Rights Act of 1965 on Negro Voter Registration in Mississippi (Unpublished Master's thesis, Mississippi State University, January, 1969).

2. Donald R. Mathews and James W. Prothro, "Social and Economic Factors and Negro Registration," *American Political Science Review*, XVIII (March, 1963).

3. U.S. Commission on Civil Rights, "Voting in Mississippi" (Washington, 1965), 60–61.

4. Pat Watters and Reese Cleghorn, *Climbing Jacob's Ladder* (New York, 1967).

5. Mathews and Prothro, *op. cit.*, p. 42.

6. The data were taken from Voter Registration, Mississippi (Atlanta: Southern Regional Council, 1964), pp. 1–8. The year 1964 was used as the base year because it is closest to the Voting Rights Act.

7. The Voting Rights Act., *op. cit.*, 1–6.

8. *Statistical Abstract of the United States* (Washington, D.C., Government Printing Office, 1972), p. 28.

9. *Ibid.*, p. 374.

10. The Voting Rights Act., *op. cit.*, 1–6.

11. *Ibid.*, p. 39.

12. This comparison was made on the basis of examination of a study completed by the Southern Regional Council. See: Marvin Wall, *The Effects of Federal Examiners and Organized Registration Campaigns on Negro Voter Registration* (Atlanta: Southern Regional Council, Inc., 1966).

13. Telephone conversation with Marvin Wall, Director of Information and Publications for the U.S. Commission on Civil Rights, October 18,1973.

14. Lester Salmon, "Mississippi Post Mortem, the 1971 Elections," *New South*, XXVII (1972), 45.

15. *Statistical Abstract, op. cit.*, p. 372

16. Telegram sent to Attorney General John Mitchell by John Lewis, Executive Director of the Voter Education Project, April 19, 1971.

17. Jack White, "Mississippi Blacks Fail to Gain Control," *Race Relations Law Reporter*, II, (Nov. 15, 1971).

18. Salmon, *op. cit.*, p. 46.

19. *Ibid.*, p. 47.

20. William Graham Sumner, *The Forgotten Man and Other Essays* (New Haven, 1919), p. 167.

21. See for example, Herbert H. Hyman, and Paul B. Sheatsley, "Attitudes Toward Desegregation," *Scientific American* (July, 1964), p. 6.

SECTION TWELVE

CONSERVATIVE BACKLASH

CHAPTER 14

The Politics of Principle
Richard Nixon and School Desegregation

By Lawrence J. McAndrews*

In many ways Richard Nixon chose a terrible time to be President. He followed an Administration which comprehensively safeguarded civil rights and financed education. Through the Civil Rights Act of 1964, the Voting Rights Act of 1965, the Elementary and Secondary Education Act of 1965, the Higher Education Act of 1965, and the Fair Housing Act of 1968, the country's leaders finally responded to the public's demand for equality of opportunity in school and society. Yet by 1968 the leaders were not meeting the extraordinary expectations raised by such legislation, and they were losing the public's trust. Nixon's challenge was therefore to realistically adjust his expectations without dangerously abdicating his leadership. If he succeeded, he could help accelerate the considerable progress which the country was making in race relations and educational achievement. If he failed, he might help alienate a generation of Americans from their leaders.

Some scholars claim that Nixon succeeded, by leading a principled assault on *de jure* school desegregation. Others claim that he failed, by orchestrating a politically expedient surrender to *de facto* school segregation. A close examination of the evidence, however, reveals that in the area of school desegregation, Nixon's record was a mixture of principle and politics, progress and paralysis, success and failure. In the end, he was neither simply the cowardly architect of a racially insensitive

"Southern strategy" which condoned segregation, nor the courageous conductor of a politically risky "not-so-Southern strategy" which condemned it. Because of his ambivalent past and his country's ambivalent present on civil rights, President Richard Nixon 'was both.

School Desegregation

In 1954, while Richard Nixon was Vice President, the Supreme Court ruled in *Brown v. Board of Education* that *de jure* segregation violated the Equal Protection clause of the Fourteenth Amendment. The next year, the Court ordered the dismantling of such segregation "with all deliberate speed," leaving implementation to lower court judges. On the tenth anniversary of the *Brown* decision, however, only one percent of African-American children in the South attended desegregated schools, so the Civil Rights Act of 1964 moved to enforce the *Brown* decision. Title IV of the Act empowered the Justice Department to litigate school desegregation cases, while Title VI permitted the Department of Health, Education, and Welfare to withdraw federal money from segregated schools. By 1968, due partly because of the Civil Rights Act, the fraction of African-American children in desegregated Southern schools had increased to ten percent.[1]

* Lawrence J. McAndrews is an Associate Professor of History at St. Norbert College, De Pere, Wisconsin.

In the same year, while Richard Nixon was a Presidential candidate, the Supreme Court ruled in *Green v. New Kent County* that "freedom of choice" voluntary desegregation plans which did not produce significant racial mixing violated the Equal Protection clause. For the next three years, on the important questions of "whether a school system must achieve a particular racial balance in order to satisfy constitutional standards and the extent to which a school board must reassign students to distant schools in order to overcome segregated residential patterns," the High Court would remain silent. But new President Richard Nixon would not.[2]

The "Southern Strategy"

Writing in *National Review* in 1964, William Rusher argued that the "Republican Party is poised to shatter the Democrats' century-old grip on the 'Solid South.'" Of the six states which Republican Barry Goldwater carried in his landslide defeat by Lyndon Johnson that year, five were in the Deep South. Four years later, Nixon campaign strategist Kevin Phillips expanded upon the Rusher thesis. "[Southern] white Democrats will desert their party in droves," said Phillips, "the minute it becomes a black party." After Nixon divided the Southern electoral vote with independent George Wallace in 1968, Phillips predicted, "We'll get two-thirds to three-fourths of the Wallace vote in nineteen seventy-two." Nixon then swept the South in his landslide victory (largely because of the outbreak of peace in Vietnam) over George McGovern in 1972. There was no denying Nixon's "Southern Strategy" in 1968 and 1972—Phillips openly admitted it. "The Right just will not learn to keep its mouth shut," wrote Garry Wills in 1970, "to work on a strategy without confessing it."[3]

Nixon's public and private statements often reflected this strategy. In the 1968 campaign candidate Nixon strongly opposed forced school busing to achieve racial balance. "I feel home environment has more to do with success in life than any amount of integrated education," Nixon would later explain. President Nixon occasionally uttered racial slurs, such as when he urged National Security Advisor Henry Kissinger to include "something . . . for the jigs" in the President's first major foreign policy address in February 1970. In 1976 former President Nixon counselled the Gerald Ford campaign, "The Negro vote's lost; don't let it lose you white votes."[4]

Nixon did not only preach the Southern strategy; he practiced it. On January 19, 1969, Secretary of Health, Education and Welfare Robert Finch announced that while the new Administration would honor its predecessor's deadline for the defunding of five segregated Southern school districts, the districts could reclaim the funds if they desegregated within sixty days of the deadline. Finch's nod toward the South gained more skeptics than followers in the region, however. At a meeting with Nixon Administration representatives, Republican Party Southern State Chairmen suggested that Nixon "take a hard look at existing (school desegregation] guidelines; advise Republican leadership if funds are to be cut off in a district; [and] have HEW review the overall situation before any further action is taken." When told that the President would not carry any Southern state in the Electoral College if he continued the Johnson policies, Nixon aide Bryce Harlow reassured them, "We were desperately sandbagged by the previous Administration. Finch is trying—which is more than the previous Administration did. . . . There will not be a continuation of the policies of the Johnson Administration."[5]

Harlow's words were prophetic. In a March 14 meeting with Finch and Attorney General John Mitchell, Nixon noted that most of the letters received by his Administration were "very critical" of the Johnson guidelines. A month later, two of Nixon's staunchest supporters, Republican Senators John Tower of Texas and Howard Baker of Tennessee, told the President that the defunding of segregated Southern school districts had created a rift between the federal government and Southern schools. "Both Senators are up for re-election in 1972," Harlow had reminded Nixon before the meeting. "Both therefore actively share your interest in a strategy that will carry Southern states."[6]

In July this strategy helped produce a measured federal retreat on school desegregation. Mitchell and Finch called for "full compliance" with the Johnson Administration's autumn 1969 deadline for full desegregation throughout the South, except in majority-black districts (given until 1970) or areas with inadequate facilities. They added, however, that "in some districts there may be sound reasons for some limited delay. . . . Examples of such problems would be serious shortages of necessary physical facilities, financial resources, or faculty." The Department of Justice would join HEW in enforcing this desegregation. Liberal Republican Senator Jacob

Javits of New York called the new policy "disastrous." Roy Wilkins, Executive Director of the National Association for the Advancement of Colored People, accused the Administration of "breaking the law." Nixon's own appointees on the U.S. Commission on Civil Rights assailed this deferral of justice.[7]

The Administration nevertheless moved to implement its new procedure. When the Fifth Circuit Court of Appeals granted a four-month delay to thirty-three Mississippi school districts facing an August 11 desegregation deadline, White House aide Harry Dent noticed that for the first time, "the Department of Justice was seated at the table with the South rather than with the NAACP." Two months later, when the Supreme Court unanimously overturned the Fifth Circuit decision and ordered the immediate desegregation of the Mississippi schools, Dent consoled Nixon, "The reaction we are getting today regarding the Supreme Court decision yesterday is that this is working in our favor at the moment . . . The Supreme Court is being blamed." Finch followed a similar line in preparing a response to Alabama Democratic Governor George Wallace's January 19, 1970 appearance on CBS-TV's *Face the Nation*. To Wallace's contention that "we had freedom of choice up unto Mr. Mitchell went into the Fifth Circuit Court of Appeals," Finch replied, "it was not Mr. Mitchell but the Supreme Court that . . . held freedom of choice plans unacceptable if they prove effective. Mr. Mitchell was merely enforcing that decision."[8]

Despite this judicial setback, Nixon pressed forward with his "Southern strategy." Two weeks before Georgia Democratic Senator Richard Russell warned Nixon of "HEW people going around stirring up trouble," Nixon fired Assistant HEW Secretary Leon Panetta for his overly aggressive pursuit of school desegregation. On February 11 Nixon publicly reiterated his opposition to "compulsory busing of school children to achieve racial balance," cited the importance of "neighborhood schools" and "quality education," and offered his support for the concept, if not the substance, of Mississippi Democratic Senator John Stennis' disingenuous amendment calling for "uniform application" of desegregation enforcement throughout the country. On February 16 Nixon bowed to segregationist South Carolina Republican Senator Strom Thurmond in forming a Cabinet Committee on Education. The committee, nominally headed, by Vice President Spiro Agnew, aimed to ease the burden of Southern desegregation through reassuring words and targeted monies.[9]

Nixon's major address on school desegregation on March 24 in many ways embodied the "Southern strategy." "Where school boards have demonstrated a good-faith effort to comply with court rulings," the President observed, "the courts have generally allowed substantial latitude as to method." He added, "When there is racial separation in housing, the constitutional requirement has been held satisfied even though some schools remained all black." He concluded, "Transportation of pupils beyond normal geographic school zones for the purpose of achieving racial balance will not be required." Panetta and his former assistant, Paul Rilling, denounced the speech's "perpetuation" of segregation and "slick rationalization for retreat." "Anonymous government civil rights lawyers" concurred with this criticism in press reports, prompting Nixon to demand their names and resignations.[10]

In June HEW Secretary Finch, whom Thurmond had earlier implored to "keep his mouth shut," became Special Counsellor Finch. "Finch [is] a poet," Nixon aide John Ehrlichman would write, citing the need for "prose guys" to "get things done." In August Nixon's prose assured a New Orleans audience that Southerners were not "second-class citizens" and condemned "those from the North that point the finger at the South."[11]

In September Southern concerns came north, as Nixon and Mitchell conferred with Congressman Charles Jonas, armed with the anti-busing petition of the Concerned Parents Association of Charlotte. Mitchell explained that in a case pending before the Supreme Court the Nixon Administration supported Charlotte "in principle, in that we are taking the position that the Fourteenth Amendment does not require racial integration as a matter of law." But seven months later, Charlotte and the Administration lost. In a unanimous ruling in *Swann v. Charlotte-Mecklenburg School District*, the Supreme Court ordered the busing of students between white suburban and black in ner-city schools to reverse the effects of pre-1954 *de jure* segregation within the district. (The average one-way trip lasted an hour and fifteen minutes, and exceeded fifteen miles.) Asserting that the "busing problem has now turned against us and can do us considerable harm," Nixon explored ways to "get clearly on the record again by being against busing in spite of the court decision."[12]

But the judiciary was not finished. In January 1972 in Richmond, Virginia, and in June in Detroit, federal judges ordered the busing of schoolchildren across school district lines to overcome residential segregation patterns. Asserting that "I totally disagree with those decisions," Nixon insisted, "I am for action now; I prefer the legislative route to do it; but if we can't that way, I will go for a constitutional amendment [to outlaw busing]." The President then signed education legislation amended by Michigan Republican Representative William Broomfield to prohibit future court-ordered busing until all appeals, or the time for all appeals, had elapsed; and amended by Ohio Republican Representative (and Presidential candidate) John Ashbrook to outlaw federal spending for busing. Anticipating a legal challenge to the sweeping language of the former provision, Nixon decried the "manifest Congressional retreat from an urgent call for responsibility," and promised more specific anti-busing legislation.[13]

Congress "retreated" further in October, when a Senate filibuster led by Democrats Edmund Muskie of Maine and Philip Hart of Michigan sank an Administration bill which would have compelled the courts to implement specific desegregation plans, to limit busing to the next closest school to a pupil's neighborhood, and to reopen court orders which exceeded these restrictions. In March 1974 the House of Representatives, by 293–117, passed an anti-busing addition to H.R. 69, the Elementary and Secondary Education Act Amendments of 1974. The rider, sponsored by Michigan Republican Marvin Esch, "prohibited federal courts or agencies from ordering busing of students to any but the school closest or next closest to the student's home" and "provided that any school district under a federal court order or desegregation plan in effect on the date of H.R. 69 could ask that the case be reopened and made to comply with the provisions of Title II." The Senate passed H.R. 69 but rejected the Esch Amendment, 46–47. The conference report on the bill adopted the Senate amendment prohibiting busing "beyond the school next closest" to a student's home "but allowing courts to mandate additional busing" if it were required to guarantee the student's civil rights." The conferees also replaced the House reopener provision with language permitting "parents or the school district to reopen a case only if the time or distance travelled was so great as to endanger the health of the student or impinge on the educational process." Whereas the House bill had *required* the termination of a busing order if a federal court determined that desegregation had been achieved, the conference report merely *permitted* such a termination.[14]

Before the H.R. 69 conference report could come to a vote, Nixon signed a bill prohibiting Federal Legal Service offices from using public or private funds to litigate school desegregation cases. Then, on July 25, 1974, the Supreme Court, in overturning the Detroit busing plan, "refused to recognize a power in the federal courts to order the amalgamation of urban and suburban school districts to obtain a desirable racial mixture in the schools, where *de jure* segregation existed only in the urban district." Encouraged by this rare judicial victory in *Milliken v. Bradley*, the House adopted the H.R. 69 conference report, 323–83, with Esch among the fifty-eight anti-busing Representatives who rejected the bill's moderate language. After the Senate adopted the conference report, 81–15, it reached President Nixon's desk on August 7. While "the bill's busing provisions fall short of your desire to retain the House provisions," HEW Secretary Caspar Weinberger wrote Nixon, the measure does "strengthen the existing law against busing and certains many of the provisions you originally sought." Noting the "obdurate attitude of the Senate and the size of the House vote accepting this compromise," Weinberger recommended that Nixon sign the legislation. But when Nixon resigned (due to the Watergate scandal) on August 9, the busing controversy fell to President Gerald Ford, who signed the legislation August 21.[15]

The Not-So-Southern Strategy

While many contemporary critics would have ended the story of Nixon and school desegregation here, the "Southern strategy" cannot fully explain the politics of busing. The President and the issue were far more complicated than that.

Richard Nixon traced his respect for civil rights to his Whittier College football coach Wallace "Chief" Newman, an American Indian. "It did not occur to me at the time," Nixon would recall, "But Chief taught us a lot about civil rights forty years before that movement became popular on college campuses." When Nixon attended Duke University Law School in the Jim Crow South, "I saw for the first time two nations, black and white, in twentieth-century America." When he ran for Vice President in 1952, Nixon committed himself to one nation: he was against the poll tax, against segregation in the District of Columbia, and in favor of anti-lynching legislation. As Vice President he endorsed the *Brown v. Board of Education* decision of 1954, lobbied hard for the Civil Rights Acts of 1957 and 1960, and spearheaded the Eisenhower Administration's effort to eliminate discrimination in the issuance of government contracts. He defended Eisenhower's dispatch of federal troops to enforce the desegregation of Central High School in Little Rock, Arkansas, in 1957 as the "moral" thing to do. Nixon refused to sign a restrictive covenant on his home, and the Quaker Vice President sent his two daughters to the desegregated Sidwell Friends School.[16]

Martin Luther King Jr. saluted Vice President Nixon's "assiduous labor and dauntless courage" as a civil rights advocate. Martin Luther King Sr. endorsed Nixon for President in 1960 after the candidate, in Jonathan Aitken's words, "held out for the most liberal platform on civil rights ever to be accepted by the Republican Party." Four years after receiving one-third of blacks' votes in his narrow loss to John Kennedy, Nixon urged Southern Republicans not to "climb aboard the sinking ship of racial injustice." In 1968 Nixon chose Maryland Governor Spiro Agnew as his running mate, in part because he had very good credentials as a moderate Republican [who] had defeated a racist Democrat." As a Presidential aspirant in 1968, Nixon championed "black capitalism," and as President he overcame the opposition of organized labor and a Senate majority to introduce the Philadelphia Plan, an affirmative action system for training and hiring black construction workers. Nixon Urban Affairs Advisor D. Patrick Moynihan recalled that "there weren't any more race riots under Nixon because of the hope generated in the black community by his welfare reform, revenue sharing, and job training proposals." White House Aide Robert Brown, an African American, remembered Nixon's record number of black appointees and "eightfold increase in the budget for civil rights enforcement." Kenneth Cole, assistant to Ehrlichman and liaison to Nixon's Domestic Council, observed that liberal ideas often attracted Nixon. Martin Anderson, deputy to White House Counsel Arthur Burns, added that Nixon's ideology was highly vulnerable to political influences from the left as well as the right. Finch recalled that

the "Southern strategy" did not necessarily foreclose attracting liberals and minorities to the Republican Party.[17]

At a time when "liberal Republican" was not an oxymoron, there indeed was much in the Nixon policies which the Left could embrace. Nixon's Task Force on Education, which issued its report on January 3, 1969, correctly predicted that the new Administration would face "continuous pressure" to "adopt a lower standard of policy generally with regard to desegregation than that enunciated by the Supreme Court." But it urged the Nixon White House to "do all in its power to assure that the Constitutional rights of children as defined by the courts are fully protected." The task force concluded that the Administration should augment the "woefully inadequate" funding required for enforcing school desegregation." The Administration would largely accept the task force's counsel. A July 1969 sit-in in Mitchell's office by thirty African Americans from four Southern states ended when Mitchell encouraged them to "watch what we do instead of listening to what we say" on school desegregation. At the same time, warnings to Nixon from Republican Governor Winthrop Rockefeller of Arkansas and Republican Senators Hugh Scott of Pennsylvania and Marlow Cook of Kentucky helped lead to the July 3 Mitchell-Finch statement expressing general adherence to the Johnson Administration guidelines.[18]

Nixon's "not-so-Southern strategy" also emboldened Finch to argue to Nixon privately in September that the Administration was actually "for busing" in many instances, then to oppose publicly in October a House-passed anti-busing amendment sponsored by Democrat Jamie Whitten of Mississippi. Finch contended that the measure, which would have prohibited HEW from spending federal money to force busing, was unconstitutional because "where racial isolation or segregation exists as a result of discrimination, the courts have required affirmative action based on constitutional principles to correct the situation." Finch's explanation hardly satisfied Thurmond, who admonished the Secretary, "Things like this do not go well in the South."[19]

Confusing? Well, yes—deliberately so. At a January 8, 1970 meeting Nixon told Finch that the Administration strategy on school desegregation was to "keep it confused." Nixon's straddle of the Stennis Amendment prompted this exchange between the President and the Attorney General at a February 18 Cabinet meeting:

Nixon:	"Mr. Attorney General, are you here?"
Mitchell:	"I think so."
Nixon:	"I thought you were out with Finch working on the Stennis Amendment. Which side are you on?"
Mitchell:	"In the right place: right in the middle."[20]

"The middle" meant lukewarm rejection of the Stennis Amendment coupled with lukewarm acceptance of a substitute sponsored by Hugh Scott. In a letter to Scott, the Administration wrote:

It is unfortunate that confusion has arisen over the Administration position in this matter. . . . Several days ago, the President indicated support of the concept of Senator Stennis' amendment to the extent that it could encourage equal application of the law throughout the country. The Administration has proposed, alternatively, the revised language which you have submitted for the reason that it would not prejudge *de facto* segregation [as the Stennis Amendment would] but would validate it in the south as elsewhere as long as the courts have not held such segregation unconstitutional.[21]

The Administration's ambivalence, while encouraging the defection of enough Republicans to pass the Stennis Amendment in the Senate in February, insured that it would go no farther. The "confusion" which the White House had disingenuously lamented to Scott was in fact quite intentional. "It's true that our current posture has an overlay of fuzz," Nixon aide Bryce Harlow wrote the President on February 23. The Administration posture is a calculated waffle."[22]

But this ambiguity risked fatally alienating the South, warned White House aide Patrick Buchanan. "My great concern," wrote Buchanan, "is that the people of the South will start to say that President Nixon is a fair weather friend; he clearly agrees with us, and yet he will do nothing to help us." Buchanan implored Nixon to emphatically and publicly state the "current case against continuing compulsory integration anywhere." Yet HEW Assistant Secretary James Farmer, an African-American, conveyed to the President "the prevalent feeling among Negroes that [the] Administration is embarked upon a Southern Strategy designed to slow down school desegregation to the detriment of Negro children."

He urged Nixon to "make a public statement putting [the] Administration unequivocally on record in support of court-ordered desegregation."[23]

For all the attention paid to Nixon's acceptance of Southern "good faith" and aversion to "unreasonable" busing, his March 24 school desegregation address sounded closer to Farmer than to Buchanan. "Some have interpreted various Administration statements and actions as a backing away from the principle of *Brown*" said the President. "We are not backing away. The constitutional mandate will be enforced." Nixon continued, "Deliberate racial segregation of pupils by official action is unlawful wherever it exists. In the words of the Supreme Court, it must be eliminated 'root and branch'—and it must be eliminated at once."[24]

African-American Republican Senator Edward Brooke of Massachusetts praised the speech's "unequivocal commitment" to school desegregation and Nixon's allocation of $1.5 billion to help enforce it. Yale law professor Alexander Bickel wrote approvingly in *The New Republic*, "The President's statement on school desegregation cannot have gladdened Senators Stennis and Thurmond." Professor James Coleman of Johns Hopkins University, a leading authority on school desegregation with whom Nixon consulted before the speech, applauded the enforcement monies as "an incentive to desegregate rather than an incentive not to."[25]

While Nixon was announcing his policy on school desegregation, his aides were formulating his policy on school resegregation. In the fall of 1969, Internal Revenue Service Commissioner Randolph Thrower had quietly begun to avoid ruling on applications by private schools for tax-exempt status. By 1970, several Southern private schools had filed suit against the IRS, demanding tax exemption. Assistant to the President Peter Flanigan then organized a working group which included Thrower, Dent, and Finch, among others. The group presented the President with three options: 1) privately grant tax exemption to Southern private schools which discriminated on the basis of race, evade press questions on the subject, and await a Supreme Court decision on the matter; 2) publicly grant tax exemptions to schools which clearly did not discriminate, tax schools which clearly discriminated, and leave unclear cases to the courts; and 3) publicly grant tax exemption to schools which professed and adopted non-discriminatory policies, tax schools which did not, and dispatch federal officials to enforce the policy.[26]

The "Southern strategy," and Buchanan, argued for Option 1 or 2: "What possible good can come out of denying the tax exemption? . . . There is no reason for the President to take this action—it would be a political error for which we would reap absolutely nothing in return." The "not-so-Southern strategy," and Harlow, chose Option 3: "I recognize the temporary political expediency to be served by Option 2. But I think this is an ephemeral advantage. It will not persuade the South, who will know better, and it surely will further abrade the President's relations with the blacks and whites who fondly regard civil rights . . . The failure to stand up to this issue will be a total loss on all sides."[27]

Nixon's selection of Option 3 on July 10 reversed his previous private opinion, conflicted with his Justice Department's position in federal court two months earlier, moved him to the left of his predecessor, and enraged his erstwhile Southern allies. Calling the decision "arbitrary, vindictive, and anti-South," Thurmond predicted Nixon's electoral defeat in 1972 unless he abruptly reversed course (he would not).[28]

On January 14, 1971, Finch's successor as HEW Secretary, the equally liberal Elliot Richardson, declared victory for the Nixon Administration's school desegregation efforts. Eighty percent of black children in eleven Southern states attended public schools with whites. More black children attended predominantly white public schools in the South than in any other region of the country.[29]

The verdicts of his biographers on President Nixon's school desegregation record, like the contemporary assessments, have tended to extremes. Contemporary critic-turned-sympathetic biographer Tom Wicker of *The New York Times* called Nixon "the right President at the right time," and desegregation "probably the outstanding domestic achievement of his administration." Joan Hoff argued that the "Southern strategy" all but died by the spring of 1970, after the failed Supreme Court nominations of Southern conservatives Clement Haynsworth and Harrold Carswell, and she concluded that Nixon, however reluctantly, surpassed the civil rights achievements of the New Deal and the Great Society. At the other extreme, Herbert Parmet wrote of Nixon and civil rights: "There was probably no other single subject about which Nixon so thoroughly compromised his convictions. . . . His positions on both school busing and 'forced' racial balancing were strongly with the dominant

view, and just as sharply opposed to a series of court decisions." Stephen Ambrose concurred: "Nixon had to be dragged kicking and screaming into desegregation on a meaningful scale, and he did what he did not because it was right but because he had no choice."[30]

Nixon deserves less credit than Wicker and Hoff have accorded him. If "the key to leadership" is, as Nixon aide Leonard Garment argued in 1972, "knowing what the speed limit of social change is," then Nixon was a brilliant leader on school desegregation. After all, he reassured many Southern blacks by opposing *de jure* segregation and heartened many Northern whites by accepting *de facto* segregation. But if leadership involves raising or lowering such limits, Nixon was less than brilliant. Not only did Richardson's desegregation statistics invite challenge, but their timing was suspect as well. "I completely agree with the strategy to complete this process now," Nixon told Finch, Mitchell, Harlow, and aide Edward Morgan on August 20, 1970, "rather than later, nearer the 1972 elections." Despite his later listing of school desegregation as a major domestic achievement, Nixon told his aides at the time to "stop bragging of past achievements, which get us no votes in the North while gravely abrading the entire South." While Nixon was, as Wicker and Hoff contend, the victim of Lyndon Johnson's procrastination on school desegregation, to assail Johnson is not necessarily to applaud Nixon. A President Hubert Humphrey, with impeccable civil rights credentials and without a Southern strategy, likely would have met the autumn 1969 school desegregation deadline and achieved a civil rights record at least as impressive as Nixon's.[31]

Amid all the political machinations, one can find a coherence to Nixon's school desegregation policies: in favor of desegregation [*Brown*] but against busing [*Swann*]. Yet most of the time, the latter position muffled the former—just as the President intended. An August 4, 1970 memorandum from aide H. R. Haldeman to Nixon revealed this imbalance: (on desegregation) "You wanted to emphasize [that] . . . all people concerned are to do only what the law requires, and they are to do it quietly without bragging about it"; (on busing) "Hit hard on the Administration position against busing at every opportunity." Ehrlichman remembers, "His [Nixon's] political compass told him to stay away from the whole subject of race: And if he could not stay out of it, the best political position was on the side of the white parents whose children were about to get on those hated buses." So despite all his heartfelt resentment of the "hypocrisy" of Northern liberals in condemning racial segregation in the South but tolerating it in their backyard, Nixon firmly safeguarded *de facto* segregation. When Senator Abraham Ribicoff, a liberal Connecticut Democrat, called Stennis' bluff and supported his "uniform application" amendment, Nixon warned his Cabinet, "He [Ribicoff] is trying to force this Administration to visit the troubles of the South on the North.... The cynical Northern liberals who don't have any problem with the civil rights issue in the coming elections will try to needle this Administration to enflame [sic] the situation."[32]

Whereas Wicker, Hoff, and Nixon's supporters blur the distinction between principle and politics. Parmet, Ambrose, and Nixon's detractors exaggerate it. Nixon's efforts to delay implementation of the *Brown* decision were unprincipled, but they were also unpopular in most of the nation. Seventy-four percent of Americans favored school integration in 1970. Nixon's attempts to undermine implementation of the *Swann* decision were popular among the public (only two percent of Americans favored forced busing to achieve racial balance in 1969), but they were also principled (Nixon had *always* opposed forced busing to achieve racial balance) and unpopular in Congress. "Never in fifteen years of testifying up on the Hill," said Richardson, had he encountered the degree of resistance which Nixon's anti-busing legislation engendered. Nixon's instincts on tax-exempt Southern "academies" were political, but his actions were based on politics *and* principle. In choosing "Option 3," Nixon not only accepted Harlow's counsel that the "straddle" offered by "Option 2" would be politically expedient in the short term, but he also agreed that in the long run, "it is certain to play pluperfect hell throughout the South," while following "no principle at all."[33]

To condemn the Richard Nixon who vigorously opposed *de jure* school segregation in the 1950s for timidly perpetuating *de facto* school segregation in the 1970s is to overlook two important realities of those two decades: the country had changed, and Richard Nixon had changed. From 1950 to 1970, the fraction of African-Americans living in the South had declined from one-half to one-fourth. As blacks arrived in Northern cities and whites departed for Northern and Southern suburbs, New York went from ten to twenty-one percent black,

Chicago from fourteen to thirty-three percent black, and Washington, D.C. from thirty-five to seventy-one percent black. In 1972 only twenty-three percent of African-American school children attended integrated schools. So when Vice President Agnew opined that "massive rioting" might result from a federal assault on such *de facto* segregation, Nixon concurred, citing the "many schools in which full-time policemen are stationed in the halls and classrooms. . . ." To his critics, "law and order," like "neighborhood schools," and "quality education" were racial code words. But to Richard Nixon and to most Americans of whatever color, they were legitimate priorities. And busing was not. "The ideal is a situation in which race is irrelevant to [school] assignment," wrote African-American journalist William Raspberry. "Preoccupation with mathematical precision, unfortunately, is not the way to achieve that ideal." Even Hubert Humphrey had come to that conclusion by 1972. So unless and until the courts forced him to act—in enforcing the *Brown* decision after October 1969 and in seeking a moratorium on busing after the *Swann* decision of March 1971—Nixon was largely content to uphold the status quo.[34]

"Most of the present population," Vice President Richard Nixon had predicted in 1956, "[will] live to see racial integration accomplished in the nation's public and private schools." Then Nixon witnessed the assassinations of John and Robert Kennedy, Malcolm X, and Martin Luther King; observed three waves of race riots in Northern cities; and read gloomy analyses by Johnson's Assistant Secretary of Labor Moynihan of the deterioration of the black family, Coleman of the dubious value of school desegregation, the Kerner Commission of the country's widening racial gulf despite *de jure* desegregation, and Bickel of the limitations of federal desegregation efforts. His defense of civil rights hardly helped in his defeat by Kennedy in 1960, and his ambivalence toward civil rights did not hurt in his victory over Humphrey and Wallace in 1968. So by 1970, President Richard Nixon decided that "integration is not the wave of the future," after all.[35]

Nixon's own view of his Presidential legacy on civil rights offers fodder for friends and foes alike. He boasted that the Philadelphia Plan was "the right kind of affirmative action—a specifically targeted plan, temporary in nature, designed to remedy a specific, clear denial of equal opportunity. And it worked." He pointed with "justifiable pride" to "what we accomplished in the area of peacefully desegregating schools in the South." "That we have failed to turn this principle into reality in every respect," Nixon wrote of desegregation twenty years later, "does not mean we should abandon it." But he inaccurately claimed that the Philadelphia Plan avoided racial quotas; implicitly absolved himself from the "total failure of the Great Society" domestic policy of Lyndon Johnson (which Nixon kept largely intact); frankly admitted to settling for a "moderate balance" on civil rights; and sadly concluded, twenty years after his Presidency, that the United States remained a racially divided nation. And just like President Nixon, former President Nixon preferred to talk a lot more about relations between nations than relations between races.[36]

"There may be some doubt as to the validity of the *Brown* philosophy that integrating education will pull up the blacks and not pull down the whites," Nixon wrote in January 1972 . . . but there is no doubt whatever . . . that education requiring excessive transportation for students is definitely inferior." Two decades in the life of the United States and the career of Richard Nixon had culminated in this marriage of principle and politics. And two more decades of unpopular court orders and festering racial wounds have vindicated Nixon's judgment then, without erasing his share of responsibility for the ambiguous legacy of school desegregation in the United States now. [37]

Endnotes

1. Davison Douglas, ed., *School Busing: Constitutional and Political Developments,* vol. I (New York, 1994), pp. ix–x.
2. *Ibid.* pp. x–xi.
3. Garry Wills, *Nixon Agonistes* (New York, 1979), pp. 244–245, 249, 251; Joan Hoff notes, however, that Nixon himself refused to acknowledge such a strategy when she interviewed him January 26, 1983, in Joan Hoff, *Nixon Reconsidered* (New York, 1994), p. 79.
4. Richard Nixon, *RN: The Memoirs of Richard Nixon* (New York, 1990), p. 444; Roger Morris, *Uncertain Greatness: Henry Kissinger and American Foreign Policy* (New York. 1977). p. 131; Robert Sam Anson, *Exile: The Unquiet Oblivion of Richard M. Nixon* (New York, 1984). p. 148.
5. Hoff, *Nixon Reconsidered,* p. 74; Memorandum from Fred LaRue to Bryce Harlow, 18 February 1969, White House Central Files, White House Special Files, Box 35, Richard M. Nixon Presidential Project, National Archives, Alexandria, VA, p. 2.
6. Memorandum from Alexander Butterfield to the Attorney General and the Secretary of Health, Education and Welfare, 14 March 1969, White House Central Files, Subject Files, Box 8, RMNPP; Memorandum from Bryce Harlow to the President, 13 April 1969, White House Central Files, Subject Files, Box 8.
7. Statement by the Honorable Robert H. Finch. Secretary of the Department of Health, Education and Welfare, and the Honorable John N. Mitchell, Attorney General, 3 July 1969, White House Central Files, Subject Files, Box 11. RMN, p. 8; "A Debt to Dixie," *Newsweek* 74 (14 July 1969), p. 24; "Spelling it out in Black and White," *Newsweek* 74 (22 September 1969), p. 24.
8. Dent, former Republican Party state chairman in South Carolina, had joined the Nixon Administration in January, and by June had moved his office from the Executive Office Building to the White House. Nixon owed much to Dent's mentor, segregationist Senator Strom Thurmond, for his victory in South Carolina and other Southern states in 1968. "Whenever the White House seems to drift to the right or placate Southern interests, Presidential Aide Dent is thought to be deeply involved," in "Up at Harry's Place," *Time* (11 July 1969), p. 15; Tom Wicker, *One of Us: Richard Nixon and the American Dream* (New York, 1991), p. 493; Memorandum from Harry Dent to the President, 30 October 1969, White House Central Files, Subject Files, Box 8, RMNPP; Memorandum from Robert Finch to John Ehrlichman, 23 January 1970, White House Central Files, Subject Files Box 9, RMNPP.
9. Memorandum from Bryce Harlow to Staff Secretary, 21 February 1970, White House Central Files, Subject Files. Box 9, RMNPP; "Nixon Administration Statement," 11 February 1970, White House Central Files, Subject Files, Box 9, RMNPP; John Osborne, "Chicken, Southern-Fried," *The New Republic* (21 February 1970). pp. 13–14.
10. "Nixon on Desegregation." *U.S. News and World Report* 68 (6 April 1970), pp. 90–87; G. C. Thelen, "Nixon-School. (Tops 44)," attached to Memorandum from John Brown to John Ehrlichman, White House Central Files, Subject Files, Box 35, RMNPP.
11. Letter from Strom Thurmond to Bryce Harlow, 21 October 1969. White House Central Files, Subject Files, Box 11, RMNPP; John Ehrlichman, "Notes of Meetings with the President," 19 August 1970, White House Central Files, White House Special Film, Box 5, RMNPP, Roy Reed, "Nixon Reassures South on Schools," *New York Times*, 15 August 1970, sec. 1. p. 11.
12. Memorandum from Edward Morgan for the President's Files, 21 September 1970, President's Office Files, Box 82, RMNPP; Archibald Cox, *The*

Court and the Constitution (Boston, 1987), p. 264, Memorandum from H. R. Haldeman to John Ehrlichman, 22 July 1971, White House Central Files, Box 35, RMNPP.

13. Gary Orfield, "Congress, the President, and Anti-Busing Legislation, 1966–1974," in Davison Douglas, ed. *School Busing: Constitutional and Political Developments,* vol. 2 (New York, 1994), pp. 25–29; Memorandum from Patrick Buchanan for the President's File, 17 March 1974 President's Office Flies, Box 88, p. 1.

14. Orfield, *Ibid.,* p. 31; "Anti-Busing Amendments Added to Education Bill," *Congressional Quarterly Almanac,* 1974, James Cannon Files, Box 5, Gerald R. Ford Presidential Library, Ann Arbor, MI, pp. 15–16.

15. Orfield, *Ibid,* pp. 31, 36, 37; Bernard Schwartz, *A History of the Supreme Court* (New York. 1993), p. 323; "Anti-Busing Amendments Added to Education Bill," p. 16; Memorandum from Caspar Weinberger to the President 5 August 1974, David Lissy Files, Box 4, GRFPL, p. 2.

16. Richard Nixon, In the Arena (New York, 1990), pp. 105–106; Stephen Ambrose, *Nixon: The Education of a Politician, 1913-1962* (New York. 1987), pp. 269, 434–436; Julie Nixon Eisenhower, in *Pat Nixon: The Untold Story* (New York, 1986), p. 170, writes, "When Tricia graduated from public Horace Mann in 1958, my parents debated whether at not she should be enrolled in private school. Politically it was important that the Nixon children be in public school so that no one could accuse the Vice President or not believing in Washington's integrated institutions." But because the Washington public schools were "inadequate," Eisenhower writes that "in the fall of 1958, Tricia and I were enrolled at Sidwell Friends, a coeducational private school which was not only integrated but also highly respected academically." The extent of racial integration at Sidwell Friends at the time is uncertain, as the school did not keep records of the racial composition of its student body, in Telephone Interview of Amy Fitch, Archivist, Sidwell Friends School, by author, 29 April 1997.

17. Jonathan Aitken, *Nixon: A Life* (New York, 1993), pp. 248. 271, 324, 355–356, 375; Hugh Davis Graham, *The Civil Rights Era* (New York, 1990), p. 340; Herbert Parmet, *Richard Nixon and His America* (Boston, 1990), pp. 266–268; Hoff, p. 78; Robert Brown, "Nixon's Legacy to African-Americans," n.d., Richard Nixon Presidential Library, Yorba Linda, CA. p. 2; Interviews of Kenneth Cole, 21 December 1977, p. 2; Martin Anderson, 3 January 1978, p. 1; and Robert Finch, 3 March 1978, p. 6. by James Reichley, GRFPL.

18. "Report of the Task Force on Education," 3 January 1969, RMNPP, p. 11; "The Administration: Tenuous Balance," *Time* 94 (11 July 1969), p. 14.

19. John Ehrlichman, "Notes of Meetings with the President," 10 September 1969; "Statement of Robert H. Finch, Department of Health, Education, and Welfare," 14 October 1969, White House Central Files, Subject Plies, Box 11, RMNPP; Thurmond to Harlow, 21 October 1969.

20. John Ehrlichman, "Notes of Meetings with the President," 8 January 1970; Memorandum from Jim Keogh for the President's File, 18 February 1970, President's Office Files, Box 80, RMNPP.

21. Letter to Senator Hugh Scott, 17 February 1970, White House Central Files, Subject Files, Box 9, RMNPP.

22. Memorandum from Bryce Harlow to the President, 23 February 1970, White House Central Files, Subject Files, Box 9, RMNPP.

23. Memorandum from Patrick Buchanan to the President, 28 February 1970, White House Central Files, Subject Files, Box 11. RMNPP, pp. 1, 3; Memorandum from Robert Brown for the President's File, 5 March 1970, President's Office Files, Box 90, RMNPP, p. 2.

24. "Nixon on Desegregation," pp. 80, 86.

25. "Senator Brooke on Nixon Message," 24 March 1970, p. 1; Alexander Bickel, "Realistic, Sensible II)." *The New Republic* 162 (April 4 and 11, 1970), p. 14; Robert Semple, "President Asks for Funds for School Desegregation," *New York Times,* 22 May 1970, sec. 1, p. 20.

26. Memorandum from John Ehrlichman to the President, 7 July 1970, White House Central Files, Subject Files. Box 2, RMNPP, pp. 1, 3.

27. Memorandum from Patrick Buchanan to the President 7 July 1970, White House Central Files, Subject Files, Box 2, RMNPP, p. 1; Memorandum from Bryce Harlow to the President, 17 June 1970, White House Central Files, Subject Film Box 7, RMNPP, p. 1.

28. Ehrlichman wrote on January 8, 1970, "President favors exemption" for private schools, in John Ehrlichman. "Notes of Meetings with the President," p. 2; Ehrlichnian wrote Nixon on July 18, "You will recall that you were surprised and curious that Bryce Harlow's position which [sic] was that option 3 should be accepted," in Memorandum from John Ehrlichman to the President, 18 July 1970, White House Central Files, Subject Files, Box 2, p. 1; Kenneth Crawford, "Thurmond Threatens," *Newsweek* 76 (3 August 1970), p. 25.

29. John Osborne, "Call it Desegregation," *The New Republic* 164 (30 January 1971), p. 12.

30. Wicker, *One of Us.* pp. 487, 496, 498, 507; Hoff, *Nixon Reconsidered,* pp. 79, 49; Haynsworth, of South Carolina's Fourth Circuit Court of Appeals. lost 45–55 on November 21, 1969; Carswell, of Florida's Fifth Circuit Court of Appeals, lost 45–51 on April 8, 1970.

Nixon, blaming their defeats in part on "the fact that they were born in the South," then successfully nominated Harry Blackmun of Minnesota. Nixon did not give up on the South, however—he successfully nominated Lewis Powell of Virginia in October 1971, in Stephen Ambrose, *Nixon: The Triumph of a Politician, 1962–1972* (New York, 1989), p. 471.

31. Theodore White, *The Making of the President, 1972* (New York, 1973), p. 227, "Desegregation: How Much Further?" *Time* 96 (26 October 1970), p. 56; Memorandum from Bryce Harlow to Staff Secretary, 20 August 1970, White House Central Files. Subject Files, Box 9, RMNPP, p. 1; Hoff, p. 20.

32. Memorandum for the President from H. R. Haldeman, 4 August 1970, White House Central Files, Subject Files, Box 9, p. 1; John Ehrlichman, *Winess to Power* (New York, 1982), p. 235; Memorandum from Keogh for President's File, 18 February 1970, p. 3.

33. Graham, *The Civil Rights Era*, p. 565; Parmet. *Richard Nixon and His America,* p. 596; Memorandum from Patrick Buchanan for the President's File, 28 March 1972, Personal Office Files, RMNPP. p. 1; Memorandum. from Bryce Harlow to Peter Flanigan, 12 May 1970, White House Central Files, Subject Files, Box 9, RMNPP, p. 2.

34. Jack Rosenthal, "Major Integration Test Confronts U.S. in 1972," *New York Times*, 19 January 1972, sec. 1, p. 20; Alexander Bickel, "Desegregation: Where Do We Go From Here?" *The New Republic* 162 (7 February 1970), p. 20; Memorandum from Bryce Harlow to Staff Secretary, 21 February 1970, White House Central Files, Subject Files, Box 9, RMNPP, p. 2; William Raspberry, "Massive Busing: A Waste," *Washington Post*, 26 February 1972, in Douglas, *School Busing: Constitutional and Political Developments*, vol. 4 p. 67; Marjorie Hunter, "Nixon's Plan Splits Rivals; Ervin Leads Busing Attack," *New York Times*, 19 March 1972, sec. 1. p. 1.

35. Milton Bracker, "Nixon Optimistic on Integration," *New York Times*, 19 October 1956, sm. 1, p. 1; The analyses were *The Negro Family in America* (1965) by Moynihan (later Nixon's Urban Affairs Advisor), *Report on Equal Educational Opportunity* (1966) by Coleman, The Report of the National Advisory Commission on Civil Disorders (1968), chaired by Governor Otto Kerner of Illinois, and "Desegregation: Where Do We Go From Here?" (1970), a *New Republic* article written by Bickel; In 1960 Nixon won thirty-two percent, and in 1968 thirteen percent, of blacks' votes, in Hoff, Nixon Reconsidered, p. 78, and Parmet, *Richard Nixon and His America*, p. 631; John Ehrlichman, "Notes of Meetings with the President," 19 March 1970,

36. Richard Nixon, **Beyond Peace** (New York, 1994), pp. 187, 191, 227–228; Nixon, RN: *The Memoirs of Richard Nixon*, pp. 436, 445.

37. Nixon, *RN: The Memoirs of Richard* Nixon. pp. 444–445.

The Affirmative Action Cases

Bakke, Weber and Fullilove

David W. Bishop*

In the broad survey of American constitutional development, the period from 1937 to the present was one in which the United States Supreme Court gradually departed from its protection of property rights, with supportive laissez-faire doctrines, to a new era of Court protection of civil and political rights. The Warren Court, with its judicial activists, easily emerged as the renowned protectors of individual liberties.[1] As far back as 1938, the Supreme Court introduced legal concepts for the new era when it observed: "prejudice against discrete (e.g. blacks) and insular minorities" may be a special condition for more searching judicial inquiry.[2] With this premise, the Warren Court eventually developed a methodology and legal guideposts for racial discrimination cases as a means for implementing the Civil War amendments.

Prior to the 1960s, rarely did the United States Supreme Court utilize the equal protection clause of the Fourteenth Amendment outside racial discrimination cases. The Warren Court, however, embraced a rigid two-tier attitude in its "new" equal protection cases, which expanded the list of interests to be protected by the Fourteenth Amendment.

In the first tier, the Court reasoned that some racial and ethnic minorities had been isolated and very often unable to effectively influence the majoritarian processes, therefore, all legal restrictions curtailing the civil rights of those groups were immediately "suspect."[3] Government practices or statutes which restricted "fundamental rights," or which were designed to "invidiously discriminate" against discrete and insular minorities or which had "suspect classifications" were to be subjected to "strict judicial scrutiny." Additionally, those aforementioned government practices could be justified only if they furthered a "compelling" government purpose.[4] Most of the equal protection cases involving racial discrimination came under the first tier. In all other challenges involving whites, economics, voting, criminal appeals, interstate travel etc., a second tier of attitudes developed, and the Court used a deferential formula called the "rational basis" test. With this test, the Court merely determined whether the program was rationally related to legitimate state goals, provided no constitutionally protective right was involved or invidious discrimination was evident.[5] The model did not require scrutiny of legislative motivation; it merely required the Court to assess the rationality of means as related to state ends. This tradition, of course, is as old as *McCulloch v. Maryland* (1819).

According to Gerald Gunther, the Warren Court used this rigid two-tier attitude too aggressively in some situations, so much so that it was "strict in theory and fatal in fact," and "in other contexts, the deferential 'old' equal protection reigned, with minimal scrutiny in theory and virtually none in fact."[6] Several justices of the Warren and Burger Courts sought an intermediate position, but the Burger Court was "reluctant to expand the scope of the new equal protection ... clause."[7] Both Justices Thurgood Marshall and Lewis Powell searched for new formulas or an overarching interpretation applicable to "all" equal protection cases. In one of his dissenting opinions, Marshall urged the Court to:

> scrutinize particular classifications, depending on the constitutional societal importance of the

* David W. Bishop is Professor of History at North Carolina Central University, Durham North Carolina.

interest adversely affected and the recognized invidiousness of the basis upon which the particular classification is drawn . . . , that is, an approach in which concentration [is] placed upon the characters of the classification in question, the relative importance to individuals in the class discriminated against of the governmental benefits that they do receive, and the asserted state interest in suspect of the classification.[8]

Under Marshall's intermediate approach, the Court would evaluate the gains and losses of a particular minority admission program in order to assess its possible detrimental or good effects. The ultimate goal would be to increase minority membership in the professions. Marshall would have the Court concentrate on individuals within a group status, constitutional and societal importance, governmental benefits and state interest.

In the midst of these legal traditions, the American people found themselves confronted with the "Black Revolution" or the "Second Reconstruction" during the 1960s. It became increasingly clear that prior efforts to rely on the various Fair Employment Practice Committees and Executive Orders to improve the employment conditions for blacks were not sufficient nor were the laws prohibiting employment discrimination. Therefore, President John F. Kennedy issued Executive Orders 10925 and 11114 in 1961 authorizing, for the first time, affirmative action as a remedy. The President's Committee on Equal Employment Opportunity (CEEO) was established. But the most effective Executive Order was 11246 issued by President Lyndon B. Johnson in 1965 and amended in 1967 and 1969. These Orders mandated an end to discrimination in employment. In regard to affirmative action, Professor John Fleming observed: "The affirmative action requirement means that employers will do more than remain neutral, but will undertake a special effort to recruit, employ and promote qualified members of groups that had heretofore been excluded, even if excluded inadvertently."[9]

The Office of Federal Contract Compliance, under the Secretary of Labor, was given authority to implement Executive Order 11246. That office delegated the responsibility for enforcing affirmative action in higher education to The Department of Health, Education and Welfare (HEW). Institutions of higher learning opposed affirmative action for blacks and other minorities, and proposals to HEW were at a snails pace. By 1975 only

thirty-two affirmative action plans in higher education had received tentative approval, and only one had received final approval in grants and contracts by HEW. Thus, the thrust for aggressive support for affirmative action was woefully missing from institutions of higher education, and without the initial aggressive support for affirmative action the entire program could become a temporary phase in the "Second Reconstruction."[10]

Ominous signs were prevalent when Congress enacted Title VI Section 601 of the Civil Rights Act of 1964 which prohibited discrimination in any federally financed program.[11] It is within the aforementioned milieu that one must consider the three affirmative action cases.

On October 10, 1977, the United States Supreme Court began hearing oral arguments in the case of *The Regents of the University of California v. Bakke.* Allan Bakke, then forty-one, who previously was denied admission to several medical schools, including the new medical school at Davis, California, because admission officials considered other whites more qualified than *Bakke* or because, as in the Davis medical school, there was a special program designed to increase the number of medical doctors among blacks, Chicanos and other minorities, thereby, reducing the total number of whites admitted to Davis. Sixteen of the one-hundred seats were reserved for blacks and insular minorities. The California State Supreme Court had ruled in favor of *Bakke,* and the case went to the United States Supreme Court on *writ of certiorari.*[12] A record fifty-one *amici* briefs were filed with the Court either in support of or in opposition to *Bakke.*

Arguments before the Court indicated that the respondent's lawyer, Reynold H. Colvin, insisted that Bakke, as an individual and not one of group status, had been invidiously discriminated against because of his race, and that the California Supreme Court had correctly used the "strict scrutiny" tier method, traditionally used in behalf of discrete and insular minorities, because the degree of judicial scrutiny did not depend upon membership in a particular racial or ethnic group.[13] The purpose here was to present a single formula to the Court applicable to all equal protection cases, a formula Justice Powell eagerly sought. Archibald Cox, petitioner's attorney, argued that the Davis program did not constitute "individious racial discrimination"; it did not injure a suspect class; and it did not infringe on a fundamental right of *Bakke* as an individual.

Consequently, Cox argued, the California Supreme Court erred in its use of the "strict scrutiny" tier, and that it should have used the "rational basis" standard because "the rationale for its application is absent when the [Davis] program at issue assists rather than harms discrete and insular minorities."[14] Indeed, Cox warned the Court, *Bakke* had none of the attributes which caused "strict scrutiny," and to apply "the suspect classification doctrine to defeat the Davis program would stand the equal protection clause on its head."[15] This is precisely what Justice Powell did in writing the ruling of the Court; the equal protection clause of the Fourteenth Amendment to the Constitution now stands upside down in a condition of utter confusion. For the third time within ninety-seven years, the amendment which was designed to facilitate the inclusion of blacks into the American system was again used by the Court to impede black progress and to benefit whites.

The Court was asked for the first time by petitioner to adopt a more restrictive view of the equal protection clause "and hold that discrimination against members of the white 'majority' cannot be suspect if its purpose can be characterized as 'benign'."[16] However, Justice Powell observed that innocent white persons might be so outraged at preferential treatment for blacks and Chicanos that they might perceive their denial of equal rights as invidious racial discrimination, thus requiring "strict judicial scrutiny" of these preferential treatment programs as at Davis. Powell showed little patience with the Court's two-tier attitude, and he offered his own formula, as had been suggested by briefs in support of *Bakke*:

> It is the individual who is entitled to judicial protection against classification based upon his racial or ethnic background because such distinctions impinge upon personal rights, rather than the individual only because of his membership in a particular group, then constitutional standards may be applied consistently.[17]

Powell concluded with this emphasis: "All legal restrictions which curtail the rights of a single racial group are immediately suspect," and the courts should subject them to rigid scrutiny. Once the methodology question was settled, the Court could readily rule in favor of *Bakke*, who seemingly had suffered so long (about six years) from invidious racial discrimination. The Court of course ruled

against the fixed number of sixteen at Davis: ". . . that portion of the California court's judgment holding petitioner's special admissions program invalid under the Fourteenth Amendment must be affirmed." It was observed that there had been no history of racial discrimination practiced at Davis. However, the Court sanctioned the use of race as an influential factor in admissions.[18] The last point was Orwellian and innocuous. If such influential factors as race, geography, gender, grades, tests, etc. are used as criteria for admission to professional schools, then some factors will be more influential than others; no brilliance is required to determine the least influential factor.

What is implied by the *Bakke* decision is the continuing unwillingness of the American people to develop and sustain viable programs to correct palpable social injustices done to blacks and other minorities. The black experience is replete with short-lived corrective or remedial programs. Could ten years (1867–1877) of rhetorical "Reconstruction" correct 200 years (1652–1867) of the demeaning effects of slavery and incomplete freedom? Could sixteen years of the *Brown* era (1954–1970) remedy the psychological, sociological and economic deprivations done to black individuals and black groups during fifty-eight years of "separate but unequal?" As Justice Thurgood Marshall stated in his dissenting opinion:

> In light of the sorry history of discrimination and its devastating impact on the lives of Negroes, bringing the Negro into the mainstream of American life should be a state interest of the highest order. To fail to do so is to ensure that America will forever remain a divided society.[19]

Justice Lewis Powell's conclusions in regard to the black experience was that one could not turn the clock backwards and offend white individuals by having preferential treatment for blacks. In god-like fashion, he ignored the historical narrative which impugned the social, economic, political and psychological effects of the American system on blacks, and he began black history with the period following *Brown v. Board of Education* in 1954. Accepting the Jewish and East European-Americans' arguments, Powell implied that blacks and Chicanos sprang forth full-grown from the head of Zeus in 1954; consequently, the merit test should be the prime criterion for entrance into professional schools. On the contrary, the American Civil Liberties Union's brief observed: "The United States cannot remedy the egregious wrongs that blight the nation's history by leaving the victims of racism where *Brown v. Board of Education* found them."[20] The American Bar Association advised the Court that minority students would be motivated to develop their academic skills once they began to aspire for professional roles, and this process would result in upward mobility and a more integrated society.[21]

The *amici* briefs in support of *Bakke* and the majority Court opinion acknowledged attentiveness to the polls. A Gallup Poll of March, 1977, indicated that eighty-three percent of the American people opposed preferential treatment for women and minorities in higher education and employment, and they favored merit tests despite past discrimination.[22] A 1976 Harris Poll found only twenty-eight percent of Americans favored some integration in some areas of life. The consensus seemed to have been that whites believed that blacks had been discriminated against in the United States, but they did not believe blacks were treated unfairly. Whites were asked in a 1977 poll to choose among several explanations as to why blacks had fewer jobs, poorer housing and lower incomes than whites. Sixty-five percent of the whites believed that blacks did not have the motivation or willpower to get out of poverty. This was the heart of white opinion; they deeply resented what they believed was the unwillingness of blacks to live by white middle-class standards. Every two years since 1970, the Center of Political Studies at the University of Michigan has asked Americans to choose between two alternative positions: (1) The government in Washington should make every possible effort to improve the social and economic conditions of blacks and other minorities or (2) Do you think that the Washington government should not make any special efforts to help minority groups; rather, they should be expected to help themselves. After each biennium, more people agreed on minority self-help than on government special programs. Dr. George Gallup remarked in 1977 that rarely had public opinion been so united as it was against quotas and special preference for minority groups.[23]

With this careful observation of public opinion polls by Americans and the Court's decision in *Bakke*, perhaps Mr. Dooley's aphorism needs updating: The Supreme Court "Gallops" with the polls. These public opinion polls certainly reveal consistencies and confusion among whites, i.e., racism,

ambivalence and ambiguities. The Court has a sophist teacher.

Historically, the issue of quotas had different connotations for different ethnic groups and women. Beginning with the National Origins Act of 1924, East Europeans witnessed the discriminatory effects of the American quota system. The combined quotas of Poland and Greece were less than that of Sweden; similarly, the combined quotas of Italy and Russia were less than that of Norway. It was not until 1965 that Congress finally eliminated quotas based on race or national origin. Through it all, East European Americans and Jews regarded quotas as invidious, demeaning and a means of exclusion. Simultaneously, white women and blacks used the quota system as a vehicle for inclusion in the political arena.[24] In addition, Stokely Carmichael and Charles V. Hamilton in their book *Black Power: The Politics of Liberation in America* called upon blacks to demand the quota system in every facet of American life.[25] The advantages of the use of quotas were expressed before the United States Supreme Court in an *amicus* brief by the Honorable Patricia Schroeder, Member of Congress, *et al*:

> Specific numerical hiring quotas succeed where non-discrimination injunctions fail because they provide a mechanism for addressing precisely those aspects of discrimination that are based on 'entrenched' behavior and beliefs. First and most important numerical goals provide specific benchmarks by which non-discrimination can be measured. Second, it is well documented that women and minorities are deterred from even seeking employment by their conviction that no jobs are available to members of their class. Public awareness of a commitment to hire . . . a specific number of women and blacks may begin to reduce the built-in discouragement that years of negative experiences have created. Finally it is only when a specified number of women and blacks are brought into a workplace that the stereotypical assumptions of their co-workers and supervisors will be challenged.[26]

To some, quotas are too rigid and goals are more flexible. Regardless of the pro and con arguments, goals and timetables are mechanisms to measure the "rate of progress" on the journey to equal opportunity.[27] In regard to the advocates of the merit system, Dr. Mary Berry, former Chancellor of the University of Colorado and former HEW Assistant Secretary of Education, observed: "at the very least, twenty percent of the mediocre white males now employed on university faculties initially obtained and now retain their jobs solely because they did not have to compete with minorities and women, or even other men for them."[28] Thus Afro-Americans and white women rejoiced in the use of quotas in politics as a means of inclusion in the system. Therefore, hyphenated Americans, blacks and women were already divided on the issue of quotas long before *Bakke*. The "native" Americans who advocated the quota system for East Europeans and Orientals were the same people who denounced quotas for blacks and women, and they used every derogatory adjective available to justify exclusion of these groups. Such words or phrases as filthy, ignorant, innately inferior, dead Indians, Chink-Chink, bastards, syphilitic M . . . F . . . , rice eaters, atheist, communist, Pollacks, Jew, etc., were commonplace in "native" American folklore.

The tragedy of *Bakke* is not that the Court rejected quotas, but that American racists used Jews and East European-Americans to dissolve a workable coalition and to forthwith impede the increasing social mobility of blacks, Chicanos and other minorities into the mainstream of American life. Self-interest became self-serving, and *Bakke* marched magnificently on its head from the courtroom to the classroom.

Seemingly, the hardest question Jews and East-European-Americans had to answer was that if quotas were used in these preferential programs for blacks and other minorities, which ethnic group(s) will be sacrificed or excluded from professional schools? The following organizations from the above ethnic groups filed *amici* briefs in support of *Bakke*: The American Jewish Committee, American Jewish Congress, Anti-Defamation League of B'Nai B'rith, Jewish Labor Committee, National Jewish Commission on Law and Public Affairs, UNICO National (the largest Italian American organization in America), Italian-American Foundation, Chicago Division of UNICO, Hellenic Bar Association of Illinois, Ukrainian Congress Committee of America, Polish American Affairs Council and Polish American Educators Associations.

According to Leonard Fein, a professor at Brandeis University, Jewish organizations supported affirmative action on paper but they opposed quotas vigorously elsewhere. Jews favored the merit system because no other ethnic group has benefited more from that system than Jews, especially in higher education. They were not willing to sacrifice a place in medical schools for disadvantaged blacks. Jews believed, continued Fein, that for some to overcome others would be forced to undercome. They believed that the *American economy could not accommodate the aspirations of excluded minorities,* wrote Fein; consequently, the allocation of seats for blacks and Chicanos meant an unfair shift of those seats away from Jews. Finally, Fein concluded, there is no single liberal reform movement in Western Civilization that has benefited Jews more than the American promise to include Jews in their system on the condition that Jews drop their Jewishness as a group and that individual Jews adhere to the American merit system, otherwise they would revert to group status just like all blacks who have group status.[29] There is an undercurrent message in the *amicus* brief filed by Jews and East European Americans in support of *Bakke.*

> At issue here is a basic question of broad social policy with direct and fundamental constitutional implications: Shall racial preferences in admission to medical school be accorded selected racial and ethnic minorities in order to increase the number of medical students and doctors who are members of these preferred groups above the level which might exist absent such preference? This is a question which goes far beyond the admission policy of any one school. . . . Its implications can change the very character of our society. So significant a decision cannot and should not be left to the judgment of individual institutions. . . .[30]

The brief indicated that the Davis Task Force doctors were not competent to handle such a problem. Therefore, the Jews and East European-Americans devised a suggested rationale, which probably would take a hundred years and thousands of litigations to improve the physician ratio of blacks and other minorities.[31]

During the two decades of the 1950s and 1960s when blacks were crusading to desegregate and integrate the schools, restaurants, hotels, public facilities, etc., hyphenated East European-Americans and Jews joined the "March of Washington" and the "Stride toward Freedom," but in the 1970s when blacks and other minorities sought real economic and professional benefits of a higher order, Jews and East European-Americans became the devil's advocate, and Satan never had better allies. They unwittingly assisted American racists in returning the "spook" to the door.

In June, 1977, shortly before the *Bakke* decision, 100 black executives representing their companies whose aggregate wealth was $900,000,000, met in the White House so President Carter could inform them of his policies and the direction of his administration as they affected black economic well being. The euphoria derived from this first of its kind meeting was short lived stated Earl G. Graves, publisher and editor of *Black Enterprise*, because in that same month the *Bakke* decision was announced. Graves was aware of numerous white business acquaintances who considered affirmative action programs dead, and that the decision would encourage them to stop their hiring efforts. Regarding the future, Graves advised blacks to insist on the continuation of currently engaged affirmative action programs; to encourage companies to continue doing business with black entrepreneurs; and that blacks must see to it that the Carter administration kept its commitment to triple federal contract procurement no matter what was decided in *Bakke*.[32]

The *Weber* case began in Gramercy, Louisiana in 1974 after the Kaiser Aluminum and Chemical Corporation and the United Steelworkers of America had agreed to voluntarily establish an affirmative action program for black craftsmen. The objectives were to redress a statistical racial imbalance due to past discrimination against blacks in craft unions and to harmonize the percentage of blacks in the crafts with the local labor force, which was two percent and thirty-nine percent respectively. A Gramercy management training program was created to select trainees on the basis of seniority within their racial groups, but fifty percent of the positions were reserved for blacks. During the first period, seven blacks and six whites were selected. Since there had been previous discrimination against blacks in the craft unions, some of the junior black trainees had less seniority than some of the white workers whose applications were rejected.[33]

Brian F. Weber was one of the rejected white workers; therefore, he brought suit against Kaiser and the United Steelworkers of America on the legal contention that the Kaiser affirmative action program violated Title VII of the Civil Rights Act of 1964 because it gave preferential treatment to blacks *vis a vis* whites. Both the Federal District Court and the Court of Appeals agreed with Weber, and the case went to the United States Supreme Court on a *writ of certiorari*.[34]

Title VII Section 703(a) of the Civil Rights Act of 1964 reads:

> It shall be an unlawful employment practice for an employer—to fail or refuse to hire or to discharge any individual, or otherwise to discriminate against any individual with respect to his compensation, terms, conditions, or privileges of employment, because of such individual's race, color, religion, sex, or national origin; or to, limit, or classify his employees in any way which would deprive or tend to deprive any individual of employment opportunities or otherwise adversely affect his status as an employee, because of such individual's race, color, religion, sex, or national origin.[35]

Section 703(c) of Title VII prohibited labor organizations from discriminating against any individual, or to limit, segregate or classify its membership because of race, color, etc. Section 703(d) prohibited employers, labor organizations or joint labor-management committees from discriminating against any individual in on-the-job training programs. Section 703(h) prohibited employers from using different standards of compensation or "different terms, conditions or privileges of employment pursuant to a bona fide seniority or merit system . . . because of race, color, etc."[36] Section 705(a) authorized the creation of an Equal Employment Opportunity Commission which had the power to investigate complaints and to cooperate with state and local officials and private individuals and to refer matters to the United States Attorney General.[37] Additionally, Executive Orders 11246 and 11478 by Presidents Lyndon B. Johnson and Richard M. Nixon, respectively, authorized affirmative action in government contracts and equal employment opportunities in the Federal government.[38]

There were twenty-seven *amici curiae* briefs filed with the United States Supreme Court in the *Weber* case. This was twenty-four less than those in the *Bakke* case.[39] Thirteen of those *amici* briefs asked the Supreme Court to reverse the lower courts decisions—included were briefs filed by the NAACP Legal Defense and Educational Fund, Inc., with Howard University, and the National Urban League, the NAACP, several affiliated AFL-CIO labor unions, the American Civil Liberties Union and a joint brief by twenty-eight women's organizations. Five *amici* briefs asked the Court to affirm the lower courts decisions—among them were the Anti-Defamation League of Bnai B'rith, the

National Jewish Commission on Law and Public Affairs, the Ukrainian Congress Committee of America and UNICO National, the largest Italian American organization in the United States.[40] For some strange reason, not a single black organization filed an *amicus curiae* with the lower federal courts; yet, the two leading Jewish Organizations filed briefs in behalf of *Weber*.[41]

The *Weber* case differs from *Bakke* because it involves the voluntary actions of two purely private parties to develop an affirmative action program in accordance with acts of Congress and two executive orders; whereas, in *Bakke* the question concerned alleged unlawful discrimination by a state governmental entity and, thus, the constitutional proscription by the Fourteenth Amendment. Additionally, the legal precedents on issues similar to *Weber* were quite different from the "strict scrutiny" tradition prior to *Bakke*. For *Weber*, the statutory interpretation becomes exclusive, and it is vital to review the history and purpose of Title VII.

The legislative history of Title VII of the Civil Rights Act of 1964 is both complex and deceptive.[42] At the close of the American Civil War, blacks constituted 80% of the skilled craftsmen in the South, and Southern whites envied their favored position. Northerners resented free black workers more than their Southern counterparts. With the emergence of big business and big labor within an environment of racism, the scales gradually tipped in favor of the white skilled craftsmen, and blacks were relegated to the low paying "Negro jobs." The American Federation of Labor, under the skillful leadership of its founder Samuel Gompers, an immigrant Jew, led the successful movement to exclude blacks from the skilled crafts by the devious device of the ritual. After the Great Depression of 1929, the Congress of Industrial Organizations compounded the problem by resorting to an equally deceptive technique—the seniority of tenure in promotions.[43] Consequently, one-hundred years after emancipation blacks faced deliberate practices designed to restrict them to specific positions in the job market. During those years, blacks relied almost exclusively on private, race-conscious voluntary action by charities and foundations as the only major redress available to fight against discrimination.[44]

Prior to 1964, Fair Employment Practice legislation was a dismal failure. Attacks on the system came in the early 1960s with demonstrations, legal action by the NAACP and other civil rights organizations and the influential March on Washington in 1963. President John F. Kennedy, on June 19, 1963, requested Congress to pass "Fair and Full Employment" legislation, especially for blacks in the areas of jobs and skills.[45] Pursuant thereof, Congress passed the Civil Rights Act of 1964 which was the first comprehensive civil rights legislation of this century directed toward alleviating the lingering legacies of racism and discrimination.

Title VII of the 1964 Act had a separate origin; it developed out of the House Education and Labor Committee, and it was concerned only with the private sector. Bipartisan politics affected the purpose and intent of every aspect of Title VII as well as other titles of the Act. Southern Democrats were almost intransigent in their opposition to any civil rights bill; several legislators in both houses of Congress were steadfastly opposed to federal regulation of private business—even the liberals joined them in insisting that management prerogatives and union freedoms be left undisturbed except to correct discrimination practices. The quota bogus elicited the usual bigotry, intolerance and prejudice in congressional debates. Opponents of the bill contended regularly that Title VII would cause businesses to hire on a quota basis, and the sponsors consistently gave assurances that they had no intent to impose quotas on unwilling employers or unions.[46] In a brief filed in behalf of *Weber*, Senator Joseph S. Clark, floor manager of the bill, was quoted as having said that "Quotas are themselves discriminatory," and Senator Hubert S. Humphrey was similarly quoted: "The Title does not provide that any preferential treatment in employment shall be given to Negroes or any other persons or groups. It does not provide that any quota system may be established."[47] But, as Senator Humphrey later remarked: "The crux of the problem of job discrimination is to open employment opportunities for Negroes in occupations which have been traditionally closed to them.[48]

After reviewing the congressional debates and briefs filed before the Court, it seems that Congress did not intend for Title VII to prohibit private industry and unions from using voluntary affirmative action involving numerical goals and quotas. The law simply prohibits employers and unions from engaging in discrimination because of race, sex, religion or ethnic origin. This means that Title VII offers no meaningful federal solution to the crux of the problem—the blacks. The law is a political hodgepodge designed to pacify some demonstrators while at the same time politicians can claim victories before their constituents. Rarely in American history have interest groups and businessmen voluntarily offered effective programs for blacks. If no individual can be sacrificed in order to help blacks, then the black problem will continue. As Charles T. Schmidt, Jr., observed:

> . . . this title [VII] is wholly inadequate to meet even the minimum demands of the *Negro*. . . . The problem of job discrimination is the *Negro*— the problem in unemployment is the *Negro*—the problem in skilled craft unions is the *Negro*— the problem in apprenticeship and training is the *Negro*—the problem in job referrals and promotion is the *Negro*—the one internal national force that threatens to extinguish this nation is the *Negro*, and extinguish *he will* unless his demands for jobs, employment and training are fulfilled immediately . . . without qualification.[49]

As aforementioned, the legal precedents on issues involving blacks and the private sector were quite different from those legal precedents concerning blacks and state action. When Title VII became effective, it prohibited the application of discriminatory seniority rules which had served in the past to exclude blacks from certain craft jobs. Three interpretations of the Title were advanced relative to the competitive standing between black and white workers in regard to correcting past discrimination. The "status quo" approach was advanced first, and it would have left white seniority rights intact and blacks would not have been able to improve their status. Secondly, there was the "rightful place" theory which held that the "status quo" violated Title VII; therefore, it was suggested that an incumbent black worker could bid for openings in "white" jobs of equal tenure on the basis of one's full length of service with the employer. "Freedom now" was the last approach, and this theory held that if seniority rights under the "rightful place" theory did not foster a preferential solution, then senior black workers would have priority over senior white workers in unfilled jobs even if white incumbents were displaced.[50]

The United States Supreme Court and lower federal courts accepted the compromise "rightful place" approach primarily because it did not result in the displacement of white workers in order to help blacks or a "robbing [of] Peter to pay Paul." In 1976, the Second Circuit Court of Appeals rejected a "quota" remedy because it meant that some

whites would have lost their jobs.[51] A federal court observed in 1970 that the problem was ". . . how to reconcile equal employment opportunity *today* with seniority expectations based on yesterday's built in racial discrimination." The court then ruled against Crown Zellerback's job seniority because they had not equated black seniority with white seniority; however, the court warned: "White incumbent workers should not be bumped out of their present position by Negroes with greater plant seniority. Plant seniority should be asserted only with respect to *new job opening*."[52] In 1976, the United States Supreme Court approved retroactive seniority to the date of the individual job application by blacks who claimed that their employer discriminated against them because of their race in violation of Title VII.[53] In *Griggs v. Duke Power Company* (1971), the Supreme Court voided the use of tests as a prerequisite for promotion. Thus on several occasions the federal courts have sanctioned "ratio hiring" or "quota hiring" in order to eradicate past discrimination and to facilitate equal opportunity in employment in the private sector.

In the *Weber* case, the United States Supreme Court concurred with legal precedents which had developed after the enactment of Title VII. The Court agreed that Title VII did not prohibit voluntary affirmative action programs, even if those programs used a rigid quota system.[54] This differs from *Bakke* because in that case Jews and other whites would have been displaced by blacks and other minorities. In *Weber*, whites benefitted because new jobs were created and no one was displaced. As the American Civil Liberties Union argued in its *amicus* brief in *Weber*, the "implementation did no harm to white expectations and no claim that whites were better qualified than blacks and actually offered newer advancements for whites. . . .[55] It may be surmised, therefore, that the rigid quota system could be applied to higher education provided no Jews or whites were displaced and that professional schools should increase the number of admissions in order to accommodate blacks and minorities. On the other hand, this society seems to be saying that blacks and other minorities may be gradually admitted into the crafts by voluntary action, but graduate and professional schools may continue to procrastinate because those schools are the citadels for educating the power elite.

The *Fullilove* case developed out of Congressional response to the 1974 recession, which was the worst economic downturn since 1934. Although the national unemployment rate was 7.7 in 1976, the nonwhite unemployment rate was 13.1%. By 1977, the nonwhite unemployment rate was 13.1%. Therefore, the nonwhite unemployment rate was unchanged whereas the national unemployment rate was 7.0%. Presidents Richard M. Nixon and Gerald R. Ford were more interested in solving the problem of inflation at the risk of continuing unemployment, while Congress advocated the New Deal solution of pump-priming to reduce unemployment and risk some inflation. The Congressional viewpoint prevailed when they overrode the President's veto and enacted the Local Public Works Capital Development and Investment Act of 1976, which was an extension of the Small Business Act of 1953 as amended several times since 1968. Further, Congress amended the 1976 Act with the Public Works Employment Act of 1977 (PWEA). This amendment authorized an additional four billion dollars of federal grants to be made by the Secretary of Commerce "acting through the Economic Development Administration (EDA), to state and local governmental entities for use in public works projects.[56] Section 103(f)(2) of the 1977 Act emphasized minority business enterprise (MBE) which required that:

> . . . no grant shall be made under this Act for any local public works projects unless the applicant gives satisfactory assurances to the Secretary that at least 10 per centum of the amount of each grant shall be expended for minority business enterprises. For purposes of this paragraph, the term 'minority business enterprise' means a business at least 50 per centum of which is owned by minority group members or, in case of a publicly owned business, at least 51 per centum of the stock of which is owned by minority group members. For the purposes of the preceding sentence, minority group members are citizens of the United States who are Negroes, Spanish speaking, Orientals, Indians, Eskimos, and Aleuts.[57]

But Title VI of the Civil Rights Act of 1964 stated:

> *No person* in the United States shall, on the ground of race, color, or national origin, be excluded from participating in, be denied the benefits of, or be subjected to discrimination under any program or activity receiving Federal financial assistance.[58]

The MBE section of the PWE Act of 1977 was sponsored by the black Congressman, Representative Parrem Mitchell, during debate in the House, and black Senator Edward Brooke sponsored the Senate version. The opponents of MBE claimed that there was little legislative history to the amendment. Since this amendment never went through congressional committees, the MBE provision failed the "strict scrutiny" test because no compelling governmental interest was shown.[59]

In 1977, the Secretary of Commerce stipulated regulations governing the administration of MBE grant programs. In November 1977, H. Earl *Fullilove* and nine other building contractors filed a complaint in the United States District Court for the Southern District of New York seeking injunctive relief from the MBE provision. They claimed that the MBE 10% requirement imposed economic difficulties and injuries and that it violated the Equal Protection clause of the Fourteenth Amendment and the Due Process clause of the Fifth Amendment as well as several antidiscrimination statutory provisions. Both of the lower federal courts rejected the injunctive relief sought by the contractors.[60]

A total of nineteen *amici curiae* briefs were filed with the Supreme Court. Fourteen asked the Court to affirm the lower courts decisions—included among them were the NAACP, NAACP Legal Defense and Educational Fund, Inc., with Howard University, the Asian American Legal Defense and Education Fund, Inc., the Mexican American and League of United Latin American Citizens and the Alpha Kappa Alpha Sorority, Inc. Four interest groups asked the Court for a reversal of the lower courts decisions—among them were the Anti-Defamation League of B'nai B'rith and the Pacific League Foundation. Conspicuously missing were all of the East European-American groups who formerly supported the Jewish position. Not one ethnic group continued its support of the Jews against blacks and other minorities in the *Fullilove* case. One *amicus* brief by the Equal Employment Advisory Council took a neutral position because of split opinions by the lower federal courts.[61] Chief Justice Warren J. Burger delivered the Court's six to three opinion.

The affirmative action issue in the *Fullilove* case was quite different from those issues in *Bakke* and *Weber*. The latter two cases were limited to the areas of academic admissions and employment; whereas, in *Fullilove* the Court, for the first time, considered the legality of affirmative action in the marketplace. The United States government, as a major consumer and purchaser of commodities and services, had used its power and influence to hasten the development of minority business enterprises in the marketplace of the construction industry.[62]

Several arguments were presented to the Court in opposition to and for the MBE legislation. The General Building Contractors argued that the MBE law failed the strict scrutiny test; that Congress had not shown discrimination against blacks and minorities on the part of construction contractors; that the meager legislative history of MBE did not demonstrate that the 10% plan would alleviate the problems of blacks and minorities.[63] Members of the Jewish B'nai B'rith argued that the MBE closed out disfavored racial, ethnic and language groups, and that the government was engaging in a racial "Inquisition" similar to the Third Reich because of their imprecise definition of blacks, Indians, Orientals, etc. Consequently, the criterion for racial classification would be "I-know-when-I-see-one."[64]

Proponents for MBE presented the historical background of the original Small Business Act of 1953 and several executive orders, especially President Richard Nixon's Executive Order 11458 in 1969 which created the first Minority Business Enterprise Program. Proponents argued that despite the actions by both the Congress and the Executive, very little was accomplished to get government contracts for blacks and minority businesses. Therefore, the 10% plan was a legitimate means to an end.[65] The NAACP Legal Defense Fund found similarities between Congressional attacks on the "First Reconstruction" and the Congressional attacks on the "Second Reconstruction." In 1864, opponents of the Freedmen's Bureau condemned the bill as class legislation, since there was no comparable legislation for whites. They chided Congress to establish a Bureau of Irishmen's affairs, a Bureau of Dutchmen's affairs or a Bureau for Those of Caucasian Descent. They saw no need for special legislation for blacks since it would be to the detriment of those poor, unfortunate whites.[66]

The Supreme Court, after hearing arguments, decided to use judicial restraint in upholding the role of Congress to redress past discrimination by use of a specified 10% quota.[67]

Justice Thurgood Marshall, joined by Justices William Brennan and Harry Blackmun, wrote the separate concurring opinion. Marshall reaffirmed his dissenting opinion in the *Bakke* case, and he applauded the Court for its full swing-around-the-circle in *Fullilove*. He reaffirmed the contention

that "a government practice or statute which . . . contains 'suspect classification' is to be subjected to 'strict scrutiny' and can be justified only if it furthers a compelling government purpose. . . ." Concurrently, Marshall reiterated the conception "that racial classifications are prohibited if they are irrelevant. . . ." or that they stigmatize. He concurred in the Court's opinion that the purpose in the 10% plan was to remedy the effects of past racial discrimination and that the 10% set-aside quota did not stigmatize qualified contractors. He reiterated that the remedial effects of past discrimination would not be effective without acknowledging race and race-conscious programs.[68] Both Marshall and Justice Powell recognized that the 10% set-aside was inadequate. Minority contractors would be allocated only $400 million of the $4 billion or .25% of the yearly construction appropriation. Finally, the 10% set-aside would end with PWEA unless amended.

Justice John Paul Stevens made several astute observations in his dissenting opinion. In Solomon like fashion, Stevens called upon the Court to exercise evenhanded justice to the injured class and not to all minorities. Racial discrimination against blacks, Stevens reasoned, was no justification for granting reparations to Eskimos and other minorities involved in the case. Blacks were forced into America, and they subsequently witnessed discriminatory laws and racism; whereas, the Eskimos, Indians and Aleuts were already in America free to exploit her natural resources. Moreover, Spanish-speaking Americans voluntarily came to the New World with an equal opportunity in the market place. Therefore, Stevens asked, how could these ethnic groups be entitled to the same reparations from the United States government as blacks? This point of view reemphasized the argument that the central problem involved black people and not minorities. Stevens continued in his dissent by accepting many ideas from the Anti-Defamation League of B'nai B'rith's argument against vague racial definitions, and he concluded with his opposition to the legislative trend of granting special privileges to a variety of influential ethnic, religious and racial groups in the absence of accurate measurements of past discrimination against minorities accompanied by reparations to all minorities in an evenhanded way.[69]

In these three cases *Bakke*, *Weber*, and *Fullilove*, I have examined and analyzed ideas and interest groups supportive and opposed to affirmative action for blacks and other minorities. If one reflects on legislation, executive orders and attacks on the two "Reconstructions" (1867–1877 and 1960–1977), the paraphrase of a popular song may be helpful— twice is not enough. For one-hundred years, blacks have witnessed a multiplicity of innocuous and meaningless programs of short duration to compensate for the wrongs of slavery and segregation. Opposition to the "Second Reconstruction" was similar and as ludicrous to that of the "First Reconstruction."

During the "First Reconstruction," the emphasis was on survival, civil and political rights and a functional educational program geared for a separate but unequal existence. There were a series of unfortunate Supreme Court decisions, which impaired the implementation of those inadequate programs. [*United States v. Reese*, 1876; *United States v. Cruikshank*, 1876; *Civil Rights Cases of 1883*; and *Plessy v. Ferguson*, 1896]. There were no significant attempts to develop effective economic programs for blacks during this period. Therefore, one may conclude that the grand design was incomplete assimilation which would enhance emotionalism and perpetuate a sub-culture for Afro-Americans.

Our "Second Reconstruction" seems to offer an affirmative action in education and professional schools; and for the first time private enterprise, labor unions and the federal government are attempting to implement compensatory programs which will increase the number of blacks in the crafts and in the marketplace. Unlike the "First Reconstruction," today the federal government recognizes the importance of economic factors and quality education. Although these programs were hastily enacted, morbid and inadequate, one at least knows that a snail is moving. The Supreme Court has restricted only a portion of those compensatory programs, and the Jewish and East European-American coalition seems to be waning for lack of unified support.

In all of the cases discussed, it seems that the most viable measuring mechanism is a rigid quota. Now that the Supreme Court is obviously leaning toward judicial self-restraint, it seems that there is an urgent need for a strong and liberal Chief Executive or a progressive Congress or both if there is going to be meaningful and sustaining compensatory programs for blacks. Through it all, one must never forget that the crux of the problem is the blacks race and not those deceptive, diluting and associated words like minorities and/or women.

Endnotes

1. See Rocco J. Tresollni and Martin Shapiro, *American Constitutional Law* (New York, N.Y.: Macmillan Company, 1970), pp. 14–25.
2. United States v. Carolene Products Company, 304 U.S. 144, 152 (1938).
3. Korematsu v. United States, 323 U.S. 214, 216 (1945).
4. As indicated San Antonio Independent School District v. Rodriquea, 411 U.S. 1, 16–17 (1973); Loving v. Virginia, 388 U.S. 1, (1967); Gerald Gunther, "Forward: In Search of Evolving Doctrine on a Changing Court: A Model for a Newer Equal Protection," *Harvard Law Review* 86 (1972):1–48; Albert Broderick, "Preferential Admissions and the *Brown* Heritage," *North Carolina Central University Law Journal* 8 (1977):124. Broderick has an interesting analysis. He argues that there are two competing constitutional principles in apparent conflict, which concerns coverage of nonracial matters—the "any person" principle and the suspect class" doctrine. *Ibid.* pp. 124–129 and N. 131–132.
5. Gunther, p. 8.
6. *Ibid.*, p. 12 Cf. Kent Greenawalt, "Judicial Scrutiny of 'Benign' Racial Preference in Law Schools Admissions," *Columbia Law Review* 75 (1975): 559–606. "In cases dealing with economic rights, the Court has applied the rational relationship standard with great indulgence, straining to find legitimate purposes when illegitimate purposes are much more plausible and accepting almost any speculative rational for why a classification serves an end that permissible. The result has been virtually complete judicial abdication to legislative decision." *Ibid.* p. 562.
7. Gunther, pp. 12, 15–18.
8. San Antonia Independent School District v. Rodriquez 411 U.S. 1, 99 (1973) and Dandridge v. Williams 397 U.S. 520–521 (1970).
9. John E. Flaming, *The Lengthening Shadow of Slavery* (Washington, D.C.; Howard University Press, 1976), p. 123. Also see John Fleming, Gerald R. Gill and David H. Swinton, *Affirmative Action for Blacks in Higher Education. A Report* (Washington, D.C.: Howard University Press, 1978), pp. 32–41.
10. Fleming, *Lengthening Shadow*, pp. 124–128.
11. Civil Rights Act of 1964, Title VI, sec. 601, 42 U.S.C., sm. 2000(d) (1976).
12. Phillip B. Kurland and Gerhard Cooper, ed., *Landmark Briefs and Arguments of the Supreme Court of the United States: Constitutional Law*, 100 vols. (Washington, D.C.: University Publications of America, Inc., (1978), "Brief of the American Bar Association" 99 (1978): 448. Note: I am using the page numbers in *Landmark* and not those of the actual briefs.

13. Regents of the University of California v. Allan Bakke, 438 U.S. 266, 57 L. Ed. 769 (1978).

14. Kurland, *Landmark*, "Brief for Petitioner" 99 (1978): 182–184.

15. *Ibid.*, p. 181.

16. California v. Bakke, pp. 773–774.

17. *Ibid.*, p. 777.

18. *Ibid.*, p. 771. Regents of the University of California v. Allan Bakke, 439 U.S. 320, 266, 267 (1977).

19. California v. Bakke, p. 772.

20. Kurland, *Landmark*, "Brief of the American Civil Liberties Union," *et. al.*, 99 (1978): 462.

21. *Ibid.*, "Brief of the American Bar Association" 99 (1978): 445–446.

22. *Ibid.*, Brief of the American Jewish Committee, *et. al.*" 99 (1978): 529.

23. See William Schneider, "An Emergence of National Consensus," *The New Republic*, October 1978, pp. 4–7.

24. Maldwyn Allen Jones, *American Immigration*, The Chicago History of American Civilization (Chicago: University of Chicago Press, 1960), pp. 272–276. Hugh A. Bowe, *American Politics and the Party System*, fourth edition (Now York, McGraw Hill 1971), p. 161. Also see: *Plan of Organization Democratic Party of North Carolina*, 1970.

25. Stokley Carmichael and Charles V. Hamilton, *Black Power: The Politics of Liberation in America* (New York, N.Y.: Vintage Books, 1967). pp. 34–36.

26. Kurland, *Landmark*, "Brief of Honorable Patricia Schroeder, et. al.," 112 (1979): 833–835.

27. Fleming, *Affirmative Action*, p. 48.

28. *Ibid.* p. 40. Mary Berry, "The Mythology of Equal Treatment," Learning and the Law, Spring 1975, p. 24, quoted in Fleming, *Affirmative Action* p. 40.

29. Leonard Fein, "The War Inside the Jews," *The New Republic*, October 1978, pp. 16ff.

30. Kurland, *Landmark*, "Brief of the American Jewish Committee, *et. al.*," 99 (1978): 523.

31. *Ibid.*, p. 522–524.

32. Earl G. Graves, "Bakke and other moments in History," *Black Enterprise*, August 1977, p. 7.

33. Brian F. Weber, *et. al.* v. Kaiser Aluminum and Chemical Corporation, *et. al.* 563 Federal Reporter, 2d Series 216–238 (1977). Kaiser Aluminum and Chemical Corporation, *et. al.* v. Brian F. Weber. *et. al.* 443 U.S. 193 (1979)

34. *Ibid.*

35. Civil Rights Act of 1964, Title VII, sec. 703(a), 42 U.S.C., sec, 2000(e) (1976).

36. *Ibid.*

37. *Ibid.*

38. Equal Opportunity in Federal Employment, Executive Orders 11246 and 11478, 42 U.S.C. sec. 2000(c) (1976).

39. Kaiser v Weber, 443 U.S. 196–197 (1979).

40. *Ibid.* See Kurland, *Landmark* vol. 112 (1980).

41. See Weber v. Kaiser, 563 Fed. Rep., 219 (1977) and the dissent of Judge Minor Wisdom with this comment: "In the district court no one represented the separate interests of the minority employees of Kaiser, the only people potentially interested in showing past discrimination." p. 231.

42. Francis J. Vaas, "Title VII: Legislative History." *Boston College Industrial and Commercial Law Review* 7 (1966): 431–432.

43. Sterling Spero and Abram Harris, *The Black Worker* (Columbia University Press (1931) pp. 4–59; Herbert Northrup, *Organized Labor and the Negro* (Harper & Brothers, N.Y., (1944)), pp. 1–16.

44. Kurland, *Landmark*, "Brief of the NAACP Legal Defense and Education Fund, Inc." pp. 702–743.

45. Vass, "Title VII," pp, 431–432. Just five months earlier the President in a special civil rights message to Congress did not request legislation in regard to private employment. p. 432.

46. Kurland, *Landmark*, Brief of United Steelworkers of America, A.F.L., C.I.O., C.L.C.," pp. 88–93. See: H. Rep. No. 914, 88 Congress 1st Session p. 150 (1963).

47. Kurland, *Landmark*, "Brief of Respondent Weber, On Writ of Certiorari. . . ." p. 209.

48. Kurland, *Landmark* ,"Brief for Petitioner United Steelworkers of America" p. 110.

49. Charles T. Schmidt, Jr., "Title VII; Coverage and Comments," *Boston College Industrial and Commercial Law Review* 7 (1966): 460.

50. "Notes: Title VII, Seniority Discrimination, and the Incumbent Negro," *Harvard Law Review* 80 (1967).

51. Chance v. Board of Examiners, 534 Fed. Rep. 2nd Series 993 (1976)

52. Local 189, *et. al.* v. United States of America, *et. al.*, 416 Fed. Rep. 2d. Series 982, 983 and 988 (1970). The court endorsed the "rightful place" theory.

53. Franks, *et. al.*, v. Bowman Transportation Company, Inc. *et. al.* 424 U.S. 747–751 (1976). See also International Brotherhood of Teamsters v. United States, *et. al.* 431 U.S. 324–394 (1977). The case involved seniority discrimination against Blacks and Spanish surnamed persons in the trucking industry. For a discussion on affirmative action and the law, see Fleming, *Affirmative Action*, pp. 29–44.

54. Kaiser v. Webber, 443 U.S. 193–225 (1979).

55. Kurland, *Landmark*, "Amicus Curiae Brief of the American Civil Liberties Union and The Society of American Law Teachers," p. 416. Similar arguments were in other amici briefs.

56. H. Earl Fullilove, *et. al.* v. Klutznick, Secretary of Commerce, *et. al.*, p. 1. (1980) Please note: All footnotes relative to the Fullilove case are taken from "Slip Opinion" in the U.S. Supreme Court Library, Docket no. 78–1007.

57. Public Works Employment Act. 91 *Stat* 116 (1977),42 USC A, sec, 6705 (1977).

58. Civil Rights Act of 1964, Title VI, sec. 601, 42 U.S.C., sec. 2000(d) (1976).

59. "Brief of H. Earl Fullilove, *et. al.* v. Juanita Kreps, *et. al.*," pp. 7–11. I am using the actual page numbers in the brief located in the Supreme Court Library. Dr. Kreps was Secretary of Commerce when this brief was filed.

60. Fullilove v. Klutznick, p. 3. The Court of Appeals rejected this argument because the government's main purpose was to remedy racial and ethnic discrimination. See 584 Fed. Rep. 605–609 (1978).

61. I have examined all nineteen briefs in the Supreme Court's Library.

62. Amicus Curiae Brief of the National, Bar Association, Inc. *et. al.*," p. 10.

63. "Brief for Petitioner, General Building Contractor of New York State, Inc. *et. al.*," pp. 7–13.

64. "Brief of the Anti-Defamation League," pp. 9–10.

65. See "Briefs of ACLU," pp. 13–22 "NAACP Legal Defense" pp. 9–18 and Lawyers' Committee for Civil Rights, pp. 96–97.

66. "Brief NAACP Legal Defense," pp. 9–10.

67. Fullilove v. Klutznick, pp. 34, 35 and 40.

68. *Ibid*. pp. 1–7 and 20.

69. Justice John Paul Stevens, "Dissent," *Slip Opinion*, pp. 1–23 (forthcoming in U.S. Reports).